INTRODUCTION TO POLITICAL SCIENCE

THIRD EDITION

INTRODUCTION TO POLITICAL SCIENCE

CARLTON CLYMER RODEE, Ph.D.
Late Professor of Political Science
University of Southern California

TOTTON JAMES ANDERSON, Ph.D.

CARL QUIMBY CHRISTOL, LL.B., Ph.D.

THOMAS H. GREENE, Ph.D.
Department of Political Science
University of Southern California

McGRAW-HILL BOOK COMPANY

New York   St. Louis   San Francisco   Auckland   Düsseldorf
Johannesburg   Kuala Lumpur   London   Mexico
Montreal   New Delhi   Panama   Paris
São Paulo   Singapore   Sydney   Tokyo   Toronto

INTRODUCTION TO POLITICAL SCIENCE

Copyright © 1957, 1967, 1976 by McGraw-Hill, Inc.
All rights reserved.
Printed in the United States of America.
No part of this publication may be reproduced,
stored in a retrieval system, or transmitted,
in any form or by any means,
electronic, mechanical, photocopying,
recording, or otherwise,
without the prior written permission of the publisher.

34567890VHVH79

This book was set in Times Roman by Black Dot, Inc.
The editors were Lyle Linder, Jean Smith, and Susan Gamer;
the cover was designed by Nicholas Krenitsky;
the production supervisor was Charles Hess.
Von Hoffmann Press, Inc., was printer and binder.

Library of Congress Cataloging in Publication Data
Main entry under title:

Introduction to political science.

    Earlier editions by C. C. Rodee, T. J. Anderson, and C. Q. Christol.
    Includes bibliographical references and index.
    1. Political science. 2. Comparative government. I. Rodee, Carlton Clymer, II. Rodee, Carlton Clymer. Introduction to political science.
JA66.R59 1976   320   75-12588
ISBN 0-07-053376-8

Contents

Preface ... ix

Chapter 1
The Nature and Scope of Political Science ... 1
What Is "Political Science"? ... 1
The Development of Political Science ... 4
The Subject Matter of Political Science ... 5
The Uses of Political Science ... 12
Study-Guide Questions ... 12
References ... 13

PART ONE
CONCEPTS AND IDEOLOGIES

Chapter 2
The Nature of the State ... 17
Origin of the State ... 18
Theories Concerning the Origin of the State ... 18
Essential Elements of the State ... 20
General Characteristics and Attributes of the State ... 27
Study-Guide Questions ... 28
References ... 28

Chapter 3
The Forms of Government ... 29
Classification: Government by One, Few, and the Many ... 29
Monarchy ... 31
Government by the Few ... 32
Government by the Many ... 35
Classifying States: A Continuum ... 36
Institutional Forms of the State: Parliamentary Government ... 37
Institutional Forms of the State: Presidential Government ... 38
Institutional Forms of Government: Unitary States ... 40
Institutional Forms of Government: Federal States ... 41

v

Study-Guide Questions	42
References	42

Chapter 4
Law and Government 45
Law 46
Schools of Law 47
Ethics and Justice 48
Sources of Law 50
Stages in Legal Development 51
Legal Systems 51
Some Characteristics of Law 56
Other Bases for the Classification of Law 58
By Way of Summary 59
Study-Guide Questions 60
References 60

Chapter 5
Liberalism and Democracy 61
Ideology 61
Democracy versus Authoritarianism: First Assumptions 62
Classical Liberalism 63
Neoliberalism 64
Conditions Necessary for the Success of Democracy 66
Criticisms of Democracy 68
Study-Guide Questions 70
References 70

Chapter 6
Marxism and Communism 73
Communism before Marx 73
Marxism 74
Leninism 79
Trotskyism 80
Stalinism 81
Anti-Stalinism 82
Chinese Communism 85
Castroism 87
Communism as an Ideal 89
Study-Guide Questions 89
References 89

Chapter 7
Ideologies on the Left, Center, and Right 91
From Left to Right 91
Anarchism 92

Communism	94
Socialism	95
Liberalism	104
Conservatism	106
Fascism	109
Study-Guide Questions	113
References	113

PART TWO
INTRODUCTION TO COMPARATIVE POLITICS

Chapter 8
Revolution or Stable Democracy? 117
Comparing Nations 117
Ten Best-governed Nations 117
Characteristics of Stable Democracy 118
Revolution and Modernization 118
The Institutions of Stable Democracy: The Suffrage 121
Representation 122
The Legislative Body 126
The Executive Branch 130
The Judicial Branch 133
Study-Guide Questions 136
References 136

Chapter 9
Politics in the United States: I 137
Colonial Beginnings 137
The Revolutionary Era 138
The Making of the Constitution 139
The American Federal System 144
Congress 148
The Presidency 155
Study-Guide Questions 164
References 164

Chapter 10
Politics in the United States: II 167
The National Judiciary 167
Judicial Review 172
Liberties and Rights 173
The Dynamics of National Government: American Politics 178
State and Local Government 182
Study-Guide Questions 184
References 185

Chapter 11
Politics in Great Britain 187
Building a Stable Democracy 187
The Evolution of British Political Institutions 190
The British Constitution 191
The Executive Branch 192
The British Parliament 197
British Political Parties 204
Study-Guide Questions 210
References 210

Chapter 12
Politics in Western Europe 211
A Conceptual Framework 212
Italy: Cleavages Almost Everywhere 222
France: Cleavages in Decline 227
West Germany: Toward Stable Democracy 236
A Note on Politics in the Postindustrial Society 241
Study-Guide Questions 242
References 242

Chapter 13
Government in the Soviet Union: Politics or Antipolitics? 245
A Cultural Polyglot 246
Continuity 246
Historical Background 247
The Revolutions of 1917 250
The Period of War Communism: 1918 to 1921 251
The New Economic Policy: 1921 to 1927 251
The Soviet System of Government 252
The Structure of the Soviet State 256
The CPSU 259
The Soviet Planned Economy 265
Trends and Projections 269
Study-Guide Questions 271
References 271

PART THREE
STATE AND CITIZEN: GOVERNMENT IN ACTION

Chapter 14
The Voice of the People: Public Opinion 275
Political Socialization 278
Personality, Attitudes, and Opinions 280
The Public-Opinion Environment 282
Distribution Patterns: Consensus and Conflict 286
Patterns of Political Linkage 289
Summary 291
Study-Guide Questions 292
References 292

Chapter 15
Political Participation: The Individual and the Political Environment 295
The Behavioral Movement in Political Science 295
The Group Approach 297
Interest Groups 300
Aspects of the Political Environment 306
The Process, Content, and Techniques of Propaganda 309
Study-Guide Questions 314
References 314

Chapter 16
The Organization of the People: Political Parties 315
The Political Party 317
Party Systems 320
Contemporary Party Systems 322
The Party within the System 328
The Party at Work 332
Study-Guide Questions 338
References 338

Chapter 17
The Impact of Science and Technology: New Challenges and Problems 339
A New Social Complex 339
The Twentieth Century and the Emergence of New Problems 341
The Difference between Pure Science and Technology 341
Science, Technology, and Business 342
Science, Technology, and Labor 343
Science, Technology, and Human Relations 344
Science, Technology, and Agriculture 346
Science, Technology, and National Defense 347
Science, Technology, and Law 349
Science, Technology, and Education 350
Science and Technology in the Soviet Union 351

Science, Technology, and the Art of
    Government   352
Study-Guide Questions   354
References   354

Chapter 18
Public Administration: Performing the Tasks of the Modern State   355
The Nature of Public Administration   355
The Scope of Public Administration   360
Recent Trends in Governmental
    Organization   361
Administrative Relationships   363
Administrative Regulation   364
The Government Corporation   371
Study-Guide Questions   373
References   373

Chapter 19
The Nature of Foreign Policy   375
Principles Governing the Selection of Aims
    and Goals   376
Factors Conditioning Foreign Policy   379
The Constitutional Framework: Official
    Agencies that Formulate Policy   383
The Process of Formulating Policy   387
Political Dynamics and Foreign Policy   390
The Execution of Foreign Policy:
    Instruments and Tactics   393

Study-Guide Questions   396
References   396

Chapter 20
Relations between States: The International System   397
The State System   398
Two Models: Political Power and Political
    Interdependence   401
Strategy and Tactics in International Politics   403
Patterns in International Politics   405
Soviet Foreign Policy   410
United States Foreign Policy   413
Current Problems of International Politics   418
Study-Guide Questions   420
References   421

Chapter 21
International Law and Organization   423
International Law and International Politics   423
International Law and International
    Organization   424
International Law   424
International Organization   433
Study-Guide Questions   451
References   451

Index   453

Preface

Almost all of you reading these words are not likely to have had any choice in the matter. You were asked to buy this book before you knew it existed. And you have been urged to read it without knowing very much about its contents. You presumably have some interest in political science, or at least in learning more about the political world around you. But your understanding of what "politics" is all about is likely to be fairly vague. The authors of this book are quick to admit that their understanding of "politics" may be only a little less vague than yours. In an important sense, then, the following chapters are a joint adventure in inquiry and a joint experiment in understanding. We must work at it together, and without deluding ourselves with the assumption that we have either complete understanding or any certain answers.

Our refusal to make sweeping claims for the authority of our work reflects our perspective on events since the first edition of this text appeared in 1957. Even since the second edition, published in 1967, the world has turned round many times. Both the practice of politics and the study of politics have been revised and transformed, sometimes beyond the recognition of older generations of politicians and scholars. There is more than partial truth in the Malay proverb "Huge though the world is, I always miss when I hit at it."

From our vantage point in the mid-1950s, and again in the mid-1960s, it was difficult to foresee that the world might soon sag dangerously under the burden of problems so severe that cautious optimists might appear to some as utopian dreamers. Political leaders even in the most stable constitutional democracies now confront a lengthening list of challenges that might have overwhelmed the most skillful leaders of any previous era of government. Unemployment that used to be associated with economic depression is now a characteristic of runaway inflation. Despite our technological sophistication, much of today's world is hungry and diseased, and the specter of uncontrolled population growth and a worldwide energy shortage threatens the earlier accomplishments of both science and government. But science and technology also pose a challenge that more traditional styles of politics seem hard pressed to cope with. Mounting rates of political violence and revelations of corruption in high public office only compound the difficulties of responsible policy makers, whose tentative successes may be more a measure of their good luck than a sign of their political competence.

Why, then, should you be asked to read this book? In part, so that you might be more informed as you think about the art and science of government. And however one may regard "politics" or "politicians," thinking about them is inevitable, if only because so much of our daily life is affected by the decisions and behavior of political leaders. This book is also written for those who represent a new generation of citizens and leaders, so that they might succeed where others have failed. And we write for a younger generation of students who, with additional study and intellectual growth, might be able to correct our errors and shortcomings with new insight and understanding.

A review of the table of contents of this book will show how we have attempted to reach these goals. Part One deals with the fundamental concepts and principles of political organization and with the major ideologies that have agitated the modern world. We begin with systems of ideas and values because they inevitably structure the way we think and act politically. They help us to understand the more superficial events of our day-to-day life. And if today our political understanding and actions are misguided or wrong, we must base our hopes for the future on a better understanding of our ideological past and present.

Part Two deals with the political realities of modern government. Here we focus on the United States, Great Britain, Western Europe and the Soviet Union, as compared with each other and with some of the major patterns of politics characterizing the less developed countries of the contemporary world. We thereby enhance our understanding of the principles and ideologies of government from not only an empirical perspective but a *comparative* perspective. Nor can this part of our study be divorced from an understanding of the relevant past: thus we refer to the historical background of these countries, thereby hoping to redress an imbalance that marks so many other introductory texts in political science.

Part Three examines the functions, operations, policies, and problems of modern government as well as the forces which structure the principal alternatives that are available to contemporary policy makers. Here the student is introduced to the more specialized and technical details of the political process, including those related to political parties, public opinion, propaganda, public administration, foreign policy, international politics, international law and organization, and the effects of science and technology on the already complicated tasks of modern states.

While we have retained most of the organizational format of the earlier editions of this book, we have critically reexamined, revised, and updated all the textual material. This is in keeping with our obligations to new students and to new scholarship. But the major revisions of this third edition also represent a necessary response to the untimely death of our senior colleague; and we wish to dedicate this new edition to the memory of Carlton Clymer Rodee, 1899–1973. Professor Rodee's scholarship and his vigorous defense of individual freedom serve as a continuing inspiration, and much of his work is still apparent in the first and second parts of this book.

Responsibility for the revision of Part One (with the exception of Chapter 4) and Part Two, however, has been assumed by our new coauthor, Professor Thomas H. Greene. He has completely rewritten Chapters 6 and 12; he has rewritten almost all of Chapters 1, 3, and 7, and he is responsible for the greater part of Chapters 5, 11, and 13. As in the earlier editions of this book, Professor Anderson is responsible for Chapters 14, 15, 16, 19, and 20, and Professor Christol for Chapters 4, 17, 18, and 21.

We also wish to record here our sincere appreciation to the editors of the McGraw-Hill Book Company for their encouragement and forbearance: Robert P. Rainier and Jean Smith have been espe-

PREFACE

cially helpful in the preparation of this new edition. And we note with sadness and regret the death in 1974 of Ronald D. Kissack, who supervised the second edition and provided valuable assistance in the early stages of the present revision.

The pages that follow are the result of the coordinated efforts of these and many others who share our commitment to the education of a responsible citizenry. We now invite the reader to join with us in working toward an improved understanding of ourselves as citizens, in our own country and in the world.

Totton James Anderson
Carl Quimby Christol
Thomas H. Greene

Chapter 1

The Nature and Scope of Political Science

WHAT IS "POLITICAL SCIENCE"?

When the authors of this book were in college, they asked this same question of the fellow student or academic adviser who recommended a course in "Polly Sigh." Everyone had heard of history, law, economics, philosophy, and even psychology and sociology. But what was political science? Today's students, however, are likely to be more politically aware and more conscious of the importance of their government and its impact on their own lives and plans than their parents were during their more tranquil college days. Students today are also more likely to be aware of their society's political, social, and economic problems, especially as these problems mark the lives of cultural and racial minorities within the larger society. A long and bitter war abroad and a major struggle concerning the appropriate powers of the presidency have contributed to the political maturation of a new generation of both students and citizens. An awareness of at least some of the hard facts of political life is inescapable in a society whose political leaders are assassinated and in which the integrity of those who survive is compromised by sensational allegations of wrongdoing, corruption, or just plain bad judgment—bad judgment that can negatively affect the lives of millions of citizens.

But government and politics, in health or infirmity, are not synonymous with political science. Is there a "science" of politics—a body of laws, rules, or principles bringing political phenomena within the range of control and prediction? Can one speak of the laws of political behavior, the principles underlying the state, or the rules for establishing and maintaining the most just and efficient government? In the sense of the precision that is attributed, often mistakenly, to such sciences as physics, mathematics, chemistry, zoology, and botany, perhaps political science is not a science. Any confusion over the meaning of "science" is understandable in an age when tyrants have used the term to justify the state's suppression of unconventional beliefs and ethnic minorities and when advertisers have used it to argue the merits of the latest laundry detergent.

This ambiguity is implicit in the Latin origin of "science," which means simply "to know" (*scire*). And as man's knowledge of the physical and social environment has developed over thousands of years of observation and reflection, "science" has come to mean any body of systematic knowledge about a well-defined area of inquiry. Consequently, political scientists are faced with two questions as they attempt to explain what they do and why their efforts deserve the label of "science": How systematic is their knowledge of politics? And what defines their area of inquiry, or—in short—what is "politics"? We must answer the last question before we can answer the first.

"Politics"

The Greeks understood "politics" in a very broad sense. The word itself comes from the Greek word for "city-state" (*polis*), and Aristotle began his famous *Politics* with the observation that "man is by nature a political animal." By this he meant that the essence of social existence is politics and that two or more men interacting with one another are invariably involved in a political relationship. Aristotle also meant that this is a natural and inevitable predisposition among men and that very few people prefer an isolated existence to one that includes social companionship. As men seek to define their position in society, as they attempt to wring personal security from available resources, and as they try to influence others to accept their points of view, they find themselves engaging in politics. In this broad sense, everyone is a politician. Aristotle concluded, however, that the only way to maximize one's individual capabilities and to attain the highest form of social life was through political interaction with others in an institutionalized setting, a setting designed to resolve social conflict and to set collective goals—the state. All people are politicians, then, but some (public officials) are more political than others.

Between the sixteenth and early twentieth centuries, "politics" was understood more narrowly than it was by the Greeks. Jean Bodin (1530–1596), a French political philosopher, coined the term "political science" (*science politique*). But Bodin was also a lawyer, and his focus on the characteristics of the state gave political science an abiding concern for the organization of institutions related to law. This more formal and restricted definition of politics was reinforced by another French philosopher, Montesquieu (1689–1755), who argued that all the functions of government could be encompassed within the categories of legislation, execution, and the adjudication of law. These categories found their way into the Constitution of the United States along with Montesquieu's assumption that liberty was best assured by the distribution of these different functions among separate institutions of government (in the United States, the Congress, the executive branch, and the courts). Given this perspective, it is understandable that political scientists should have concentrated, almost exclusively and until very recently, on the organization and operation of institutions which make law, which enforce it, and which settle controversies arising from different interests and various interpretations of the law.

But this clearly is not the whole story of the "political process." The term itself, which has been accepted by an ever-larger number of political scientists since the 1950s, implies a recognition that legislatures, executive agencies, and courts do not exist by themselves, that they do not operate independently of either one another or of the other political organizations in society. These latter include, primarily, political parties and interest groups (or pressure groups, or lobbies). Together with the more formal institutions of the state, they constitute the "political system," a term meant to suggest that politics is indeed a complex process involving citizen attitudes and interests, group organization, electioneering, and lobbying, as well as the formulation, implementation, and interpretation of law. In short, contemporary political scientists recently have moved back toward the Greeks' understanding of politics and most of them consider any aspect of society that directly or indirectly affects the institutions of the state to be appropriate subject matter for their tools of inquiry.

"Science"

We return, then, to our first question: To what extent can one be systematic in a study of the political process? How "scientific" is political science? This is not the sort of question that can be answered with a "yes" or "no." It really is a matter of "more" or "less." And none of the social sciences, including political science, sociology, psychology, anthropology, and economics, can ever hope to attain the scientific status enjoyed by physics, chemistry, geology, physiology, astronomy, or any of the other disciplines of the natural sciences. Students and citizens who insist on certainty in the understanding of their environment are bound to be disappointed as they shift their attention from natural to social phenomena. Especially in the study of politics, a presumption of certainty is very likely to be an illusion designed to support one's own value prejudices.

Even among the social sciences, however, there are important differences in the scientific potential of their subject matter, the methodologies of their research, and the analytical rigor of their findings. Historically, economics was the first social science, emerging in France and England after the mid-eighteenth century. It was no coincidence that the development of economics as a well-defined discipline of study coincided with the commercial and industrial revolutions and was furthest advanced where industrialization appeared first and where it proceeded at a relatively rapid rate. Compared with economics and all the other social scientific disciplines, political science probably ranks among the lowest in terms of scientific potential. But most political scientists would argue that their discipline is more scientific than history, philosophy, or any of the other disciplines we commonly include in the "humanities." What accounts for these striking differences?

A fundamental test of the scientific potential of any discipline is its capacity for clearly classifying its subject matter in terms of discrete and mutually exclusive categories. These categories in turn must readily lend themselves to the construction of variables; a *variable* is any given set of phenomena that have measurable properties (for example, gravitational force, electrical charge, the social class of legislators, or a citizen's party identification). The more scientific a particular discipline is, the more observable these variables are, the easier it is to measure changes in their properties, the more susceptible the variables are to quantitative measurement, and the better able the researcher is to manipulate his variables in a controlled environment. In a highly scientific field of study (for example, physics), almost all researchers agree on the appropriate categories for classifying the phenomena they study. The relatively great observability of the variables drawn from these categories (they can be identified with one or more of the five senses) is likely to yield precise measurement of their variations over time and from one environment to another. It thus is easier to formulate hypotheses that predict the effects of one variable on another variable. The findings are more likely to be expressed in quantitative terms, and it is relatively easy for the findings of one researcher to be replicated and tested by other researchers in different places at different points in time.

This should help to explain the relatively low scientific standing of political science. Political scientists do not agree on the appropriate categories for classifying the phenomena of politics. This disagreement reflects the difficulty of observing and the frequent impossibility of quantifying the variables that political scientists do manage to identify. They do not enjoy the advantages of the economist, who measures a society's change over time in terms of gross national product, its wealth in terms of per capita income, and the substance of all economic interaction in terms of dollars and cents or some other unit of monetary exchange. Political scientists seldom have the advantages of the psychologist, who can test his hypotheses in a controlled laboratory setting with a relatively small number of subjects. Political scientists typically deal with large numbers of people in an uncontrolled setting where each individual has many behavioral options open to him. And how does one define, much less measure, political power and influence—the very substance of the political process?

But it would be wrong to conclude that political scientists are constrained to describe in nonhypothetical terms the bare-bones outline of institutions and the written codes that guide their operations. Political science itself is not an undifferentiated discipline of research and analysis; there are many *sub*disciplines of political science, and these in turn vary significantly in terms of their scientific potential and demonstrated accomplishments. Before considering the various subdisciplines of political science, however, the reader should have a more detailed perspective of the development of political science as a whole. And enough has already been said to make it clear that what is today called "political science" did not emerge intact from the brow of Zeus, or even from the brows of Plato and Aristotle.

THE DEVELOPMENT OF POLITICAL SCIENCE

Contemporary political science has evolved from many related fields of study, including history, philosophy, law, and economics. Once a part of these various disciplines, political science finally reached the point (in the United States, during the first and second decades of the twentieth century) where it could properly declare its independence—just as many of these related fields had earlier freed themselves from philosophy and religion. But despite the recent development of political science as a special field of study, the theoretical and practical study of the state and of politics dates back at least to the ancient Greeks (about 500 to 300 B.C.).

Early Trends in the Study of Politics

Plato may be considered the father of political *philosophy,* and Aristotle the parent of political *science,* at least in the West. Both viewed the state from the perspective of the philosopher to whom all knowledge was an integrated whole. In the Aristotelian threefold division of sciences, politics represented the practical, as distinguished from the theoretical and productive, sciences. Aristotle, moreover, was the father of the scientific method; he studied existing governments and claimed to base his conclusions upon these empirical observations. Actually, Aristotle began these observations with several preconceived ideas and values, many of which he had acquired from his teacher, Plato. Neither Plato nor Aristotle thought much of democracy. Plato's ideal republic was to be ruled by wise, just philosophers; Aristotle's "best practical state" was to rest on a combination of oligarchy and democracy—a compromise between wealth and numbers. Both rejected the notion of human equality; their low opinion of the populace was both caused and confirmed by the unhappy and unstable cycle of governments in ancient Athens, where democracy degenerated into "mobocracy" and then into tyranny.

The legacy of ancient Rome to political science consisted chiefly of contributions in the fields of law, jurisprudence, and public administration, all of which bore the imprint of Stoic notions of human equality, the brotherhood of all men, the fatherhood of God, and the unique value of the individual, who, however lowly, had within him a spark of the divine reason animating the universe. The philosophy of democracy, with its assumptions of human rationality, morality, and equality and its concepts of natural law and natural rights, owes much to Stoicism and to Cicero, who incorporated Stoic philosophy into Western political thought.

During the Middle Ages, the state was less important than the church, which, indeed, came to assert its power to crown and depose princes and to dictate public policy. Political philosophy was little more than a subordinate branch of theology; political controversies were resolved by appeals to authority, i.e., religious writings, rather than to empirical or practical considerations. However, the medieval age left a legacy of concepts that are still vital parts of modern political thought, such as the ideal of world unity and a body of ethicoreligious restraints upon political action, including what Christian philosophers called the "peace of God," the "fair wage," the "just price," and the idea of a "higher law" that was necessarily superior to the commands of a ruler or the state. In fact, any citizen today who claims a right to resist the authority of government, whether in terms of military induction, peaceful or violent demonstration, the payment of taxes, or the forfeiture of property, implies by his resistance some notion of a higher law.

Modern Trends in the Study of Politics

The Renaissance brought a revival of interest in the learning of ancient Greece and Rome, including the works of their great political philosophers. As the rising national states of Western Europe shook off the shackles of both pope and Holy Roman emperor, and especially when the Reformation led to the establishment of national churches dependent upon strong monarchs for their existence, the medieval hegemony of the church was overthrown, and a new balance was established between secular and spiritual authority. Niccolò Machiavelli, whose name has unjustly become a synonym for ruthless duplicity, broke with the Middle Ages by divorcing politics from religion. Considerations of national unity, security, and interest took primacy over subordination to pope and to dogma.

The era of the religious wars produced penetrating inquiries into the origin of the state, the citizen's duty to obey and his right to revolt, the obligations of the prince to his people, and the nature of liberty. The "social contract" theory of state origin,[1] although implied in the writings of Cicero, was first stated by Lutheran and Calvinistic writers in the latter part of the sixteenth century. The rights of passive disobedience and active resistance, first asserted on behalf of subjects whose princes' commands were deemed contrary to the law of God, were soon extended to nonreligious matters, giving rise to the doctrine that citizens might properly overthrow an unjust prince to restore the original sovereignty of the people.

During the period of history commonly termed "modern" (beginning approximately with the fifteenth century), the subject matter and methods of political science thus changed considerably. Just as Plato and Aristotle had sought to discover political laws and truths to match the findings of their contemporaries in physics or astronomy, so modern political scientists have been impressed and influenced by new discoveries and theories in the many other fields of human knowledge. Newton and Descartes actually contributed not only to physics and mathematics but to political science as well; the preoccupation, in the latter part of the eighteenth century, with such concepts as the separation of governmental powers and checks and balances represented an attempt to apply mechanical and mathematical principles to the structure of government.

This new attitude toward government and politics led to greater use of the empirical method, observing actual human institutions and processes in order to discover fundamental political laws. However, the earlier deductive approach of Plato and the rationalists, who started with certain premises or assumptions regarded as self-evident and then deduced conclusions as to what was politically right or natural, displayed remarkable tenacity, particularly in the United States.

In the mid-nineteenth century, Darwin's theory of evolution began to exert a powerful influence upon political science; biology came to reinforce history in the study of political institutions, which were seen as the product of historical change and, apparently, organic evolution. The development of sociology, especially after the nineteenth century, prompted political scientists to give more attention to the impact on government of social forces not defined with reference to the institutional outlines of the state. The industrialization of previously agricultural societies and the sharpening clash between classical and Marxist economic theories, and between new social classes forged on the anvil of industrial development, compelled a closer study of economic facts, forces, and trends, as these produced political problems and helped to shape political behavior.

THE SUBJECT MATTER OF POLITICAL SCIENCE

Thus for nearly 2,500 years there has been speculation, study, and argument concerning the state—its origin, justification, limits, functions, processes, and problems. With academic independence and with the sophistication of its methods of observation and measurement, and not least because of an ever-increasing number of trained political scientists, political science has developed many fields or subdisciplines. But not all political scientists will agree that the following listing is either complete or sufficiently exact, and this in turn is a cogent comment on the problems of making the study of politics "scientific."[2]

1 Political Philosophy

Every political act implies some underlying political value. It is appropriate, then, that the principal preoccupation of political scientists, from Plato to the early twentieth century, was with the values that were regarded as essential to the good citizen and the just state. What is justice? What makes political power and its exercise legitimate? What is

---

[1] See Chap. 2.

[2] For a more detailed listing, unannotated, of the various fields of specialization within political science, see American Political Science Association, *Biographical Directory,* 6th ed., Washington, 1973, pp. v–vi. The *Directory* identifies eight general categories of political science, which together subsume a total of sixty fields of specialization.

the sanction for rebellion against the authority of the state? How should property and the other forms of material possession be distributed among citizens? (If the student has never given it any thought, he or she should now consider what the justification is for *private* property—an institution that is fundamental to modern Western civilization.) Under what conditions, if any, are social and economic inequalities legitimately supported by the police and legal apparatus of the state? To what extent should citizens be entitled to participate in the decision-making processes of government? Should elected legislators be the rubber-stamp representatives of the opinion of a majority of their constituents, or should they be entitled to vote according to their own good conscience and their interpretation of the public interest?

Answers to these and similar questions have been and will continue to be endlessly debated because the "answers" are in terms of *value*, not facts. Individuals may use both fact and logic to support their values, but ultimately these values must stand or fall according to their inherent self-evidence—their appeal to other people with, apparently, equivalent rational endowment. Thomas Jefferson clearly understood this principle when he wrote in the Declaration of Independence about the political "truths" which "we hold . . . to be self-evident." They could not be demonstrated by empirical observation, mathematical deduction, or an exercise in logic.

By its very nature, then, political philosophy is the least scientific subdiscipline of political science. It is concerned with the *normative* implications of political organization and behavior—the way the state and society *ought* to be organized and the way the citizen *ought* to behave, given certain fundamental human values. This alone suggests that insofar as the other subdisciplines of political science lose sight of the value implications of their research and findings, they are likely to stray from the humane values of political life that are the ultimate justification for their very existence. Science without philosophy is not the servant of man, but his master.

2 Judicial and Legal Process

Along with political philosophy, this subdiscipline of political science has been among the main pillars supporting the edifice of the discipline. How do constitutions affect the operations of government, and how do the operations of government affect the development of constitutions? How are the laws administered, interpreted, and enforced? How are conflicts between several laws relevant to the same area of activity resolved? What are the rights of citizens under the law? If the constitution of a state is the supreme law of the land, which agency of government has the final word in determining the meaning of the law—in fact as well as in theory? How are conflicts between the legislative, executive, and judicial branches of government resolved? How are the jurisdictions of federal and state governments defined?

Contemporary students of the judicial and legal process ask these and many other related questions, and some have succeeded in introducing an analytical dimension that has gone beyond the earlier emphasis on institutional description and historical narrative of the development and application of the law. Laws that regulate the activities of businesses, corporations, or labor unions may be studied in terms of the interest groups that are invariably involved in the legislation and adjudication that affect their interests. The decisions of judges may be classified in terms of the interests affected or the issues raised by the particular case. Judges' decisions may be evaluated according to their liberal or conservative or their proregulatory or antiregulatory content. These findings may be explained with reference to the social and political background of the judges before their judicial appointment, or they may be used to predict future decisions in similar cases and controversies. In this way the subdiscipline of judicial and legal process has come to mean much more than the study of constitutions, the statutory enactments of legislatures, and their implementation by executive and judicial branches of government.

3 Executive Process

The most visible symbol of a state is its chief executive. How is he selected? What are his formal and informal responsibilities? How does he exercise the powers inherent in his office, and to what extent can he generate additional powers from his many roles in the political process? What are these roles, and how do they complement or conflict with one another according to the personality of the president, his ambitions and goals, the issues he confronts, his public image and his image among the leaders of foreign states, the strength of his party in the legislature, and many other variables that help to make the study of the executive process an especially fascinating subdiscipline of political science?

As these questions suggest, however, kings, prime ministers, premiers, and presidents have all required staffs of executive assistants for the performance of their duties in office. And government has become so complex that no head of state, whether it be president, governor, or mayor, can expect to carry out all the responsibilities of office without the assistance of a large number of political and administrative personnel. The study of the executive process, then, is in large part the study of bureaucracy—the way it is organized and the way it functions. And one of the most obvious characteristics of an urban society with an industrial economy is a far-flung bureaucratic apparatus with awesome powers over many of the details of each citizen's everyday life.

How, then, are personnel selected for the many executive positions that make up the state's bureaucracy? How do they define their own administrative position and role, and what are the resources available to them as they attempt to maximize their own influence over subordinates and superiors? What are the relationships between executive and legislative branches of government—an especially critical area of study in light of the increasing domination of the executive over the legislative branch? In an age when the executive elites of the state hold in their hands the instruments of war and peace and exercise sweeping control over the nation's economy, it is appropriate to ask whether even the most constitutionally representative system of government is in fact anything other than an administrative establishment. It is of obvious importance to ask also how this establishment can be made responsible to rank-and-file citizens and how executive elites can control the many departments and agencies of government that may be only nominally subordinated to the chief executive's authority.

4 Administrative Organization and Behavior

The study of these last questions leads inevitably to the study of administrators themselves, at all levels of the bureaucratic hierarchy. Current research in this subdiscipline is concerned not only with the formal characteristics of administrative organization, but also with the patterns of behavior that appear to coincide with particular administrative roles, responsibilities, and personality types. How are decisions actually made? How is it that the best-made plans of administrators often produce unintended results, or no results, as the plans are interpreted and implemented by other administrators in other agencies of government or by administrators in the lower echelons of the agency that initiated the plan? Why is the clearest "line organization" of administrative personnel frequently irrelevant to the actual distribution of influence within the administrative hierarchy and to the actual process of decision making? Not responsible to voters, perhaps enjoying the professional security of a civil service appointment, how can an administrator be motivated to perform his tasks with a sense of responsibility to the public interest?

To help answer these difficult and important questions, researchers in this subdiscipline often rely on detailed case studies that trace the interaction of administrators in the formulation and implementation of a specific governmental program. Interviews with participating personnel and studies of documents that derive from a series of issue-related decisions may help to clarify the administrative process that, in modern society, affects all forms of social organization—not only government but also the business corporation, the trade union, the university, and all groups of people with a common interest who are brought together for a collective purpose.

5 Legislative Politics

How are laws made, and how are they made not only in terms of constitutional prescription or the unwritten conventions of the legislature but also in terms of the clash of interests inside and outside the legislative arena? How do the rules and procedures of the legislature, its system of committees and subcommittees, affect the substance of legislative policy? How is power distributed among the legislators themselves? And how is influence over the legislative process related to party and committee membership, seniority, and personal relationships with the chief executive and with other members of the legislature?

Aided by interviews with legislators and by the

analysis of their declared position on roll-call votes, one can usually determine their regard for their party's national program, their relationship to the chief executive and to other party leaders, and their sensitivity to the interests of their constituents and particularly to the special interests that may have supported and financed their election. But how should each of these variables be "weighted" in a legislator's voting on matters related to foreign affairs and national defense; international trade; government aid to business, labor, and agriculture; welfare spending; civil rights; or the more strictly political questions including legislative organization, patronage distribution, and government controls on campaign contributions and spending?

And if it is true that legislatures have lost their policy-making initiative to the executive branches of government, what are the principal functions of legislative institutions? If they function primarily as watchdogs over the executive, how successful are they in monitoring the operations of executive agencies and in maintaining the political responsibility of administrators to rank-and-file citizens through their elected representatives? How is it possible for legislators to be informed about all the far-flung activities of the administrative state? How well do legislators attend to the diverse needs of their many constituents? And what are the implications of any shortcomings in these categories for the traditional notions of popular representation and democratic government?

6 Political Parties and Interest Groups

Many political scientists view the legislative branch of government as primarily an institution that structures the conflict of interests and demands expressed by political parties and other politically oriented groups in the society. From this perspective, the more important questions of politics are in terms of the organization and behavior of these groups, which find in a congress or parliament a means of formalizing their political, economic, and social claims on one another. Especially from the standpoint of "group theory," a law passed by the legislature expresses simply the prevailing distribution of influence among competing groups, each of them seeking to advance its own particular interests.

It is appropriate to ask, then, about the kinds of interests represented by these groups, the characteristics of their leadership and membership, their strategies and tactics for influencing public policy, and the nature of their access to decision makers. In the case of political parties, how are their membership, political access, and policies structured by the electoral system, by their role in the legislature, and by their majority or minority position in the legislative and executive branches of government? To what extent are the electoral supporters of the various parties drawn from the same or from different socioeconomic categories in the society? Do their policies and programs differ? What are the career patterns of their leaders? How frequently, and under what conditions, do they alternate with other groups in controlling or influencing the legislative and executive process—at all levels of government (national, state, and local)— and how does their influence vary from one issue to another? With regard to the groups themselves, we also should ask how they make decisions, how they select their leaders, how they recruit new members, how they raise money, and to what extent power is concentrated or diffused throughout the organizational hierarchy. Answers to these last questions are likely to vary according to the timing of elections and the prominence of particular issues in government and in the mind of the public.

7 Voting and Public Opinion

What is the "mind" of the public? How do the opinions, attitudes, and beliefs of citizens affect the policy making of political elites? What motivates citizens to vote (or not to vote), and why do they vote the way they do? Are voters oriented more toward issues or toward the personality of particular candidates, or is their vote an expression of long-standing loyalty to a particular party, regardless of its candidates or position on the major issues of the day? If voters perceive a discrepancy or inconsistency between these various categories (e.g., between party loyalty and the party's candidate), how are they likely to behave? And how do the various orientations of voters relate to their level of formal education; the extent of their political knowledge; their age, sex, race, religion, profession, income, and place of residence; and the opinions of their close friends?

What explains a voter's shift in political allegiance between elections or his willingness to vote for candidates of different parties in the same election? And what accounts for changes in public opinion on salient issues over time—for example, on the rights of black citizens in a white-dominated society, on the proper role of government in the economy, or on the appropriate foreign policy for combating guerrilla insurgency abroad? To what extent are changes in public opinion on major issues reflected in the decisions of political elites? Or is it the other way around: Do changes in the decisions of political elites precede changes in public opinion? And how does this relationship vary from one issue to another? It is obvious that the recent development of this particular subdiscipline of political science has depended heavily on the sophistication of the science *and* art of survey research—the inference from a small sample of respondents of opinions and characteristics representative of the entire population.

8 Political Socialization and Political Culture

Survey research has also been indispensable in attempts to learn how citizens do acquire the opinions, attitudes, and basic beliefs that help to determine their political behavior. If both my parents (for example) are loyal Republicans and if they consider labor unions an unfortunate blight on the economic landscape, what are the chances that I will vote Democratic and regard businessmen as self-serving profiteers who compromise the public interest? To what extent do people acquire their political opinions from their family, school, church, close acquaintances, and professional colleagues, and how do these patterns of socialization vary from one individual to another according to age, education, income, and many of the other variables already cited?

The characteristics of political socialization and the clusters of opinions, attitudes, and beliefs that make up a society are in turn a part of the society's political culture. And the characteristics of a particular political culture are important variables in helping to answer some fundamental and enduring questions of political science: What accounts for a society's political stability or instability? As Machiavelli well understood, the answer is partly in terms of the extent to which the actual conduct of politics and the "moral habits" of citizens coincide with the norms of behavior prescribed by the state's constitution.

9 Comparative Politics

Any or all of the above subdisciplines may be integrated into a comparative framework. When political scientists look at the political parties or socialization processes of two or more societies, they are able to clarify their generalizations about a particular political system because its characteristics are highlighted by comparison with those of other political systems. Comparative political analysis is also an aid in understanding and identifying those characteristics which may be universal to the political process, regardless of time or place.

In fact, it may be argued that no hypothesis or theory of politics deserves credibility unless it has been tested in several different societies—i.e., cross-culturally. And while the traditional approach to comparative politics tended to describe only the institutional details of several foreign states, more recent trends have been in terms of specific system characteristics compared cross-culturally. It is possible to learn more about executive domination, for example, by looking at executive-legislative relationships not only in the United States but also in Great Britain, in France, and in other countries that represent different stages of socioeconomic development and different types of culture.

It should also be noted here that even for political scientists who concentrate on politics in the United States, a comparative dimension lends their findings a degree of certainty that would otherwise be lacking. This research advantage has long been enjoyed by specialists in state and local politics, even within the framework of the American political system, and these particular fields of inquiry should be identified as additional subdisciplines of political science. From the perspective of comparative politics, new fields of research also have been developed, including comparative studies of political elites, political violence, and political corruption. Political socialization, political culture, and the more traditional areas of study, including political parties and interest groups, have been substantially strengthened by their inclusion within a comparative framework of analysis. Political scientists can help to compensate for the relative lack of scientific precision in their scholarly efforts by broadening their interests beyond the narrow confines of their own social and political setting.

10 Political Development

Especially after World War II, however, it became apparent that students of comparative politics had overlooked a vast reservoir of potential knowledge about the political process. The earlier focus had been on the more developed and modernized states, especially the United States and the countries of Western Europe. But an ever-growing number of political scientists, the emergence of newly independent countries all over the world, the financial support of government institutions and private foundations, the development by American and European researchers of language competence in non-Western cultures, and the increasing sophistication of our research methods and tools of analysis have meant an explosion of interest and knowledge that transcends our own cultural boundaries. Students of political development are today concerned with the effects of urbanization and economic development on political organization and behavior; with the relationship of literacy, education, and the other variables of political culture to citizen behavior and institutional performance; with the way in which political change and socioeconomic development affect the more fundamental differences between various ethnic and religious groups within the same society; and with the ways in which a sense of national identity is created in the place of more traditional loyalties to family, clan, village, tribe, religion, and caste.

The study of less developed states has helped us to understand that the institutions and the supporting attitudes and behavior that define "democracy" do not emerge suddenly from the informed intellect and goodwill of those who choose to write democratic constitutions. And, in fact, all societies may be understood to be in the process of political development. They consequently can be differentiated according to their varying stages of "modernization": the extent to which all citizens have been mobilized by socioeconomic development and cultural change for participation in politics; the extent of national identification by all citizens with the symbols and institutions of a centralizing state; and the capabilities of existing political organizations for accommodating the interests and demands of citizens, thus providing them with a sense of participation and efficacy in the functioning of government. That all states, including the United States, fall short of these ideals does not come as a surprise to students of comparative politics and political development.

11 International Politics and Organization

Because war and peace dramatize the existence of the state and are among the most visible manifestations of political decision making, the study of international politics has been one of the long-standing concerns of political scientists. The focus in this subdiscipline is on the resources that help to explain differences in the distribution of international power; the circumstances that contribute to a balance of power between competing states or to a breakdown in the balance of power; the characteristics of the communications process between foreign states; the interests represented by alliances between states and the patterns of conflict and cooperation between blocs of aligned and nonaligned states; the relationships stimulated by economic trade and interdependence; the efforts toward arms control and disarmament; and those institutions devoted to improving the chances of peace and international cooperation (for example, the League of Nations, the United Nations, and the European Economic Community).

The tendency of most (although not all) students of international politics to treat states as discrete units of analysis, like so many self-conscious individuals on a single stage, has sometimes led to a separation of this subdiscipline from the other subdisciplines of political science, not only in terms of methodology and conceptual styles, but even within the academic hierarchy of the same university. Except for those who study the decision-making process related to foreign policy and international organizations, students of international politics are concerned more with the foreign policies that emanate from the state's institutions, and the impact of those policies on the foreign policies of other states, than they are with the many variables that contribute to an explanation of the structure and functioning of the state itself. Like those political scientists who are presently associated with an emerging subdiscipline identified as "policy analysis," students of international politics are concerned more with the "output" than with the "input" dimensions of the political system.

12 Political Theory and Methodology

One sign of the increasing maturity of a field of knowledge is its explicit, frequently agonizing concern with the problems of theory development within the discipline. The term "political theory" is used here to mean something significantly different from "political philosophy." Philosophy deals with fundamental questions of values, and it studies the logical relationships between normative propositions. Its "truths" are thus not immediately relevant to problems of fact. Unlike a philosophical system of moral principles, a theory can be tested empirically. It consists of propositions that are expressed hypothetically, and the hypotheses in turn predict the relationship between variables that can be observed and measured, however imprecisely. (But the more precise the measurement, the more systematic—and therefore scientific—the theory and its related discipline.) Theories can be proved or disproved or, more formally, "confirmed" or "disconfirmed." A particular philosophy is there for the taking—or the leaving.

It is important to remind the reader again that this is not meant to minimize the important role of political philosophy, which is always at least implicit in political analysis and which enables political scientists to evaluate the implications of their findings in terms of "good" or "bad" and "just" or "unjust." Nor do the authors mean to confuse the issue here by observing that there is a great deal of political theory in the thought of the great political philosophers; i.e., they were concerned not only with the basic value implications of certain styles of political organization and behavior but also with the observation of relationships between such variables as economic and political structures (Plato and Marx), social structure and political stability (Aristotle), and political culture and political authority (Machiavelli and Hobbes). More contemporary political scientists, however, have drawn a sharper line between political philosophy and political theory, and those concentrating on the latter have made clear their intent to render political science as scientific as possible.

"Traditionalists" and "Behavioralists" From this perspective, however, it would be wrong to argue that there is an irreparable split between traditional and behavioral political scientists. The former are no less committed than the latter to precise observation of political phenomena, to the clear definition of categories that help to order these phenomena conceptually, to dispassionate analysis of data, and to the clear communication of findings that help to enlighten students, citizens, political leaders, and professional colleagues. The much-celebrated or much-bemoaned division of political science into traditionalism and behavioralism conceals the extent to which practitioners in both categories share many of the same research interests, advance the same generalizations in their particular subdisciplines, subscribe to the same political and ethical values, and demonstrate a common devotion to academic excellence.

The debates between traditionalists and behavioralists, which were especially intense in the late 1950s and early 1960s, reflected the rapid growth of the discipline following World War II, the proliferation of its fields of inquiry, and the emergence of a new generation of political scientists. This new generation, more so than its predecessors, has been sensitive to the growth in scientific potential of the related social sciences, especially sociology and psychology. New kinds of data have been generated, and not only from the more traditional sources (speeches by public officials, legislative and executive acts, judicial decisions, international agreements, election results); census records and other types of aggregate data, opinion polls, and controlled experiments with a limited number of subjects (including the simulation of political events and relationships) have all helped to enlarge the resources of political scientists committed to improving our understanding of the political process.

The development of new types of data has coincided with the popularization of new analytical techniques: content analysis, model building, factor and regression analysis, and other techniques designed to lend more precision to our findings—without ever threatening to take the place of the scholar's own good judgment. Behavioralists, then, are more likely to use statistical techniques in their study of politics; to be more intent on elaborating testable hypotheses that consist of measurable variables (*not necessarily* susceptible, however, to quantification and statistical measurement); and to be less content with the knowledge that comes from the study of only the formal characteristics of political institutions.

The interest generated among political scientists after the late 1950s by "systems theory" and "structural functionalism" illustrates especially well this last-cited concern of the so-called behavioralists. The new jargon was meant to call attention to the various ways in which all societies, large and small, primitive and modern, organize and carry out the political process. States and their institutions come and go, but the basic "functions" of the political process (e.g., interest articulation and aggregation, political socialization, recruitment, and communication) remain the same. And while the structures performing these functions may vary, all the structures are integrated into a single unit—the political "system." That systems theory is not really theory but simply another way of looking at politics has become increasingly evident, especially to students of comparative politics who have found the gross categories of the systems approach to be less useful than was originally assumed. A measure of the vitality of political science, however, as well as an indication of its relatively low standing as "science," is the continuing search for new sources of data, new tools of analysis, and new perspectives that might impart a little more coherence to the complicated puzzle that we call "politics."

THE USES OF POLITICAL SCIENCE

Political science is a part of man's continuing effort to understand himself. This in turn suggests that the study of political science belongs to the academic tradition that is associated with an education in the liberal arts. A liberal education is meant to prepare individuals to think more clearly about themselves and about their relationships with others, to be more tolerant of diversity, to be less hasty in their judgments of the unfamiliar, and to get more meaning out of life regardless of where they are or what they do.

What students of political science do with their education, then, is wide-ranging and frequently far-reaching. Approximately one-third to one-half of those who major in political science in college go on to law school, and a degree in law opens the way to many professional opportunities that are not directly related to the practice of law. Depending upon the college or university and the characteristics of its students, another 5 to 25 percent of undergraduate political science majors continue their education in graduate school. They may seek a Ph.D. in political science and subsequent employment on a university faculty, or they may earn an M.A. in business, economics, or public administration as a prerequisite to the higher executive positions in business and government. But students with a B.A. in political science also may be found in the executive hierarchies of business corporations, in organized labor, in consumers' and special-interest-oriented groups, in public and private schools as teachers and administrators, and at all levels of government as civil service employees or as staff personnel associated with particular political leaders or their party organizations.

The student of political science is no more assured of a respected niche in society than any of his student colleagues in most of the other academic disciplines. But the very characteristics of the discipline, including the conceptual challenge to make some sense out of the complexity of its subject matter, should help to equip the persevering student of political science with intellectual resources that are not found among most citizens, or even among most college graduates. And then there is the drama and excitement of dealing with materials that relate to the ways in which we live; whether we like it or not, politics defines the basic conditions of social life, within which we define ourselves. Some of the many ways that politics impinges upon us, in terms of what we do and what we think, are the subject matter of the chapters that follow.

STUDY-GUIDE QUESTIONS

1 Why are the natural sciences more "scientific" than the social sciences?
2 How does the study of politics today differ from the study of politics in the Middle Ages?
3 How would you distinguish between the study of political philosophy and the study of voting and public opinion?
4 What is a variable? Identify a variable in physics and one in political science. How would you "measure" these variables?
5 Assume that you are carrying out survey re-

search among samples of voters, legislators, and public administrators. Write several questions that you would want to ask the respondents in each of these three categories. What do you hope to learn from the responses to your questions?

REFERENCES

American Political Science Association: *A Guide to Graduate Study in Political Science,* 2d ed., Washington, 1973.

Bluhm, William T.: *Theories of the Political System,* 2d ed., Prentice-Hall, Inc., Englewood Cliffs, N.J., 1971.

Dahl, Robert A.: *Modern Political Analysis,* 2d ed., Prentice-Hall, Inc., Englewood Cliffs, N.J., 1972.

Easton, David: *A Systems Analysis of Political Life,* John Wiley & Sons, Inc., New York, 1965.

———: "Political Science," in *International Encyclopedia of the Social Sciences,* Crowell Collier and Macmillan, Inc., New York, 1968, vol. 12, pp. 282–297.

Eulau, Heinz: *The Behavioral Persuasion in Politics,* Random House, Inc., New York, 1963.

——— and James G. March (eds.): *Political Science,* Prentice-Hall, Inc., Englewood Cliffs, N.J., 1969.

Hacker, Andrew: *The Study of Politics: The Western Tradition and American Origins,* 2d ed., McGraw-Hill Book Company, New York, 1973.

Irish, Marian D. (ed.): *Political Science: Advance of the Discipline,* Prentice-Hall, Inc., Englewood Cliffs, N.J., 1968.

Lasswell, Harold: *Politics: Who Gets What, When, How?* McGraw-Hill Book Company, New York, 1936.

———: *The Future of Political Science,* Atherton Press, Inc., New York, 1963.

Shively, W. Phillips: *The Craft of Political Research: A Primer,* Prentice-Hall, Inc., Englewood Cliffs, N.J., 1974.

Somit, Albert, and Joseph Tanenhaus: *American Political Science: A Profile of a Discipline,* Atherton Press, Inc., New York, 1964.

Sorauf, Francis J.: *Political Science: An Informal Overview,* Charles E. Merrill Books, Inc., Columbus, Ohio, 1965.

Strauss, Leo: *What Is Political Philosophy?* The Free Press of Glencoe, Inc., New York, 1959.

Van Dyke, Vernon: *Political Science: A Philosophic Analysis,* Stanford University Press, Stanford, Calif., 1960.

PART ONE

CONCEPTS AND IDEOLOGIES

Chapter 2

The Nature of the State

Political science has been variously defined as the study of life in an organized community, as the study of the state (whether the ancient Greek city-state or the nation-state of modern times), and as the study of power relationships between individuals and groups, i.e., what we call "politics" ("who gets what, when, and how."). However, during most of the history of the discipline known as "political science," the emphasis has been placed upon the modern *national* state—its institutions, laws, and processes. Hence no introduction to political science can ignore an analysis of modern nation-states—the framework within which the domestic political process operates and among which conflicts of national ambition pose the question of human survival.

Just what *is* the state? Is it a natural or an artificial institution? How did it originate? Could men get along without it today? Did they ever do so in the remote past? Is the state divinely ordained, or was it conceived in sin? Is it a force working toward good or toward evil? Does it promote progress or restrain it? How much power should the state have, and in what spheres of human activity? Where should the political authority of the state be located—in the hands of one man, of a few, or of the many? Is the essential character of the state to be found in the force that it wields or in such ethical attributes as justice and law?

These bewildering questions have been the concern of political philosophers at least since the days of ancient Athens. The more we learn from the widening researches of anthropologists, the more it would appear that the state—in at least a rudimentary form—has existed for as long as man has inhabited this planet. Even where explicit theorizing about the state is lacking, anthropological evidence indicates that the actual governmental structures and laws of primitive peoples reflect their ideas about the role of the state in human society. Conscious efforts to formulate principles concerning the state—in other words, political philosophy—began, in the Western world, with the ancient Greeks. Thus it is sometimes said that, for Western civilization, the study of the institutions and principles of politics starts with the Greeks because they "invented" it.

ORIGIN OF THE STATE

Down through the centuries, political thinkers have wrestled with the question: How did the state begin? Lacking adequate historical or anthropological evidence, they were compelled to invent various explanations. Thus the state has, in times past, been thought to have derived from the will of God, the fall of man in the Garden of Eden, the social contract (by which men consciously established the state), the processes of evolution (the state having developed like a living organism), the family (the patriarchal model), the institution of private property, or simple force or conquest.

On the basis of existing knowledge, it would appear that the state originated with the family, which later developed into the clan and the tribe, with habits of obedience carrying over from the father to the tribal council of elders. A more formal organization of government, in the sense of explicit rules and established procedures for resolving social conflict, seems to date from the rise of a pastoral economy and the institution of property. Both these presented problems calling for stronger social controls and leadership—the latter usually exercised by a chieftain whose rule frequently became hereditary.

At a later period, when population began to outrun the supply of food, many previously nomadic peoples settled upon fertile lands that could be cultivated. With the rise of an agricultural economy, the territorial state came into being; territorial attachment supplemented the earlier bond of kinship. War and conquest seem also to have played an important role in the rise of the state and government, their importance obviously varying in different times and places. Thus the state is the end product of many factors—biological, economic, cultural, and military. Like all human institutions, it cannot be explained in terms of any single factor, nor is its development described by an unbroken line of progressive evolution from the past to the present.

THEORIES CONCERNING THE ORIGIN OF THE STATE

Only in very recent times, and with the aid of the researches of archaeologists and anthropologists, has it become possible for us to draw even the very hazy sketch, outlined above, of the development of political institutions. Down through the centuries speculation was the rule, and even today, despite conflicting evidence, many old theories continue to have their supporters.

The Divine Theory

Perhaps the oldest of all theories of the origin of the state is that God ordained and established it. This notion prevailed in the ancient Oriental empires, where the rulers themselves were regarded as the descendants of gods. The early Hebrews thought that the Lord had created their government, and the early Christians believed that God had imposed the state upon man as a punishment for his sins, as represented by Adam's fall from grace in the Garden of Eden. Centuries later, Thomas Paine, the pamphleteer of the American Revolution, expressed much the same idea when he declared: "Government, like dress, is the badge of lost innocence." These ideas, in slightly different form, still mark some of our conventional wisdom today, especially when we dismiss all politics as "dirty" or describe government as a "necessary evil."

Throughout the Middle Ages, the divine origin of the state went unquestioned, although the struggle for supremacy between the popes and the Holy Roman emperors indicated disagreement as to whether temporal rulers derived their authority directly from God or indirectly through the pope.

The Protestant Reformation strengthened the claims of national monarchs that they had received their authority directly from God, and soon many of them came to assert not only that temporal government was of divine origin but also that they themselves, as persons, ruled "by the grace of God." This theory of the "divine right of kings" was even more emphatically asserted later on when the rising middle classes began to advance the doctrine of popular sovereignty. The revolutions of the seventeenth and eighteenth centuries were waged in the name of the people against the divine pretensions of royal absolutism.

The Social Contract Theory

The theory of popular sovereignty, which ultimately triumphed over that of the divine right of kings, was based in large part on the notion that men had originally created the state by means of a social contract to which each individual had consented. Many different versions of the social contract theory were advanced during the period of the religious wars and in the course of the popular revolutions in England, the United States, and France. Two of the best-known and most influential social contract theorists were Thomas Hobbes (1588–1679) and John Locke (1632–1704). Hobbes outlined a social contract by means of which man surrendered his natural right of self-government to an absolute sovereign (either king or parliament—although Hobbes preferred a monarchy). Locke described an agreement under which man retained almost all his natural rights under a limited, parliamentary type of government responsible to the "people"—or at least to the propertied upper classes of England.

Once an accepted view of the origins of the state, however, the notion of social contract was ready at hand for later and more democratically oriented thinkers (including Jean-Jacques Rousseau) simply to enlarge the category of people defined as "citizens." And by the early twentieth century in most of Western Europe and in the United States, neither property ownership nor religion nor sex was an accepted criterion for restricting political participation. As Rousseau (1712–1778) had argued, the people were sovereign, and Rousseau's sovereign was as absolute in its exercise of authority as Hobbes's was. But the definitions of "people," "citizenship," and "political participation" were not restricted to a narrow socioeconomic oligarchy, as they had been by Locke. Unlike both Hobbes and Locke, Rousseau insisted on the right of *all* the people to participate in the affairs of government. What was the ethical justification for this democratic orientation? Rousseau answered that political authority was not legitimate unless it was exercised directly by the people: The only law that individuals must obey is the law they give to themselves. Are they bound to obey laws that have been made by representatives they have elected? Rousseau answered "no" to this difficult question, but he then admitted that under such a principle of political organization, it would be impossible for true democracy to exist (especially when the number of citizens in the state was large).

Not wanting to be impaled on the doctrinal horns of either anarchism or authoritarianism, more contemporary political philosophers have been hard pressed to give a convincing answer to the question concerning the relationship between legitimate authority and political representation. But Rousseau clearly described the outlines of the dilemma, and he also made it clear that legitimate political authority originates in the social contract between citizens and government. In this sense he followed Locke in concluding that a government act that is contrary to the original contract is illegitimate and that citizens are consequently entitled to resist, even rebel. This part of the social contract theory remains fundamental to the principles of democratic government and to any notion of civil liberties that derive from "natural rights"—rights that are inherent in people as individuals, regardless of the acts of government.

The Force Theory

Another theory holds that the state originated in conquest and coercion. Early writers often argued that the state was based upon injustice and was essentially evil; the strong had imposed their will upon the weak and then had thrown the cloak of pretended legitimacy over their disregard for the rights of others. The early Christians so regarded the Roman regime, and medieval church writers also stressed the role of force in the establishment of the power of secular rulers of whom the church disapproved. In the eighteenth-century era of revolution, absolutist governments were similarly denounced, though in secular terms.

Not all writers, however, regarded force—or the state that it had produced—as necessarily evil. In the latter part of the nineteenth century, as nationalism became an increasingly powerful force, a school of thought arose in Germany which argued that force was the most characteristic attribute of the state, that "might made right," and that power was its own justification. Hence physically powerful peoples were the "best" peoples, and the state, *as* power, was superior to other forms of human association and above the ordinary run of moral considerations. This view was by no means confined to German theorists, however. Note that this argument concerning the origin of the state, wherever it may be advanced, does not sanction any resistance to the acts of government, nor does it preserve to the citizen those "natural rights" of "life, liberty, and the pursuit of happiness" that most social contract thinkers reserved exclusively to the individual.

The Natural Theory

The ancient Greeks viewed man as inseparable from the state, which they considered to be not only a necessity for human survival but also the means whereby man could achieve the "good life." Aristotle declared that man was "by nature a political animal" who could fulfill himself only through the state; man outside the state was, indeed, not a man at all, but either a god or a beast.

This concept of the state as a natural, growing, inevitable, and beneficent institution was carried further in later ages by the impact of historical and scientific research. Although many writers, such as Herbert Spencer, sought to interpret the idea of evolution so as to minimize and discredit the state, others came to look upon the state as almost a living organism, evolving into higher and better forms. The English "idealist" school of the late nineteenth century did much to revive the Aristotelian idea that the state was natural, not artificial, and that it was a force for progress toward the good life rather than an evil—necessary or otherwise.[1]

The implications of this view, however, were inevitably conservative: What exists must exist for a good reason, or otherwise it would not exist. The state has evolved out of a complex set of human needs, and neither these needs nor the characteristics of the state can be totally understood through human reason. People should be extremely reluctant, then, to tamper with existing institutions and social relationships. (This argument was perhaps most persuasively expressed by the English political thinker and statesman Edmund Burke [1729–1797].) Unlike the notions of social contract, the natural theory of the state was not a sanction for the assertion that citizen rights exist independently of governmental authority. The individual's only rights are those which are prescribed by the state and the long-standing traditions of society. These latter may act as a restraint on the actions of the state, but, again, citizen liberties are not an "automatic" right of the individual in a political context. Nor does the natural theory of the state guarantee to citizens any necessary rights of participating, however indirectly, in those political decisions which affect their lives and living conditions.

A comparison of the principal characteristics of these several approaches to explaining the origin of the state points up the critical importance to democratic government of the ideas of social contract and natural right.

ESSENTIAL ELEMENTS OF THE STATE

The modern state has four essential elements: people, territory, government, and sovereignty (or independence). Each of these essentials requires more extended discussion.

People

Numbers To say that the state is made up of people is to affirm the obvious, but further questions immediately arise. How many people are needed? Can a state have too small or too large a population? In any particular state, is the population increasing, decreasing, or remaining stationary? What are the factors influencing population changes? What roles are being played by food supply, technology, urbanization, religion, education, and war? Should public policy be directed toward stimulating, retarding, or ignoring the rate of population change? While some modern states (e.g., the United States, the Soviet Union, and Canada) are still underpopulated relative to area, resources, and similar factors, others (e.g., Italy, Egypt, and India) are confronted by the problem of a population that is expanding too rapidly for their natural or technological resources. Should these

---

[1] For an excellent exposition of this view, see Thomas Hill Green, *Lectures on the Principles of Political Obligation*, R. L. Nettleship (ed.), Longmans, Green, London, 1885–1888, 3 vols.; see also John R. Rodman (ed.), *The Political Theory of T. H. Green*, Appleton-Century-Crofts, Inc., New York, 1964.

latter states encourage birth control, try to increase their production of food and other essential commodities, or go to war to wrest land and resources from richer neighboring states?

On the other hand, a state with a very small population may find it difficult or impossible to maintain its independence against states with greater manpower. While technological progress by a small state may serve to balance the scales against a populous but backward rival, the spread of technical knowledge to the latter may ultimately become fatal to the smaller nation. At least until the mid-1950s, the lack of significant population growth in France contributed to the decline of France as a world power and, in relation to France's resources, to a relatively slow rate of economic growth—especially in comparison with both East and West Germany. The ideal of national self-determination (that each distinct nationality is entitled to govern itself as an independent state, free from foreign domination) poses the practical question of whether a state that is small in population and territory can make good its bid for independence against, for example, a political colossus like the Soviet Union or Communist China. And where small states have survived in the apparently hostile presence of one or more of the greater powers (Switzerland during World War II, for example, or contemporary Austria and Finland), they have been able to do so because the greater powers have usually found it economically and diplomatically useful to perpetuate the smaller states' independent status.

Characteristics What has just been said serves to introduce other aspects of the state that relate to its people. What kind of people constitute a particular state? Are they literate, well educated, and culturally and vocationally advanced? Are they skilled in modern technology? Cultural levels are as important as numbers—probably more so, under modern conditions. Are they a homogeneous people, made up of one rather than many nationalities, and do they speak a single language? Do they have, perhaps, a common religion and subscribe to the same body of political and cultural traditions? Homogeneity is an important factor in state survival; a homogeneous people is likely to be more fully agreed on the fundamentals of its political system and hence better able to communicate and to live harmoniously together. On the other hand, a state made up of peoples of diverse races, nationalities, religions, languages, and customs may be subjected to greater internal cleavage and stress in periods of domestic or international difficulty. It must be observed, however, that various factors can produce deep disunity among a homogeneous people, while, on the other hand, a state made up of heterogeneous elements (e.g., the United States, the Soviet Union, and Switzerland) may display a surprising degree of unity, particularly when confronted by external danger.

Nationalism The element of nationality, just referred to, requires further explanation. It is a modern concept, dating from the rise of the national state itself. In ancient times the state was either a city-state, such as Athens, Sparta, or early Rome, or a far-flung empire, such as those of Macedon and Persia. Even at this early date, peoples were aware of their racial or cultural differences, and each people tended to regard itself as superior. The term "barbarian" was first employed by the Greeks to designate non-Greeks; the Jews considered themselves a chosen people. But such ethnocentric feelings were not the same as the modern spirit of nationalism, which has made its appearance concurrently with the rise of the national state as a new form of political organization. As Spain, France, and England were transformed from clusters of feudal principalities into national monarchies, their peoples gradually came to regard themselves as Spaniards, Frenchmen, or Englishmen, rather than as Andalusians, Burgundians, Gascons, Yorkshiremen, or other provincial inhabitants. In other words, the enlargement of territory under a single ruler was matched by a larger loyalty, first to the ruler as a person, and then to the nation thus brought into being. The new sense of nationalism—of belonging to a homogeneous, unified group—was the result of many factors. The invention of the printing press, the development of vernacular (native, popular) languages, wars to secure or maintain the nation's independence, a national church, the building up of a common history and tradition—all these and many other forces combined to produce this modern attitude or spirit called "nationalism."

The basic ingredients of nationalism are common

or related blood, a common language, a common religion, a common historical tradition, and, above all, common customs and habits. Custom has been called the "amalgam" that cements and holds together the other ingredients. Not all these ingredients need to be present among a people to produce the spirit of nationalism; again, Switzerland, the United States, and the Soviet Union may be cited as examples of countries that are pervaded by a strong sense of national unity despite differences in national origins, language, religion, and culture patterns. Hitler claimed that race (or blood) was the only real basis of nationality and that language and environmental conditioning had nothing to do with "making a German." This idea has been generally rejected in favor of the notion that a nationality is the product of the varied influences mentioned above.

Thus a nationality is a culturally homogeneous group; such a group, however, may not enjoy political independence, but may be merely a part of a larger state or empire. Many nationalities were included within the old Austro-Hungarian Empire, which was dissolved at the close of World War I; today approximately 100 nationalities are included within the Soviet Union. National minorities are to be found in many other states, since no amount of devotion to the principle of national self-determination can achieve so perfect a drawing of state boundaries that each state will contain only people of a single nationality. It is impossible to unscramble the ethnographic omelet resulting from countless centuries of migration and intermarriage. However, if a nationality achieves political unity and independence, it becomes a nation or nation-state.

Territory

How much territory is necessary for the maintenance of the state? In the modern world there are presumably sovereign, independent states of all sizes and shapes ranging from the Soviet Union (one-sixth of the land surface of the globe) to such tiny principalities as Luxembourg and Monaco (which are slightly smaller in total land area than the state of Rhode Island). According to international law, independent states are equal in rights and status, regardless of inequalities in area and population. Yet in reality a tiny state finds itself in a precarious position, and it usually must seek protection from one or more of the Great Powers in order to maintain its existence. Though small states may be nominally and legally sovereign, they could not continue today without the toleration or active assistance of greater powers. Some small states have been permanently neutralized by international agreement (Switzerland); others occupy the status of protectorates; still others are known as "client states" of greater powers or as belonging to a cluster of states gathered under the aegis of one of the Great Powers.

The trend toward national self-determination has increased the number of small states at the very time when technological and economic developments have emphasized the advantages of larger, rather than smaller, political units. Each new national state means more barriers to international trade, another national currency, probably intensified national antagonisms and new minority problems, and further fragmentation of land and other resources essential to subsistence.[2] While not even such gigantic states as the Soviet Union and the United States are entirely self-sufficient (in the sense of possessing within their own borders all the raw materials and other resources they need), such Great Powers are far more self-reliant than tiny states that lack enough land, industrial materials, power resources, or other essentials for independent survival. Even some major powers (most notably Great Britain) are unable to produce enough food to feed their populations and must consequently rely on heavy agricultural imports from other countries. (See Figure 2.1, where GNP, or gross national product, is a measure of the total market value of goods and services annually produced.) Both Italy and Japan are examples of

---

[2]The European Economic Community (or Common Market) was established in 1957 and by 1973 it included nine full members: Belgium, Denmark, France, West Germany, Great Britain, Ireland, Italy, Luxembourg, and the Netherlands. The Common Market was organized in order to reduce and eventually to eliminate tariffs and other trade obstacles among the member nations, to coordinate the monetary and fiscal policies of their governments, and to rationalize the distribution of economic and manpower resources in Western Europe. Similar international trading organizations, none as successful as the Common Market, have been established for countries in Eastern Europe, Latin America, southern Asia, and sub-Sahara Africa.

THE NATURE OF THE STATE

Figure 2.1 Gross national product in U.S. dollars and total imports as percentage of GNP in Italy, the United Kingdom, and the United States, 1970.

modern countries that import substantial amounts of food, iron, coal, oil, and most other basic industrial commodities to keep pace with the needs of their industries and their people. The smaller, less economically developed states are, on the other hand, usually one-crop or one-product countries that are very dependent on fluctuations in the international market and on those states which are the major customers for their products. And economic dependency usually means political dependency.

Resources, Technology, Climate Thus resources are as important as area—indeed, more important. Little England and medium-sized Germany became Great Powers because of their industrial development, which in turn was possible only because of rich natural resources to which technology could be applied. Climate is part and parcel of the resource picture; a mild, temperate climate, coupled with adequate rainfall on fertile soil, means abundant crop yields. Moreover, peoples inhabiting temperate areas are likely to be healthier and more energetic than those living in the tropics. It is no accident that peoples living under favorable climatic conditions (Greeks, Romans, English, French, etc.) have left a deep imprint on world history.

Geography Location is also an important factor in a state's survival and growth. Whether a state occupies an island, a peninsula, or an entire continent; whether it has access to the sea or is landlocked; whether it is protected by natural barriers, such as oceans, seas, rivers, mountains, or deserts; whether it has powerful, aggressive neighbor states—these and similar considerations will affect its economic, political, and military policies. Island powers like Great Britain and Japan developed strong navies, whereas continental powers like Russia, Germany, and France typically relied on the military strength of their land armies. Peninsular powers usually engage in foreign trade but must keep navies to protect them from attack. The United States, a continental power with two long coastlines and outlying island dependencies, first developed as a naval power. Its unusual geographic security (now ended with the development of nuclear weapons delivered by long-range bombers, missiles, or orbiting satellites) made it possible for the United States to devote its energies to the domestic development of its abundant economic resources without fear of foreign invasion. At the same time, these fortunate circumstances fostered among many United States citizens (especially those living in the Midwestern states and those of German ethnic origin) an attitude of indifference or aversion to United States involvement in the world wars and to international affairs in general.[3]

Government

Government is the important—indeed, indispensable—machinery by means of which the state maintains its existence, carries on its functions, and realizes its policies and objectives. But government is never identical with the state because the latter is the entire community of persons, whereas the government includes only a relatively small proportion of the population. Moreover, the state is a continuing, virtually permanent entity, while a particular government may be completely obliterated (as by revolution) without destroying the existence or rights of the state as such. While states may disappear as the result of conquest by other states and while new states may be formed out of old states or out of their colonies, such developments are very different from the internal changes in forms of government that have occurred so frequently in the present century. Italy, as a state, has endured through constitutional monarchy, Fascist dictatorship, and democratic republic; Germany, through autocratic empire, Weimar Republic, the Nazi regime, and post–World War II bifurcation; and France, through absolute monarchy, republic, empire, limited monarchy, republic (again), empire (again), republic (again), foreign occupation, the Fourth Republic, and the Fifth Republic. Clearly, these states (and others that have passed through revolutionary transformations) are more than, and distinct from, their governments at any given moment. The rights and obligations of states under international law are not canceled or altered by revolutionary changes in their governments. Governments may change, but—as the Dutch philosopher Hugo Grotius put it in the seventeenth century—"states are immortal."

Sovereignty

The fourth essential element of the state is sovereignty. The word "sovereignty" denotes supreme and final legal authority, above and beyond which no further legal power exists. Jean Bodin defined sovereignty as perpetual, indivisible, and inalienable (meaning that the sovereign authority cannot surrender or delegate any of its powers). Sovereignty, then, has at least two dimensions: *internal* supremacy within the territory of the state and *external* independence from direct political control by any other state or political authority, e.g., an international organization. One could scarcely speak of a state which did not possess adequate powers to control and regulate affairs within its borders or which was at the mercy of irresponsible groups; similarly, in international law, the term "state" is reserved for independent, sovereign entities and is not used with reference to colonial or other dependencies.

In this connection, it is important to note the gradual evolution, between the sixteenth and mid-twentieth centuries, of the British *Empire* into the British *Commonwealth of Nations.* During the course of the evolution from empire to commonwealth, many British colonies were granted successive installments of self-government, followed later by dominion status; this was first achieved by Canada in 1867 and later extended to other British possessions. Today, the nations of the Commonwealth are fully sovereign states, and their sovereignty is all the more obvious as they argue among themselves about the appropriate economic, diplomatic, and even military policies to adopt with regard to the remnants of racism in Africa (especially in Southern Rhodesia and South Africa). For many years, however, their sovereignty was a matter of scholarly dispute, particularly with respect to their foreign relations, which were heavily influenced by the British government's calculations of its own national security. This in turn demonstrates the difficulty of drawing a hard-and-fast line between the several dimensions of sovereignty.

---

[3] The development of nuclear weapons and intercontinental delivery systems has revolutionized traditional policies of national defense. Today there is no place to hide. Area, population, resources, and technology are still important, but no spot on the globe is immune to nuclear destruction. Isolationism is as obsolete as the crossbow.

Actually, there is no such thing as absolute, utterly unqualified power, and hence no absolute sovereignty, whether in domestic or international affairs. Even the most powerful kings, dictators, and presidents have been constrained by events, circumstances, and political forces that they could not control, as well as by the practical limits of public patience under oppressive measures. In international affairs, even the mightiest nation must shape its policies in accordance with the realities of the international situation, and smaller states find their range of possible action seriously circumscribed. Many so-called sovereign states—legally independent and equal members of the family of nations—are actually dependent in military or economic matters upon one or more of the Great Powers.

Internal Sovereignty With respect to domestic or internal sovereignty, there are wide variations among states as to the location and scope of sovereign power. In theory, sovereignty is indivisible, and yet all *federal* systems rest upon at least an implied assumption that sovereignty can be divided between the nation on the one hand and the states or provinces on the other. Even among states that accept the doctrine of popular sovereignty, there are marked discrepancies as to how frequently and in what manner the sovereign people may express their power. In the United States, for example, there is no national referendum, even to pass upon proposed amendments to the federal Constitution, and in Great Britain no provision whatever is made for the initiative, referendum, or recall.

Sovereignty has been a useful concept of political science, particularly since the rise of the nation-state, which really gave birth to the idea. However, it is a legal—and philosophical—concept and should not be regarded as a literal description of the composition and incidence of *political* power. Discrepancies can always be noted between the legal sovereign (whether king or people) and those who actually possess political power, e.g., cabinet ministers, party leaders, or powerful interest groups. However, the idea of the state requires this further concept of ultimate legal authority because no matter what forces or pressures have determined the content of a law, only the sovereign power of the state can legitimately proclaim it as law, invest it with dignity and prestige, and support it with sanctions in order to secure observance.

Development of the Concept of Sovereignty The concept of sovereignty was developed in conjunction with the rise of the modern nation-state. It is significant that the Middle Ages produced discussions of the limits of secular, as against spiritual, authority, but not in the terminology of *state* sovereignty—because the state, as we know it, did not then exist. It is also noteworthy that the word "sovereignty" is derived from "sovereign" (king or monarch), thus reflecting the fact that early writers on sovereignty were attributing powers to the king rather than to the state as such. In many countries, kings were struggling to assert their authority against the nobility on the one hand and against the church on the other. Even after the Reformation, when national churches were being established under the aegis of the state rather than that of the papacy, monarchs were often still forced to contend with the clerical power.

The so-called father of the modern theory of sovereignty was Jean Bodin, the French political philosopher already referred to in this chapter and the preceding one. Bodin was not only a lawyer but also a supporter of strong monarchical government, which, for Bodin, was not synonymous with arbitrary despotism. He was instead dedicated to providing the French monarchy with a philosophical basis for exerting state power over those institutions and practices supported by the common law. *Common law* consists of the decisions made by judges as they settle cases and controversies according to precedent over a prolonged period of time. Bodin argued that the common law was not superior to the law promulgated by government (meaning the king), and by asserting the primacy of the monarchy in law making, he sought to strengthen the king in his struggles with the French nobility and also to bring to an end the protracted conflict between French Catholics and Protestants. Because the king was *sovereign,* nothing could legitimately restrain his law-making power—at least in these areas of state policy.

In his *Six Books of the Commonwealth* (1576),

Bodin described sovereignty as supreme and perpetual power over subjects and their possessions, unrestrained by existing law in its promulgation of new law. With more than a little inconsistency in his argument, however, Bodin also insisted that the sovereign power was limited by divine law (which comes from God), natural law (which is perceived through reason), international law, the *leges imperii* (laws of the realm, or perhaps the constitution), and the rights associated with private property. Despite Bodin's use of words like "absolute" and "unrestrained," then, he clearly contemplated a limited, constitutional monarch instead of an absolute tyrant. It remained for later philosophers, including Rousseau, to redefine sovereignty in terms of the *people* rather than a king.

The concept of sovereignty was also influenced, but in a different manner, by the writings of Niccolò Machiavelli (1469–1527). At a time when the petty princes of Italy were objecting to church claims of domination in temporal matters, Machiavelli prepared a series of recommendations for his prince, Lorenzo de Medici of Florence. Among them was the suggestion that the prince had the right to throw off the shackles of the church and to avoid outside domination by the Papal State. Machiavelli's advice meant that the temporal prince might disregard external control. This laid a foundation for the second phase of sovereignty, that of the *external* independence of the state. In this sense the concept means that the state is to be entirely independent of external control, whether spiritual or temporal.

The Implications of Sovereignty for International Politics Although he could not have foreseen the results of his argument, Machiavelli thus laid the basis for *international* conflict between sovereign states, none of them subordinate to any agency or principle transcending their own self-interest. And one of the major problems for political philosophers today is to determine the extent to which the state ought to be free to make war on other states, to intervene in their internal affairs, and to exploit their resources and oppress their citizens, directly through political control or indirectly through economic penetration.

It was Hugo Grotius who first responded to the problem of defining the rights *and* responsibilities of states in international politics. For Grotius, there is a natural law that ought to regulate the affairs of nations, just as there is a natural law that ought to limit the power of government over its citizens. This natural law can be perceived through informed reason, and in both domestic and international politics it ought to serve as a restraint on the exercise of political power.

Again it becomes clear that the vague but essential principles of natural law and natural rights are fundamental to any attempt to check arbitrary authority in the regulation of human affairs. And the reader might well pause at this point to consider what the specific content of natural law is and how—once discovered—it might be implemented, thereby putting international peace and domestic tranquillity in the place of war and domestic strife.

Sovereignty in the United States Who, or what, is sovereign in the United States? A ready answer would be "the people," since our democratic government is based on the principle of popular sovereignty. Yet not all the people may or do vote; moreover, the voters participate only slightly, if at all, in the actual day-to-day work of government, such as legislation, administration, and adjudication. In a popular referendum the voter may participate in the making of state or local (but not federal) law or in the amendment of his state's constitution or his city's charter. To this extent he is exercising, respectively, legislative or constituent (constitution-making) sovereignty. But under our federal system sovereignty is theoretically divided between the national government and the states, with each supreme in its sphere of powers, as these powers are delineated by the United States Supreme Court. Today it is doubtful whether the states are truly sovereign; they may be more aptly described, to use the language of the Court, as "quasisovereign."

Hence the voter's direct participation in legislation and constitutional amendment at the state or local level does not affect the federal governmental process or answer the question of the sovereignty of that government. Where, in the federal government, does *its* sovereignty reside—in Congress, the president, the Supreme Court? Actually, none of these branches of government is sovereign, although to each has been delegated the *exercise* of some portion of sovereignty. Congress apparently exercises legislative sovereignty, but only within constitutional limits as determined by the Supreme Court. Some writers have argued that the Court most closely approximates the supreme, sovereign agency of our government because it can pass upon the constitutionality of legislative, executive, and administrative actions and does in effect "make" the Constitution by deciding what its phrases mean and how they should be applied. Yet judges are appointed; presidents, congressmen, and senators are elected; and the Congress and president can and have set limits on the jurisdictional authority of the courts. Thus we are brought back to the idea that the people who elect these officials are, after all, sovereign—at least at election time.

To this concept of *electoral* sovereignty must be added the admittedly indirect share that the voters have in *constituent* sovereignty. Ultimate sovereignty in the United States is to be found in the body—or, rather, bodies—that together amend our federal Constitution. Collectively, the two houses of Congress and the legislatures (or special conventions) in the several states amend the Constitution and are therefore sovereign. But in the ultimate analysis, the voters who choose the members of these bodies indirectly hold the ultimate, final power to determine the form of the government under which they are to live. Such constituent sovereignty, rather than ordinary *legislative* or *electoral* sovereignty, would appear to be that "supreme power" to which Bodin referred.

GENERAL CHARACTERISTICS AND ATTRIBUTES OF THE STATE

As was observed at the beginning of this chapter, the state has always been a controversial subject. Even today, when people no longer entertain fanciful notions about how the state originated, they differ as sharply as ever in their judgments of it. To many, the state appears as an evil, whether necessary or otherwise—a force tending toward corruption, impeding economic and social progress, and constantly threatening human liberty. To as many others, the state represents the highest of human impulses: Its purpose is viewed as the raising of ethical standards; its hallmark, as justice; and its essence, as law, based upon right reason and popular consent.

Attitudes toward the state have, of course, been largely influenced by the behavior of particular states at particular periods in history. The ideas of Plato and Aristotle reflected events in ancient Athens; the Stoic aversion to political participation was an outgrowth of the collapse of the Greek system of city-states. Early Christianity viewed the state as punishment for man's original sin, and eighteenth-century philosophers and radicals denounced all states as evil because the states of their day and age were absolute, corrupt monarchies. By the beginning of the nineteenth century, the pendulum of political thought had reached a point at the extreme opposite from Aristotle's view of man as a naturally social being; the state was now considered unnatural—an artificial contrivance to be kept weak lest it destroy men's liberties. Toward the close of the nineteenth century, at least in England and Germany, the philosophic tide began to turn, and extreme doctrines of hostility toward the state were qualified by a growing appreciation of the good, constructive achievements of the modern state, such as public education and health, the amelioration of evil social and economic conditions, and the uplifting of moral as well as material standards.

Evaluating the Performance of the Modern State

It seems clear that our current attitude toward the state is far more pragmatic than attitudes in past periods of history. In general, states are judged by their works, with some rated "good" and others "bad." The world's contemporary criteria are largely those of democracy and humanitarianism, although the governments that proclaim their pursuit of these ideals frequently follow strange and contradictory paths. Even most "authoritarian" regimes (or those which severely restrict opposition to the existing government) profess their devotion to democracy and human welfare and claim to be governing in the interests of all their citizens. The question is no longer whether the state is good or bad in the abstract, but rather how well it does its job—and, speaking broadly, its job is conceded to be the promotion of the welfare of its inhabitants and a decent respect for the rights of other peoples and states. Only visionaries believe that modern man could get along without state and government, and even the most rugged of individualists concede the necessity for much state regulation and control in order to cope with the myriad problems of our complex technological era. Thus the controversy is not in terms of state or no state, control or no control. Rather, it concerns the degree of state intervention, its precise form, and the methods of administration necessary to bring about the desired objectives of public policy.

But it should be remembered that the ways in which Americans choose to resolve these last-cited problems of government are not necessarily applicable to other societies or even to this society at different points in time. Given their pronounced tendency to judge others by themselves, American citizens *and* policy makers should be especially careful to avoid the "fallacy of projection"—deciding that what works here will also work elsewhere. The following chapters will consider the various methods employed by different types of states to attain such universal ends as national security, order, welfare, and whatever else in a particular country might be viewed as progress. Closely tied to the problem of the *scope* of state authority over the individual and group is the question of *where political authority should be located.* Consequently, we shall survey the principles and practice of contemporary democracy, communism, and other types of political beliefs and political systems, which should put us in a better position to understand others as well as ourselves and to answer the perennial question of how best to make the state serve its citizens.

STUDY-GUIDE QUESTIONS

1 Is there any justification for resisting political authority? Under what circumstances would you feel justified in rebelling against the authority of the state?
2 What is the meaning of "natural right"? Where do natural rights come from? What do they specify? What are their implications in terms of the relationships between citizen and state?
3 Consider the characteristics of territory and population. What combination of characteristics in these two categories is likely to maximize the state's chances for international security and domestic stability?
4 What is "sovereignty"? Where is sovereignty in the United States? Is the notion of the "sovereign people" more myth than reality? Why or why not?
5 What do you think ought to be the role and functions of government (or the state) in modern society?

REFERENCES

Barker, Ernest: *Social Contract: Essays by Locke, Hume, and Rousseau,* Oxford University Press, New York, 1962.

Dahl, Robert A.: *A Preface to Democratic Theory,* Phoenix Books, The University of Chicago Press, Chicago, 1963.

Deutsch, Karl W.: *Politics and Government: How People Decide Their Fate,* Houghton Mifflin Company, Boston, 1970, part I.

Jouvenel, Bertrand de: *Sovereignty: An Inquiry into the Political Good,* The University of Chicago Press, Chicago, 1963.

MacIver, Robert M.: *The Web of Government,* rev. ed., The Macmillan Company, New York, 1965.

Sabine, George H.: *A History of Political Theory,* 3d ed., Holt, Rinehart and Winston, Inc., New York, 1961.

Tinder, Glenn: *Political Thinking: The Perennial Political Questions,* 2d ed., Little, Brown and Company, Boston, 1974.

Wolff, Robert Paul: *In Defense of Anarchism,* Torchbooks, Harper & Row, Publishers, Incorporated, New York, 1970.

Chapter 3

The Forms of Government

Although it has already been noted that the state is not synonymous with its government and that the former is greater and more enduring than the latter, it also must be admitted that states are commonly distinguished according to their *forms of government.* People like to reassure themselves of their knowledgeable grip on world affairs by applying hard-and-fast labels: This state is a democracy; that state is a dictatorship; this state is governed by the people; that state is governed by a narrow and self-interested elite. Political reality, however, is usually more complex than the simple pictures of the world around us that we fix in our minds. This chapter is intended to lend some precision to the labels we invariably use when we compare states according to their forms of government and when we attempt to answer those larger questions about the justice or injustice of particular states.

CLASSIFICATION: GOVERNMENT BY ONE, FEW, AND THE MANY

The reader may remember that one of the measures of the relatively low standing of political science as "science" is the unending dispute over the appropriate categories for classifying political phenomena. Conceptual disagreement also has marked man's efforts, at least since the time of the ancient Greeks, to distinguish states according to their forms of government. But it is not possible to evaluate a political system without comparing it with others, and one cannot compare two or more political systems without inventing some meaningful scheme for classifying their various characteristics. Thus it is necessary to begin with at least some rudimentary typology of governments, and one that has enjoyed an unusually long life may be found in

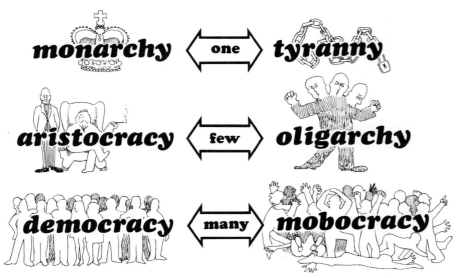

Figure 3.1 Good and bad forms of government, according to rule by one, few, and the many.

the political thought of Plato and Aristotle, the Romans (especially Polybius and Cicero), and thinkers of the Renaissance (Machiavelli), the Enlightenment (Montesquieu), and even more contemporary times. The argument here is that any state may be classified according to the distribution or location of political power within it: Power is exercised by *one* person, a *few* people, or *many* people (meaning most or all citizens). Governments by one, few, or the many may in turn be distinguished as "good" or "bad" forms of government; each good form has its bad counterpart. The result is a *six*fold classification of governmental types. (See Figure 3.1.)

One man might rule the state, then, but it is not a foregone conclusion that his rule will be either good or bad. This question is answered in terms of whether he rules in his own self-interest or in the interest of the whole society. The same criterion is applied to government by the few and the many; in each case it must be asked whether the rulers make their decisions in the interest of the general welfare or in their own private interest. (It remains to be seen whether rule by the many according to each citizen's calculation of his or her own private gain actually results in the welfare of all.) Because wielders of political power never admit to making decisions that benefit only themselves and their political or business associates, it is not easy to resolve this particular question, and the answer also is likely to vary from one issue to another for the same form of government. For example, political leaders who operate in the general interest when they formulate policies for national defense may act in their own private interest when it is time to give the taxpayers' money to defense contractors.

It may have been this potential confusion inherent in the classification scheme that induced Plato, Polybius, and others to conclude that each form of government tended to be transformed by its own inertia into other forms. Democracy, the least stable and therefore the least desirable "good" form of government, tended to degenerate into "mobocracy," which was more undesirable than all the other forms of government, good and bad; but mobocracy tended to give rise to tyranny, or—according to a metaphor favored by the French—to the "man on horseback" who could put order in the place of apparent anarchy. Tyranny was the "best" form of "bad" government, but those who subscribed to this classification scheme agreed that the best of all possible forms of government was enlightened monarchy. And it was no coincidence that sovereignty in Plato's ideal state was concentrated in the person of the "philosopher-king."

MONARCHY

Plato argued that the rule of law was at best an imperfect way of settling disputes and reconciling differences between citizens. By their very nature, laws are general and are designed to apply to one or several of the many categories of social relationships. But the problems of a society are expressed in particular terms; they pertain to individuals in different social contexts, and these social contexts also change over time. Enlightened monarchy was consequently the most efficient and the most just way of ruling a state; it guaranteed that the basic guidelines of the society would be implemented according to changing circumstances and particular needs.

Supporters of monarchical government, even in contemporary times, also have argued that this type of government maximizes the chances of political stability, especially in the context of sweeping social and economic change. In fact, the student of comparative politics must be impressed by the relatively high stability of contemporary states that have retained their monarchical institutions, in some cases over centuries of time. Great Britain, Sweden, and Denmark are the obvious examples, but one should also include in the category of present-day monarchies those of Holland, Norway, Belgium, Luxembourg, Morocco, Jordan, Afghanistan, Japan, Thailand, Saudi Arabia, and Iran. There also is the promise of a return to monarchy in Spain after the death or resignation of General Franco. In striking contrast to the relative stability of almost all these states, monarchies in the twentieth century have been eliminated in Russia, Germany, Austria, Hungary, Turkey, Portugal, Spain, Italy, Yugoslavia, Bulgaria, Rumania, Albania, Egypt, and—in the 1970s—Greece, Libya, and Ethiopia. Rule by one man, then, is not a guarantee of political stability. What explains the variations in these findings?

Monarchy and Political Adaptation

A large part of the answer to this question (although not all of it) has to do with the ability or willingness of particular monarchs and their successors to accept a progressive reduction in their political power. The classic example is that of England following the establishment of William and Mary on the throne in 1689. Their coronation was contingent on their acceptance of parliamentary supremacy over the monarchy in the critical areas of public policy, including taxation, military organization and command, and the religion adopted by the monarch. (This agreement between the English Parliament and the monarch may be thought of as a "social contract," although it was a social contract that excluded the participation of the people.) Much of the subsequent political history of Great Britain is the story of the increasing powers of Parliament, especially the House of Commons, and its progressive democratization, along with the declining power of the monarchy.

Today it is fair to say that the British king or queen reigns rather than rules and that the primary functions of the monarchy are symbolic: It represents the continuity of British traditions and serves as a focal point for the loyalties of British citizens. The monarch's political responsibilities are almost exclusively formal, for example, reading the government's legislative program at the outset of each new term of Parliament—a program that may be written by a socialist party—or approving (but never disapproving) the enactment of parliamentary legislation or the dissolution of the House of Commons and the calling of new elections as determined by the Government. But on some occasions the monarch may exercise important political *influence*, especially when the king or queen has enjoyed a long tenure on the throne, has remained well informed on political affairs, and has the constitutional opportunity to designate a new prime minister, following the death or resignation of the previous prime minister, on the advice of competing leaders of the majority party. In Sweden in late 1973, King Carl XVI Gustaf participated in the various attempts to resolve the partisan standoff that resulted from parliamentary elections in September. It is far more right than wrong, then, to conclude that contemporary monarchies have remained important institutions in their societies because a succession of kings and queens have reconciled themselves to declining political significance.

This contrasts vividly with the histories of monarchical institutions in France during the eighteenth and nineteenth centuries, in Russia during the first decades of the twentieth century, and in Egypt and Greece in the mid-twentieth century. In these and the other countries that have eliminated their monarchies, royal authority proved unable or unwilling to alter its political functions along with political and social change. Typically, the monarch clung tenaciously to power and failed to encourage the development of parliamentary autonomy and the exercise of executive authority by political leaders not accountable to the throne. The king's reward for his intransigence was the loss of his throne and occasionally the loss of his life and the lives of his family and loyal supporters.

The fate of the Russian tsar illustrates the point. Forced by the revolution of 1905 to convene a parliament (Duma), Tsar Nicholas II nevertheless manipulated its representation to get the results he wanted, censored the speeches of its delegates, and refused to take the advice of his government ministers. The tsar's insistence on ruling according to the outdated notion of the "divine right of kings" (which made him accountable only to God) was especially intolerable in the context of his mismanagement of Russia's military involvement in World War I. In fact, we might hypothesize that the more a monarch resists any reduction in his authority, the more likely he is to be replaced by a revolutionary regime that employs widespread violence to root out the vestiges of monarchical and aristocratic domination. This hypothesis helps to explain events as widely separated as those in England in 1640, in France in 1789 and 1848, in Russia in 1917, in Egypt in 1952, and in Ethiopia in 1974.

GOVERNMENT BY THE FEW

Even when the divine right of kings was an accepted formula for legitimating royal authority, it was nevertheless true that the monarch depended on the support of a loyal cadre of advisers and bureaucrats to carry out his policies. It was the gradual evolution and institutionalization of the roles of advisers and civil servants that, in France and elsewhere, led to the establishment of parliament (advisers) and the state's administrative apparatus (civil servants). An awareness of these historical trends, along with the conviction that democratic institutions are an illusion that conceals the political domination of a minority, has convinced some twentieth-century political scientists (notably Gaetano Mosca and Robert Michels) that government everywhere and always has been the affair of a few—neither one nor the many.

In this context, "aristocracy" means government by an elite of the society that has high social status, wealth, and political power. These advantages are passed from one generation of the aristocracy to another. Status, power, and wealth are inherited. We also may say that in aristocratic societies status is allocated according to "ascriptive" rather than "achievement" norms: Your place in society is determined by who you are (or who your parents are) rather than by what you do. Who you are is indicated by your styles of speech, dress, and comportment; your family background; where you were educated (even more than what you learned); and your ability to live a comfortable life without having to work for it. No wonder that workers, peasants, and intellectuals in most societies throughout history have registered such a low regard for aristocrats and aristocratic institutions.

Where an aristocratic class is politically dominant is also where, invariably, monarchical institutions will be found. In England in 1820, for example, the monarchy was still a politically significant institution, the upper house of Parliament (the House of Lords) exercised major influence in the legislative process, and fewer than 500 citizens, most of them peers in the House of Lords, were able to elect a majority of members to the House of Commons. Even after the passage of the Reform Bill of 1832, the suffrage did not extend to more than 12 percent of all adult males in England. But after the Reform Bill of 1867, 30 percent of all adult males were enfranchised, and it may be said that at this point in time the politics of Great Britain were controlled less by an aristocracy than by an oligarchy. *Oligarchy* means government by a minority of the society, a minority that is not necessarily distinguished by aristocratic title or privilege. But in the mid-nineteenth century Great Britain also could have been described as a *plutocracy*—rule by the few who are rich.

Aristocracy and Political Adaptation

Like monarchs, aristocratic elites have survived only where they have not resisted fundamental political and social change, especially the gradual democratization of political authority and the development of new sources of wealth along with economic growth and industrialization.

In England, for example, the aristocracy proved receptive to capitalism, in part because the land was early given over to the raising of sheep for the profitable wool trade and in part because only the firstborn male could inherit his father's property and aristocratic title (primogeniture). In England there were consequently many sons and daughters of the aristocracy who were without inherited title and wealth, and they frequently made alliances in business and through marriage with an enterprising bourgeoisie, or middle class.

In most of the continental countries of Europe, however, the land remained under the plow for the production of cereal crops. This in turn induced the landed aristocracy to insist on the maintenance of its traditional feudal controls over the peasantry. And, in most of Europe, aristocratic title was transmitted to, and the wealth divided among, all the family's heirs, which in turn contributed to a rigid separation of the society's social classes.

These traditional social patterns help to explain the relative political stability of Great Britain (and the survival to this day of the British aristocracy) and the relative instability and the disappearance of the aristocracy in most of the rest of Europe. And where the aristocracy was swept away by war or revolution (or both, as in France and Germany), the swelling proletariat found few champions to intercede on its behalf with the growing capitalist classes. In England before the rise of working-class parties, the aristocracy and even the traditional Tories proved responsive to the demands of workers for improved living conditions and employment security. This also helps to explain the willingness of socialist governments in Great Britain to tolerate, however grudgingly, the continued privileges and high social status of the British aristocracy.

Government by the Few: Authoritarianism

By their very nature, governments by the few are authoritarian governments. It will not come as a surprise to students of history that most of the governments around the world and throughout history deserve to be classified as "authoritarian." Monarchies (rule by one), aristocracies (rule by the titled few), oligarchies (rule by the untitled few), and plutocracies (rule by the rich) are all authoritarian because the majority of citizens do not have any direct or institutionalized role in policy making; they do not participate in elections, and they are not organized into political parties or clearly identifiable interest groups.

As Greek and Roman political philosophers argued, however, government by the few does not mean that policy making will always be inconsistent with the interests and demands of the many in the society. In the past, for example, authoritarian governments have reduced or eliminated the influence of religious institutions over the social and economic lives of citizens; they have encouraged business investment and economic growth along with introducing basic welfare programs for the lower classes; they have physically transported cultural minority groups to new areas where, for perhaps the first time in history, the individual members of these groups could live in peace with their neighbors; they have resolved long-standing conflicts which aroused the passions of mutually hostile groups in the society and which no popularly elected government was strong enough to grapple with; and they have eliminated the threat of famine for millions of people, curtailed economic exploitation by moneylenders, and given citizens their first opportunities for health care and education. However critical one may be of the methods and ethical foundations of authoritarian governments, it is important not to overlook their occasionally significant and humanitarian accomplishments. Given the prominence of authoritarianism in the history of the world, it would be a sad comment on the fate of mankind if the record of authoritarianism were categorically dismissed as all bad. In politics, unlike religion, nothing is either all good or all bad.

Authoritarianism and One-Party Rule In the contemporary world, it also is true that authoritarian governments are almost everywhere identified by the presence of only one political party. Instead of classifying states according to the location and scope of political power, it may in fact be more useful to classify them according to the number and characteristics of their political parties. And there should be little doubt that a government that permits only one party to operate in the political system is an authoritarian government: No organized political opposition exists, there is no alternative set of political leaders who can take the place of existing elites for the purpose of implementing new programs, political communication is strictly according to what the government and its ruling party allow, and alteration of governmental personnel and policies must take place within the single party, typically only after the death or purging of the dominant leader.

Generalizations such as these are difficult to understand without some concrete examples. It is likely that in reading through the above characteristics of authoritarian or one-party states, the reader thought of one or more contemporary countries: the Soviet Union? China? East Germany? Cuba? Yes. According to the above criteria, these four countries definitely qualify as authoritarian states. But what about Yugoslavia, South Vietnam, Egypt, Mexico, Tunisia, Spain, France, or (after September 1973) Chile? These and many other countries like them are also characterized by a weak or nonexistent political opposition and by oligarchic rule that enjoys a monopoly on political communications and policy making. Clearly, then, some countries are more authoritarian than others, and it is appropriate to think of authoritarianism in terms of a *continuum* of regime types instead of insisting on the dichotomous categories of "either-or." Later in this chapter we shall return to the concept of a continuum in the classification of states.

Totalitarianism Since the 1950s some scholars have argued that the most extreme type of authoritarianism is best described as "totalitarianism."[1] In addition to the characteristics of authoritarianism already cited, totalitarianism also implies "an official ideology which members of the society must adhere to and which covers all aspects of life in the society"; "a system of terroristic police control which supports, and supervises on behalf of, the leader, and which is directed against the 'enemies' of the State"; and "central control and direction of the entire economy."[2] We could add other characteristics of totalitarianism: the subordination of the arts and sciences to the interests of the political elite and to the specifications of the ideology and the organization of youth groups, labor unions, cultural associations, the educational system, and other intermediary social structures for the purposes of broadening the elite's political and social control and supporting its ideological objectives. And while there is a sophisticated apparatus for communicating the elite's demands to the population, there are no institutional channels for assuring feedback communications from the population to the elite. In short, authoritarian governments are content to control the overt behavior of the citizen and to eliminate any sign of organized opposition. Totalitarian governments attempt to control not only the citizen's behavior but his thoughts as well. In this sense, many religions—including Judaism and early Christianity—were among the first manifestations of totalitarian government.

It is important to remember, however, that the characteristics of totalitarianism are the result more of deductive logic than of empirical observation. Totalitarianism is an *ideal* type; i.e., it exists only or primarily in the mind. While the term "totalitarianism" may be useful in clarifying definitions, it should be remembered that it seldom, if ever, has existed in fact. It is no coincidence, for example, that as students of communist societies have collected more data and as they have looked more closely at the details of communism, they have been almost unanimous in abandoning the label of "totalitarianism." It may be argued that Nazi Germany and Stalinist Russia (the latter in the mid-1930s, the late 1940s, and before Stalin's death in 1953) came close to representing, in reality, totalitarianism, but it would be wrong to conclude that the political, ideological, economic, and social characteristics of these two societies closely resembled each other. And if there can be such variation in the characteristics of the totalitarian type, then it has almost no conceptual utility at all.

It also is doubtful whether Fascist Italy (the word "totalitarianism" appears to have been invented by Mussolini), the Soviet Union under Khrushchev and Brezhnev, Castro's Cuba (or Batista's Cuba), Franco's Spain, or even Maoist China should be labeled "totalitarian." And the label is obviously misleading with respect to contemporary Poland,

---

[1] For example, see Carl J. Friedrich and Zbigniew K. Brzezinski, *Totalitarian Dictatorship and Autocracy*, Harvard University Press, Cambridge, Mass., 1956; and Gabriel A. Almond, "Comparative Political Systems," *Journal of Politics*, vol. 18, pp. 391–409, August 1956.

[2] Friedrich and Brzezinski, op. cit., p. 9.

Hungary, Yugoslavia, South Africa, the two Vietnams and the two Koreas, and many other authoritarian countries that are only insulted rather than described by the epithet "totalitarian." The degree of authoritarianism characterizing these states varies significantly from one to another *and* for the same state from one point in time to another. One should not allow a liking for quick and easy labels to take the place of a commitment to careful inquiry and dispassionate analysis. But it also is clear that a government by the few, however brutal or benign its authoritarian rule, does not fit the traditional understanding of "democracy."

GOVERNMENT BY THE MANY

Appeals for careful inquiry and dispassionate analysis apply with equal force to the understanding of "democracy." The word derives from the Greek words for "people" and "to rule." But just how do the people rule?

Direct Democracy

Ideally, in a direct democracy all citizens would be able to assemble together in order to discuss and resolve their common problems. But immediately, even under these ideal conditions, some difficulties become obvious. Who sets the time and place for convening the meeting? How is the meeting's agenda prepared, and by whom? What are the rules for debate? How are decisions made—by a simple majority vote, by a majority vote of all citizens in the society, or by a majority vote of only those attending the meeting? If, as democrats, we agree that I am obliged to obey only those decisions which I consent to obey, how can a majority force me and others in the minority to obey the will of the majority? Under conditions of majority rule, an oppressed minority may perceive little difference between democracy and authoritarianism. As the French aristocrat and political theorist Alexis de Tocqueville argued in the mid-nineteenth century, a majority of the many may be just as tyrannical as an oligarchy of the few. But assuming that a decision is made by the assembly of all citizens after "sufficient" debate on a particular issue, how is the decision to be implemented? How do we enforce citizen compliance? Even a little reflection on these difficult questions should help the reader understand why any sustained interaction between people inevitably gives rise to politics, the institutions of the state (including bureaucracy), and complex rules and procedures for decision making and administration.

But on rare occasions in history and in relative isolation—for example, in parts of Greece, Switzerland, and New England—states have been established with forms of government that approximated direct democracy. What can be learned from these noble political experiments? First, usually only a minority of citizens participated in decision making. In one instance in the history of the Athenian city-state, slightly less than 10 percent of the 40,000 Athenian citizens eligible to participate in the meetings of the *ecclesia* actually attended. A large number of citizens, of course, works against the realization of the ideal of equal access to policy makers and equal influence on policy making. In the contemporary kibbutzim of Israel, the average percentage of kibbutz members attending the meetings of the general assembly declines as the number of members in the kibbutz increases over time—from 50 to 100 and, in the case of some kibbutzim, to 500 and even 1,000 or more. As citizens lose the opportunity for face-to-face interaction with others, the majority develop interests that are not immediately relevant to politics, and a minority of citizens—by virtue of their interest and perhaps their talent—become the political elite. The history of experiments in direct democracy also indicates that this type of government is unlikely to survive under conditions of crisis (including war or the threat of war) and that it also is likely to wither away as the economy of the society loses its agrarian character and gives way to commerce and trade, with the consequent introduction of socioeconomic, and thus political, inequalities between citizens.

Representative Democracy

As new residents increased the number of citizens in the early New England towns of the United States, and especially as new immigrants introduced cultural cleavages into these once all-white, Anglo-Saxon, Protestant communities, the direct democracy of the New England town meeting disappeared. Why? This occurred partly because there were simply too many people to participate directly in policy making and partly because the older resident citizens correctly understood that continued direct democracy threatened their control of local government. By instituting elections and by delegating policy making to elected representatives (a town council), the chances of continued control by the more established citizens were much improved. The writers of the United States Constitution also knew that by providing for the *indirect election* of the president and members of the Senate (qualified citizens voted for electors, who in turn selected these public officials), they were most likely to prevent policy making from falling into the hands of the "irresponsible" elements in society (meaning the lower socioeconomic classes). And, strictly speaking, the United States and other contemporary "democracies" are *republican* governments in which citizens participate in policy making through elected representatives.

In fact, the ancient Greeks well understood that the *election* of public officials almost invariably worked against true democracy. In the glory days of the Athenian city-state, public officials were selected from among all the citizens by *lot* and were quickly rotated with other citizens through public office. To institute elections meant to disqualify most citizens from equal access to public office: The more articulate, the more personally appealing, the better organizers, and the richer citizens inevitably had (and have) superior advantages in an election contest. The candidate's personality, appearance, and family and private life can and do affect voters' attitudes, but these characteristics of the candidate have no immediate relevance to his or her qualifications for public service. For the ancient Greeks and for many other political thinkers in more recent times, elections and representative democracy invariably led to government by the few and rule by a self-interested oligarchy.

Assessing the "Representativeness" of Representative Democracy In large nation-states composed of many citizens with different cultural backgrounds and socioeconomic interests, it is inevitable that the few will rule and that the many will be ruled. But the truth of this commonsense observation should not mislead us in our evaluation of the representativeness—or, more popularly, the degree of democracy—characterizing any particular state.

What is at issue is the extent to which (1) all socioeconomic and cultural sectors of the society are represented in the policy-making process; (2) access to decision makers is equally distributed among all citizens; (3) policy making coincides, at least in the long run, with the distribution of public opinion on salient issues; (4) the political elite is organized into competing factions or parties with differing political programs; and (5) citizens have regular opportunities for electing alternative government personnel and, through them, implementing new programs. Democratic states might also be distinguished from one another and from authoritarian states according to the communications and public-media access enjoyed by competing groups with differing views on public policy. These criteria for distinguishing between representative forms of government figure prominently in what follows.

CLASSIFYING STATES: A CONTINUUM

It again is obvious that states claiming to be democratic cannot be classified in terms of "either-or" categories. Some states are more democratic than others, just as some are more authoritarian than others. The question is one of degree, and the extent of democracy characterizing any given state will vary according to time and the particular issue (some issues will be settled more democratically than others).

It is perhaps best to think of a continuum that ranges from democracy to authoritarianism, as long as it is understood that no single state represents an ideal type of either democracy or authoritarianism. And if we draw from the more or less impressionistic judgments of those who are well informed on contemporary comparative politics, our picture of some of the world's states, distributed along a continuum of democracy and authoritarianism, might look like Figure 3.2

The picture portrayed in Figure 3.2 should not be taken too literally. The precise distribution of countries along the continuum is likely to vary from one researcher to another according to the criteria selected for evaluating the countries and according to the researcher's own ideological bias. But the figure presented here should stimulate discussion of these basic analytical problems, and it also helps to dramatize the point that few states can be classified as entirely democratic or authoritarian. Even in the

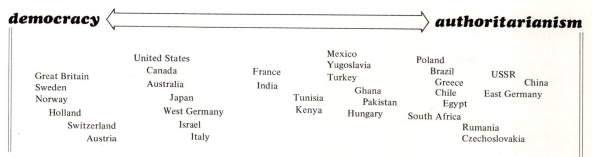

Figure 3.2 Approximate distribution of selected states along a continuum of democracy and authoritarianism.

most authoritarian states there are frequent instances of policy-making conflict among competing factions of the ruling elite, and there are occasional examples of major reversals in public policy that appear to respond to the changing interests and demands, however informally expressed, of rank-and-file citizens. With regard to the United States, the figure also illustrates what is likely to be the judgment of most scholars and citizens who are informed about world events and who have lived or traveled abroad: In comparison with the governments of other countries, the government of the United States is better than most but not as good as some.

INSTITUTIONAL FORMS OF THE STATE: PARLIAMENTARY GOVERNMENT

Of the 34 countries represented in Figure 3.2, approximately three out of every four have a parliamentary form of government. Citizens in these countries do not vote directly for a chief executive. They vote for legislative representatives, or members of parliament, who are organized into one or more political parties. This in turn suggests that the parliamentary form of government, by itself, is not an index of the democracy or authoritarianism characterizing any given state. But all parliamentary systems have in common a close institutional relationship between the executive and legislative branches of government. The chief executive is a prime minister (as in Great Britain) or a premier (as in Italy). He (or she, as in Israel and India during the prime-ministerships of Golda Meir and Indira Gandhi) selects the other ministers of government, who constitute the cabinet. Each cabinet minister is responsible for administering a particular department of government—education, labor, foreign affairs, justice, defense, treasury, and so on. And the cabinet as a whole (referred to as the "government") is voted into or out of executive office by a majority of the parliament.

Executive and Legislature in Parliamentary Government

This explains one of the major strengths of the parliamentary system. Executive personnel and policies closely approximate the distribution of opinion and interests represented in the legislature. If the government advances a program that does not command the support of a majority of legislators, the government can be removed from executive office and replaced by a new government that is committed to a different program. In France during the Fourth Republic (1946 to 1958), this in fact happened on the average of every six months. Political observers consequently were moved to lament the "instability" of French politics. But this is the way the parliamentary system is supposed to work: to search constantly for governments whose public-policy positions enjoy the support of a majority in the legislature. It would be wrong to conclude that the governmental "stability" that accompanies the frequent deadlock between executive and legislative branches in the presidential system marks this as a necessarily superior form of government. In this instance, stability may signal stagnation.

In the event of a deadlock between the government and the legislature in a parliamentary system, the executive also enjoys the advantage of being able to dissolve the legislature, thereby calling for new parliamentary elections. There is likely to be a constitutional requirement that limits the tenure of the legislature (frequently five years), but elections may be called at any time during this period. The timing of elections in parliamentary systems, then, is more a function of the patterns of political conflict in the society than it is a response to the automatic dictates of the calendar. And by taking his case to the electorate, a prime minister whose position is threatened by a flagging majority in parliament can win the support he needs to implement his program. If he loses (meaning that his parliamentary support is further weakened by the election), a new government is formed that more closely represents the distribution of opinion in the electorate and partisanship in the parliament.

Leaders and Parties in Parliamentary Government

A major characteristic of parliamentary systems is the partisan experience and identification of the chief executive and his cabinet ministers. The prime minister is not only the head of government but also the leader of his party and, consequently, the leader of the parliamentary majority. His cabinet ministers are likely to have substantial experience in party politics and parliamentary debate, and thus they too are recognized party leaders. Indeed, they may spend an important part of their time maneuvering against one another for the position of successor to the top party leader. But the close relationship between members of party, parliament, and executive government in the parliamentary system helps to improve the chances of government action in an age when government inaction may be tantamount to catastrophe or, less dramatically, widespread economic and social distress among the population.

It is also important to note the relative openness of political conflict in the parliamentary system. The heads of state sit in the legislature and must frequently undergo intensive questioning by the parliamentary opposition. Visitors to the Senate or House of Representatives of the United States and to the Parliament of Canada or Great Britain are likely to be struck by the dramatic contrasts in open policy conflict. Most government leaders in a parliamentary system are able to articulate their points of view and defend their positions with conviction and intelligence. And the more notable chief executives of parliamentary history, instead of avoiding open political confrontation, seem to have thrived on it. The contrast with the presidential system of government is all the more vivid when a president (e.g., Lyndon Johnson in 1967-1968 and Richard Nixon in 1972-1974) prefers uncontested communication with citizens through the public media to undergoing the rigors of an open and unrestricted press conference. Even when it is operative, however, the press conference in the presidential system is no substitute for the institutionalized challenge to an existing government and its policies that is represented by an opposition party in parliament.

INSTITUTIONAL FORMS OF THE STATE: PRESIDENTIAL GOVERNMENT

It should be apparent from the above that the presidential system of government tends to isolate the chief executive from the legislature and that the chief executive, if he chooses, may in turn isolate himself from the people. Unlike the parliamentary system, presidential government is characterized by very few institutional channels for communication between legislative and executive branches. Much of the story of the "constitutional" development of presidential systems hinges on the informal procedures that are established by successive administrations for bridging the communications gaps between the several branches of government: private meetings between the president and legislative leaders and the building of a network of personal loyalties between legislators and administrators. Such informal liaisons are all the more important when one political party controls the presidency and another (or a coalition of opposition parties) controls the legislature. Under these conditions, policy making is very definitely a function of political compromise and bargaining, and the formal specifications of the constitution may have little to do with the actual conduct of politics.

The Separation of Powers in Presidential Government

The informality of these procedures also reflects the political philosophy that underlies the entire presidential system of government, especially in the United States. The assumption is that the chances of tyranny or dictatorship are reduced insofar as legislative and executive (and judicial) branches of government are separated in terms of both institutions and personnel. In the United States, the principle of checks and balances (for example, the president's authority to veto legislation or the Senate's authority to approve or disapprove presidential appointments) is actually a corollary to the more fundamental principle of separation of powers. By distributing a part of the powers of each governmental branch to the other branches of government, the writers of the Constitution intended to provide each branch with the means of ensuring its constitutional integrity. The record of parliamentary government, however, makes it clear that the principle of separation of powers is not essential to democracy; some parliamentary systems (including those of Great Britain and Scandinavia) are more democratic than most, if not all, presidential systems of government. It is necessary to look elsewhere for explanations of the extent of democracy (or authoritarianism) characterizing a particular state. Presidential systems, like parliamentary systems, may be relatively democratic, or they may be relatively authoritarian.

Executive and Legislature in Presidential Government

In the relatively democratic presidential system, the chief executive is chosen by the people—not by the legislature (as in a parliamentary system). He selects his cabinet officers, in most cases with the routine approval of the legislature, and they in turn are accountable to him and not to the legislature. The legislature of course cannot dismiss the government, except under the unusual circumstances of conviction of the president following impeachment by the legislative branch, and even then the impeachment process (as in the case of President Nixon) is not likely to relate directly to partisan or institutional differences over public policy.

In the overwhelming majority of cases, then, the president is assured of continued tenure in office, regardless of his relationships with the legislature and at least until the next election. And one of the important measures of the extent of democracy in a presidential system is the frequency of an alteration in partisan control of the presidential office. In Mexico, a principal accomplishment of the revolution of 1910 was the imposition of a six-year limit on presidential tenure, but the limitation on presidential personnel has not impeded control of the Mexican presidency by a single political party.

In the United States, the presidency has evolved from the largely passive role in policy making envisaged by the writers of the Constitution to one of high visibility and activism within the American political system. This reflects the fundamental transformation of the United States from a rural and agricultural society to a highly industrialized and urban one. The functions of government have changed accordingly, and it has fallen to the president to play a major role not only in coordinating the functions of government but also in initiating policy changes and securing their legislative enactment. But the institutional separation of legislative and executive branches immensely complicates his task, even when the presidency and Congress are controlled by the same political party. Coincident with these changes in American government and society, however, is the democratization of the electoral process by which the president is chosen, and it is a tentative measure of the democracy of the United States that this eminently powerful office is filled only according to the votes of rank-and-file citizens.[3]

Presidents and Politics in Presidential Government

Where there is presidential government outside the United States, it usually is the case that there will also be a fragmented party system, weak political institutions, or both. In France after 1958, in Pakistan after 1962, and in Chile before the military coup d'état of September 1973, a strong presidential office existed for the principal purpose of imparting cohesion and direction to the political process. President Ayub Khan of Pakistan argued that Pakistan's earlier parliamentary institutions were so weak, and the need for modernization of Pakistan's

[3] Presidential selection in the United States is a complicated part of the American political process, as will be seen in a subsequent chapter. It should also be noted here that a presidential office exists in several other countries, but the organization of the government in these countries is basically parliamentary. (Italy, India, West Germany, and the French Fourth Republic are examples.) The president is not directly elected by the people, and his functions are more akin to those of a reigning and occasionally influential monarch than they are to the functions and powers of a chief executive.

socioeconomic structures so compelling, that power had to be concentrated in a single political office. And it is typical of newly independent states with underdeveloped economies that government is initially organized along the lines of a presidential system—until the military intervenes and removes the civilian politicians from power.

In the underdeveloped world and where civilian politicians continue to rule within the constitutional parameters of a parliamentary system (as in India), there is likely to have been a long tradition of parliamentary government inherited from the mother country that previously ruled the colonial society. But in the relatively modernized setting of France, Charles de Gaulle instituted a popularly elected president precisely for the purpose of relocating political power from a divided parliament (in which no single party could command a majority) to a centralized and strengthened executive. One of the conditions for ensuring a strong French presidency after de Gaulle's departure from office was the institution of the popular election of the president, a result of de Gaulle's national referendum on presidential selection in 1962; only the president, then, could claim to speak for a majority of the French people, and this was likely to enhance his bargaining relationship with a traditionally intractable parliament.

The recent political histories of France and Pakistan, however, and of Indonesia, Ghana, Egypt, Brazil, Argentina, and many other countries with presidential systems suggest that a presidential form of government is a frequent precondition for authoritarianism, even within the context of apparently democratic elections. These findings are another reminder that in order to understand and evalute the political process of any particular country, one must look behind the institutional facade represented by the "forms of government."

There is no denying the fact, however, that the forms of government can have a determining impact on politics, on who rules and who does not rule, and on what gets done and what does not get done. In this sense, the institutions that are invented to carry out the work of government structure political styles of interaction, perceptions of policy needs, and opportunities for bargaining and compromise. And among the more determining institutional characteristics of government, together with the parliamentary or presidential form, is the way in which the state itself is organized: How centralized or decentralized is the state, or is it unitary or federal? In considering the following, it also is important to remember that unitary or federal states may have either presidential or parliamentary forms of government; these variations will in turn reflect the particular society's political traditions, its geographic size, and the demographic and cultural characteristics of its population.

INSTITUTIONAL FORMS OF GOVERNMENT: UNITARY STATES

A *unitary state* is one in which the central or national government is supreme, possessing complete governmental power. No spheres of governmental action are assigned by the constitution to smaller units of government, such as states or provinces. In a unitary state the national government may, and usually does, delegate many duties to cities, counties, or other local or regional units. However, this authority is delegated by an ordinary statute enacted by the national legislature—not by the constitution—and it may be withdrawn with equal facility.

In comparison with federal states, a unitary state enjoys some obvious advantages, including uniformity of laws and administration, which enable the nation as a whole to adapt to new conditions and problems. In a federal system, some individual states may be progressive, while others may pursue antiquated and harmful policies (e.g., in education, public welfare, or health). On the other hand, a unitary state frequently suffers from overcentralized administrative control over local affairs. The unitary form is particularly ill adapted to large or culturally heterogeneous nations in which local problems usually require special rather than standardized policies. Even in relatively small and highly homogeneous nations, such as France, overcentralized administration has resulted in what one authority aptly terms "paralysis at the extremities and apoplexy at the center." It is noteworthy that while, on the one hand, there seems to be a trend toward centralization in most federal states, there is also a conscious effort in many unitary states toward decentralization. The 1946 constitution of Italy contains provisions (finally implemented in

1970) aimed at decentralization that set up regional governments to assume some of the functions previously carried out by the national government and also to aid in developing a spirit of initiative and popular participation in local governmental affairs. Even in Great Britain, where centralized government and a unitary state are long-standing traditions, there now are pressures from political leaders in Wales and Scotland for more economic and political independence from London.

While it is sometimes argued that the unitary state discourages popular interest in public affairs and leads to the creation of a large, centralized bureaucracy, it is nevertheless true that Great Britain, France, Norway, Sweden, Denmark, New Zealand, and many other unitary democracies have avoided these pitfalls. Unitary government can be as democratic as federal government; popular interest and participation depend upon many factors entirely apart from the form of government. About 80 percent of British voters, for example, regularly exercise their right to vote, while the record of American voters usually lags far behind.

INSTITUTIONAL FORMS OF GOVERNMENT: FEDERAL STATES

A *federal state* signifies a division of governmental powers between the national government and constituent units (states, provinces, republics, regions, or cantons). Such a division of powers is specified in the constitution. Although the constitution can be amended, the amending procedure is invariably more difficult than the enactment of ordinary laws. In almost all federal systems, amendments require favorable action by both the federal or national government and a large majority of the state or provincial governments. In the United States, amendments are usually proposed by a two-thirds majority vote in both houses of Congress and become effective if and when they are ratified by simple majority vote of the legislatures (or specially chosen conventions) in three-fourths of the states.

The federal system of government is particularly well adapted to states embracing wide areas, with sectional diversities due to geography, climate, resources, economic factors, and social conditions, as well as to heterogeneity of race, nationality, language, or religion. The list of federal states includes the United States, Canada, India, Australia, the Soviet Union, Brazil, and Mexico. On the other hand, medium-sized countries like West Germany and Yugoslavia and extremely small nations such as Austria and Switzerland are also federal. Yugoslavia includes at least six distinct nationalities and several religions and languages, while Switzerland, despite her strong nationalism, is a composite of German, French, and Italian cultures; is religiously divided between Protestants and Catholics; and has three "official" languages.

In most federal states, the component units (cantons, provinces, or states) existed before the establishment of the federal regime and voluntarily came together to form a union for the advantages it would provide, e.g., greater military security, a customs union, or free trade. Often the federal union followed a *confederation,* a type of organization in which the member states retain their full sovereignty and must act together unanimously on all major questions of policy and on amendments to the confederation's basic law. The United States, Switzerland, and Germany went through this intermediate stage between complete separateness and federal union. Other federal states have been more abruptly and deliberately created—e.g., India, Canada, Australia, and Pakistan.

Advantages and Disadvantages of Federalism

Among the advantages of federalism are the following. The powers and functions of government are divided between the national or federal government and the component units, thus permitting national and international problems to be dealt with by the central government, while matters of local or regional concern are left to the states. In other words, federalism secures uniformity where needed, while at the same time permitting diversity where sectional or local conditions make it desirable. The component units may experiment with new legislative and administrative approaches to the constantly changing problems presented by a technological age, and often such laboratory experiments by a single state serve as a guide for later federal legislation.[4] However, it is much easier to

[4]Recent examples in the United States include individual state experiments with welfare administration, health insurance, pollution control, penalties for narcotics possession, regulation of election campaign financing, and no-fault automobile insurance.

talk in general terms about a division of powers based on general or national interests as distinguished from local matters than it is to spell out such lines of demarcation in actual practice. Moreover, what was of purely local concern a century ago (e.g., education, health, traffic regulation, and social security) has often become a matter for state or even federal action today.

Among the disadvantages of federalism is the lack of uniform state legislation on a lengthening list of matters in which basic uniformity grows increasingly advisable. These include standards of public education, labor legislation, commercial regulations, marriage and divorce laws, and social security. Federalism also presents the problem of overlapping federal and state jurisdiction in many fields, with consequent duplication of administrative agencies and personnel and therefore additional costs to the taxpayer. In some federal states, such as Switzerland, the federal government does not maintain its own administrative machinery, but requires cantonal officials to enforce federal laws. Many governmental problems exist in a "twilight zone," where the federal government may lack constitutional authority to act and yet where action by individual states may be futile without concerted action by all of them. Such uniform state action is difficult if not impossible to achieve, particularly where individual states see short-run advantage in nonconformity. Some American states profit by substandard laws on such matters as the labor of children and women, the chartering and supervision of corporations, public education, gambling, divorce, and prostitution.

Centralizing Trends in Federal States

There is no constant ratio between federal and state powers in a federal system; some federal governments are relatively weak, and others decidedly strong. It is impossible to say at what precise point the growing powers of a strong federal government may overstep the boundaries of federalism and usher in a unitary system. The federal government usually possesses power over foreign relations, war and peace, the armed forces, the currency, interstate and foreign commerce, immigration and naturalization, the postal system, and patents and copyrights. In some federal states, the central government enjoys additional powers in the spheres of economic and social control. The taxing power is, of course, a tool that enables all federal governments to intervene in the economic and social affairs of individual states.

In a world whose tempo has been startlingly accelerated in recent years, there has been a steady trend toward expanding both the powers and the responsibilities of federal governments. On balance, this trend cannot be said to have weakened democracy in either theory or practice. Indeed, citizens commonly show greater familiarity with, and interest in, the national government than they do with regard to state and local units; moreover, they go to the polls in greater numbers in national elections. Modern problems are forcing new divisions of powers and functions between federal and state authorities; while federal governments grow relatively stronger, with consequent administrative centralization, this does not necessarily mean bureaucratic regimentation and loss of individual liberty, particularly where the trend toward centralization is matched by an increasingly informed and more politically active citizenry.

STUDY-GUIDE QUESTIONS

1. What circumstances appear to coincide with the dissolution of monarchical institutions? In the context of modernization, how would you advise a king to behave in order to retain his throne?
2. Distinguish "authoritarianism" from "totalitarianism."
3. What are the prerequisites for "direct democracy"? Why are examples of direct democracy so unique in political history?
4. What are the principal advantages of parliamentary over presidential forms of government? What are the principal disadvantages?
5. What are the characteristics of any given society that would lead you to predict its adoption of a federal (rather than a unitary) form of government?

REFERENCES

Bachrach, Peter: *The Theory of Democratic Elitism: A Critique,* Little, Brown and Company, Boston, 1967.

Bowie, R., and Carl J. Friedrich (eds.): *Studies in Federalism,* Little, Brown and Company, Boston, 1954.

Buchanan, J. M., and G. Tullock: *The Calculus of Consent: Logical Foundations of Constitutional Democracy,* The University of Michigan Press, Ann Arbor, 1962.

Duchacek, I. D.: *Comparative Federalism: The Territorial Dimension of Politics,* Holt, Rinehart and Winston, Inc., New York, 1970.

Elazar, Daniel J.: "Federalism," in *International Encyclopedia of the Social Sciences,* Crowell Collier and Macmillan, Inc., New York, 1968, vol. 5, pp. 353–365.

Epstein, Leon D.: "Parliamentary Government," in *International Encyclopedia of the Social Sciences,* Crowell Collier and Macmillan, Inc., New York, 1968, vol. 11, pp. 419–425.

Friedrich, Carl J. (ed.): *Authority,* Harvard University Press, Cambridge, Mass., 1958.

———: "Constitutions and Constitutionalism," in *International Encyclopedia of the Social Sciences,* Crowell Collier and Macmillan, Inc., New York, 1968, vol. 3, pp. 318–326.

———: "Monarchy," in *International Encyclopedia of the Social Sciences,* Crowell Collier and Macmillan, Inc., New York, 1968, vol. 10, pp. 412–414.

———: *Limited Government: A Comparison,* Prentice-Hall, Inc., Englewood Cliffs, N.J., 1974.

Jenkin, Thomas P.: "Oligarchy," in *International Encyclopedia of the Social Sciences,* Crowell Collier and Macmillan, Inc., New York, 1968, vol. 11, pp. 281–283.

Lowi, Theodore J. (ed.): *Private Life and Public Order: The Context of Modern Public Policy,* W.W. Norton & Company, Inc., New York, 1968.

Michels, Robert: *Political Parties: A Sociological Study of the Oligarchical Tendencies of Modern Democracy,* Dover Publications, Inc., New York, 1959.

Mills, C. Wright: *The Power Elite,* Oxford University Press, Fair Lawn, N.J., 1956.

Neustadt, Richard E.: "Presidential Government," in *International Encyclopedia of the Social Sciences,* Crowell Collier and Macmillan, Inc., New York, 1968, vol. 12, pp. 451–456.

Peabody, Robert L.: "Authority," in *International Encyclopedia of the Social Sciences,* Crowell Collier and Macmillan, Inc., New York, 1968, vol. 1, pp. 473–477.

Price, Don K., and Harold J. Laski: "A Debate on the Parliamentary and Presidential Systems," in Roy C. Macridis and B. E. Brown (eds.), *Comparative Politics: Notes and Readings,* The Dorsey Press, Homewood, Ill., 1961, pp. 365–381.

Schlesinger, Joseph A., and Harry Eckstein: "Political Parties," in *International Encyclopedia of the Social Sciences,* Crowell Collier and Macmillan, Inc., New York, 1968, vol. 11, pp. 428–452.

Stammer, Otto: "Dictatorship," in *International Encyclopedia of the Social Sciences,* Crowell Collier and Macmillan, Inc., New York, 1968, vol. 4, pp. 161–168.

Verney, Douglas V.: *The Analysis of Political Systems,* The Free Press of Glencoe, Inc., New York, 1959, especially chap. 2, "Parliamentary Government"; chap. 3, "Presidential Government"; chap. 9, "Elite Theories"; and chap. 10, "The Iron Law of Oligarchy."

Wheare, K. C.: *Federal Government,* Oxford University Press, New York, 1964.

Chapter 4

Law and Government

The nation-state's internal sovereignty—its claim of right to exercise a supreme will over individuals, groups, or other entities located within it—is most obviously manifested through its monopoly of law. This is the Law[1] that the state recognizes, proclaims, and enforces. Indeed, the Law is regarded by many political and legal philosophers as the hallmark—the very essence—of the nation-state. Although we commonly speak of scientific, divine, natural, economic, or social laws, the concept of "the Law" connotes, to the political scientist, the processes, principles, standards, and rules which govern the relationships and which help resolve the conflicting interests of men and institutions in a cohesive society.

[1] "The Law" is here used in a broad sense to take into account what has come to mean the rule of law or the supremacy of law. It does not refer to mere statutes, e.g., laws. They compose only a part of the Law.

In the United States, we speak of international, constitutional, national, state, county, and city or municipal law. Treaties between nations constitute the most formal source of international law; decisions of the United States Supreme Court proclaim the meaning of the provisions of our national Constitution; congressional statutes govern the areas of human affairs that the Constitution has entrusted to national authority; laws passed by state legislatures blanket the remainder of such relationships, except where the states have conferred law-making authority over certain matters upon counties, districts, cities, and other municipalities.

It is impossible to conceive of a modern society operating without benefit of law—without the carefully formulated principles, standards, and rules that keep our involved social complex from disintegrating. No rational person believes that the intricate problems arising in an urban-industrial society could be dealt with in the absence of statutes, courts, legislatures, executives, administrators, policemen, and penalties. Such a society constitutes a seamless web of important and conflicting interests, and the concept of law is central to it.

Government does not rely solely upon the Law to achieve its objectives, but government without Law is like "*Hamlet* with Hamlet left out." To govern means to control, and control in the political sense within a nation-state requires principles of conduct embedded in legal principles, standards, and rules and enforced by sanctions, whether civil or criminal.

Government is concerned with broad legal *principles* as well as with the minutiae of legal *rules*. It uses legal standards to bridge the gap between them. It is generally conceded that the goal of democratic government is the attainment of justice; law exists to help reach this goal, although in practice results often fall short of the ideal. It is interesting to recall that St. Augustine declared that justice was the only feature that distinguished the state from a band of brigands. Like the state, brigands might occupy territory, hold people in subjection, and successfully defy external authority, but their power would be arbitrary, probably capricious, and certainly devoid of legitimacy and regularly established principle. This is true because force, uninformed by the principles of law, is the negation of law. Force in negating law also destroys the civilized values that give meaning and direction to law and to laws.

Law also encompasses the do's and don'ts of man's routine experiences. Let him park on the wrong side of the street, dispose of rubbish in a forbidden way, play his radio or television set too loudly or too late, insult or punch his neighbor in a fit of temper, or fail to file his income tax return or apply for a license for his dog, and legal sanctions will fall upon his shoulders—heavily or otherwise, according to the nature of his offense.

Not only the student of political science but every adult person as well needs to understand his or her country's basic legal system and the philosophy of law behind it. It is also important to learn something about the legal systems of other countries—not only how, but why, they differ from one's own. The growing complexity of life in the modern state has necessitated many extensions of governmental control over, or management of, activities, and every new extension of control or management implies a new law and sometimes a new agency for its enforcement or administration.

Americans are very law-conscious. We are prone to engage in litigation. When we encounter a social problem, we are likely to say, "There ought to be a law!" On reflection we may conclude that we should be spared the extension of legal authority. Despite many signs to the contrary, especially in times of deep social unrest, we hold the rule of law in the highest esteem, as evidenced by our traditional respect for reason and for duly constituted authority. Nonetheless, we are quick to criticize the terms of specific statutes and legal holdings that we consider to be adverse to our imagined personal and national interests. Above all, we view our Constitution as a higher law, the ark of our political covenant, to be venerated as the British revere the institution of monarchy. Thus, for Americans, a consideration of the nature and utility of law is peculiarly appropriate.

LAW

Bacon begins his *Essay on Truth* by making reference to a familiar question: "'What is truth?' said jesting Pilate, and would not stay for answer." What is law? The term is one of the most ambiguous and fluid known to man. There is little agreement as to its meaning, and it may be that there is no final answer. A basic difficulty is that "law" means so many different things to so many different persons at so many different times and in so many different places. Justice Oliver Wendell Holmes once said: "A word is not a crystal, transparent and unchanged; it is the skin of a living thought and may vary greatly in color and content according to the circumstances and the time in which it is used."[2] This is true of law.

Many problems present themselves when one attempts to arrive at a meaning for this important and traditional word. The individual who attempts a definition of law may be guided by his or her own subjective understanding of its character. For example, some individuals conceive of law as provid-

[2] *Towne v. Eisner,* 245 U.S. 418, 425 (1918).

ing fixed and immutable precepts connected with a given set of values and favorable to policies and programs in which they believe. Other persons, however, armed with another set of values, may regard law as a device to give support and status to *their* beliefs. Traditionally, most Americans have abhorred those who claim a right to take the law into their own hands. Again, individuals acting in an intuitive manner and basing their conclusions upon limited individual experience may fall into the error of believing there is only a single approach to an understanding of law.

SCHOOLS OF LAW

In fact, there are many approaches to an understanding of law, each somewhat different from the others, although including some elements common to all. These various approaches can be grouped into what may be called "schools of jurisprudence." One widely used classification recognizes the following schools: the positivist or imperative school; the "pure science of law" school; the historical school; the sociological school; the functional school; and the philosophical or teleological school. A summary description of these six approaches to law will set the stage for further analysis.

The Positivist School

The positivist or imperative approach (sometimes known as the analytical school) may be traced back to Jeremy Bentham (1748–1832), an English writer on legal subjects and the father of British utilitarianism. He sought to understand reality, and much of his writing was devoted to analyses of legal terms in an effort to demonstrate what such terms meant in practical, factual situations. Thus he was vitally interested in the mechanics of the legal system. Of equal importance, he, as a utilitarian, wished to examine all laws to determine whether in actual application, they contributed to the "greatest happiness of the greatest number." Thus he provided an early example of a writer who analyzed both the processes and the purposes of the law (and consequently he could be termed both "analytical" and "philosophical").

Bentham ridiculed the notion of natural law, which presumably laid down self-evident principles of right and wrong, and he conceived of sovereignty in much the same fashion as his fellow Englishman John Austin (1790–1859), who is regarded as the leading exponent of the positivist-imperative-analytical school. This approach conceives of law as the command of a sovereign to those under his jurisdiction, with a sanction or penalty available for noncompliance. Austin viewed law as the relationship existing between a superior and inferiors who are in a condition of habitual obedience. The rightness of such commands is irrelevant; what is important is the element of authority behind them.

The "Pure Science of Law" School

An important contemporary application of the positivist-analytical approach to law is the pure science of law of Hans Kelsen (1881–1973). Kelsen adopted that part of the imperative approach which conceives of law as a command, but instead of looking to a known sovereign, as Austin did, Kelsen found the source of law in an assumed *Grundnorm,* or basic norm, from which all other legal norms are derived. The legal order is thus a hierarchy of norms. The pure science of law requires that law be cleansed of all extraneous elements. To Kelsen, law implies no moral principles or standards; it plays no favorites concerning specific kinds of conduct. Many modern approaches to law, according to Kelsen, are too heavily laden with notions of justice and natural law; modern law has been overcoated with a metaphysical "mist" compounded of subjective moral values. This metaphysical mist must be eliminated if one is to develop a pure science of law. Law, for Kelsen, has little or nothing to do with history, sociology, ethics, or ideals of justice. However, most legal scholars disagree with Kelsen and believe that law cannot stand apart from the social sciences, especially history and sociology, and cannot avoid questions of ethics and justice. While the positivist-analytical and pure legal theorists have added significantly to our understanding of law, they have not produced suitable answers to such questions as: What is law and what are the goals of law?

The Historical School

The historical approach to law seeks to ascertain how law came into being, and it contends that law is intimately related to the social complex in which it has developed. Savigny (1779–1861), an exponent of this school, was not concerned with law as a sovereign command, nor did he seek to divest it of its normative aspects. While admitting the importance of custom as a condition precedent to the existence of formal or positive law, the historical school stressed mankind's intuitive feelings about right and wrong. Men in given environments—at various times and places—were said to react instinctively because of their inherent sense of right. Thus the historical school contended that a sovereign's command to a moral society to perform a dishonest or dishonorable act could not constitute true law. By the same token, legislation that did not conform to standards of right was doomed to failure. Strong links exist between this and the philosophical school.

The Sociological School

The sociological school emphasizes the relationship between law and the needs and institutions of society. A leading exponent of the sociology of law was Eugen Ehrlich (1862–1922), who wrote *Fundamental Principles of the Sociology of Law*. He regarded law as merely one manifestation of society. Put in other words, this school's explanation of law places emphasis upon the need for popular acceptance of law before it can be true law. The living law is the law that is popularly accepted. To the extent that custom meets this test, it receives the approval of the sociological jurist. The most obvious defect of this approach to the law is the attempt to equate law with society itself; law is much narrower in scope. However, the sociological school takes into account both law and society, placing the greater emphasis on formal sources of law such as constitutions, legislation, and judicial opinions.

The Functional School

The leading American exponent of the sociological approach to law was Roscoe Pound (1870–1964), longtime dean of the Harvard Law School. Pound's approach has sometimes been called the "functional approach" to law, for it assigns primary importance to what the law does and how it works—an analysis of function, and most frequently the judicial function. Law, for Pound, is concerned with balancing conflicting and competing social interests. Pound's formula, which recognizes that law, as construed and interpreted, possesses policy value, seeks the realization of maximum wants with a minimum of social friction. Hence law is not really a matter of form or authoritative source, as it was for the analytical theorists, or of intuitive preferences, as it was for the historical jurists. Rather, it is the result of the judicial or administrative balancing of competing interests in society. This has sometimes been referred to as "social engineering."

The Philosophical School

This school is concerned primarily with the rightness of law and the extent to which it aids society in attaining goals conceived by human reason. Thus the standard for the appraisal of law must be found in a philosophy of social life—in a set of social ideals. Law must be studied both as the product of culture and as a means for advancing it. Law is essentially a social means to a social end, which, in the final analysis, is the achievement of social justice. The elements of command and coercion in law are subordinated to the purpose of law. Several jurists of the philosophical school regard law as being independent of, having existed before, and standing above, the state. The test of law is not its official source but its conformity to the community's sense of right.[3]

ETHICS AND JUSTICE

Lawyers, it has been said, are experts in making distinctions. Law is conventionally distinguished from ethics and from justice, although there are those who maintain that such delineations are unreal, that each influences the content of the other, and that if governments and peoples were but willing, ethics and justice could also be law. In support of this point of view it has been suggested that the provisions of the Ten Commandments and other historic religious formulations containing much of morality and justice have been incorporated into the warp and woof of the law. Even a very casual examination of legal principles and statutory rules would clearly support such a conclusion.

[3]Francis W. Coker, *Recent Political Thought*, Appleton-Century-Crofts, Inc., New York, 1934, chap. 19, "Law and the State," pp. 527–541.

Ethics may be distinguished from law. Ethics are concerned with individual morality. They involve motive as well as action, for the area of ethics suggests that motive, no less than action, affects the character of the individual. Ethics encompass rules that describe basic goodness and rightness. They embody the absolute ideal upon which man should pattern his conduct. Voluntary adherence by the individual to such ideal rules, it is assumed, will necessarily promote the good life.

While ethics are essentially personal, they guide, influence, and perfect law. The uniform ethical code of a mass of individuals creates a community standard. It is of itself a view of correct behavior. Such views, if held vigorously by a sufficiently influential number of the group, necessarily will guide the development of law. Failing incorporation into law, ethics are nonetheless a tremendously beneficial influence on human behavior.

However, until society, acting through a legal order, declares itself in favor of the ethical rule that has been imposed by man upon himself, such a rule is not law. A breach of the moral code may lead to widespread censure, but until it is recognized as violative of law, the state takes no notice and imposes no sanctions.

Justice may also be distinguished from law. Law, from the point of view of ideals, is less highly developed than justice. Law, and particularly the administration of law in the courts, is confronted by the requirement that decisions be made. In a hurried, practical world such decisions may not emphasize or even give much attention to justice. Statutes may be uncertain, and the contest may have many ramifications. Perhaps the prize sought may not be readily distributed among the contestants. Rough rather than incisive distinctions as to what is just may be the only ones that, from a practical viewpoint, are available. The fable in which two men quarrel over possession of an oyster illustrates this point. It will be remembered that the arbiter solved the dispute by eating the oyster and giving to each of the disputants the remaining and fairly equal, but certainly not identical, oyster shells.

Law can be unjust. A certain but unjust rule of law may at times receive the support of those who make decisions, in preference to just but uncertain rules. The factor of certainty may prevail over other contending ideas. It has been with this view in mind that judges sometimes declare that it is better that a case be decided than that it be decided right. Further, any movement, according to the laws of physics, results in friction. A change in a well-established, known, and unjust legal rule must overcome social inertia and offer persuasive evidence that it will promote a more just result. Arguments for change may be generally persuasive but unacceptable. Arguments in favor of the status quo may support injustice and yet may contribute to the certainty and stability of the legal apple cart. Moreover, the powers of judges are limited—they are sworn to uphold the law and often look to legislatures to obtain a higher correlation between law and justice.

Nevertheless, Salmond has given abundant proof that justice is the ultimate guide by which law is judged and that law is a basic technique by which justice may be achieved.[4] In this sense, justice is a guide to the moral, fundamental, civilized expectations of man. The purpose of an ideal system of law is, or ought to be, justice. Justice means the existence of ideal relations between men and between men and the state.

Justice ultimately depends upon a scale of social values. In the democratic state, justice is characterized by an emphasis on personal liberty and equality. But in the totalitarian state, where the state rather than the individual is of chief significance, justice is equated with preserving the existence and furthering the will of the state. Here, more than in any other community, justice proves itself lacking in morality.

Where there is conflict as to social values, there will be conflict as to the meaning of justice. There may also be conflict as to the proper group that is to administer justice. For example, in a highly integrated totalitarian state, justice may be the monopoly of the ruling group through party controls or through the influence of the executive branch of the government. In a democratic society, the public shares in the administration of justice through the jury system and through its influence over the various branches of government. No matter what the composition of the dominant group may be, it will attempt to foster and preserve its own set of social values. It is in this sense that law has

---

[4] Sir John Salmond, *Jurisprudence*, 10th ed., Glanville Williams, Sweet and Maxwell, London, 1947, p. 41.

frequently been described as a living institution in a living society.

Today, in the United States, the administration of justice is conducted through several important public bodies and one significant private technique. Although legislative bodies once participated in the administration of justice, constitutional provisions against bills of attainder have entirely eliminated this historic process. However, in England, the House of Lords still functions as the supreme court of appeal in very important cases. While legislatures still establish standards of justice, the primary instrumentality for implementing such standards is the judicial branch of government. In recent years the work of the judiciary, aided by the jury system, has been supplemented by fast-growing administrative agencies. In the area of criminal law, executive clemency serves to soften the decisions of the courts. Finally, in order to secure justice, even beyond the area of law, private disputants now make frequent use of private arbitration panels.

No matter what precise form the decisional component may take, the search for justice will remain of primary importance, at least in democracies. Its goals will always be to establish an ideal relationship between men, based upon their reasonable, civilized expectations and a maximum of "free individual self-assertion,"[5] as well as to establish an ideal relationship between man and the state. Without justice as a fundamental objective, social control through law would rest essentially upon the sterile grounds of pure authority. Justice in its proper context is antithetically opposed to pure authority.

Law, as has been suggested, is related to social control and to justice. Law has so many other aspects that in order to comprehend more fully its true character, it will be well to set forth a scheme of classification.

SOURCES OF LAW

Law may be classified and interpreted from the point of view of its sources, both formal and informal. Where does law come from? Here the two broad categories undoubtedly are natural and positive law.

Natural law is ideal law and as such is a philosophical concept. Hence, if one were attempting to identify its source, one would not look to statutes, judicial decisions, executive orders, or administrative rules and regulations. It is referred to as the "right reason" of man, and while this concept is simple enough, dealing as it does with the assumption that law is the product of universal common agreement based on human intelligence and understanding, there are almost as many views as to the nature, validity, content, and purpose of natural law as there are meanings of law itself.

Much dispute centers around the fundamental characteristics and concepts of natural law. Its very vagueness contributes to varied usage. It may be, and has been, cited by revolutionists as the basis for the rights of man and by fascists in order to support their preference for statism. Conflict exists regarding its allegedly universal character and divine authentication. There is also disagreement as to whether natural law is static and invariable or whether it possesses a dynamic, changing content.

Since man's perception of natural law as an impulse toward good, even when subject to the test of right reason, has failed to provide the ultimate guide in disputes on specific details, does it then follow that natural law should be abandoned? In the history of thought, natural law has a long and well-founded justification.[6] Significant use may be made of its concepts. Its role of providing direction or guidance to positive law—of being an informing agent, a kind of traffic manager for positive law—is manifestly a strategic one. In order to meet criticism, some proponents of natural law speak today of "natural law with variable content." This suggests a relative approach to the substance of law, with given views conforming to right reason at one time and with other, and possibly opposed, views conforming to right reason at a subsequent time.[7]

Positive law, on the other hand, consists only of that thinking, right or wrong, which has received

---

[5]Roscoe Pound, *Justice According to Law*, Yale University Press, New Haven, Conn., 1952, p. 21.

[6]Justice Frankfurter expressed this point of view in his concurring opinion in *Adamson v. California*, 332 U.S. 46, 59–68 (1947). In a dissenting opinion in the same case, Justice Black criticized the "natural-law" theory of the Constitution.

[7]Even those who refuse to accept the notion of natural law recognize that human beliefs as to rightness and wrongness have great influence upon the decisional process.

the express approval of the decision-making authority of the state. The approval is manifested in constitutions, statutes, treaties, administrative rules and regulations, executive orders, and judicial decisions. The foremost exponent of positive law, John Austin, described it as the command laid down by a sovereign (political superior) to a political inferior. Austin's superior habitually received the obedience of the bulk of the community and was not in the habit of obeying any other person or body of persons. Authority, rather than right reason, is the primary characteristic of this concept. The source of positive law is readily identifiable. Its substance or content, however, can be, and frequently is, as variable as that of natural law.

STAGES IN LEGAL DEVELOPMENT

Law may also be classified from the point of view of its maturity or lack of it, or according to the stage of its development. From the historical point of view, the earliest law was primitive law, characterized by slow progress. Its principal and approved technique for ending disputes was self-help. However, a system of courts began to supplant individual strife as a means for the settlement of disputes during this period.

Paton suggests that primitive law was followed by the law of the middle period, which was a period of legal growth. In it there was emphasis at first upon rigidity and technicality. However, the law of the middle period employed fictions, i.e., "as if" reasoning, and equity to modify the technicalities that were characteristic of it at the beginning. During this period recourse to the courts rather than self-help was much expanded.[8]

The next period may be called the "era of classical law," during which law made much progress, taking into account the results of rapid social development. Emphasis was placed on the search for, and the formulation of, general principles.

The final stage of law (if there can be such a stage) would reflect the maturity of law. It is to be hoped that this period might achieve a fusion of ethics, justice, equity, logic, experience, and practical considerations, to the further glorification of systematic law. During such a period the role of law would be particularly important and would provide guidance to men and to their governments. Ideally, it would be dynamic, thus accommodating new social situations; at the same time it would be stable, and through contact with the past it would follow traditional practices in order to protect well-established social and individual interests. Such merging of the new and old would be accomplished through orderly processes.

A new facet of legal development has appeared with the emergence of the underdeveloped nations of Africa and Asia. By Western standards, their legal systems are very primitive and are, for the most part, based on authoritarian cultures. Some of these countries (e.g., India) have had a background of caste and religious stratification inimical to the growth of a concept of egalitarian justice, which, however imperfect, has been the essence of Western jurisprudence. Stoic, Christian, and Anglo-Saxon notions of law, based on popular consent, on the equality of all men, on due process of law, and on fairness and impartiality in the judicial process, are still somewhat alien to many of the cultures of Africa and Asia. Many decades of social and institutional development are the necessary prerequisite to a full understanding and successful implementation by these peoples of the legal concepts of the Western world.

LEGAL SYSTEMS

Law may also be classified from the point of view of geographic areas. Thus we may distinguish international or world law (for the entire world community) from the law of separate nations or, more precisely, from a series of more or less separate systems indigenous to certain cultures. The most influential of these separate systems at the present time are the Roman, civil, Anglo-American, and Soviet.

International Law

International law is a significant area of law and, within limits, is very effective. It is a body of generally accepted principles, standards, and rules regulating or controlling the conduct of nation-states, individuals, and international organizations. Today, the International Court of Justice, estab-

---

[8]G. W. Paton, *A Textbook of Jurisprudence,* Oxford University Press, Fair Lawn, N.J., 1951, pp. 41–46.

lished by the Charter of the United Nations, is charged with the adjudication of controversies arising under the Charter and international law.[9]

Roman Law

Roman law sought to systematize and standardize all the legal rules of the Roman world. It was essentially formalistic rather than equitable in character. Unlike the law of ancient Greece, which individualized cases so that real justice might be achieved, Roman law emphasized strict adherence to stated rules and principles, and it opposed variables and fine distinctions.

Roman law was characterized by its emphasis upon classification. It stressed the notions of order, uniformity, certainty, and inflexibility, and it blended the essential elements of logic and experience. It succeeded in ordering human conduct and in keeping the peace with a minimum of social friction and waste.

It has been described as classical. It has, to a large extent, impressed a classical and invariant character upon the judicial process. Its weakness has been its lack of realism in the face of changing conditions. Both its strengths and its weaknesses have influenced the development of current legal systems. It has provided many of the substantive foundation stones upon which Anglo-American law now rests. It has, for example, greatly influenced our present views as to the nature of contract and the rights of property.

Civil Law

The term "civil law" has many meanings. It has been used to identify that area of the law involving civil, as distinguished from criminal, actions. Here civil law would include suits between legal persons involving torts (civil wrongs), contracts, mortgages, and wills, for example, rather than criminal prosecutions for crimes, such as murder, arson, and traffic-law infractions.

However, civil law has a much broader meaning. One may speak of a civil-law system. Such a system began to develop during the Middle Ages, and as it grew it applied a modified Roman law to the legal problems, legal systems, and customs of the Western European continent.[10] Civil law, in the sense used here, is the important legal system found in continental European countries, especially those possessing a Latin heritage. It is one of the two great legal systems of the modern Western world. As such, it may be contrasted with the great common-law system, also possessing Roman antecedents, which now is fundamental to Anglo-American jurisdictions.

The civil-law system is characterized by emphasis upon statutes and also upon codes of law. Much of the civil law may be traced back to the code prepared for the Roman Emperor Justinian and known as the Justinian Code of 533 A.D. One of the more famous civil codes is that of France, prepared for the Emperor Napoleon in 1804 and known as the Code Napoléon.

In a civil-law country (for this system exists in a number of countries), the role of the legislature is emphasized over that of the courts. Statutes are assumed to constitute a complete, original statement of the social will of the community. The expectation in civil-law countries that the social will could be stated in its entirety at one time in statutory form has proved to be unfounded and an inadequate basis for law. Consequently, the civil-law codes as represented in the Corpus Juris Civilis (a term used since the seventeenth century to describe the digest, institute, code, and novels of Justinian) have always been the subject of much judicial interpretation, explanation, and construction.

Under the civil-law system, primary responsibility for such interpretation has fallen to the teachers of law. In fact, their role in giving final meaning to the codes has been more important than that of the judges. The textbooks of the teachers have become the significant guides to the meaning of civil law.

Civil-law codes deal with typical legal subjects. Examples are civil procedure, criminal procedure, commercial law, maritime law, property, and wills. The civil-law system has emphasized an objective legal order protecting private rights on an equal basis. All individuals in a common situation in a civil-law system stand before the law on the basis of equality.

---

[9] See Chap. 21.

[10] The Roman law was modified by canon or church law, feudal law, and existing primitive and barbaric customs.

Civil law, like common law, is a taught tradition, but on the other hand, it has not been able to rely upon judicial pronouncements as a source of growth. In civil-law countries, judicial decisions are regarded as merely persuasive, rather than as precedents entitled to more than usual respect. Civil law, then, is essentially the product of the legislator and the professional commentator rather than of the judge.

The role of the judge in a civil-law country is interesting. Decided cases provide rules, not principles, and such cases are not very valuable to the judge during the gestative period of the decisional process. Nonetheless, he must arrive at a decision, even where the code either is vague or makes no reference at all to the issue in dispute. Failure to decide a case may make the judge criminally liable for a denial of justice. In such circumstances the civil-law judge, upon the urging of the *avocat* (lawyer), readily reasons by analogy from a convenient legislative command or precept. Thus reliance on the command of the state, manifested through the legislative process rather than through the courts, is fundamental to the civil law.

From a realistic point of view, legislators embroiled in serious political differences rarely have the time or the inclination to close awkward gaps in existing legislation. Consequently, even in the civil-law countries, the judge is frequently called upon to legislate in fact, if not in legal theory.

Common Law

The common law is another of the world's great legal systems. It is characterized by the concepts of the supremacy of law and of man's equality before it. Common law is judge-made law. Under the common-law system, cases decided by judges are regarded as a valid, major source of law. Common law originated in England and is based on the case law built up by the itinerant justices of the king's superior courts, who were sent out from London to apply common or general customs to litigation in various parts of the realm. Common law depends upon a centralized system of courts following established methods. The common-law system supposes a uniform judicial approach to the interpretation of legislative, executive, judicial, and administrative determinations. The common-law judge may look to legislative enactments, to traditional or customary law, and to the consensus of reasonableness in arriving at his decision. As an instrumentality of government he may effectually proclaim rights and provide remedies.

Both the substantive rules and the techniques of the common-law system are in use in the United States and in most of the English-speaking nations. The common-law system was brought to the American colonies at an early date and was readily adapted to conditions somewhat different from those existing in England. Its rules and techniques are basic to the administration of justice in the United States.

The essence of the common-law system is the judicial process. The lawyer initially and the judge subsequently, in order to ascertain the law to be applied to a dispute, are obliged to consider previously decided cases. Prior judicial expressions are highly significant as to the meaning of the law. Since no two cases can be precisely the same, the lawyer and the judge must make comparisons between earlier cases and the one under consideration in order to analyze their similarities and differences. If the judge can find significant similarities, through a process known as "analogy" (which consists of making comparisons), he accepts any applicable rules or principles found in previously decided cases. Usually the judge's research enables him to find an earlier, reasonably analogous situation that serves, both fairly and logically, as a precedent in the problem case.

However, where legislation has not been enacted to clarify or protect rights, the courts may provide judicial protection for reasonable conduct. Ultimately, if the judge can find no guidance in cases, he may have to improvise and may create law out of his deeper sense of what is just and reasonable under the circumstances. The occasions are rare when a judge must go this far.

The common-law system is concerned with more than simply finding the authoritative law to be applied in a particular case. Also present is the problem of shaping old law to meet new social conditions. There is also the need to formulate general principles that will serve as stabilizing influences in human relations. The judge must be an observer of emerging social values and a translator of such observations into law.

The judge, as a public official with the force of the state behind his proper actions, may in his opinions systematize and organize the law. Such opinions provide a known and accessible source of law. Further, common law with its appellate judicial processes can be used to unify the valid, and avoid the provincial, attitudes of the lesser courts.

While the common-law system has been a unifying factor in the economic and political life of the United States, its mere existence has not resulted in the acceptance of common legal principles throughout the entire nation. Louisiana, for example, follows the civil-law system, having based much of its law on the Code Napoléon. Excluding Louisiana, the technique of judge-made law is uniformly accepted in the United States, and it has not been without influence in Louisiana.

Diversity also exists among the common-law states because differing views on a given legal problem are to be expected in a country as large and diverse as ours. Thus the states of the American union are usually divided in their support between majority and minority rules of substantive law.

As a technique for the administration of justice, the common-law system has achieved notable results. Involving as it does the central role of the judge, the system can be no better than its judges. The common law assumes that the judge will adhere to reasonable precedents with reasonable frequency and that he will not be unfair or arbitrary. However, in actual fact, a judge may decide cases incorrectly, as through a misunderstanding of existing law or through the application of unsupportable general reasoning to a unique situation. A dissatisfied litigant may usually appeal from the decision of a trial court on the grounds (among others) that the trial court erred in construing existing law or that it decided a case without having the required jurisdiction over it.

Appellate courts enjoy a wider latitude than trial courts insofar as adherence to precedent is concerned. While generally seeking to maintain legal stability by following precedent, our state and federal supreme courts recognize their responsibility for the adaptation of earlier legal rules to accommodate the strains and stresses imposed by changing conditions in the entire social complex.

Probably the greatest merit of the common-law system is to be found in this adaptability to a shifting environment. Common-law flexibility in judicial hands permits a gradual, steady growth and accommodation, very different from the periodic and extensive legislative overhaulings required by systems of code law. Legal lag is less pronounced in common-law countries, where broad principles, originally formulated in an agricultural society, have been adapted to a complex, industrial economy. However, since this capacity for growth depends on the wisdom of judges, a basic question arises: How much latitude should judges have in shaping the law? In answering this question, a distinction must be noted between two areas of law: public law and private law. Although the judge enjoys considerable latitude in both fields, the range of judicial discretion is distinctly wider in the public-law field.

Public law, in the common-law system, is that area of the law affecting the rights of the individual in which the state is dominant and the individual occupies a subordinate position. Public law is often concerned with great issues of public policy, although a public-law question would exist if even a minor issue affecting the power of the state over the individual were the sole problem before the court. Constitutional law, for example, falls within the area of public law, and when the United States Supreme Court is confronted with a case in which it must determine the effect of the federal war power, the federal taxing power, or the federal power over interstate commerce, it is then concerned with both public law and broad issues of public policy. A decision relating to the use of the war power could conceivably be vital to national security and even national survival, as well as to an individual's rights. The civil and political rights and liberties of citizens fall within the area of public law. Within our democratic tradition it is a principal function of courts to protect individuals against abuses emanating from public officials and private persons. In the policy area of individual rights the courts possess much latitude. Here there is less regard for judicial certainty and uniformity. Such exercises of judicial discretion sometimes provoke the charge that the courts (and especially the United States Supreme Court) are superlegislatures.

Private law, on the other hand, deals with relationships between individuals in which they are equals. In this area the latitude of the common-law judge is considerably more restricted. In such fields as contracts, mortgages, and the law of property, where the business community has become accustomed to established rules and methods and where the need for judicial change is less pressing, judges are much less inclined to assume the legislative role. In the realm of private law, adherence to precedent is the usual, but not the exclusive, approach; here the legislature performs the major task of modernizing and rehabilitating the law.

Barring the occasional eccentric, highly opinionated, or ignorant judge, the judicial response to public- and private-law situations tends to be rather uniform. Judges are the product of a fairly uniform system of legal education, the roots of which go deep into the past. Judges, as lawyers, have shared many common experiences. They are all much influenced by the guiding force of a continuous tradition. As a result, they generally react rather uniformly to the legal situations that confront them. The fact is that judges think and act alike because they are judges. The judicial tradition tends toward an organic growth of the law, which tends to become a fairly consistent whole. However, if it were not for judges who are persuaded, rightly or wrongly, of the need to break existing legal images, there would be no occasion for surging changes in the direction taken by the law. However, the occasional modification of legal imagery is a far cry from a shattering of the entire legal structure.

Judicial latitude in significant policy situations has led to the observation that certainty is the greatest myth of the law. The common-law system permits judicial invalidation or overruling of previously decided cases. The need for occasional overruling of earlier decisions was clearly seen by the late Justice Cardozo, who wrote that judges who misinterpret the mores of their day should not be permitted to tie, in helpless submission, the hands of their successors.[11]

The conflict between the need for legal certainty and that for judicial flexibility is of long standing. With uniformity in the law, based on the general practice of following the rules laid down in reported cases, the lawyer is able to advise his clients. They in turn can make important decisions and act upon them. Confidence in the legality of one's actions is reassuring to everyone and is especially conducive to stability in the business community. However, the broader needs of society may from time to time require courts to modify or discard previously announced rules. The judge, as guardian of the common-law system, possesses the latitude to continue earlier traditions or, within limits, to embark upon new paths that he expects will more closely promote the common welfare.

The common law suffers from several limitations. The judge brings his learning to bear only after an event has happened. His decision discloses what the litigants should have done. At least one and perhaps both of the parties may have acted at their peril, although they may have consulted legal counsel who offered guidance after examining previously decided cases. Although the attorney may have been conscientious and capable, the court may decide that the earlier cases have lost their vitality and should be disregarded or overruled. Admittedly, this is an uncertainty that the common-law system cannot protect against.

On the other hand, courts may adhere to old cases decided during times long since outmoded. There is often a time lag between the demands of social expediency and corresponding changes in judge-made law. This is attributable partly to rather conservative thought patterns among our judges and partly to certain defects of form in the common-law system. Here one is confronted with a superabundance of materials, consisting of literally hundreds of thousands of decided cases, with the consequent and very real problem of integration and reconciliation. Myriads of tiny but necessary changes are constantly being made by judges to eradicate small spots of organic decay in the law. This leads to the charge that the common-law system creates a wilderness of single instances and that essential guiding rules and principles are all too painfully lacking.

Other criticisms bear out the point, already made, that the common-law system is not perfect. Important decisions may not be entirely clear. The essentials of the judicial opinion must be separated from its incidentals. The cases themselves must be interpreted. This is not made easier by the loquacious judge or by the judge who occasionally writes more

---

[11] B. N. Cardozo, *The Nature of the Judicial Process*, Yale University Press, New Haven, Conn., 1928, p. 150.

for his own enjoyment or advantage than for the benefit of the litigant.

The prejudices of individual judges also affect individual decisions. Our system of appeals permits rectification of unfair decisions, although one should not lose sight of the high cost of appeals and of the half-humorous description of the United States Supreme Court as the court of final appeal and ultimate error. At the trial stage, crowded court calendars may result first in delay and then in hasty decisions. Further, the court, in a certain sense, is passive. It must wait for litigants to bring cases to it. It is not permitted to initiate inquiries into critical areas of conduct. Despite all these criticisms of the common-law system—and there are others, for example, the occasional corrupt judge—it is fair to say that this system accords to the individual a standard of justice probably not attained or obtainable elsewhere in the civilized world.

Soviet Law

The Soviet Union has a distinctive legal system. As will be pointed out in Chapter 13, Soviet law possesses a special character. Lenin once said, "Law is politics," and the law of the Soviet Union is declared to be "class" law, "proletarian" law, rooted in materialism and environmental factors. Rejecting universal concepts of law and justice, Soviet jurisprudence views law as one more instrument for the realization of national, class, and ideological policy.

In the Soviet Union, many traditional Western principles and rules have been blended with the newer demands of the Soviet state. It is as though the Soviets had erected a new structure, employing old bricks but new mortar. They regard international law, as they do all law, as an instrumentality to advance the Soviet program.[12]

Differences between Soviet and Western Law

Soviet law contrasts sharply with Anglo-American, Roman, and civil law. In the first place, the Soviets regard their legal system as an instrument dedicated to the final victory of the toilers in their inevitable class struggle. Soviet law is not supposed to be neutral; its objective is to build a communist socie-

[12]Andrei Y. Vyshinsky, *The Law of the Soviet State*, The Macmillan Company, New York, 1948, pp. 11, 50.

ty and a special economic order. The other systems seek no such comparable objectives; their professed goal is impartial justice.

Second, because Soviet law is viewed as a tool or technique available to the state for the achievement of its objectives (both domestic and international), it is highly flexible, adaptable to circumstances, and subservient to changes in the Communist party program. Other systems are both more democratically oriented and more stable.

Third, while Soviet law may be, and is, used to protect common interpersonal relationships, its dominant concern is the protection of the Soviet regime and the ruling Communist party. Collective rights transcend individual rights. Other legal systems place greater emphasis upon the equal status and rights of citizens and accord to the individual more effective protections against interference by government.

A final difference to be noted is the allegedly *temporary* character of Soviet law. When (and if) the Soviet Union achieves its goal of pure communism, laws and the state itself may be expected to "wither away." (See Chapter 6 for further discussion of this theory.) Needless to say, all other legal systems are viewed as permanent.

SOME CHARACTERISTICS OF LAW

In consequence of the great variety of views toward law, it is not an easy task to summarize its essential characteristics. Nonetheless, in a democratic society several important elements can be identified.

Interrelationships

First, to understand law, one must realize that it deals with interrelationships. Law is alert to relationships of many kinds, and its essential function is to mediate between and among opposing and often conflicting relationships. It may mediate between an individual and another individual or between groups, one of which may be the largest social group—the state. These are relationships external to, but encompassed by, the law. In another sense, law consists of internal relationships, such as the relationship between its own principles, standards, and rules. These, too, are in need of balancing.

Principles, Standards, and Rules

Second, law distinguishes between its three major components—principles, standards, and rules. The *principles* of law are general, eternal, theoretical, and broad to the degree of being almost all-encompassing. A few such legal principles are as follows: Agreements should be kept; no one should benefit from his own wrong; a person is presumed innocent of guilt.

Standards constitute the connective tissue between broad and possibly inoperative principles and specific and possibly extremely harsh rules. It is the function of the standard to mediate between such concepts by interposing considerations of reasonableness, fairness, and compassion. A standard other than reasonableness is that of the "public interest, convenience, and necessity."

The interrelated *rules* are particular, more or less permanent (but may be extremely short-lived), practical, limited, and specific. Formal rules usually contain sanctions, although conformity with rules rests more frequently than not upon the habit of obedience. For example, a person who is convicted of murder may be sentenced to death or life imprisonment; one who is convicted of speeding must pay a fine or be imprisoned. It is easier to comply with rules than to exert oneself to the point of engaging in violations. Compliance is more frequent than violation; violations are more frequent than sanctions. The state's monopoly of legal force enables it to employ a great variety of sanctions. In proper cases such sanctions, or threats to impose them, undoubtedly do possess real, if sometimes short-range, effectiveness. From the foregoing it may be concluded that the part of law dealing with rules, sometimes referred to as "lawyer's law," has the quality of being restricted to fairly narrow and exact boundaries. This kind of law is less than the totality of the social complex and permits a distinction to be drawn between law and morals, law and religion, or law and social customs. All these influence human conduct to a substantial extent.

Sources

A third characteristic of law relates to its sources. As pointed out above, the two major sources of law are its *formal* and *idealistic* elements. The formal source is the positive law, which, like rules, deals with the law that actually exists. Formal sources include constitutions, statutes, administrative orders, and judicial decisions, among others. These illustrations point to the need for specific rules and for certainty in their interpretation in order to achieve stable, harmonious individual and social interrelationships. The result may be conformity to old, fixed rules even though there may be doubt as to their fairness today.

The idealistic or normative source of the law is natural law, which, like principles, seeks to determine what law ought to be. Guided by the doctrine of right reason, it is concerned with the ends or goals of law. It stresses justice, fair play, and the constant improvement of man as a social and moral being.

Paradoxes

Fourth, law reflects many inconsistencies and paradoxes. It is at once both dynamic and static; it exists in an environment of ceaseless change, and yet it is characterized by inertia and is subject to the restraining influences of those forces which support the status quo. On the whole, law is perhaps more dynamic than static and has come to be regarded as a living institution in a living society. Justice Holmes once referred to law as a point on the line of time, and more recently the late Supreme Court Justice Robert H. Jackson observed, "No alert lawyer doubts that the law he works with is constantly being reshaped and at any given moment represents a point at which contending forces have temporarily come to balance."[13]

Conflicts

Fifth, specific legal rules can be in sharp conflict with one another, just as opposing principles may compete for acceptance by judges, legislators, and the body politic. It has been said, for example, that legal rules travel in opposite or opposing pairs. This means that in the interpretation of the law—in the balancing of competing points of view—the role of the judge or other policy maker is to choose. In this context, customs and traditions are of major significance. Just as principles, standards, and rules are interconnected, so one must seek for harmony or

---

[13]Robert H. Jackson, *Jurisprudence in Action*, Baker, Voorhis & Company, Inc., New York, 1953, foreword, p. iv.

for preferences within the rules. This results in emphasizing the importance of the kind of choice exercised by judges and others who have a part in the decisional process. It is well known that the principal function of judges is to exercise choice. Their options are many. They can choose between competing legal concepts, they have a choice as to the facts they will use, and they may elect between competing values and value systems. It is for judges to determine whether their tribunals have jurisdiction to hear cases presented to them. Undoubtedly, judges' most important and most personal choices concern their perception of their function—activism or judicial self-restraint.

The Role of the Community

Sixth, law permits (indeed, compels) its interpreters to refer to the community—more particularly to the particular community—for guidance in the making of choices. National law reflects the national community; international law is restricted by the limited development of an international community. Law inevitably derives its qualities (simple or sophisticated, rude or barbaric) from the nature of the community in which it arises.

Other Characteristics

Finally, law possesses other characteristics, such as its capacity to accept any kind of legal dispute, even one that may arise in a political context. Law cannot exist without reference to a legal order, i.e., a government in some form, centralized or decentralized. Although law is usually held to be general in its context and impersonal in its application, there are many exceptions. It is able to effect all manner of classifications and distinctions, so that in reality it does take significant differences into account. The law is able to particularize on account of age, sex, and mental capacity. Recently it has begun to abandon distinctions based on color and place of residence.

OTHER BASES FOR THE CLASSIFICATION OF LAW

Law and Equity

In Anglo-American jurisprudence a distinction is commonly made between law and equity. Originally equity was a process to soften the harsh rules that had become a part of English common law. It was employed by the king's chancellor, who, as a churchman, had been trained in canon law. Originally the chancellor's conscience, as influenced by his whole outlook on temporal matters, led to broad departures from the rigors of the common-law system. Equity, at its inception, emphasized fairness and justice. However, as the system of equity matured, it lost much of its early flexibility and capacity for change. Today, while still stressing fair play and good conscience, equity is limited to such matters as suits for the specific enforcement of special contracts, the reformation or rescission of unfair contracts, and the securing of injunctions requiring acts that in the absence of court order, persons have been unwilling to perform.

Equity can also be distinguished from law in the sense that equity deals with remedies, while law deals with rights. One person, for example, may have a valid claim against another. Law determines the nature of the right and may require one party to pay damages to the injured person. Equity provides the remedy of specific enforcement of contracts rather than monetary damages for nonperformance. Equity, with its greater emphasis on remedies, seeks more closely to approximate the terms of original understandings and their fair implementation.

Law as the Protection of Interests

Law may also be classified from the point of view of the interests protected. Here the basic areas of interest are individual and social. In this classification there is an assumption that at certain points, individual interests may be in conflict with those of other individuals and also with the interests of society.

Individual interests include personal interests, such as physical protection and freedom from slavery; family interests, such as marriage and the rights of children; economic interests, e.g., the right to property and economic security; and political interests, including participation in politics and the right to vote and to be elected. Social interests encompass such matters as the existence of an effective legal order, including laws and a judicial system; national security, including a code of military justice; the economic welfare of society, including opportunities for employment; the protection of religious, moral, humanitarian, and intellectual values, including constitutional guarantees of civil rights and liberties; and the maintenance of a strong and healthy population, including activity falling within the broad range of public health, safety, morals, and welfare. While the points of conflict between society and the individual are sometimes emphasized, the areas of agreement are broader and more significant.

BY WAY OF SUMMARY

From the foregoing it may be concluded—at least with reference to a democratic society—that law cannot be regarded as merely an arbitrary order impressed upon an undiscerning and unresisting public. Nonetheless, law occupies a dominant and central position in the state; it is the ultimate evidence of the state's final power and authority. Law is not, and cannot be, a simple thing with "one simple meaning."[14] Law cannot be equated with legislative statutes and nothing more. Such statutes are indeed laws, but the law is more than statutory enactment. The law is to be found in constitutions and in all the formal regalia of governments. But law is also to be found in human behavior and attitudes, for it is through such means that the primacy of the rule of law is acknowledged as a viable alternative to force in the resolution of opposing claims.

Law is not a universal whole. In federal states there is normally a lack of wholly consistent and uniform laws. A number of problems arise in the implementation of laws, such as competition among different governmental agencies for the authority to promulgate or administer laws; the misinterpretation of, or a misapprehension respecting, the nature of existing laws; or the retention of obsolete laws under modern conditions. However, the presence of difficult dilemmas does not vitiate the overall importance of the law in organized society.

In spite of all these problems, the central idea in law is that of control. Control in this sense does not necessarily relate to a restriction upon conduct. Control may, in fact, enlarge as well as restrain conduct. While law establishes affirmative rights for individuals, such as subsidies, pensions, and other money grants, and while it enlarges man's freedoms through protection of free speech, press, and worship, it also limits human action through interdicting murder, arson, rape, and even some forms of speaking, writing, and religious activities.

Law deals with and is the product of the conduct of man in society. It is a control that concerns relationships existing between man and man, between man and groups of men, between man and the state, between states themselves, and even between states, individuals, and international organizations. While its scope is large, it is not all-encompassing, and there are many areas in which law has not ventured to establish firm patterns of conduct, such as styles of dress, family courtesies, diction, posture, and certain religious observances.

The search for the meaning of law is a never-ending one because the substance of law is both large and ever-changing. The search for ultimate rules has been complicated by views held in foreign countries and in alien cultures and by the ever-present factor of change. In France, for example, the important and traditional word is *droit,* which contains heavy overtones of right and justice as well as law. American law, on the other hand, does not necessarily concern itself with notions of justice, although Anglo-American law is much guided by justice as an ideal. This complicates the search for universals.

In short, law is a relational science. It is a device allowing the achievement of orderly change. It is a means facilitating unification of the social order. But in its largest and most important sense, law is obliged to mediate among the often vague, difficult, and contending interests of individuals and groups. Charged with high missions, the law should listen attentively to the advice of former Chief Justice Earl Warren, who said: "In these trying times when much of the world has not made up its mind whether it will abide by the force of law or adhere to the law of force, it is our great mission both at home and abroad to keep the terms law and justice synonymous."[15]

A Definition of Law

In view of what has been said, the difficulty of arriving at a definition of law is readily appreciable. Nonetheless, for the purpose of stimulating more thought on the subject, a working definition is here suggested: In a democratic society, law is a process

---

[14]Pound, loc. cit.

[15]Earl Warren, "Convocation Address," *University of Illinois Law Forum*, 1956, p. 278.

with a purpose; it is an institution contributing to the realization of balanced individual and social value-oriented goals.

It has been said that law possesses a statecraft all its own, that it has the quality of improvability. As a living institution it participates in man's aspirations for a better, brighter world. It is also the heritage of proud men who seek the total unfolding of man's true potential. Properly employed, law is an achievement of the first order of importance.[16]

STUDY-GUIDE QUESTIONS

1 On what grounds is it possible to justify the view that law is not, and cannot be, a simple thing with one simple meaning?
2 What are the arguments for and against the view that the enforceable orders of a band of brigands can constitute "law"?
3 Have you, in your own personal experiences, been able to observe the working of law and the judicial process from the perspectives set forth in this chapter?
4 What are some of the reasons why law cannot be equated with universal justice?
5 In the United States, justices of our Supreme Court occasionally observe that the courts are not the only branch of government that has the capacity to govern. From your reading can you offer an opinion on why such judicial observations are made?

REFERENCES

Cahn, Edmond N.: *The Moral Decision: Right and Wrong in the Light of American Law,* Indiana University Press, Bloomington, Ind., 1955.

Cardozo, Benjamin N.: *The Nature of the Judicial Process,* Yale University Press, New Haven, Conn., 1928.

Cohen, Morris R., and Felix S. Cohen: *Readings in Jurisprudence and Legal Philosophy,* Prentice-Hall, Inc., Englewood Cliffs, N.J., 1951.

Coker, Francis W.: *Recent Political Thought,* Appleton-Century-Crofts, Inc., New York, 1934, chap. 19.

Frank, Jerome: *Courts on Trial,* Princeton University Press, Princeton, N.J., 1950.

Friedrich, Carl J.: *The Philosophy of Law in Historical Perspective,* The University of Chicago Press, Chicago, 1958.

Hurst, J. W.: *The Growth of American Law,* Little, Brown and Company, Boston, 1950.

Paton, George W.: *A Textbook of Jurisprudence,* Oxford University Press, Fair Lawn, N.J., 1951.

Pound, Roscoe: *Justice According to Law,* Yale University Press, New Haven, Conn., 1951.

Rostow, Eugene V. (ed.): *Is Law Dead?* Clarion Books, New York, 1971.

Wolff, Robert P. (ed.): *Rule of Law,* Clarion Books, New York, 1971.

---

[16]Dean Pound considers law to be social control through the systematic application of the force of a politically organized society. Edward H. Levi, formerly of the University of Chicago Law School and in 1975 appointed Attorney General of the United States, has defined law as a set of principles dealing with justice and a set of normative rules regulating human behavior. Huntington Cairns has said that law is the "means through which the community maintains itself and achieves its end." Huntington Cairns, "The Community as the Legal Order," in Carl J. Friedrich (ed.), *Community,* The Liberal Arts Press, Inc., New York, 1959, pp. 31–49. All stress the view that law is a device of social control.

Chapter 5

Liberalism and Democracy

IDEOLOGY

A first principle of political life is that power seeks legitimacy. Whether the head of a family or the chief of state, the wielder of power attempts to justify his acts in terms of some ethical principle: the father's knowledge of what is necessary for the child's healthy growth, or the president's authority that derives from an electoral majority and constitutional procedure. Few men in history have sought to legitimate their power by relying exclusively on their superior strength or greater wealth. They invent or subscribe to formulas, myths, superstitions, or metaphysical sanctions to make it appear that they are the agent of some greater and more impersonal force at work in human affairs. It also is true that political stability and governmental efficiency depend in large part on the willing compliance of citizens who believe that the institutions, personnel, and policies of government are legitimate—that government has the right to do what it does. "Ideology," then, refers to the values or principles that those who exercise or seek political power refer to in order to lend legitimacy to their acts. In this sense "ideology" is a neutral term, and it is misleading to say (for example) that those who are democratic have philosophy, while those who are authoritarian have ideology.

Functions of Ideology

By providing government with legitimacy, ideology justifies the status quo. But ideology also may be used by reformists or rebels to attack the status quo. While governments may sanction their oppression of citizens by citing the "divine right of kings" or "historical inevitability," rebellious citizens may legitimate their own acts of violence by appealing to principles of "natural right" or the "consent of the governed." An ideology that is identified with the apparent interests of the working class may be used to challenge the authority of the bourgeois state, and, subsequently, the same ideology may be

61

used to legitimate dictatorial control over the working class.

By imparting an ethical basis to the exercise of political power, ideology also helps to cohere citizens of the state or followers of a movement who seek to change the state. Ideology facilitates symbolic communication between leaders and the led, and it enables them to struggle with each other in terms of principles instead of personalities. Ideology serves as a guide to policy choices and political behavior. And ideology explains to all those who consult it and believe in it the meaning of their existence and the purposes of their action. The success of a particular ideology, then, is at least as much a matter of faith as it is the result of rational conviction. And this applies with equal force to both democratic and authoritarian ideologies.

DEMOCRACY VERSUS AUTHORITARIANISM: FIRST ASSUMPTIONS

What is the nature of man? There is no way to answer this question "scientifically." No matter how many facts we have before us that purport to reveal various facets of human personality and motivation, our conclusions about human nature are invariably the result of a conceptual arrangement of the data, and this in turn is likely to be mixed together with our own value prejudices. We are asking a question that is fundamentally philosophical, and there may well be as many answers as there are philosophers. Most philosophers who have speculated on the nature of man have assumed that their conclusions apply to all men in all places at all times. But most philosophers also have derived their conclusions from unsystematic observation of their own narrow cultural and social setting.

Whatever our view of human nature, it has immediate implications for our political preferences. And however we choose between democratic and authoritarian options, our choice automatically implies a view of the nature of man. Thus most political philosophers have been compelled to argue that there is such a thing as "human nature," that we can observe its various manifestations, and that each individual has a right to develop his personality and talents insofar as this does not inhibit similar efforts by others. Surprisingly, both authoritarians and democrats agree on these fundamental points, and the assumption of an inherent right of individual development may be construed as an almost universally accepted "natural right" of human existence. What divides democrats from authoritarians is their conclusion about the following: the extent to which each individual is capable of self-development without the aid of superior authority.

Thus the authoritarian has a dim view of what man can accomplish on his own. Plato, for example, considered that most men were uninformed about their natural capabilities. Without enlightened guidance from absolute political authority, they were unable to develop their capabilities, and they consequently were unable to ensure their own happiness and the justice of the larger social order. Christianity has traditionally viewed man as a sinful creature, living a temporary and mortal existence as punishment for his sins and as a test to determine whether he is eternally damned or saved. To improve the chances of salvation, mortal man is in perpetual need of the authoritarian guidance of God's divine law, which is interpreted and administered in an equally authoritarian manner by the religious institutions that God has ordained on earth. Both communism and fascism, with their sights fixed on the here and now instead of the hereafter, also agree that the individual, by himself, is capricious; without the guidance of the party or state, man is doomed to a meaningless life that neither fulfills his own potential nor achieves the more meaningful goals that are associated with membership in a particular class or cultural group.

The democrat, on the other hand, regards man as a basically rational creature, neither mired in sin nor dependent on a superior social order for the fulfillment of his individual potential. The individual himself, argues the democrat, is best able to understand his own needs and interests. He is the most likely to know, if only through trial and error, what actions are appropriate to the attainment of his particular objectives. The individual's continuing efforts to improve the circumstances of his life are also likely to contribute to the betterment of the whole society, and this in turn explains why "progress" is a major characteristic of those societies in which men are free to define and to pursue their own welfare. Some democratic philosophers have admitted that this may not always be the case, but they quickly reply that there is no way of determining when and under what conditions the individual or the society is most likely to benefit from authoritarian guidance. It does not follow logically, they say, that authoritarianism in the family justifies authoritarianism in the state. For the democrat, then, most of the "truths" of social existence are relative, and our admission of uncertainty as to ultimate truths commits us to a policy of tolerating differences in both opinion and behavior. Society and government, in short, are most properly structured in terms of the principles of "liberalism."

CLASSICAL LIBERALISM

The early development of liberal ideology is closely tied to the ideas of the Enlightenment and the French Revolution of the late eighteenth century. It is important to remember that liberalism thus began as the ideology of a particular class that identified the interests of all mankind with its own particular interests. In part, the universal and absolute characteristics of Enlightenment thought and liberal ideology were a response to the heavy-handed censorship of the French monarchy, which prevented discussion and debate on the specific details of French politics and social organization; unable to talk in terms of particular reforms, Enlightenment thinkers tended to generalize with sweeping abstractions. But "liberty, equality, and fraternity" referred to the aspirations of the French bourgeoisie—the rising middle class of businessmen, shop owners, merchants, bankers, intellectuals, and professionals (lawyers, doctors, journalists, engineers)—who felt constrained by the institutions of an aristocratic society ruled by absolute monarchy.

The French bourgeoisie of the eighteenth century sought an end to outmoded economic controls (identified as "mercantilism") on trade, capital investment, and business growth; it sought the elimination of the role of the Catholic Church as a major property-owning and economic institution in French society; it wanted a reduction in the powers of the monarchy or—according to the dictates of revolutionary events—its complete dissolution; and it urged the abolition of inherited privilege and social status that distinguished the aristocracy from the bourgeoisie. In the place of monarchy the bourgeoisie wanted parliamentary institutions that were controlled by the bourgeoisie; in the place of mercantilism it wanted an economic system of free trade based on capitalism and the principles of laissez faire (no economic intervention by the state); and instead of inherited privilege and social status it wanted all men to enjoy the same opportunities for self-development, at least at birth, unencumbered by differences in title or rank.

Equality

The frequent debates over the meaning of "equality" in liberal ideology, then, have usually missed the point, and they still do so today. The writers of the American Declaration of Independence and the French Declaration of the Rights of Man did not mean to say that "all men are created equal" in virtue, talent, rational insight, and business ingenuity. Indeed, it was apparent to the early liberals in France, England, and the United States that there are substantial differences between people in these and many other categories of social life.

The point was that all individuals ought to have an equal opportunity to demonstrate their particular capabilities and that their circumstances of birth should not jeopardize their chances of proving whether they have these capabilities—that, in short, everyone should have an equal opportunity to show how unequal he is. The assault of liberalism on the bastions of aristocratic privilege should not be interpreted as an argument in defense of either social sameness or economic equality. In fact, the *political* values of classical liberalism represented the conviction that economic *in*equality was not only inevitable but also a good thing for all concerned.

The Ruling Elite

The liberals argued that political power ought to be in the hands of those who own property and those who, through their own ingenuity and hard work, have demonstrated their superior capacity for governing. The argument was not entirely new to the history of political philosophy.

Aristotle, in fact, had declared that the best practicable state (the "polity") was based on property ownership, with the middle classes of the society dominating the political system. His argument was in part a response to Plato's opposing view that the combination of economic power and political power was detrimental to both rulers and ruled; good public policy was most likely to emanate from political leaders who had no economic stake in their political decisions. And, for Plato, policy makers should not have any property at all. The argument seems especially relevant to a society that, in the early 1970s, is agitated by the corruption of even its senior public officials.

Plato's unorthodox views, however, have been clearly in the minority, and the point is underlined by the important influence of Protestant thought on liberal ideology. Especially for John Calvin in the sixteenth century, the justification for political authority was in the economic success of God's "elect." Men prosper only according to the will of God, argued Calvin, and their prosperity is a clear sign that God has chosen them for salvation. It follows that those who are divinely blessed ought to govern. The close association of Protestantism, capitalism, and the political philosophy of liberalism was hardly coincidental.

The Functions of Government

Classical liberalism, then, not only implied a union of economic and political power but also assumed that the functions of government should be minimal because rational men pursuing their economic self-interest are only handicapped by governmental intervention. The "wealth of nations," as the English liberal economist and philosopher Adam Smith put it in 1776, results from each individual's working for his own economic advantage. "Private vice equals public virtue" was the accepted formula, and Smith's concept of the "invisible hand" was meant to reassure liberals everywhere that the general welfare was a function of their own acquisitive instincts. Good government was limited government, and the best government was the government that governed least because government was an evil—albeit a necessary evil.

The proper and primary role of government was to ensure for each individual his natural right to private property. A government that transgressed against this natural right, as John Locke had argued in the late seventeenth century, broke the social contract, which was the government's only source of legitimate power. Individual freedom and liberty, then, were equivalent to an absence of institutional restraint. And it probably is true that, in their particular time and place, the principles of classical liberalism were essential to the economic betterment and political liberalization of societies with inefficient economies and autocratic governments.

The ideas that were appropriate for preindustrial societies in the eighteenth and nineteenth centuries, however, are not necessarily appropriate to the industrial or even the economically underdeveloped societies of the twentieth century. And classical liberalism, in effect, was an ideology justifying the authoritarian control of the whole society by the middle class. Compared with its ideological predecessors, it was unquestionably a step in the direction of what we mean today by "democracy." And the very generality of its principles of "liberty, equality, and fraternity" lay ready at hand for later and more liberal thinkers who wanted to extend the privileges of the bourgeoisie to everyone in the society, regardless of property-owning status.

NEOLIBERALISM

In the contemporary United States, and at least since Franklin Roosevelt's New Deal programs of the 1930s, "liberalism" has come to mean the intervention of the state in the affairs of citizens, and not only in their economic relationships. The ultimate end of both classical liberalism and neoliberalism remains the same: to secure for all citizens an equal opportunity for individual self-development. But the *means* to that end have changed, and government is understood by contemporary liberals to be a necessary instrument for maximizing individual opportunity. In an age when liberalism has come to mean "one man, one vote" instead of political domination by a property-owning bourgeoisie, it has fallen to liberals in government to ensure that equal access to policy makers is a working reality as well as a natural right. And in an age of giant business corporations, the free market is no longer a guarantee of economic efficiency or the "wealth of nations." The "invisible hand" may have been operative in an economy with many essentially equal competitors, but it has little relevance to an economic system in which the decisions of a few conglomerates, and of government, affect the income, employment opportunities, and price level of consumer expenditures of virtually every citizen.

The Functions of Government

Neoliberalism, then, implies a concern for the political and social, as well as the economic, rights of all citizens, not only the middle classes, and the rights especially of those citizens who are prevented by circumstances beyond their control from beginning the footrace of life from the starting line. Increasingly, the modern "service state" seeks to enlarge economic, social, and cultural opportunities through the enactment of such laws as those making education more widely available; establishing social insurance systems; regulating the hours, wages, and working conditions of labor; restricting the labor of children; and curbing monopolistic, fraudulent, and other antisocial business practices. While each new intervention is usually assailed (by those who are restrained) as the destruction of liberty and the harbinger of dictatorship, the trend toward such legislation in democratic nations grows steadily stronger and as yet shows no signs of being accompanied by curtailments of political or civil liberties. Thus in Great Britain, despite extensive public ownership and governmental regulation of industry, the British heritage of democratic government and civil liberty remains intact.

Later the reader will be in a better position to consider whether, as some contend, liberty in all its forms must stand or fall as a unit or whether the various liberties are distinct and separable. According to the former view, restrictions of economic liberty will inevitably make government "master of people's souls and thoughts" because "economic freedom cannot be sacrificed if political freedom is to be preserved."[1] The opposing school of thought insists that liberty is merely a convenient designation for a totality of specific and separate liberties and rights established through centuries of struggle toward human emancipation; that many civil liberties, such as freedom of religion, antedated economic liberty; and that an expansion, rather than a diminution, of civil and political liberties has accompanied the increased social and economic legislation of the past century. It is further pointed out that such legislation represents a reallocation of social and economic liberties, rights, and opportunities, restraining some and freeing others, and that liberty is really a distributable commodity that society reapportions among groups and classes from time to time in the light of changing needs and demands. There is, it is argued, no precise and static structure of relationships that can be permanently identified with liberty. "There is no sacred totality called 'the liberty of the individual,' for men are bound together in such a network of relations that in many respects the greater liberty of one is the lesser liberty of another."[2]

The fact that these two opposing concepts of liberty are current today and that emphasis has shifted from one aspect to another serves to illustrate the changing character of liberty and to indicate the impossibility of precise definition. Today it appears that the earlier *negative* notion of liberty as the mere absence of state interference—and of liberalism as a doctrine and movement opposing such intervention[3]—is being supplanted by the *positive* concept of liberty as the presence of opportunity—opportunity that must frequently be provided by purposeful governmental action, which the liberalism of today urges and supports.

A major problem of democracy is the reconciliation of liberty with authority. Democracy traditionally exalts freedom and frowns upon authority except insofar as it is clearly necessary. The eighteenth-century concept of government as an evil, albeit a necessary one, still shapes much of our thinking. Yet it is obvious that the powers of a democratic government must be commensurate with its tasks if it is to survive. Just as the needs of citizens change with social and economic modernization, so do the functions of democratic government change in response to citizen needs. A free people may elect political leaders who choose to define the functions of government in terms of restraint; they may also elect political leaders who understand that responsible government in the modern world is a government of action. The actions of government may work to the advantage of more equal opportunity for all. Government is not *necessarily* an evil. And the extent of democra-

---

[1]Herbert C. Hoover, *The Challenge to Liberty*, Charles Scribner's Sons, New York, 1934, pp. 203, 204.

[2]R. M. MacIver, *The Web of Government*, The Macmillan Company, New York, 1947, p. 201.

[3]For the classic statement of this view, see John Stuart Mill, *On Liberty* (1859), reprinted in *The World's Classics*, Oxford University Press, Fair Lawn, N.J., 1933, vol. 170.

cy in a liberal society is measured less by the substance of government policies than it is by the procedures employed in making and implementing those policies.

CONDITIONS NECESSARY FOR THE SUCCESS OF DEMOCRACY

The institutional structures and problems of democratic government will be discussed in later chapters. At this point we should briefly consider the conditions commonly regarded as necessary—or at least extremely helpful—for the establishment and maintenance of democracy.

Economics and Politics

Aristotle drew attention to the economic basis of politics. And since Aristotle, the interdependence of economics and politics has been generally accepted throughout the course of Western political thought, even long before Marx and Marxism. Medieval writers, who were invariably members of the clergy, recognized the obligations of monarchs to advance the economic and social well-being of their subjects. Feudalism was a unified system embracing economic, social, and political relationships. The revolutions of the seventeenth and eighteenth centuries brought about extensive economic, as well as political, changes. The framers of the United States Constitution were fully aware of the importance of property relationships and their effect upon government. James Madison saw factions arising in part from the extremes of wealth and poverty. The Founding Fathers did not, indeed, aim to establish a democracy, but rather a mixed system in which democratic elements (the House of Representatives) would be offset by an essentially oligarchic body (the Senate) representing the interests of property. The resulting balance was intended to minimize popular interference with established economic relationships. In his early writings Thomas Jefferson wished to keep the United States an agrarian nation—a nation of sturdy, independent farmers, whose ownership of land would provide the economic foundation for political democracy. He feared that industrialization and urbanization would produce extremes: a very rich class and a propertyless rabble, which would be constantly at war with each other, to the great detriment of the nation.

More recently, grave concern has been expressed as to whether political democracy can thrive in those nations where ownership or control of the economy has become concentrated in the hands of a relatively small number of persons. Even the more moderate critics of modern capitalism stress the dangers inherent in the development of larger and more powerful corporations, interlocking directorates, holding companies, chain stores, trade associations, international cartels, and many other devices tending to restrict competition and to narrow the opportunities of small business. Many recent studies indicate that large, powerful aggregates of capital in the United States own much of the national wealth, receive a large share of the national income, account for a large part of the national product, and employ large numbers of the nation's workers.[4]

Such a situation creates a dilemma: an increasingly powerful economic oligarchy and an expanding political democracy within the same society. Oligarchy and democracy tend to clash; powerful economic interests seek to shape public policy to promote their own purposes, while the popular majority just as naturally tries to use its political power to improve its own economic and social status. Thus the question arises of whether popular sovereignty can be a reality in any society where an increasing number of the sovereign people lack economic independence and job security.

Property Ownership and Democracy In all industrialized nations, and especially in those with a liberal heritage, the growth of private monopoly has stimulated demands for the public ownership of public utilities and, in Great Britain, France, and

---

[4]These concerns were expressed by representatives of government even before World War II. See the *Hearings, Monographs,* and *Report* of the Temporary National Economic Committee to Investigate the Concentration of Economic Power in the United States, 75th Cong., 3d Sess., Pub. Res. 113, 1938–1941, especially "Economic Prologue," *Hearings*, vol. I. See also the early views of A. A. Berle, Jr., and G. C. Means, *The Modern Corporation and Private Property,* The Macmillan Company, New York, 1932. More recent research by the People's Policy Center, whose president is former Senator Fred R. Harris of Oklahoma, has found that 4.4 percent of the United States population owns 60 percent of all corporate stocks, 71 percent of all federal bonds (except savings bonds), 77 percent of state and local bonds, and virtually all the corporate bonds and foreign bonds. This same 4.4 percent of the United States population has a third of the nation's personal cash, a fourth of the real estate, and 40 percent of all noncorporate business assets. See the summary of the center's findings in the *Los Angeles Times,* Sept. 24, 1973.

Italy, of many other basic industries. The movement in democratic nations toward partial nationalization of the economy, coupled with national planning and regulation of other important business, raises the question of whether private property in the instruments of production, distribution, and exchange—i.e., capitalism or free enterprise—is essential to the preservation of democracy. On the one hand, it is contended that democracy is impossible without private property and freedom of business enterprise.[5] On the other, it is claimed that political democracy and liberty will be realities only when they are supported by economic and social democracy—that no society can be politically democratic if there are extreme differences in the distribution of wealth.

In the light of continuing experiments with democratic government since the days of ancient Athens, however, and despite the economic and social transformations wrought by technological development, it would be erroneous to accept any dogma concerning the inevitable or necessary relationship between democracy and a particular economic system. To argue that the economic system necessarily determines the characteristics of the political system is to fall into the trap of a vulgarized Marxism. Great Britain, the Scandinavian countries, and New Zealand may be cited as examples of countries that, although more or less socialist in their economic structures, are nevertheless politically democratic. A distinguished political scientist has written that "a democracy may approve a collectivist program or may reject it";[6] another believes that "free political and industrial systems, such as ours, are the most flexible" and that such a system can change "without abandoning its basic principle of the consent of the governed and its protection of human personality and the common good."[7]

We should conclude, then, that private property—not necessarily unlimited—is desirable for democracy and that democracy will be stronger where the ownership of property is widely and rather evenly distributed. This was precisely the argument advanced by Aristotle. And it is also significant that democracy appears particularly secure in those countries, such as Switzerland, Norway, Sweden, and Denmark, which are not characterized by great extremes of wealth and poverty. In Italy, on the other hand, and also in India and in several individual states of the United States, such extremes have been and still are very conspicuous, and democracy in these various political systems has made slow and halting progress.

Politics and Society

In evaluating the conditions essential to successful democratic government, it is also necessary to consider some important *non*economic factors, including the characteristics of culture. It is generally agreed that democracy cannot be transplanted successfully among people who do not understand it and whose political leaders are unaccustomed to the resolution of their conflicts through political compromise and bargaining. Democracy cannot be served up intact on a platter of authoritarian traditions. The unhappy fate of the countries of Eastern, Central, and Southern Europe after World War I and of many of the newly independent nations illustrates the difficulty of spreading the democratic gospel and, even more, of implementing it. Only after a long period of education and democratic experience can these peoples and their political leaders be expected to make democracy work. The success of democracy is dependent upon the presence of what one writer has called the "democratic vision," which inspires the citizenry to work earnestly for the realization of democratic goals.[8] This is closely related to what another writer terms a "civic" sense among the people—"a rational like-mindedness and an imaginative sympathy that in some degree transcend economic and cultural differences."[9] It is also said that there must be within the community "a certain balance between the forces of cohesion and the forces of individualism."[10]

Most contemporary students of comparative politics also hold that a consensus on fundamentals is necessary to the smooth working of democracy and

---

[5]F. A. Hayek, *The Road to Serfdom*, The University of Chicago Press, Chicago, 1944, presents the classic statement of this point of view.

[6]MacIver, op. cit., p. 207.

[7]C. E. Merriam, *What Is Democracy?* The University of Chicago Press, Chicago, 1941, p. 15.

[8]David Thomson, *The Democratic Ideal in France and England*, Cambridge University Press, New York, 1940, p. 5. See also MacIver, op. cit., p. 190.

[9]Francis W. Coker, *Recent Political Thought*, Appleton-Century-Crofts, Inc., New York, 1934, p. 372.

[10]Thomson, op. cit., p. 5.

that consensus is in large part a function of a relatively homogeneous society and culture; where there are major racial, linguistic, or religious cleavages, there are also very likely to be political instability, a tendency toward authoritarian politics, or both. This is especially true where political parties or governmental institutions (e.g., a popularly elected presidency) do not exist or do not cut across the various cultural, social, and economic cleavages in the society.

Another generally recognized precondition for successful democracy is a literate and reasonably well-educated citizenry. This can be achieved only by means of "a system of general education, an intelligent and independent press, and freedom of association and discussion."[11] While well-educated peoples are not necessarily democratic, it is clear that democracy develops successfully only where there is a high degree of literacy, a public reasonably well informed on civic matters, and adequate and open channels of communication. Democracy arrived earlier in England, France, and the United States than it did in Italy or Spain, where illiteracy was widespread.

Moreover, if education is mainly factual and vocational, failing to encourage independent and critical thinking about public questions, it will not produce the civic interest and awareness on the part of the citizenry upon which the success of democracy ultimately depends. An informed but indifferent public is as dangerous as an illiterate one. It is also important that vigorous public discussion be encouraged and facilitated by means of institutional arrangements and constitutional safeguards that assure full opportunity for association, meeting, communication, and orderly protest. Without these safeguards even a literate and educated citizenry cannot provide adequate protection against the abuses and excesses of an authoritarian regime, but may become merely its pliant subjects.

CRITICISMS OF DEMOCRACY

Like all human arrangements, democracy is far from perfect, and it has accordingly been subjected to severe attacks for its shortcomings. The very nobility of democracy's goals seems to evoke an especially caustic type of criticism; the gap between theory and practice becomes all the more conspicuous. Despite the manifest difficulties of operating under the rules of the democratic system (it is so much easier to give orders than it is to win agreement), democratic governments are all too frequently held to impossibly exacting standards of performance. The most common complaints against democracy are those relating to its failure to operate efficiently, promptly, and honestly. It is often assumed, by contrast, that dictatorships, monarchies, and aristocracies are much more efficient and that they are therefore able to do many things that a democracy cannot accomplish because of its inherent limitations.

Democracy and Efficiency What are the criteria upon which a judgment of this sort may be based? What is it that people expect from their government? What do they want most? Security? Order? Freedom? Opportunity for self-development? People do not value an efficient, prompt government as an end in itself, but rather as a means toward other, higher ends. They do not really want efficiency; they want other things from government, though they would of course prefer to have them efficiently provided.

The word "efficiency," as applied to government, implies competence, adequacy in operation or performance, or general capability. As applied to a machine, efficiency is the ratio of the work done or energy developed by such a machine to the energy supplied to it—i.e., the ratio of output to input. The difficulty in employing this term where government is concerned lies in the fact that there is no agreement as to what the output—or, for that matter, the input—is or how it is to be measured. How can the services of government be evaluated? Many such services are unique; they are not available from other agencies. Thus there is no market in which the value of these services can be determined through competition. Nor can national defense, education, social security, health protection, and similar services be measured by cost alone or by the number of persons engaged in rendering them. The best government is not necessarily the cheapest or that which operates with the smallest staff of employees. Similarly, it can scarcely be said that the speed with which government acts is, by itself,

[11]Coker, op. cit., p. 373.

proof of that government's superiority. Promptness is, of course, desirable—but so are wisdom and justice.

Democracy and Mass Society It is also contended that, inasmuch as the average human being is unintelligent, uninformed, prejudiced, emotional, and resentful of superiority in others, a government controlled and directed by the majority is likely to reflect the attitudes of such average persons and therefore will not pursue the most intelligent and forward-looking policies. Critics claim that the legislation enacted in democratic nations discloses a preference for standardization and uniformity and shows hostility and distrust toward variation, invention, and superiority in any form. It is said that democracies seek to "level down," not up, and that the masses make heroes of demagogues and scoundrels rather than of great and wise men. Middle-class virtues are exalted, especially the virtue of conformity, and the spirit of toleration is conspicuous by its absence.

Some critics contend that democracy is in fact a visionary ideal, impossible of realization. These writers say that all so-called democracies have been and are, in reality, oligarchies of one sort or another; political power is always actually exercised by some small ruling group or class. One author defines democracy as government *of* the people by an elite sprung *from* the people.[12] The people do not really govern themselves, but merely choose at intervals between or among rival leaders and programs. The extent of nonvoting in democracies is cited to prove that the people do not really want self-government, with its attendant responsibilities, but prefer leaders to follow and heroes to worship.

The Demands of a Technological Age Much current criticism holds that democracy is unworkable under the complex conditions of modern life. The democratic process of debate and discussion is held to be too slow for today's problems; more power should be given to experts; the public is too susceptible to propaganda. Walter Lippmann diagnosed the "malady of democratic government" as a "derangement of powers" between the executive or "governing" function and "the assemblies and the mass electorates," which "have acquired the monopoly of effective powers."[13]

Such views imply that democracy's day may be over; that however well suited to an earlier epoch, democracy is too slow, too lacking in expertise and competence, to meet the rapid-fire challenges of the age of technology and the era of nuclear power. Even some who devoutly support democracy are tempted to wonder whether the responsibilities it imposes today upon the average citizen, or even upon most policy makers, are not too much for the capacity of the human mind.[14]

The Flexibility of Democracy The heaviest attacks are concentrated on the practice, rather than on the ideals, of democracy. Critics often misstate the ideals of democracy, setting up straw men to demolish. Actually, democracy's basic assumptions are qualified and practical; man is not assumed to be perfect or always to act in a rational or moral manner. Faith in democracy does not require the believer to deny the existence under democracy of problems such as political intrigue and corruption, individual and group selfishness, and popular indifference.

Moreover, the principles of democracy are sufficiently flexible to permit the incorporation of many of the better features of aristocracy into democratic government. Virtually every democratic government in history has contained some elements of aristocracy or oligarchy. Many if not most legislative upper houses were or are designed to give added weight to age, wealth, conservatism, or social status. Judicial review of the constitutionality of legislation, which is based upon a deep veneration for the wisdom and probity of judges, might be regarded as an American version of aristocracy. Where the citizens of a democracy elect the well-born and well-to-do to represent them in legislative bodies, and where such men feel a duty to serve the government as legislators, diplomats, judges, and

---

[12]Maurice Duverger, *Political Parties,* John Wiley & Sons, Inc., New York, 1954, p. 425.

[13]Walter Lippmann, *The Public Philosophy,* Little, Brown and Company, Boston, 1955, pp. 54–57. Lippmann argues that the "effective powers" to govern must be concentrated in the executive branch of government, with its exercise of power restrained as much by considerations of natural law and natural right as by periodic elections.

[14]See Chap. 17 for an assessment of the impact of science and technology on modern government and politics.

civil servants, the result may well be a fusion of the best features of democracy and oligarchy.

Great Britain still operates under such a mixed system, and in some parts of the United States the scions of distinguished families are consistently returned to public office. British democracy operates successfully without direct popular election of executive or administrative officials and without the initiative, referendum, or recall, thus avoiding the charge of too much meddling by the masses in the operations of government. The American movement toward the short ballot—away from the Jacksonian idea that every executive or administrative officer (from president to surveyor or coroner) ought to be directly elected—is a step in the same direction. The growing recognition that the executive branch must be strengthened (as in the item veto for state governors and the reorganization of federal executive agencies) indicates a trend toward making our democracy more effective and responsible, but no less democratic. Modern democracies are actually utilizing the abilities of persons of superior talents and show greater willingness than democracies in days past to heed the advice of experts. Of course, there is still room for improvement, but democracy, more than any other system of government, has demonstrated its ability to draw upon all segments of society and upon all its members' diversified gifts to make their particular contributions.[15]

The defender of democracy is most effective when modest in his claims. At the very least, he can point to a going concern, which has weathered attacks from many quarters. Democracies have survived two world wars; on the other hand, royal autocracies and fascist dictatorships have fallen. There is no body of historical evidence proving that any other system of government is superior to democracy. There is no valid scientific foundation for theories of inherited superiority of individuals, classes, nations, or races. Emphatically, there is none supporting the notion that particular abilities, such as those of the statesman or citizen, are inheritable. Aristocracy is an appealing, but elusive, doctrine; elites often turn out to be, as in Fascist Italy and Nazi Germany, bands of mere adventurers. If the majority errs, so do kings, dukes, titans of industry, and dictators. It would be difficult to conceive of greater national disasters than those brought down upon the German and Italian peoples by their "infallible" leaders.

We may conclude by admitting that all forms of government are imperfect in one way or another. In this sense, the characteristics of government simply reflect the characteristics of man. But government and ideology are as inevitable a feature of the social landscape as the struggle for power is a constant factor in human relationships. To recite a cliché made famous by Winston Churchill, "Democracy is the worst form of government—with the exception of all the rest."

STUDY-GUIDE QUESTIONS

1 Are your assumptions about human nature consistent with your preferences for political organization? How is human nature likely to be viewed by someone with authoritarian preferences?
2 What did classical liberalism mean by "all men are created equal"?
3 Summarize the views of classical liberalism and neoliberalism on the appropriate functions of government.
4 How does the distribution of wealth in a society affect the distribution of political power?
5 How might the best characteristics of aristocracy and democracy be institutionally combined to produce a government of wisdom and justice?

REFERENCES

Almond, Gabriel A., and Sidney Verba: *The Civic Culture: Political Attitudes and Democracy in Five Nations,* Little, Brown and Company, Boston, 1965.
Berlin, Isaiah: *Four Essays on Liberty,* Oxford University Press, New York, 1969.
Davies, James C.: *Human Nature in Politics: The*

---

[15]Former Senator J. William Fulbright of Arkansas stated the problem eloquently when he wrote: "The case for government by elites is irrefutable insofar as it rests on the need for expert and specialized knowledge. The average citizen is no more qualified for the detailed administration of government than the average politician is qualified to practice medicine or to split an atom. But in the choice of basic goals, the fundamental moral judgments that shape the life of a society, the judgment of trained elites is no more valid than the judgment of an educated people. The knowledge of the navigator is essential to the conduct of a voyage, but his special skills have no relevance to the choice of whether to take the voyage and where we wish to go." *The Elite and the Electorate: Is Government by the People Possible?* Center for the Study of Democratic Institutions, Santa Barbara, Calif., 1963, pp. 4–5.

Dynamics of Political Behavior, John Wiley & Sons, Inc., New York, 1963.

Eckstein, Harry: *Division and Cohesion in a Democracy: A Study of Norway,* Princeton University Press, Princeton, N.J., 1966.

Galbraith, John Kenneth: *The New Industrial State,* 2d ed., Houghton Mifflin Company, Boston, 1972.

Girvetz, Harry K.: *The Evolution of Liberalism,* Collier Books, The Macmillan Company, New York, 1963.

Laski, Harold J.: *The Rise of European Liberalism,* Unwin Books, Barnes & Noble, Inc., New York, 1962.

Lipset, Seymour Martin: *Political Man: The Social Bases of Politics,* Anchor Books, Doubleday & Company, Inc., Garden City, N.Y., 1963.

Mason, Alpheus T. (ed.): *Free Government in the Making,* 3d ed., Oxford University Press, New York, 1965.

Mosca, Gaetano: *The Ruling Class,* McGraw-Hill Book Company, New York, 1939.

Rodee, Carlton C.: "Defenders and Critics of American Capitalism and Constitutionalism: Conservatism and Liberalism," in J. S. Roucek (ed.), *Twentieth Century Political Thought,* Philosophical Library, Inc., New York, 1946, chap. 18.

Schumpeter, Joseph: *Capitalism, Socialism and Democracy,* Harper & Brothers, New York, 1947.

Spitz, David: *Democracy and the Challenge of Power,* Columbia University Press, New York, 1958.

Tawney, R. H.: *Equality,* Capricorn Books, G. P. Putnam's Sons, New York, 1961.

Chapter 6

Marxism and Communism

COMMUNISM BEFORE MARX

The classical liberal's assumption that government is a necessary evil reflects some very old Judeo-Christian ideas. Before man's "fall" from God's grace, there was no government, nor was there any private property. The existence of government after the fall of man was not only a "badge of lost innocence" (Thomas Paine) but also a sign of the passing of a more perfect social order—communism.

The Old Testament

The book of Genesis in the Old Testament teaches that all things are derived from God and that man has no inherent rights of possession. In fact, the Hebrew word for property, *nachala,* connotes moral inheritance, social obligation, and material assets that man enjoys only as a trust, not as a right. The social order of the ancient Hebrews thus attempted to maintain an element of communism, as noted in Leviticus, chapter 25: "The houses of the villages which have no wall around them shall be reckoned with the fields of the country . . . the fields of common land belonging to their cities may not be sold." Deuteronomy, chapter 15, explains the "year of release," which comes every seven years, a time when "every creditor shall release what he has lent to his neighbor"; in other words, all debts (among the Jewish people) are automatically canceled every seven years. And Leviticus, chapter 25, describes the "year of jubilee," which occurs every fifty years, a time when all the accumulated inequalities of land distribution are eliminated and the land is redistributed according to the original principles of equality among the Hebrew tribes.

Much of the fury of the Hebrew prophets, beginning in the eighth century B.C., was directed against the breakdown of the old social order and the erosion of its egalitarian, welfare, and communist norms. Micah, chapter 2, says: "Woe to those who devise wickedness and work evil.... They covet fields, and seize them; and houses, and take them away; they oppress a man and his house, a man and his inheritance" (meaning what God had given man as a *trust* rather than as a means of investment and profit). And in Micah, chapter 3: "Hear this, you heads of the house of Jacob and rulers of the house of Israel, who abhor justice and pervert all equity, who build Zion with blood and Jerusalem with wrong. Its heads give judgment for a bribe, its priests teach for hire, its prophets divine for money." Isaiah, chapter 32, repeats the same accusations and, in promising a return to social justice after the Day of Judgment, gives a concise picture of the divinely blessed society: "Happy are you who sow beside all waters, who let the feet of the ox and the ass range free." In short, there is no private property, and all things are held in common.

Christianity and the Utopians

The hope for a return to a more just society and an end to corruption and greed inspired the social organization of the early Christians. They also sought to realize these ideals through the communist principles traditional to their religious and cultural ancestors, the ancient Hebrews. Thus chapter 2 of Acts of the Apostles (the only book of the New Testament that describes Christian society immediately after the Crucifixion) says: "And all who believed were together and had all things in common; and they sold their possessions and goods and distributed them to all, as any had need."

After the sixth century, the growth of Christian monasticism represented a repudiation of the worldly concerns of the church and an attempt to return again to the ancient principles of equality and the spirit of brotherhood that were associated with the possession of things in common. The persistent belief in an earlier "Golden Age" when all things were shared also inspired the periodic efforts toward communist social organization by medieval peasants and, on occasion, even urban artisans.

The development of capitalism after the sixteenth and seventeenth centuries stimulated many philosophers, both religious and secular, to write of utopian societies organized according to communist principles. The most notable writers of such utopian tracts were Robert Owen in England and Charles Fourier and Saint-Simon in France. In some instances, especially in the United States during the nineteenth century, these utopian plans were put into practice with, inevitably, varying degrees of success. Those utopian communist communities which were entirely or primarily agricultural and whose members were devout believers in some fundamentalist variety of the Christian faith, were exclusively male and celibate, and were guided by a charismatic leader were the most likely to endure in the midst of a rapidly changing and decidedly *un*utopian world.

A society organized according to communist principles, then, was not the invention of Karl Marx, and the principles of communism antedate those of classical liberalism by at least 3,000 years. The more recent experiments in communal living by participants in the "counterculture" of the contemporary United States and by members of kibbutzim in Israel also express many of these same social and humanistic ideals, ideals that are as old as Western civilization.

MARXISM
Early Capitalism

In England in the sixteenth century, attempts to build factories and to operate them at a profit proved premature. The industrialists of the day lacked sufficient capital (wealth available for investment in the production of goods or services), and peasants, artisans, and other potential factory workers "refused to exchange the freedom of their homes for the discipline of the factory."[1] But by the time Karl Marx and Friedrich Engels wrote the *Communist Manifesto* (in 1848), the factory system was well established:

> Against the competition of machine-made goods, the handworker struggled in vain, and he was left with no resource except to enter the hated factory. The workman of today who has known nothing else but the factory can have only a feeble idea of what it cost the domestic worker to submit to factory discipline.[2]

---
[1] Arthur Birnie, *An Economic History of Europe, 1790–1939*, Methuen & Co., Ltd., London, 1962, p. 8.
[2] Ibid.

It is even more difficult today for privileged students in a generally privileged society to understand the incredible hardships of men, women, and children (the last frequently fed into factories at the age of six or seven) who worked sixteen or eighteen hours a day, six days a week, in the choking dust of the textile mills and coal mines, who lived in crowded urban slums occasionally swept by killing epidemics, who had been cut off from the social security of the small community, and who were periodically unemployed as the economic cycle fluctuated between boom and bust—the vast majority of them without any hope of escaping the clutches of the company store, the company town, the leather straps of factory overseers, or the whirling machines that tore limbs from workers as readily as the pressures of factory production split the family apart, reducing men, women, and children to a numbing struggle for bare survival.

While classical liberals justified these social evils in terms of individual freedom and economic progress, early socialists recoiled before the horrors of industrialism and attempted to advance the interests of a degraded humanity. Thus the French sociologist Émile Durkheim described socialist thought and politics as fundamentally a "cry of pain." And more recent scholars of the writings of Karl Marx have argued that beneath the gloss of economic laws and political sociology that characterizes Marx's work is a philosophy of humanism—especially a concern for the *alienation* that separates the individual's creative needs from the forces of nature, the structure of society, and ultimately from the individual himself.[3] Like the biblical communists of ancient times, Marx and the Marxists have searched for a more just way of organizing society and of ensuring that the satisfaction of economic needs does not contradict the fulfillment of human needs.[4]

Marxist Materialism

For Marx, however, an understanding of human needs and the structure of society necessarily begins with an understanding of man as an economic being. "Economic" not only referred to the production, distribution, and exchange of goods and services but also described the inescapable condition of human existence—that man is first and foremost a *biological* entity with basic requirements that must be met if his survival is to be ensured:

> We must begin by stating the first premise of all human existence, and therefore of all history, the premise, namely, that men must be in a position to live in order to be able to "make history." But life involves, before everything else, eating and drinking, a habitation, clothing, and many other things. The first historical act is thus the production of the means to satisfy these needs, the production of material life itself. And indeed this is a historical act, a fundamental condition of all history, which today, as thousands of years ago, must daily and hourly be fulfilled merely in order to sustain human life.... The first necessity therefore in any theory of history is to observe this fundamental fact in all its significance and all its implications, and to accord it its due importance.[5]

The "scientific" study of history is thus the study of the way in which man has responded to the material challenge of his physical environment. Seeking to maximize his chances for survival, man has progressively improved the technology of production and adapted the structure of his society to the demands of changing technology. The first major breakthrough was in replacing *self-sufficiency*—whereby each man struggled to produce all that he needed to survive—with *specialization of task,* which enabled one man to concentrate (for example) on the production of food and another to specialize in the making of clothing, another to specialize in building, and another to specialize in the manufacture of tools, while others eventually specialized in trade and finance.

Economic Class But with specialization of economic task came social differences in status, wealth, and political power—however primitive the society or its political system. Economic classes developed that were distinguished primarily be-

---

[3] See especially Robert C. Tucker, *Philosophy and Myth in Karl Marx,* Cambridge University Press, London, 1961.

[4] Educated in Germany in a period dominated by Hegelian philosophy, Karl Marx (1818–1883) and Friedrich Engels (1820–1895) spent most of their lives in England, where Marx's prolific writing and activities on behalf of international labor organization were largely supported by Engels, a successful industrialist.

[5] Marx and Engels, *The German Ideology* (1846), reprinted in Lewis S. Feuer (ed.), *Marx and Engels: Basic Writings on Politics and Philosophy,* Anchor Books, Doubleday & Company, Inc., Garden City, N.Y., 1959, p. 249.

tween those who owned property and the means of production and the workers who were essential to the functioning of the means of production. The inevitable result was conflict between these classes, or class struggle, which in fact was the major characteristic of historical development.[6]

The class structure of industrial society was marked by the domination of the bourgeoisie, or property-owning middle classes, and the exploitation of the numerically larger but economically inferior working classes, or proletariat. The struggle between these two classes was bound to intensify as the productive potential of the bourgeoisie exceeded the consumption potential of the proletariat. Workers kept at or below a subsistence level of life were unable to buy the goods that the capitalists needed to produce in order to maximize their wealth. Thus revolution was inevitable.

The Dialectic

The "determinism" that characterizes Marx's thought derives from this assumption: The way in which people organize the means of production necessarily determines the broad outlines of their social structure, their political system, and even the ideologies (religious or secular) they invent to justify or attack the status quo.[7]

In this sense, "dialectic" refers in part to the interrelationships of all phenomena, and any particular phenomenon can be understood only in terms of its more general context. One cannot understand the characteristics of capitalism, for example, without understanding its initial development in the context of feudalism and mercantilism. Nor can one understand the behavior of the proletariat without reference to its peasant origins or to the demands and interests of the bourgeoisie. From the perspectives of the dialectic, the more complete (or "scientific") knowledge is the knowledge of phenomena as they interact with other phenomena; nothing can be understood by itself, according to its isolated characteristics abstracted from reality.

Thus each man defines himself only as he interacts with nature (the material demands of his environment) and with the social reality around him. And "dialectical materialism" (a term Marx never used, but one that aptly describes his thought) may be understood as an early statement of twentieth-century existential philosophy.

As the above examples suggest, dialectical relationships are inevitably antagonistic relationships. History is properly understood as the working out of tensions and contradictions between nature and man, ever more efficient means of production, competing social classes, and opposing ideologies. At any point in time it is possible to identify a specific characteristic of social life as a *thesis* (for example, feudalism and economic restraint), which is eventually confronted by an *antithesis* (capitalism and free trade), with the contradictions generated by the clash of thesis and antithesis leading to a *synthesis* of the best attributes of each (socialism, which enables man to enjoy the efficiency of production developed by capitalism, but in the context of the social harmony and stability that characterized feudalism).

The dialectic is thus a means of conceptualizing any set of interrelated phenomena (social forces or ideas); it also describes a real process, a process of antagonism and contradiction, that is inherent in all phenomena. And the principal motor of *historical* development is class struggle, which conveniently summarizes all the material and intellectual contradictions peculiar to each historical epoch.

Economic Class and Political Power As one class comes to dominate another, it captures control of the state. The distribution of political power in any society is thus a function of the distribution of economic power. As economic power shifts from a landowning aristocracy to an enterprising bourgeoisie, the political domination of king and nobility gives way to parliamentary institutions controlled by the owners of new wealth and their political representatives. The ideology of divine right is replaced by the ideology of classical liberalism. The ideology justifies the use of the institutions of the state and their most characteristic expression—law—as a means of consolidating and perpetuating the socioeconomic domination of the bourgeoisie.

---

[6]The famous opening sentence of part I of the *Communist Manifesto* declares: "The history of all hitherto existing society is the history of class struggles." See Feuer, op. cit., p. 7.

[7]For Marx, however, religion (and especially Christianity) invariably supported the status quo. By inducing the faithful to look to the hereafter instead of to the here and now for social justice, religion was a major instrument of class domination; it was thus the "opiate of the masses."

Thus the state, its supporting ideology, its laws, and its police and judicial apparatus are the instruments that enable one class to enforce and legitimate its exploitation of other classes in the society. (And, again, it is dialectical analysis that helps one understand the complex interrelationships of all these phenomena.) But the fallacy of every class ideology before that of socialism has been to assume absolute right and universal applicability. History, however, shows that what has typically been taken as a permanent feature of the social landscape has been doomed to pass away as the horizons of man are extended by both economic change and intellectual inquiry. Dialectical analysis, then, also enables one to understand that capitalism, like feudalism, is only a temporary phenomenon.

Revolution, Socialism, and Communism

The fundamental contradiction of capitalism, according to Marx, is its socialization of the means of production (or the creation of worker interdependency through the factory system), at the same time that the distribution of wealth has continued according to the principle of private interest and personal advantage. This contradiction inherent in capitalism is best understood in the context of feudalism and socialism and the characteristics of the dialectic (see Table 6.1).

Marx distinguished his thought from the ideas of the utopian socialists by arguing that they had an undialectical view of history. This meant in part that the utopians had failed to recognize the inevitability of capitalism; they also had failed to understand that capitalism was, up to a point, a *positive* stage in historical development and a definite benefit to mankind. The utopians had wanted to reverse the march of history by repudiating capitalism before it had run its necessary course, and many of them had proved downright reactionary by seeking to return man to the conditions of an agrarian society. For Marx, however, the capitalists had developed technology and organized the means of production with immense ingenuity and unparalleled efficiency. Man in capitalist society had finally come to grips with nature and had in his hands the means for eliminating poverty and want and for ensuring the survival of the species in terms of biological necessity.

Table 6.1 The Organization of Production and the Principles of Distribution in Feudalism, Capitalism, and Socialism, According to the Marxian Dialectic

	Feudalism (thesis)	Capitalism (antithesis)	Socialism (synthesis)
Organization of production	Private	Social	Social
Principle of distribution	Private	Private	Social

Exploitation and Surplus Value But capitalist society was also a society of immense inequality, and by simply looking around him, Marx could justly conclude that the majority of men, women, and children suffered from poverty and want. Those who worked the machinery of production were those who suffered most from the effects of industrialism. They also were those who received the least amount of what they produced. There was something economically *and* morally wrong in a society where the few who did not perform manual labor enjoyed most of the wealth produced by manual labor. And the only way of determining the value of a given commodity was by computing the labor that was necessary to produce it (the "labor theory of value"): Because the capitalist was not a worker, he did not produce value, but the worker was not compensated for the total value of the commodities he produced; what was taken from the worker by the capitalist was "surplus value," a concept introduced by Marx to describe the exploitative relationship between capitalist and worker. Even as capitalism had advanced man's mastery over nature, then, it had aggravated the alienation and exploitation that—in the final analysis—marked all men in bourgeois society; even the capitalist, in his headlong pursuit of profit, was exploited by his own materialistic ambitions and was unable to give free rein to the diverse interests and creative potential that complicate the human condition in a society of private property.

Economic Crisis and Political Change The very basis of capitalist production, however, was the bringing together, or socialization, of many workers in large factories. This social fact of capitalism contrasted vividly with the isolated circumstances of workers in small workshops or workers employed in the cottage industries of the precapitalist period. Under capitalism, the workers' close association with one another raised their sense of class identity and helped to prepare them for the moment when the capitalist machinery of production—for want of a market for its output—would simply grind to a halt.

Writing the *Communist Manifesto* in 1848, in the context of violent revolutions that were sweeping across Europe from Copenhagen to Palermo and from Paris to Budapest, Marx and Engels naturally tended to think in terms of an abrupt and violent transition from capitalism to socialism. Events proved them wrong, but Marxist thinkers have always argued that the method of dialectical analysis allows for constant revision of the details of Marxist theory in the light of historical development, even while the broad outlines of dialectical materialism remain intact. And in their writings after 1848, Marx and Engels substantially modified their views on the characteristics of the socialist revolution. They admitted that the transition to socialism would vary according to the particular political culture, and they cited England, Holland, and the United States as examples of countries where the substitution of socialism for capitalism might be relatively peaceful and extended in time.

The Dictatorship of the Proletariat Whether socialism was the result of peaceful transition or violent change, it was inevitable that the proletariat would rise to power and, for the first time in history, that the institutions of the state would be transformed into the instrument of majority rule. It was only under the "dictatorship of the proletariat" that true democracy would become a working reality. Through its political dominance, the proletariat would be able to bring under state control all the means of production, nationalizing industry, land, business, communications, transportation, and commerce; controlling distribution and exchange; abolishing the rights of inheritance, which, in any event, were inconsistent with liberal ideology; instituting a heavy and progressive income tax; eliminating the factory labor of children; and ensuring "free education for all children in public schools" (according to the *Communist Manifesto*).

Capitalism had enabled man to conquer nature; socialism would enable all men to become meaningful participants in society. It is important to note that Marx neither advocated nor justified the dictatorship of the few over the many.

The End of Alienation "Communism" was the label adopted by Marx and Engels to distinguish their ideas from those of the early utopians. It also described the final stage of social development, a stage following socialism and the dictatorship of the proletariat in which (1) the role of the state is minimal in socioeconomic organization; (2) classes have ceased to exist, and consequently political instability and socioeconomic conflict are relics of the past; (3) the distribution of goods and services is according to individual need and without regard for the individual's labor or productivity; (4) international boundaries and state sovereignty have disappeared; and (5) a "cultural revolution" has effected a change in consciousness whereby men come naturally to identify their interests with the collective good and general welfare of the entire society. Under the conditions of communism, not only is man in control of nature and society, but he is also finally able to realize his particular ambitions for creative development and self-fulfillment—and not at the expense of others. In short, communism ensures the end to man's alienation from himself, and he finally returns to the Golden Age that has been the inspiration of political philosophers since people were first moved to speculate on the causes of social injustice.

The Meaning of Marx

It may be argued that as Marx attempted to prophesy the future, he became a utopian himself and revealed how thoroughly he was influenced by the basic liberal ideals of individual freedom and equal opportunity for self-development. But it should be quickly added that Marx, in the great body of his writings, has relatively little to say about the characteristics of socialism and much less to say about communism.

His attention was focused on capitalism. He sought to describe the way capitalism had developed and the way it worked or failed to work. His visions of the future, when they were offered, derived from his attempts to extrapolate apparently major trends in capitalist society, including the tendencies toward monopoly capitalism, the division of capitalist society into two major classes (bourgeoisie and proletariat), and the progressive "pauperization" of the proletariat, and the apparently inexorable movement of capitalism in the direction of catastrophic depression.

Other trends were overlooked: the intensity of nationalist and patriotic sentiment, which compromised class solidarity along economic lines; the extension of the suffrage and the development of political democracy in most industrialized states; and the increasing willingness of the "bourgeois" state to intervene in the economic and social lives of citizens to help smooth the abrasive effects of unregulated capitalism.

But on one point Marx was adamant as he looked into the future: Democratic and humanistically inspired socialism could not come about until capitalism was fully developed and all the technological potential of capitalism had been realized. This was essential not only to the economic efficiency of socialist society but also to the development of a social consciousness among citizens that was the very basis of democratic socialism and communism.

Subsequent political thinkers and activists, including those discussed below, have been hard pressed to explain how the "socialist" revolution could develop in the context of an *underdeveloped* capitalist society, where the major classes were peasants and landowners instead of proletarians and an urban bourgeoisie. And it well may be that, in the twentieth century, those who have called themselves "Marxist" and "communist" have been neither Marxist nor communist.

LENINISM

Marxism was exported from Western Europe to tsarist Russia in the late nineteenth century, where it exercised its curious charm on only a small circle of intellectuals. Among these were the founders of the Russian Social Democratic Labor party, which was established at a secret congress convened in Minsk in 1898. In addition to their problems with the tsar's secret police and network of informers, the Russian Social Democrats were troubled by the following question: When and how should the socialist revolution come to Russia? At the party's second congress in 1903, convened first in Brussels and then in London, the Social Democrats split into two factions. The Mensheviks (or members of the minority faction) accepted the necessity of a prolonged period of capitalist development in Russia before socialism could become a viable alternative, and they called for the organization of a loosely structured and mass-based political party. The Bolsheviks (or members of the majority faction) argued instead that the socialist revolution need not be postponed and that its arrival could be hastened by the organization of a highly centralized and disciplined core of professional revolutionaries.

The Party The political and ideological leader of the Bolsheviks was Vladimir Ilyich Lenin (1870–1924, born Ulyanov). In a pamphlet published in 1902 and entitled *What Is to Be Done?* Lenin urged the organization of the kind of tightly knit revolutionary party that in fact came to characterize the Bolsheviks—who were to adopt the "communist" label after the Russian Revolution of October 1917.

For Lenin, the revolutionary party was likely to be most effective if it was composed not of workers but of intellectuals dedicated to pursuing the interests of the working class. That such a party was essential was made clear by the repressive autocracy of the tsarist state, which prohibited working-class organization. And, in any event, the workers—if left to their own resources—were very unlikely to transcend what Lenin called "trade union consciousness"; concentrating on higher wages, on shorter working hours, and on only superficial improvements in their immediate circumstances, the workers required the leadership of a revolutionary party in order to develop revolutionary consciousness.

Lenin, in effect, was arguing that the socialist revolution was inevitable only if the party made it so. For Marx, on the other hand, the socialist revolution was a largely impersonal process propelled by the contradictions in capitalist economic development. Lenin substituted the personal intervention of the Leninist party for the objective forces of Marx's history. And in the process of turning Marxism upside down, Lenin insisted that the socialist revolution was inevitably violent and an abrupt departure from the past. These ideas may have been appropriate to the task of fomenting revolution in Russia, but then tsarist Russia was not exactly Marx's idea of a model capitalist state.

Imperialism Thus Lenin was compelled to explain why the socialist revolution had failed to materialize in the advanced capitalist states of Western Europe, as Marx had predicted, and why the revolution might first appear in backward Russia. In 1916 Lenin published *Imperialism: The Highest Stage of Capitalism,* in which he elaborated Marx's earlier argument that monopoly capitalism inevitably attempts to ensure its further development by absorbing foreign territories and exploiting their resources and native peoples. In this sense, too, politics—even international politics—was to be explained primarily in terms of underlying economic interest.

Lenin argued that the advanced capitalist countries had temporarily postponed catastrophic economic crisis by finding new markets in the underdeveloped countries of the world. The expropriation of "surplus value" from workers had been internationalized through the spread of colonialism. The world war that began in 1914 should be understood as an imperialist war waged by the Great Powers in the interest of greater colonial domination. Imperialist expansion also enabled the bourgeoisie to buy off its indigenous proletariat through distribution of some of the profits expropriated from foreign and less class-conscious workers. And the war was a temporary boon to the flagging capitalist economies, enabling the bourgeoisie to appeal to the proletariat in terms of more secure employment as well as patriotic devotion. The consequences, for Lenin, were obvious: The proletariat of Western Europe had been "duped" and was most appropriately characterized by "false consciousness."

The Weakest Link Where was revolution most likely to occur, then? Lenin answered with his "theory of the weakest link." Russia was the weakest link in the chain of European capitalism. The least developed of the capitalist states, Russia was also the least advanced in the imperialist race for foreign markets. Its proletariat was consequently more susceptible to revolutionary mobilization, and in alliance with the Russian peasantry and led by the Bolshevik party, the Russian working class could be the first to inaugurate a socialist regime. And soon after the Bolshevik coup in Petrograd in October 1917, Lenin bravely announced his intent before the Second All-Russian Congress of Soviets: "We will now proceed to construct the socialist order." But how could *Marxian* socialism be constructed in an economically underdeveloped and largely peasant society?

TROTSKYISM

Leon Trotsky (1879–1940, born Lev Bronstein), along with Lenin, was the essential leader in the revolutionary success of the Bolsheviks in Russia and in the Red Army's subsequent victory over the counterrevolutionary Whites during the Russian civil war of 1918 to 1920. It may even be true that without Trotsky's impassioned rhetoric, incisive logic, and brilliant tactical leadership (admitted even by his enemies), bolshevism would merit only passing reference in the history of the modern world. Thus it is all the more ironic that Trotsky did not consider himself a Bolshevik throughout most of Russia's prerevolutionary period; that during the dramas of the Russian Revolution of 1917 he concluded that, instead of his converting to Leninism, Lenin had adopted his (Trotsky's) views on socialist revolution; and that Stalinist and post-Stalinist history in the Soviet Union has denied that Trotsky was anything other than a traitor to the Russian Revolution.

Permanent Revolution Ideologically, however, it was Trotsky who had explained how revolution in backward Russia could result in socialism, but socialism on a necessarily international scale of political and economic change. Trotsky's doctrine of "permanent revolution" held, first, that the revolution could succeed and sustain its socialist ambitions only if it were extended beyond the borders of Russia, eventually overwhelming the forces of capitalism elsewhere in Europe. And after the Bolsheviks' seizure of power, Trotsky believed that news of their success would be an important catalyst in eliminating the false consciousness of workers in the more advanced capitalist countries. With the aid of the Red Army and with the indigenous cadres of dedicated revolutionaries in each country, workers in Poland, Germany, Austria, Hungary, and

France could become a potent force for revolutionary change in their own societies.

The failure of Communist revolutionary efforts in Europe in 1918 and shortly thereafter, however, induced Trotsky to argue that the international proletarian revolution was only temporarily postponed and that continuous efforts should be undertaken to raise the revolutionary consciousness of the workers. In the meantime, he repeated his contention that there was a second dimension to the principles of permanent revolution, that of "telescoped revolution": In Bolshevik Russia, the foundations of socialism could be laid even while the state encouraged the economic development and cultural transformation that elsewhere had resulted from capitalism and the efforts of an enterprising bourgeoisie. While the Russian working class was being enlarged and socially educated through state-sponsored industrialization, agricultural production should be collectivized—thereby hastening the development of a socialist spirit among the peasantry. Thus Trotsky opposed the quasicapitalist New Economic Policy (NEP) implemented by Lenin in 1921 and continued by Stalin until 1928. For Trotsky, the NEP's failure to collectivize the peasantry and its encouragement of the bourgeois spirit among small entrepreneurs represented a setback in the development of socialism in Russia.

The Revolution Betrayed   And there was no doubt in Trotsky's mind that socialism in Russia was impossible insofar as it was not supported by working-class revolutions elsewhere in Europe. It also was impossible insofar as political power was concentrated in the hands of a narrow state bureaucracy that, in fact, only intensified the exploitation of the working class. Because of these views and because of his failure to win the intraparty struggle with Stalin after Lenin's death in 1924, Trotsky was exiled from the Soviet Union in 1929 and assassinated in Mexico in 1940. His martyrdom has helped to lend conviction to the handful of Trotskyite intellectuals who may be found today in many countries throughout the world (including those in the Socialist Workers party in the United States) and who are affiliated with the Fourth International founded by Trotsky in Mexico City in 1937, all of whom share Trotsky's views on the "statist" characteristics of the Soviet Union. They argue that the Soviet Union is not really a socialist state, nor are its communist allies, and they remain committed to the organization of proletarian revolution wherever there is an opportunity for advancing the cause of socialism and, ultimately, communism.

STALINISM

A clear measure of the irreconcilable differences between Trotsky and Stalin was their attitude toward the proper role of the Communist International (Third International, or Comintern), founded in Moscow in 1919. Trotsky viewed the Comintern as a vehicle for coordinating revolutionary activity throughout the world—or the institutional expression of his concept of "permanent revolution."[8]

In opposition to Trotsky's position, Joseph Stalin (1879–1953, born Dzhugashvili) sought to subordinate the Comintern to Soviet national interests instead of to the cause of worldwide proletarian revolution. Especially by the mid-1930s, it was clear that Stalin, firmly in control of both the state and the party, understood that Soviet national interests were not served by the international extension of the Bolshevik Revolution. "Stalinism," then, represents in part an extreme suspicion of revolutionary adventure, either at home or abroad. Communist parties in France, Germany, Spain, Italy, Latin America, or wherever they were subordinated to Moscow consequently talked about revolution, even while the tasks of revolution were left to Trotskyites and others committed to the interests of the masses instead of to the interests of the Soviet state. In the hands of Stalin, Soviet self-interest became the antithesis of Marxian internationalism.

---

[8]The First International, formally named The International Workingmen's Association, was organized by Marx in London in 1864. Its purpose was to bring together workers from all countries in order to advance the cause of socialism. But the Association's brief history was marked by intense factional struggles, particularly between Marx and its anarchist members, notably Bakunin. Its last congress was held in 1874 in Philadelphia, where Marx had moved the organization when he determined that it no longer served its original objectives. The Second International was founded in Paris in 1889 and included most of Europe's socialist parties. With the outbreak of World War I in 1914, national loyalties proved stronger than international proletarian solidarity, and the Second International disintegrated.

Socialism in One Country For Stalin, however, this was explained and justified by the doctrine of "socialism in one country."[9] Soviet Russia was to become the "bastion of socialism," a model of socialist development that would inspire socialists throughout the world. After 1928, Stalin thus collectivized agricultural production in the Soviet Union (thereby following Trotsky's program after Trotsky had been purged from the party) and initiated the first of a series of five-year plans designed to make the Soviet Union an industrial and military power. These programs signaled Stalin's liquidation of opposition elements in the party and the state bureaucracy (identified with Trotsky on the left and with Nikolai Bukharin on the right) and made obvious his commitment to rapid economic development even at the cost of millions of lives of Russian citizens, especially peasants.

The 1936 constitution of the Soviet Union declared that "socialism" had been achieved along with the elimination of classes opposed to the proletariat. But contrary to the stipulations of Marx, Engels, and even Lenin (in *The State and Revolution,* written in the late summer of 1917), the apparatus of the state had not begun to "wither away" with the establishment of socialism. "Capitalist encirclement," Stalin said, threatened the security of the Soviet Union and intensified as the socialist state advanced toward communism. Instead of withering away, the state consequently had been and would continue to be strengthened. And today, "Stalinism" also is meant to denote an extreme bureaucratic centralization of political power in the hands of a single leader who dominates both the party and the state; the ideology becomes a dogma that stifles dissent, and "socialism" is more the manipulation of definitions than it is a reflection of the objective relationships between society and the forces of production.

ANTI-STALINISM

Much of the troubled history of communist ideology and politics since World War II is the direct result of the tensions created by efforts toward "de-Stalinization." Trotsky and his supporters were among the first to denounce the bureaucratic excesses, ideological rigidity, and antirevolutionary orientation of Stalinism. But the extension of communist power in Eastern Europe and Asia after World War II laid the basis for new divisions among those who continued to proclaim their fidelity to the principles of Marxism-Leninism. And it was no coincidence that the most serious challenge to Stalinism came initially from Yugoslavia, where Tito's partisans, operating against the German occupation of Yugoslavia after 1941, succeeded in capturing power without the aid of the Soviet Army. Elsewhere in Eastern Europe, the presence of Soviet military power ensured the communist leaders' subordination to Moscow and Stalin, at least until Stalin's death in 1953. The case of Yugoslavia, however, was dramatically different.

Titoism

Marshal Tito was born Josip Broz in 1892. A soldier in the Austro-Hungarian Army during World War I, he was captured by the Russians, was converted to bolshevism, and distinguished himself as a soldier in the Red Army during the civil war of 1918 to 1920. He subsequently returned to Croatia, was employed as a metalworker, and gained prominence as a union organizer. He was imprisoned for his political and trade union activities between 1929 and 1934. In 1937 the Comintern gave Tito responsibility for reorganizing the weak and fragmented Yugoslav Communist party. The German invasion and occupation of Yugoslavia during World War II provided Tito with the necessary ideological appeal and political base for recruiting a large number of supporters. With the aid of the Soviet Union, and eventually even the military and political support of Great Britain and the United States, Tito emerged after the war as the dominant political leader of Yugoslavia. A major part of his domestic program was the creation of a federal state that promised cultural autonomy to the many Yugoslav ethnic groups that had long been dominated by Serbia.

Tito against Stalin From his vantage point after the war, Tito believed that the opportunities for communist revolution were not limited to the zone of operations of the Soviet Army and that many of the countries of Europe (including Greece, Italy,

---

[9]Stalin's principal ideological contributions to Marxism-Leninism may be found in his *Foundations of Leninism* (1924) and *Problems of Leninism* (1934).

France, and Belgium) were vulnerable to the forces of indigenous communism. As Tito and his partisans had demonstrated, power could be seized through superior military organization, competent political leadership, and—if necessary—civil war. (Nor did this seem to represent "Marxism.") But Tito's implicit variation on Trotsky's "permanent revolution" met with the conservative opposition of Stalin, who was content to consolidate the Soviet Union's control over Eastern Europe. For the moment, however, Stalin was not in a position to direct all the activities of foreign communists, especially the activities of Tito.

The Comintern had been formally dissolved by Stalin in 1943 in deference to the ideological sensitivities of Russia's wartime allies. But Tito and other communist revolutionaries sought a new international communist organization, and the founding of the Communist Information Bureau (Cominform) in 1947 represented a modest victory in their struggle against Stalin's antirevolutionary position. Tito and the militant Soviet ideologist Andrei Zhdanov immediately used the first meeting of the Cominform as a platform for strongly denouncing the bourgeois collaborationist policies of the Western European communist parties, which, according to Tito, had failed to take advantage of their revolutionary opportunities. The call went forth for violent confrontation with the institutions of the bourgeois state. But wherever the communists responded affirmatively to the Cominform's directive (as in France), the coercive apparatus of the state proved more than capable of putting down the challenge, and striking workers—threatened with military conscription—returned to their jobs (and many also destroyed their membership cards in the Communist party).

The Titoist adventurism of the Cominform thus ended almost as suddenly as it had begun. In 1948, Stalin asserted control: Zhdanov died in Russia under mysterious circumstances, and Yugoslavia was expelled from the Cominform. All the communist parties vented their wrath on the "renegade" Tito, who was accused of collaborating with the Germans during the war and of instituting a "fascist" state in Yugoslavia. Stalin was reported as saying, "I will bend my little finger, and Tito will be no more."

The political, diplomatic, and economic isolation that suddenly descended on Yugoslavia forced a major shift in Tito's policies, especially as the threat of a Soviet military invasion loomed on the Yugoslav horizon. In the United States, the Truman administration understood that a division in the ranks of communism and a Yugoslavia that was independent of Moscow represented major victories in the mounting struggles of the cold war. And United States economic and military aid to Yugoslavia between 1949 and 1955 (which amounted to $1.2 billion) played an important role in assuring the survival of Titoism. Titoism today thus denotes the very opposite of revolutionary adventurism.

Revisionism and Reform Titoism has come to represent a nonaligned foreign policy that does not consistently support the position or interests of either the communist or the noncommunist states. It follows logically that the Soviet Union is not a compulsory model for socialist development, and the Yugoslavs have argued that, in some cases, the transition from capitalism to socialism may be a largely peaceful process carried out by parliamentary institutions and working-class parties.

Titoism also represents a relatively noncoercive style of communist government. Yugoslavia is a federal state with planning and other administrative functions distributed among the six states, which are defined along the lines of culture and language. There is a relatively free exchange of ideas, and Yugoslav citizens and foreign tourists easily travel back and forth across Yugoslavia's borders. Privately operated farms dominate the agricultural sector, and where Yugoslav peasants have been collectivized, it is the result of economic inducement rather than terror or coercion. The right of workers to strike is acknowledged by the government, which represents a major civic and economic right unavailable to workers in other communist states. Workers elect representatives to "workers' councils," who participate, with varying degrees of influence, with management in the decision making that affects the operations of the factory. Local or commune governments are encouraged to exercise substantial authority in the regulation of local affairs. Law courts enjoy a significant degree of independence from other state institutions. The state itself, contrary to Stalin's views on the matter, is supposed to have begun the process of withering away, although the Communist party will remain as a general guide to policy choices—but more through education than command. And Yugoslav ideology admits that, even under socialism, antagonisms and conflicts may arise between workers, management, and the state. There consequently is a sincere concern for reducing and eliminating the excesses of bureaucracy.

Especially in the light of Yugoslavia's experiments with worker participation in factory management, Titoism represents a relatively humanistic approach to industrial organization that approximates the original spirit of Marxism. And in the contemporary world Yugoslavia stands as one of the most important political, social, and economic laboratories for testing alternative solutions to a problem that transcends national borders and ideology—bureaucratic control of citizen life.

Anti-Stalinism in the Soviet Union[10]

The death of Stalin in March 1953 also marked the end of a dark chapter in the history of Russia, with the exception of those pages which describe the Soviet Union's spectacular economic growth during Stalin's reign and the national resurgence that accompanied the defeat of Hitler's armies during World War II. But these accomplishments were achieved at the expense of great loss of life and only through the imposition of a heavy-handed constraint on individual and public initiative—constraint that was inconsistent with the principles of Marxism, Leninism, and even Trotskyism and Titoism. In fact, some of the revisionism that characterized Titoism eventually found its way into Soviet policy.

Power in the Party First was the issue of political power and the extent of its concentration in the person of the party leader. There could be no doubt that the Communist party of the Soviet Union (CPSU) was to remain the controlling institution of that country, using the apparatus of the state as a means of implementing policy established by the party. But the disappearance of Stalin and his forceful personality and the influence that derived from his close identification with Lenin meant that no subsequent party leader was likely to concentrate in his hands the sweeping powers exercised by Stalin.

Shortly after Stalin's death the new Soviet leaders, Malenkov, Bulganin, and Khrushchev, announced their commitment to the principle of "collective leadership" and moved decisively to curb the powers of the secret police (Beria, its chief, was executed in December 1953). References to "collective leadership," however, declined as the power struggle within the new triumvirate was resolved in Khrushchev's favor, and his position as first secretary of the CPSU gave him a marked advantage in the maneuvering for party support. Nevertheless, Khrushchev's authority ultimately remained in the hands of the more than 100 members of the party's Central Committee. It was the Central Committee that ratified Khrushchev's consolidation of power over the Molotov "antiparty" group in 1957 and was also responsible for Khrushchev's removal from power in 1964, The subsequent rise of Brezhnev and Kosygin, and the former's undoubted preeminence after the Twenty-fourth Party Congress in 1971, also depended on the distribution of support and opposition within the higher echelons of the party's hierarchy. The point is that, in contrast to the concentration of power characteristic of Stalinism, power in the Soviet Union after Stalin has been a function of those norms of bargaining and coalition building which are not unfamiliar to students of politics in more democratic societies.

Purging Stalinism The most dramatic—and the most sensational—assault on Stalinist power was launched by Khrushchev himself at the Twentieth Party Congress in 1956. Khrushchev detailed the aberrations of Marxism-Leninism worked by Stalin's "cult of the personality" and promised a new era in citizen liberties and policy-making procedures. He also denied that the Soviet Union represented a compulsory model for other communist parties and states, admitted the possibility of peaceful roads to socialism, and emphasized the international importance of "peaceful coexistence."

Thus the way was opened for new foreign policy initiatives helping to reduce the tensions of the cold war (symbolized in 1956 by the dissolu-

---

[10] Some of the themes elaborated in Chap. 13 are briefly anticipated here.

tion of the Cominform) and for some major and largely consistent efforts to broaden the civil liberties of Soviet citizens—within the limits set by the state's ideology. Greater attention was given to the needs of Soviet citizens as consumers as well as producers, and the extensive welfare provisions in education, health, and employment security were expanded. Important economic reforms were introduced after the early 1960s allowing for more individual initiative in implementing the programs of a modestly decentralized planning establishment. The party program adopted at the Twenty-second Party Congress in 1961 envisaged the laying of the foundations of "communism" by the 1980s. These trends have been largely continued by the post-Khrushchev regime, although progressively less attention has been given to the ideology's specifications for the "communist" stage of social development.

Economic Growth and Peaceful Coexistence It is even appropriate to say that, since Stalin's death, European communism (with the tentative exception of communism in Yugoslavia) has increasingly lost sight not only of Marx's but also of Lenin's ideals for socialist-communist development. Communism in Europe is now dedicated primarily to raising the living standards of citizens, through the efforts of the state as directed by the party, beyond the living standards of citizens in the so-called capitalist states.

It is in this sense that communism continues to wage its *ideological* battle with the industrialized states of the West. But advanced economic development in the European communist states depends heavily on international détente between the world's superpowers, which is the precondition for technological development and heightened living standards within the communist societies themselves. Peaceful coexistence, international trade, a reduction in military expenditures at home, and increased technological interdependency between capitalism and communism are all essential to the efforts of existing communist elites to raise the living standards of their citizens, and a steady rise in the levels of production and consumption has now become the basis for the claims of communist elites to political legitimacy.

There consequently is little reason to doubt the Soviet Union's interest in peaceful coexistence on a global scale. Occasional conflicts on a regional scale (as in the Middle East) do not contradict this basic principle, and such conflicts are typical of the rivalries between Great Powers throughout history. The Soviet Union continues to justify its commitment to peaceful coexistence in terms of the balance of world nuclear power, which, it is argued, makes sustained international conflict unthinkable. Domestically, the complement to peaceful coexistence abroad may be found in the Soviet Union's equally sincere commitment to improving the quality of citizen life, which also demonstrates its willingness to allow status differences to continue to develop among citizens according to individual initiative and productive talent.

From these perspectives, de-Stalinization was the logical outcome of advancing economic development; coercive bureaucratic controls and rigid centralization proved counterproductive to the basic goal of economic abundance. "From each according to his ability, to each according to his work" will continue to be the guiding principle of European communist social organization. But it is precisely the social inequality implicit in this principle and the antirevolutionary orientation now institutionalized by peaceful coexistence that have helped to lay the basis for the intensifying hostility that has marked Soviet and Chinese Communist relationships since the late 1950s.

CHINESE COMMUNISM

Is Chinese communism, or "Maoism," more Marxist-Leninist than Russian communism? It is a foregone conclusion that the Chinese Communists have answered this question with a resounding "yes." The Soviets have been equally adamant in the negative. As befits the complexity or ambiguity of the question, the answer would seem to be both "yes" and "no."

The Chinese Revolution
After the Bolshevik Revolution in Russia, and with the impetus imparted by the founding of the Comintern, the Chinese Communist party (CCP) was organized in 1921 by professors at the University of Peking. The small circle of intellectuals directing the CCP gave the party a Leninist orientation; its

ideological appeal and organizational efforts were directed at the members of China's proletariat, a relatively small social class in a society where 80 percent of the population was made up of peasants, and the CCP was considered to be the necessary revolutionary vanguard both for capturing power and for constructing socialism. Between 1923 and 1927, and following the directives of the Comintern in Moscow and its agents in China, the CCP was allied with the Kuomintang, or Chinese Nationalists, who had initiated China's republican revolution in 1911. The growing political and military strength of the Nationalists, whose leader after 1925 was Chiang Kai-shek, led to a dissolution of the alliance with the CCP and Chiang's liquidation of many Communist cadres. In 1927 the CCP lost its principal stronghold in Shanghai. The party's position in China's urban areas and among the Chinese workers appeared to be hopeless, and it was in this context that Mao Tse-tung captured the leadership of the CCP and gave the party an almost exclusively agrarian orientation. At this point it was difficult to conclude that Chinese communism was either Leninist or Marxist.

Mao's strategy was to build a peasant-based army and to secure "liberated" areas in the Chinese hinterland where the CCP could enhance its appeal to the peasantry through agrarian reform. Especially in northern Shensi province, where Mao and his followers ended their epic "long march" of 1934–1935, the CCP carried out programs of land redistribution (to the advantage of the poorer peasants), limited the exploitation of the peasantry by landlords and moneylenders, instituted progressive tax and welfare programs, built factories, and strengthened Communist political and military organization. The civil war with the Nationalist armies continued, but it was the territorial extension of Japan's military occupation of China after 1935 that laid the principal cornerstone for the eventual victory of Chinese communism. The Communists proved more effective than the Nationalists in fighting the Japanese, and Japan's defeat at the end of World War II opened the way for the advancing Red Armies, which finally forced the Nationalists to flee mainland China for the island of Taiwan in 1949. It also is difficult to argue that the victory of communism in China followed either Marx's or Lenin's scenario for the socialist revolution.

Building Communism in China

Nor has the Chinese Communist regime's continuing struggle to carry out basic industrialization and to augment agricultural production through collectivization reflected Marx's understanding of socialist construction. It will be recalled that, for Marx, "socialism" is possible only after the social and cultural transformations worked by mature capitalism and, subsequently, the dictatorship of the proletariat. For the Chinese Communists, on the other hand, "communism" should be more broadly defined, and its ultimate test is in the communalization of the production process and the elimination of private incentive in worker motivation.

In the "Great Leap Forward" of 1958, the CCP attempted to win the race with the Soviets to pure communism by communizing agriculture, which entailed the elimination of all forms of private property (some of which remain in the Soviet collective farm system) and the organization of all workers into production brigades, presumably inspired by the collective good of the whole society. The setback to these high hopes, due in part to natural disaster and—admittedly—overly optimistic planning, worked to the advantage of those CCP elites who advocated a slower rate of economic development and more incentive for the individual producer. More incentive, however, meant greater reward differentials, and by the middle of the 1960s Mao was faced with both a weakening of his control over the party and the development of a Chinese social structure that, in its growing status inequalities, was beginning to parallel that of the Soviet Union.

The Chinese Cultural Revolution The "Great Proletarian Cultural Revolution" of 1966 to 1969 (and with occasional reverberations into the 1970s) was thus a major effort in two directions: first, to reestablish Mao's political authority and the dominance of his most fervent supporters by eliminating the influence of the party—the party itself was to be rebuilt along the lines dictated by the youthful and militant Red Guards and, especially, the Chinese Red Army—and, second, to inculcate in the collective consciousness of Chinese citizens the necessity of total social equality along with the socialist spirit of all for one and one for all.

Consistent with this spirit is the rotation of

students, office workers, party bureaucrats, and other privileged strata of Chinese society through periodic job assignments in the rural communes and factories. Technological skills are to be transmitted universally; e.g., an agricultural brigade in a peasant commune elects a representative who receives advanced education in the latest techniques of agricultural production, and he (or she) then returns to the commune to educate other peasants in the uses of the new technology. In the process, differences of status and rank are presumably eliminated or minimized. Even in the Red Army, rank is supposed to be eliminated, at least among the lower and middle echelons of soldiers and "officers." It of course remains to be seen whether any large social structure can carry out industrialization and economic modernization without the differences in reward, privilege, and status that have characterized all societies undergoing socioeconomic change—including the Soviet Union.

The Sino-Soviet Conflict

These fundamental ideological differences between Communist China and the Soviet Union have been reflected in their conflicts over de-Stalinization and peaceful coexistence. Any attack on Stalin's cult of the personality and the highly centralized authority of Stalinism was also an attack on Maoism, and it was no coincidence that Mao Tse-tung was among the first to resist Khrushchev's efforts toward de-Stalinization. While peaceful coexistence reflected the Soviet Union's interests in improving its political and economic relationships with the West, the same principle—for the Chinese Communists—represented a betrayal of the revolutionary aspirations of underprivileged peoples throughout the underdeveloped world.

Thus the Soviet Union's willingness to join with Great Britain and the United States in signing the Nuclear Test-Ban Treaty in 1963 signaled to the Chinese the Soviet Union's commitment to "big-power chauvinism"—the attempt to retain a monopoly of nuclear weaponry in the hands of those superpowers who pursued only their own national self-interest. For the Chinese Communists, it is essential to advance the cause of world socialism through wars of liberation, beginning in the underdeveloped areas of the world. But the CCP has consistently argued that China's role in such revolutionary undertakings must be limited to diplomatic and occasional economic support and that the tasks of liberation in each country fall to the people themselves.

That the Sino-Soviet conflict has more than ideological implications has been dramatized by the periodic confrontation of Russian and Chinese armies along mutually contested borders. The Soviet military threat, as perceived by Peking, in turn induced the Chinese leadership to seek a détente with the United States in 1972. The lesson is obvious: It is not easy to construct a communist society, as Marx well understood, in a world of antagonistic ideologies and competing nation-states—a communist society that is communist in substance as well as in name—or to build communism in a world where, in fact, there are as many kinds of communism as there are communist states with different cultural backgrounds; at different stages of economic, political, and social development; and with different views of what represents the best interests of humanity, both at home and abroad.

CASTROISM

Fidel Castro's father was a wealthy plantation farmer and representative of Cuba's provincial upper classes. The advantages of birth, plus his own intellectual, oratorical, and leadership talents, enabled Castro (born in 1926) to graduate from the University of Havana as both a lawyer and a leader of Cuban liberals who were opposed to the dictatorship of Fulgencio Batista. Batista had seized power in Cuba just before the presidential elections scheduled for 1952, and his authoritarian and corrupt regime enjoyed significant support from the government of the United States. Business interests in the United States had been deeply involved in the Cuban economy and in Cuban politics since the Spanish-American War of 1898, when Cuba won independence from Spain only to find itself economically and politically subordinated to the colossus 90 miles to the north.

The Cuban Revolution

Convinced that the Batista government could not be reformed by constitutional and nonviolent methods, Castro resolved on revolutionary action. On

July 26, 1953, he led an attack on the Moncada army post in Santiago de Cuba, but he was captured and imprisoned. Released under the terms of a general amnesty for political prisoners, Castro then went to Mexico and organized the 26th of July Movement, which received political and economic support from prominent Cuban exiles, also hostile to the Batista regime. Castro's declared intent was to raise a popular revolt against Batista that would return Cuba to democratic and constitutional government, thereby restoring basic civil liberties to the Cuban people and improving the economic opportunities for businessmen who were frustrated by prevailing inefficiencies and political corruption. And before the collapse of Batista's government in January 1959, Castro received the support of a wide array of Cuban business and professional groups and sympathy from across the spectrum of Cuba's economic and social classes.

Castro's early strategy for revolution in Cuba, however, continued to be defeated by events. An urban uprising, planned to coincide with the amphibious landing of Castro and eighty armed men in southwestern Oriente province in 1956, failed to materialize. Of the landing party, only twelve escaped the initial encounter with Batista's militia—among them Fidel and Raul Castro and Che Guevara, a medical doctor born in Argentina. This small band of intellectuals and urban-oriented revolutionaries took refuge in the mountains of the Sierra Maestra, and, more by necessity than design, they began to cultivate the support of local peasants—especially "squatter" peasants who did not hold legal title to the land they worked.

Like Mao before him, Castro thus was forced by initial defeat to rethink his strategy for revolution, and what emerged was a program of agrarian reform coupled with the tactics of guerrilla warfare. Batista's inability to root out the guerrillas enhanced their popular appeal, and these frustrations contributed to Batista's launching in 1958 of a campaign of indiscriminate terror against the Cuban population. The number of Batista's supporters, including those among the military, rapidly declined as the terror campaign continued and as the guerrillas succeeded in their military advance toward Havana. But Castro's guerrilla army never numbered more than 2,000, and its victorious entry into Havana in January 1959 was the result more of Batista's accumulated weaknesses than of the guerrillas' military capabilities.

Castroism in Cuba

Once in power, the Castro government imprisoned and executed those who were closely identified with the Batista regime, initiated the collectivization of Cuban agriculture, and nationalized all domestic and foreign-owned industries and business enterprise. By the 1970s, and through rigorous economic planning, Castro's charismatic leadership, and Soviet economic aid, the Cuban population had made important gains in housing, welfare, and education; the government was firmly in place, and it appeared to enjoy the support of the large majority of Cubans who had not emigrated abroad. But the initial actions of the Castro regime heightened the hostility of the government of the United States toward the Castro revolution, and that hostility was dramatized in 1960, when the Eisenhower administration canceled the Cuban sugar quota.

Just as the threat of the Soviet Union forced a major alteration in Yugoslavia's foreign and domestic policies after 1948, the imperatives of revolutionary government and the hostility of the United States forced a major redefinition of "Castroism." In order to ensure the cooperation of the administrative, military, and trade union structures of Cuban society with his revolutionary programs, Castro took advantage of the disciplined and ideologically dedicated members of the Cuban Communist party. The Cuban Communists had registered their support for Castro only when the 26th of July Movement appeared to be headed for victory. But by purging the Communist party's top leadership, Castro assumed control over the party, whose militants were then infiltrated into the critical centers of Cuban government and society. And, anxious to demonstrate its time-honored commitment to revolution, the Soviet Union proved willing to subsidize the struggling Cuban economy. Thus in December 1961, after the abortive Bay of Pigs invasion supported by the United States, Castro declared himself a Marxist-Leninist. Like Castro's earlier changes in revolutionary strategy, however, his declaration appeared to be a function more of unanticipated events and circumstances than of prior doctrinal conviction. And, indeed, it was not clear what there was in Castro's revolution that might be qualified as either Marxist or Leninist.

Castroism in Latin America

That Castroism represented a unique ideological and political phenomenon was also suggested by the revolutionary ideology that eventually emerged from the Cuban revolution, especially as elaborated by Che Guevara and Régis Debray—the latter a young French intellectual who became a confidant of Castro and his close associates. To the constant embarrassment of the Soviet Union, which remained committed to the extension of its diplomatic and economic influence rather than to revolutionary adventure, Castroism became identified with peasant-based revolution throughout Latin America.

The principal assumption was that the millions of impoverished Latin-American peasants were ready to revolt and that the primary instrument of peasant revolution was the presence of armed guerrillas (or the guerrilla *foco*), who progressively enlarged their scope of military activity against the existing government. Contrary to both Leninist and Maoist (and Vietnamese Communist) principles, the political arm of the revolution was to be subordinated to the military, and it was events in the countryside (as determined by the military) rather than in the city that were ultimately to determine the success of the revolution.

As a program for revolution in Latin America, however, Castroism proved to be a superficial reading of the complexity of the Cuban revolution itself, and it seriously overestimated the revolutionary potential of Castroite guerrillas and peasants elsewhere in Latin America. It also underestimated the effectiveness of counterinsurgency techniques developed in Latin America (with the help of military equipment and training from the United States) after Castro's revolution in Cuba. These points were dramatically underlined by the extreme difficulties and eventual defeat encountered by Guevara and his followers in Bolivia between 1966 and 1968.

COMMUNISM AS AN IDEAL

History, however, is filled with examples of noble ends poorly served by inappropriate or corrupted means. In politics, especially revolutionary politics, no one is innocent. But if it is true that even man's notable accomplishments inevitably fall short of his ideals, it also is true that, without ideals, nothing notable is accomplished. Greater social justice for all is likely to continue to be the principal ideal of the large majority of mankind. And in part because of the very ambiguity of their meaning, "Marxism" and "communism" are likely to remain an inspiration to those reformers and revolutionaries who seek to build for the future what the biblical prophets understood to be a Golden Age of the past.

STUDY-GUIDE QUESTIONS

1 From the Marxist point of view, why do economic classes develop? What are the social and political effects of class divisions?
2 Why did Marx think that the socialist revolution was inevitable? What did Marx mean by "revolution"?
3 Was Lenin really a Marxist?
4 In what ways did Stalin's ideological and programmatic contributions to communism contradict Trotsky's notions of the "permanent revolution"?
5 Which most closely approximates Marxism: Titoism, Maoism, or Castroism? Why?

REFERENCES

Avineri, Shlomo: *The Social and Political Thought of Karl Marx,* Cambridge University Press, London, 1969.

Borkenau, Franz: *World Communism: A History of the Communist International,* Ann Arbor Paperbacks, University of Michigan Press, Ann Arbor, 1962.

Committee of Concerned Asian Scholars: *China! Inside the People's Republic,* Bantam Books, Inc., New York, 1972.

Debray, Régis: *Revolution in the Revolution? Armed Struggle and Political Struggle in Latin America,* Monthly Review Press, New York, 1967.

Deutscher, Isaac: *The Prophet Armed: Trotsky, 1879–1921,* Oxford University Press, New York, 1954.

Draper, Theodore: *Castro's Revolution: Myths and Realities,* Frederick A. Praeger, Inc., New York, 1967.

Feuer, Lewis S. (ed.): *Marx and Engels; Basic Writings on Politics and Philosophy,* Anchor Books, Doubleday & Company, Inc., Garden City, N.Y., 1959.

Fromm, Erich: *Marx's Concept of Man,* Frederick Ungar Publishing Co., New York, 1961.

Hoffman, George W., and Fred Warner Neal: *Yugoslavia and the New Communism,* The Twentieth Century Fund, New York, 1962.

Johnson, Chalmers (ed.): *Change in Communist Systems,* Stanford University Press, Stanford, Calif., 1970.

Mallin, Jay (ed.): *Che Guevara on Revolution,* University of Miami Press, Coral Gables, Fla., 1969.

Meyer, Alfred G.: *Marxism: The Unity of Theory and Practice,* Harvard University Press, Cambridge, Mass., 1954.

———: *Leninism,* Harvard University Press, Cambridge, Mass., 1957.

Schram, Stuart: *Mao Tse-tung,* Penguin Books, Inc., Baltimore, 1967.

Stojanović, Svetozar: *Between Ideals and Reality: A Critique of Socialism and Its Future,* Oxford University Press, New York, 1973.

Treadgold, Donald W. (ed.): *Soviet and Chinese Communism: Similarities and Differences,* University of Washington Press, Seattle, 1967.

Tucker, Robert C.: *Philosophy and Myth in Karl Marx,* Cambridge University Press, London, 1961.

Wilson, Edmund: *To the Finland Station,* Anchor Books, Doubleday & Company, Inc., Garden City, N.Y., 1940.

Chapter 7

Ideologies on the Left, Center, and Right

Over the last several centuries, the organization and conduct of politics have been complicated by the development of political parties and specific institutions for legislation, administration, and adjudication. In earlier days, static social structures, agrarian economies, and a largely self-sufficient community of citizens required few services from a central government. Government was simple when society was simple. Today, however, it is no coincidence that "big government" is found where the society is highly urbanized, where the economy is geared primarily to industrial production, and where many categories of citizens turn to government for the services once provided by the family, the church, and the agrarian community. The opportunities for political conflict have increased as economic development has created new values, attitudes, and interests, and the proliferation of ideologies reflects these fundamental changes in our ways of life and in the organization of our society and government.

FROM LEFT TO RIGHT

In everyday political parlance, and especially where there are more than one or two political parties, we inevitably try to impart some conceptual order to our understanding of political competition. Thus we frequently describe a particular government, ideology, individual, or group as "leftist," while others are "centrist" or "rightist." Where do these terms come from, and what do they imply?

The conceptual dichotomy between ideological left and right probably derives from earlier days of political organization when the king, sitting in council, arranged his closest supporters near his right hand (typically the stronger of the two hands). These included his most trusted advisers and those

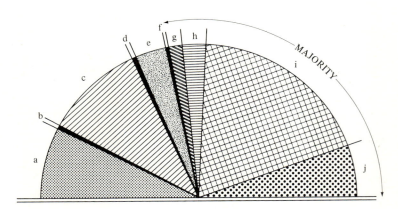

Figure 7.1 Partisan distribution of seats in the French National Assembly, following the parliamentary elections of March 1973.

responsible for various administrative tasks of state. Those seated to the king's left were not necessarily hostile to his rule, but it may be surmised that they frequently represented alternative points of view on governmental policy.

After the French Revolution of 1789 was under way, and while king and parliament struggled for supremacy, the deputies seated in the National Assembly distributed themselves in the chamber according to the extremism of their views. The most antiroyalist deputies sat on the far left, the king's strongest supporters sat on the far right, and those groups with more moderate views sat in between. Even today in the French parliament and in other houses of parliament throughout the world, the governing party and its cabinet officers sit to the right of the speaker, while opposition parties sit to the speaker's left. In multiparty legislatures where seating is distributed in a semicircle around the speaker's chair, a visitor to the chamber gallery can always identify the Communist delegates (if there are any); they are seated on the speaker's extreme left. And, from the speaker's vantage point, the Socialists are to the right of the Communists. In France, where the extent of a party's leftist traditions is an important symbol in political conflict, parliamentary delegations have occasionally engaged in bitter debate over who should be seated where. In politics, as in religion, symbols and ritual may frequently overshadow the substance of policy and belief. (See Figure 7.1.)

The distinctions between political left, center, and right really imply a *continuum* of ideologies, and such a continuum may help us to understand that one ideology is likely to share some values and assumptions with other ideologies to its immediate left or right. Again we are concerned with categories that are elaborated in terms of "more or less" instead of "either-or." And if we organize the continuum according to an ideology's prescriptions for socioeconomic equality and political authority, we are likely to agree on the following distribution of political ideologies, which will then serve as the chapter outline for what follows. (See Table 7.1.)

ANARCHISM

The Haymarket riot in Chicago in 1886, the assassination of President William McKinley in 1901, and other tumultuous events attributed to anarchist violence around the turn of the twentieth century have left us with the impression that the anarchist is best depicted with flowing hair, shaggy beard, a knife between his teeth, and a lighted bomb in either hand. The violent strain in anarchist ideology may be attributed largely to Mikhail Bakunin (1814–1876), who was born of the Russian aristocracy but who came to believe that complete individual freedom could be realized only after the violent destruction of the state and its supporting institutions. It was appropriate that anarchist violence was perpetrated almost exclusively by individuals acting under their own inspiration rather than by groups or organizations following the outlines of some comprehensive plan for revolution and the establishment of anarchism.

The association of anarchism with violence, however, is an inaccurate characterization of a philosophical tradition which has been largely *nonviolent* and which can be traced back to Zeno of Citium and to some of the tenets of early Stoic philosophy in ancient Greece. As it has developed over the centuries, anarchism has come to represent an extreme view of individual liberty and the possibility of social organization without hierarchy or authority; the word "anarchism," in fact, comes from the Greek and literally means "having no government." In this sense, anarchism approximates Marx's vision of the ideal communist society. It may also be interpreted as a logical extension of classical liberal principles on the necessary autonomy of each individual—whose subordination to authority is justified only by the individual's specific and continuing consent.

Authority Anarchism, however, denies that consent justifies political authority. The only authority that has moral and legitimate force is the authority people give to themselves. Individuals cannot be constrained to perform any act unless the act derives from their own independent will. Following Rousseau's concept of the "general will," contemporary anarchists in France (associated with the journals *Le Monde libertaire* and *La Libération*) have argued that the individual's right to legislate for himself is inalienable; it cannot be delegated. The *administration* of law may be delegated, but not the making of law. Legislation and policy making are the exclusive right of each individual as he reflects on his own interests and needs. "Each citizen his own legislator" would be an apt characterization of the anarchist position.

Freedom and Equality Anarchism, then, stands opposed to any institutional restraint that compromises individual freedom. And, by definition, all institutions compromise individual freedom; these include religious institutions, capitalism, private property, and (as in the case of classical liberalism) the state. If man is to be truly free, these institutions must be abolished. How? The emphasis in

Table 7.1 Continuum of Ideologies, Left, Center, and Right—According to Prescriptions for Socioeconomic Equality and Political Authority

Left	Center	Right
	Communism	Classical liberalism	
Anarchism	Socialism	Conservatism	Fascism
	Neoliberalism		

anarchist thought is less on violence and direct action than on education and a universal awareness of the apparent nature of man. In the small village society of southern Spain in the nineteenth century, where peasant anarchism was particularly strong, anarchists might be asked: "How would the great change come about? Nobody knew. At bottom the peasants felt that it must somehow come about if only all men declared themselves for it at the same time."[1] Knowing the truth would make all men free, and a major tenet of anarchist truth and a necessary condition for freedom was equality. It thus is understandable that the mass base of anarchism's appeal has been among the lowest strata of workers and peasants, particularly peasants in southern Spain and Italy (including Sicily).

Cooperation How should the new society be organized? Insofar as there is any organization at all, anarchism insists on the free and spontaneous association of citizens. In the eighteenth and nineteenth centuries, William Godwin in England, Pierre Proudhon in France, and the Russian-born Piotr Kropotkin and Mikhail Bakunin contributed to anarchist thought the assumption of a progressively enlightened mankind, ever more informed through the use of human reason and ever less dependent on the restraints of institutions suited to more primitive times and less rational behavior. Drawing from his studies and field observations in the natural sciences, Kropotkin (1842–1921) also disputed the classical liberal's argument, particularly as advanced by Herbert Spencer, that species' survival and evolutionary development depend on

---

[1] E. J. Hobsbawm, *Primitive Rebels: Studies in Archaic Forms of Social Movement in the 19th and 20th Centuries,* W. W. Norton & Company, Inc., New York, 1959, p. 88.

competition and self-interest. For Kropotkin and anarchism in general, the survival of each animal species and the social progress of mankind depend on mutual aid and cooperation. Men are not free when they pursue their own self-interest; they only end by falling on one another's throats.

Thus the highest social order, and the only moral one, derives from each man's enlightened understanding of his interdependency with others. And in the free and unfettered working out of this interdependency, the only legitimate source of authority is the individual himself.

COMMUNISM

As noted above, communism and anarchism share the ideals of socioeconomic equality and individual autonomy. The former is the necessary condition of the latter. The individual's unrestrained development of his creative potential, however, is also contingent on his consciousness of his social obligations. Thus the "self-interest" that motivates citizens of anarchist and communist societies is qualitatively different from the ego-oriented self-interest of bourgeois citizens in capitalist societies.

The anarchist, however, tends to view the possibilities for anarchist social development as immediate: the new world awaits only our recognition of its inherent justice and rationality. And in the new world of anarchist social organization (or *non*organization) there is, of course, no room for the institutions of the state. On the other hand, the communist—at least of the Marxist variety—argues that the ideal society evolves over an extended period of time marked by substantial economic change. The collective consciousness of communist existence, however autonomous the free and creative individual, emerges only after substantial changes in the objective conditions of life, and not suddenly from a flash of rational insight. And while the state ceases to function as an instrument of class repression, the communist does not deny the necessity of some institutional means for coordinating the production and distribution of goods and services in communist society. Economic abundance still entails social interdependence, even though communist man is no longer alienated from his nature by material necessity and coercive social organization.[2]

Party and State Contemporary communism, even in Yugoslavia, is unwilling to leave the affairs of society exclusively in the hands of workers. Not only is the *Communist party* the necessary instrument for capturing political power and initiating the construction of the ideal society (which again separates communism from anarchism), but it also remains as a "guide" to policy making and exercises controlling authority in the event of decision-making conflict. Or, more properly put, the party continues to function as the institutional setting for the resolution of conflict, however decentralized the administrative hierarchy of the state.

That we can even refer to a "state" in the discussion of communist social ideals testifies to the problems of reconciling ideals with reality. Self-declared communists today exercise political power; anarchists have never exercised political power, and, at best, they have provided ideals for only a particular segment of a few societies and have exerted factional influence over a decided minority of the labor movement. Their depiction of the ideal future has consequently remained vague, and the future has been projected in universal terms. But confronted with the reality of political power and economic development in a highly fragmented world, communist ideology has implicitly abandoned its universalistic aspirations. Khrushchev's much-publicized and little-understood threat to the United States in particular and "capitalism" in general ("We will bury you") was intended as a promise of ideological not military struggle. He was saying, in effect, that the ideology and socioeconomic system of communism will endure, while that of capitalism will prove its own inadequacies with the passage of time and will eventually pass away of its own accord.

But even this style of ideological posturing seems to have faded with time, especially as communist economies have shown their increasing interdependence with the economies of more advanced industrial and noncommunist states. The realities of

---

[2]The varieties and characteristics of communist ideology have already been discussed in greater detail in Chap. 6.

political power thus have forced contemporary communism to lose sight of the ideal future of an autonomous man in a universally egalitarian world society. Uncontaminated by the exercise of power, anarchism has never had to contend with the sobering problems of actual social organization, and its universalistic ideals have consequently remained more intact. If, as Lord Acton observed, power tends to corrupt, it also tends to make obvious the incompatibility that exists between high ideals and harsh reality.

SOCIALISM

As a label, socialism is the least specific of all the isms used in political discourse, partly because socialism may subsume anarchism, syndicalism, and communism and may even shade across the ideological continuum to include neoliberalism. This genial ambiguity of the socialist label also helps to account for its political prominence throughout recorded history; most societies and most ideologies have had a socialist bias. This is also to say that there are many types of socialism, in terms of both political organization (authoritarian or democratic) and economic system (highly centralized and directly regulated or largely decentralized and only indirectly regulated). It is manifestly wrong to argue that socialism necessarily implies political dictatorship or heavy-handed controls on individual and corporate economic activity.

Man as a Social Being   The prominence of some form of socialist thought and practice over time and around the world probably results from the very nature of society: men, women, and children living together in families, villages, tribes, cities, and nation-states. Any practical definition of individual rights has had to take into account social obligation. By the very nature of human existence, those who live in society are not isolated individuals. The way in which people behave invariably affects the opportunities for self-development of others. The state or analogous institutions of government arise to regulate the inevitable conflicts of interacting citizens, and this in turn requires a definition of individual rights in terms of their social implications. And, in essence, "socialism" means simply the subordination of the individual's welfare to the welfare of the whole society. The many are likely to benefit most if the interests of a few are not taken to represent the well-being of everyone. In both thought and practice, however, the actual working out of these general principles has taken many forms, including the following.

Doctrinaire Socialism

After the mid-nineteenth century and in the context of industrial society, socialist thought had a strong Marxist motif. As has been pointed out already in Chapter 6, however, Marxism itself contained many ambiguities, and consequently there were many interpreters who disagreed on the meaning and contemporary relevance of Marxism, even as they called themselves Marxists or recognized Marx as the ideological godfather of modern socialism.

Those who insisted on a rigid application of Marx's principles may be called "doctrinaire" or "orthodox" socialists (although the latter term may incorrectly imply that there is one, and only one, appropriate interpretation of socialist or Marxist principles). Chief among the doctrinaire socialists was Lenin, although it has been shown how Lenin's interpretation of Marx was made to fit Lenin's understanding of the characteristics of tsarist Russia. The problem of rigorously applying Marxism to contemporary reality was also apparent in the ideological and political struggles of doctrinaire socialists in Western Europe; the notable ideologues in this category were the Frenchman Jules Guesde (1845–1922; his last name is pronounced gĕd) and, in Germany, Karl Kautsky (1854–1938). Even more than Lenin, they were troubled by the implications of parliamentary participation by elected socialist deputies. But Guesde, Kautsky, and their doctrinaire comrades were less willing to tamper with the principles of Marxism than were the revisionist socialists, discussed below.

Strategy and Tactics   The doctrinaire socialists, then, adhered closely and conscientiously to Marx's theories and predictions. Although they doubted the validity of Marx's theory of value (by this time the labor theory of value had been repudiated by virtually all schools of economic thought in favor of the theory of marginal utility), they clung steadfastly to his materialistic interpretation of history, his pessimistic predictions regarding the future of capitalism, and his insistence that the condition of the working class under capitalism would grow steadily worse. They accepted the idea of the class struggle and hence the ultimate necessity of revolution; however, this was construed to mean revolution at the right time, not constant uprisings. The doctrinaire followers of Marx recognized the need for political organization of the workers to "win the battle of democracy," but they disagreed among themselves concerning the propriety of participation by socialist deputies in government coalitions. In general, they tended to oppose such participation in principle, but to support it in practice, usually on the ground that their refusal would bring reactionaries into power.

They were also at odds over socialist support for ameliorative or welfare legislation when such legislation was introduced by a nonsocialist government. On the whole, the doctrinaire socialists were inclined to depreciate the value of such immediate but nonsocialist reforms because they felt that the effect of such measures would be to make capitalism more palatable to the workers and hence weaken their class-consciousness and revolutionary ardor. Reform legislation was to be supported only if it strengthened the workers in their struggles with the capitalists; obviously, it was difficult to determine in advance the probable effect of such proposed measures. Proposed extensions of public ownership (e.g., of the agencies of transportation and communication) did not necessarily warrant the support of socialist deputies because public ownership would still mean capitalist control unless the workers were in control of the state and the government.

The general policy of doctrinaire socialist parties and their leaders was one of obstruction. They were not disposed to assist in repairing capitalism or in remedying its inefficiencies and injustices, preferring instead to remain aloof in order to hasten its collapse. Concerning war, they were in disagreement among themselves; on the whole, they were not as internationalist as Marx had been. Many doctrinaire socialist leaders approved of wars of national defense, and they spoke of the need to preserve the cultural heritages of their particular nations. While they praised and desired peace, they sought it through the socialization of each country rather than through a sweeping policy of pacifism. But the socialist parties in the Second International were never able to reach agreement on a resolution pledging all member parties to resistance and a general strike in the event of war. The outbreak of World War I found most socialists rallying to their countries' colors; the spread of socialism had been more than matched by the intensification of nationalism.

Toward Revisionism Among doctrinaire socialists there was also the apparently inevitable gap between ideology and practice. Although the ideologues and some of the party leaders might advocate socialist opposition to liberal reform measures, the party rank and file and especially the trade union membership frequently demanded immediate reforms, including the eight-hour working day, social insurance, and other ameliorative legislation beneficial to labor. These demands were made in both France and Germany. In Germany, the Erfurt program adopted by the Social Democratic party in 1891 included a call for many such reforms. Even Karl Kautsky, who had become the recognized leader of the doctrinaire socialists after the death of Engels in 1895, felt compelled to approve many of the welfare enactments of the German government—which at the time was neither liberal nor socialist.

Despite denunciations by Kautsky and other doctrinaire leaders of the conciliatory policies of the revisionist wing of the socialist movement, they themselves thus veered steadily toward revisionism in actual practice. There was more than a little truth in the derisive charge, made later by the Bolsheviks, that Kautsky and his followers "talked a good revolution," even while they scrupulously avoided doing anything to hasten its arrival. And a major problem for all doctrinaire socialists (including the communist parties of the industrialized world) has been to reconcile the revolutionary principles of their ideology with the antirevolutionary implications of their political involvement. With growing support in the trade union movement and in the electorate, the doctrinaire socialists became increasingly reluctant to risk their political influence and organizational strength through revolutionary adventure. The point seems clear: Where doctrinaire socialists were consistently denied the opportunities for trade union organization and political participation (as in Russia), they remained irrevocably committed to revolution. But where the state proved responsive to working-class interests, the pressures on socialists for ideological revision usually proved impossible to resist.

Revisionist Socialism

A major difference between the socialist and the anarchist is the former's belief that the state, under certain conditions, may be an instrument of good rather than evil. The socialist does not mean to eliminate the state, but rather to transform it in the interests of, first, the working class and, ultimately, all men in the society. Socialism, in its concern for the appropriate role of the state, focuses more on the here and now and does not look as far into the future as anarchism and communism do. What separated doctrinaire from revisionist socialists, however, was the question of how the state should be transformed: by revolution and direct action or by political organization and electoral competition. Although doctrinaire socialists in Western Europe preached the former while practicing the latter, revisionist socialists recognized the necessity of squaring ideology with practice.

The State and Evolution An early effort in the direction of reconciling ideology and practice came from Ferdinand Lassalle (1825–1864), who organized the first workers' party in Germany in 1863 and who viewed socialism as largely the result of government action within the territory of each individual state. This clearly was a fundamental revision of the internationalist ethic imparted to socialism by Marx. But in their struggle with the doctrinaire socialists, the revisionists also were moved to challenge Marxian orthodoxy on a number of other points. And in the process, the revisionists—as ideologists and party leaders—have generally directed their movement toward more and more moderate, democratic, and evolutionary methods of achieving socialism.

These trends, especially obvious after World War I, are now even more pronounced. And the revisionist content of socialism is manifested not only in practice but also in thought. Revisionists have declared themselves willing to accept socialism in installments, through social legislation, progressive taxation, and schemes of limited, partial public ownership. They thus have directly challenged or rejected many of Marx's assumptions and conclusions. Even in the late nineteenth century, Eduard Bernstein (1850–1932), the founder and leader of revisionist socialism, rejected the labor theory of value and qualified the materialist interpretation of history. Bernstein argued that noneconomic factors, including the ideals of men, were equally important in shaping history. And revisionists have generally held that noneconomic forces would grow more influential as the material life of mankind was increasingly enriched along with industrial progress.

Changes in Capitalism Bernstein also took sharp issue with Marx's negative prognosis for capitalism, contending that the middle class was not disappearing and that the diffusion of ownership of the stock of industrial corporations tended to create more, not fewer, capitalists. The appearance of giant corporations, then, did not necessarily imply greater concentration of the ownership of the means of production. Revisionists also argued that the rate of capitalist concentration varied in different industries, that economic crises were becoming less frequent and less severe, and that the collapse of capitalism was not imminent.

An important factor in the preservation of the capitalist system was said to be the tendency (almost unknown during the early stages of the factory system) toward curbing the ruthless and exploitative excesses of capitalism by means of social welfare and labor legislation. Jean Jaurès, a French revisionist and socialist leader, argued that the condition of the proletariat was growing better, not worse. Many revisionists also wondered aloud (the unuttered thought was heresy to the doctrinaire socialists) whether the proletariat actually was increasing in size and was becoming more class-conscious. Some argued that, in fact, proletarian class-consciousness was on the decline.

Politics instead of Revolution The upshot of revisionist appraisals of capitalist tendencies in an era of widening democracy was the conviction that although revolution might be ultimately necessary, the time for it was not yet ripe; moreover, ameliorative legislation and other advantages to be secured from the existing nonsocialist state would help—not hinder—the workers in their preparations for such a final revolution. Revisionists insisted on the necessity of proletarian socialist parties and on their gaining control of the governments of their respective countries, but the socialism to be thus established would be more moderate and limited than the sweeping transformation of society urged by the doctrinaire socialists. Most revisionist leaders seemed willing to accept partial rather than complete socialization of production and urged reform programs consisting largely of such progressive proposals as universal suffrage, electoral reform, the initiative and referendum, social security legislation, broadened educational opportunities, and taxation based upon the individual's ability to pay. While they reiterated their devotion to an *ultimately* "complete transformation of the capitalist system" by means of the "necessary and progressive substitution of social property for capitalist property," industries were to be nationalized only "as fast as they become ripe for social appropriation."

Revisionists also believed it proper for socialists to accept ministerial posts in a liberal government and to support all democratic reforms designed to promote justice. Some revisionist writers laid their chief emphasis upon the ethical goals of socialism, stressing cooperation rather than class struggle. Others expressed apprehension over the sheer magnitude of the task of socializing complex modern societies. And as these apprehensions have proved to be well-founded, revisionist socialists have concentrated on the state's control of fiscal and monetary resources instead of urging direct control by workers or the state of the production process.

Democratic Socialism: Great Britain

As governments became more sensitive to the problems of unregulated capitalism and more open to working-class representation, socialism became more democratic. And it already is obvious that doctrinaire socialism was strongest in Russia, less strong in Germany and France, and weakest of all in Great Britain and the United States. Only in Russia did the state (under the tsars) absolutely refuse to allow trade union organization and industrial strikes, to encourage the systematic provision of welfare services, and to extend the suffrage beyond the privileged minorities of a highly stratified society. In the context of a destructive war and military defeat, the Russian state thus proved vulnerable to capture by revolutionaries who represented the epitome of doctrinaire socialism.

Compromise and Pragmatic Reform In Great Britain, by contrast, the Chartist movement of the mid-nineteenth century and the guild and Fabian socialists of the early twentieth century all rejected revolutionary techniques. They opted instead for the extension of the suffrage (the Chartists), for trade union organization (the guild socialists), for the formation of working-class political parties (the Fabians), for education rather than agitation, and for the reform of the policies of the state instead of the overthrow of its institutions.

And, happily for the development of democracy, the state responded affirmatively to these general demands. In Great Britain, the traditions of monarchy, aristocracy, and mercantilism helped to soften the impact of early capitalism and also served as precedents for governmental controls imposed during the more advanced stages of capitalist development. The idea of noblesse oblige impelled many members of the British landed aristocracy to protest against slums and inhuman working conditions for factory laborers. Even the Whig (later known as the Liberal) party, which represented the rising class of factory owners and merchants, sponsored the first Factory Act (1833) and poor-law reform. By the early twentieth century, the Liberal party, then supported by the votes of miners and factory workers, enacted the first unemployment insurance law (1911), the Labor Exchanges Act of 1909, and the Trade Boards Act (a minimum-wage law), also in 1909.

Meanwhile, steady steps were taken toward public ownership of such enterprises as water supply, docks and harbor installations, the telegraph (1868), and the telephone (1911). The growth of municipal ownership of electric power facilities led to the establishment in 1926 of the Central Electricity Board to fix rates and coordinate public and private power systems; by 1939, two-thirds of British cities owned their electric power services. In 1926, radio broadcasting became a national government monopoly, administered through the government-owned British Broadcasting Corporation; in 1933, the London Passenger Transport Board took over London's system of subways, buses, and trolleys.

The nationalization and extensive social security programs enacted into law by the Labour government (1945–1951) therefore rest upon foundations laid by both Conservative and Liberal predecessors. With typical British practicality and compromise, economic and social problems have been met on the plane of workability rather than dogma. Such words as "socialism" and "collectivism" have little scare power in England. The empirical character of British socioeconomic policy is shown by the fact that such programs as those for public housing, the national health service, the extension of educational opportunities, and even the nationalization of coal, civil aviation, and gas were either recommended or actually started during the tenure of Conservative governments. Despite Conservative enactment of legislation to denationalize certain sectors of iron and steel and inland transport, Conservatives as well as all other Britons accept as final the nationalization of the Bank of England, coal, civil aviation, all telecommunications, electricity, and gas. Moreover, regulations covering the use of land (especially farmlands) and controlling industrial plant expansion, raw material imports, types of products to be manufactured, markets to be cultivated, and mergers under governmental planning and supervision are now supported or were originated by Conservative or coalition governments.

Consensus on Socialism Thus democratic socialism is less a theory than an accepted practice in Great Britain. The paucity of British treatises on the subject, when compared with the voluminous writings of American New Dealers, is mute testimony to British reluctance to belabor the obvious. The British idealist doctrines, elaborated in the late nineteenth century by Oxford intellectuals as an ethical protest against the harsh materialism of individualism and classical liberalism, helped to influence the thinking of several generations of upper-class Englishmen and, therefore, later public policy. The intensity of American feeling during the controversy over the New Deal can be matched in recent British history only by the struggles from 1909 to 1911 over David Lloyd George's budget, tax, and social-reform proposals. Despite occasional intemperate language during the height of political campaigns (e.g., Winston Churchill's claim during the 1945 elections that a victory for Labour would turn Britain into a police state—and Churchill lost the election), the British people judge the activities of government by the results rather than by the semantic labels attached to them by political factions. They are more likely to ask, "Does it work?" or "How much does it cost?" rather than, "Is it socialism?"

Democratic Socialism: Continental Europe

In view of the widespread American tendency to call modern Britain "socialistic" because of its partial (about 20 percent) nationalization of industry and its extensive health and social security programs, it is not strange that the nations on the Continent (with the possible exception of West Germany) are viewed in many American quarters as hopelessly enmeshed in the tentacles of statism, collectivism, or Marxism, the precise term depending on the vocabulary of the critic.

A Tradition of Government Controls Speaking historically, continental European nations never went through a period of thoroughgoing laissez faire comparable to the American era of rugged individualism. Lacking our broad territory, our unparalleled natural resources, our economic opportunities afforded by free land and frontier, our international security (provided by oceans and friendly national neighbors), and our further advantage of small population, European states found it necessary to impose many economic controls not required in the United States. Strong monarchical regimes and landowning aristocracies with their roots in feudalism were slow to remove mercantilist restrictions merely to benefit merchants and industrialists. Bounties, subsidies, monopolies, import-export controls, tariffs, and other, similar devices were common. Capitalism on the Continent, especially in autocratic states like Germany, really began as monopoly, cartel capitalism, aided and controlled by the government for nationalistic and imperialistic purposes, rather than as small-scale, free, competitive, individual enterprise. Also, the prevalence of mixed enterprises, combining both private and government capital, tended toward state capitalism.

European businessmen have for a long time preferred mergers, combinations, cartels, and pools to the rigors of competition, particularly for purposes of foreign trade, which is often government-subsidized. Central banks (e.g., the Bank of France or the German Reichsbank) have also, under governmental direction, exerted powerful influence on financial activities and trends. Long before socialist parties or trade unions were in any position to force concessions, autocratic rulers or their prime ministers frequently established schemes of social insurance, public housing, and municipal ownership that many Americans today still regard as socialistic. Bismarck was no socialist, and yet he shrewdly took these and other steps to keep the German people happy and comfortable. In other countries, paternalism on the part of monarchs and aristocrats brought many benevolent interventions by the state.

European Socialist Parties Today It is important to note that just as the doctrinaire followers of Marx became revisionists in practice, so have the revisionists of today ceased to be Marxists at all. The Socialist party of France and the Social Democratic and Labor parties of West Germany, Italy, Switzerland, Holland, Norway, Sweden, and Denmark are really parties of social and economic reform along the lines of revisionist and democratic socialism.

Not all these parties, including the British Labour party, are exclusively proletarian, but typically include between 20 and 40 percent of non-working-class voters within their electorates. They advocate and practice moderation, political bargaining, and programmatic compromise, entering governmental coalitions with nonsocialist parties without the tremors of class treason that troubled the doctrinaire socialists of an earlier day. On many issues of public policy (e.g., social security, housing, and public ownership of utilities, transport, and key industries), the moderate socialists take a position scarcely distinguishable from that of the Christian Democratic parties of Italy and West Germany, and their methods are those of peaceful, gradual reform through the democratic parliamentary process. They neither advocate nor support the struggle of classes, revolution, the liquidation of capitalism, or the abolition of private property.

Society as a Living Organism Naturally, ideological justifications of revisionist socialism, or "empirical collectivism," have varied from one European country to another. In France, the concept of human society as the highest stage in organic evolution helped to inculcate the idea that the state's function and duty are to maintain the solidarity of the society. Some writers described society as a living organism or superorganism, whose ideas and sense of unity are institutionalized by the state. And, in fact, the *organic analogy* of society, from Plato through political philosophers of the Middle Ages to modern times, has always represented an essentially socialist definition of citizen rights and obligations: Each member of the body politic has meaning and function only in association with all other members, and each is consequently subordinate to the well-being of all. Along similar lines, French moral philosophers have stressed the interdependence of individuals and groups, the necessity of their cooperation, and a sense of reciprocal obligation in order to maintain the organic unity of society. The so-called solidarity school of writers on the Continent and the Oxford idealists in Great Britain sought to mark out a middle position between the pure individualism of classical liberalism and the pervasive collectivism of doctrinaire socialism in order to harmonize both the rights of man and the interests of society.

In Germany, the so-called academic state socialists of the late nineteenth century followed similar lines of thought. They argued that the democratic state had a duty to curb abuses, protect the weak, provide cultural facilities for the many, and in general throw its weight onto the scales in order to tip the balance toward social justice. And in Italy and other Catholic countries, the trend toward a democratic and socialist society may be traced, in part, to the organic characteristics of the church itself and to the social philosophy that emerged from the papacy beginning in the late nineteenth century.

The Social Philosophy of the Church Especially the now-famous papal encyclical of Pope Leo XIII in 1891, *Rerum Novarum,* and the *Quadragesimo*

Anno of Pope Pius XI in 1931 pointed to the necessity of putting a collective and social responsibility in the place of the self-seeking materialism of classical liberalism. Alarmed by the plight of workers under capitalism and the consequent inroads made by socialist parties, Leo XIII and his successors attacked the domination and power of wealth accumulated in the hands of a few, but also condemned Marxism as inconsistent with Christian principles and reminded workers and employers of their duties toward one another, emphasizing the latter's Christian obligation to pay a "just wage" and to refrain from greedy exploitation of the poor. Criticizing "an economic science alien to the true moral law" (i.e., the classical liberal doctrine of laissez faire), but without specific recommendations for appropriate government policy, the church has continued to urge united Christian action toward the "greater common good."

This growing sensitivity to the material and spiritual needs of all citizens in contemporary society demonstrates the trend toward some form of socialist thought and organization in almost all the countries of the modern world, even though some people, particularly in the United States, are pleased to give socialism another name or prefer to ignore the problem altogether.

Democratic Socialism: The United States

While the nations of Western Europe are today socialist by American standards, they have reached this stage by a route very different from that traveled by the United States. Europe's transition has been essentially from the old collectivism of absolute monarchy, aristocracy, mercantilism, and state capitalism to the new collectivism of democracy leavened by revisionist socialism.

In the United States, on the other hand, a virgin continent, settled by colonists who feared and resented government and who particularly abhorred monarchies and aristocracies (benevolent or otherwise), felt the full impact of the industrial revolution uncushioned by paternalistic traditions and was able to develop a capitalistic economy in an extremely favorable and secure environment. Principles of laissez faire and classical economics were more nearly implemented in the United States than anywhere else, although even here a gap always existed between ideology and practice.

In the United States, "socialism"—and even "empirical collectivism" or "pragmatic collectivism"—are consequently loaded labels that usually trigger more violent debate than reasoned analysis. But even the relatively rugged "individualism" of fifty or seventy-five years ago, along with protective tariffs, subsidies to industry, and large corporations whose enterprise was not strictly a function of the free market, would have appeared collectivist to the English classical liberal Adam Smith.

It also is essential to distinguish clearly between authoritarian socialism and democratic socialism, with the latter implying a process by which the people or their elected representatives decide on the appropriate policies for regulating the economy and providing social security in order to "promote the general welfare" (according to the Preamble of the Constitution). And, semantics aside, it would appear today that all democratic and industrialized states are socialistic, having been forced to intervene in economic and social matters if only because of technological development. Certainly the United States is among the least self-consciously socialistic nations in this category and the most determined in its adherence to the phraseology of classical liberalism and individual free enterprise.

The Role of Government in American Capitalist Development And yet, beginning with Alexander Hamilton's proposals for protective tariffs and for taxes on liquors and luxuries and continuing through the era of land grants and railroad subsidies, the federal government has aided and regulated such vital sectors of the economy as transportation, public utilities, banking, the stock market, trusts and monopolies, labor relations, and many others. State governments, exercising their police power for the promotion of public health, safety, and morals, dealt with such problems as child labor, minimum-wage laws, limitations on the hours of labor, and prohibition.

During the era of Theodore Roosevelt and Woodrow Wilson, much new regulatory and social legislation was enacted, not to hasten collectivism for dogmatic, doctrinal reasons, but, on the contrary, to restore genuine individualism. The central theme was to outlaw monopolies, regulate or prohibit antisocial business practices, curb the powers of privilege and special interests, help the farmer and the laborer, and in general make the United States once more the land of competitive but equal economic opportunity.

Important parts of the Progressive and Wilsonian programs failed of legislative enactment at that time. The New Deal of Franklin D. Roosevelt (who said the name was a combination of Wilson's New Freedom and Theodore Roosevelt's Square Deal) made realities of such Progressive objectives as unemployment relief, collective bargaining, a national minimum wage, the ending of child labor, social security, aid to agriculture, and more effective regulation of public utilities, the stock market, and banking. Far from being a revolution, the New Deal represented no more than a speeding up of earlier trends, necessitated by the Depression, and brought the national government, with its vast financial resources, to the rescue—rather than the destruction—of our "quasicapitalistic" or "mixed" economy.

Principles of the New Deal Because of its very empiricism or pragmatic style, the political ideology of the New Deal defies precise statement; New Deal writers and supporters differed among themselves in this regard. However, the following ideas might be considered basic: (1) Government must intervene by democratic processes to solve pressing economic and social problems; (2) government bears the responsibility for providing for innocent victims of economic depression; (3) agriculture is entitled to equal treatment with industry; (4) labor has the right to organize and to bargain collectively; (5) our economy should be so directed as to provide full employment and assure everyone at least a minimum standard of living; (6) the spirit of social cooperation between groups can and should replace the philosophy of ruthless competition; (7) the centrifugal tendencies of excessive individualism should be balanced by a greater sense of individual and group responsibility to promote the welfare of society as a whole; (8) all our contemporary problems, however acute, can be resolved without revolution, within the framework of democracy; (9) governmental institutions, as well as policies, can and should be modified and modernized to cope with current problems; and (10) American governmental machinery requires increased federal powers, more authority in the executive branch, wider use of experts, and further delegation of quasilegislative and quasijudicial powers to administrative agencies.

Continuing the New Deal The Fair Deal of President Truman was essentially an adaptation of the New Deal to the conditions and problems of the postwar era. Even the election of President Eisenhower in 1952 represented only a change of command and personnel instead of a change in fundamental policies or direction. President Kennedy's New Frontier and President Johnson's Great Society were extensions of the policies of Presidents Roosevelt and Truman. Such New Deal policies and programs as parity payments to farmers, social security, minimum wages, and collective bargaining have become so deeply ingrained in the fabric of the American economy as to defy eradication by any change of administration. And even while continuing these programs and trends, as emphatic an antisocialist as President Richard Nixon introduced price and wage controls in the early 1970s in order better to achieve the *government's* definition of an economically healthy society.

Distasteful as the thought doubtless is to rightwing elements in both political parties, a return to the halcyon (and largely imaginary) good old days of laissez faire is a political and literal impossibility. The modern generation of American voters, many of whom cannot remember the president who preceded Franklin D. Roosevelt, is so habituated to social security, veterans' benefits, public housing, FHA loans, aid to education, varying degrees of socialized medicine, farm price supports, and direct and indirect subsidies to business that no political party advocating the repeal of such programs is likely to win at the ballot box. The Republican party's nomination of Senator Barry Goldwater in 1964 may be seen as an attempt to move back toward laissez faire. But it is significant that since the Depression, the Republicans have been able to capture the presidency only through candidates who did not stand for a reversal of long-established trends of government involvement in the economy.

It is unrealistic, then, to picture neoliberals and Democrats in the United States as collectivists or socialist schemers or to think of conservatives and

Republicans as extreme individualists and laissez faire liberals. Nothing could be more terrifying to certain business groups than the prospect of a repeal of protective tariffs, zoning restrictions, the Taft-Hartley Act (which limits the right of labor to strike), farm price supports, building codes, railroad and utility rate regulation, fair-trade laws (which allow price-fixing), and the myriad other forms of "government interference" that, in fact, protect businessmen from the rugged individualism, free enterprise, competition, and struggle that they publicly praise but secretly dread. In our modern, interdependent economy, the removal of the present network of socioeconomic support and control by government would result in economic and social chaos rather than genuine freedom for even a few. The citizens of a modern industrial society, unlike their pastoral, agricultural, and feudal predecessors, seem destined to "hang together or else hang separately." And by understanding the extent to which we hang together, both socially and economically, we may be better able to understand the apparently inevitable trends toward varying degrees of socialism that describe the contemporary world. If only from this perspective, Marx's understanding of the fate of *unregulated* capitalism may be more right than wrong.

The Future of Socialism

Those who today call themselves democratic socialists, however, would hasten to add that the state's provision of welfare services and governmental regulation of the broad outlines (and, increasingly, the intimate details) of the economy do not guarantee the realization of basic socialist goals.

Fundamental Needs In Scandinavia, Western Europe, Japan, and the Anglo-American countries, the great majority of citizens (but not everyone) need no longer fear for their physical survival. Most citizens are assured of an adequate diet, basic educational opportunities, a habitable dwelling, a tolerable working environment, annual vacations, varying cultural levels of entertainment, private or public means of transportation, and protection against the hazards of unemployment, infirmity, and old age. These are major accomplishments, especially as one surveys the conditions of life of most people in the industrialized world of only a few decades ago.

In the less industrially developed nations, however—which are inhabited by the vast majority of mankind today—these fundamental needs and safeguards of life are still largely lacking. This helps to explain the decided socialist orientation of most governments in the contemporary underdeveloped world; their meager resources and the desired rapidity of economic development prompt almost all these governments to intervene in the economic affairs of citizens. In this sense, it is fair to say that *all* governments presently engage in varying degrees of economic planning and governmental control over the means of production. Even in the United States, at the levels of federal, state, and local government, extensive planning takes place—as may be discerned from only a casual inspection of the data base, fiscal policies, and monetary expenditures projected by the annual budgets of each governing institution.

Toward Humanist Society? But to what extent is truly equal opportunity for self-development and creative personal fulfillment a reality for even a narrow majority of citizens in the industrially advanced countries of the contemporary world? If these countries have effectively eliminated the threat of catastrophic depression and unemployment, how far have they advanced in the direction of a humanist society in which each individual's worth is measured by what he does instead of by who he is or how he lives?

Contemporary democratic socialists therefore emphasize the continuing importance of organization, especially of citizens as consumers, white-collar workers, professionals such as schoolteachers, and state employees, as an additional means of influencing the policies of government. They also are sensitive to the dehumanizing impact of massive bureaucracies in all areas of life, including those associated with the welfare establishment of the state. They now tend to dismiss the nationalization of industry as a heavy-handed means for ensuring the social responsibility of business, and they note correctly that government ownership or economic subsidies may serve only as a guarantee of corporate profits and a reduction in the risks of business competition. They do not seek to "level" the income of citizens, but they do point to the inequities of "progressive" tax systems that favor the superrich over the factory wage earner and salaried middle classes. In fact, since World War II, the welfare state and prevailing tax systems in the United States and in most countries of Western Europe have contributed to only a slight redistribution of wealth among the middle classes themselves; the wealthy and the underprivileged minorities—the latter frequently locked into their fate by racial discrimination—have been relatively unaffected by the welfare programs that have been introduced over the course of industrial development.

This is also to say that, from the perspective of the democratic socialist, much remains to be done before the fundamental goals of socialism become more a reality than a promise. But it also is true that the democratic socialist, in reflecting on the necessary course to follow, may derive some useful guidelines from a body of doctrine that, in the context of early industrial development, was initially more coherent and better articulated than socialism—the ideology of liberalism.

LIBERALISM

In Chapter 5 the characteristics of liberalism were discussed largely in terms of its historical circumstances; beginning as a class-based ideology seeking to put bourgeois privilege in the place of aristocratic privilege, liberalism in the modern world has become the doctrine most clearly associated with popular sovereignty and democratic government. This chapter, however, will focus briefly on the characteristics of liberalism that both identify and distinguish it from other ideologies, mainly those along the ideological continuum and to the left of liberalism.

Individualism, Rationality, and Political Power

First, liberalism plainly prefers to judge the extent of social justice from the perspective of the individual rather than from that of the society as a whole. The individual is the liberal's unit of social analysis, and the extent of social justice is determined in part by the extent of freedom allowed the individual in order to demonstrate his particular virtues and capabilities. For the classical liberal, the actions of government invariably compromise individual freedom. But government is essential to maintain the security of the society, both at home and in its relations with foreign states. Government also is essential, as John Locke argued, to the creation of a means of monetary exchange that facilitates the accumulation of wealth.

And there can be no doubt that classical liberalism—the ideology most closely associated with laissez faire capitalism—defines individual virtue and capability in terms of economic enterprise and business acumen. *Rational* behavior itself is demonstrated most clearly by the superiority of profit to loss at the bottom of the investments ledger. And because virtue, talent, and rationality are unequally distributed among men, wealth, status, and political power also should be unequally distributed. The state may be organized politically according to elections and representative government, but the suffrage should be restricted to those who have demonstrated their superior rationality, usually through material accumulation; and, in any event, policy makers—drawn from the propertied classes —should be largely autonomous from, and unrestrained by, the narrow interests of the society's lower classes. If there is a "social contract" that restricts the actions of government, the parties to the contract are drawn from the same social classes that in fact make up the government. A just society is not a society of equality, but a society in which reward differentials faithfully reflect the differences inherent in each and every citizen.

The Role of Government and the Survival of the Fittest

Like all the ideologies discussed above, then, liberalism insists upon equal opportunity for individual self-development. The differences between liberalism and more leftist ideologies—and they are important differences—derive from the liberal's assumption about what is *necessary* for individual self-development. For the classical liberal, all that the individual needs in order to succeed is to be found within himself—a secularized expression of Christ's teaching that "the Kingdom of God is within you." This is a surprisingly "spiritual" theme in liberalism, given its otherwise materialistic bias. But like Protestant Christianity, especially Calvinism, liberalism regards the fruit of a man's labor as the most important measure of his inherent endowment, whether his endowment is self-generated or a gift from God. Whatsoever we mix our labor in is therefore ours by virtue of our inalienable and natural right to our own labor power (the labor theory of value). Government, then, has no authority to expropriate the fruit of our labor, whether directly through the nationalization of the means of production or indirectly through taxation.[3]

It is especially obvious to the classical liberal that the state's intervention in the economy and its provision of social welfare seriously distort the natural opportunity structure inherent in unregulated social relationships. By taking from the rich to give to the poor, for example, government penalizes the rich for demonstrating their own superior talent. And, as the English philosopher Herbert Spencer (1820–1903) argued, government intervention also upsets the evolutionary balance of nature that perpetuates the human species through competition and the survival of those most fit to survive. Spencer even went so far as to attack compulsory smallpox vaccinations because such programs for public health compromised the evolutionary principle by preventing the survival of the fittest. No one has ever accused Herbert Spencer of failing to take his argument to its logical extreme.

Self-Interest and Utilitarianism Early classical liberal thought also was eager to demonstrate the necessary social harmony that results from each individual's pursuit of his own self-interest. What motivates individual behavior? The French philosopher Claude Helvétius (1715–1771) and the English social philosopher and political reformer Jeremy Bentham (1748–1832) replied that men inevitably seek to maximize pleasure and to minimize pain. What men do and what they call "good" are necessarily a function of their calculations derived from the pleasure-pain principle. Motivation is the result of "utility," or, more simply, men do what they think will be useful to their self-interest.

The principles of utilitarianism were thus designed to link the self-interested behavior of the individual to the resulting harmony of general interests that characterized the good society. Social harmony did not mean a lack of competition; on the contrary, it was in part the result of competition, but competition that took place within those boundaries of nonviolence and respect for property which were maintained by the state. It was in this sense that classical liberalism described the state as a *necessary* evil. And in the good society this was the state's principal function: to be, in essence, the policeman on the corner whose very presence reminds citizens to keep their aggressive, if not their acquisitive, instincts in bounds. In this context, self-interested behavior would work toward the most just distribution of wealth, status, and power (distributed in proportion to individual talent); toward the most efficient exploitation of national resources (or, as Adam Smith put it, the "wealth of nations"); and toward the utilitarian's definition of what constituted "the greatest happiness of the greatest number."

Revising Early Liberalism: John Stuart Mill

John Stuart Mill (1806–1873), however, eventually came to doubt that utilitarianism was as scientific as its founding fathers had assumed. Mill argued that by attempting to reduce all motivation to a single hedonistic principle of pleasure versus pain, utilitarianism had grossly oversimplified human behavior. The differences between types of pleasure were more qualitative than quantitative, and there were degrees of morality in behavior that made the definitions of "good" and "right" a problem for philosophy rather than mathematical calculation. The justice of a society also had to be determined with reference to the values that were independent of economic freedom and material progress. There ultimately was the liberty of conscience, thought, opinion, and expression that defined the true quality of a man; his individual abilities were reflected less by the contents of his wallet than by the content of his mind.

Mill also argued that, however unequally talent might be distributed, a system of laissez faire was no guarantee that each individual would receive his

---

[3]The position of classical liberalism on consent and majority rule has always been ambiguous, if not downright inconsistent. The problem derives from the necessity for some pragmatic principle of government and decision making—thus majority rule. But majority rule is clearly incompatible with any notion of inalienable natural rights—which remain the basis for judging the extent of legitimate political authority. Can the majority take away private property? The classical liberal obviously wants to answer "no," but he does so at the expense of other important parts of his argument (notably those of consent and majority rule).

just reward. Looking at British society in the mid-nineteenth century, Mill was convinced that reward was frequently in "inverse proportion to work," that basic social and political reforms *through government* were essential, that the exploitative conditions of workers and women demanded ameliorative legislation, and that education and the organization of farm cooperatives and labor unions were among the appropriate means for raising the level of justice in society. Thus Mill appeared to be aware of the importance of defining the individual's liberty in terms of his social context and to realize that classical liberalism had erred by abstracting man from his environment before identifying his nature, motivations, and apparent rights. And, indeed, it was obvious that the basis for the classical liberal's argument on behalf of an absolute right to private property—derived from Locke's labor theory of value—was expressed in terms of man in a state of nature rather than man in an economically interdependent society.

Ends and Means In this sense, John Stuart Mill was a transitional figure between the antigovernment individualism of classical liberalism and early utilitarianism and the increasing collectivism and democratic socialism that finds tentative expression in neoliberal thought. The ethical *end* of individual opportunity remained the same; the understanding of what *means* were necessary to that end changed over time, and it has continued to change, until it is difficult to determine where the line should be drawn to distinguish neoliberalism from democratic socialism.

The difference may be largely one of historical perspective and cultural context. Thus in the United States "socialism" is used as an epithet to be hurled at enemies on the left, while the principal ideologies and participants in the American political process are distinguished as either "liberal" or "conservative." It has already been pointed out, however, that "liberalism" is not easily defined. And to complicate the picture even further, the following section will show that "conservatism," while easily defined, is frequently misused. The reader is reminded that nothing in politics is simple and that nothing political is precisely what it appears to be.

CONSERVATISM

Properly speaking, those who wish to *conserve* what exists, to perpetuate the status quo with little if any change in the foreseeable future, are "conservatives." Thus conservatism is less a body of belief than it is a point of view or a state of mind. It cannot be identified with a particular place and time or with a specific school of thought. There have always been conservatives, and there will always be conservatives. The generic opposite of conservatism is radicalism, but what is radical in one context (for example, classical liberalism in France before 1789) may be conservative in another (classical liberalism in England after John Locke and the Glorious Revolution of 1688). A citizen of the contemporary United States is likely to regard a Communist administrator in the Soviet Union as a radical, but the same administrator may be regarded as a conservative by the new generation of Soviet economists who urge the administrative decentralization of economic planning.

Limits on Reason

But it also is true that one can find some common ground underlying the arguments and actions of most of the self-conscious conservatives of more recent history. And especially from the work of the most widely recognized spokesman for conservatism—the English philosopher and politician Edmund Burke (1729–1797)—it is possible to identify immediately a major theme that radically distinguishes conservatism from the ideologies already discussed.

Anarchists, communists, socialists, and liberals all assume that human reason is capable of understanding the nature of man and the nature of society. Perceiving an inconsistency between man's nature and his social condition, they at least imply that reason is a largely infallible guide in helping us to set things right. If reason informs us that all men ought to be free, that they ought to have an equal opportunity for self-development, and that they have an inalienable right to the product of their labor, then reason also can tell us how to organize the just society, and this may require revolution and the complete restructuring of society and all its social relationships. From Edmund Burke's point of view, this is exactly what the French revolutionaries of 1789 had assumed and attempted, and the resulting chaos, terror, and widespread destruction of property and loss of life were the inevitable—and predictable—result.

The Complexity of Society For the conservative, reason is an aid but not an infallible guide to understanding the nature of man and society. There are too many imponderables, and there is too much complexity in the fabric of any given society for reason to be capable of fully comprehending what motivates men or how society works. The interaction of state, family, religion, language, race, class, and cultural norms over time is different for every society, and what is thought to be appropriate for one is likely to be inappropriate for another.

The revolutionary or radical consequently deceives himself and those who follow him when he pretends to know what ails society and how society can be healed. The results of a radical departure from the past and present are always unpredictable, but they are likely to entail more suffering and hardship than would a continuation of what exists. The conservative, however, does not deny that there is injustice in the world or that there may be substantial injustice even in his own society. He simply denies that his intelligence or the intelligence of anyone else is capable of understanding all the causes and characteristics of the injustice or of providing a foolproof remedy.

Initiating Change

The conservative is consequently very reluctant to initiate change. Especially the long-established institutions of the society—its church, socioeconomic structures, and political institutions—ought to be regarded with religious reverence, and their details altered, if at all, only with extreme circumspection. The initiation of new public policies or the reform of old ones should be undertaken only after careful reflection and extensive discussion and debate. Good public policy is a function of cautious experimentation; orderly procedure is more important than lucid reason, and a judgment based on practical results is more reliable than one derived from moral principles.

Tradition In effect, the conservative argues that what has worked in the past carries with it its own moral sanction for the future. Thus the conservative is not troubled by the weakness in the classical liberal's argument for natural rights and private property. For the conservative, there are no natural rights, and there is no absolute right to private property, although the substance of these principles may have moral sanction if the long-standing traditions of the society have institutionalized the rights to life, liberty, and property. Where property has been the basis of social organization for generations of citizens, there is no need for an abstract argument such as the labor theory of value. Time and survival are the principal tests of any institution's legitimacy. And to attempt to provide a justification drawn from abstract reason for any long-standing institution or practice is to threaten the credibility of tradition itself. It was according to this logic that James I of England (1566–1625) denounced attempts to study too closely the principle of divine right: To question the logic behind the authority of absolute monarchy was to weaken monarchical government, and the consequent weakening of norms of obedience laid the basis for political division and social chaos.

The Natural Aristocracy

But societies do undergo change, and new policies have to be initiated. On whose shoulders should such monumental responsibility be placed? The conservative is not only suspicious of rapid procedures and hasty innovation but also unwilling to allow the relatively unenlightened masses of the society, inevitably inexperienced in statecraft, to have anything other than the most indirect influence on policy making.

The Spanish philosopher José Ortega y Gasset (1883–1955) was explicit about the probability of social chaos if the masses were allowed to rule themselves. Self-government by the people was certain to lead to their own disadvantage and distress. If it is true that the effects of policy making are always difficult to calculate, it also is true that the risks of policy making are minimized when the policy makers have a feeling for the complex nature of their society and are sensitive to their heritage from the past and their obligations to the future. This kind of balanced judgment is not likely to characterize the decision making of lower classes of citizens, who are more preoccupied with their own circumstances and interests than with the continuity of the society's cultural "genius" (in Burke's sense of the word). The contemporary French conservative philosopher Bertrand de Jouvenel has expressed grave concern over the rise of popular sovereignty and the parallel decline in any restraint on the exercise of governmental power. Edmund Burke also argued for the necessary independence of the elected parliamentary representative, who must always consult with his constituents, but who must never allow his own good judgment to be influenced by popular whim or by the understandable aspiration for continued reelection. Conservative thinkers have thus subscribed, at least implicitly, to the concept of a "natural aristocracy" of citizens, an elite whose authority is based on demonstrated good judgment and experience and in whose hands the affairs of state should be concentrated.

Inequality and Social Responsibility The conservative, then, tends to see the "just" society as a society of social, economic, and political inequality, if only because these are the characteristics of all societies throughout recorded history. But pervasive inequality is not synonymous with a society of irresponsible government, and one of the justifications of elite status is the natural aristocracy's continuing concern for the welfare of the whole society. Unlike classical liberalism, conservatism has not been so presumptuous as to identify the well-being of all citizens with the conservative's own self-interest. Elite status carries with it an obligation to others of inferior status, an obligation that is not unlike the obligations of noblesse oblige in aristocratic societies of an earlier day. And it is no coincidence that in Great Britain the Tories stood more solidly for social reform and restraints on capitalist enterprise than the early Liberals and that the Conservative party in twentieth-century Great Britain has continued and even initiated some of the regulatory and welfare legislation supported by the British Labour party.

Conservatism in the United States

In the United States, then, to what extent is the Republican party most appropriately identified as "conservative"? As the term has been defined here, it is clear that there are many conservatives in both the Republican *and* Democratic parties and that there also is substantial overlap among their electorates in terms of a basic predisposition toward conservatism. In many respects, the history and political process of the United States are most appropriately classified as conservative. Apparently radical breaks with the past, as in the War of Independence against Great Britain and President Roosevelt's New Deal programs, had many points of continuity with what went before and did not represent abrupt departures for uncharted horizons.

The Republicans: Barry Goldwater It also is true, however, that the Republican party, over time, has been more reluctant than the Democratic party to experiment with new programs and that it has proved far more hostile to the growth of a welfare state and governmental intervention in the economy. But Republican resistance to these trends has declined as voters have expressed their support for welfarism and as government intervention in the economy has proved responsive to the interests and demands of business, especially big business.

Nevertheless, among the recent and most vocal Republicans expressing opposition to these trends is Senator Barry Goldwater, who in 1960 published a forthright statement of his views in a book entitled *The Conscience of a Conservative.* But as one reads Senator Goldwater's book and assesses his political actions, it becomes very apparent that Senator Goldwater is more of a classical liberal than a conservative. He does not advocate continuity with the recent past and cautious experimentation in the immediate future. On the contrary, he seeks a major break with the past and the present by calling for the establishment of a free market economy and by urging the elimination or reduction of welfarism, government subsidies to producers, and government programs designed to extend civil liberties and civil rights to minority classes of citizens. His initial recommendation that the social security contributions of employees be made voluntary signaled his intent to dismantle the entire social security system in the United States—a radical rather than a conservative proposal. And he clearly advances a notion of natural rights, while his concept of freedom is the classical liberal's definition of freedom in terms of an absence of restraint on individual activity.[4] Senator Goldwater thus assumes that his own reason and the rational endowment of those who agree with him are capable of providing an understanding of the nature of man and of bringing about a resolution of the problems that beset the United States.

The Republicans: Everett McKinley Dirksen

Senator Goldwater's views, then, not only are *mis*represented by the label of "conservatism," but also clearly do not reflect the mainstream of Republican ideology and public policy, as exemplified by the presidencies of Eisenhower, Nixon, and Ford and the acts of leading Republican politicians.

For example, probably the most self-conscious conservative of recent Republican history was the late Senate minority leader Everett McKinley Dirksen (1896–1969). As a member of the House of Representatives in the 1930s, Dirksen was critical of New Deal legislation, but he eventually came to accept the welfare and regulatory establishment elaborated by the Democrats in response to the Depression. He also acknowledged the appropriate role of government in extending the rights and liberties of American citizens, and in opposition to Goldwater, he voted for, and was a major architect of, the landmark Civil Rights Act of 1964, which was enacted during the Johnson administration.

And yet Dirksen remained skeptical of the ability of government to understand fully and to organize rationally the affairs of citizens. In his criticism of the Great Society programs initiated by President Johnson after 1964, Dirksen remarked: "When you begin to tamper too much with the economy of a complicated country, and you start letting decisions be made in Washington, D.C., instead of in the marketplace, you are going to develop imbalances and trouble."[5] Faith in the self-regulatory efficiency of the "marketplace" is a cardinal principle of classical liberalism, and Dirksen's comment suggests the extent to which important parts of classical liberalism have in fact been incorporated into contemporary American conservatism. But Dirksen's more fundamentally conservative orientation, and that of the Republican party in general, is also apparent in both his actions and his thought; even orderly constitutional procedure and constant reference to what has worked in the past are no guarantees of either augmented efficiency or improved social justice—regardless of the party in power. Society is too complex for any man or any group of men to understand the full impact of governmental action, and "tampering" by government is bound to lead to "imbalances and trouble."

The conservative thus stands opposed to the assumptions and prescriptions of the ideologies on his left, which are viewed as both too presumptuous and too utopian. But the conservative also stands opposed to ideologies on his right, namely, fascism, which represent some of the same basic presumptions—although not the same prescriptions—as leftist ideologies. This is also to make the point that contemporary American leftists demonstrate their own bad judgment and lack of political understanding when they identify conservatism with ideologies on the extreme right.

FASCISM

The Effects of War and Depression

Italy fought on the side of the victorious Allies during World War I. But at the Paris Peace Conference, Italy was denied its principal territorial claims, and many Italian citizens and political leaders consequently shared a sense of international betrayal. After the war, Italy's domestic situation also was troubled. By the fall of 1920, at least 100,000 Italian citizens were unemployed, and the

---

[4] See the foreword to Goldwater's book, where he writes that "the people's welfare depends on individual self reliance rather than on state paternalism," that "individual liberty depends on decentralized government," and that "these principles are derived from the nature of man, and from the truths that God has revealed about His creation." *The Conscience of a Conservative*, Hillman Books, New York, 1960.

[5] Quoted by Arthur Krock (a distinguished American journalist and political conservative) in the *New York Times,* Jan. 11, 1966.

Italian Fascists were a small but strident extremist party. By early 1922 there were 600,000 unemployed, Italian Fascist membership was growing rapidly, and in October the Fascists' "march on Rome" ended with Mussolini's appointment by the king as premier. Without altering the structural outlines of Italy's political institutions, the new premier proceeded to transform the Italian republic into a personal dictatorship based on the Fascist party's monopoly of political power.

As one of the defeated Central Powers in World War I, Germany's treatment at the Paris Peace Conference was far more severe than Italy's. The Treaty of Versailles forced the new republican government, founded in Weimar in 1919, to admit Germany's responsibility for the war; German territories were ceded to France, Poland, Denmark, and Belgium; and the Rhineland area of western Germany was occupied—in part to ensure Germany's payment to the Allies (especially France) of massive reparations for war damages. These circumstances fueled the fires of international bitterness and domestic division, and among the many extremist groups organized in Germany after the war was the National Socialist German Workers' party (NSDAP, or "Nazi," from the German pronunciation of the first two syllables of "National"). The Nazi party, however, proved to be neither socialist nor based on the German working class, and under Hitler's leadership it directed its militant appeals to all sectors of German society—with the notable exception of German Jews.

Encouraged by Mussolini's success in Italy after the war, Hitler's small band of extremists attempted a coup d'état in Munich in 1923 (the "beer-hall putsch"). The failure of the coup, Hitler's temporary imprisonment (when he wrote *Mein Kampf*), and especially Germany's postwar recovery, beginning with economic stabilization after 1923, brought the Nazis to a low point of membership recruitment and political activity. But with the beginning of the worldwide Depression in 1929, which hit the German economy with devastating force, Nazi fortunes immediately improved. As unemployment in Germany increased from 2 million to 6 million, Nazi membership rose from 100,000 in 1928 to 1.4 million in 1932, and the Nazi electorate grew by a staggering 5.5 million voters between 1928 and 1930. An enfeebled government eventually turned to Hitler, who was appointed chancellor (or prime minister) in January 1933. As Mussolini had already done in Italy, Hitler intimidated the political opposition and engineered parliamentary and electoral support in order to become dictator.

The Spread of Fascism The success of the Nazis in Germany was quickly followed by fascist and semifascist coups in Europe from Finland to Greece. In Austria in March 1933 and in Bulgaria in early 1934, weak democratic institutions were replaced by fascist-type dictatorships. In Spain in 1936, the Fascists under General Francisco Franco began their successful military revolt against the Spanish republic. Since the 1930s and World War II, the "fascist" label also has been applied to militarist, nationalist, and dictatorial regimes in Asia (Japan), the Middle East (Egypt), sub-Sahara Africa (Ghana, South Africa), Latin America (Argentina, Brazil, Paraguay), and, in more recent times, Greece (between 1967 and 1974) and Chile (since September 1973). This is not a complete listing, but the variety of societies and regimes characterized as "fascist" begs the obvious questions: What precisely is fascism, and what are the circumstances that appear to contribute to the success of fascist movements?

Institutional and Cultural Preconditions

In ancient Rome, the *fasces* (a bundle of rods tied around an ax) symbolized political authority supported by the unity of the nation. The symbol was an apt representation of what Benito Mussolini (1883–1945) understood to be essential to Italy's recovery of the greatness of imperial Rome. In Weimar Germany, Adolf Hitler (1889–1945) also pointed to the weakness of democratic institutions, the intense factionalism of many competing political parties, the apparent dangers of socialism and communism on the extreme left, and the hostility of foreign states intent on reducing Germany to servile status. And like Mussolini, Hitler also urged the reconciliation of classes instead of class struggle and the subordination of all citizens to the greater good and higher ideal of the state.

Nationalism It may be no coincidence that in both Italy and Germany, political unification was achieved relatively late in modern European history (in 1871 for both countries). German and Italian political thought consequently emphasized the historical importance of building state institutions that expressed the common cultural identities of peoples who, for centuries, had lived in separate political jurisdictions. German and Italian ideology, then, invariably focused on the nation instead of on the individual and on the necessary superiority of the state to the citizen. Thus there was never the emphasis on individuality, natural rights, and social contract that characterized political thought elsewhere in Western Europe and in the United States. But where the political unity of the state was well established before the onset of industrialization, social change, and intensive military conflict, classical liberalism and democratic socialism had an opportunity to develop and to mark out a domain of individual activity that was meant to protect the citizen from the authority of the state.

Authoritarianism The success of fascism also seems to depend on a fundamentally authoritarian political culture. The hallmark of fascist organization is rigid hierarchy and the rank subordination of followers to the authority of a single leader. The leader exercises charismatic appeal that reinforces his claim to infallible judgment and unquestioning obedience. The political culture that supports this style of political and social organization is uncongenial to the patterns and norms of participation that characterize more democratic societies. In those political cultures susceptible to fascism, decision making in the family, church, and workshop; in all forms of social organization; and in the institutions of the state is distinguished more by command than by compromise, more by dogmatic assertion than by bargaining.

And it is notable that most fascist movements have arisen in Catholic countries, where the authoritarian norms of the church had been transmitted throughout the society over a long period of time and where the church resisted the development of a secular state, the organization of political parties, and the growth of electoral competition through the extension of the suffrage to all citizens. These trends were correctly viewed by the church as a major challenge to its dominant, and authoritarian, position in the society. Where the principal institutions (including church and state) and prevailing cultural norms were opposed to democratic styles of regulating social conflict, the roots of fascism were planted.

Industrial Development and Social Status To grow and flourish, however, fascism also depended on other circumstances, and not only on weak political institutions whose already low level of legitimacy was further undermined by apparent military setback and economic depression.

The initial base of fascism's appeal is in the society's middle and lower middle classes, and thus the society must have experienced a significant degree of industrial development. The success of fascism has in fact been interpreted as largely a consequence of the middle classes' fear of declining social status, a fear that is all the more compelling when the middle classes are confronted by economic crisis and the simultaneous mobilization of the lower classes. The threat of the lower classes is made especially apparent by the presence of a strong trade union movement and a communist party that loudly proclaims its allegiance to socialist revolution and proletarian supremacy.

Fascism, then, may be understood as a means of continuing industrial development without jeopardizing the status of already privileged groups in the society. Their status is apparently protected by the fascist movement's emphasis on the interests of the state and nation—an ideological orientation that replaces the economic interests of the lower classes with the illusion of their comradeship in the forging of national greatness. The extent to which rightist extremism feeds on leftist extremism is also a dramatic comment on the occasional operation of a "dialectic" in political conflict.

Charismatic Authority and Ideology

It is far more correct than incorrect, then, to say that fascism is a largely *negative* expression of a variety of individual fears and social divisions. Compared with the other ideologies discussed in this chapter, fascism emphasizes what is wrong with existing society and has much less to say about how to make it right; the correctives for all that is wrong are to be found in the wisdom of the leader, and fascist followers are notable for their religious-type faith rather than their intellectual commitment.

Thus the lack of rational coherence and logical consistency in fascist ideology; the focus is on the lowest common denominator of citizen allegiance—on the nation as the expression of a pure and noble race—and on action rather than thought. Emotion is thought to be much more determining in human behavior than rational judgment. Mussolini put it succinctly when he shouted in his typically belligerent manner, "Action! Deeds! These alone matter. Leave theory to the scribblers!" Mass rallies, waving banners, beating drums, blaring horns, repeated slogans, uniforms and decorations, precision marching, and raucous singing are calculated to dull the mind and to raise emotions to fever pitch as one and all find their collective unity and personal identity in the impassioned rhetoric and physical presence of the leader.

And physical prowess is indeed the measure of an individual's quality, just as the military power of the nation is the surest sign of the society's strength and the basis of its claims to glory. The competitive instinct and the will to power of the individual must be welded into a cohesive national force, and one of the more significant differences between fascism and communism is the former's reliance on international conflict for the generation of national solidarity, while the dynamic of communism is derived from its emphasis on domestic economic growth. Communism also is careful to subordinate the military to civilian control, and its commitment to raising the living standards of the society's lower classes (peasants and workers) contrasts vividly with fascism's perpetuation of existing inequalities in the society.

Violence in the Pursuit of Power The ideology and trappings of fascism, then, were admirably suited to its techniques for capturing power and for exercising it. While fascist parties might participate in the electoral process, much of the force of fascist movements came from the threat and actual employment of physical coercion, which weakened opponents while lending cohesion to the fascist rank and file. In Weimar Germany, the Nazis organized their own paramilitary units and unleashed them against Socialists, Communists, uncooperative public officials, trade union organizers, Jewish merchants and shopkeepers, and all those who subscribed to the norms of a more civilized society. In Italy, Mussolini's "march on Rome" was preceded by the Fascists' seizure of power in Tuscany. In both Germany and Italy, then, the gloss of legality that attended the Fascists' accession to constitutional authority covered only superficially their blatant use and threat of violence against political opponents and the state itself.

Once in power, Fascists in Germany, Italy, and elsewhere centralized the state; reduced or eliminated the autonomy of provincial and local governments; declared illegal all non-Fascist parties and organizations; eliminated civil rights and liberties and muzzled the press and other media of public communication; imprisoned and liquidated enemies of the state; imposed controls on the internal migration and employment of citizens; subordinated labor unions to state authority and eliminated their rights to organize, strike, and bargain collectively; created a multitude of youth, professional, and cultural organizations in order to mobilize the population in the interests of the political elite; and eventually brought business and industrial enterprise under state control—especially for the purposes of production and mobilization for war.

The Aftermath of Fascism

Just as military defeat can lay part of the foundation for fascist strength, it also is the typical end of the fascist state. Ironically, the growth of fascism in Italy, Germany, and Japan, and its subsequent defeat, may be viewed as functional to the construction of more durable democratic institutions from the ashes of World War II. While the basis of fascist strength, especially in Europe, was in the middle classes (fearful of the upward mobility of the lower classes), fascism came to power with the overt and covert support of members of the old aristocracy—distributed among the landed oligarchy and in the society's bureaucratic and military hierarchies. It was precisely these sectors of the old society which had proved most resistant to democratic institutions and procedures. Their defeat, along with the military catastrophes wrought by fascist leaders, helped to pave the way for more enlightened political elites, committed to the principles and norms of the more egalitarian and democratic ideologies discussed in the preceding sections of this chapter.

STUDY-GUIDE QUESTIONS

1. Why are anarchists considered more extreme in their leftist orientation than communists?
2. How would you distinguish between "doctrinaire" and "revisionist" socialism?
3. Do you think that the United States is an essentially socialist society? Why or why not?
4. Distinguish between liberalism and conservatism in terms of their respective views of man's rational capabilities.
5. Define "fascism." What are some of the preconditions for strong fascist movements?

REFERENCES

Arendt, Hannah: *The Origins of Totalitarianism*, 2d ed., The World Publishing Company, Cleveland, 1958.

Bernstein, Eduard: *Evolutionary Socialism*, Schocken Books, Inc., New York, 1961.

Buckley, William F., Jr.: *Up from Liberalism*, Hillman Books, New York, 1961.

Burke, Edmund: *Reflections on the Revolution in France*, Henry Regnery Company, Chicago, 1955.

Carsten, F. L.: *The Rise of Fascism*, University of California Press, Berkeley, 1967.

Cole, G. D. H.: *A History of Socialist Thought*, Macmillan & Co., Ltd., London, 1961, vol. II, *Socialist Thought: Marxism and Anarchism, 1850–1890*.

Crosland, C. A. R.: *The Future of Socialism*, rev. ed., Schocken Books, Inc., 1963.

Evans, M. Stanton: *The Future of Conservatism*, Anchor Books, Doubleday & Company, Inc., Garden City, N.Y., 1969.

Harrington, Michael: *Socialism*, Bantam Books, Inc., New York, 1972.

Hayek, F. A.: *The Road to Serfdom*, Routledge & Kegan Paul, Ltd., London, 1962.

Hobhouse, L. T.: *Liberalism*, Oxford University Press, New York, 1964.

Jouvenel, Bertrand de: *Power: The Natural History of Its Growth*, Batchworth, London, 1952.

Kirk, Russell: *The Conservative Mind: From Burke to Santayana*, Henry Regnery Company, Chicago, 1954.

Lane, David: *The End of Inequality? Stratification under State Socialism*, Penguin Books, Inc., Baltimore, 1972.

LaPalombara, Joseph: *Politics within Nations*, Prentice-Hall, Inc., Englewood Cliffs, N.J., 1974, chap. 14, "The Future as Politics."

Lippmann, Walter: *The Public Philosophy*, Little, Brown and Company, Boston, 1955.

MacPherson, C. B.: *The Political Theory of Possessive Individualism*, Oxford University Press, London, 1962.

Stephen, Leslie: *The English Utilitarians*, Augustus M. Kelley, Publishers, New York, 1968.

Tawney, R. H.: *The Acquisitive Society*, Harcourt, Brace and Howe, New York, 1920.

Woolf, S. J. (ed.): *The Nature of Fascism*, Vintage Books, Random House, Inc., New York, 1969.

PART TWO

INTRODUCTION TO COMPARATIVE POLITICS

Chapter 8

Revolution or Stable Democracy?

COMPARING NATIONS

In any area of inquiry, understanding is impossible without generalization, and to generalize means inevitably to compare. One can understand the velocity of a falling body, the brightness of a distant star, or the characteristics of human pathology only with reference to some absolute standard that gives meaning to one's observations.

Where knowledge is less systematic and understanding is more difficult, as in the study of politics, there are few, if any, absolute standards for measurement and comparison. Part of the problem, then, is to identify patterns of regularity or uniformity that distinguish one set of phenomena from another. By comparing the characteristics of stable societies with those of unstable societies, for example,

we improve our understanding of revolution and political stability. The one concept has meaning primarily with reference to the other.

TEN BEST-GOVERNED NATIONS

What can be learned, then, from the findings of the American Institute of Public Opinion (the Gallup poll), which in 1970 put the following question to a scientifically selected sample of persons listed in *The International Year Book and Statesmen's Who's Who:* "Omitting your own country, what nation of the world do you think is best governed?"[1] Respondents were drawn from forty nations and included the world's leading statesmen,

[1] Reported in the *Los Angeles Times*, June 25, 1970.

117

scientists, jurists, business executives, publishers, and educators. The results of the poll are as follows:

1. Switzerland
2. Great Britain
3. Sweden
4. West Germany
5. Canada
6. The United States
7. Denmark
8. The Netherlands
9. Australia
10. Japan

There are some obvious differences between the ten countries included in this list. Five countries (Switzerland, West Germany, Canada, the United States, and Australia) have a federal form of government; the others are unitary in structure. Only one country (the United States) has a presidential system of government; the rest are parliamentary systems, with the chief executive drawn from the majority party or coalition in the legislature. While most of these countries have a bicameral legislature (Denmark's is unicameral, and Sweden established a unicameral parliament in 1970), only Switzerland and the United States have two chambers that are essentially co-equal in the legislative process. Citizens and foreign policy makers in the United States thus should not assume that "freedom," "democracy," and "responsible government" are synonymous with the particular institutions and principles operable in the United States. A popularly elected chief executive, the separation of powers, checks and balances, federalism, bicameralism, and judicial review are apparently not essential to stable democracy.

CHARACTERISTICS OF STABLE DEMOCRACY

But the similarities between these ten "best-governed" countries of the world are much more striking than the differences, and it is these similarities which help one to understand some of the preconditions for stability and instability, democracy and dictatorship. All these countries have competitive elections and three or more political parties, but one or two of the parties are politically dominant. All these countries have an elaborate system of interest groups and professional and semiprofessional organizations that aggregate the interests of a sizable percentage of the population. None of these countries has a recent history of colonial domination, and thus their contemporary politics have not been troubled by a prolonged or violent struggle for political independence, either at home or abroad. With the exceptions of Japan and West Germany, they all have a long record of political stability and, with the exception of West Germany, a modern history of national unity. The culture and politics of these countries have not been subordinated to the influence of a national and state-supported church (as in most Catholic countries), and, with the exception of Japan, the majority of the population in each country is Protestant. There is a high degree of racial homogeneity in each country, and with the important exceptions of Switzerland and Canada (which will be discussed in Chapter 12), there is one dominant language in each country.

Perhaps most obviously, all these countries are highly industrialized and urbanized. They also have extensive welfare systems, high per capita income, professionalized bureaucracies, well-developed institutions of primary and higher education, virtually universal literacy, and sophisticated networks of public and private communication. The reader can probably name other similarities between the ten countries besides the ones listed here, but these characteristics are probably fundamental to stable democracy, and it is very likely that any country in the world that is found lacking in the majority of these categories will be authoritarian, politically unstable, or both. This in turn helps to explain the high incidence of authoritarianism and political instability in the contemporary world and, indeed, throughout history.

REVOLUTION AND MODERNIZATION

Between 1937 and 1941 the sociologist P.A. Sorokin published his massive four-volume study of instability in eleven political communities, from ancient Greece and Rome to Western Europe and Russia over a period of 2,500 years. Sorokin studied a total of 1,622 "internal disturbances"; 70 percent of these "involved violence and bloodshed on a considerable scale." Sorokin also found that for every five years of relative stability, there was one year of "significant social disturbance."[2]

Political Instability since World War II

Sorokin concluded his research shortly before the full impact of World War II, but his observation that the twentieth century was "the bloodiest and the most turbulent period" in history has been dramatically confirmed by subsequent events. Between the end of the war and 1969, 40 of the approximately 100 states in Asia, Africa, and Latin America recorded at least one successful military coup d'état.[3] Between 1948 and 1967, almost all the countries of Latin America, two-thirds of the countries of Asia, and one-half of those African countries independent by 1962 experienced at least one successful or unsuccessful attempt to alter their governments by unconstitutional means.[4] For the shorter time period of 1946 to 1959, the *New York Times* reported more than 1,200 incidents of "internal war," including "civil wars, guerrilla wars, localized rioting, widely dispersed turmoil, organized and apparently unorganized terrorism, mutinies, and *coups d'état*."[5] And an ominous note for the future was sounded in 1971 by the United Nations secretariat; in its *Report on the World Situation* it concluded that most of the countries of the contemporary world face "sharpening polarization and conflict" in the decade ahead, as well as a "critical period of social change."[6]

Patterns of Instability

Most historians and political scientists studying the characteristics of instability agree that *social change* is, in fact, one of the major preconditions for political violence and revolution. The critical period in a country's history appears to coincide with fundamental economic change that carries with it basic transformations in the society's social structure. Since at least the Middle Ages, for example, a typical pattern of socioeconomic and violent political change would include the following:

1 A subsistence-oriented agricultural economy is rapidly transformed by the introduction of new technology along with monetary exchange and the production of commodities for sale on an open and competitive market.
2 Old social classes break down as new wealth is generated by a growing capitalist class in both agriculture and commercial enterprise.
3 Growing inequality in the distribution of land (exaggerated by rapid population growth) is paralleled by rapid industrial development and urbanization; an impoverished peasantry, an urban proletariat, and a growing bourgeoisie place new demands on antiquated social and political structures.
4 The institutions of the old order are unable to adapt to the demands of newly mobilized social classes; in essence, change from "below" has outstripped the capacity for change from "above."
5 The chances of violent political conflict also increase as the society is fragmented by different racial, linguistic, or religious groups; socioeconomic change inevitably aggravates the differences and hostilities between these groups.
6 Especially where societies with the above characteristics are subordinated to the colonial domination of a foreign power, revolutionary movements and political violence are highly probable, and they may be precipitated by any or all of the following "accelerators":
   a Military defeat, of either the colonial or national army
   b Economic crisis, especially catastrophic depression, which is likely to accompany military defeat
   c Violence perpetrated by the government against various sectors of the population, especially students or intellectuals
   d The government's attempts to centralize the state or, ironically, to initiate needed socioeconomic reforms
   e Increasing fragmentation and dissension within the society's dominant elite, which frequently results from attempts at socioeconomic reform
   f The outbreak of violence, revolution, or anticolonial movements in *other* societies with

---

[2]See Sorokin's summary of his findings in "Fluctuations of Internal Disturbances," in George A. Kelly and Clifford W. Brown, Jr. (eds.), *Struggles in the State: Sources and Patterns of World Revolution*, John Wiley & Sons, Inc., New York, 1970.

[3]Fred R. von der Mehden, *Politics of the Developing Nations*, Prentice-Hall, Inc., Englewood Cliffs, N.J., 1969, p. 92.

[4]Charles Lewis Taylor, "Turmoil, Economic Development and Organized Political Opposition as Predictors of Irregular Government Change," paper presented to the Sixty-sixth Annual Meeting of the American Political Science Association, Los Angeles, Sept. 8–12, 1970.

[5]Harry Eckstein (ed.), *Internal War: Problems and Approaches*, The Free Press of Glencoe, Inc., New York, 1964, p. 3.

[6]As reported in the *Los Angeles Times*, Jan. 25, 1971.

similar political and socioeconomic characteristics (sometimes referred to as the "demonstration effect")

Traditions of Violence In those societies where violence has become a frequent means of political change and upward mobility for underprivileged or threatened social groups, the chances of developing stable political institutions and norms of bargaining and compromise are extremely limited. Two-thirds of those countries which, after World War II, achieved political independence only after a long and violent struggle experienced a successful coup d'état following their attainment of independence.[7] The difficulties of mobilizing those economic resources which do exist in the country, the impossibility of meeting popular expectations and demands stimulated by independence from the colonial power, the heightening conflict between different ethnic or (especially in Africa) tribal groups confronted by economic change and the organization of new political institutions, the incompetence of an inexperienced civil service, and the apparently inevitable corruption that marks the political and economic activities of most underdeveloped countries all contribute to a life that—for most citizens and most governments—is, in Thomas Hobbes's words, "solitary, poor, nasty, brutish, and short."

Instability and Authoritarianism in the Underdeveloped World

In Ghana, for example, a military coup d'état in January 1972 overturned one of the few parliamentary governments remaining in postcolonial Africa. The civilian elite had been faced with falling agricultural production. The international market for Ghana's principal export (cocoa) was declining. These trends in turn contributed to a rising imbalance in Ghana's foreign trade, a massive foreign debt, and increasing rates of unemployment and inflation. To reduce its economic commitments, the government launched a program of fiscal austerity and devalued the national currency by almost half of its current value. The government also cut expenditures for the civil service, the police, *and* the army—thereby sealing its own fate.

Faced with monumental problems associated with economic underdevelopment and recent political independence, and without the decades, even centuries, that smoothed the modernization process of most contemporary democratic and industrialized states, the countries of the underdeveloped world are reluctant or unable to establish the institutions enjoyed by citizens in the ten "best-governed" countries listed above. The legitimacy of the political system in underdeveloped countries is a function more of the personalities of temporary leaders than of long-established institutions, and this in turn contributes to the instability of the government.

The concern for rapid economic development also reduces or eliminates the ruling elite's willingness to tolerate opposition parties and a free and independent press. "In a developing area like Africa," according to Robert S. Matano, Kenya's Minister of Information, "we can ill afford to use our limited resources for publishing destructive press statements."[8] And, today, of the thirty-six independent black African nations, only three (Botswana, Gambia, and Mauritius) retain a semblance of parliamentary government with competing political parties. Of the 230 million citizens of independent black Africa, more than 90 percent live under an authoritarian regime, and 135 million are ruled by military dictatorship.[9]

Poverty and Politics

When one studies the best-governed countries of the world, then, and—as in the following sections of this book—when one focuses on the political institutions and processes of the United States, Great Britain, and Western Europe, inevitably only a small minority of the peoples and governments of the contemporary world comes under investigation. Approximately 80 percent of the 4 billion people alive in the world today live in a rural village. Most of them lack educational opportunities and the necessary sanitation and health care facilities for curtailing disease (their average life expectancy is about twenty-six years, and one of every two children born in the world today will die before his or her sixth birthday), and they obviously lack

---

[7]von der Mehden, loc. cit.

[8]Quoted by Stanley Meisler in the *Los Angeles Times*, Aug. 12, 1973.
[9]Ibid.

opportunities for meaningful and sustained political participation.

These data alone help to explain the frequent strength of radical movements in the contemporary underdeveloped world, including those movements which call themselves "communist."[10] In fact, where communist parties have been able to monopolize the issues of agrarian reform and anticolonialism (especially in Asia), they have proved to be an almost unbeatable force. And, in terms of the characteristics of democracy and revolution outlined above, it is not difficult to understand the vulnerability of anti-communist governments in South Vietnam—where 80 percent of the population is made up of rural peasants; where the literacy rate does not exceed 20 percent; where the political elite was traditionally drawn from a small, wealthy class that lived in the major cities; where there are prominent ethnic and cultural cleavages, including those between the economically and politically dominant—before 1975—Catholic minority (about 8 percent of the total population) and the Buddhist and Taoist majority; and where the country's history is marked by protracted and violent struggle against foreign invaders and their political agents in the capital.

India: An Exception The problems of building stable democratic institutions in Vietnam, and in most of the rest of the underdeveloped world, are highlighted by a comparison with India, considered relatively stable and democratic, at least before mid-1975. India's independence movement was initiated *before* the organization of communist parties following the Bolshevik Revolution, and the movement was far less violent than movements in most of the other countries colonized by the European powers. Thus an early foundation was laid for peaceful political confrontation and bargaining.

This also suggests that there was some advantage to being a colony of Great Britain (as compared with being a colony of, for example, France, Belgium, or Portugal), and the British in India left behind a well-organized system of national transportation, a professional civil service recruited largely from the indigenous population, and well-established and functioning institutions of national and local government. After independence in 1947, India also benefited from the long tenure of enlightened charismatic leadership (notably that of Jawaharlal Nehru, prime minister from 1947 to 1964) and from a relatively slow rate of economic growth that did not immediately generate popular demands or social change in excess of institutional capabilities.

Focus on Modernity

The sections and chapters that follow will concentrate on some of those best-governed societies which developed political institutions over a relatively long period of time. Time itself is a legitimating force, and where political institutions have survived and evolved through time, they are likely to endure the more temporary problems associated with economic or military setback and the occasional incompetence or unpopularity of political leaders. These societies do not represent the majority of the peoples or governments at work in today's world, but it is fair to say that they represent the aspirations of the many, if only the realization of a fortunate few.

The sections immediately following also focus more on the *institutions* than on the cultural or behavioral characteristics of the best-governed societies. In stable democracies the organization and operation of institutions have a more determining impact on behavior than is the case in the more authoritarian and unstable societies of the world—where the values and behavior of political or military elites may tell the whole story of a particular country's fate.

THE INSTITUTIONS OF STABLE DEMOCRACY: THE SUFFRAGE

Because democracy implies popular sovereignty, a democratic state must maintain a system of universal, or nearly universal suffrage. In actual practice, even in the most advanced democratic nations, certain groups of persons—children, aliens, and inmates of penal and mental institutions—are usually prohibited from voting. The most common requirements are citizenship, attainment of a minimum age (which may mean almost any age between

---

[10] A line that appears in Bertolt Brecht's *Three-Penny Opera* is appropriate here: "First comes the bread, then come the morals."

eighteen and thirty-five),[11] residence in the country and in the voting district, and registration as a voter. Until recently, women were not allowed to vote; until 1971, democratic Switzerland (the best-governed country of all, according to the Gallup poll of 1970) barred women from the national suffrage. However, beginning with New Zealand in 1893, almost eighty countries have extended the vote to women. Racial barriers (overt or covert) still exist in some democratic countries; property qualifications have persisted during the nineteenth century and into the twentieth. Religious qualifications, once widely prevalent, have practically disappeared. The idea behind the requirement of property ownership survived indirectly in the poll tax, which was required in a few of the American states until the 1960s, and also in the suggestion that persons receiving public relief be disfranchised.

Women's Suffrage The exclusion of women from the suffrage originated when the electorate was restricted to those who bore arms, and it was further perpetuated by the general economic and legal dependence of women. The increasing employment of women in factories, stores, and offices; their admission to the professions; and their equal access to educational opportunities have removed the principal foundations for the earlier discrimination against them. While the adoption of women's suffrage has not had the uplifting and purifying effect upon democratic politics that was optimistically predicted by its early advocates, it is altogether in accord with democratic principles. It is significant that the activities of women in both world wars had the effect of strengthening the movement for women's suffrage. Also, the findings of psychologists have exploded many earlier notions about women's "innate inferiority" to men. In the United States, women's votes have tended to be distributed among parties, candidates, and issues in virtually the same proportions as the male vote, although it was widely believed that women had voted for General Eisenhower in 1952 and in 1956 in greater proportion than men. Women are increasingly active in both major parties, and more and more women are seeking and securing public office. After the 1972 congressional elections there were no women senators, but fifteen women were representatives in the House (thirteen of them were Democrats).

Ending Racial Discrimination in Voting Substantial progress also has been made toward overcoming racial barriers to voting, especially in the United States. The Supreme Court outlawed the use of the white primary in 1944; the payment of a poll tax as a requirement for voting has been outlawed by the Twenty-fourth Amendment to the United States Constitution (ratified in 1964) with respect to voting for president, vice president, United States senators, and representatives in Congress. Civil-rights legislation passed in 1957 and 1960 authorized federal officials to intervene to prevent interference with the right to vote and even in certain cases to register qualified black citizens who have been refused registration in segregated areas. The Civil Rights Act of 1964 made the completion of the sixth grade in an elementary school a rebuttable presumption of literacy for voting in any federal election, and the Voting Rights Act of 1965 suspended literacy tests for state and local elections.

But universal suffrage is meaningless unless the voter has a genuine choice between or among candidates, parties, and programs. Hitler retained the suffrage laws of the Weimar Republic, and the Soviet Union holds "elections," but unless the voter may express his or her desire to change the incumbent administration and its policies without fear of the concentration camp or lesser forms of political reprisal, democracy does not exist. Indeed, the freedom to vote for a change in government is one of the prime essentials of democracy.

REPRESENTATION

There are two forms of democratic government—direct and indirect. In a direct democracy, all the qualified voters assemble at stated times to enact laws and decide issues; the New England town meeting is a good example. Obviously, this method is possible only in very small communities; indeed, in ancient Athens, it was believed that the city-state

---

[11]Until 1971, the voting age in the United States was twenty-one in all the states except Georgia and Kentucky (eighteen), Alaska (nineteen), and Hawaii (twenty). Eighteen-year-olds voted for the first time on a national basis in the presidential elections of 1972, and the partisan distribution of their vote generally approximated that of older citizens.

should have no more citizens than could assemble and hear the voice of the orator.

The application of democracy to the large nation-state has been made possible by the device of representation, resulting in indirect democracy. The voters elect representatives to legislate for them; in some countries the voters also choose executive, administrative, and judicial officers to carry out various specialized tasks of government. In a system of indirect democracy the average citizen's official participation in the governmental process is confined to voting for elective officials (usually at regular intervals), to jury and military service, and, in a few countries, to voting in referendum elections to decide specific questions submitted for the verdict of the people. However, it would be a mistake to assume that the citizen's influence on government is limited to casting a ballot. Citizens may also write or personally contact their representatives; through the many organizations to which they belong they may bring collective pressure to bear; they may attend the many open hearings held by public bodies (e.g., the school board and the city council); they may write letters to the editors of newspapers; and they may campaign energetically for the candidates and policies of their choice. Elected representatives in a "responsible" political system pay heed to citizens' letters and telegrams, as well as to the published reports of public-opinion polls. Citizens of a democracy can be sure that their elected representatives have their ears to the ground to catch the rumblings of civic approval or resentment. In addition, many citizens are called upon to participate in the process of government by serving on advisory boards and committees, which are widely used by all levels of government.

Representative legislatures rest, in the ultimate analysis, on the assumption that the people can delegate the exercise of the legislative portion of their sovereign power to elected deputies or representatives. This assumption has been challenged, notably by anarchists and the great eighteenth-century political philosopher Jean-Jacques Rousseau. Rousseau considered sovereignty to reside in the general will of the nation and argued that this will could not be delegated to, or formulated by, representatives; therefore, he disapproved of representative democracy and advocated only the direct form.

Geographic Representation: The Single-Member District

Another question arises concerning the proper basis of representation: Are representatives to be elected from geographic areas roughly equal in population or on the basis of economic or occupational groupings? Most countries with representative governments follow the geographic principle, dividing the country into districts of approximately equal population, each district electing a single representative by the vote of a majority or plurality in the district. The effects of any electoral system are advantageous to some political parties and disadvantageous to others. The "single-member district, simple-plurality" electoral system (used, for example, in the United States and Great Britain) is invariably based on geographic representation. Its principal effects are to *under*represent minority parties in the legislature and to *over*represent the majority. Thus in a recent nonpresidential national election in the United States, the Democratic candidates for Congress received 56 percent of the total vote, but Democrats won 65 percent of all congressional seats. This electoral system also discriminates with a vengeance against third-party movements, which have no chance of placing their representatives in the legislature unless the party's electoral strength is geographically concentrated. This system also is equitable only if district boundaries are frequently and fairly redrawn to take account of the growth and shifting of population. In most American legislative bodies, as in England before the reforms of 1832, 1867, 1884, and 1918, rural areas have been accorded undue weight, while urban populations have been seriously underrepresented. Such inequities were written into many state constitutions;[12] in addition, state legislatures have deliberately manipulated the boundaries of both state and congressional districts to enable the

---

[12]In the United States, however, there have been some important changes. In *Baker v. Carr,* 369 U.S. 186 (1962), the United States Supreme Court decided that questions of state legislative apportionment involving charges of a denial of constitutional equality *could* be decided by the Court. In *Wesberry v. Sanders,* 376 U.S. 1 (1964), the Court held that congressional districts within a state must also be substantially equal in population, thereby reducing the advantage previously enjoyed by representatives from rural districts. These were major decisions by the Supreme Court, and it should be noted that they effected important changes in American political institutions without direct reference to elected representatives or the amending process of the Constitution. In effect, the Court made new law.

party in power to capture as many seats as possible. This practice, known as "gerrymandering," produces districts that are weird in shape and grossly unequal in population. One remedy is to take redistricting out of the hands of the legislature and place it in the hands of a nonpartisan body; this has been done in Great Britain, resulting in a virtually continuous redistricting process that produces districts remarkably equal in population.

The single-member district system, as it operates in the United States, has resulted in the practice of electing to the legislative body only residents of the district. This narrows the list of candidates available to the voter and discourages many able men from running for office. Moreover, it makes the representative a mere agent, who is expected to secure every advantage for his locality rather than to advance the public interest. Thus state and national policies are entrusted to men with a "ward politics" outlook. Another criticism arises from the fact that even under a two-party political system, the minority voters in a district go unrepresented; the single representative regards himself as the emissary of the dominant majority party. Where there are additional minority parties and groups of so-called independent voters, the situation grows worse; the successful candidate may have received a mere plurality rather than a majority of the vote cast, and the bulk of the electorate is not represented at all.

Proportional Representation

To remedy this last defect, various methods of "proportional" representation have been proposed, and several countries and municipalities have put such plans into operation. Many Americans assume that our system is one of proportional representation because it is proportional to population. However, the idea in proportional representation (or PR) is to assure, by distributing votes rather than voters, that the number of seats in the legislative body won by a political party or group will be as nearly as possible in proportion to the popular vote cast for that party or group. In recent elections to the Italian Chamber of Deputies (elections organized according to proportional representation), the Communists received 25.3 percent of the popular vote and 27 percent of the Chamber's seats; the Socialists received 13.8 percent of the vote and 14 percent of the seats; the Christian Democrats received 38.3 percent of the votes and 41.5 percent of the seats; and the Liberals received 7 percent of the votes and 6 percent of the seats. To make representation in the legislature conform perfectly to the distribution of votes, it is necessary to organize the entire country into one, and only one, electoral district; Israel, in fact, employs such a system in its election of members to the 120-seat Knesset.[13]

Proportional representation contributes to ideological rigidity and tightly organized political parties. It tends to create a multiparty system in which the formation of a government depends on the successful building of coalitions across two or more political parties, however ideologically opposed to each other they might be. Proportional representation is strongly supported by minority parties and those who identify with independent or ideologically extreme candidates; it is opposed (naturally enough) by strongly entrenched political organizations, which profit from the electoral distortions of the single-member district, simple-plurality system.

Pros and Cons of Proportional Representation

There has been much controversy over the merits of proportional representation. Its advocates point out that it will eliminate the need for the primary election and also the necessity for reapportionment and redistricting (thus removing the incentive for gerrymandering). They further contend that the majority principle rests upon the assumption of a two-party system, which no longer really exists in such traditional biparty countries as Britain and the United States. The Hare system is said to provide the only method for the expression of the views of the independent voters. The defenders of PR claim that lobbying will be largely eliminated under proportional representation because all interest groups

[13]New York City elected its council by PR (using a modified form of the Hare system) between 1936 and 1947, when it was eliminated from the city charter by an amendment approved by a majority of the voters in a referendum election. This change in the electoral system eliminated the multiparty representation on the city council (which included representatives from the American Labor party, Liberals, and Communists); in the 1949 municipal elections, the Democrats won twenty-four of the twenty-five seats, while the Republicans elected only one councilman. It was a perfect example of the effects of the single-member district, simple-plurality system—"winner take all." See B. Zeller and H. A. Bone, "The Repeal of P.R. in New York City: Ten Years in Retrospect," *American Political Science Review*, vol. 42, no. 6, pp. 1127–1148, December 1948.

will be directly represented in the legislative body, which becomes a true mirror of the nation.

Critics point out that PR tends to encourage the formation of small "splinter" parties, thus making all cabinets necessarily coalitions that lack the solidarity requisite for effective national leadership and the formulation of coherent government policy. Critics of PR also argue that it emphasizes divisive, centrifugal forces in the society, thereby contributing to ideological rigidity rather than programmatic compromise. And, indeed, democratic government rests on the assumption that the various sectional, economic, cultural, and other groups can reach workable compromises—that they can widen the area of agreement rather than the area of conflict. Virtually to invite each minority and each dissident group to organize as a political party is to help to crystallize and perpetuate minor differences that might otherwise be accommodated in a larger political party.

Defenders of the Anglo-American party system believe that a true political party is essentially different from, and broader than, a special-interest or pressure group and that PR tends to obliterate this distinction and to substitute narrow group interests for the public welfare that a truly national, broadly based political party seeks to promote. Proportional representation has also been blamed for the excessive number of political parties in Weimar Germany, which at one time totaled over thirty in a Reichstag election. Some claim that PR was a major factor in discrediting parliamentary government in Germany and that it facilitated the rise of the Nazis to power. It must be remembered, however, that Germany, France, and Italy developed multiparty systems *before* PR was established. Political parties reflect cleavages in the body politic; an electoral system may aggravate, but does not cause, such conflicts of interest.

In defense of the single-member district system, it should be noted that it has the advantage of encouraging compromise, rather than hairsplitting, on the part of both parties and candidates, as well as the further merit of usually producing a government that can govern. Here, however, much will depend upon the number and attitudes of the political parties. The chief defect of this system is the possibility that many representatives will be chosen by a plurality rather than a majority of their constituents. Such defects as gerrymandering and electing only residents of a district are not inherent in the system, as British practice proves.

Obviously, proportional representation is suitable only for elections to *legislative* assemblies—national, state, provincial, or local. It is clearly impossible to "draw and quarter" a president, governor, mayor, or other executive officer. However, in a democratic system it is the legislature that should ultimately determine public policy; the executive may indeed propose, but should not dispose. Besides, under the widely prevalent parliamentary system, the voters do not choose the chief executive; they choose the party—and its legislative representatives—that best reflects their views on public policy. Granting the many advantages of the two-party system (which is sustained by the majority-plurality method of voting), modern society is so complex and so many-sided that public issues cannot really be resolved by the dichotomized "either-or" approach, which the geographic single-member district requires. Attitudes on public questions cannot always be neatly compartmentalized as "for" or "against," and proportional representation allows the independent or "in-betweener" an opportunity to be heard.

Functional Representation

The other major criticism of the prevalent system of geographic representation is based on the contention that people do not, in reality, share common interests merely because they happen to reside in the same area and that they would be more accurately represented on the basis of economic or occupational groups. The proposals for such "functional representation," as it is called, show little agreement regarding the particular groups to be represented, the distribution of representation among them, or the relationship of such an economic parliament or council to the geographically and politically elected legislature (if any). Opponents of functional representation stress the difficulties of defining the groups, determining in which group each individual belongs, allocating representation among the groups in an equitable manner, and ensuring that basic, general interests of public safety, health, and order will be adequately protected.

Again, no unassailable conclusions may be

drawn. Functional representation has been experimented with to only a very limited extent. The corporative state in Italy developed a Fascist and Corporative Chamber based on occupational groupings, but it was devoid of any representative character in the democratic sense because of the complete absence of elections. The German Nazi regime established a system of estates for basic economic groupings, but these were not utilized as the basis for selecting a legislative chamber. They served merely to facilitate the operation of the thoroughly regimented economic system.

Several democratic countries have experimented with national economic councils possessing merely advisory powers, including France, Italy, Holland, and Japan. France today has an Economic and Social Council appointed by the executive branch and advising it with respect to economic and social problems. The membership of the Council includes spokesmen for the different economic and social interests and the professions, as well as a variety of experts. The National Recovery Administration, set up during the early days of the New Deal, utilized trade associations and other occupational groups in formulating and administering codes of business practices. The modern interest or pressure group serves to provide effective representation for particular interests in its dealings with government, but this does not necessarily ensure the effective representation of all interests or all citizens.

The Role of Elected Representatives

There are differences of opinion concerning the responsibility of representatives to their constituents. American and French practice tends to make representatives delegates of those who elected them, while the traditional British doctrine, persuasively expounded by Edmund Burke and John Stuart Mill, holds that representatives ought to exercise their own independent judgment rather than merely obey, literally, the wishes of their constituents.[14] This latter view emphasizes the duty of representatives to promote the national welfare rather than the interests of their particular locality.

[14]See John Stuart Mill, *Considerations on Representative Government* (1861), chap. 12. It is interesting to note that Edmund Burke's constituents once declined to reelect him precisely because he had insisted on following his own judgment rather than their wishes. True to his conservative convictions, however, Burke refused to abandon his principles for political expediency (see the discussion of conservatism in Chap. 7).

Because in England members of Parliament are not required by either law or custom to reside in the constituency in which they seek election, they are more free from local control than the French deputy or the American representative in Congress, both of whom are required (by custom rather than by law) to reside in the district they represent. However, the development of political parties and the increasingly firm discipline exerted by them upon representatives, in Britain and in other European countries, tend to substitute accountability to the party for accountability to the local voters.

The independence of elected representatives is therefore an ideal rather than an actuality. Whether complete independence of judgment is desirable is open to question. Much depends upon the ability and integrity of representatives themselves. Some authors contend that this American (and French) attitude is more in accord with the democratic ideal than the "lofty and seductive theories" of Burke;[15] however, most students find it difficult to reach any final conclusion and favor an intermediate position. They believe that representatives should be neither supine nor officious toward their constituents and that they should try to protect and advance legitimate local interests insofar as these are compatible with the general welfare—a compatibility of which they should be the judge.

THE LEGISLATIVE BODY

In the modern democratic state a national legislature—elected by, and responsible to, the people—is an indispensable part of democratic machinery. Even in those countries (and those states of the American Union) which make extensive use of the popular initiative and referendum, there is no thought of abolishing the legislative body; these popular checks upon the legislature serve to control, but not to preclude, the exercise of discretion by the people's elected representatives.

Bicameral and Unicameral Legislatures

Most national legislatures are bicameral—that is to say, they consist of two houses or chambers. Originally, the development of parliamentary bod-

[15]David Thomson, *The Democratic Ideal in France and England*, Cambridge University Press, New York, 1940, especially pp. 54–56.

ies consisting of two (or three) chambers reflected the stratified societies of an earlier period. Thus in England the nobility and the higher clergy formed the House of Lords, while the knights and lesser clergy grouped themselves with the burgesses (representatives of the boroughs or towns) to form the House of Commons. In France and other continental countries the clergy formed one estate, the nobility formed another, and the common people's representatives became yet another chamber known as the "Third Estate."

The survival of bicameralism after the establishment of democracy is due partly to tradition and imitation and partly to other factors. Where a national state is formed (as the United States, Germany, and Switzerland were) out of states or cantons that were previously sovereign and independent, a bicameral parliament is adopted as a means of representing state or local interests in the upper house and national interests in the lower house and of achieving balance and harmony between these interests. In other countries, such as France, bicameralism has been deliberately established to provide a check by a conservative upper chamber upon the presumably rash, ill-advised, or radical legislation emanating from the popular chamber. Upper chambers commonly rest upon some basis other than that of direct popular election. Some have a hereditary membership (the House of Lords); some are appointive for life (the senate of Canada and that of Italy before and during fascism); and others are elected indirectly (the senates of Ireland and of the French Fifth Republic and the United States Senate prior to the adoption of the Seventeenth Amendment in 1913). Members of upper houses are usually required to be older than representatives elected to the popular chamber; in some countries (Canada) they must own a minimum amount of property or belong to one of several specified functional categories, such as administrative officials, scholars, scientists, noted literary figures, or large taxpayers (as in the old Italian senate).

Bicameralism is defended on several grounds. It is maintained that it (1) is essential to a federal system; (2) ensures thorough, careful consideration of legislation; and (3) prevents the undue concentration of political power in a single body, which might, if unchecked, become arbitrary and despotic, thus threatening the liberties of individuals and minority groups. It is further contended that a single, all-powerful legislative chamber can too readily dominate the executive branch and thereby nullify, in practice, the separation of powers widely regarded as essential to the proper working of democratic government. This argument seems, however, to be refuted by the fact that the British Parliament is today virtually unicameral and yet shows no tendency toward excessive legislative dominance over the Cabinet. In fact, the trend has been in the opposite direction, and concern has been expressed over what some regard as the extreme power of the executive over the House of Commons.[16]

Reforming Bicameralism Advocates of the unicameral legislature point out that a truly representative, popularly elected body should not, in a democracy, be subjected to checks and delays interposed by an upper chamber elected or appointed on an undemocratic basis. Moreover, as the complex problems of the industrial age placed heavier burdens upon government, the two-house legislature showed marked defects. Deadlocks frequently occurred between the two chambers, especially where the upper chamber was avowedly aristocratic or conservative in composition. The division of legislative responsibility encouraged each house to blame the other for failures and delays. Where (as in the Third Republic of France) the cabinet had been made responsible to both chambers, this situation contributed to the weakness and instability of the entire governmental system, tending to refute the claim that the bicameral scheme was a greater guarantee of balance and harmony.

As the ideals of democracy won wider acceptance, the obviously undemocratic character of many second chambers led to demands for their reform or abolition. In England, the obstructive tactics of the House of Lords toward progressive

---

[16] The first constitution offered to the voters of France by a constituent assembly following World War II proposed a strong unicameral parliament and a weak executive. The rejection of this draft constitution by the French people on May 5, 1946, was attributable at least partly to the fear that a single, powerful chamber might become a tool whereby the Communist party could dominate France. However, the constitution finally adopted established such a weak upper house that the lower chamber still had the power to overthrow ministries in irresponsible fashion. Under the present Fifth Republic, the Senate occupies a much stronger position (see Chap. 12).

social and economic legislation led to the Parliament Act of 1911, which deprived the Lords of all power over financial legislation and rendered them unable to do more than delay other legislation for two years.[17] Various proposals have been advanced to reform the House of Lords by making it smaller and more broadly representative of elements outside the ranks of the peerage, but the only progress in this direction took the form of an act of 1958 creating an indeterminate number of life peerages, which could be conferred on women as well as on men.

In the United States, the Seventeenth Amendment provided for direct popular election of United States senators, replacing the original method of election by state legislatures. Many of the new nations established at the close of World War I adopted the unicameral system;[18] several Latin-American states did likewise.[19] Since World War II, several of the newly emerging nations have established unicameral parliaments.[20] In other countries, the upper chamber has been reduced to a distinctly secondary position, with the lower chamber empowered to override it; such provisions were incorporated into the constitutions of the German republic, Czechoslovakia, Poland, and Austria following World War I.

Unicameralism has long been the rule in municipal government in both the United States and Europe. Most European states have established single-chamber legislatures in their provinces, cantons, or other regional areas of government. All the Canadian provinces except Quebec are unicameral. The preference for bicameralism shown by the states of the American Union has been broken by Nebraska, which installed a unicameral legislature in 1937. Movements in favor of unicameralism are under way in other American states, and in still others demands are being made that the state senate be drastically reconstructed.

Size

Another problem of the modern legislature is the question of its proper size. In general, large assemblies are criticized as unwieldy and inefficient; they are forced to work largely through committees or to delegate much authority to a cabinet or president or to various administrative bodies.

Yet there seems little disposition to reduce the size of national legislatures; the House of Commons numbers 635 members; the National Assembly of France, 487 (a drop from 626 under the Fourth Republic); and the United States House of Representatives, 435. To reduce the size of the legislative body would necessitate enlarging the district (as was done in France) and thus the number of voters represented by the legislator. Most constituencies are already so large and populous as to impair if not destroy the personal relationship between voters and their representatives. The French deputy represents an average of 107,000 people; the British member of Parliament, about 89,000; and the United States congressional representative, about 490,000. In the modern democratic state, the political party and the pressure group have arisen to maintain contact between the legislature and the people. However, such organizations fail to present the wishes of unorganized voters and often exaggerate the claims of their own members for special legislative consideration.

Functions of Legislatures

A vital question is that of the proper functions of the national legislative body in a democracy. Americans, accustomed to the doctrine of the separation of powers among distinct executive, legislative, and judicial branches of government, believe that the chief function of the legislative body is to enact laws. However, legislatures have many other functions to perform. Among these are participation in the process of amending the constitution; control of national finances through taxation, borrowing, and appropriations; and supervision of administration. In some instances, a legislative chamber shares the power of appointment to important executive and

---

[17]In December 1949 the Labour government secured the passage of a law that reduced this period of possible delay to one year. It should also be noted that for many years the Labour party had urged the outright abolition of the House of Lords.

[18]Finland, Latvia, Lithuania, Estonia, and Yugoslavia. Other European nations with unicameral national legislatures are Bulgaria, Rumania, Denmark, and Sweden.

[19]Costa Rica, the Dominican Republic, Salvador, Honduras, and Panama.

[20]Ghana, Sierra Leone, Tanganyika, Western Samoa, Pakistan (1962), Gambia, Mauritius, Laos, Israel, Dahomey, Ivory Coast, Senegal, Togo, Mali, Mauritania, and Niger. New Zealand joined the ranks of unicameral countries in 1951.

judicial offices;[21] one or both chambers frequently participate in treaty making.[22] It is customary for legislative bodies to exercise certain judicial powers, such as deciding contested elections, expelling their own members, passing upon the qualifications of their members (thus in effect adding to the qualifications stated in the constitution or statute), and bringing impeachment actions against public officials or trying cases of impeachment.[23]

Supervising the Executive Under the parliamentary system, a major function of the popular chamber is the supervision and control of the cabinet. Since the cabinet or ministry must have the confidence of the chamber, no government can be formed or continue in office without parliamentary support. Legislative control is exercised through questions addressed to ministers, amendment or rejection of government bills (including the budget), and votes of "no confidence" that compel the ministers to resign—unless, as in England, they can secure the dissolution of Parliament, in which case the people will decide in the election that follows whether they approve the program of the ministry or that of Parliament. In the United States, legislative control over the executive operates through congressional committee hearings on legislative proposals (including the budget) and especially by means of congressional investigating committees.

Legislative-Executive Relationships In the American system of government, the doctrine of the separation of powers presumes rather clear-cut differentiation among the tasks of the legislative, executive, and judicial branches and seeks to avoid encroachment by one upon another. Yet the equally respected American notion of checks and balances, incorporated in the provisions of our federal and state constitutions, gives the legislative branch a share in such executive functions as appointments and treaty making and permits it to control administration by withholding funds for certain agencies or by abolishing such agencies outright. Thus, although the legislature neither chooses the chief executive[24] nor removes him (except by impeachment) and although it frequently happens that the president belongs to one political party while one or both houses of Congress are controlled by the other, the two branches do in fact impinge closely upon each other. Sometimes the executive branch seems stronger than the legislative, and sometimes the situation appears to be reversed; the relationships depend upon the ability and energy of the leaders involved and upon the attendant circumstances.

The increased tempo of modern life and its greater demands upon government have raised other questions concerning the proper role of the legislative body. Because of the increasing scope and technical character of government programs, there is a tendency for the legislature to delegate some of its authority in law making to executive departments and to what are commonly known as "quasilegislative" agencies, boards, and commissions.[25] The legislature enacts a law stating the broad objectives to be accomplished and the general principles, rules, and limitations, and it empowers the executive officer, board, or commission to fill in the details in the form of regulations that have the force of law. Such delegated legislation is on the increase in all countries; it is especially marked in Great Britain. There is considerable criticism in some quarters of this tendency on the part of the legislature to abdicate its functions; critics contend that this development leads to arbitrary and irresponsible government by bureaucrats and means the decline of representative government and true democracy. On the other hand, it is pointed out that

---

[21]The United States Senate must confirm appointments of federal judges, diplomatic and consular officers, and a host of other federal officials.

[22]The United States Senate must approve a proposed treaty by a vote of two-thirds of the senators present.

[23]In the United States federal government, the House of Representatives initiates impeachment proceedings, while the Senate tries all cases of impeachment. A president is removed from office only if convicted by a two-thirds vote of the Senate, following a majority vote for impeachment by the House of Representatives. (In both instances, the required vote is in terms of the number of members present and voting, assuming a quorum.) President Andrew Johnson was impeached by the House in 1868, but the Senate failed to convict him by one vote. President Richard M. Nixon resigned in August 1974 after a bipartisan majority of the House Judiciary Committee voted to recommend impeachment to the full House and when it became apparent that Nixon's impeachment by the House and conviction in the Senate were inevitable.

[24]Unless no presidential candidate receives a majority of electoral-college votes. See the discussion of the electoral college in Chap. 9.

[25]See the discussion in Chap. 18 under Public Administration: Performing the Tasks of the Modern State.

legislators lack the expert knowledge required for the enactment of detailed laws regarding, for example, railroads, the marketing of investment securities, civil aviation, banking, or the radio-television industry and that the experts in these fields, appointed to appropriate regulatory commissions and presumably freed from political influences, will produce better and more workable regulations.

Whatever the merits of this perennial controversy, it poses the crucial question: Should the modern legislature attempt to legislate on every detail embodied in public policy? It is increasingly argued that the most effective role of the legislature, under modern conditions, is that of ultimately approving or rejecting broad legislative policies initiated, in most instances, by the executive and administrative experts. Such executive accountability to the legislature, coupled with the responsibility of the legislators to the voters, will, it is claimed, preserve the basic principles of the democratic process without slowing down and obstructing legislation through legislative preoccupation with minor details.

Recourse to Direct Democracy The power and responsibility of state legislatures in the United States have been weakened in recent years by the rise of initiative and referendum. Both devices, by bringing the electorate into participation in the legislative process, represent a modern attempt to regain some of the advantages of direct democracy. Their spread has also been due to popular dissatisfaction with the operation of the legislative body, which has been regarded as slow, unresponsive to public opinion, subservient to special interests, excessively partisan, and sometimes corrupt. Although useful as safeguards against a corrupt or indifferent legislature and as an educational experience for the voter, neither the initiative nor the referendum is indispensable to democracy. Indeed, average voters are often poorly qualified to pass judgment on the complex issues submitted to them, and their votes may be determined by the massive advertising and public-relations campaigns organized by those who use the initiative and referendum as a means of securing their own special interests. The initiative and referendum cannot be indiscriminately employed (as is done in some states) without seriously impairing the power and usefulness of American political parties and legislative bodies. "Direct democracy" may sound appealing, but—like any other institution or procedure in the political process—it may be misused by those who, under the banner of popular government, enhance their private advantage by circumventing the institutions and procedures of representative government.

THE EXECUTIVE BRANCH

The role of the executive branch of government has already received some attention in Chapter 3, where presidential and parliamentary systems of government were discussed. This is the appropriate place, however, for emphasizing the most important trends in the recent development of stable democratic government—trends, however, that do not necessarily guarantee the survival of democracy as it has traditionally been defined.

Growth of Executive Power

In the modern democratic state, the chief executive not only is responsible for law enforcement and general administration but also is increasingly regarded as chief legislator. He is expected to provide legislative leadership for the parliament or congress, suggesting in considerable detail the main lines of foreign, domestic, and fiscal policy. Today the messages and recommendations of the democratic chief executive to his legislature approximate the dimensions of a comprehensive national plan submitted for legislative approval.

Early Opposition to Executive Power Such a tendency seems all the more remarkable when one recalls the fear and suspicion with which the executive power was regarded during the period following the American and French Revolutions. It was natural that men who had only recently freed themselves from arbitrary and oppressive monarchical rule should view all executive power as dangerous and should seek to limit its scope and subject it to restraints imposed by other branches of government. In the United States, this attitude was reflected in the extremely limited powers and short terms of the early state governors, in the very absence of a national chief executive under the Articles of Confederation, and in the constitutional checks placed upon the president. Until recently, the American people have been inclined to fear any increase in the powers of mayors, governors, or the president; the press has sometimes stigmatized proposals looking in this direction as dictatorship bills. Yet marked progress is being made toward the eradication of such apprehensions regarding executive power; proposals for federal reorganization are now discussed objectively and with few signs of our ancient phobia.

Trends toward Executive Power The reasons for this change in attitude are not difficult to find. On the one hand, the earlier enthusiasm for the wisdom and competence of representative assemblies has declined; on the other, a century and more of experience with popularly elected (or popularly controlled) executive power has dissipated earlier suspicions and established confidence. Moreover, the rapidly multiplying problems and functions of democratic government have virtually compelled the transfer of many powers from the legislature to the executive. The growing need for prompt governmental action in the field of both domestic and foreign policy has caused the modern legislature to delegate much legislative authority to the executive, subject, as a rule, to guiding principles and limitations set forth by the legislature. In some instances the legislature reserves the right to set aside the action taken by the executive. Thus the United States Congress has empowered the president to revise tariff duties upward or downward within established limits and for prescribed periods of time and to negotiate reciprocal trade agreements without submitting them to the Senate. The long intervals between legislative sessions (during which governmental action may be imperative), the inability of the legislature to provide in advance and in detail for all possible contingencies, and the notorious delays incident to the partisan and acrimonious debate often characteristic of the legislative process combine to justify the conferring of wider discretion, in matters of policy, upon the executive branch. A further reason for the expansion of the power of the American president is the realization that he is the representative chosen by the people of the entire nation, whereas congressmen and senators too often espouse sectional or other special interests that may be in conflict with the national welfare.

Dependency on the Presidency If, in the United States, the president does not or will not represent the national welfare (in actions as well as in words), the public interest is served more by chance than by design. Unlike Great Britain and other democracies in which the chief executive is not directly elected by the people, the United States lacks a cohesive national party system that can interpret the will of an elected majority into official public policy. In the United States, a weak president or one who is the agent of special interests (whether trade unions or giant, multinational corporations) almost inevitably leaves the definition of the national welfare to the self-interested activities of pressure groups. And it is a significant finding of comparative political studies that where political parties are weak, interest groups are strong. Nor is it correct to assume (as James Madison did in the *Federalist No. 10*) that a large number of special interests will contribute to the general interest by ensuring that no group is dominant. While the general interest or national welfare on any particular issue is seldom easy to define, one cannot assume that it will magically emerge from the competition of groups (an assumption that is the *political* equivalent of Adam Smith's economic "invisible hand"). In fact, they may silently agree to trade off their special advantages and political access and show no interest whatsoever in establishing a competitive balance of power in the distribution of government money and favors.

In a presidential system with relatively weak political parties (as in the United States), the chief executive is the ultimate source of political responsibility to the general public. But this in turn is not without grave risks to the balance of power among politicians and between the public and government. The centralization of power that appears to be essential to responsible government in the modern world may also lead to irresponsibility in the actual exercise of power. The well-being of citizens is ever more dependent on the enlightenment and political choices of elected elites, regardless of the ways in which formal political power is organized.

Scope and Nature of Executive Power

The democratic chief executive is invested with such powers as the conduct of foreign relations, the appointment and supervision of administrative officials, the command of the military establishments, and the granting of pardons and reprieves. In countries having the parliamentary system, these powers are nominally assigned to the chief of state, whether elected president or limited monarch, but are actually exercised by the responsible ministry. Under the presidential system, the president is both the formal and actual chief executive. However, even under this system, the chief executive must rely for advice and assistance upon the heads of the executive departments and administrative agencies. The vital difference lies in the fact that under the presidential system, the president does not need to take the advice offered, nor is the validity of his signature dependent upon countersignature by a responsible minister, as is the case under the parliamentary system.

Foreign Relations In the exercise of these executive powers under either system, the executive is by no means free from legislative control. Thus in the sphere of foreign relations, while the executive is charged with the direction of the diplomatic and consular services, the appointment and transfer of such personnel, the negotiation of treaties, and the formulation of the principal lines of foreign policy, the legislature of the modern democratic state must approve some or all treaties (by vote of one or both houses) before they become effective, provide funds to carry out foreign policies, and sometimes share the power of appointment of high-ranking diplomats. It alone has the power to declare war.

In practice, the executive can, by its conduct of foreign relations, create an international situation that leaves the legislature little choice other than a declaration of war. The longest "war" in the history of the United States, however, was fought in South Vietnam between 1961 and 1973 without a formal declaration of war by the Congress. Presidents Kennedy, Johnson, and Nixon were able to escalate United States military involvement in Southeast Asia almost at will, claiming that Congress's continuing votes for money appropriations to fight the war (and the Gulf of Tonkin Resolution of 1964) constituted legislative authorization for the executive's war policies. With the Vietnamese war uppermost in its mind, the Congress in late 1973 thus passed legislation limiting the power of the president to commit United States troops to foreign battle without explicit authorization from Congress. But even the most "dovish" members of Congress admit that in a nuclear age, diplomacy and foreign policy decisions that may risk the lives of millions of citizens must frequently be made without direct reference to their elected representatives in the legislature. In this sense, the technology of modern communications and weapons systems supersedes the constitutional requirements for decision making.

Executive Authority and Legislative Prerogative
Other executive functions are also subject to varying degrees of legislative control. Executive officers may engage in only those activities authorized by law, and they are subject to a vast body of legal directions and restrictions, which the legislature revises from time to time. The administration of each department is reviewed annually by the legislature when its budget is voted, and funds may be cut if the legislature disapproves its administration. Legislative investigations constitute another potent weapon of legislative control. In the United States, legislative approval is required for appointment to the more important executive and administrative positions. In all democratic countries, the adoption of civil service laws has placed many lesser positions beyond the reach of executive discretion by requiring competitive examinations of all applicants. Although the power of the executive to issue orders, rules, regulations, and ordinances is extensive and constantly expanding in all democracies, it is circumscribed by either the legislature or the courts. Under the parliamentary system, the legislature, which grants such power, can reprimand or remove a government that exceeds or misuses it.

The democratic chief executive (either nominal or actual) also performs many traditional functions in the legislative sphere, such as calling the legislature into session, adjourning or dissolving it, summoning special sessions, sending messages, introducing legislation or causing it to be introduced, and vetoing bills. Detailed provisions vary from country to country. Some democratic governments are still characterized by legislative supremacy over the executive; Italy is a good example of this type of relationship. However, the power of dissolution provided by the 1946 constitution curbs legislative irresponsibility. Great Britain is usually described as having a government dominated by the Cabinet rather than by Parliament. In the American federal government the balance shifts from time to time; a strong president may dominate Congress, while a weaker one may be overridden by it.

How Democratic Chief Executives Are Chosen

All democratic chief executives are elected, directly or indirectly. Indeed, most present-day dictators, despite the fact that they may owe their positions to revolution, seem to take pleasure in claiming that they wield their absolute powers with the full consent and enthusiastic support of their peoples.

In democratic states, there are three methods of electing the chief executive: (1) direct popular election, (2) indirect election by an electoral college, and (3) election by the national parliament. The United States belongs theoretically in the second category, but actually in the first. The German Weimar Republic employed direct popular election to choose its president; so does the French Fifth Republic, following the referendum of November 7, 1962. Direct election of the chief executive, since World War II, has been practiced in twenty-nine countries (some of which, however, are not genuine democracies),[26] in all the American states, and in most American cities.

Indirect election by an electoral college or special convention is found in only six nations: Finland, India, Lebanon, Pakistan, West Germany, and the United States. Election by both houses of the national legislature is the method in eight countries (Italy, Switzerland, Austria, the Soviet Union, Guatemala, Burma, Turkey, and Egypt). In forty-one countries, many of which are dominated by a communist party, the chief of state is elected either by a unicameral parliament or by the lower house alone. In Yugoslavia, the constitution proclaimed in 1963 made Tito president for life.

It is obvious that direct popular election is the most democratic method of choosing the executive; it imposes an additional responsibility upon the voters, thus providing them with a desirable experience in citizenship, and it provides a responsible chief executive who can speak for the whole people. On the other hand, the electorate has not always chosen wisely (as in the election of Louis Napoleon in France in 1848); hence conservatives generally incline toward indirect election, which, however, is both undemocratic and also conducive to providing a weak executive, particularly where he is chosen by the legislature and is dependent on it. An electoral college can easily be transformed by the party system into the equivalent of direct popular election.

THE JUDICIAL BRANCH

We have already considered in broad outline the nature, sources, and main systems of law. We must now give attention to the role of the judicial establishment in a democracy.

Judicial Independence

The judiciary of a democratic state occupies an especially eminent position and exercises extremely important functions. Basic to democratic doctrine is the principle that the judicial branch must be independent. This is interpreted to mean that judges must be impartial and must be protected from political influence or other pressures that might affect their decisions. Hence judges usually hold office "during good behavior"—which in practice means life tenure—and they can be removed only for serious offenses and by a difficult process. Adequate salaries and social prestige also help to render the judge immune to economic and social temptations. In all democratic countries members of the judiciary, especially of the higher courts, are accorded great popular respect and esteem— usually far more than is manifested toward the political branches of the government.

In the United States, where one of the most cherished principles is that of a "government of laws and not of men," we have strengthened the independent position of the judiciary by means of the doctrine of the separation of powers. Our state and federal constitutions expressly provide for a judicial establishment as one of the three coordinate branches of government. Our constitutions go even further by establishing particular courts, conferring jurisdiction upon them, and often providing

---

[26]These are Algeria, Bolivia, Brazil, Chile, Colombia, Costa Rica, Cyprus, Dominican Republic, Ecuador, Ghana, Guatemala, Guinea, Haiti, Honduras, the Republic of Ireland, Liberia, Mexico, Nicaragua, Panama, Paraguay, Peru, the Philippines, Portugal, Salvador, Sierra Leone, Tunisia, Uruguay, and Venezuela.

for the number, qualifications, and selection of judges. In England, Parliament can, and in France under the Third Republic parliament could, by statute create, alter, or abolish courts and determine all other judicial matters, such as jurisdiction, procedure, and the selection and tenure of judges. Despite this apparent legislative supremacy, custom prevented improper legislative or political encroachments. The English judiciary is thoroughly independent and free from political or other interference, and the judiciaries of most other democratic nations also enjoy comparable degrees of independence. However, under the present Fifth Republic in France, judges appear to lack complete independence from either local popular pressures or central government influence.

Overlapping Authorities As was pointed out in Chapter 3, it is impossible to achieve, in practice, a literal and perfect application of the principles of the separation of powers and of checks and balances. Many activities of government cannot be classified as clearly and exclusively legislative, executive, or judicial. Accordingly, each branch is usually assigned duties that do not strictly belong within its sphere. Thus the courts often perform functions that are not strictly judicial in nature, such as appointing certain officials, redrawing the boundaries of election districts when the state legislature has failed to reapportion its membership, administering estates, appointing receivers for bankrupt businesses, and issuing injunctions and other writs to prevent or compel certain actions by other public officials. Similarly, the principle of checks and balances seldom if ever ensures a perfect balance of power among the executive, legislative, and judicial branches; moreover, the checks that each can exert upon the others are seldom completely reciprocal. Therefore, as has already been noted with regard to legislative-executive relations, one branch of government tends, because of forces and conditions present in a particular country, to become predominant over the other branches. In the United States there exists what some writers have called "government by judiciary." This judicial supremacy is based on the power of the United States Supreme Court to declare federal and state laws invalid if they conflict with the Court's interpretation of the Constitution. Since 1937, however, the United States Supreme Court has undergone what some have termed a "revolution," adopting a much broader view of federal powers; in recent years very few legislative acts have been held invalid, and the Supreme Court—in its interpretation of the Constitution—has concentrated more on the redefinition of civil liberties as affected by the actions of police and other administrative bodies.

The Judicial Process

Even where the greatest care is taken in democracies to secure the services of high-minded, impartial judges, the human element creeps inevitably into the judicial process. Judges, however distinguished, are still men—not gods sitting upon Olympus and judging the controversies of mortals with complete detachment. Judicial decisions are subtly influenced by the educational backgrounds, experiences, and philosophies of the judges, even when they are consciously striving to be impartial. The judicial process is not purely rational, mechanical, and legalistic. It involves more than the mere weighing and counting of precedents on either side of the controversy. Precedents are not always clear in their meaning; they can be interpreted in many ways. The legal vocabulary is filled with broad terms and phrases that are subject to many divergent interpretations. It is the function and duty of the democratic judiciary, especially in a common-law country (where law is developed over time and is based on judicial precedent), to interpret the law and to determine its meaning when new problems and situations arise. New conditions and changing judicial personnel will produce varying interpretation of what the law is. This is inevitable and, indeed, desirable.

The Rule of Precedent Judicial realization of the need for flexibility in the law is shown by the reluctance of courts to overrule earlier precedents explicitly; the courts much prefer to base new rulings on distinctions that they find in the case before them, thus leaving the earlier decision for future use as a precedent, should the need arise. When this is done, the court has many alternatives open to it: the old rule, a conflicting rule, and exceptions to both.

When a court in a common-law country is dealing with a case, it can follow precedents established in previous decisions (if any); it can overrule (reject) such precedents (unless it is an inferior court and hence compelled to follow rules laid down by the higher, or appellate, tribunal); or it can distinguish those cases or precedents which stand in the way of the decision at which the court wishes to arrive. "Distinguishing" a case means pointing out how and why the precedent does not apply to the instant case and, therefore, why it does not constitute a precedent that the court is obliged to follow. Any lawyer worthy of the name is adept at this process, and an experienced judge is a past master of the art.

For example, under Chief Justice Marshall (chief justice from 1801 to 1835), the Supreme Court interpreted the commerce clause of the Constitution as giving Congress unlimited authority to regulate commercial activities involving two or more states and also to regulate the transportation of goods crossing state boundaries. Subsequent Supreme Court decisions, beginning with those of Chief Justice Taney (chief justice from 1836 to 1864), progressively limited congressional authority in these areas, and the "laissez faire" Court of the late nineteenth and early twentieth centuries consistently declared unconstitutional the efforts of state and federal legislatures to regulate interstate commerce. After 1937, however, the Supreme Court rapidly withdrew from this area of judicial activism, declaring that Congress had plenary authority to regulate interstate commerce and even *intra*state commerce (which inevitably had an impact on interstate commerce). The words of the Constitution remained the same throughout this checkered history of judicial interpretation of the commerce clause: "The Congress shall have power . . . to regulate commerce . . . among the several states . . ." (Article I, Section 8). But there were obviously some major alterations in constitutional interpretation along the way.

Judicial Argument

An important influence upon judicial argument in the United States has been the development of the Brandeis-Goldmark type of brief and its extensive use by lawyers in presenting cases to the courts. Named after the late Justice Brandeis of the United States Supreme Court and his wife (whose maiden name was Goldmark), this brief emphasizes economic and social data rather than judicial precedents. The brief was developed when Mr. Brandeis was an attorney representing labor and other less privileged groups and when his wife was active as a social worker. Both had come into intimate contact with the human consequences of bad housing, low wages, child labor, excessively long hours of labor, night work by women, the sweatshop, and other aspects of uncontrolled industrialism. When Attorney Brandeis argued before the courts in support of legislation aimed at remedying these and other social evils, he filled the pages of his briefs with statistics showing how industrial accidents increased during night hours or toward the end of an excessively long working day and how the health of workers was impaired because of the lack of healthful working and living conditions.

This type of legal argument has become widespread in recent years and has compelled judges to give more attention to existing conditions and to place less emphasis on judicial precedent. In its landmark decision of 1954, which declared unconstitutional a state's maintenance of racially segregated schools, the Court also relied on the substantial evidence presented by attornies to the Court; sociological and psychological findings demonstrated that "separate but equal" schools were in fact "inherently unequal."

Judicial Review

Chapter 10 will consider the question of judicial review of legislation. The idea that a national supreme court should have the power to declare void those laws deemed in conflict with the national constitution is essentially an American invention—one of our major contributions to modern democratic government. Hence it is appropriate that judicial review be discussed as an essential part of the American governmental system.

At this point, however, it is well to note that several other nations have also empowered a supreme judicial tribunal to declare the acts of their national parliaments unconstitutional. Among such nations are Australia, Canada, the Federal Republic of Germany, India, Ireland, Italy, and Turkey. In France a constitutional council exercises a limited type of judicial review; organic laws must, and ordinary laws may, be submitted to it. Moreover, the president must consult the council concerning his emergency decrees, but he need not follow the council's advice. At least superficially, the judiciary's authority to invalidate legislation appears to be a serious compromise with the formal principles of representative government. But it may also be true that the preservation of responsible and democratic government leans heavily on the great authority of an independent judiciary.

STUDY-GUIDE QUESTIONS

1 What explains the relative stability and democracy of India, in comparison with most of the rest of the countries of the underdeveloped world?
2 What type of electoral system is used for electing representatives to legislatures in the United States? What would be the effects of electing representatives according to proportional representation?
3 Distinguish between the parliamentary and presidential systems of government. Which do you prefer? Why?
4 How would you characterize the prevailing trends in executive-legislative relationships? How do you explain these trends?
5 How is it possible to reconcile the power and role of national judiciaries, which are almost invariably composed of nonelected and life-tenured judges, with the principles of democracy?

REFERENCES

Apter, David E. (ed.): *Ideology and Discontent*, The Free Press, New York, 1964.
Banks, Arthur S., and Robert Textor: *The Cross-Polity Survey*, The M.I.T. Press, Cambridge, Mass., 1963.
Barnard, Chester I.: *The Functions of the Executive*, Harvard University Press, Cambridge, Mass., 1971.
Birch, A. H.: *Representation*, Frederick A. Praeger, Inc., New York, 1972.
Black, C. E.: *The Dynamics of Modernization: A Study in Comparative History*, Harper & Row, Publishers, Incorporated, New York, 1966.
Blondel, Jean: *Comparative Legislatures*, Prentice-Hall, Inc., Englewood Cliffs, N.J., 1973.
Burns, James M.: *Presidential Government: The Crucible of Leadership*, Houghton Mifflin Company, Boston, 1966.
Corwin, Edward S.: *Court over Constitution: A Study of Judicial Review as an Instrument of Popular Government*, Peter Smith Publisher, Gloucester, Mass., 1957.
Duverger, Maurice: *Political Parties*, Methuen & Co., Ltd., London, 1954.
Eisenstadt, S. N.: *Modernization: Protest and Change*, Prentice-Hall, Inc., Englewood Cliffs, N.J., 1966.
Greene, Thomas H.: *Comparative Revolutionary Movements*, Prentice-Hall, Inc., Englewood Cliffs, N.J., 1974.
Heeger, Gerald A.: *The Politics of Underdevelopment*, St. Martin's Press, Inc., New York, 1974.
Huntington, Samuel P.: *Political Order in Changing Societies*, Yale University Press, New Haven, Conn., 1968.
Koenig, Louis: *The Chief Executive*, rev. ed., Harcourt, Brace & World, Inc., New York, 1968.
Kornberg, A. (ed.): *Legislatures in Comparative Perspective*, McKay Publishing Company, New York, 1973.
Kothari, Rajni: *Politics in India*, Little, Brown and Company, Boston, 1970.
LaPalombara, Joseph: *Politics within Nations*, Prentice-Hall, Inc., Englewood Cliffs, N.J., 1974.
McCord, William: *The Springtime of Freedom: The Evolution of Developing Societies*, Oxford University Press, New York, 1965.
Moore, Barrington, Jr.: *Social Origins of Dictatorship and Democracy: Lord and Peasant in the Making of the Modern World*, Beacon Press, Boston, 1966.
Polsby, Nelson W. (ed.): *Congressional Behavior*, Random House, Inc., New York, 1971.
Rustow, Dankwart A.: *A World of Nations: Problems of Political Modernization*, The Brookings Institution, Washington, 1967.
von der Mehden, Fred R.: *Politics of the Developing Nations*, 2d ed., Prentice-Hall, Inc., Englewood Cliffs, N.J., 1969.

Chapter 9

Politics in the United States: I

COLONIAL BEGINNINGS

When the first shipload of British colonists set sail for America, they carried with them an invisible cargo of old traditions and new hopes. The traditions included the ideas underlying Magna Carta (e.g., jury trial and due process of law), other basic rules of British common law, the social pattern of seventeenth-century England, and notions of representation and parliamentary government. Their hopes were centered on self-improvement—materialistic rather than idealistic. The colonists, who came largely from the middle class, hoped to improve their economic and social status in the New World.

The Role of Religion The Puritans who settled in New England sought to escape the disabilities imposed by the British government on dissenting religious sects, and yet they had no thought of establishing a society characterized by religious toleration. Instead, they sought to make theirs the established church, which indeed became as intolerant as the Anglican and developed into a theocracy, i.e., a government by ecclesiastical authorities and godly persons.

There were religious qualifications for voting and for public office. Only members of the established (Congregational) church were legally freemen and as such entitled to vote; in 1650, only about one-fifth of the adult male population enjoyed this status. The church was a closed corporation; the members of the congregation were less than eager to share their political power with those seeking admission, and they quite understandably adopted an exclusive attitude. The clergy was predominant in public affairs; the annual election sermon by the reigning preacher (such as Cotton Mather, Increase Mather, or John Cotton) determined the political outcome. The preacher was more powerful than the governor; a citizen was once fined £40 for daring to criticize a minister. The civil arm of the state was employed to enforce church dogma, and Calvinist standards of personal behavior were written into law and enforced upon all citizens, regardless of their religious beliefs. Freedoms of speech, the press, and assembly were conspicuous by their absence, and the government's control over economic as well as moral matters was complete.

However, the seeds of future democracy were present in early Puritanism. The internal government of the Congregational church was democratic, at least in principle; each congregation was a tiny republic, electing its pastor and church officers independently of other congregations. Each New England town and village enjoyed local self-government through the town meeting, in which all qualified voters participated directly. As in ancient Athens, such church or village democracy was confined to a minority of the adult population, but it served as a precedent for the future spread of the democratic idea.

The social contract doctrine, already discussed, provided another sturdy seed of democracy. The principle was familiar in the colonies and had, indeed, been put into practice in the Mayflower Compact. Roger Williams, the religious rebel who left Massachusetts to establish Providence Plantations (later Rhode Island), accepted the social contract idea and used it to support his then novel notions of separation of church and state, religious toleration, and popular sovereignty. The Fundamental Orders of Connecticut, in 1639, provided a concrete instance of a new community founded upon a social contract. The progressive governmental arrangements in Rhode Island (including the popular referendum and recall, a unicameral legislature, and a highly flexible constitution) and the more limited democracy set up in Connecticut served as examples to be followed elsewhere, though not until much later. The suffrage continued to be based on property ownership long after religious qualifications began to recede; eloquent Revolutionary orations about the sovereign people obscured the fact that in most colonies, only those who owned a substantial amount of real property could vote in 1776.

THE REVOLUTIONARY ERA

Despite certain differences, the thirteen colonies had developed along broadly similar lines, particularly with respect to their common English heritage, political philosophy, governmental organization, and attitude toward the mother country. English traditions and customs had been modified by the frontier environment, as in the adaptation of many rules of the common law to meet American conditions. The political ideas of the colonists on the eve of the Revolution reflected political events, controversies, and writings in England and France, as well as in America, during the seventeenth and eighteenth centuries. Colonial concepts of the social contract and popular sovereignty had been reinforced by the English revolution of 1688 and the writings of John Locke; ideals of civil liberty had been reaffirmed in the English Bill of Rights of 1689; notions of natural law and natural rights had found support in French philosophical writings; and William Penn's ideas of democracy had been shaped in part by the English Levelers. Even more specific political concepts, such as rotation in office, the separation of powers, and checks and balances, had found their way into American thought through the writings of Harrington and Montesquieu. Ideas of limited government, a distrust of executive power, and talk of judicial supremacy and of a "government of laws, not of men" were as much the result of English as of American developments.

Toward Independence Grievances against England varied somewhat among the colonies, with the Northern seaboard area rather more aroused than the agricultural South over British trade restrictions. Yet when the mother country adopted a clearly coercive attitude and decided to station British troops in the colonies at the latter's expense, the thirteen colonies united in resistance. At first, colonial protests consisted mainly of legalistic arguments based on the language of colonial charters or the spirit of the British constitution. Their rights as Englishmen were said to include trial by their peers (i.e., for violations of the Navigation Acts), no taxation without representation, and freedom from arbitrary decrees.

When such arguments proved unavailing, colonial spokesmen turned to broad philosophical arguments concerning the natural rights of man, the social contract theory (of Locke, not Hobbes), popular sovereignty, the consent of the governed, and the corollary right of revolution. As this stage was reached, leadership was increasingly assumed by more liberal and radical elements, displacing earlier spokesmen for conservative commercial interests. Samuel Adams and Thomas Paine roused the artisans, laborers, tenants, and poor farmers by their appeals to the people to achieve not only independence from England but the realities of democracy in America, thus sharpening the social conflict between privilege and poverty already evident in England as well.

Early Constitutions As armed struggle began, the colonies (now states) reconstructed their governments along democratic lines. New state constitutions contained affirmations of popular sovereignty and bills of rights and cut the power of government to the bone. The desire for weak government and broad individual liberty left a large sphere of anarchy within, as well as among, the newly independent states. The state governor was reduced to virtual impotence; in most states he was elected by the legislature for a one-year term and possessed neither the power of veto nor that of independent appointment of lesser officials. The fear of executive power, born of arbitrary monarchs and their colonial appointees, remains an American political stereotype. Ever since 1776, an uphill struggle has been necessary to confer upon governors, mayors, and presidents even the irreducible minimum of executive authority needed for effective government.

By contrast, the early state legislatures were viewed with greater confidence; as the repositories of popular sovereignty, they exercised most of the limited powers enjoyed by state governments. Bicameralism was continued in eleven of the original thirteen states, both houses now being popularly elected. However, despite the influence of revolutionary propaganda for democracy, the suffrage remained restricted to property owners. The court system set up during the colonial period was left virtually intact, except that election of judges by the state legislature (in five states) replaced the earlier method of appointment. The practically inseparable doctrines of the separation of powers and of checks and balances found expression in all the new state constitutions.

THE MAKING OF THE CONSTITUTION
Background

The Declaration of Independence had asserted that "these colonies are, and of right ought to be, free and independent states." Each state thus became completely sovereign. The need for concerted action during the Revolutionary War and the general need for government, regardless of military circumstances, eventually led to the adoption of the Articles of Confederation. They provided a semblance of national government, although unanimity among the states was required to amend the Articles. There was neither a national executive branch nor a national judiciary; all the very limited governmental powers conferred on the Confederation were exercised by the Continental Congress. In this body, each state had one vote; its members were appointed and recalled by the various state governments.

Weak as the state governments were, the Confederation was even weaker; indeed, on paper it resembled the ill-fated League of Nations rather than a national government. The Congress of the Confederation had no power to levy taxes, regulate interstate or foreign commerce, or pass laws directly affecting individuals. It could not compel the states to honor either their own promises or the treaties made by Congress, and in the absence of a national executive with such powers of enforcement, the states went their several ways with only coincidental concern for the general welfare.

Economic Problems The Revolutionary War had disrupted earlier patterns of trade and commerce, particularly with foreign nations. Further economic dislocations resulted from the conflicting legislation passed by state legislatures, several of which were controlled by radical and debtor-farmer elements. State tariffs caused the collapse of both interstate and foreign trade. Thirteen different—but equally worthless—state currencies also helped to strangle all commercial and credit activities. The depreciated paper money of one state was refused in all its sister states and by European merchants. Interstate debts could not be collected because of the lack of a national judiciary and because the state courts seldom accorded justice to a "foreigner" from another state. Despite the easy bankruptcy laws and inflationary currency measures passed by debtor-dominated legislatures, actual violence was resorted to by a mob of debtor farmers in Massachusetts (Shays' Rebellion) to prevent farm foreclosures.

The impact of these developments on the conservative propertied classes can readily be imagined. All credit dried up, except that the well-to-do speculated in paper money and other public obligations (in the hope of their ultimate redemption at face value) and also in Western public lands. There was growing discussion among solid citizens of the need for a national government strong enough to maintain order, protect property, and promote business development. It is significant that the movement resulting in the making of our Constitution was clearly a demand for stronger, not weaker, central government and for a government with new and considerable powers over the economic life of the emerging nation.

The Constitutional Convention

Virginia and Maryland, as a consequence of their efforts to settle certain questions concerning the navigation of the Potomac River, invited other states to participate in broader discussions of common problems. Only five states sent representatives[1] to a gathering held in September 1786, which thereupon drew up a resolution proposing that delegates from all the states meet in Philadelphia in May 1787 to consider the entire problem of government. The Congress of the Confederation endorsed the proposal, and on May 25, 1787, the convention held its opening session.

The call for the convention had made no reference to drafting a new constitution, and the fifty-five delegates[2] (not one of whom had been elected by the people) carried instructions confining their powers to consideration of possible revisions of the Articles of Confederation. Nevertheless, the delegates soon discovered that a new frame of government was necessary.

The fifty-five delegates constituted a small body for such a momentous task; the average attendance at sessions was about thirty or thirty-five. Rhode Island refused to send a delegation to such a conservative gathering, and New Hampshire was late in sending its. Moreover, the delegates were not truly representative of the country as a whole; most of them came from urban, not rural, areas, and almost all came from the well-to-do classes. "Not one was a frontiersman or a wage-earner, and only one had a small-farmer background."[3] Forty delegates owned public securities; fourteen held land for speculation; twenty-four were moneylenders; eleven were in mercantile, manufacturing, or shipping businesses; and fifteen were slave owners.[4] Many of the most active delegates were young men; e.g., James Madison was thirty-six, and Alexander Hamilton was thirty. Only twelve were over fifty-four; six were under thirty-one. About half were college graduates. Only eight of the delegates had been among the signers of the Declaration of Independence. A new, conservative leadership had replaced the revolutionists of 1776, and the desire for order and stability caused liberty to be quoted at a discount.

As for democracy, only Benjamin Franklin (almost eighty-two) held it in high favor. Almost every one of the convention's leaders spoke of democracy's dangers and evils, not of its virtues. Such democrats as Patrick Henry, Thomas Jefferson, John Hancock, Samuel Adams, and Thomas Paine were absent.

Main Characteristics of the Constitution

There is neither space nor need to repeat here the well-known details of the various compromises arrived at by the convention to reconcile conflicts

---

[1] Nine states appointed delegates, but only those from five appeared.

[2] Seventy-four delegates were originally designated to attend, but only fifty-five actually did so.

[3] F. A. Ogg and P. O. Ray, *Introduction to American Government*, 12th ed., Appleton-Century-Crofts, Inc., New York, 1962, p. 20.

[4] The American historian Charles A. Beard declared that at least five-sixths of the delegates "were immediately, directly, and personally interested in the outcome of their labors at Philadelphia, and were to a greater or less extent econimic beneficiaries from the adoption of the Constitution." *An Economic Interpretation of the Constitution of the United States,* The Macmillan Company, New York, 1913, p. 149.

between the large and the small states, over slavery, over the regulation of commerce, and over the taxation of imports. However, it is important to note the spirit and character of the arrangements embodied in the Constitution. Its outstanding characteristics were (1) its conservatism, (2) its emphasis on stability rather than change, and (3) the significant powers that it conferred upon the new federal government.

Conservatism Conservatism was manifest in (1) the suffrage arrangements, (2) the series of checks placed on popular legislation, and (3) the device of judicial review. The federal suffrage was left to be determined by the states, wherein property and other qualifications made voting the privilege of perhaps 6 percent of the total adult male population. Only persons qualified to vote for the more numerous house of their state legislature were to vote for members of the federal House of Representatives—the only federal officials to be popularly elected.[5]

Even a 6 percent democracy was viewed with deep apprehension by the framers. The presumably rash legislation emanating from the House would be checked by a Senate, which, in addition to providing equal representation for both large and small states, would be composed of older and presumably wealthier men, chosen (for longer terms) not by the people but by state legislatures. If the Senate concurred with the House, both could be blocked by the presidential veto, made difficult to override; the president would be chosen neither by the people nor by Congress, but by an electoral college intended to be independent of political pressures. Thus legislative proposals would need to clear three successive hurdles: a House chosen by a restricted electorate, a Senate indirectly elected through state legislatures, and a chief executive chosen by yet another process. Pervading these arrangements was the apparent belief that delay, and even deadlock, was preferable to hasty action.

Judicial review was to provide a further check on legislation, in addition to maintaining the balance of the federal system. A long dispute among scholars as to whether the framers of the Constitution intended the Supreme Court to have the power to nullify federal and state legislation seems finally to have been resolved in the affirmative. Precedents for such judicial review had been provided during colonial times by decisions of the Judicial Committee of the Privy Council in London and, after 1776, by several decisions by state supreme courts holding state laws unconstitutional. Alexander Hamilton, writing in *The Federalist* (a magnificent piece of political propaganda published to secure the ratification of the Constitution), declared that constitutional limitations on legislative authority "can be preserved in practice no other way than through the medium of courts of justice, whose duty it must be to declare all acts contrary to the manifest tenor of the Constitution void."[6]

The Emphasis on Stability Stability of governmental institutions and policies has been a desideratum of many eminent political philosophers, beginning with Plato and Aristotle, and thus the Founding Fathers found themselves in impeccable company as they spelled out arrangements to spare the new American system from the convulsions of confusion and rapid change. These arrangements fall under three main headings: (1) the separation of powers, coupled with checks and balances; (2) the difficult method of amending the Constitution; and (3) the new powers of the federal government, which, as already indicated, were in themselves a significant feature of the new American political system.

Already embodied in the new state constitutions, the principles of separation of powers and of

---

[5] Some estimates place the figure even lower than 6 percent. It has been stated that in our first national election (in 1789), "only about one out of every thirty adult Americans was legally eligible to vote." Hugh A. Bone and Austin Ranney, *Politics and Voters*, McGraw-Hill Book Company, New York, 1963, p. 7. The conservative and economically elitist orientation of the Founding Fathers, first documented by Charles A. Beard (cited above), has been challenged by the interpretations of several more contemporary scholars, notably Robert E. Brown, *Charles Beard and the Constitution*, Princeton University Press, Princeton, N.J., 1956. But statistical support for Beard's arguments may be found in Lee Benson, *Turner and Beard: American Historical Writing Reconsidered*, The Free Press of Glencoe, Inc., New York, 1960. And earlier research, by E. Wilder Spaulding, *New York in the Critical Period, 1783–1789*, Columbia University Press, New York, 1932, also confirms Beard's findings, although Spaulding's study is ignored in Professor Brown's book. While the details may be debated, there is ample evidence to support the generalization that political participation in the early United States was reserved to a privileged minority.

[6] *The Federalist*, No. 78.

checks and balances were carried over to the new federal governmental structure, but without explicit affirmation in the actual language of the Constitution. However, Article 1 deals with the legislative power; Article 2, with the executive branch; and Article 3, with the judiciary—and in such plain terms that the Supreme Court, from the very beginning, assumed and declared these maxims to be basic to the American system of government. With each of the three branches chosen in a different way, abrupt or extreme changes in public policy would be very difficult, and to judge from the views of Hamilton, Madison, and John Jay as expressed in *The Federalist,* the scales of the check-and-balance system were to be tipped against the legislature and in favor of the executive and judicial branches. Hamilton, in particular, favored a strong executive branch ("Good government requires energy in the executive") and did not want to see the executive and legislative check each other too far because this would make impossible the development of the strong federal government he desired. There is, indeed, a paradox in the adoption of the separation of powers and of checks and balances by men who, with few exceptions, wanted a strong central government with ample powers, economic as well as political. Apparently the fear of debtor-class legislation caused the framers to choose the risk of stalemate rather than that of possibly radical legislation, even though the existing suffrage laws seemed certain to put the well-born and well-to-do in firm control of the new national government.

A second device to ensure stability was the difficult method of amending the Constitution. Actually, four possible methods were provided, but all were equally difficult to implement. Of the twenty-six amendments thus far adopted, the first ten were ratified by state conventions, as was the Constitution itself. All the rest except one were ratified by majority vote of the legislatures of three-fourths of the states. The Twenty-first Amendment, which repealed the Eighteenth (Prohibition) Amendment, was ratified by majority vote of specially chosen conventions in the several states. Up to and including the Twenty-sixth Amendment, all amendments adopted have been proposed by a two-thirds vote of both houses of Congress. This same procedure was followed in the proposal and ratification of what was likely to become (in 1975 or 1976) the Twenty-seventh Amendment to the Constitution: "Equality of rights under the law shall not be denied or abridged by the United States or by any state on account of sex."

Nevertheless, there has been much criticism of the amending process ever since the Constitution was adopted; some critics believe that it is too slow and difficult, others claim that it is too easy, and still others think that it is not sufficiently democratic, particularly in view of the fact that minorities can control the fate of proposed amendments. Any combination of thirteen states can defeat an amendment; the thirteen least populous states, which contain slightly over 4 percent of our total national population, could defeat the will of the remaining 96 percent. Fortunately, this has never happened, but the mere possibility proves the undemocratic character of the amending procedure. By contrast, in every one of the fifty states, constitutional amendments must be submitted to a popular referendum. Of course, the Founding Fathers feared democracy; yet even such a staunch Federalist as Chief Justice Marshall called the amending process "unwieldy and cumbrous." Although the total of twenty-six (or twenty-seven) amendments refutes the charge of utter rigidity, one may well doubt whether governmental adaptations to not only the technological but also the nuclear era can indefinitely be accomplished through methods devised by men afraid of social change.

New Governmental Powers The new powers of the federal government represented not only a stabilizing check upon the supposedly impetuous innovations that the states might undertake but also a long step toward national unity, centralized government, and (however unpalatable the thought may be in some circles today) economic and social collectivism. The powers of Congress to tax, to regulate interstate and foreign commerce, to coin money and regulate its value, to admit new states, to administer the territories, to maintain military and naval forces, to borrow money, to establish uniform bankruptcy laws, and to make all laws necessary and proper for carrying into execution the foregoing powers—all these, particularly as interpreted by the Supreme Court, have produced a new leviathan, sovereign not only in the international but also in the internal sphere.

The Founding Fathers wanted stability and economic security; they saw its realization in a powerful central authority that they created and at first controlled. They were—almost to the man—mercantilists. The idea of laissez faire capitalism, as enunciated by Adam Smith in *The Wealth of Nations* in 1776, required three or four decades to become part of the American climate of opinion. The language of the Constitution (especially such words as "commerce" and "regulate") should be interpreted in accordance with the dictionaries of that day, not ours. If these old lexicons are consulted, it becomes clear that commerce included manufacture and, indeed, everything except the production of articles to be consumed within the family. Hence the congressional power to regulate commerce was originally virtually unlimited. A century later, a Supreme Court subservient to commercial interests seeking complete independence from both state and federal control narrowed the definition of interstate commerce almost to preclude federal regulation.

The new powers of the federal government were matched by significant restrictions upon the states, which were forbidden to coin money; issue bills of credit; enter into treaties; pass bills of attainder, ex post facto laws, or laws impairing the obligation of contracts; keep troops or ships of war in time of peace; or impose duties on imports or exports. The prohibitions relating to currency, credit, and contract impairment plainly reflected the preceding era of inflation and easy bankruptcy laws; the ban on state-imposed duties was designed to prevent roadblocks to interstate and foreign trade.

The Struggle over Ratification

Because of the demonstrated difficulty (if not impossibility) of amending the Articles of Confederation under the rule of unanimity, and also because of considerable criticism of the convention and the proposed constitution, the framers provided that the new document was to go into operation when ratified by nine states acting through conventions specially chosen for this purpose. Conventions were to be employed rather than state legislatures because many of the latter were still controlled by radical elements.

Even with this reduced requirement of only 70 percent, rather than all, of the states, the new constitution was by no means assured of ratification. In particular, it seemed very doubtful for a time whether such important states as Virginia and New York would ratify. In the Massachusetts state convention, flattery was necessary to win John Hancock and Samuel Adams over to the proratification side; even then, the victory turned on the slim margin of nineteen votes. In New York, the masterly skill of Hamilton, Madison, and Jay in *The Federalist* was necessary to turn the tide in favor of ratification, which carried by only a three-vote margin. With the announcement that nine states had ratified, the remainder followed suit; even Rhode Island, which had sent no delegates to Philadelphia, brought up the rear of the procession by ratifying early in 1790.

Legitimacy of the Constitution Although the question has long since become purely academic, it is interesting to ask whether our Constitution was itself constitutional in the manner of its adoption. Delegates without authority to do more than amend the Articles of Confederation, and representing only twelve of the thirteen states, had brought forth a proposed new constitution. Amendments to the Articles required ratification by all the states before becoming effective. The Constitution was proclaimed as in effect after the ninth state had ratified; thus at this point—and despite later additional ratifications—it *was* an unconstitutional constitution. Some writers have described the Constitutional Convention as marking the second American revolution; others have termed it a coup d'état engineered by conservative interests.

Both characterizations are extreme and unwarranted, but they serve to emphasize an important fact: The framers of the Constitution were not interested primarily in legalisms or in whether their proposals were strictly in accordance with the proprieties of the Articles of Confederation. They were, however, deeply concerned with the political, economic, and social dilemmas plaguing the country and were determined to bring order out of the chaos surrounding them. To say that they were practical and business-minded is no reproach; they knew they were confronted by conditions, not theories, and acted accordingly. They built a government whose powers were to be commensurate with its problems; unlike Thomas Jefferson, they did not believe that the least government was necessarily the best government.

Significance and Contributions of the Constitution

The United States Constitution, by the simple fact of its adoption and implementation, became a landmark along the road of modern government. Its mere existence was a contribution to the science of government; it proved that written, republican constitutions were feasible and real—that they could be transferred from the pages of philosophical writings to animate the institutions and processes of actual political life. Probably the three chief American contributions to political science have been (1) the demonstration of the practicality of a written constitution, (2) large-scale federalism, and (3) judicial supremacy. To these might well be added the later proof that popular government, combined with the representative principle, could be applied to a large area (virtually a continent), contrary to the earlier notions of both ancient Greek and eighteenth-century writers, who held that democracy was possible only in small city-states or tiny communities.

Institutionalizing the Rule of Law As has already been noted, written constitutions are no more than a core around which, with the passage of time, accretions of custom, judicial interpretation, and political practice tend to accumulate. Quite apart from formal amendment and explicit judicial rulings, our Constitution has developed many understandings, informal precedents, and accepted habits that are in many ways analogous to the conventions or customs of the British constitution—not legally enforceable, but observed as faithfully as the law of that constitution. American examples would include the transformation of the electoral college by the rise of political parties, the custom of insisting that a representative reside in the district in which he seeks election, and the development, as a collective body, of the presidential cabinet. The Constitution today reflects a growth that has been due more to custom, judicial interpretation, congressional statutes filling out and completing constitutional provisions, and accepted practices of all three branches of the federal government than to formal amendment.

Undoubtedly the most significant thing about our Constitution is not so much the fact that it is written as the fact that it expresses the belief in the supremacy of the Constitution over all mere government. This is explicitly stated in Article 6: "This Constitution . . . shall be the supreme law of the land." Thus all government, state and federal alike, and all officers of the government, up to and including the president, were to be restrained by this higher law—now a *written* embodiment of the concepts of natural law, right reason, and limited government that had long been part of the heritage of European (and particularly English) political thought. Constitutionalism—synonymous with limited, as opposed to arbitrary, government—was now spelled out with clarity, simplicity, and admirable brevity. The continuing force of these principles could be demonstrated no more dramatically than by the Supreme Court's unanimous decision, in 1974, that not even appeals to executive privilege or national security can elevate a president above the law.

THE AMERICAN FEDERAL SYSTEM

The nature, advantages, and defects of federal states have already been discussed. Federalism was not an American invention, but it had never before been attempted on such a vast territorial scale. The new federal government was made one of enumerated powers (some granted expressly, others by implication), whereas the states that had formed and entered into the Union retained powers that were original and inherent, stemming from their sovereignty as proclaimed in the Declaration of Independence. The Tenth Amendment declares that "the powers not delegated to the United States by the Constitution, nor prohibited by it to the States, are reserved to the States respectively, or to the people." Thus all residual powers remained with the states, except insofar as the necessary and proper clause (Article 1, Section 8, final paragraph) empowered Congress to make all laws that might be necessary and proper to implement congressional or other federal powers.

Significantly, under the American political system no government possesses unlimited powers; both the national and state governments fall short of sovereignty in the sense of absolute, unlimited authority. Each is theoretically sovereign in its own particular sphere, and yet in reality *neither* is fully sovereign. The numerous constitutional prohibitions against federal as well as state action operate to create a sphere into which no government may intrude. The Ninth Amendment declares that the enumeration in the Constitution of certain liberties shall not be interpreted "to deny or disparage others retained by the people."

Governmental Powers and Limitations

Three categories of powers and three categories of prohibitions against the use of certain powers are to be found in the Constitution or in its amendments: (1) certain powers (called "exclusive" powers) are given to the national government *only*, e.g., regulation of interstate and foreign commerce, management of foreign relations, and control of the currency; (2) a broad range of power is recognized (but not enumerated) as properly and inherently possessed by the states, e.g., their police power to enact legislation to promote public health, safety, and morals, including the bulk of civil and criminal law, such as the law of property, contracts, and marriage; and (3) certain powers, which were originally possessed by the states and which they may continue to exercise except where forbidden to do so by the Constitution, are shared with the federal government (so-called concurrent powers), e.g., taxation of personal and corporate incomes, enactment of laws within the jurisdiction of each, maintenance of courts, ownership of property, and the power of eminent domain.

The three categories of prohibitions follow the pattern of the categories conferring or recognizing powers: (1) the national government is constitutionally barred from doing many things that the states may do, e.g., levying direct taxes without apportionment among the states according to population and bringing a person accused of a capital or otherwise infamous crime to trial except on indictment by a grand jury; (2) a longer list of "thou shalt not's" restrains the states from actions that may be taken by the federal government, e.g., coining money, making treaties with foreign powers, passing laws impairing the obligation of contracts, taxing imports, and denying the equal protection of the laws; and (3) the realm of individual liberty is further protected against encroachment by means of prohibitions running against both national and state governments—e.g., both are forbidden to pass ex post facto laws or bills of attainder, to grant titles of nobility, or to deprive any person of life, liberty, or property without due process of law.

Growth of Federal Power Great changes have occurred in the pattern of American federalism since 1789. Our original orientation toward strong national government under the aegis of the Federalist party was continued by Chief Justice John Marshall and other Federalist judges long after the party was swept from power in the election of 1800. A series of decisions by Marshall firmly established the principle of judicial supremacy over Congress, the supremacy of the federal government (through the doctrine of implied powers), and the sanctity of private property against encroachment through state legislation. The broad construction of federal powers was supplemented by very strict construction of those of the states.

The Democratic-Republican party of Thomas Jefferson favored states' rights and a strict construction of federal powers, but even Jefferson and his Republican successors (Madison, Monroe) could not turn back the clock. The growth of the nation, the rise of industry, and international events all tended to push out the frontiers of federal power. Jefferson's purchase of Louisiana from France in 1803 was an act of wise statesmanship, but it was also a violation of the dogma of strict construction. Moreover, the longevity of Marshall and other Federalists on the Supreme Court made new constitutional interpretations impossible for more than a third of a century. By the time of Andrew Jackson's appointment of Democratic Roger B. Taney as Marshall's successor, the federal government's powers had become too firmly consolidated to be destroyed or reduced by judicial reinterpretation. Also, with the appearance of new Western states, which, as territories, had developed the habit of looking to Washington for assistance, the states no longer presented a solid opposition to developing national powers.

The Trend toward Centralization

The Civil War, the spanning of the continent by railroads, the rise of huge industrial and financial corporations, the growth of monopoly, the rise of labor and social problems in the wake of technology, and the emergence of the United States as a world power—all exerted pressures toward more centralization in government. Problems that were once easily handled by local governments (e.g., public health, education, roads, and law enforcement) became matters of state concern; others, once within the reach of state regulatory authorities (e.g., railroad and utility rate regulation, child labor, wage-and-hour legislation, and conservation), similarly came to require federal action. New, rapid means of transportation and communication, by increasing human mobility, caused local problems to spread out in their effects, thereby necessitating greater cooperation between cities, states, and the federal government. Criminals and epidemics alike could quickly get beyond the reach of local authorities, and the mobility of both labor and commodities in a nationwide market rendered state regulation of labor and business ineffectual. The clamor, for example, for national laws forbidding child labor or establishing maximum working hours or minimum wages arose because goods produced in a state having humane legislation on such matters would be forced to compete in the national market with the products of states that had not provided such protection. Similarly, corporations chartered and securities issued in states with lax requirements in such matters caused difficulties for safer and sounder businesses in other states—and for the investor as well.

Federal Aid The states have always been markedly unequal in area, population, and resources. Consequently, the more prosperous states have been able to provide good roads, schools, public health services, charitable institutions, police protection, and the like, while the poorer states have lagged behind in meeting these and other social needs of vital national importance. Recognition of the national interest in these and other matters has led to a system of federal grants-in-aid, under which the national government appropriates money to aid certain services or activities falling within the scope of state authority. Such grants are apportioned among the states, presumably on a basis reflecting need, but the states may spend such federal money only for the purpose specified; moreover, they must also appropriate sums for the same purpose (in most cases in amounts equal to the federal grant), and they must submit to inspection and the setting of minimum standards by appropriate federal authorities. Federal aid is now provided for more than sixty varied state or local government activities, including highways, the state militia (now the National Guard), forest-fire prevention and control, vocational education and rehabilitation, public (state) employment offices, old-age assistance (i.e., noncontributory pensions), help for crippled and needy children, and help for the blind. At the present time federal aid is being extended into other fields, such as assistance for elementary, secondary, and university education, although the fear of unduly centralized control over education has produced strong resistance.

Regulatory Authority Despite the traditional American fear of centralization and the persistent belief that democracy is strongest and safest at the local or state level, the trend toward stronger federal control over ever-widening areas of our national life seems bound to continue. Centralization in economics leads to centralization in politics; big business and big labor produce big government. The present inadequacy of the states in the fields of economic and social regulation stems in part from the fact that there is no correlation between the political boundaries of the states and boundaries of the problems to be met. Many problems are too big to be handled—often in contradictory fashion—by several states and at the same time are not big enough to warrant national regulation. However, there is no intermediate governmental unit, such as the long-proposed regions (ten or twelve in number) to be based on natural geographic, social, and economic lines of demarcation.

Hence any problem that grows too large for the states is inevitably dumped into the lap of the national government, with an equally inevitable hue and cry over regimentation and bureaucracy in Washington and dire predictions about the imminent disappearance of the states and of democracy along with them. Those who raise the issue of states' rights are opposed to certain federal policies or programs and seek a legal justification for their opposition. Thus when the Supreme Court was striking down New Deal legislation, it was regarded as the ark of the covenant by conservatives and attacked by liberals; later, when it handed down civil-rights decisions, the liberals came to its defense, and conservatives became its severest critics. The administration of President Eisenhower indicated an intention to slow down, if possible, the trend toward federal centralization, but little was, or has been, accomplished in this direction. Once a bureaucratic apparatus has been established and once the lower levels of government have become dependent on money and services provided by the higher levels of government, the great majority of politicians and administrators—regardless of partisan label or ideological orientation—tend to resist any basic change in ongoing programs or the relationships between the various levels of government.

Centralization and Democracy The centralizing trend has caused the states, in turn, to assume many functions that were formerly in the hands of units of local government. In terms of the number and scope of their activities, the states are doing more than ever before. Actually, federal, state, and local governments have all grown in power and importance because of the multiplicity of problems and tasks thrust upon them by technological progress. The pull of centralization and control reaches down to the very roots of the body politic; the individual citizen is confronted by government wherever he turns.

While such controls *may* conceivably diminish democracy, there is no reason why this *must* happen. Significantly, the trend toward centralization has been matched by the extension of the suffrage and of popular education; our originally oligarchic federal republic has become a democratic republic. If citizens avail themselves of information at their disposal and exercise their power as voters, they can control the national government as readily as that of a state, county, or municipality. Even so ardent an advocate of states' rights and local home rule as Thomas Jefferson felt that if the federal government must grow powerful, it must be controlled by the people themselves, in which case their liberties would remain secure. Today, however, it is also clear that democratic government depends not only on an informed citizenry but also on well-organized and responsible political parties. Political parties may be associated with authoritarian government, but there can be no democracy without them.

Recent Developments

The controversy between the advocates of states' rights and those who wish to expand the functions of the national government is a hardy perennial, although the subject matter of the argument varies from decade to decade. In the 1930s the burning question was whether the national government or the states ought to deal with the economic and social problems arising from the Great Depression; in 1952 it was whether a few states or the nation should have title to tidelands oil deposits. The two major political parties sometimes change sides on this issue. During the New Deal era the Democrats abandoned their historic stand in favor of states' rights and supported national legislation to cope with the Depression. The Republican party, which formerly favored national powers, now viewed with alarm the prospect of effective regulation of business practices by the national government and picked up the banner of states' rights dropped by the Northern and urban-oriented Democrats.

In the 1960s the struggle centered on such issues as the civil rights of black Americans; medical care for the aged under the social security system; federal aid to higher education, both public and private; and the establishment of a Cabinet-rank department of urban affairs and housing. More recently, political debate and legislative action have revolved around the issues of medical insurance for citizens of all ages, the reduction of unemployment through manpower retraining programs, the federal government's sharing of revenue with state governments, the provision of a guaranteed minimum annual income, and, in general, the extension of welfare and regulatory programs already administered by the federal government.

Economic Regulation In 1970 Congress responded to the Nixon administration's concerns over mounting inflation by passing the Economic Stabilization Act. Direct control over wages and prices was thereby added to the federal government's already existing authority to regulate the economy indirectly through such mechanisms as business and agricultural subsidies, tax allowances, government spending and purchasing policies, and the arsenal of fiscal and monetary weapons for economic regulation available to all modern governments. Wage and price controls were imposed by the Nixon administration between 1971 and 1973—with varying degrees of success or failure, depending on the critic's particular perspective. And while President Nixon's Cost of Living Council was abolished in June 1974, one of President Ford's first acts was to secure from Congress in August 1974 legislation that established a Council on Wage and Price Stability. The new council was empowered to "monitor" wages and prices and, inevitably, to advance "guidelines" designed to encourage wage and price restraint.

It is typical of the frequent ironies of politics that it was the Republicans who first made use of these powers, powers that were irreconcilably opposed to the spirit and principles of laissez faire and the free market. But it was probably no coincidence that in November 1972 the United States Chamber of Commerce, the nation's largest business federation and solidly Republican in partisan orientation, went on record as favoring the federal government's implementation of wage and price controls and its continued exercise of some form of direct or indirect authority over the nation's economy.

Modern Society and Big Government This impressive *bipartisan* responsibility for the development of the modern welfare and regulatory state is paralleled in the United States by the extensive cooperation between federal and state governments in the administration of public policy; cooperative federalism is replacing the earlier spirit of competition. Such federal-state cooperation is especially conspicuous in the enforcement of criminal justice, in the administration of programs related to highways and agriculture, and in selected aspects of health and welfare. It also is essential in the context of a modern society, where the economic *inter*dependence of citizens has replaced the relative independence characterizing citizen life in an agrarian society of long ago.

In the United States, the complex role of modern government is perhaps best indicated by the findings reported in 1971 by Tax Foundation, Inc.: One of every three United States citizens was receiving some form of income maintenance support from federal, state, or local government, including 15.7 million government employees and military personnel; 13.8 million recipients (including 7 million children) of varying forms of public assistance; 8.4 million persons on state or local government retirement rolls who were not covered by old-age, survivors', or disability insurance; 5.5 million veterans or their survivors; 2.1 million unemployed; and 1 million persons on the federal government's civil service retirement rosters. The trend toward increasing government involvement in the nation's social life and economy is also dramatically illustrated by the following: Total spending by federal, state, and local government represented 9.5 percent of total national income in 1900; 11.9 percent in 1929; 22.7 percent in 1940; 25.2 percent in 1950; 32.8 percent in 1960; and 39.1 percent in 1970. There is no doubt that an important part of what is meant by "modern living" refers to the characteristics and role of modern government.

CONGRESS

It is obviously impossible to include between the covers of this book a full description of all the complexities of American government. Moreover, this text is designed to introduce the student to all fields of political science and is not intended as a text in American government. Nevertheless, the American political system is so outstanding as an example of democracy in operation that a brief outline of American national government seems clearly in order. Following the tripartite arrangement in the Constitution itself, we shall consider the main features of Congress, the presidency, and the judiciary, in that order.

A bicameral legislative body was adopted by the Constitutional Convention for several reasons. The precedent of the British Parliament, as well as of the colonial legislatures, pointed to a bicameral system. It also permitted an essential compromise between the large and small states on the subject of representation, and in addition, as has already been noted, it provided for a conservative upper house as a check on the popular chamber.

The House of Representatives

Beginning with sixty-five members, the House of Representatives has been enlarged through successive acts of Congress to reach its present size of 435. However, Congress can, if it wishes, further increase or decrease the size of the House. Following the admission of Alaska in 1958 and of Hawaii in 1959, each of these states was temporarily assigned one representative, thus bringing the total membership of the House to 437. The number of representatives was reduced to 435 in 1960, and subsequent population changes in the United States are to be reflected in the redistribution of the 435 House seats among the several states. By the terms of the Constitution each state, no matter how small, must have at least one member. Four states—Alaska, Nevada, Vermont, and Wyoming—have less population than the average number required for a member. According to a law of 1929, the 435 House seats must be reapportioned among the states after each decennial census, which means that rapidly growing states will gain seats at the expense of others. After a census, one seat is assigned to each state, and the 385 seats remaining are then distributed in proportion to state populations.

Gerrymandering However, the number of seats assigned to a state does not guarantee an equitable distribution of congressional representatives *within* that state. Each state legislature bears the responsibility for drawing the boundaries of its congressional districts because, although a few congressmen are elected at large (i.e., from the state as a whole), most of them are chosen from districts. State legislatures, bent on achieving the maximum advantage for the party in power and on maintaining the chronic overrepresentation of rural as against urban areas, all too often gerrymander the districts. This term refers to the practice of so drawing district boundaries as to give the party in power a majority in as many districts as possible. The result is to produce districts grotesque in shape and markedly unequal in population and to make the House of Representatives a badly distorted mirror of the nation. On the basis of the present national population (211 million in 1974), the average population of a congressional district should be approximately 485,000. Actually, as the result of gerrymandering, many congressional districts were initially created that had substantially less than the average, while other districts had far larger populations. In 1964 the smallest district had 177,431, while the largest had 951,527.

Judicial Intervention In 1962 the United States Supreme Court held that the federal courts had the power and the duty to consider the constitutionality of the distribution of seats in state legislatures. The Court said that some apportionments could be so unfair as to violate the clause of the Fourteenth Amendment which forbids any state to "deny to any person within its jurisdiction the equal protection of the laws."[7] In 1964, in *Reynolds v. Sims* (377 U.S. 533), the Court held that both houses of a state legislature must be based on population alone. And by the late 1960s most of the fifty states had adopted reapportionment plans fairly well in line with the principle of "one man, one vote."

Early in 1964 the United States Supreme Court, in a six-to-three decision, held that the Constitution requires that *congressional* districts within a state also be substantially equal in population. Justice Hugo Black, who wrote the majority opinion, further said in a comment from the bench that "the people should have one vote for one man as nearly as that is possible." Justice Black's opinion found the Constitution's requirement for population equality in the language of Article 1, Section 2, paragraph 1, which states that the House of Representatives shall be chosen "by the People of the several States." He declared that "it would defeat the principle embodied in the Great Compromise, equal representation in the House of equal numbers of people, for us to hold that, within the states, legislatures may draw the lines of Congressional districts in such a way as to give some voters a greater voice in choosing a Congressman than others."[8] In his dissenting opinion, Justice John M. Harlan expressed the view that the majority decision would cast doubt on the constitutional status of 398 representatives from thirty-seven states. But the majority's landmark decision still stands, again demonstrating the decisive impact of the Supreme Court on the political process and citizen life as it plays the role of supreme *legislator*—as well as supreme adjudicator of cases and controversies.

---

[7] *Baker v. Carr,* 369 U.S. 186 (1962). This suit was brought by a group of voters in Nashville, Tenn.
[8] *Wesberry et al. v. Sanders et al.,* 376 U.S. 1 (1964). See also the *New York Times,* Feb. 18, 1964.

Suffrage Restrictions Suffrage restrictions also impair the representative character of the House. Some states have required the payment of a poll tax as a condition of voting, and several have imposed literacy tests; three have prohibited voting by paupers. The Twenty-fourth Amendment, ratified on January 23, 1964, bars poll taxes as a qualification for voting in federal elections. The Civil Rights Act of 1964 makes the completion of a sixth-grade education a rebuttable presumption of literacy for voting in any federal election. The Voting Rights Act of 1965 declares that literacy tests and other voter-qualification devices are suspended. Moreover, in states in which less than 50 percent of the residents, qualified by age, are registered to vote or did vote in the November 1964 presidential election, federal voting examiners may be appointed to supervise and control registration and voting. On March 7, 1966, the United States Supreme Court upheld the constitutionality of several key sections of this law.[9]

American citizenship is now required in all states, and the usual residence requirement is one year in the state and shorter periods in the county and voting district. The right to vote is conferred by the states, rather than by the national government; however, the Fifteenth and Nineteenth Amendments forbid the states to deny the right to vote because of race, color, previous condition of servitide, or sex, and the Fourteenth Amendment has been interpreted by the Supreme Court to prohibit other restrictions deemed to involve a denial by the states of the equal protection of the laws or the privileges and immunities of citizenship.

Candidates and Members According to federal law, members of the House of Representatives are elected by districts, by secret ballot, and on the Tuesday following the first Monday in November of each even-numbered year. The two-year term is prescribed by the Constitution itself. A candidate for the House must be at least twenty-five years old, must have been a citizen for at least seven years, must be a resident of the state from which election is sought, and must not be a holder of any other federal office, civil or military. The residence requirement has been narrowed by custom to residence in the particular district that the candidate seeks to represent. In fact, though not in legal theory, additional qualifications have sometimes been added; each house of Congress is declared by the Constitution to be the judge of the elections, returns, and qualifications of its own members, and on various occasions both House and Senate have refused to seat duly elected members deemed unpatriotic, polygamous, or otherwise unacceptable. It is easier for Congress to refuse (by simple majority vote) to seat a newly elected member than to expel him later; the Constitution requires a two-thirds vote for expulsion.

Members of the House and Senate are constitutionally protected against suits for libel or slander based on remarks made in the course of speech or debate in their houses. They are not immune from prosecution for violations of criminal law; however, they cannot be subpoenaed as witnesses or impaneled for jury service.

Salaries for congressmen and senators have long been the subject of controversy. An act of 1946 raised their salaries to $12,500 plus a tax-free expense allowance of $2,500. Early in 1955 this salary was increased to $22,500 a year, and it was raised to $30,000 a year in 1965; eight years later the annual salary for members of both the House and the Senate stood at $42,500.

The Senate

The Senate consists of 100 members, two from each state. Equality of state representation in the Senate was a political necessity in 1787, and its abolition is a political impossibility today. However, the present disparity in population among the states (e.g., California with 20 million as against Alaska with about 300,000) makes the Senate far less representative than in 1789. The direct popular election of senators established by the Seventeenth Amendment could not equate the populations they represented.

Representation Like most state legislatures, and especially their upper houses, the Senate of the United States for a long time underrepresented the urban, industrial centers of population and overrepresented the sparsely populated farming and graz-

---

[9]*South Carolina v. Katzenbach*, Case No. 22 (original), *Law Week*, vol. 34, no. 34, p. 4207, Mar. 8, 1966. Chief Justice Warren delivered the opinion of the Court, relying on the Fifteenth Amendment, Section 2.

ing areas. Small-state senators often wielded a legislative influence out of all proportion to the number of people they represented; obviously, the opportunities for pressure-group influence on such senators were vastly greater than in states with more diversified economic and social structures.

On the other hand, the Senate has proved in most instances since the 1950s to be a more liberal legislative body than the House, in part because the senators from large urban and industrial states must be sensitive to the interests and needs of cities and workers; and, since World War II, most states have developed major urban-industrial centers. It is no coincidence, then, that the liberal Republican Senator Jacob Javits is from New York and the conservative Republican Senator Barry Goldwater is from Arizona. The more liberal orientation of the Senate as compared with the House is also a dramatic reversal of the Founding Fathers' intent to make the House a vehicle for lower-class interests and the Senate a force for conservative restraint.

The term of senators is six years, in contrast to the two-year term of representatives. They are elected from the state as a whole, not from districts. Under the constitutional provision dividing the first senators into three equal groups, with one third retiring after two years, the second third after four years, and the last third after six years, one-third of the total of 100 senators comes up for election every two years. Sometimes this figure is increased as a result of vacancies caused by death or resignation. Suffrage requirements are identical for the election of senators and representatives.

A senator is required to be thirty years of age (at the time of taking his seat), nine years a citizen of the United States, a resident of the state for which he is chosen, and not a holder of any other federal office. He enjoys the same privileges and immunities as a member of the House and receives the same salary, but he gets a larger allowance for administrative and secretarial assistance (approximately $150,000 each year).

Rules and Organization: The Filibuster The Senate differs from the House in many respects. It is smaller and hence less formal in its rules and organization. It has seventeen standing committees, while the House has twenty-one; senators are likely to serve on more committees (at least two or three) than members of the House. The lack of an effective method of limiting Senate debate has resulted in the filibuster, the practice of talking interminably either to defeat a measure by never permitting it to come to a vote or to force its supporters to add desired provisions. Filibusters are sometimes individual projects, but in recent years they have tended to be collective undertakings by groups of senators seeking a common objective. Unlike the House, the Senate permits unlimited debate, which, however admirable as the practice of democratic discussion, too easily degenerates into pompous long-windedness and sheer obstructionism. A device for closure (limitation of debate) adopted in 1917 is usually unworkable in practice, having been successfully invoked only sixteen times in fifty-seven years. However, in 1964 the Senate adopted a new rule that requires that at least three hours of each day's debate be confined to the business at hand, thus ensuring that the day will not be completely wasted on irrelevant and dilatory tactics. The Senate filibuster is another means by which those seeking to prevent change can impose their will on the majority. It has typically been used to frustrate civil-rights reform, and in the closing hours of the congressional session of 1973 it was used to prevent major changes in the methods of campaign financing. But the filibuster is likely to remain a sacrosanct privilege of United States Senators; most would admit that they can foresee circumstances under which they would want to take advantage of the obstruction and delay afforded by the possibilities of unlimited debate. And any senator who attempts to change the rule on unlimited debate may be frustrated by the use or even the threat of a filibuster.

Tenure and Independence Senators from the larger states are more broadly representative than congressmen chosen from districts and hence are not quite so parochial in outlook. Because of their longer terms, senators are somewhat less constrained to please their constituents at all times and are less frequently distracted by campaigns for reelection. Most senators are reelected, and many have served three or four terms. The result is greater and more continuous experience in legislative affairs. However, when coupled with the seniority rule regarding committee assignments and chairmanships, such continuity in office may produce government by senility. Another consequence is the greater independence of a senator from party control, as contrasted with a representative. The Senate is distinctly less predictable than the House when it comes to giving solid support to party measures. Another contrast arises from the fact that the Senate has been a continuous body since 1789; it has no need to organize itself and elect its officers every two years, as is the case with the House. Its presiding officer, the vice president, is prescribed for it by the Constitution, and only the newly elected third of its members need to be assigned to its committees every two years.

Precedent and tradition are very strong in the Senate, which behaves in many respects like a gentlemen's club. Though its members are by no means always well behaved, the upper chamber hesitates to discipline them. However, in December 1954 the Senate voted 67 to 22 to condemn the conduct of Senator Joseph R. McCarthy of Wisconsin, who had won notoriety for his unproved allegations of communist infiltration into government. The Senate resolution declared that certain specific actions and statements of the senator were "contrary to Senatorial ethics and tended to bring the Senate into dishonor and disrepute." Much the same concern was expressed more recently by the Senate when it voted to censure Senator Thomas Dodd of Connecticut for financial improprieties with campaign contributions. In the cases of both Senators McCarthy and Dodd, formal Senate criticism of their behavior effectively ended their political careers.

But for those senators who learn the rules of the senatorial game, who understand the importance of deference to colleagues and the necessity of compromise and bargaining, and who stay around long enough to accumulate seniority, there is both privilege and power. Probably the most influential senator in modern history was Carl Hayden of Arizona, whose forty-two years in the Senate (from 1926 to 1968) earned him the chairmanship of the powerful Senate Appropriations Committee, membership on the Senate Policy Committee (with control over the Senate's agenda), membership on the Rules and Administration Committee (which, among other perquisites desired by most senators, controls the Senate Contingency Fund), and the position of president *pro tempore,* or presiding officer of the Senate in the absence of the vice president. There was consequently no member of the Senate who could do without the friendship and support of Carl Hayden; such is the nature of power in the American Congress, where parties are relatively weak and where, as a consequence, the distribution of power often has little to do with the climate of public opinion.

The Legislative Process

The Constitution requires Congress to convene in regular session at least once a year; the Twentieth Amendment, ratified in 1933 for the purpose of preventing legislation by a lame-duck Congress (consisting of members recently defeated for reelection), specifies the third day of January unless Congress by law selects a different day. In addition, special sessions of one or both houses may be called by the president, who may also fix a time of adjournment if the houses cannot agree on a date.

Distributing Power After each congressional election, the House of Representatives must organize as though for the first time, electing a presiding officer (known as the "speaker"), a clerk, a sergeant at arms, and other officers, as well as adopting rules of procedure and electing members to its various committees. The American speaker, unlike his British counterpart, is definitely partisan and employs his powers (within the limits set by the rules of the House) to aid his own political party. He is invariably a senior ranking member belonging to the party in control of the House. His powers are still extensive, though far less so than before the so-called revolution of 1910 to 1911, when the House took from the speaker the chairmanship of the important Rules Committee and the power to appoint members of all standing committees. He still has (among others) the power to recognize members wishing to speak and the power to decide points of order, interpret the rules, and assign bills to the appropriate standing committees.

There are at present twenty-one standing committees of the House, ranging in size from nine to fifty members each, with the average around thirty. Before 1946 there were forty-seven standing committees; reducing the number has meant that any one member is normally required to serve on only two rather than several committees. However, there are about 130 subcommittees (five to ten for each standing committee), and so the burden of committee work is at least as heavy as ever. Members are assigned to the various committees by their respective party organizations in the House, although they are formally elected to their committee posts by vote of the House itself. Each committee reflects the distribution of party strength in the House; the party in power always has a majority on every standing committee and formally designates the committee chairman.

Committee chairmanships, however, are assigned on the basis of seniority, and this same principle also applies to all committee assignments. The more senior members are invariably from "safe" constituencies (where continued reelection is almost a certainty), and these constituencies are usually found in the more rural areas of the country. Thus the congressional leadership, more often than not, is relatively conservative—especially in comparison with the president, whose electoral base is usually in the more populous and industrial states. Regardless of partisanship, then, there is a built-in conflict that marks the relationships of the executive and legislative branches, and this conflict may be a more effective block to concerted action than any separation of powers devised by the Founding Fathers.

The less senior congressmen are those who are newly elected and those from "close" constituencies (usually more urbanized), where the turnover of elected officials is more frequent. They are first assigned to less important committees and, if continually reelected, will work their way up the ladder of responsibility and power. In the House of Representatives, the most important and powerful committee has frequently proved to be the Rules Committee, which has used its *procedural* authority to influence the substance of legislation. The Rules Committee can expedite or block legislation (usually the latter), it can prevent consideration of a bill approved by another standing committee by refusing to recommend a special rule whereby the bill may be brought to the floor for debate and a vote, and it can report a bill to the floor of the House with rules that limit the bill's chances of passage. The House Rules Committee is in many respects a functional equivalent to the filibuster rule in the Senate; in both cases, conservative minorities are able to exploit the rules and procedures in order to defeat, delay, or emasculate legislation supported by a majority of citizens *and* representatives.

Making Law Apart from the speaker, committees, and other official House machinery, each party maintains its own House organization, including the caucus (consisting of all the members belonging to a particular party), a steering or policy committee, and the floor leader (one each for the Republicans and Democrats). Speaking broadly, the caucus shapes party policy and chooses party leaders (speaker, committee members, etc.); the steering committee of the party in power selects and pushes through desired legislation; and the floor leader maneuvers against his opposite number in the course of debate. The House of Representatives normally receives as many as 15,000 bills in the course of its two-year life. Although more than half of all important legislative proposals originate with the executive branch (being actually introduced in Congress by members known to be administration spokesmen), the private member retains his indefeasible right to introduce a bill on any subject conceivably within the purview of the federal government. In most instances, however, such bills are inspired by interest groups, which usually draft them and hand them to a friendly member for introduction. In some instances the congressman or senator may introduce a bill marked "by request," thus renouncing responsibility for the ideas it embodies.

The course of a bill through the legislative mill may be outlined as follows. After being dropped into a box on the desk of the clerk of the House (or the secretary of the Senate), a bill is given a first reading (by title only) and is at once referred to the appropriate standing committee. If there is doubt as to which committee should receive the bill, the presiding officer resolves the question. The committee then considers the bill, with or without holding public hearings, and may report it out with or without amendments. Indeed, bills are often pigeonholed because the party or faction dominant on a particular committee opposes them. To force a committee to report a bill back to the House requires an absolute majority vote (i.e., 218), which cannot be taken until the committee has had the bill for thirty days. In practice, it is virtually impossible to get such a vote; hence many bills are "killed" by committees.

After a bill has been reported out, it is placed on one of the three calendars of the House. However, bills are by no means necessarily taken up in the order in which they are listed on these calendars. The steering committee of the majority party can select bills that it deems important, whereupon the Rules Committee may bring in special orders giving such bills priority. A bill receives its second reading at this stage. For the consideration of certain kinds of bills, especially financial measures, the House resolves itself into a Committee of the Whole, whereupon the speaker is temporarily replaced by a special chairman, 100 members constitute a quorum (instead of 218 required for the House as such), no one may speak for more than five minutes without unanimous consent, and most of the House's time-consuming maneuvers (e.g., roll-call votes and motions to postpone) are forbidden. Actions taken by the Committee of the Whole must be reported back to the House as such, which normally accepts the report. This procedure shortens debate, gives everyone a chance to speak, permits consideration of many criticisms and amendments, and bypasses most legislative technicalities. It is an ironic but appropriate comment on the structure of the House that in order to transact business efficiently, it must suspend many of its rules. When the rules are enforced, the legislative process moves slowly, if at all. As in the exercise of political power, the effects of enforcing the rules are not neutral, and the principal effect is to aid those who resist change. (The reader may here recall the discussion of conservatism in Chapter 7.)

After debate in the House, a motion is made that the bill be read a third time; if this carries, the bill receives a third reading (usually by title only), followed by a vote on final passage, which is normally a matter of course at this point. If passed, the bill is signed by the speaker and sent to the Senate.

The reader should note that with the exception of bills for raising revenue, which are constitutionally required to originate in the House, legislation may be started in either of the two houses. If a bill has its origin in the Senate and is later sent to the House, the sequence outlined here is merely reversed.

In the Senate, the bill is referred to one of its standing committees, which may or may not hold hearings on it, and this in turn is likely to reflect the interests and ideological orientation of the committee chairman. If favorably reported by the committee, it is placed on the Senate's calendar, although it can be taken up in or out of its proper order. It must go through the formality of three readings, of which the second is the most important. The Senate does not use the committee-of-the-whole procedure. After debate and possible amendment the bill, if passed, is returned to the speaker of the House.

Rarely indeed does a bill of any consequence that has passed the House emerge unscathed from the Senate. If amended by the Senate, such a bill goes back to the House and usually to the standing committee that originally sponsored it. If the House is unwilling to accept the Senate's amendments, the bill goes to a conference committee made up of an equal number of senators and representatives. If and when this committee agrees on a compromise version, it is reported to both houses, which usually accept it.

It thereupon goes to the president. If he approves and signs it, it becomes law; if he disapproves, he is required by the Constitution to return it to the house in which it originated with his reasons for rejecting it. Only by a two-thirds vote of both houses can Congress override a presidential veto, with the result that most vetoes prove final. The president may allow a bill to become law without his signature, provided Congress remains in session ten days or more after the president receives the bill. If Congress adjourns within such a ten-day period, the bill lapses and does not become law; this is called the "pocket veto."

Congressional Shortcomings

Before leaving the subject of Congress, it is well to note a few of the many criticisms leveled at it. First of all, the House is said to be too large and unwieldy for effective debate. Also, the two-year term is considered too short to allow the representative time to learn his job before hurrying home to try to get reelected. In fact, this term is shorter than that of a member of the lower house of any other important national legislature. Early in 1966 President Johnson recommended that the term of members of the House be lengthened to four years and timed to coincide with presidential elections. This would tend to smooth out relationships between president and Congress, but some members of Congress feared that it would deprive Congress of some of its independence and importance and unduly enhance the influence of the chief executive. Such a change would require an amendment to the Constitution.

The practice of requiring the representative to reside in the district in which he seeks election has also come in for criticism. The rule of seniority for assigning committee memberships and chairmanships in both House and Senate has drawn fire because it often results in chairmen who are too old and infirm to discharge their duties effectively. The formalities of the seniority rule were modified in 1973, but it is very likely that the great majority of committee chairmen will continue to be selected according to seniority. The rules of procedure in both houses also are declared to be outmoded; in the House such rules tend to stifle debate without achieving much legislative speed, while in the Senate the filibuster too frequently nullifies the advantages of full, unrestricted discussion of public policy. The introduction of too many bills, especially those inspired by irresponsible pressure groups, clogs the legislative machinery and makes for too much haste in the passage of really important measures. Also, because political party organization and discipline are weak on the national level, party leaders in the House and Senate often cannot hold their followers together to carry out platform promises. Thus responsible party government, so essential to democracy, is conspicuously absent from the national legislative process. Congress does not always produce legislative leadership, as the British House of Commons does. Although ready to apply the name "dictator" to a strong president who aggressively pushes his legislative program, Congress often flounders helplessly when it is *not* pushed.

THE PRESIDENCY

The Founding Fathers vested the executive power of the United States in a president, who with a vice president is elected by an electoral college for a term of four years. The office of president can be held only by a natural-born (as distinguished from a naturalized) citizen of the United States who is at least thirty-five years old and has resided in the United States for fourteen years. Since no mention is made of the sex of the candidate, women as well as men are eligible, although the thought would doubtless have startled the framers.

Presidential Tenure

The Constitution was originally silent regarding reelection and the number of presidential terms. The long tradition against a third term was broken by the reelection of Franklin D. Roosevelt to not only a third term but also a fourth. This event aroused the fear that presidential powers might be still further expanded. The result was the Twenty-second Amendment, ratified in 1951, which limited future presidents to two full terms and, at the maximum, one-half the term of a previously elected president. This amendment tends to weaken a president's legislative and party leadership during his second term because in his bargaining relationships with other political activists, inside Congress and out, he can pose neither as a threat nor as a promise for reelection. A popular president, however, may sustain his political influence by playing the role of power broker in his party's selection of a presidential successor. It thus is important for the president to play his cards close to his chest, refusing to reveal his personal nominee until the last possible moment; if he keeps his party colleagues guessing, he may keep much of his political influence throughout his second term in office. (This is an important lesson in the intangible quality of political power, which is much more than the sum of authority conferred by the Constitution or by legislative statute.) It is true, however, that the limitation on presidential tenure may deprive the nation of the services of an able president after eight years of service. There are no corresponding limitations on the terms of state or national legislators, some of whom have held office for twenty years or more. In New York State, Nelson A. Rockefeller enjoyed the powers of the governorship for fifteen years, from 1959 through 1973.

Presidential Succession

If the president dies, resigns, is unable to perform the duties of the office, or is removed by impeachment, the vice president succeeds to the presidential office for the remainder of the term. The Twenty-fifth Amendment, adopted in 1967, provides that the vice president becomes acting president when the president notifies the presiding officers of the two houses of his inability to discharge the powers and duties of his office and that he remains acting president until the president transmits a written declaration that he is able to resume his duties. The amendment further provides that if the president has not notified Congress of his inability to discharge the duties of his office, the vice president and a majority of either the heads of the executive departments or of some other body, as Congress may provide, may transmit to the president a written declaration that he is unable to discharge the duties of his office.

The amendment further specifies that if and when the president wishes to resume his duties, his written declaration of such intention will bring this about, *unless* the vice president and the other officers referred to above notify Congress within four days (in writing) that they consider the president unable to return to his duties. Congress must then assemble within forty-eight hours to decide the issue; twenty-one days after it has received the written declaration of presidential disability or twenty-one days after it has assembled (if not previously in session), Congress is to determine by a vote of both houses (voting separately) whether the president is able to resume his duties. If the Congress decides by a two-thirds vote of both houses that the president's disability still continues, the vice president continues as acting president.

The Twenty-fifth Amendment also stipulates that whenever there is a vacancy in the office of vice president, the president shall nominate a vice president who takes office upon confirmation by a majority vote of both houses of Congress. It was according to the terms of this amendment that President Ford nominated Nelson A. Rockefeller to the vice-presidency in 1974 and that Ford himself had replaced Spiro Agnew as vice president in 1973. Agnew resigned after admitting income tax improprieties, one of the first signs that the troubled Nixon administration might not live out the entirety of its second term. But the specific details of the Twenty-fifth Amendment were elaborated in the context of an earlier and prolonged threat of political crisis; following President Kennedy's assassination in November 1963 and Vice President Johnson's accession to the presidency, there was no nationally recognized political leader who stood in the line of succession to the presidency in the event of President Johnson's death or resignation—a constitutional failing that endured for more than a year.

If both the president and vice president should die, resign, or be impeached, the presidential succession is to be determined by Congress, which has passed several laws on the subject. The law of 1947, now in effect, provides that the next in line after the vice president is the speaker of the House of Representatives, followed in order by the president *pro tempore* of the Senate; the secretaries of the Departments of State, Treasury, and Defense; the attorney general; the postmaster general; and the secretaries of the Interior, Agriculture, Commerce, and Labor.

Salaries and Benefits

The salaries of the president and vice president are fixed by Congress, but may not be reduced during their terms of office. The president's salary today is $200,000. Following elaboration of a law passed in 1958, Congress has provided lifetime pensions of $60,000 a year for former presidents and $20,000 a year for their widows. By resigning instead of submitting to probable impeachment and conviction, President Nixon assured his retention of these pension rights, which include up to $96,000 a year (for life) in government funds for staff and office expenses. The salary of the vice president is $62,500, while the secretaries of the executive departments receive an annual salary of $60,000. In all these cases, the salary is supplemented by allowances for expenses, including staff assistance, and the sum of both salary and allowances is taxable. But it is clear that the financial advantages accruing to executive leaders are not only a function of statutory benefits; at the beginning of his first presidential term, Richard M. Nixon declared his net worth as $307,141; on May 31, 1973, his declared net worth was $988,522. The unhappy fate of the Nixon presidency also suggests the wisdom in Plato's argument that good public policy is likely to come only from those who have no financial stake in the decisions they make.

Nomination and Election of the President

The framers devised the electoral college to avoid the dangers of both popular election and election by

Congress. Each state was empowered (Article 2, Section 1, paragraphs 2 and 3) to appoint, in any manner designated by its legislature, a number of electors equal to the number of representatives and senators that the state then had in Congress. At first, state legislatures themselves tended to select the electors, frequently from among their own members. With the rise of political parties and the broadening of the suffrage, the electors came to be chosen by the voters on the basis of party affiliation. Political parties began to put up slates of electors pledged to support the presidential and vice-presidential nominees of the party organizations, and the voters regarded their ballots for electors as really being cast for president and vice president.

The Constitution is silent on the method of nomination, as well as on the subject of political parties. The founders apparently expected the electors to perform the tasks of both nomination and election. With the rise of parties, the members of each party in Congress (the caucus) at first selected the party's presidential and vice-presidential nominees. In 1831 the first national nominating convention was held, and this method was soon adopted by all political parties.

For many years the national nominating conventions of the Republican and Democratic parties were held in June or July of a presidential election year; in 1956, however, both conventions were scheduled in August, ostensibly to shorten the overlong campaign. Each party makes its own rules covering the composition and procedure of its convention unless state laws regulate the methods of choosing delegates; there are no national laws on the subject. Between 1968 and 1972, the Democratic party made major efforts to reform its procedures for selecting delegates in order to democratize the nominations process and to ensure that the characteristics of convention delegates would more closely approximate the characteristics of the general population—especially in terms of blacks and women as a percentage of the total population. After the decisive defeat of Senator George McGovern's presidential candidacy in 1972, however, the Democratic National Committee rejected the strict application of "quotas" in the allocation of delegate seats at the national convention. This policy was reaffirmed in a historic midterm convention of the Democratic party, convened in Kansas City in December 1974; more than 2,000 delegates agreed on a charter to govern party organization and procedures and adopted "affirmative action" guidelines to assure more equitable representation of youth, women, and minority groups in party affairs. Thus the Democrats had challenged the Republicans to help reform the nominations process in order to reduce the role of old-line party bosses in presidential selection. But it was not at all certain that a more democratized nominations procedure would improve on the won and lost record of the party bosses, whose presidential choices have usually been a function more of the candidate's chances of being elected than his ideological or programmatic orientation. And it was typical of such reform efforts that the party initiating the reforms was out of office and struggling to get back in. As in athletic competition, political organizations are reluctant to tamper with their personnel and procedures when they have hit upon a winning combination.

How Delegates Are Chosen More than one-third of the delegates are chosen by state (or state and district) party conventions; the remainder, by primary elections. The original idea behind the primary was to democratize the convention and further the nomination of candidates desired by the party rank and file rather than the bosses. Thirty states have presidential primaries in which the voters may vote for their favorite candidate for the presidential nomination, but the other states have not adopted the system. The practical impossibility of binding the convention delegates after the balloting gets under way (e.g., after it appears that the man they were pledged to support has no chance) has lessened enthusiasm for the primary. However they are selected, the rank and file have little voice in the selection of the nominees for president and vice president or the policies that will be written into the party platform. The real decisions have traditionally been made by the party leaders and are usually the result of bargains or deals reached at private conferences. The perennial criticism of national conventions of both parties is that they are run by party bosses who meet in smoke-filled rooms and make the real decisions, which are then noisily ratified by the convention itself. The *ratify-*

ing functions of the national convention and the critical importance of *pre*convention maneuvers by party professionals are made clear by the findings of Professor Donald R. Matthews, a political scientist at the University of Michigan; of the twenty Democratic and Republican national conventions held between 1936 and 1972, fifteen of them selected as the presidential nominee the man who was the party's leading contender six to eight months before the convention.

The Convention in Action Large cities bid vigorously for the honor (and profit) of playing host to national political conventions. In addition to the delegates, an equal number of alternates, the families and friends of both, and the representatives of press, radio, and television, thousands of people flock to watch convention proceedings, which, whatever their shortcomings, add up to one of the greatest shows on earth.

A convention traditionally lasts four or five days; sometimes, when it is certain to renominate an incumbent president, matters seem to drag. On other occasions, every moment is crammed with suspense. A convention is called to order by the chairman of the party's national committee. He presents the list of temporary officers prepared by the committee, who are elected forthwith. The temporary chairman delivers the keynote speech, which points with pride or views with alarm, according to whether the party is in or out of power. The convention then elects its four main committees: one on credentials, which is very important in cases such as the 1952 Republican and 1972 Democratic conventions, when bitter fights developed over the appropriate distribution of seats within particular state delegations; one on permanent organization; one on rules and the order of convention business; and one on the convention's resolutions and platform.

Party platforms and responsible government The convention platform is supposed to serve as the program of the presidential candidate and, if he is elected, of the party in both the presidency and the Congress. In this way, effective party cohesion can transcend the separation of powers specified by the Constitution; separate legislative and executive institutions may be united behind a single program by a unified party that controls both the presidency and the Congress.

In fact, this may be taken as the principal measure of "*responsible* government"—the ability of a political party to implement the program that it adopts in convention and presents to the voters. The weak structure and low level of cohesion characterizing political parties in the United States, however, are measured in part by their frequent inability to legislate the program for which they have campaigned. This may be attributed to the differences between parties in convention and parties in Congress. The former want to win an election, and party cohesion is consequently relatively high, especially if the presidential nominee looks like a winner in November. But the party in Congress is marked by low cohesion; only very infrequently do two-thirds or more of a party's legislators vote the same way on a major issue of public policy. According to findings made available by *The Congressional Quarterly,* for example, there were 684 roll-call votes in the House and Senate during the 1970 legislative session; on only 219 (32 percent) of these votes did a *majority* of voting Democrats oppose a *majority* of voting Republicans, which vividly illustrates the complexity and bargaining characteristics of American politics. Unlike the party in convention, then, the congressional party concentrates less on winning an election than on maintaining each member's status in the congressional power structure and in the home district. To repeat an important point: The party in Congress is not the same as the party in convention, in terms of both personnel and political motivation. This in turn helps to explain the relative irresponsibility of government in the United States, especially as compared with the governments of most of the other ten best-governed countries identified in Chapter 8. It is in this sense that the decision-making process of the nominating convention often represents ritual more than substance.

Balloting and selection Balloting on the convention's nominees proceeds by a roll call of the states, with the chairman of each state delegation announcing that delegation's vote. Sometimes other members of a delegation challenge the chairman's figure, thus necessitating a poll of the delegation. In both Republican and Democratic conventions, a majority of all the delegates is required to choose the presidential nominee. The Republicans give freedom to state delegations to divide a state's votes among different candidates. The Democrats have traditionally favored the unit rule, under which a state convention may require a delegation to vote en bloc for a single candidate, or the delegation itself may decide by majority vote to bind all delegates to vote for the majority's choice. More than one ballot is usually necessary unless the convention of the party in power is renominating an incumbent president. The record was set in 1924, when the Democrats required 103 ballots to nominate John W. Davis. In 1952 General Eisenhower was nominated by a shift of votes, after the first ballot showed him to be only four votes short of a majority of the Republican delegates; Governor Stevenson was similarly nominated by a rush of changed Democratic votes when the third ballot showed that he had missed nomination by only 2½ votes. In 1960 both Senator Kennedy and Vice President Nixon received their nominations on the first ballot; in 1964, 1968, and 1972 the presidential nominees of both parties also were nominated on the first ballot, again underlining the importance of *pre*convention politicking.

In the nomination of a vice-presidential candidate, the convention follows the same sequence of roll call, nominating and seconding speeches, and voting. The vice-presidential nominee is usually selected to represent a different section of the country or wing of the party from those represented by the presidential candidate. In the past, little attention was paid to his qualifications for becoming president, but the death of President Franklin D. Roosevelt, the illness of President Eisenhower, and the assassination of President Kennedy have dramatically emphasized the need to select vice-presidential nominees with the greatest care. That much remains to be done in this area of the American political process was demonstrated by the embarrassment of both President Nixon and Senator McGovern during and after the 1972 presidential elections; their vice-presidential running mates were forced to withdraw from the campaign or (in the case of Vice President Agnew) from public office after disclosure of information not previously known to the presidential candidates or to the nominating conventions.

A national nominating convention has no counterpart in any other country. Foreign visitors are invariably amazed by our quadrennial political circus. Even American citizens who have fancied themselves rather hardened about politics were startled (and often angered) by the spectacles of the national conventions in 1952, 1956, and, to a lesser degree, 1960 and 1964. However, the hope that televising convention proceedings would lead to their improvement seems as vain as the similar hope when they were first broadcast over radio. The trite and banal phrase, the threadbare cliché, the tub-thumping pomposity, the hackneyed nominating speech in which the name of the candidate (already known to all) is withheld until the orator, with his last gasp, announces that his perfect candidate is Aloysius Q. Throttlebottom—all this is seemingly part of an unchangeable ritual, to be accepted at face value only by the politically naive. But in politics, as in religion, ritual is important, and it well may be that the American people would withhold from any presidential aspirant or officeholder the stamp of complete legitimacy if he had failed to undergo the baptismal rites of the nominating convention.

The Campaign The campaign, which stretches between convention and ballot box, starts slowly, but closes in a frenzy of praise and vituperation. Campaign rhetoric is likely to become more moralistic and politically irresponsible as the candidate is shown by the polls to be an almost certain loser. Money plays an increasingly important part when radio and television time is so expensive; equal opportunity to propagandize for one's party is qualified by the ability to pay. The steamroller tactics of the party organizations gain overwhelming momentum in the living room of the voter, who is bombarded at thirty-minute intervals by charge and countercharge.

The vitality of American democracy and the common sense of the American voter are nowhere better vindicated than during a presidential campaign. Presidential elections are not always won by a preponderance of dollars, newspapers, radio commentators, or television personalities on one side or the other. Political prognosticators have more than once been confounded by results refuting expert predictions.

Yet the cost of a presidential campaign is tremendous. The sheer size of the electorate (over 77 million voters in 1972) makes effective campaigning very expensive. If money does not guarantee a candidate's election, it also is true that he or she cannot win without money. It has been estimated that $6.5 million would have been required to print and mail one circular to each of the 67 million voters registered in 1948. Estimates of the cost of the 1952 campaign ranged from $32 million to $100 million. Expenditures on behalf of *all* candidates for *all* public offices ranged between $165 million and $175 million in 1960 and amounted to $200 million in 1964.[10] In 1972 President Richard M. Nixon and his supporters raised more than $60 million for the presidential campaign alone; more than one-sixth of the amount came from only twenty-eight contributors (typical of Republican campaign financing), many of whom had major financial interests in the United States petroleum industry.

Although huge expenditures are not in themselves proof of improper use of funds, public concern lest election victories be too consistently won by money alone has led to the enactment of several laws to limit expenditures in national campaigns and otherwise to regulate the solicitation, acceptance, and disbursement of campaign funds. Up until at least 1974, however, national legislation on this subject proved particularly ineffective. But aroused by the illegal fund-raising and spending practices of the Nixon reelection campaign of 1972, Congress passed legislation in 1974 that provided up to $20 million in government funds (raised by the $1 income tax checkoff previously in effect) to finance the general election campaigns of Republican and Democratic presidential candidates in 1976. Additional money was authorized for the major parties' primaries and national conventions. In both the general election and primary campaigns, minor parties receive funds in proportion to their voting support in the preceding national election. Limits are placed on campaign spending by a candidate for the House of Representatives (approximately $70,000), and a candidate for the Senate cannot spend more than approximately $150,000 in the general election campaign ($100,000 in the senatorial primary). Campaign contributions by individuals are limited to $1,000 for any one candidate, and organizations (business corporations, trade unions, etc.) can contribute no more than $5,000 to any one candidate. An individual cannot contribute more than a total of $25,000 to all candidates in one election, but no limit is imposed on the campaign contributions of organizations. The legislation also established a full-time independent commission to enforce the new campaign finance law; two of the eight commissioners are appointed by the leadership in the Senate, two by the leadership in the House, and two by the president, with all six of these commission members subject to confirmation by both the Senate and the House. The secretary of the Senate and the clerk of the House serve as nonvoting members of the commission.

This historic legislation, reluctantly signed into law by President Ford, was a welcome first step toward reducing the emphasis on vast sums of privately donated money that had increasingly characterized American elections. But many political observers pointed out that the legislation would tend to reinforce the already privileged position of incumbent politicians; a limit on campaign expenditures may constitute a severe handicap to relatively unknown candidates who wish to challenge the existing political establishment. It was significant that no provisions were made in the final bill for government funding of congressional and Senate elections. And the disbursement of government funds to presidential candidates threatened even further the already weak structure of the parties' organizational apparatus.

Thus if young political activists want to introduce major changes into United States politics without resorting to confrontation or violence, there may be no better place to start than in the wholesale reform of campaign financing. It also may be true that political bossism, corruption, and conflict of interest can be eliminated or minimized only if government imposes a limit on all campaign expenditures *and* provides for campaign financing through the distribution of tax moneys. Compared with the operations of other competitive political systems, the machinery of American politics is heavily greased by the money advanced by "fat-cat" con-

---

[10]See *Financing Presidential Campaigns: Report of the President's Commission on Campaign Costs,* Government Printing Office, Washington, 1962, p. 9. The Commission made several specific proposals for coping with the problem; Adlai Stevenson also offered suggestions about meeting broadcasting costs, which accounted for more than one-third of total expenditures. Ibid., p. 25. California voters approved a referendum proposal in 1974 that may serve as a tentative model for other states and even the federal government. Strict limits were imposed on campaign expenditures, with challengers allowed to spend 10 percent more than incumbents, and lobbyists were flatly prohibited from contributing to candidates or influencing any campaign donations.

tributors. And this again may be taken as another indication of the relatively weak structure of American political parties.

The Election: Popular and Electoral The voters go to the polls on the Tuesday following the first Monday in November. Legally and constitutionally, they are voting for the presidential electors of their respective states, although in thirty-one states (and the District of Columbia) the names of these electors do not even appear on the ballot. Presidential electors are chosen by the respective party organizations, sometimes in a state party primary, and a party may require electors so chosen to promise to cast their electoral votes for the candidates nominated by the party's national convention. In the absence of such a pledge, the electors are legally free to vote for anyone they choose, and this has happened on a few occasions. In the 1960 election, one Republican elector defected and voted for Senator Harry Byrd of Virginia, thus joining fourteen unpledged Democratic electors (eight from Mississippi and six from Alabama) who also voted for Senator Byrd. Ordinarily, however, the electors do the bidding of their parties when they assemble at the various state capitals on the first Monday after the second Wednesday in December.

However, the popular vote is distorted in the electoral college because all a state's electoral-college votes go to the party whose presidential candidate received a mere *plurality* of the popular vote. In effect, Americans elect a president according to the electoral system of single-member district and simple plurality—winner take all in each of the fifty states (and in the District of Columbia). When third parties are major contenders, as was true in 1912, 1948, and 1968, the margin of popular-vote victory in certain states may be very narrow. Even when only the two major parties are involved, the party that wins a slight majority captures all the electoral votes of a populous state and may thereby win the presidency. There are now 538 votes in the electoral college (the total of 435 representatives and 100 senators plus 3 electoral votes for the District of Columbia), of which 270 are necessary for election. It is significant that the twelve most populous states account for 277 electoral-college votes, so that a narrow popular margin of victory in each of them could elect a candidate rejected in the other thirty-eight states.

Effects of the electoral system Although this extreme situation has never arisen, there have been nine presidents who received less than a majority of the total popular vote cast in the nation, as well as many others whose electoral victory assumed landslide dimensions out of all proportion to the popular vote. In 1964, for example, Lyndon Johnson received 61 percent of the popular vote, but 90 percent of the electoral-college vote. In 1972, Richard Nixon also received 61 percent of the popular vote, but 97 percent of the electoral vote. As in almost all elections organized according to the single-member district, simple-plurality system, the majority's position is overrepresented. In the case of American presidential politics, the usual result is to induce presidential contenders to focus their attentions on the more populous states. This also means that under normal circumstances (notably those of peacetime), no presidential candidate is likely to win if he ignores the interests and demands of the middle and lower middle classes of citizens in the urban areas of the nation. This in turn helps to explain the frequent conflict between Congress and the president; the electoral base of the latter predisposes him toward change and innovation, and the power structure of the Congress predisposes it toward conservatism and the status quo. As President John F. Kennedy put it, the president usually wants to sail, while the Congress wants to "anchor down."

The Powers of the President

The president of the United States is unquestionably the most powerful elected executive in any democratic nation. He represents all the people as no representative or senator can do, and he reflects national rather than sectional, state, or local interests. The president is more than a chief executive; his legislative functions have increasingly tended to overshadow his executive duties. He is really elected as a legislative leader, whose views on broad issues of public policy seem to be in accord with those of a majority of the voters, and he is held responsible for the success or failure of his administration's program. For this reason we may consider his legislative responsibilities before taking up his executive powers.

Legislative Powers The president is authorized by the Constitution to call special sessions of one or both houses of Congress, to send or deliver to it messages on the state of the union and to recommend legislation, and also to adjourn both houses if they cannot agree on a date of adjournment. The Budget and Accounting Act of 1921 gives him power over the preparation of the national budget, which he submits with his annual budget message early in January.

To his power to veto bills directly or by pocketing them should be added the *threat* of veto, which often induces Congress to amend bills to meet presidential objections. However, the president cannot veto mere parts of bills or items in appropriation bills of which he may disapprove; he is therefore sometimes compelled to sign appropriation bills containing distasteful items in order not to deprive other government agencies of necessary funds.

The president's power to appoint federal officers also enables him to influence legislation, particularly during the early months of a new administration, when there are many such vacancies to be filled. A president traditionally appoints persons selected by, or at least acceptable to, the senators and representatives from the states in which the appointments are to be made. This privilege of legislators virtually to make federal appointments in their states and districts is known as "patronage" and is highly important to their political status at home. The president can withhold (or threaten to withhold) patronage from legislators who oppose his legislative program, thus exerting powerful legislative leverage.

Presidential conferences with congressional leaders of both parties and appeals to the country through the public media are also among the weapons in the president's legislative arsenal. Moreover, he is, by virtue of his office, the titular head of his party, and as party leader he can crack the whip over his subordinates. He chooses the chairman of his party's national committee and has much influence over the party platform and the choice of a nominee to succeed him. Much depends, of course, upon the president's qualities of leadership and his determination to exert them upon Congress and the country. We have had strong, weak, and mediocre presidents; some (like Taft and Coolidge) have believed that Congress should lead itself, while others (such as Wilson and the two Roosevelts) have felt it their duty to provide legislative leadership. The steady growth of presidential powers, many of which have been conferred by Congress (e.g., the president's power to revise tariffs within prescribed limits), indicates a general recognition of the increasing need for stronger presidential leadership under present-day conditions.

Congress sometimes retaliates against what it considers undue presidential pressures or encroachments by a counterinvasion into executive territory. The administration of President Eisenhower was marked by several striking congressional attempts to limit executive powers, including efforts by congressional investigating committees to force the executive branch to disclose secret or confidential data and the proposed Bricker amendment, which sought to restrict the power of the president to conclude executive agreements with other nations. The increase in the powers granted to the president during Franklin D. Roosevelt's terms, first to cope with the greatest depression the country had ever witnessed, and later during World War II led to many charges that Congress had been reduced to a rubber stamp. These additional powers were reluctantly granted to the president by Congress, usually for only temporary duration.

A reaction set in against this enhancement of executive power, but did not reach its peak until President Eisenhower took office. Against a president striving hard to be cooperative rather than aggressive, congressional leaders sought to take control of many phases of foreign relations and law enforcement. Although this was not the first time Congress had sought to dominate a president, this invasion of the executive domain constituted, in the words of a seasoned political observer, "the constitutional crisis of our time." President Kennedy also had difficulty in getting broader authority to negotiate tariff reductions and to make long-range foreign-aid commitments. But it was the accumulated impact of the prolonged war in Southeast Asia that finally induced the Congress to impose limits on a major domain of executive authority; in 1973 the Congress restricted the authority of the president to commit United States troops to foreign combat (for a period in excess of ninety days) without the explicit approval of Congress. In this sense, recent legislation has restored a part of the Constitution to its original meaning.

The separation-of-powers principle, so often invoked against presidential domination, needs to be asserted against Congress also. Quite apart from tradition, Congress is inherently incapable of the proper discharge of executive and administrative functions; this was made abundantly clear under the Articles of Confederation, when committees of the Congress sought to manage foreign affairs and perform other executive tasks. It should be remembered that foreign relations, by their very nature, have always represented an executive, rather than a legislative, responsibility. Secrecy and discretion, so necessary in diplomatic negotiations, are not easily maintained in a large legislative body or its committees; leaks of information—deliberate or inadvertent—can readily nullify delicate international understandings. Firm international agreements, economic or military, are next to impossible if their continuance is at the mercy of frequent changes in the mood or political complexion of Congress. Similarly, the operations of the FBI and other intelligence agencies of the government are endangered if their secret files can be subpoenaed and the contents revealed by politically minded legislators in quest of new headlines. As in guarding the nation's military security, however, it is important for political elites to maintain a delicate balance between what the law prescribes and what common sense dictates. When the two are in conflict, the safety of citizen and state leans heavily on the good judgment of political leaders, and in the United States this invariably includes the president. If he is unable or unwilling to lead or if his leadership is incompetent, the whole society is likely to suffer. By concentrating so much responsibility and authority in the office of the president (instead of in the Cabinet or in the majority party of a parliamentary system), the presidential system of government runs grave risks in an age when governmental action is imperative and inaction is an admission of defeat.

Executive Powers But how is the president able to lead? If he is the most powerful figure in the world's most powerful state, what are the sources of his power? The president's executive powers are derived from the Constitution, from statutes, and from the implications of his office. The Constitution makes him commander in chief of the Army and Navy and of the militia (now the National Guard) of the states when called into the service of the United States; it empowers him to require the opinion, in writing, of the principal officer in each of the executive departments, thus giving him control over the Cabinet; it vests in him the power to grant reprieves and pardons for offenses against the United States, except in cases of impeachment (it was this constitutional authority that President Ford relied upon in September 1974 when he pardoned former President Nixon for his role in the Watergate cover-up—although Nixon had yet to be indicted or convicted, and thus President Ford's action interfered with the traditional requirements of the judicial process); it declares that he shall have power, with the advice and consent of two-thirds of the senators present, to make treaties; and it empowers him to appoint, with the advice and consent of a simple majority of the senators present, ambassadors, ministers, consuls, federal judges, and all other officers of the United States whose appointments are not otherwise provided for in the Constitution. If vacancies occur in such offices while the Senate is not in session, the president may fill them until the end of the next session of the Senate; these are known as "interim appointments."

The power to appoint, according to Supreme Court interpretation, includes the power to remove. Thus the president alone may remove officials for whose appointment senatorial confirmation was required; however, this removal power, as applied to members of quasilegislative or quasijudicial agencies such as the Federal Trade Commission, is subject to regulation by statute. Therefore the president can dismiss a member of such a commission only for reasons specified by Congress in the law governing that commission. The power to appoint also involves much consultation with senators belonging to the president's party; the rule of senatorial courtesy decrees that the Senate will refuse to confirm the president's nomination of an appointee in a particular state if either senator from the state objects.

It should be noted that the Cabinet, as a collective body, is not mentioned in the Constitution and has no status as a policy-making body. Made up of the president's personal choices, it is completely subordinate to his wishes. The president can force any Cabinet member to resign or to pursue particular policies within his department. Lincoln is reputed to have put a question to his Cabinet and called for a vote; Lincoln voted "aye," and all the rest "no," whereupon Lincoln declared, "The 'ayes' have it!"

Broad construction of the president's constitutional duty to faithfully execute the laws, coupled with the power to remove federal officers, provides the basis for the broad presidential powers over administration, including the power to issue rules and regulations covering all branches of the government service—civil, military, naval, domestic, and foreign. Not only the making of treaties but also the management and direction of American foreign relations thus fall within the purview of the president.

The president's constitutional and statutory powers are broad and impressive, but they still do not tell the whole story of presidential power. A president's ability to influence others is ultimately a function of both tangible and intangible qualities: his personality and persuasive capabilities, his knowledge of the issues of public policy and the details of the political process, his popular standing at home and abroad, his past record and future promise as a winner, his ability to maximize information from diverse sources and to multiply his options in decision making, and the extent of his control over rewards sought by others. Somewhere along the line, most politicians and citizen leaders will want something that only the president can give them, or they will find that their ability to get what they want is likely to be immensely facilitated by the cooperation of the president. The successful president is in part the man who understands these opportunities and who knows how to take advantage of them—not in terms of his own personal interest, but in terms of his understanding of good public policy. If the public requires the president *to appear* to be "above politics," it also is true that without a shrewd political sense, the president is bound to be overwhelmed by his job, perhaps even crushed by the wheels of the political grind.

STUDY-GUIDE QUESTIONS

1 To what extent was the United States Constitution an embodiment of long-standing traditions (from both England and colonial experience) or a response to current conditions and problems as perceived by the Founding Fathers?
2 How would you explain the expansion of governmental power in the United States since the adoption of the Constitution? What have been the principal causes? What have been the effects on "individual freedom"?
3 What are the institutional rules and procedures in the American political process that enable minorities to frustrate the will of a majority?
4 How democratic is the selection of presidents and vice presidents in the United States? How might the selection process be made more democratic?
5 How would you define "presidential power"? How can the president maximize his chances of successfully enacting his program?

REFERENCES

Beard, Charles A.: *An Economic Interpretation of the Constitution of the United States,* The Macmillan Company, New York, 1967.
Benson, Lee: *Turner and Beard: American Historical Writing Reconsidered,* The Free Press of Glencoe, Inc., New York, 1960.
Charles, Joseph: *The Origins of the American Party System,* Torchbooks, Harper & Row, Publishers, Incorporated, New York, 1961.
Corwin, Edward S.: *The President: Office and Powers, 1789–1957,* 4th ed., New York University Press, New York, 1957.
DeGrazia, Alfred (ed.): *Congress: The First Branch of Government,* Doubleday & Company, Inc., Garden City, N.Y., 1967.
Donovan, John C.: *The Policy Makers,* Pegasus, New York, 1970.
Fenno, Richard F., Jr.: *The Power of the Purse: Appropriations Politics in Congress,* Little, Brown and Company, Boston, 1966.
———: *Congressmen in Committees,* Little, Brown and Company, Boston, 1973.
Harris, Joseph: *Congress and the Legislative Process,* 2d ed., McGraw-Hill Book Company, New York, 1972.
Hofstadter, Richard: *The American Political Tradition and the Men Who Made It,* Alfred A. Knopf, Inc., New York, 1948.
Jewel, Malcolm E., and S. C. Patterson: *The Legislative Process in the United States,* Random House, Inc., New York, 1966.

Lipset, Seymour Martin: *The First New Nation: The United States in Historical and Comparative Perspective*, Anchor Books, Doubleday & Company, Inc., Garden City, N.Y., 1967.

Neustadt, Richard E.: *Presidential Power: The Politics of Leadership*, John Wiley & Sons, Inc., New York, 1964.

Polsby, Nelson W.: *Congress and the Presidency*, 2d ed., Prentice-Hall, Inc., Englewood Cliffs, N.J., 1970.

——— (ed.): *Congressional Behavior*, Random House, Inc., New York, 1971.

Reedy, George E.: *The Twilight of the Presidency*, World Publishing Company, New York, 1970.

Wildavsky, Aaron (ed.): *The Presidency*, Little, Brown and Company, Boston, 1969.

Chapter 10

Politics in the United States: II

The oldest constitutional democracy, the United States was bound to invent procedures of government that were unique in their time, although eventually imitated by other nations also moved to experiment with democratic government. But the most unique, and the least imitated, has been the American judicial system, which was given heavy responsibility for maintaining the integrity of constitutional government and the men who run it. Only through the most indirect channels of accountability were the men of the high judiciary linked to citizens and elected officials, but their noble record testifies to the real possibility of making the rule of men conform to the rule of law. Daniel Webster observed that "Justice is the great interest of man on earth." Explaining how American democracy has attempted to ensure justice in the interest of citizens of the United States is the intent of what follows.

THE NATIONAL JUDICIARY

Jurisdiction

It is important to remember that federal court jurisdiction (the judicial power of the United States) is limited by the Constitution to only certain types of legal questions or to cases arising between certain kinds of parties. Thus cases involving interpretation of the federal Constitution, national laws, treaties, or admiralty law come within federal court jurisdiction because of their *subject matter.* Cases to which the United States government is a party, cases between two or more states or between citizens of different states, and cases between a state or its citizens and foreign states or citizens come under federal court jurisdiction because of the nature or status of the *parties involved*. Also in this latter category are cases affecting ambassadors and other public ministers and consuls and cases in which a state sues citizens of another state. Since the Eleventh Amendment was added in 1798, a citizen of one state cannot sue the government of another state in the federal courts, nor, by later judicial interpretation, may he sue the government of his own state in the federal courts.

The fact that a case *may* be tried in a federal court does not mean that it *must* be tried there. The Constitution says merely that federal jurisdiction "shall extend" to certain cases, but such jurisdiction need not be *exclusively* federal unless Congress has conferred exclusive jurisdiction over certain cases upon the federal courts. Congress has done so with respect to all admiralty, maritime, patent, copyright, and bankruptcy cases; all cases of crimes under federal statutes; all civil actions wherein the United States or a state is a party (except cases between a state and its own citizens); and all cases affecting foreign diplomats and consuls as defendants. In the absence of such congressional action, a case within federal court jurisdiction may begin in either a state or a federal court.

If such a case is started in a state court, the defendant may, under certain circumstances, request that it be transferred to a federal court. He may do so, for example, if the parties are citizens of different states and he is not a citizen of the state in which the suit is brought.[1] Other cases go to the United States Supreme Court on appeal from a state supreme court; e.g., if a litigant claims that a state law is contrary to provisions of the federal Constitution, the state supreme court may decide the question, but if it upholds the state law, the defeated party has a right of appeal to the United States Supreme Court. With respect to other types of cases involving federal questions, the Supreme Court has discretionary power either to grant or to deny the request for an appeal. Its decision to grant or deny the writ of certiorari (which directs the lower court to send the case to it) is usually based on the importance of the constitutional principle involved.

Federal court jurisdiction includes both criminal and civil cases; the latter, in turn, include cases at law and those in equity. Equity originally developed as a special branch of Anglo-Saxon jurisprudence and for several centuries was administered in England by a separate system of courts. The central idea in equity is to grant relief in cases where the law alone will not provide substantial justice. For example, if A contracts to sell to B a famous painting at an agreed price and later refuses to do so, a court sitting in equity may issue a "writ of specific performance" ordering A to carry out his bargain. In such a case, where the subject matter of the contract is unique (e.g., there is only one *Mona Lisa*), it is impossible to determine the amount of damages in terms of money, which would be the only remedy available in a suit at law.

Court Structure

The Constitution specifically established only one federal court, the United States Supreme Court, but authorized Congress to establish inferior federal courts. These inferior courts are of two levels: district courts and courts of appeal. Today there are ninety-four of the former and eleven of the latter (one of which operates in the District of Columbia). More federal district judges are needed in the more populous districts; the total number today is about 366. Similarly, the courts of appeal are manned by some ninety-two judges.

District Courts Except for cases over which the Constitution gives original jurisdiction to the United States Supreme Court, all cases starting in a federal court begin at the district level. These district courts have no appellate jurisdiction and are simply trial courts. Their procedure is regulated by Congress except where covered by provisions in the Constitution or its amendments (jury trial, due process, etc.).

Courts of Appeal These courts have only appellate jurisdiction; no cases begin before them. They hear appeals from federal district courts and review rulings made by many quasijudicial federal agencies, e.g., the National Labor Relations Board.

---

[1] However, civil suits between citizens of different states may not be started in, or transferred to, a federal court if the amount involved is less than $10,000.

Every case before a court of appeals must be heard by at least two judges; if this court declares a state law invalid, there is a *right* of appeal to the United States Supreme Court.

The United States Supreme Court

Size The Founding Fathers did not specify the size of the Supreme Court. Congress first provided for a chief justice and five associate justices; the number has been gradually increased to the present total of nine, including the chief justice. Like all federal judges, the justices of the Supreme Court are appointed by the president with the advice and consent of the Senate and hold office during good behavior. They can be removed only by impeachment.

Qualifications Curiously, the framers of the Constitution established no qualifications whatsoever for federal judges, whether of age, citizenship, literacy, period of residence in the United States, legal training, or judicial experience. This omission stands in sharp contrast to the detailed qualifications set down for president, vice president, representatives, and senators. Such an oversight implied no disrespect for the bench, but rather an assumption that proper care would be exercised in making judicial selections—an assumption that has, on the whole, been vindicated. However, some of our most distinguished Supreme Court justices had little legal training or experience when they were appointed to our highest tribunal.

Salaries The Constitution expressly forbids any reduction in the salary of a federal judge during his continuance in office. Until recently, judicial salaries were low in view of the importance of the judicial function. However, Congress has increased the salaries of federal judges, raising that of the chief justice of the United States Supreme Court to $62,500, those of the eight associate justices of the Supreme Court to $60,000, and those of federal district judges to $40,000. Long overdue, this action partially remedied the disparity between low judicial salaries and the high level of competence that Americans expect of judges. Any man or woman worthy of sitting on the Supreme Court can easily earn, through the practice of law, far more than even the present salary paid to the justices. Helping to compensate for the lower salaries is the sense of prestige, of public service, and of contributing to American constitutional development. In all aspects of government; in business, the university, and law enforcement; and in every niche of organizational life good salaries do not guarantee good personnel, but low salaries are almost certain to attract the incompetent and self-serving.

How the Court Functions The Supreme Court begins its annual term on the first Monday of October and usually ends it the following June. Its time is spent hearing oral arguments, studying briefs and other printed materials, conferring to decide cases, and writing opinions. The chief justice assigns the writing of a particular opinion to one of his colleagues, or he may write it himself. An effort is made to distribute the work load fairly, although justices who are known to be specialists in certain fields may find themselves very busy if cases in their areas are numerous during a particular term of court. A Supreme Court opinion sets forth the facts in the case, the legal or constitutional issues involved, and the reasoning on which the Court's decision is based. If the justices are unanimous, no names will be appended to the opinion except that of the justice who wrote it. However, the Court often divides on important cases; in such an event, one or more justices write dissenting opinions, giving their reasons for not following the majority's decision. Sometimes justices agree with the majority decision but not with the reasoning behind it; in this case they may write concurring but separate opinions. Both dissenting and concurring opinions are often cited in later decisions; sometimes an earlier dissent is adopted by a later Court and becomes the law of the land. In this sense, too, the Supreme Court plays a major role in legislating new law, despite the rigid logic of the separation-of-powers doctrine.

A quorum of the Court to hear argument on a case is six; a binding decision requires a majority of a quorum, which may mean as few as four justices. If the Court divides evenly (e.g., if only six or eight justices hear the case), the decision of the lower court is automatically upheld. One reason why some justices are absent when certain cases are heard is a firmly established ethical rule that a justice shall take no part in deciding a case in which he, his former law partners, or members of his family have been retained when the case was being tried or heard in a lower court or in which the justice has a financial interest.

The Supreme Court's Jurisdiction The Supreme Court has original jurisdiction only in the few cases designated in the Constitution: those affecting ambassadors, other public ministers, and consuls and those to which a state is a party. Congress cannot enlarge this original jurisdiction. The Court has appellate jurisdiction over all other cases coming within the federal judicial power, subject to "such exceptions and under such regulations as the Congress shall make." This is the only formal power that Congress can wield to restrain the Court; it was invoked just after the Civil War to prevent a test of the constitutionality of the Reconstruction Acts, but has since fallen into disuse. Its regular employment by Congress would entail the risk that if one Congress should exclude the Court from hearing appeals involving, say, the constitutionality of laws regulating business, another Congress might bar the Court from appellate jurisdiction over cases involving civil liberties. Congressional pressure on the Supreme Court thus invariably takes on more subtle forms, and not only through participation in the appointments process.

Judicial Appointments From the outset, presidents making appointments to the Supreme Court have been largely influenced by political and ideological considerations rather than by the judicial stature of prospective appointees. John Marshall, for example, was appointed chief justice mainly because he had been a loyal, able Federalist politician. Similarly, President Andrew Jackson named Roger B. Taney chief justice to succeed Marshall largely because of Taney's prior political services in Jackson's Cabinet. When President Grant was about to fill a Supreme Court vacancy, he first wrote letters inquiring about the views of prospective appointees regarding the constitutionality of the Legal Tender Acts passed during the Civil War and declared unconstitutional by the Supreme Court. Grant wanted this decision reversed, and the justices he appointed helped to bring the reversal about when a new case was presented. One president after another has appointed justices not only from his own political party but also from among men holding political, social, and economic views in harmony with his own. Theodore Roosevelt and Woodrow Wilson sought to put "trustbusters" on the Court, and Wilson appointed Justice Brandeis because both favored social-reform legislation. The Harding-Coolidge era produced conservative appointments to the Supreme Court; the Roosevelt New Deal, liberal appointments.

Whether the Court's viewpoints will change slowly or rapidly is determined largely by changes in its membership, which depend on judicial longevity (coupled, today, with the possibility of retirement on full salary at the age of seventy). Some presidents have had the opportunity to appoint several Supreme Court justices; others, few or none. Calvin Coolidge did not make any Supreme Court appointments; during his twelve years as president, Franklin Roosevelt made eight appointments; and President Nixon was able to appoint four justices to the Court during his first term in office. If many deaths or resignations occur during a single administration and if young justices are chosen to fill such vacancies, the course of American constitutional interpretation may be fixed for several decades to come.

The Supreme Court, Congress, and the President
Reference has been made to the struggles between Congress and the president and the implications for the principle of the separation of powers. During several periods in our history, a comparable issue was raised between the Supreme Court, on the one hand, and the "political" branches (Congress and the president), on the other. Such clashes occurred under Jefferson, Jackson, Lincoln, Theodore Roosevelt, Franklin D. Roosevelt, and others. The Dred Scott decision in 1857 provoked criticism of the Court every whit as bitter as that later provoked by the decisions striking down many of the major early New Deal enactments. Such conflicts, whoever may be the parties at any particular moment, illustrate the mythical character of the notion of checks and balances among the three coordinate branches of government. The American system is unquestionably one of checks, but these are not sufficiently reciprocal to achieve a balance among president, Congress, and Court. The effectiveness of any check (e.g., Senate confirmation of appointments or

judicial review of legislation) depends ultimately upon the political affiliation, integrity, competence, energy, drive, and independence of the individual persons involved. A strong president may dominate a Congress and Court willing to be dominated; a strong Court may stubbornly resist the will of president, Congress, and electorate; and a Congress led by determined, power-seeking legislators can readily shoulder a weak president aside.

All these situations have occurred at one time or another; far from being balanced and coordinate, our three branches of government are constantly changing their relative positions, with some one branch on top. After the Civil War (or War Between the States) and during the period of so-called reconstruction, the Congress imposed its vengeful will on the other branches of government and on the states of the old Confederacy. In the 1920s and early 1930s the Court was supreme as it struck down federal and state legislation designed to adapt the role of government to the new realities of an urban-industrial society; between 1937 and 1945 the president was dominant, in part because of the inevitable concentration of power that is associated with the waging of war. Congress became more assertive under President Eisenhower; the legislative and executive branches were divided by partisanship (some of Eisenhower's major policies depended on Democratic support for enactment), but Eisenhower also appeared to be unwilling or unable to exert presidential leadership. Presidents Kennedy and Johnson, however, restored the presidency to a position of leadership. President Nixon's preoccupation with foreign policy, his lack of interest in initiating new domestic programs, the scandals associated with his administration, and the natural partisan conflict between a Republican president and a Democratic Congress tipped the power balance back in the direction of Congress. Before President Nixon resigned from office in August 1974, the Congress had placed limits on the president's war powers, had restricted his authority to impound funds appropriated by Congress, and had challenged the power of the White House Office of Management and Budget by establishing a congressional budget office to oversee and coordinate the budgetary process and federal spending.

But Congress is not really in a position to stake out new directions or to initiate major new policies, either foreign or domestic. It is fair to say that if the president does not or cannot lead the country, the country is leaderless. And this, again, is a sobering comment on the relative weakness of the major political parties in the United States and the vulnerabilities of the presidential system of government in the contemporary world.

Restraining the Court Even presumably reciprocal checks do not operate simultaneously; with respect to the Supreme Court, any control by president and Senate ceases the moment a new justice is sworn into office. Although the Court can check Congress, executive and administrative officers, and state legislatures, the Court itself is harder to control. Justice (later Chief Justice) Harlan Fiske Stone once said that the only real restraint on the Court was its own sense of self-restraint (dissenting opinion in *United States v. Butler,* 297 U.S. 1, 1936). However, Congress can sometimes enact statutes that will meet or override the Court's objections, and as "Mr. Dooley" (Finley Peter Dunne) once observed, Supreme Court justices *do* read the election returns.

Congress also has the constitutional authority to restrict the appellate jurisdiction of the Supreme Court; this power, however, has not been exercised since reconstruction days. But Supreme Court justices also read the *Congressional Record* and are alert to the content of the public media. Thus they are likely to understand when a Court decision has aroused public indignation and inflamed congressional oratory. The Court has no means of enforcing compliance with its decisions other than through the goodwill and customary deference of citizens, politicians, and government officials. If the Supreme Court wishes to maintain its high status in the political system, it must—in the long run—strike a balance between the ideological convictions of its members and the society in which it operates.

In this sense, the Supreme Court is no less immune to the pressures of the political process than the other and more explicitly political institutions of government. The Supreme Court's 1974 decision that invalidated President Nixon's claim of executive privilege to withhold tape recordings related to a criminal investigation came at a time when a clear majority of congressmen and citizens (through the opinion polls) had declared their opposition to the Nixon presidency. In the same year a new majority on the Court also modified the Court's previously strong stand in favor of enforced busing to achieve "racial balance" in the public schools; nor did this decision run counter to public opinion. Thus the Supreme Court is not as far removed from the dynamics of popular government as a simple reading of the Constitution would suggest.

JUDICIAL REVIEW

Most Americans regard judicial review as a necessary and indispensable part of democracy's institutional apparatus. They would view their cherished rights as very insecure if the Supreme Court were to lose its power to declare federal and state laws null and void when deemed in conflict with the Constitution, although others feel insecure because the Court *can* nullify. Simply stated, the case for judicial review of legislation amounts to this: Since the courts must apply the law to cases that come before them, they must, if there is a conflict of laws, determine which law is superior to the other, and they must apply and uphold that higher law—which, in the United States, is the federal Constitution as interpreted by the United States Supreme Court.

A further reason for judicial review in a federal system is the necessity of an arbiter to keep both the national and state governments within their proper constitutional spheres of power, to resolve conflicts between them, and to settle disputes between or among the states themselves. Judicial review is also necessary to maintain the separation of governmental powers among legislative, executive, and judicial branches.

Apart from direct criticism of judicial review, it must be noted that several democracies—and especially Great Britain—have adhered strictly to constitutional limitations, preserved individual liberties, and maintained thoroughgoing democracy without it. As will be seen in Chapter 11, the respect that the British people accord to tradition and established principles and practices (whether written or unwritten) constitutes a bulwark against despotic or arbitrary government that—for them, at least—is every bit as effective as the accumulated decisions of all our Supreme Courts.

Attacks on the Court

Inevitably, the Supreme Court has been unable to please all of the people all of the time. Both major political parties and persons of all shades of opinion have denounced the Court at various periods in our history. Those who praised it for invalidating the early New Deal legislation berated it when it reversed such decisions. The Court moves too slowly for some and too rapidly for others. A new grievance was provided by two decisions in the early 1960s; one held unconstitutional the (noncompulsory) recital of a nondenominational prayer; the other, the required reading of the Bible in the public schools. Both rulings were based on the First Amendment, as extended to the states by the Fourteenth.[2]

Other recent decisions have provoked public demands and congressional proposals to alter the Court's policies and to curb its appellate jurisdiction, e.g., over cases involving the questioning of witnesses by congressional investigating committees, those involving the authority of a state to regulate admission to the practice of law in the courts of the state, and those concerned with the rights of suspects apprehended by the police, the definition of "obscenity" in the censorship of films and printed media, the legality of religious prayer in the public schools, the busing of schoolchildren to achieve "racial balance," and the right of states to enact their own laws against subversive activities. Recently proposed constitutional amendments would deprive the Supreme Court of jurisdiction in cases involving apportionment of state legislatures and would create a Court of the Union, which could review Supreme Court decisions involving federal-state relations.

Continuity of the Court

Clearly, criticism and defense of judicial review have not yet become purely academic in the United States, and yet there is no conceivable possibility that Americans will abandon a governmental device which they gave to the world, which several other nations (including West Germany, Austria, Japan,

---

[2]*Engel v. Vitale,* 370 U.S. 421 (1962) (prayers); *School District of Abington Township, Pennsylvania et al. v. Schempp et al.,* 31 *Law Week* 4683 (June 17, 1963), 374 U.S. 203 (1963) (Bible reading).

Italy, and India) have recently adopted, and which has served the country well for two centuries. Not the least of the Supreme Court's achievements has been its protection of civil rights and liberties, and it must be admitted—especially from the standpoint of minority groups in the United States—that the Supreme Court has been a more vigorous supporter of the basic values of democracy than any of the other branches of American government. It may be the case that the Court can stake out for itself this progressive, even visionary, role precisely because its members are removed from the electoral process—which makes legislators and presidents more sensitive to the self-interest of the dominant groups in the society.

LIBERTIES AND RIGHTS

Liberty is fundamental not only to the principles of democracy but also to its practice. Unless citizens can freely exchange information and opinions through all the available media of communication, unless they can form parties and associations to promote their political and other group interests, and unless they can hold public meetings, urge the adoption of policies at variance with those of the government, and support candidates of their own choosing, democracy cannot exist. This is not to say that no restrictions whatever may be placed upon the manner in which these basic liberties may be exercised. "The most stringent protection of free speech would not protect a man in falsely shouting 'fire' in a theatre and causing a panic."[3]

The claim of freedom of religion, as another example, cannot be allowed to defeat society's right to prohibit practices deemed prejudicial to public morals (e.g., polygamy) or to thwart the operation of laws held necessary to the protection of the public health (e.g., compulsory vaccination). Freedom of the press does not include immunity from the law of libel, nor is the right of association held to extend to organizations that proclaim their contempt for democratic methods and flaunt their intention to employ force to achieve their aims. Liberty of contract and business enterprise is subject to regulations designed to protect and promote the public health, safety, and morals. No one's liberty includes the right to deny the equal liberty of others. Freedom implies responsibility; the rights recognized and safeguarded by a democratic society are matched by duties owed to that society by those enjoying such protection.

Defining "Liberties" and "Rights" The term "civil liberty" in its most general usage "connotes the freedom of the individual with respect to personal action, the possession and use of property, religious belief and worship and the expression of opinion."[4] This freedom implies a right of protection against infringement by government or by private persons or groups. Other definitions of civil liberty mention "liberty as defined by law," "personal security," and the "lawful rights which result from the existence of organized government."[5] The term is very nearly synonymous with "civil rights," except that the latter refers to "rights enjoyed and protected under positive municipal law."[6] In other words, civil rights are specific, enumerated rights derived solely from the state; civil liberties, on the other hand, are sometimes actually enjoyed and respected without precise formulation in constitutions and bills of rights. Civil rights accrue to individuals by virtue of what they *are*—citizens, for example, born in a particular country and with the right to vote after attaining a certain age. Civil liberties relate more to what people *do*—speaking publicly, for example, or publishing their beliefs and attempting to organize other citizens who support their point of view in order to influence government.

Historical Background

Whether referred to as liberties or rights, these human freedoms have evolved out of a past in which they were not recognized at all, and they are presently undergoing a further expansion that is projecting them into the economic and social sphere. Civil liberties, as we know them, are of modern origin. The first civil liberty to secure

---

[3]Dissenting opinion of Justice Holmes in *Schenk v. U.S.*, 249 U.S. 47 (1919).

[4]Robert E. Cushman, "Civil Liberties," in *The Encyclopaedia of the Social Sciences,* The Macmillan Company, New York, 1930, vol. 3, p. 509.

[5]E. C. Smith and A. J. Zurcher (eds.), *Dictionary of American Politics,* Barnes & Noble, Inc., New York, 1944, p. 54.

[6]John Dickinson, "Civil Rights," in *The Encyclopaedia of the Social Sciences,* The Macmillan Company, New York, 1930, vol. 3, p. 513.

widespread recognition was freedom of religious worship. Beginning with Magna Carta in 1215, successive English constitutional documents enlarged the scope of civil liberties to include protection against the quartering of soldiers in private homes, the trial of civilian offenders by martial law, imprisonment without a proper trial, excessive bail, royal suspension of law, and royal interference with parliamentary elections or freedom of debate. The doctrine of civil liberties was further developed in the United States through the colonial charters, which spelled out relationships between the colonists and the mother country, and also as an outgrowth of the philosophy of the "natural rights of man," which gained wide support in both Europe and the United States during the seventeenth and eighteenth centuries. This concept, of Stoic origin, held that all men, regardless of race, creed, or color, were endowed by nature or by God with natural rights with which the state could not justifiably interfere. As was noted in Chapter 2, John Locke's version of the social contract doctrine held that the individual retained virtually all these natural rights after consenting to the establishment of government, especially the rights of life, liberty, and property, which were declared to be inalienable.

Institutionalizing Liberty Locke's philosophy was embodied in the American Declaration of Independence and in the bills of rights of the early state constitutions. It was subsequently reflected in the Bill of Rights appended to the United States Constitution at the demand of several state ratifying conventions. Although the framers of the United States Constitution did not intend to establish a democratic system of government, they sought to safeguard certain liberties by means of provisions incorporated in the body of the Constitution. The guarantee of jury trial in federal criminal cases (Article 3, Section 2), the definition of treason (Article 3, Section 3), the guarantees of the privileges and immunities of citizens (Article 4, Section 2) and of a republican form of government for every state (Article 4, Section 4), and the protection against bills of attainder, ex post facto laws, and suspension of the writ of habeas corpus—all were safeguards of individual liberty.

Many additions to these early enumerations have since been made. Later amendments to the Constitution of the United States prohibited human slavery; extended the suffrage by forbidding state voting restrictions based upon race, color, previous condition of servitude, or sex; and prohibited the states from abridging the privileges or immunities of citizens and from depriving any person of life, liberty, or property without due process of law or denying anyone the equal protection of the laws. While most of these provisions were designed to protect the then newly emancipated black citizens of the United States, judicial interpretation has diffused their application in many directions; one of the most important consequences has been the broadened meaning of due process of law to include not merely procedural matters such as a fair trial but also the substantive content of legislation. In this way the Supreme Court has made itself the protector of civil liberties against state—as well as federal—encroachments.

American Liberties Today

It is impossible to make a neat, tidy list of all the rights enjoyed under the American system of government. Some rights are specifically protected by our federal Constitution against impairment by the national government; others, against impairment by the states; and still others, against impairment by either. Other rights are specifically protected by state constitutions. Among the more important civil rights enjoyed by Americans today (each being relative rather than absolute and also subject to judicial interpretation) are the following: freedom of religion, speech, the press, peaceable assembly, association, and petition; security against unreasonable searches and seizures; protection against double jeopardy (being tried twice for the same offense); protection against self-incrimination (being compelled to testify against oneself); protection against deprivation of life, liberty, or property without due process of law; and protection against having private property taken for public use without just compensation; the right to a speedy and public trial by an impartial jury; the right to choose counsel for one's defense, to subpoena witnesses in one's favor, and to have a trial that is fair in all respects and in accordance with due process of law; security against excessive bail or fines and against cruel and unusual punishments; the equal protection of the laws; protection against slavery, involuntary servitude, ex post facto laws, bills of attainder, unwarranted suspension of the writ of habeas corpus, and changing legislative definitions of treason; and, finally, various guarantees related to taxation—uniformity of indirect federal taxes, fairness in tax classification, and firmly established Supreme Court precedents holding that all taxation must be for a public purpose, i.e., not calculated to aid one group at the expense of another.

Extending the Definition of Liberty In recent years, as a consequence of the problems presented by the era of technology, the discussion of liberties and rights has turned increasingly toward the need to proclaim and protect economic and social rights. Where the statesmen of earlier centuries were preoccupied with establishing and safeguarding political and civil liberty, today's emphasis falls on such rights as those to a job, to education, to a living wage, to decent housing, and to security against the hazards of unemployment, ill health, and old age. It is contended that without such minimal security, neither political nor civil liberty is real or complete. Thus the 1946 constitutions of the French Fourth Republic and of the Italian republic explicitly recognized and guaranteed such rights as those of workers to organize in unions of their own choice, to bargain collectively, and to strike; equal access to education for all persons; and the guarantee of protection against the hazards of illness, unemployment, and old age. The preamble to the constitution of the French Fifth Republic, adopted in 1958, "solemnly proclaims" the "attachment" of the French people to these rights.

Besides this assumption by the democratic state of new responsibilities toward its citizens there is the growing recognition that the liberties, rights, and privileges of membership in a democracy also involve correlative duties on the part of the individual.

Protecting Civil Liberties

Democratic principles require that protection be accorded to civil liberties, but such protection varies both in method and in extent among democratic nations. In the United States, the courts, through judicial review of both legislation and administration, have become the guardians of civil liberty and, speaking broadly, have upheld it consistently despite occasional lapses. In most other democracies, the protection of civil liberties is entrusted to the national legislature. In England, civil liberties are certainly as secure as they are in the United States. In the democracies of continental Europe, the administrative courts afford protection against infringement of such rights by administrators, but not against possible invasion by the national parliament. Although the parliaments of Great Britain, France, Switzerland, the Scandinavian countries, and other nations with strong democratic traditions have shown consistent respect for civil liberty, there are many signs that European democracies are tending toward judicial review of legislation, which should provide additional protection for civil liberties.

In the final analysis, public opinion is the ultimate sanction behind all bills and declarations of individual liberties. Courts, as well as legislative assemblies, reflect (whether promptly or belatedly) the temper of the popular mind. Thus in wartime or other periods of emergency, there is a noticeable tendency to impose and justify restrictions upon freedom of speech, the press, association, assembly, and education; sometimes such restrictions affect religious groups that oppose war or ceremonies like saluting the flag. Both world wars were accompanied by a variety of restrictions upon civil liberty in the United States, Great Britain, and other democracies; in the United States, the Supreme Court upheld some, though not all, such restrictions. In the aftermath of World War I, nearly half the American states passed laws against sedition and criminal syndicalism, which were generally upheld by the state and federal courts; in the period of tension following World War II we again witnessed an attack upon civil liberties that involved the risk of seriously curtailing the liberties of innocent persons caught up in a wave of popular concern over the apparent threat of communism. The distress provoked by Vice President Agnew's attacks on the public media after 1968 reflected this long-established reluctance to allow the government to dictate what should be said and who should say it.

The Problem of Censorship Quite apart from the dangers of internal subversion, mention should be made of the tendency of well-intentioned persons and organizations to impose their concepts of decency, morality, and proper conduct by means of legislation. This tendency is particularly marked in the United States, where both the Puritan tradition and the social policies of the Catholic Church have produced many legislative attempts at censorship. Many other organizations and groups, nonreligious in nature, also agitate to secure laws imposing censorship in various fields. While the motives of all these groups may be above question, censorship tends to spread from one area of conduct to another and from the moral sphere to economic and political ideas. A militant minority sometimes succeeds in imposing its views upon an inactive majority and often places its own members upon the board of censors or other supervisory agency. A crucial question is: Who shall be the censors to determine what is immoral or indecent? Wide differences of opinion exist on this subject, among individuals and among nations. It is obvious that complete license cannot be permitted in any society, no matter how democratic. There must be social control over utterances which are clearly beyond the pale of decency or which are almost universally conceded to be injurious to the morals of young persons. However, democracies must be vigilant against legislative encroachments in the name of morality, especially where there is any considerable disagreement among the citizenry.

No hard-and-fast line can be drawn between civil liberties and the need for social control. Even a society passionately devoted to the cause of liberty must enact various social regulations that appear to encroach upon the civil liberties of certain groups. The American states possess what is called the "police power"; this is the power to pass laws for the protection of the public health, safety, morals, and welfare. Such laws usually restrict someone's liberty (e.g., to smoke marijuana or to seek an abortion without the approval of the state), and the United States Supreme Court then decides (if the results of the state's exercise of its police powers are brought before the Court) how to reconcile the public advantage sought by the legislation with the civil or other liberties alleged to be invaded. This balancing of public benefit against individual or group detriment is one of the Court's most vital functions. The Court examines the actual extent of the social evil to be remedied by the law, inquires whether the law will in fact substantially alleviate the evil, and considers the effect on the liberty of those adversely affected. Not as directly tied to public opinion as legislators, judges and Supreme Court justices have tended to be more tolerant of deviations from the social norm and thus less willing to impose the majority's notions of morality on the minority.

Legislative Investigating Committees

In the years following World War II, the fear of espionage and infiltration by international communism led to the establishment of both federal and state legislative committees to investigate "un-American" activities. At times these committees were so concerned with the dangers to public security that they failed to respect fully the rights of individuals summoned before them or mentioned in the hearings they conducted. Some chairmen and members of such committees seemed more anxious to capture headlines than subversives. As a result, many who were devoted to the preservation of civil liberties urged the complete abolition of un-American activities committees.

Investigating the Loyalty of Citizens Legislative investigating committees represent the merging, rather than the separation, of powers; they perform the functions of investigator, judge, jury, and legislator. While using the judicial powers of subpoena and contempt citation, the members of such committees enjoy immunity as legislators against suits for slander. As demonstrated by the earlier investigations into alleged subversion, this immunity allows them to make irresponsible remarks, not only about witnesses before them, but also about other persons who are not present to defend themselves and who are sometimes never given that opportunity.

Hearings before some legislative investigating committees have been conducted without due process of law. Hearsay evidence is admitted, as it would not be in a court of law; the accused is seldom allowed to confront his accusers or, in most cases, to learn their identity. Thus there can be no cross-examination of witnesses for the prosecution, nor can the accused bring witnesses in his defense.

Similar procedural defects characterize hearings held by many state and federal loyalty review boards, which pass upon dismissals of government employees as poor security or loyalty risks. Here the absence of adverse witnesses is further aggravated by the lack of specific charges that the dismissed employee and his counsel could seek to refute. It should be noted that no one has a constitutional right to be employed by any level of government, but, at the same time, all citizens are entitled to equal protection of the laws and to due process of law—regardless of their ideological orientation. A state's willingness to tolerate nonconformity is a major test of its democratic character. The strength of our commitment to democratic values is not measured by the extent to which everyone else thinks and acts the way we do.

But legislative, judicial, and popular support for congressional investigation of citizen beliefs depends largely on an international climate of hostility and confrontation. The two world wars and the wars in Korea and Vietnam were all accompanied by governmental pressure for opinion conformity, following the argument that any opposition to the government's foreign and military policies only aided the enemy and prolonged the conflict. (And this well may be one of the costs a free society must pay in order to remain free.) A major accomplishment of the first Nixon administration (1969–1972), however, was the reduction of international tension and cold-war rhetoric through its policies of consultation and tentative cooperation with the Soviet Union and Communist China. In the early 1970s the Congress still maintained its committees on "internal security," which were empowered to investigate subversion and thus were inevitably involved in confusing the differences between opposition and treason. The importance of these committees, however, seemed to be declining, especially as the one-time leader of anticommunism in the United States (Richard M. Nixon) announced the arrival of a new era of international negotiation and compromise.

Investigating the Executive: Watergate The investigative thrust of Congress has more recently been in the direction of the executive branch of government instead of toward citizens and minuscule groups with unpopular beliefs. The Watergate break-in and subsequent cover-up that troubled the second Nixon administration raised to the point of high drama questions about the meaning of the separation of powers and the appropriate relationships between Congress and the presidency. In resisting the efforts of the Senate Watergate committee and the special prosecutor to subpoena tape recordings and written memorandums related to the Watergate affair, President Nixon claimed "executive privilege" and argued that the making of public policy requires the president and his staff "to communicate among themselves in complete candor, and that their tentative judgments, their exploration of alternatives, and their frank comments on issues and personalities at home and abroad remain confidential."[7] The President was saying essentially that any cooperation with congressional investigations into the activities of the presidential office must derive from the free will of the chief executive and is not compelled by the Constitution—even under the circumstances of impeachment proceedings. Senator Sam J. Ervin, Jr., chairman of the Watergate investigating committee, responded that "there is nothing in the Constitution of the United States that gives the President the power to withhold information concerning political activities or information concerning illegal activities."[8]

The sensation and controversy associated with Watergate helped to illustrate the ambiguity of executive-legislative relationships under the United States Constitution, particularly in the context of intense political conflict. It was inevitable, then, that clarification of these relationships and the resolution of the struggle between President Nixon and Congress should turn on the intervention of the Supreme Court. In *United States of America v. Richard M. Nixon* the Court implicitly endorsed Senator Ervin's views of a president's obligations under the Constitution. The Court's unanimous decision, handed down on July 24, 1974, held that President Nixon had overstepped the boundaries of the separation of powers. Chief Justice Warren E. Burger, a Nixon appointee, wrote that executive privilege "cannot prevail over the fundamental demands of due process of law in the fair administration of criminal justice." Thus President Nixon was obliged to turn over to the Special Watergate

---

[7] Quoted from President Nixon's letters of July 1973 and January 1974 to the Senate Watergate committee, as reported in the *Los Angeles Times*, Jan. 5, 1974.
[8] Quoted in the *Los Angeles Times*, Jan. 5, 1974.

Prosecutor tape recordings which revealed that the President had lied to the American people about the extent of his knowledge of the Watergate cover-up and that he had encouraged perjury in the testimony of his subordinates, conspired in the obstruction of justice, and attempted to use the agencies of government (the FBI, CIA, and Internal Revenue Service) in the pursuit of narrow political ends. This was a chilling reminder of the extent of power that has been accumulated by the executive branch of government and dramatic testimony of the importance to responsible government of a political leader's personal values.

The lessons of Watergate But the intervention of the Supreme Court, and President Nixon's subsequent resignation from office in the face of certain impeachment and conviction, came within the context of an aroused citizenry and Congress. Without the sense of integrity that motivated less exalted government officials, a crusading free press, and an independent judiciary (especially as represented by District Court Judge John J. Sirica), it is doubtful that the investigative powers of Congress would have been fully mobilized or that the whole truth of Watergate would ever have been revealed to the American people. If it is true that "eternal vigilance is the price of liberty," one still must ask who has the specific responsibility for being vigilant. In the United States, an important part of the answer is in terms of the judicial system, but the dramas of Watergate suggested that this is by no means the entire answer.

Watergate also made clear that the separation of powers works best not when the powers of government are separated but when they are coordinated. Coordination in turn requires a willingness to tolerate (not to punish) the opposition and a shrewd political sense of bargaining that has already been referred to in the earlier discussion of presidential power (Chapter 9). Much of Richard Nixon's sad fate in fact may be attributed to his abiding suspicion of those who expressed opposition to his policies, to his consequent insistence on secrecy, and to his continuing unwillingness to deal directly with congressional leaders, party leaders, and the press. These failings were reflected in Nixon's narrow centralization of authority among his closest political advisers, none of whom had ever stood for election or occupied public office. They in turn shut him off from the flow of political communications that might have helped him to avoid the tragedy of Watergate. But Nixon himself, when he assumed the presidency in January 1969, had been out of public office for eight years and away from the give-and-take of congressional politics for sixteen years. There is no power without politics, and it may be that the fundamental error of the Nixon presidency was to try to remove politics from the exercise of power.

THE DYNAMICS OF NATIONAL GOVERNMENT: AMERICAN POLITICS

The essential nature of political parties and their role in the modern state are fully discussed in Chapter 16, thus making anything more than brief mention unnecessary at this point. However, the student must recognize the vital truth that modern democratic government is impossible without political parties—that democratic government *is* party government. The current challenge in American politics, especially at the national level, is to make such party government responsible. In Great Britain, largely because of stronger national party organization and discipline, responsible party government has been achieved. In the United States, the loose, federated character of the national party organizations, coupled with the presidential type of government, the vast extent and sectional diversity of the country, and our irrational fear of party machines (i.e., strong organizations), has thus far resulted only in partisanship, not responsible government.

The Development of American Political Parties

The Founding Fathers made no provision for political parties in the Constitution. James Madison probably reflected the opinion of his colleagues when he wrote in *The Federalist* of the evils of partisanship and "factions," as he called political parties. He defended the Constitution on the ground that the evils of factions would be curbed in a large federal government, for it would be unlikely that any party or faction would capture control of all the states or of all branches of the national government. He was at least partly correct insofar as political parties were concerned, but he was wrong with regard to pressure groups, another type of modern faction now wielding great power on the national scene.

However, the silence of the Constitution could not prevent the rise of political parties, which appeared almost at once. The Federalist party was dominant from 1789 to 1800, when it lost both the presidency and control of Congress to the Jeffersonian Democratic Republicans. The period of Democratic Republican supremacy (1801–1825) was followed by the so-called era of personal politics, during which party lines were being redrawn. The Federalist party had gone out of existence following its complete repudiation by the voters for having opposed the War of 1812, and many smaller groups—personal followers of leading political figures—filled this void. The Jeffersonian Republicans, renamed the Democratic party, held power for twenty-four of the thirty-two years between Andrew Jackson's first inauguration and that of Abraham Lincoln in 1861. Its chief opponent during this period was the Whig party (so named because of its opposition to "King Andrew"), which, however, held the presidency for only eight of these years.

The Republican party, formed in 1854 amid the political confusion caused by the issue of slavery, was the only third (or minority) party ever to achieve success in national politics. Between 1861 and 1913 it controlled the presidency for forty years, while the Democratic party controlled the office for only eight years, during the two terms of Grover Cleveland.

Presidential Parties in the Twentieth Century

Between 1913 and 1953 the presidential scales tilted in favor of the Democratic party. Woodrow Wilson held office for eight years, Franklin D. Roosevelt for twelve (the first president to break the tradition against a third term, and starting a fourth term at the time of his death), and Harry S Truman for eight. This twenty-eight-year Democratic total considerably outweighed the twelve years of Harding, Coolidge, and Hoover (1921–1933). The election of Eisenhower in 1952 returned the presidency to the Republican party after an interval of twenty years. The election of John F. Kennedy in 1960 and of Lyndon B. Johnson in 1964 made the 1913–1969 box score: Democrats thirty-six years, Republicans twenty. The Republicans' success in 1968 and 1972 coincided with serious divisions within the Democratic party and a long and costly war abroad that had embittered public opinion; indeed, the former was largely caused by the latter. Thus the Republicans, before the 1976 presidential elections, had controlled the presidency for only sixteen of the last thirty-four years.

Especially in terms of presidential politics, then, the Republicans are the weaker of the two major parties in the United States. Over the years, public opinion polls have shown a progressive decline in Republican strength: 38 percent of United States citizens identified themselves as Republicans in 1940, 33 percent did so in 1950, 30 percent did in 1960, and 29 percent did in October 1970. In mid-1973, according to the Gallup poll, 24 percent of United States citizens identified with the Republican party, 43 percent identified with the Democratic party, and 33 percent declared themselves "independents." That one in three respondents identified with neither Democrats nor Republicans again makes clear the relatively weak structure, in terms of both organization and ideological commitment, of political parties in the United States.

These data also suggest that to capture the presidency, the Republican party must capitalize on general dissatisfaction that is associated with an incumbent Democratic administration, and it must nominate a well-known candidate whose position on the major issues of the day is relatively vague. In this way, the Republican candidate can maintain the partisan loyalty of most Republican voters, capture the majority of independents, and cut into the ranks of nominal Democrats. In the context of disenchantment with United States military involvement in Southeast Asia, Richard M. Nixon turned the incumbent Democrats out of office in 1968 with only 43.4 percent of the popular vote. Nixon also benefited from the division of the remaining votes between two candidates (Hubert Humphrey received 42.7 percent, and George Wallace received 13.5 percent). The single-member district, simple-plurality system that is operable in the allocation of each state's electoral votes thus worked to Nixon's advantage in a close popular election; with only 43 percent of the popular vote, Nixon received 56 percent of the electoral-college vote in 1968.

It also must be remembered that the results of congressional elections do not always conform with the presidential vote. Popular presidential candidates sometimes run far ahead of the rest of the party ticket, especially in particular states or regions. This was the case in 1952, when Dwight Eisenhower received an impressive popular and electoral majority, while the Republican party won only a narrow victory in the House and Senate. In 1956, President Eisenhower was reelected by an even larger popular majority, but the Republicans did not win control of either the House or the Senate. Neither in 1968 nor in 1972 was Richard Nixon able to transfer his own electoral success to Republican congressional candidates, and in both instances the Congress remained solidly in the hands of Democrats. Such a *partisan* division between executive and legislative branches of government may be more effective as a "separation of powers" than any constitutional division of authority designed by the Founding Fathers. Such situations also illustrate the American tendency to vote for (or against) the man rather than the party, a tendency due partly to the paucity of clear-cut ideological differences between our two major parties. In midterm or off-year elections (i.e., when there is no presidential contest) congressional and senatorial candidates cannot ride into office on the coattails of a popular presidential candidate; not infrequently the president's party loses control of one or both houses of Congress at the midterm. This happened to President Wilson in 1918, to President Hoover in 1930, to President Truman in 1946, to President Eisenhower in 1954, and to many other presidents in the past, thus making responsible party government impossible. All too frequently (as in 1930–1932 and 1946–1948) congressional partisanship has led to deadlock, with urgent national problems neglected for the sake of political advantage.

American Parties as Coalitions

The lack of sharp ideological differences between the Republican and Democratic parties is criticized by doctrinaires and praised by pragmatists. Continental Europeans often regard our major parties as coalitions because their own parties have often been narrowly based on religion, nationality, class, economic status, or ideological persuasion. To Americans, on the other hand, the multiparty systems of France, Italy, and Germany resemble the sectional interests and pressure groups that operate within the intentionally all-inclusive major American parties. Certainly the effect of getting diverse elements inside one big party tent is to harmonize, or at least minimize, their differences; conversely, the effect of the multiparty system is divisive, with a premium placed on widening the area of difference instead of the area of agreement. Third or minor parties have provided outlets for those Americans who rebelled against "Tweedledum and Tweedledee" or to whom certain principles (or prejudices) were so important that the certainty of defeat at the polls was of little consequence. However, a few third parties have made a deep imprint on American history; the Free Soil party of 1848, the Populist party of 1890–1900, the Progressive movement of 1912 and 1924, and the Republican party itself have altered the course of our politics. Whenever the platform planks of a third party attract popular support, one of the two major parties adopts them, thus stealing the thunder of the third party and rejuvenating the old one.

The attempts of both major parties to win support from all sections and classes make them fill their platforms with conflicting promises and weasel words. Each seeks to outbid the other for the support of business, farmers, and labor, despite the obvious fact that the interests of these groups frequently conflict. Even if the national platform appears consistent (in which case it must be very vague indeed), campaign speakers often make conflicting promises in different parts of the country—even in an age of radio and television. Both major parties include diverse and antagonistic elements. Ever since the days of Thomas Jefferson and Aaron Burr (who is commonly associated with the organization and machinations of Tammany Hall), the Democratic party has been plagued by conflict between its conservative, "100 percent American," Protestant, well-to-do Southern elements and the liberal, immigrant, Catholic, working-class voters of the North. Southern Democrats urged the retention of national prohibition, while their Northern brethren campaigned for its repeal. The Republican party is as deeply, if not as conspicuously, divided within itself; its Eastern wing is staunchly pro-big-business, while its Western section (made up of farmers and small businessmen) has been markedly favorable to legislation curbing big business and big finance.

In foreign policy, the Eastern Republicans are far more internationalist than their fellow party members in the Midwest, who first clung to isolationism and then, shifting to the opposite extreme, became militant anticommunists and international interventionists. In the early 1960s the Republican party was further divided by the emergence of a right wing led by Senator Barry Goldwater of Arizona, whose views were and are diametrically opposed to those of such liberal Republicans as Nelson Rockefeller, Senator Jacob Javits of New York, Senator Charles Percy of Illinois, and others. Both major parties include right, center, and left factions; both include people who seem so nostalgically bemused by the past that they are unwilling to face the present; and both include leaders and factions who argue that the future is determined by enlightened policies and progressive programs initiated in the present.

The Functions of American Political Parties

The heterogeneity and catchall characteristics of this country's two major parties, however, may be viewed as salutary for democracy in general and the United States in particular. Democrats and Republicans thereby keep third or splinter parties in their proper place—as goads and spurs to save the major parties from political rigor mortis. The ritualistic invocations of the spirits of departed political heroes—whether Lincoln and McKinley or Jefferson, Jackson, and Franklin D. Roosevelt—conveniently ignore the fact that their respective parties have moved far afield in the interval and have embraced programs formerly unheard of and ideas of dubious political origin. Social security, public health insurance, aid to education, a guaranteed minimum wage, public funding of selected bankrupt corporations, and parity payments to farmers are now Republican by adoption though Democratic in origin.

Political parties have been potent forces working toward greater democracy in the United States. The rise of parties transformed the electoral college from a gathering of the well-born and well-to-do into the echo of the people's voice. Political party competition gave us universal suffrage; the initiative, referendum, and recall in state and local government; and innumerable other reforms (economic and social, as well as political), which, added together, equal modern American democracy. Despite "boss rule"—which is less prevalent than commonly supposed and which flourishes best where the people sleep—the political party is increasingly compelled to consider what the people want and what they will endure. Tammany Hall, which perhaps unjustifiably became a byword for the "machine," long understood the responsibility of the party to the common people—as have such comparable Republican organizations as the old Vare machine in Philadelphia and countless Republican party machines in the more rural areas of the country. Asked why Tammany seemed so bent on helping the poor, an old chieftain of the "wigwam" is reported to have said, "Because they're so grateful—and because there are so many more of them!" Even when compounded with such cynicism, the humanitarian ingredient shows through.

Both major parties have traditionally presented platforms containing something for everybody; neither is so strong in terms of sectional, class, or interest-group support that it can espouse any narrow cluster of interests without going down to defeat. This point was made dramatically in 1964 by the Republican disaster that attended the Goldwater candidacy. And in 1972 the Democrats' George McGovern also became too closely identified with narrow partisan and ideological interests and thus was unable to maintain the cohesion of even the Democratic plurality (Senator McGovern received 37.5 percent of the popular vote, compared with 60.7 percent for President Nixon).

As in England, where both Conservatives and Labourites must woo middle-class voters in order to win, both Republican and Democratic organizations must get support from the so-called independent voters to achieve victory. This may indeed lead to me-tooism, but it can help to minimize socioeconomic and cultural cleavage in the society and to maintain continuity and stability in national policy. Neither major party can entirely reverse the policy of its predecessor in office without serious consequences in the next election. Programs, however socialist in fact or conservative in label, become so enmeshed in the fabric of the national economy that to renounce them becomes equivalent to political suicide. Any party that proposes going back to something is headed offstage. The consequences also include, however, a *personality* orientation in American politics and fragmented political parties that are usually unable or unwilling to legislate the policies adopted in a national convention. That these generalizations are made in a comparative context will be apparent from the following chapter.

STATE AND LOCAL GOVERNMENT
The States

The constitutional position of the states in the American federal system has already received some attention. This is a union of equal states, and in admitting new states Congress, in principle, cannot impose conditions that would place such new states in a position of inferiority. When Congress in fact has exacted promises from a territorial legislature before admitting that territory to statehood, the Supreme Court has held that the new state may disregard such promises. The admissions of Alaska (1958) and Hawaii (1959) are noteworthy in that they have transformed a union of contiguous states into one of transcontinental and transoceanic proportions.

Federal-State Relations Federal-state relations have undergone marked changes since 1789. There are today relatively few governmental functions that are carried on exclusively by one level of government. Health, welfare, public education, highways, law enforcement, conservation, public works, hospitals, and public housing provide significant examples of federal, state, and local cooperation. Apart from grants-in-aid and other extensions of federal control, there has been a marked growth of compensatory and reciprocal state and federal legislation to cope with problems common to both levels of government. Thus the federal government, through its power to regulate interstate commerce, may establish uniform regulations among some or all of the fifty states with regard (for example) to the transportation of stolen goods, the establishment of daylight saving time, rates charged to farmers by interstate *and* intrastate carriers, and the services and travel facilities made available to all citizens, regardless of race. While the states cannot constitutionally prevent any legitimate commodity from being shipped in from another state, the federal government can do so. There has also been much cooperation in the field of taxation; the states have been permitted to tax the property and shares of stock of national banks, and the federal estate-tax law permits a credit of 80 percent for inheritance taxes paid to a state.

Uniformities and Differences The governmental structures of the states are remarkably uniform. Each state has a written constitution, a governor, a legislature (bicameral in all states except Nebraska), a system of courts and of law (based on English common law except in Louisiana), judicial review of legislation by the state's highest court, a declaration of individual rights, a system of public education (varying widely in different parts of the country), public health and welfare services (also varying widely from state to state), and a system of local government.

However, brief mention should be made of a few conspicuous differences. Until 1971, the voting age varied from eighteen to twenty-one. Until 1964, several states had laws requiring payment of a poll tax in order to vote in federal elections, and seventeen had literacy tests.[9] The term and powers of the governor are far from uniform. In thirty-one states his term is four years; in nineteen, it is two years. The governors of all but nine states have the item veto; that is, they can veto individual items in appropriation bills without rejecting the entire bill. The governor of North Carolina is the only state chief executive who has no veto power whatsoever. Methods of amending state constitutions vary considerably; thirteen states allow voters to propose amendments via the initiative, which is not possible for amendments to the United States Constitution.

Most state legislatures have traditionally over-represented rural areas, to the detriment of the large urban centers. This problem was progressively aggravated by the population trends of recent

---

[9]A federal Commission on Registration and Voting Participation was appointed in March 1963 by President Kennedy. Among other proposals, the Commission recommended that literacy tests be eliminated in determining the qualifications of voters. And, in 1965, the Voting Rights Act outlawed literacy tests, which had typically been used to disenfranchise underprivileged citizens.

decades; the 1960 census revealed new distortions. However, as noted in Chapter 9, the Supreme Court's historic decision in 1962 in *Baker v. Carr* touched off a virtual revolution in state legislative representation.

Although the organization and operation of state governments do not parallel those of the federal government—since the states are *unitary*, not *federal*, in structure—the same basic principles apply alike to both levels of government. All state governments are based on such concepts as those of the separation of powers, checks and balances, and due process of law. But there are substantial variations among the states in terms of state constitutional requirements for legislative action (especially regarding budgetary and fiscal policies), the competitiveness of state political parties, the competence of administrative personnel, the fairness of the courts, and the sources of revenue and extent of state expenditures for welfare and education, as well as differences in many other areas of state government. (In fact, these many variations among the fifty states provide a wealth of data for *comparative* political analysis, even within the context of a single national unit.) The serious fiscal problems encountered by most states over recent years have also induced the federal government to propose various "revenue-sharing" programs. In December 1973, for example, President Nixon signed into law a bill that made available to state and local governments $1.65 billion for the development and administration of manpower programs designed to combat unemployment and to retrain workers for technologically advanced employment. In the context of federal-state cooperation, the legislation also underlined the government's commitment, even under a Republican president, to play an important role in the economy and to serve as the "employer of last resort."

Local Government

Local units of government are the creatures of state, not federal, government. Each state, unless restricted by the state constitution itself, may establish, alter, or abolish any or all of its local government areas and jurisdictions, although the tradition of local home rule and self-government would make it difficult if not impossible for any state to wipe out historic units, whether counties or municipalities, no matter how outmoded by modern conditions.

The Municipality The most vital unit of local government in this age of urbanization is the municipality (city, village, borough, or town). According to the 1960 census, about 70 percent of the population lives in urban areas. The 1970 census recorded a total United States population of 204 million, and of this total approximately 41 percent lived in the thirty-four United States cities with a population in excess of 1 million inhabitants. These data alone make clear the immense changes that have overtaken American life since 1790 (when population density per square mile was 4.5 instead of the 58.9 of 1972), with consequent and radical changes in the role of government at federal, state, and local levels.

Types of municipal government American city governments may be classified under three major types or forms: (1) the mayor-council form, (2) the commission plan, and (3) the council-manager plan. Most large cities still operate under the familiar mayor-council system, with both mayor and council directly elected by the people. In some cities, however, the position of the mayor has been strengthened in recent years. The commission plan, originating in 1900, is in operation in about 300 cities; its central feature is a small commission (of three to five members) elected by the people on a citywide rather than a ward or district basis and exercising both legislative and administrative powers. Displacing the usually large and unwieldy city council and reducing the mayor to mere ceremonial status, the commission plan has speeded up and somewhat streamlined city government. This plan, however, has not worked well and has been abandoned by many cities that tried it. The elective commissioners, who head the several city departments, seldom are qualified administrators, and responsibility is hopelessly divided among the several commissioners.

The council-manager system, currently in the ascendant, is in force in about 1,865 cities—i.e., in nearly half of the cities with more than 25,000 inhabitants. Its main idea is the concentration of authority over, and responsibility for, all municipal administration in the hands of a city manager chosen by the city council, which can dismiss him at any time. This plan avoids the dispersal of administrative authority and responsibility among the numerous directly elected officers found under the mayor-council system or among lay commissioners under the commission plan. The manager, a well-paid expert in public administration, appoints, directs, and removes almost all important city administrative officials; supervises and coordinates all administrative activities; and prepares the budget—which only the city council can adopt. The council is supposed to concentrate on and decide broad questions of public policy, while the manager is concerned with carrying out and administering policies established by the council. Politics may affect the council (and usually does, even where elections are supposed to be nonpartisan), but the manager is relatively removed from the political struggle. Selected for administrative ability and experience and frequently coming from another city or state, an able manager can do much to dilute the influence of politics in municipal administration. These trends also make clear the increasing importance of professionally trained experts in the administration of governmental affairs—at every level of political life.

Reforming Local Government In 1904, Lincoln Steffens published *The Shame of the Cities*, in which he exposed the extent of corruption in municipal governments. Lord Bryce called the city the "disgrace" of American government. Great improvements have since been made, although too few citizens are aware of them. City government today is far more professional, less political in the bad sense of the word, better managed, more efficient, more honest, and more economical. The spread of civil service and the consequent weakening of the spoils system have lessened opportunities for favoritism and corruption and at the same time have produced a growing body of trained and devoted professionals in municipal administration.

It is unfortunate, however, that many Americans pay so little attention to local government affairs. The classical liberal's assumption that citizens are better governed at the local level because they know more about local government is not supported by the facts or by the substantially lower turnout of voters in municipal elections (as compared with voter turnout in national or presidential elections).

And the voters' relative lack of interest in, and knowledge about, local government—even government at the state level—makes it all the easier for special interests to gain unpublicized access to the critical centers of governmental decision making. Local politicians with a stake in perpetuating the status quo and their own jurisdictions are unlikely to participate in federal programs designed to improve the opportunities of underprivileged citizens; it was these kinds of conflicts that helped to assure that President Johnson's War on Poverty program would fall far short of its goals. And the inability of American political parties to cohere political leaders at all levels of government in the efficient administration of a complex society is another comment on the relative irresponsibility of United States government, however well-intentioned its leaders. If the United States is to succumb to chronic political crisis in the foreseeable future, the crisis is likely to begin at the local level of government, where citizen demands (in terms of welfare, municipal services such as transportation, and the quality of the social and physical environment) far exceed governmental capabilities. The observation that cities like New York are essentially "ungovernable"—regardless of the party in power or the qualities of leadership—has become so frequent that it now stands as a tragic cliché.

STUDY-GUIDE QUESTIONS

1 What is the constitutional procedure for appointing Supreme Court justices? What criteria are likely to be applied by a president when he chooses his nominees?
2 To what extent is the Supreme Court isolated from the political process? What factors help to explain substantive changes in judicial decision making over time?
3 In what ways did the Supreme Court's decision in *United States of America v. Richard M. Nixon* clarify the principles of the separation of powers?
4 What explains the ideological ambiguity or overlapping characteristics of the Republican and Democratic parties?
5 What is the meaning of "federalism" in the United States? How do the functions of state and local governments differ from those of the federal government?

REFERENCES

Adrian, Charles R.: *Governing Our Fifty States and Their Communities,* McGraw-Hill Book Company, New York, 2d ed., 1972.
——— and Charles Press: *The American Political Process,* 2d ed., McGraw-Hill Book Company, New York, 1969.
Gellhorn, Walter: *American Rights: The Constitution in Action,* The Macmillan Company, New York, 1960.
Greenstein, Fred I.: *The American Party System and the American People,* 2d ed., Prentice-Hall, Inc., Englewood Cliffs, N.J., 1970.
Hyneman, Charles S.: *The Supreme Court on Trial,* Atherton Press, Inc., New York, 1963.
Key, V. O., Jr.: *Politics, Parties, and Pressure Groups,* 5th ed., Thomas Y. Crowell Company, New York, 1964.
Mason, Alpheus T., and William Beaney: *The Supreme Court in a Free Society,* Prentice-Hall, Inc., Englewood Cliffs, N.J., 1969.
Pritchett, C. Herman: *The American Constitutional System,* McGraw-Hill Book Company, New York, 1963.
Schmidhauser, John R., and Larry Berg: *The Supreme Court and Congress: Conflict and Interaction, 1945–1958,* The Free Press, New York, 1972.

Chapter 11

Politics in Great Britain

BUILDING A STABLE DEMOCRACY

No society is without its cleavages and conflicts, and no state follows a linear path of development from traditionalism to modernity. An independent nobility, for example, does not readily give up its privileges to a centralizing monarchy, nor does a landed aristocracy welcome the growth of a middle class whose new wealth derives from trade, commerce, investment, banking, or—eventually— industrial production. A bourgeoisie that has won political representation from an entrenched aristocracy does not willingly extend voting rights to the society's lower classes. A dominant church is unlikely to encourage the organization of reformist political movements, mass-based political parties, or labor unions, correctly fearing a reduction in its popular influence and authority. Democracy, in short, is neither the logical outcome nor the inevitable successor of authoritarian government. Much depends on the enlightenment and values of political elites. But there also are some important preconditions to the development of stable democracy, as illustrated by the case of Great Britain, which help to smooth the way for political elites committed to the principles of democracy.

Change and Stability

It would be wrong to argue that the development of British democracy has been without major instances of social conflict and political instability. The ancient Celtic peoples inhabiting the British Isles were invaded and occupied by Caesar's legions, by Germanic tribes (the Angles, Saxons, and Jutes), by the Vikings, and by the Normans (from the Norman provinces of France), and they all left their imprint on the social, cultural, and political life of Great Britain.[1] The protracted violence of the Hundred Years' War, the Wars of the Roses, and the Puritan revolution helped to shape the relationships between king and nobility, Parliament and the monarchy, citizens and sovereignty. Social unrest mounted with industrialization from the late eighteenth through the mid-nineteenth centuries. In the late nineteenth and early twentieth centuries, British politics and society were agitated by the issues of Irish independence and by increasing economic conflict that reached high points during the general strike of 1926 and the Great Depression. Even in the early 1970s the conflict over Britain's role in Northern Ireland left a trail of violence through the mails and along the streets of London and Belfast; the Conservative government of Edward Heath struggled with the trade unions for control over Britain's flagging industrial economy; and the Labour government of Harold Wilson exerted itself to bring business and the unions together in a joint assault on the massive problems of inflation, while at the same time maintaining the party's influence over Labour's more radical political and trade union supporters.

The present study, however, continues in the larger context of *comparative* political analysis. And from a comparative perspective it should be noted that Great Britain's evolution toward democratic government and a responsible party system has been relatively stable over time and marked more by continuity than by abrupt departures from the past. The student of comparative politics must first be impressed by the simple observation that the principal institutions of British government—the monarchy, the House of Lords, the House of Commons, the courts, and the system of local government in a unitary state—have remained intact over centuries of sweeping socioeconomic change. The *structures* are the same; it is their *functions* and their interrelationships that have changed. These changes have in turn been facilitated by the long-standing legitimacy of British political institutions. Social conflict is less likely as reforms are implemented through existing institutions, whose substance may change even while their form remains the same.

Preconditions of Stability

But how can one explain Great Britain's capability for change within the context of stability? Some clues may be found in the earlier discussion of revolution versus stable democracy in the first part of Chapter 8. One is well-advised to look first at the cultural characteristics of the society, and the next two chapters, which discuss other European governments and the Soviet Union, will also follow this strategy.

Cultural Characteristics It is apparent at the outset, then, that British society has been and continues to be highly homogeneous in terms of the fundamental dimensions of culture. Even where another language is spoken, as in Wales and in parts of Scotland, English remains the dominant language of economic, social, and political interaction. The British people also are highly homogeneous in terms of race; only about 2 percent of Britain's 54 million people are nonwhite, and most of these immigrated after World War II under the terms of Commonwealth membership (largely from Pakistan, India, and the West Indies). It is significant, however, that as nonwhite immigration increased in Great Britain, especially in the early 1960s, the issue of race and control over immigration became prominent in British politics. But Britain clearly does not face the same magnitude of problems that is generated by racial cleavage in the United States (where blacks and other racial minorities make up 12 percent of the population) or—to cite a more extreme example—in the Sudan (where two-thirds of the population of 17 million is Arab and one-third is black). There also is substantial religious homogeneity in Great Britain; approximately 90 percent of the population is Protestant. Racial and religious homogeneity in Great Britain was even more pronounced during the critical period of early industrialization. Thus the development of potentially antagonistic economic classes was not reinforced by existing cultural cleavages in the society.

Geography and Social Structure An important part of Great Britain's cultural homogeneity can be

---

[1]"Great Britain" refers to England, Scotland, and Wales. "The United Kingdom" (UK) refers to England, Scotland, Wales, and Northern Ireland.

attributed to its island status. Relative geographic isolation has also kept Britain protected from the land wars that have periodically ravaged most of the continental countries since the very moment of their birth. Not having to maintain a large standing army in turn meant for Great Britain a low profile in domestic politics for the military—frequently a source of political instability and authoritarian politics in much of the rest of the world. Britain's island status and its dependency on agricultural imports and foreign trade also required the early growth of an enterprising middle class. And, as Aristotle observed long ago, a large and vital middle class is an indispensable pillar of support for relatively stable and democratic institutions.

Role of the Aristocracy The growth and vitality of the British middle class, within the context of early capitalism, were immensely facilitated by the characteristics of the British aristocracy. In most of the contintental European countries the aristocracy was tied to the land and the production of cereal crops, which required the perpetuation of a servile status for a large class of peasants—a potent force for radical change throughout the world. In England, however, the landowning aristocracy converted the basis of its wealth to pasturage and the raising of sheep for the profitable wool trade. This meant the effective elimination of the English peasantry *before* the onset of industrialization; thus there was no peasantry to ally with a working class for the advancement of a revolutionary program.

In England, aristocratic title was also passed from father to only the eldest son ("primogeniture"), whereas on the Continent aristocratic title was conferred on all the father's male heirs. The continental aristocracy was consequently "closed" and set apart from other social classes, more opposed to political reform, and typically hostile to employment in business or in other professional fields because it was considered demeaning to aristocratic status. The English aristocracy, however, was more "open," largely because it had a greater interest in business and trade *and* because the majority of sons with aristocratic fathers did not inherit their father's title or his wealth. Thus they were compelled to make their way in the worlds of business and politics, and they frequently made quick alliance (through marriage) with the growing bourgeoisie, thereby enlarging and strengthening Britain's middle classes.[2]

In England, the aristocracy was also an important intermediary between the laissez faire interests of capitalism and the regulatory and welfare demands of the emerging working class. Many of the first reforms directed at the social and economic evils of unregulated capitalism, and thus the beginnings of the British welfare state, were initiated by members of the aristocracy who found in politics a new vehicle for their status ambitions.

Political Adaptation British political institutions consequently proved to be more responsive to the demands of new social classes mobilized by economic change. Political adaptation was in turn aided by the relatively slow pace of industrialization. And political reform itself was extended over a relatively long period of time, thus allowing for the measured growth of political parties and for experimentation in new institutional relationships. The extension of the suffrage in Great Britain illustrates the point: In 1820, fewer than 500 men, most of them peers in the House of Lords, elected a majority of members in the House of Commons; the reform bill of 1832 gave the vote to 12 percent of all adult males; in 1867, 30 percent of all adult males were enfranchised; in 1884, 75 percent were enfranchised; in 1918, all adult males, married women, and unmarried women over thirty were given the right to vote; in 1928, all women over twenty-one were entitled to vote; and in 1969, the voting age was lowered to eighteen for all citizens.

On the other hand, where the suffrage has been extended rapidly, as in France in 1848, in Germany after World War I, and in many of the newly independent countries since World War II, the result has been political instability and authoritarian politics. In tsarist Russia (to make the contrast with Great Britain even more obvious) the suffrage was extremely limited, parliament was subordinate to the monarchy, trade unions were illegal, political parties were weak, and the state's role in providing welfare and social services was virtually nonexis-

---

[2]On the "open" and "closed" characteristics of the European aristocracy and for the social and political consequences, see Seymour Martin Lipset, *The First New Nation*, Anchor Books, Doubleday & Company, Inc., Garden City, N.Y., 1967, chap. 6 "Values and Democratic Stability," especially pp. 279–280.

tent. And, as we know, Russia underwent a cataclysmic revolution.

The building of stable democracy, then, is as much a matter of good luck as it is the consequence of good planning and noble intent. And as we focus more closely on the *institutional* development and characteristics of British politics, we should continue to look for additional clues that will help us to explain the relative success and stability of democracy in Great Britain. Especially in comparison with the United States, we also want to determine why government in Great Britain qualifies as so highly "responsible."

THE EVOLUTION OF BRITISH POLITICAL INSTITUTIONS

Responsible government, in the sense of a ministry that can be called to account or ousted by Parliament, is a British invention. And responsible government, in the sense of cohesive political parties that are able to implement programs approved by a majority of voters in a national election, is most clearly illustrated by the British political process. One country after another on the continent of Europe has attempted to import the British parliamentary or cabinet system and to adapt it to its own needs and circumstances. Most have failed, largely because they lacked the preconditions for stable democracy enjoyed by Great Britain and because their party systems varied widely from the model of responsibility exemplified in British parliamentary politics. The first such transplantation occurred after the revolution of 1789 in France; this attempt in turn served as a model for other continental countries emerging from absolute monarchy and embarking upon experiments in constitutional government. As was to be expected, each imitation or adaptation showed marked variations from the British or French system, but all versions of cabinet government have certain common features, and these may be best understood by considering first the basic institutional characteristics of British government.

Modernizing the State

The political institutions of modern Britain, as noted above, are the product of a long, slow, and mainly (though not entirely) peaceful evolution. A process of gradual change has brought the British from feudalism to absolute monarchy, then through aristocracy and oligarchy to democracy. This democracy, despite the survival of kingship, the House of Lords, and a still-stratified social system, is as genuine as any on earth.

England developed the foundations of both its monarchy and its Parliament during the Anglo-Saxon period (the fifth century), although in only the most rudimentary form. After the Norman Conquest (1066), the powers of the king (now a Norman) were increased, and the former Saxon witenagemot, or council of wise men, became two distinct bodies: the Great Council (of nobles) and the *Curia Regis* (king's court), from which both the court system and also the privy council were later derived. The latter became the parent of the modern cabinet.

Although Magna Carta (1215) laid the foundations for British civil liberties and constitutional government, its immediate significance lay in the checks imposed by the rebellious nobles of Runnymede upon the arbitrary and petulant King John. The promises that he made to the nobles were not extended to the common people—the serfs and villeins—until many centuries later.

Development of Parliamentary Supremacy The rise of Parliament began in the thirteenth century; the model Parliament convened by Edward I in 1295 repeated the precedent established in 1265 of summoning, in addition to the nobles, two knights from each shire (county) and two burgesses from each borough (town).[3] Such "commoners" were sometimes elected and sometimes not. The honor of representing one's county or town was more often shunned than sought because a summons to Parliament usually meant that the members would be told by the king of additional taxes to be imposed to support a new war. These were not glad tidings to carry back to one's neighbors.

At first, Parliament possessed neither legislative nor financial powers; in the fifteenth century, however, substantial control was established over the public purse, and an understanding was also reached regarding legislation, whereby the king

---

[3]Only those towns which had been granted royal charters enjoyed borough status; thus not all towns sent representatives to Parliament.

would not enact laws running *contrary* to the petitions laid before him by Parliament. Sessions were infrequent and often depended upon the royal pleasure; during the reigns of Henry VII, Henry VIII, and Elizabeth I, Parliament sank into obscurity and was completely overshadowed by these absolute—though popular—monarchs. The Puritan revolution of the 1640s ushered in a period of violence, confusion, and experimentation, in the course of which the monarchy and the House of Lords were abolished and a republican Commonwealth was established (1649), and from 1653 to 1660 England, Scotland, and Ireland were governed under a written constitution called the Instrument of Government. The style of this regime, headed by Oliver Cromwell as protector, was conservative, the one-house Parliament being elected only by citizens owning a substantial amount of property. The death of Cromwell in 1658 merely accelerated earlier developments toward the restoration of monarchy and a bicameral Parliament, a trend that culminated in the restoration of the Stuart dynasty, in the person of Charles II, in 1660.

This restoration was based on a compromise between a strong Parliament and a strong monarchy, under which the king, although in principle still sovereign and actually still in possession of many substantial powers, yielded the basis of sovereignty to Parliament and its ministers. While Charles II kept the bargain, his brother and successor James II did not; his Stuart stubbornness brought on the Glorious (and bloodless) Revolution of 1688, following which a special Parliament placed William, Prince of Orange, and his wife Mary (a daughter of James II) on the throne. This was done under an explicit agreement, called the Bill of Rights, enacted into law by Parliament; this document approximated a written constitution and, after listing the sins of the Stuart kings, stated emphatically that such acts were illegal. In sum, the Bill of Rights gave Britain the limited constitutional monarchy that it still has today; although the British system of government has been elaborated and refined since 1689, its foundations were the same then as now. The Bill of Rights put an end to all royal pretensions of divine right, placed the monarch under the law, made Parliament legally supreme, and laid down the principles of popular sovereignty and the rule of law, instead of the reign of monarchy.

Among the major political developments since 1689 are the reduced powers of the king, the rise and institutionalization of the cabinet system, the democratization of the suffrage and the House of Commons, a reduction in the powers of the House of Lords, the development of a competitive and largely bipartisan political party system, and the vast expansion of governmental economic controls and social services.

THE BRITISH CONSTITUTION

England provides the classic example of an unwritten constitution that is, however, as highly respected and as strictly obeyed as any written instrument of government. During the last three centuries there has been a growing tendency to reduce more and more of the understandings or customs of the constitution to written form. Today, British constitutional authorities describe the British constitution as consisting of two elements: (1) the *law* of the constitution (basic statutes, fundamental judicial decisions, certain common-law rules, and great compacts or agreements), which is enforceable in the courts, and (2) the *conventions* or customs of the constitution—hallowed by tradition and backed by public opinion—which are not judicially enforceable. Examples of such conventions are the annual sessions of Parliament, the entire cabinet system (until 1937), and much of the present position of the monarch in relation to such matters as the dissolution of the House of Commons.

It should be noted that the law of the British constitution is made by Parliament and is thus distinguishable from ordinary statutes only by its nature and importance. This is in marked contrast to the United States, where both federal and state constitutions have had their source in constitutional conventions distinct from legislatures, are ratified by special procedures, and are, moreover, amended by a process that differs sharply from that followed for ordinary legislation. Thus it is by no means an easy matter to determine exactly which of the important British parliamentary enactments should be regarded as parts of the constitution. While such great landmarks as Magna Carta, the Bill of Rights, the great suffrage-reform acts, the Parliament Act of 1911 (and its 1948–1949 sequel), the Statute of Westminster of 1931, and many others are obviously of constitutional stature, there are many that do not merit quick classification as a part of the British constitution.

The British constitution, unlike many others, grows and changes by gradual adjustments rather than by sudden and complete transformations, although many amendments—for example, the curtailment of the powers of the House of Lords—have engendered bitter controversy. Another feature of British constitutional development is the tendency for practice to precede theory—for custom to crystallize before legal recognition is granted. Thus the self-governing dominions were in fact virtually sovereign before the Statute of Westminster legally sanctioned this status in 1931; also, the cabinet system was established as the keystone of the arch of British government long before it was legally recognized in 1937. Some Americans and other foreign observers have difficulty in regarding the British constitution as truly a constitution in their sense of the term. However, it should be remembered that even the most lengthy written constitution develops unwritten and customary accretions very similar to those which have arisen in England.

Before passing to the structure and operation of British government, it should be noted that it is a unitary system, that it does not in practice adhere to the principle of separation of powers (certainly not in the American sense), that Parliament is legally omnipotent (no parliamentary statute can be declared unconstitutional by the courts), and that private rights and civil liberties consequently depend for their protection not so much upon the courts as upon the wisdom and self-restraint of Parliament, public opinion, and ingrained traditions of individual freedom and constitutional government. The responsibility of government in Great Britain is a dramatic comment on the importance of enlightened political leadership, no matter what the laws of the land or the constitutional distribution of authority. A government of law is no better than the men who make, interpret, and administer the law.

THE EXECUTIVE BRANCH

Authority of the Crown To this day, British statutes require and automatically receive the royal assent and are enacted in the name of the crown. Every act of government is performed in like manner; treaties, declarations of war, appointments, administrative orders, rules and regulations, the designation of new peers, and the convening and dissolution of Parliament, as well as a host of other governmental functions, are carried out as though at the behest of the crown. The term "crown" is not synonymous with "monarch," but refers rather to the synthesis of monarch, ministers, and Parliament (in which the ministers are predominant), which possesses executive power and shapes public policy and which has come to hold the powers formerly belonging to the monarch alone.

Functions of the Monarch As has been well said, the British monarch reigns but does not govern. Every royal act having legal, governmental effect must be performed on the advice of ministers, at least one of whom must countersign the royal document. The ministers are responsible to the House of Commons—whose members are in turn responsible to the British voters. Thus the monarch has no political powers that he or she alone may exercise. However, the sovereign performs many political functions that are inseparable from the British government system. Some of these, it is true, are chiefly ceremonial and might logically be performed by other persons. Such, for example, are the royal duties of receiving foreign diplomatic envoys, creating new peers (actually selected by the Cabinet), and reading the Speech from the Throne at the opening of a session of Parliament—a speech written by the prime minister, not by the monarch. On the other hand, only the monarch may name a political leader to form a new Cabinet, and only the monarch may issue a writ of dissolution that ends the life of a Parliament and sets in motion the machinery of a new election for members of the House of Commons. Actually, the king or queen does not have a free hand in selecting the new prime minster, but is compelled by the most rigid of constitutional conventions to designate as prime minister the recognized leader of the political party (or, sometimes, coalition of parties) having a majority of the seats in the House of Commons. Similarly, the monarch may dissolve Parliament only when the Cabinet, through the prime minister, requests it.

An able monarch, however, is not by any means a

figurehead. He or she must be consulted and kept informed by government ministers. The monarch receives the minutes of all Cabinet meetings and is usually visited by the prime minister before such meetings are held. A monarch of any considerable ability who has a genuine interest in public affairs can easily exert much influence on the Cabinet. The royal family also stands at the pinnacle of British society, setting the standards of popular taste and conduct. The monarch is a symbol of both national and imperial unity; today, when the Commonwealth nations are recognized by Britain as sovereign states, the only vestige of a legal bond between them and the mother country is their oath of allegiance to the British monarch.[4] The monarch also provides the continuity of authority necessary to a cabinet system, remaining while ministers come and go and forming the bridge between succeeding Cabinets. In the absence of a constitutional monarch, countries under the cabinet system find it necessary to establish a presidency—usually devoid of political power and not popularly elected—to provide governmental continuity and a chief executive who will stand above, or at least apart from, partisan politics and who can properly represent and express the national interest. The British monarchy serves all these purposes admirably and there is today little if any popular desire for a republic. Although the Labour party for many years urged the complete abolition of the House of Lords, it never advocated the end of the monarchy.

Ministry and Cabinet

The term "ministry" is the collective designation for all the ministers and is synonymous with the word "government" or what Americans call the "Administration," that is, the political party in power. Within the ministry, which today usually numbers between seventy and ninety, there is an inner circle consisting of the more important ministers, who are referred to, collectively, as the Cabinet. This group today numbers about twenty, the exact size (over and beyond certain offices of outstanding importance) depending upon the prime minister in office.

Cabinet and ministry differ in their roles as well as in size: the Cabinet formulates policy, while the ministry carries it out in the various executive departments. The two bodies may be regarded as concentric circles; the inner circle possesses both power and responsibility, and the outer circle, in principle, has responsibility alone. All ministers, whether or not of Cabinet rank, are collectively responsible to the House of Commons, which can vote them out of office unless, through a dissolution of Parliament and new elections, the ministry wins popular approval of its policy. Thus ministers not of Cabinet rank are bound by Cabinet decisions, in the making of which they do not participate, and they must stand or fall with their Cabinet colleagues.

Formation of a New Ministry

In the normal course of political events today, a change of ministries is likely to occur only as the result of a parliamentary election in which one party loses its majority status in the House of Commons and is replaced by an opposing party or coalition. Before political parties became well organized and disciplined, it was not uncommon for a prime minister to find himself deserted by some of his followers in a vote on an important issue of policy, with the result that a vote of no confidence might be registered against him and his ministerial colleagues. In other words, some members of the majority party might "cross the aisle" and go over to the Opposition benches.[5] Today, however, party discipline is very strict (much more so than in the United States), and for members to vote against their party and its leader is tantamount to commit-

---

[4]In 1974 the Commonwealth of Nations included thirty-three member states, including the following (with their date of entry into the Commonwealth in parentheses): United Kingdom (1931), Australia (1931), India (1947), New Zealand (1931), Bahamas (1973), Bangladesh (1972), Barbados (1966), Botswana (1966), Canada (1931), Cyprus (1961), Fiji (1970), Gambia (1965), Guyana (1966), Ghana (1957), Jamaica (1962), Kenya (1963), Lesotho (1966), Malawi (1964), Malaysia (1963), Malta (1964), Mauritius (1968), Nauru (a special-status member in the South Pacific, which became a member of the Commonwealth in 1968), Nigeria (1960), Sierra Leone (1961), Singapore (1965), Sri Lanka (1948; formerly Ceylon), Swaziland (1968), Tanzania (1964), Tonga (1970), Trinidad and Tobago (1962), Uganda (1962), Western Samoa (1970), and Zambia (1964).

[5]This expression arises from the seating arrangement in the House of Commons. Government and Opposition face each other from rows of benches running at right angles to the speaker's chair and separated by an aisle whose width is equivalent to the length of two swords. Swords are long since obsolete, but the physical arrangements persist and help to structure parliamentary exchange in terms of bipartisanship.

ting political suicide. Such "maverick" members would receive no support from—and might well be opposed by—their party organization in the next election, and under present conditions a candidate has small hope of victory without organized party backing.

Executive Stability and Party Cohesion This helps to explain why the voting cohesion of political parties in the British Parliament is so much higher than the voting cohesion of political parties in the Congress of the United States. In the United States Congress it is the exception to find two-thirds or more of the Republicans voting against two-thirds or more of the Democrats on major issues, but in the British Parliament virtually 99 percent of the Conservatives may be found in opposition to 99 percent of the Labourites on the great majority of divisions (votes).

This in turn makes more visible to public opinion the party responsible for the present state of affairs, whether good or bad. Members of Parliament, then, typically follow their party's leadership and refrain from adverse votes, despite occasional personal doubts concerning the wisdom of party policy at any given moment. Thus a prime minister with a comfortable majority need not worry about votes of no confidence and can count on a full five-year tenure of office for his government unless he himself considers it politically advantageous to schedule an election before the term of Commons has expired. He also is assured of a cohesive legislative majority with which to implement the program adopted by his party in national conference and, presumably, approved by at least a plurality of voters in the most recent national election.

Role of the Opposition An outgoing prime minister hands his own and his colleagues' resignations to the monarch, who then calls to Buckingham Palace the leader of the party or coalition that has been victorious in the election, authorizing him to form a new government. The new prime minister is in all likelihood the man who has been, during the tenure of the previous government, the leader of His (or Her) Majesty's Loyal Opposition. His opposition responsibilities include the formation of a "shadow cabinet," which is composed of ministerial counterparts to every major Cabinet post in the existing government.

In Great Britain, then, and in striking contrast to the United States, no sudden crisis or shift in electoral sentiment finds the political system leaderless or without a clear alternative to the current administration. In the United States, especially when the president defaults on his responsibilities, it is not clear who the opposition is or who ought to be held responsible for providing an alternative government. The importance of an institutionalized opposition in the formulation of British public policy is dramatized by the government's payment of an annual salary to the leader of the Opposition; in 1972, this salary (then paid to the leader of the Labour party, Harold Wilson) was set at £9,500 ($20,900).

Choosing a Cabinet The former leader of the Opposition and new prime minister must form a new government, normally drawn from among the outstanding men and women of his own party and from among those who, while in the Opposition, already informed themselves of the responsibilities of their Cabinet post. Although constitutionally free to select whom he pleases, the prime minister must in fact include the powerful personalities in his own party; show appropriate regard for its economic, social, sectional, and ideological factions; appoint men and women who are competent administrators; and, for the inner Cabinet circle, surround himself with able parliamentary strategists and speakers who can share his burdens of leadership.

The only constitutional limitation on a prime minister's freedom of choice is the requirement that every minister be a member of one or the other house of Parliament—not necessarily at the time of his designation as a minister, but before he can assume the duties of office. There are two methods by which an able man may quickly be made a parliamentary member: (1) The prime minister may ask the monarch to confer a peerage, thus making the desired minister a member of the House of Lords, or (2) a member of the House of Commons belonging to the prime minister's party and representing a constituency considered "safe" for that party's candidate (whoever he may be) may be asked to resign his seat, thus creating a vacancy for which the prospective minister will be the party's candidate in a special election, or "by-election." With the decline in the powers of the House of Lords, more and more ministers have come from the House of Commons, and today the prime minister is invariably a member of the lower house. However, inasmuch as a minister may speak only in the house of which he is a member, every ministry must include some members of the Lords. A law of 1937 requires that at least three ministerial department heads must come from the upper house, as well as a minimum number of the parliamentary undersecretaries (ministers who assist department heads). This statute, incidentally, was the first to confer legal recognition upon the Cabinet.

British Administrative Organization

British national administration is carried out through some thirty-two executive departments, each of which is headed by a minister responsible to the Cabinet and to the House of Commons. Departmental names and titles are confusing and often misleading; some are called "ministries," some "offices," and other "boards," although this variety of nomenclature has no bearing on the rank or status of the department. The titles of ministers themselves are even more misleading to non-Britishers. For example, the first lord of the Treasury (invariably the prime minister) has nothing whatever to do with the Treasury Department, and the chancellor of the Exchequer has nothing to do with the Exchequer (the British equivalent of our national government's General Accounting Office). On the other hand, the chancellor of the Exchequer *is* the head of the Treasury Department.

Treasury Control and the Welfare State The Treasury is the oldest and most important of all the departments and exercises supervisory control over the others in financial and personnel matters, serving as an agency of general administration. The Treasury prepares the governmental budget for submission to Parliament, keeps the public accounts, spends or authorizes the expenditure of public moneys, and in general is charged with the duty of formulating and executing all governmental financial policies—subject, of course, to the audits of the comptroller and auditor-general (an agent of Parliament) and being at all times responsible to the House of Commons. The chancellor of the Exchequer, then, is appropriately considered second in command to only the prime minister. It is through the budget-coordinating activities of his offices ("treasury control") that the party in power attempts to supervise and discipline the far-flung activities of the British bureaucracy.

This supervisory function becomes especially important as the state extends its regulatory and welfare roles. In the case of the latter, an official publication of the British government puts the problem succinctly as follows:

> In Britain the State is responsible, through either central or local government, for a range of services covering family allowances, national insurance, help for war victims, financial assistance when required, health and welfare services for mothers and young children, the sick, the mentally disordered, elderly and handicapped and for families in difficulties of various kinds, and the care of children lacking a normal home life . . . and for education . . . and housing. . . . Public authorities in Britain are spending nearly £9,360 million a year on this range of services, that is, over £168 a year per head of the population.[6]

Bureaucratic Growth and Power Departments other than that of the Exchequer carry on the functions indicated by their titles, although (as in the United States) some departments are charged with duties far removed from their main fields of administration. The Home Office is conspicuous as a residuary legatee, getting many odds and ends difficult to assign elsewhere. Indeed, the actual allocation of duties is due to evolution and historical accident rather than conscious planning. The newer departments, as one would expect, are more systematically organized and have more clearly defined responsibilities.

The expanding obligations of British government have led to the establishment of many economic and social departments, most of which have come into existence during the present century. World War II and the Labour government's nationaliza-

---

[6]*Britain 1971: An Official Handbook,* Her Majesty's Stationery Office, London, p. 122. £168 is equal to approximately $370.

tion program (1945–1949) have resulted in a marked growth both in the number of ministries and in the scope of their functions. Even more recently, such ministries as those for Welsh Affairs, for Technical Cooperation, and for Science have been added to the lengthening list.

In their organization, all ministries are basically alike. Below the responsible minister at the head are at least one parliamentary undersecretary and one permanent undersecretary. Several departments have two or three of the former, and many have two or three of the latter. The permanent undersecretaries are career civil servants—professionals in administration with years of experience and secure tenure. By contrast, the parliamentary undersecretaries are assistant ministers who come and go as Cabinets change. The permanent undersecretary must advise and assist a new (and often inexperienced) minister concerning the work of the department and, in matters not directly concerned with policy making, is likely to be the administrative chief rather than the minister himself. Even in the field of policy, the minister is dependent upon the permanent undersecretary, whose knowledge and experience provide the necessary factual foundations for policy determination.

In a complex bureaucratic apparatus, even as power flows from the legislature to the Cabinet, power may continue to gravitate into the hands of the permanent civil servants (in Britain, particularly the undersecretaries), who on many issues of the day may prove to be the "real power behind the throne." In modern societies and complex economies, *information* is power, and those who have the knowledge and experience of governmental operations may actually exercise influence far beyond the scope of their institutional responsibilities.

The Civil Service

The permanent undersecretary thus stands on the top rung of the civil service ladder. He holds the highest rank attainable by some 490,000 government officials and employees who have secured their positions by merit as demonstrated in competitive examinations. This top administrative grade in Great Britain is identified as the Administrative Class, which includes approximately 4,000 senior civil servants and the permanent undersecretaries.

The other classifications, in descending order of rank and salary, are the Executive Classes (90,000), Specialist Classes (85,000), Clerical Classes (127,000), Clerical Assistant Class (71,000), Typing Class (26,000), Personal Secretary Class (3,600), Minor Technical and Manipulative Classes (53,000), and Messengerial Classes (26,000). Adding those employed in the British postal system (220,000) and in the industrial civil service (230,000) gives a total of about 950,000 British citizens who are employed in the British civil service. (In the United States, there are approximately 2.1 million government employees at the *federal* level only.)

Development of the Civil Service The British civil service was established by a series of reforms beginning in 1855. Governmental positions were previously filled on the basis of patronage rather than merit. Today, the British civil service is considered to be one of the best in the world and to maintain the highest possible standards of competence and integrity. A competent and professionally dedicated civil service is an essential precondition to responsible and democratic government.

British civil service examinations, especially for the Administrative Class, are extremely rigorous. Great emphasis is placed upon what are commonly called "cultural" questions—i.e., those covering history, philosophy, literature, etc. The British believe that such questions test the applicant's intelligence, while some American critics argue that they merely reflect his educational background—which, in turn, may well be the result of his economic and social status.

By tradition and practice, civil servants enjoy permanent tenure, although they are not protected by law against removal for arbitrary or political reasons. Again, custom rules; the security of the British civil servant is, if anything, greater than that of his American counterpart, despite the elaborate legal procedures so commonly established in the United States to provide redress for wrongful removal or demotion of civil service employees.

Salaries paid to British civil servants range as high as £15,750 ($34,650) for permanent undersecretaries. Civil service salaries have usually compared favorably with salaries paid for similar work and training in private industry, although there has been some dissatisfaction within the service on this point. However, British civil servants enjoy a very considerable social prestige, and this, coupled with security of tenure, serves to attract and retain able men and women even in times when outside pecuniary rewards are higher.

THE BRITISH PARLIAMENT

An eighteenth-century French philosopher, de Lolme, once said that the British Parliament was so powerful that it could do anything except change a woman into a man or a man into a woman. In reality, of course, Parliament neither was nor is so utterly omnipotent; a wide variety of political and practical considerations limit the scope of parliamentary power. However, in a purely legal sense, the British Parliament is supreme. No court can declare its enactments void, neither monarch nor prime minister holds the power of veto, and no constitutional provisions limit or prohibit particular kinds of legislation. Indeed, Parliament may—legally speaking—so amend the British constitution as to transform the entire scheme of government. It could eliminate the monarchy and the courts, sweep away civil liberties and rights, and refuse to hold parliamentary elections. And yet the stability, democracy, and high level of responsibility of Britain's political elites make it dramatically clear that institutional checks on authority are not essential to good government. It is more a matter of men and manners. And, of course, custom and tradition are so strong in Great Britain that no Parliament would dare to tamper with the fundamentals of the democratic process or the hallowed rights of Englishmen.

The Suffrage

The real and ultimate sovereignty in Great Britain resides in the British electorate. Today the British electorate includes every British citizen who has attained the age of eighteen, who is not subject to any legal incapacity (such as insanity or imprisonment), and who resides in the district in which he or she seeks to vote. There are no racial, literacy, educational, property-owning, or tax-paying qualifications.

As was discussed above, this thoroughly democratic suffrage is a very recent accomplishment. For many centuries land, rather than persons, was represented in Parliament; property qualifications for voting persisted in one form or another until 1918. During the nineteenth century, under the impact of the industrial revolution, successsive reform acts extended the suffrage to the urban middle class (1832), the urban working class (1867), and the rural workers and miners (1884). Still, however, the voter was required to be, if not the owner, at least the occupier of real property that had a stated rental value per year. Plural voting, which permitted an individual to vote in every constituency in which he owned or occupied property, was curtailed in 1918 and finally abolished in 1948. This system had been thoroughly undemocratic and had operated to the advantage of the Conservative party. The university constituencies founded by James I, allocating twelve seats in the House of Commons to be filled by the votes of those holding degrees from Oxford, Cambridge, and other universities, were also abolished in 1948.

In the course of these extensions of the vote, the "rotten borough" system was also reformed. This term had come to be applied to very small boroughs that had declined in population but were still entitled to send their quota of two members each to the House of Commons. On the other hand, large industrial cities had sprung up that were still without parliamentary representation. Successive acts of Parliament took seats away from the smallest boroughs, consolidated others, and gave the seats thus accumulated to populous urban areas. Today each constituency contains, on the average, about 60,000 voters.

Election of the House of Commons

British parliamentary elections normally occur at five-year intervals unless this period is shortened by dissolution or lengthened because of war or other emergency. The term of five years was established by act of Parliament in 1911, but since no Parliament can bind its successor (or itself), prolongation is a simple matter. Elections were postponed because of both world wars; none were held from 1910 to 1918 or from 1935 to 1945, but two elections occurred in 1910, and there was one each in 1922, 1923, and 1924. In 1922 and 1924, the elections were forced by the withdrawal of one party from a government based on coalition; in 1923 Prime Minister Baldwin felt that he was bound by tradition to "go to the country" before his government would be justified in adopting a protective tariff program. Normally the government itself determines the timing of the elections; it usually selects a moment that looks auspicious for the party, instead of merely waiting out the full five-year interval. Since an election may therefore occur at any time and without warning, all party organizations are constantly on a "war footing," unlike national party organizations in the United States, which virtually hibernate for two- and four-year intervals. The scheduling of British elections according to the political climate (instead of the calendar, as in the United States) also reinforces the organizational integrity of British political parties.

Nominating the Candidates When a writ of dissolution is issued, it touches off a process that is both brief and intense. Nominations must be filed by the eighth day following dissolution, and voting occurs on the ninth day after nomination day. In a few constituencies only one candidate may appear; such unopposed candidates are declared elected on nomination day. Usually, however, there is a contest, with both the Conservative and Labour parties nominating candidates in the overwhelming majority of the constituencies—which in 1970 were set at a total of 635. The Liberal party has traditionally presented fewer candidates (usually around 300), concentrating them in the relatively middle-class and rural constituencies of Wales, Scotland, and southwestern England.

Nomination is a simple process. There are no primary elections; each candidate merely files a nomination paper bearing the signatures of ten registered voters in the constituency and posts a deposit of £150, which is forfeited if he fails to receive at least one-eighth of the votes cast. This rule was designed to discourage frivolous candidacies; though apparently undemocratic, it no longer has such an effect, as most deposits are made by the party organizations—which again works to the advantage of party control over individual candidates and elected representatives.

Although, at different times in the past, qualifications for candidacy included residence in the area, religious tests, and property ownership, all these have now been abolished; however, clergymen of the Church of England, the Roman Catholic Church, the Church of Scotland, and the Church of Northern Ireland; undischarged bankrupts; persons holding certain public offices; and members of public services are prohibited from seeking election. Today, any other British subject, man or woman, who has reached the age of twenty-one and is willing to take a simple oath (not religious in character) may be a candidate. Peers are ineligible.

The Election Campaign The campaign makes up in intensity for what it lacks in duration. Not only do parties and candidates hire halls, give radio and television addresses, and employ the familiar techniques of advertisements and cartoons, but British campaigning includes two features that are less familiar to Americans: street-corner speeches and doorbell ringing. Listeners heckle the speaker by interrupting him with questions that are annoying and often difficult to answer. The success of a candidate may well depend upon his ability to handle hecklers in the give-and-take of such debate. A ready wit is an invaluable asset. The doorbell ringing is done by unpaid party workers who go from house to house extolling the virtues of their particular candidates. The voter would feel slighted unless a representative of each candidate called at his home for this purpose, despite the obvious inroad upon his privacy and leisure time. However, British voters are, generally speaking, more dutiful than their American cousins; they take their politics more seriously and turn out at the polls more conscientiously. In the 1964 parliamentary elections, for example, 77 percent of the eligible voters in the United Kingdom actually voted (76 percent in 1966); the comparable figure for the 1968 presidential election in the United States was only 61 percent.

Britain has laws limiting campaign expenditures and forbidding such practices as bribery, the intimidation or impersonation of voters, the payment of canvassers, and the "treating" of voters, or the hiring of conveyances to take them to the polls. In contrast to practice in the United States, such laws are carefully conceived and effectively enforced. Campaigning is not nearly as expensive as it is in the United States, and the major campaign funding that derives from business (for the Conservatives) and trade unions (for Labour) is channeled through the *national* party organization—an important factor in explaining party cohesion in Great Britain. British elections have long been remarkably free from charges of improper practices, and it is uncommon for the results of an election to be subsequently contested. When such contests do arise, they are settled by the courts, not by Parliament.

Voting Britain uses the "short ballot," which also contributes to the central importance of British political parties. The voter elects only one officer of his national government—his MP, or member of Parliament. The ballot shows only the names of the candidates in alphabetical order, without party affiliation; it is up to the voter to know which candidate represents which party. Voting is secret, and when the polls close, the ballot boxes are sealed and taken to the city hall or other central location, where the ballots from all wards and precincts are collected together and then counted; thus no ward or precinct results are given separately, only the totals for the entire constituency.

The new Parliament usually meets within two weeks after the election, with slight percentage shifts in the partisan distribution of the vote producing major variations in parliamentary representation (the inevitable result of the single-member district, simple-majority system). British elections are typically contested on one relatively clear issue; sometimes (as in the elections of 1950 and 1964) an election is held simply because the term of Parliament is drawing to a close. But, again, the variability of the date of parliamentary elections (contrary to practice in the United States) helps to adjust the political process to the temper of the times and the ebb and flow of both issues and personalities. In British elections, however, the predominant role of the party is further reinforced by *party* voting rather than *personality* voting, the latter being a more frequent characteristic of voting behavior in the United States.

The House of Lords

The House of Lords is older than the House of Commons, having originated in the Great Council of Norman times. While the House of Commons has grown more broadly representative and democratic, the House of Lords still provides class representation for only a narrow, privileged group. It is a surviving remnant of medievalism, of parliamentary organization based on estates—these estates being the "lords spiritual" and the "lords temporal."

Membership The House of Lords consists of seven categories of members: (1) the princes of the royal blood, (2) hereditary peers, (3) representative peers of Scotland, (4) representative peers of Ireland, (5) "law lords," (6) the high dignitaries of the Church of England (the lords spiritual), and (7) a number of life peers created under the Life Peerages Act of 1958.[7] In the first group there are usually only two or three male members of the royal family who can qualify, and these almost never attend sittings. About 90 percent of the membership is found in the second group, the hereditary peers. These are persons who either have received peerages from the monarch or are the descendants of such persons. Hereditary peers are automatically members of the House of Lords, except that women who are peeresses by inheritance are not allowed seats.[8] About 80 percent of the existing peerages have been created since 1800, and over half of them since 1900; hence the peers of today are largely the commoners of yesterday who have achieved distinction in business, finance, law, politics, the army, science, literature, and the like. This is further testimony to the relative "openness" of the aristocracy in Great Britain, which, as already noted, has contributed to the development of British democracy.

The actual selection of candidates for elevation to the peerage is made by the Cabinet and is often dictated by political considerations, such as the need for stronger government representation in the upper chamber. Since the Conservative party has been traditionally—and naturally—predominant in the Lords, both the Liberal and Labour parties have found it necessary to recommend the conferring of new peerages upon their members and supporters. There is no limit to the number of peerages or to the size of the House of Lords. Thus if the Lords should stubbornly oppose certain types

---

[7]In April 1961 there were approximately thirty such life peers, six of whom were women. Their entrance into the previously all-male House was bitterly deplored by a few of its older members.

[8]Such a peeress is the eldest daughter of a hereditary peer who has no sons, but only a limited number of the older peerages may be inherited by women.

of legislation—as when they rejected the Liberals' tax program in 1909—the upper house could be packed with new peers who would support the Cabinet's measures. While this weapon has always been available, it has been used sparingly; too frequent use would tend to depreciate the peerage and to make the House of Lords (now numbering over 1,000 members) larger and more unwieldy than ever.

Declining Power of the House of Lords This difficulty has been met by reducing the legislative powers of the Lords. The Parliament Act of 1911, which was the direct result of the Lords' rejection of the Asquith government's program of increased taxation of wealth, virtually stripped the upper chamber of all power over money bills and substantially curbed its power over other types of legislation. A money bill (i.e., one relating to taxation, appropriations, government borrowing, etc.) that has been passed by Commons must be sent to the Lords at least thirty days before the end of the session of Parliament; if the Lords do not approve it without amendment within one month after they have received it, such a money bill automatically becomes law. The act of 1911 also provided that any other public bill (with one or two minor exceptions), if passed by the House of Commons in three successive sessions and if sent (each time) to the Lords at least one month before the end of the session, might become law without the Lords' approval, provided that at least two years have elapsed between the first debate on the bill in the first session and its final passage in the third.

This period of delay has since been reduced to one year, and it is now necessary for Commons to repass the measure only once over the Lords' objections; hence only two, rather than three, sessions of Parliament are required.[9] This change, proposed by the Labour government, was staunchly resisted by the Conservatives. To fend off such a diminution in the powers of the House of Lords, a committee of Conservatives, including a number of peers, proposed a reform of the composition of the upper chamber. Several such reform plans had been drawn up (e.g., the Bryce Report of 1918), contemplating a sharp reduction in size and the elimination of the hereditary basis of membership. The 1948 scheme added the idea of basing membership on outstanding public service and also of making women eligible. However, the government's bill to shorten the Lords' delaying powers became law first (over the objections of virtually all the Conservative peers); the Lords thereupon gave up all plans to reform the composition of their chamber until the passage of the Life Peerages Act in 1958.

The upper chamber still remains a political anachronism, albeit with virtually no legislative power. It retains its judicial powers, both for the trial of impeachments and as the supreme court of appeal. Its members also are free to debate the appropriate course of government policy without the haste and political pressures that are more characteristic of proceedings in the House of Commons. The House of Lords occasionally proposes useful amendments to bills already passed by Commons, and in these instances the amendments are readily accepted by the government when the bills are returned to the lower house.

The Legislative Process

The British method of law making differs sharply from the American. In the first place, the cabinet system vests legislative initiative and responsibility in the Cabinet—not in the individual members of Parliament. The latter may introduce what are known as "private member bills" (to distinguish them from "government bills"), but only a limited amount of time is allotted for their consideration; members draw lots for the privilege of introducing such bills. Hence most legislative proposals emanate from the Cabinet and are part of its overall program for the nation. A government bill is introduced, explained, and defended by the appropriate minister with the assistance of his colleagues. The prime minister himself usually launches a bill that is at the heart of his government's program.[10]

---

[9] House of Lords Reform Act of 1949.

[10] It should be noted that money bills may be introduced *only* in the House of Commons, and judicial bills *only* in the House of Lords. Also, under a rule of the House of Commons, private member bills may not call for new or increased taxes or expenditures; they may, however, propose reductions. Thus only the Cabinet actually formulates and introduces financial legislation, which may be considered essential to responsible government in an age of governmental regulation of the economy.

Role of Committees In the House of Commons, bills are not at once referred to standing committees, as is the case in the United States. Only after a bill has been given its second reading, and only after its main principles have been debated and voted upon (favorably), does the bill go to one of the standing committees. There are usually eight such committees, in contrast with twenty-one—formerly forty-seven—in the United States House of Representatives. All but one of the committees are designated merely by the first letters of the alphabet; these may receive any and all types of legislation, with no attempt at specialization. Only one standing committee, the Committee for Scotland, is specialized; all its members are Scots, and to it are referred most measures relating to Scottish affairs. British committees also differ from American in that seniority counts for very little. The distribution of political power in the British legislative process is thus more a function of *party* than it is in the United States, where power is a function of the positions occupied by specific individuals in the complex hierarchies of the Congress.

The power of British committees over bills, then, is limited; a committee cannot "kill" a bill by declining to send it back to the House, and its role is essentially to refine and improve measures that the House has already approved in their main outlines. Nevertheless, committee refinements and amendments frequently necessitate compromises between the committee and the government, which is the author of most bills. When a bill is reported back to the House, it usually passes with little, if any, delay or change. Entrenched minorities are rarely able to frustrate the will of the majority, which is not the case in the United States.

Money bills are not referred to a standing committee, but to the Committee of the Whole—that is to say, the entire membership of the House of Commons sitting as a committee and thereby avoiding the formalities and delays imposed by the rules governing sessions of the House as such. This method of handling financial legislation affords every member the opportunity—and imposes upon him the responsibility—of participation throughout the entire legislative course of such bills.

Passing a Bill: Debate and Compromise Parliamentary debate, once marked by flowery oratory (when the role of government in the society was less substantial and when, as a consequence, the legislative process was more leisurely), has in recent decades become brief and businesslike—although nonetheless combative. The presidential system of government, as in the United States, has no counterpart to the regular and institutionalized confrontation between government and Opposition that marks the legislative process in parliamentary systems. Thus, despite occasional criticism, there has been general approval of the tightening of rules designed to limit debate. While such restrictions give the "backbenchers" little opportunity to speak, the business of government goes forward more expeditiously. In any case, the power of the House to disapprove remains intact.

A bill that has gone through the stages in Commons already described (introduction, first and second reading, debate, approval in principle, reference to committee, report back to the House, third reading, and passage) is then sent to the House of Lords, where it goes through essentially the same steps, although in a somewhat simpler form. If approved by the Lords, the bill receives the royal assent and becomes law. If not, an exchange of written messages may be resorted to in order to iron out differences, although the Cabinet itself, through its members in both houses, is the most effective agency for this purpose. We have seen that Commons can today override the Lords without much difficulty, but except for very controversial bills, the government usually prefers to effect a compromise.

This in turn is an important comment on the concern of British political leaders to fashion public policy through negotiation and bargaining rather than by forcing their majority advantage on the Opposition. "Responsible government" also implies a commitment to take into account the interests of the minority. In the United States, however, the weakness of parties in Congress makes it difficult to identify clearly an opposition with whom the executive can negotiate issues of public policy. The successful American president must consequently bargain endlessly with many different personalities, ever striving to construct a majority coalition on a particular issue—a coalition that is likely to fall apart as soon as another issue is raised. This makes the policy-making process (in the United States) less visible to public opinion, and voters are hard pressed to determine the accountability of either Republicans or Democrats for the current state of affairs. It is no wonder, then, that the voting behavior of the American electorate, in comparison with that of the British electorate, is frequently marked by a personality rather than a partisan orientation.

Dominance of the Executive The British legislative process involves considerably more leadership by the executive than is the case in the United States, despite the recent growth of presidential powers in this field. The private member and the standing committee are far less important in Britain. These differences are due to the strength of the parties and the nature of the cabinet system. The whole concept of cabinet responsibility breaks down unless the Cabinet has sufficient power vis-à-vis Parliament to enact its program into law. Hence the Cabinet has control over the time of Parliament, planning the order in which legislative business will be taken up, when debate will end, and when "divisions" (votes) will be taken. As might be expected, there is criticism of allegedly high-handed maneuvers employed by the government to restrict Opposition speeches and of the enforced—and nearly complete—silence of the backbencher.

On the whole, however, all British Cabinets observe the basic rules of fair play in Parliament; tradition is very strong in this respect, and no speaker of the House of Commons would tolerate improper practices.[11] Debate is—necessarily—shortened in order to complete urgent parliamentary business, but the Opposition's leaders, at least, are always heard. It is doubtful whether any British government has ever employed the more outrageous types of "gag" and "steamroller" tactics often seen in American legislatures.

Parliamentary Oversight: The Question Hour The powers of the Cabinet over the legislative process are, of course, balanced and controlled by the power of the House of Commons to reject all or part of the Cabinet's legislative program. One device of parliamentary control over administration is the question hour. The first fifty minutes of every sitting of the House of Commons on the first four days of the week are set aside for this purpose, and any member of the House may address a question to any minister.[12] The rules of the House require that at least two days' advance notice be given to the particular minister, and they seek to ensure that the questions will not be improper (e.g., insulting). While these questions may come from the members of the minister's own party and may seek only factual information, most inquiries are likely to emanate from the Opposition and to be critical in tone. Although the ministry's answers to questions seldom lead to debate and almost never cause its downfall, the knowledge that every phase of their work may be the subject of parliamentary questioning keeps the ministers constantly on their toes. The spotlight of publicity is thrown upon the administration every day that Parliament is in session, leaving no dark corners where laziness, incompetence, or dishonesty may lurk.

The question hour is often given a major share of the credit for the exemplary integrity of British governmental officials. As a means of controlling the administration, it is superior to the occasional investigation carried out by the United States Congress. When such investigations do take place, as in the Congress's inquiry into the Watergate affair, the behavior of the government is already manifestly irresponsible; the investigation becomes a form of punishment after the fact instead of a continuing check on the responsibility of executive elites. As a check on the policies and actions of the executive, the parliamentary question hour is also a much more reliable process than the occasional press conference in the United States, which is convened at the whim of the president and usually with reluctance. Especially during the final stages of President Johnson's and President Nixon's administrations, the infrequency of the presidential press conference suggested a fundamental hostility to the probing and challenges characteristic of parliamentary government; and, in the United States, a

---

[11]The speaker in the British Parliament, unlike his congressional counterpart in the United States, plays a judicial rather than a partisan role in the legislative process. Although a member of a party when elected, the speaker assumes a posture of impartiality and never uses his authority to favor his own or any other party.

[12]The importance of parliamentary questions in Great Britain is suggested by the astonishing fact that approximately 100,000 questions are put to the government in the House of Commons and House of Lords each year.

Table 11.1 Government Majorities and Prime Ministers in the House of Commons, 1906–1974

Year	Party	Majority	Prime minister
1906	Liberal	356	Campbell-Bannerman (after Dec. 1905)
Jan. 1910	Liberal	124	Asquith (after Apr. 1908)
Dec. 1910	Liberal	126	Asquith
1918	Coalition	263	Lloyd George (Liberal; after Dec. 1916)
1922	Conservative	79	Bonar Law
1923	(No majority)	—	Baldwin (Conservative)
1924	Conservative	225	MacDonald; Baldwin (after Nov. 1924)
1929	(No majority)	—	MacDonald (Labour)
1931	Nat'l. Gov't.	425	MacDonald (Labour)
1935	Nat'l. Gov't.	247	Baldwin; Chamberlain; Churchill (Conservative)
1945	Labour	146	Attlee
1950	Labour	8	Attlee
1951	Conservative	16	Churchill
1955	Conservative	59	Eden; Macmillan (after Jan. 1957)
1959	Conservative	100	Macmillan; Douglas-Home (after Oct. 1963)
1964	Labour	4	Wilson
1966	Labour	99	Wilson
1970	Conservative	31	Heath
Feb. 1974	(No majority)	—	Wilson (Labour)
Oct. 1974	Labour	3	Wilson

president who is afraid of the press is a president who is afraid of the people.

Government and Opposition In Great Britain, the more frontal type of attack upon a government may take the form of either a vote of censure or a vote of no confidence. A vote of censure is usually aimed at a particular minister because of certain specific acts, and it may result in his resignation. Normally, however, the principle of Cabinet solidarity or "collective responsibility" prevails; the entire ministry rallies to the support of the member under attack because his actions were presumably the outgrowth of the policy adopted by the entire government. A motion of no confidence is aimed at the government's whole policy and program rather than at any specific item. If such a motion is carried, a government either resigns or "goes to the country." The Cabinet is not responsible to the House of Lords and regularly ignores adverse votes in that body (as far as Cabinet resignation is concerned). In the House of Commons, a government may make the vote on any bill a matter of confidence, whether or not the Opposition leader has introduced a formal motion for this purpose.

The strengthening of party discipline in recent decades makes votes of no confidence decidedly unlikely unless the government rests upon a coalition from which some party group withdraws. Even where—as in the case of the Labour governments elected in 1950 and 1964—a government holds a perilously slim majority, it is very difficult for the Opposition to win a vote of no confidence. Nevertheless, a government advantage of fewer than fifteen or twenty seats is considered unsafe because some majority members are almost certain to be occasionally absent because of illness or for other reasons. The death of an older MP means a by-election to fill his seat, and the election may go against the majority. On the other hand, a majority advantage of more than fifty or sixty seats heightens the chances of one or more members' defecting from the party's position during parliamentary divisions; with a comfortable parliamentary advantage, the more "maverick" MPs feel less pressure to conform to party policy on specific issues. (For variations in the government's parliamentary advantage since 1906, see Table 11.1.)

But it still is a rare event when the cohesion of the parliamentary party does not approximate 99 percent; voting cohesion declines as the party's "whips" are withdrawn, typically on those issues regarded as raising basic moral questions. Thus, for over more than half a century, only two governments have fallen because of votes of no confidence, and neither of these enjoyed a single-party majority in the House of Commons. Yet this fact does not warrant sweeping generalizations such as that the Cabinet possesses "dictatorial" power or that Commons is being "led around by the nose." There is a vast amount of compromise, of give-and-take, in working out both the general and particular aspects of pending legislation. No Cabinet would dream of drafting—let alone introducing—its bills until it had carefully ascertained and weighed the opinions of its supporters and opponents in Parliament, of important interest groups (business, labor, agriculture, and the like), and of the general public. Government measures are, to a considerable degree, modified and compromised before they begin to run the gauntlet of actual parliamentary debate. And while Her Majesty's Loyal Opposition is expected—and its leader paid—to oppose and criticize government bills, this seldom degenerates into mere partisan obstructionism. One of the justly praised virtues of the British system is that both sides usually put the national welfare ahead of party advantage.

Growth of Executive Power The confidence in which the Cabinet is universally held is shown by the steady growth of its powers in the field of delegated legislation. The increasing volume and complexity of legislation have produced, in all countries, a trend toward investing the chief executive or other executive and administrative agencies with quasilegislative powers. Congresses and parliaments tend more and more to confine their attention to broad questions of principle and policy, leaving the details (of both substance and procedure) to be filled in by the executive branch of the government. The increasing concentration of executive power is a major trend in all contemporary political systems, although the trend is most noticeable in those stable democracies with long-standing traditions of legislative autonomy. Along with industrialization, urbanization, and the increasing role of government in economic and social relationships, executive authority has increased, while legislative autonomy has declined.

In England, this means that the Cabinet and the various ministries have, over the last half century or more, been endowed with formidable legislative authority in a wide variety of fields. While ultimately subject to the overriding power of Parliament, the various ministries are to all intents and purposes the real authorities in their particular jurisdictions. They may even, in some cases, go beyond the powers conferred by Parliament, although the House of Commons' Select Committee on Statutory Instruments acts as a watchdog to call the House's attention to any irregularities or to any departures from parliamentary intent. While this trend has provoked strong opposition, a special committee of investigation appointed to study the problem and its dangers reported, in substance, that there was no real cause for alarm. Although it might appear as though the House of Commons had spent centuries wresting power from the king only to hand it over to the Cabinet, there remains the very real and all-important difference that the kings of yore were absolute and arbitrary, while the Cabinet is responsible and democratic. If it is less frequently turned out by the House of Commons than was the case a century ago, the Cabinet is far more accountable to a democratic people, now possessing and vigorously exercising universal suffrage.

BRITISH POLITICAL PARTIES

British political parties today have evolved a long way from their ancestors, the factions (Lancastrians and Yorkists, Cavaliers and Roundheads) which in earlier days plunged England into civil war. Modern political party struggles have been aptly termed a "sublimation" of civil war, and in Britain this transition may be clearly seen in the pages of history.

Development of British Political Parties

The earliest parties, as distinguished from factions, were the Tories and the Whigs, who appeared in the eighteenth century. The Tory party generally supported the king, while the Whigs tended to oppose him. Early in the nineteenth century, the Tories came to be known as Conservatives, and the Whigs as Liberals. Though at first the two parties were almost equally aristocratic in both leadership and policy, the suffrage reforms of the nineteenth century and the split in the Liberal party over home rule for Ireland had the effect of drawing the bulk of the aristocratic and wealthier classes into the Conservative party, thus tending to make the Liberals somewhat more distinctly the party of reform and change along the lines of middle-class thinking. However, it must be emphasized that British political party lines never have been, and are not now, drawn on class lines; even the Labour party, appearing in 1900 as the political expression of the trade unions and socialist societies, has broadened its base so that it today receives substantial support from the middle and even the upper classes. On the other hand, the Conservative party has adopted an increasingly "liberal" attitude on many issues, with the declining Liberal party occupying a middle position between Labourites and Conservatives.

Actually, party positions overlap; there are right, center, and left wings in all three parties. These differences reflect in part the overlapping of social classes that characterizes Britain's two major parties: Of those voters who identify themselves as middle-class, 79 percent support the Conservative party, and 21 percent support the Labour party; of those voters who identify themselves as workers, 72 percent are pro-Labour, and 28 percent are pro-Conservative.[13] Of the MPs elected to the House of Commons in 1966, 30 percent of the Conservatives and 9 percent of the Labourites had a business background, while 46 percent of the Conservatives and 43 percent of the Labour MPs were from the professions (lawyers, doctors, civil servants, etc.).[14] While class identification is an important factor in explaining British voting behavior, the sociological overlap of the parties' voters and activists *and* the effects of the single-member district, simple-majority electoral system require both the Conservatives and Labour to appeal to broad cross sections of the electorate; indeed, without such appeals they cannot hope to win a majority in Parliament. This helps to reduce any tendencies toward social and political conflict based exclusively on economic class, and it reinforces the predisposition of British political elites toward government through compromise and bargaining.

Party Competition and Social Reform

The broad trend in British politics has been toward what is commonly termed the "left," i.e., toward democratic political, social, and economic reform. Just as the landed aristocracy once wrested power from the king, so the rising commercial and manufacturing classes later became more dominant, demanding and securing legislation designed to advance their interests; during the past century, the working class has forged to the front, pushing Britain toward its own version of democratic socialism. During the first third of the nineteenth century, the Tories (then distinctly the party of the landed aristocracy) were in power; during the middle third, the Whigs were dominant and at the same time became more middle-class in membership and more reformist in policy. Under the new names, Conservative and Liberal, the two parties alternated in power between 1874 and 1915, with the Liberals having somewhat the better of it. Although the Liberals led the way in political, economic, and social reform, particularly just before World War I, the Conservatives were by no means adamantly opposed to such measures and, indeed, must be given a share of the credit for some of the major reforms of the nineteenth and early twentieth centuries.

The appearance of the Labour party in 1900 accelerated the leftward trend in British politics. In the decade before 1914, the twenty-nine Labour members of the House of Commons exerted considerable influence on the enactment of the social legislation (minimum wages, unemployment insurance, etc.) of that era. The Labour party drew many working-class voters away from the Liberals and, by splitting the non-Conservatives into two groups, not only started the Liberal party on the road to near extinction but also enabled the Conservatives to win several undeserved victories in parliamentary elections. Thus in the elections of 1922 and 1924, the combined popular vote for the Labour

---

[13]David Butler and Donald Stokes, *Political Change in Britain: Forces Shaping Electoral Choice*, Macmillan & Co., Ltd., London, 1969, pp. 76, 106.

[14]David Butler and Anthony King, *The British General Election of 1966*, Macmillan & Co., Ltd., London, 1966, p. 208.

Table 11.2 Elections and Parliamentary Representation in Great Britain, 1945–1974*

	1945	1950	1951	1955	1959	1964	1966	1970	Feb. 1974	Oct. 1974
Conservatives										
Votes (in millions)	10.0	12.5	13.7	13.3	13.7	12.0	11.4	13.1	11.9	10.4
Percentage vote	41	44	48	50	49	43	42	46	38	36
Elected MPs	213	298	320	344	365	304	253	330	296	276
Labour										
Votes (in millions)	12.0	13.3	13.9	12.4	12.2	12.2	13.1	12.2	11.6	11.5
Percentage vote	50	47	49	47	44	44	48	43	37	39
Elected MPs	393	315	296	277	258	317	363	287	301	319
Liberals										
Votes (in millions)	2.2	2.5	0.7	0.7	1.7	3.1	2.3	2.1	6.0	5.3
Percentage vote	9	9	3	3	6	11	9	7	19	18
Elected MPs	12	9	6	6	6	9	12	6	14	13

*The percentage of the total popular vote received by all minor parties in Great Britain (including the Republican Labour party, Welsh and Scottish Nationalists, Socialists, Communists, and others) typically ranges between 1 and 3 percent. Their parliamentary representation also is negligible (two MPs in 1966 and seven in 1970). The total number of seats in the House of Commons was set at 630 by the act of 1949 and at 635 by the act of 1970.

and Liberal parties exceeded that cast for the Conservatives, and yet the Conservatives won both elections. In other elections, such as those of 1931 and 1935, the Conservative-dominated national government (coalition) won a far larger number of parliamentary seats than its popular majority warranted. On the other hand, the Liberal party failed to secure its appropriate share of seats, and the long-run effects of the single-member district, simple-majority electoral system (in Great Britain as in the United States) have been in the direction of two-party rather than multiparty politics. (See Table 11.2.)

Alternation in Power

From 1924 to 1929 and from 1931 to 1940, the Conservative party was in power; during the latter period, it ruled as the dominant party of a coalition. In 1940, World War II compelled the formation of a truly national government, in which the leaders of all parties assumed ministerial posts; indeed, the post of leader of His Majesty's Loyal Opposition was declared vacant until the end of hostilities. The election of July 1945 resulted in a sweeping victory for the Labour party, which won almost two-thirds of the seats in the House of Commons and thus was able to form the first Labour government that was in power as well as in office. In February 1950 Labour's margin in the House was sharply reduced, and in October 1951 the tables were turned. However, the Labour party actually received more popular votes than the Conservatives. The virtual deadlock between these two parties was accompanied by a sharp drop in support for the Liberal party, which secured only 2.5 percent of the popular vote and 1 percent of the seats. Most of the Liberal voters apparently backed Conservative candidates, thus producing the slim Conservative victory. Because of their small majority, the Conservatives made no abrupt changes in public policy, although they did denationalize parts of the steel industry that Labour had nationalized earlier. The parliamentary elections of 1955 and 1959 were also won by the Conservative party. In the latter year the Liberal party staged an impressive comeback, more than doubling the popular vote it had received in 1955.

The election of October 15, 1964, was won by the Labour party, but only by the precarious margin of 4 seats in the House of Commons. Labour won 317 seats; the Conservatives, 304; and the Liberals, 9 (a gain of 3 over 1959). Harold Wilson, the new prime minister and Labour party leader, managed to carry on despite his slim majority and also to hold his party followers together.

Early in 1966 Mr. Wilson called a parliamentary election for March 31, 1966, hoping to win a substantial Labour majority. His hopes were realized in the election; Labour captured 363 seats; the Conservatives, 253; and the Liberals, 12. By winning an absolute majority in the House of Commons, Mr. Wilson scored the most impressive Labour victory since 1945 and achieved the opportunity to carry through the party program. However, he lost his earlier excuse for moving slowly; he could no longer point to his slim margin in Parliament.

The Labour party manifesto of March 1966 offered the voters a moderate and realistic program to cope with the economic and financial problems confronting the British government both at home and abroad. Proposals for further nationalization of industry were conspicuous by their absence. Instead, emphasis was placed on a massive program for modernizing and strengthening British industry, including cash grants to corporations expanding their production. Faced with mounting inflation, which was threatening the stability of the pound sterling and producing an excess of imports over exports, the party manifesto proposed to reduce prices and profits by increasing productivity and by making British industry more efficient and hence more competitive in the world market. However, the Labour government did not abandon Labour's traditional concern for social welfare. The manifesto gave its first priority to housing, followed by slum clearance, urban renewal, and the coordination of commuter transportation. Labour also promised to improve the condition of the farm workers and to protect the consumer against extortionate prices and poor quality. The social security system was to be strengthened, and the national health service improved; higher education was to be expanded, and the school-leaving age was to be raised from fifteen to sixteen years (which was calculated to reduce pressures on employment, especially as British industry attempted to improve its productive efficiency through automation).

The normal course of events would have required the Labour government under Mr. Wilson to hold new elections in 1971 (five years after Labour's resounding success in the 1966 elections). Public opinion polls, however, encouraged Prime Minister Wilson to dissolve the House of Commons and to hold elections in 1970, seeking to enlarge the Labour majority or at least to perpetuate its rule for an additional four or five years. The opinion polls and the confidence of the government appear to have lulled a small but significant percentage of Labour's traditional supporters into overoptimism; they failed to turn out to vote, and the Conservative party, led by a surprised Edward Heath, swept into office. As before, the *electoral system* exaggerated a slight shift in partisan voting; with 46 percent of the popular vote, the Conservatives captured 52 percent of the 630 seats in the House of Commons. In this way, the British electoral system may help to assure a *majority* government even when the leading party wins only a *plurality* of the vote.

The new Conservative government, however, continued Labour's emphasis on restoring Britain's economy to a competitive position among the world's industrial nations. To this end, the Heath government succeeded in early 1972 in negotiating Great Britain's entry into the European Common Market—a major and dramatic alteration in Britain's traditional orientation and one that had been earlier advanced by the Labour government under Harold Wilson. (But as Opposition leader after the 1970 elections, Mr. Wilson *opposed* Britain's entry into the Common Market.) And, in reality, British political parties are not far apart in their programs and policies, despite occasionally overheated campaign oratory. All British parties approach public problems in a pragmatic spirit; all are prepared to accept workable compromises rather than cling dogmatically to preconceived theories. When parties replace each other in the Cabinet, the new government seeks "to modify rather than to overturn the positions laid down" by its predecessor.[15] The course of public policy in Britain is determined by stubborn facts rather than by doctrinaire considerations, although party differences may result in

---

[15]Wilfrid Harrison, *The Government of Britain*, Hutchinson Publishing Group, Ltd., London, 1948, p. 16.

either acceleration or retardation of particular programs. As the internationally famous British cartoonist David Low has said, "The Labour men . . . like planning, while the Conservatives do it with tears in their eyes."[16]

Problems of the Seventies

The apparent similarities between Labour and the Conservatives, however, appeared to contribute to Great Britain's political crises of the mid-1970s. Rampant inflation, lagging industrial production, a chronic balance-of-payments deficit (in foreign trade), labor strikes and high wage demands, and widespread opposition to Britain's entry into the Common Market had eroded the Conservative party's position in Parliament and support in the electorate. Hoping to capitalize on labor unrest and to consolidate his parliamentary strength, Prime Minister Heath called for elections in February 1974. The results (see Table 11.2) produced Britain's first minority government in forty-five years; no party won a majority in the House of Commons. The resurgent Liberals, calling for public policies that elevated the "public good" above the interests of both business and labor, cut deeply into the voting support of both Labour and the Conservatives (especially the Conservatives). But when the Liberals refused to join Prime Minister Heath in the formation of a coalition government, he resigned, and the Queen appointed Harold Wilson prime minister.

The Wilson government, with a seventeen-seat deficit in the House of Commons, proved to be more of a "caretaker" government than a reformist government capable of restoring Britain's economic health while reducing the advantages of Britain's privileged classes. Even after several decades of the welfare state, economic planning, and the fundamentally socialist programs of all Britain's postwar governments, more than 80 percent of Britain's wealth is owned by less than 10 percent of its population. But its reformist commitments, reinforced by the Labour party's left wing, which called for more nationalization, only complicated the Wilson government's position in Parliament and in the electorate.

[16]David Low, "Clues to an Understanding of Britain," *The New York Times Magazine*, Oct. 30, 1949, pp. 9ff.

Thus new elections were held in October 1974. The Labour party succeeded in winning an absolute majority in the House of Commons, but its perilously thin margin of only three seats suggested that another round of elections would have to be held before the five-year term of the new Parliament expired. The Wilson government's weak parliamentary position only underlined the absence of a majority consensus in the British electorate, and it further compromised the capacity of Britain to cope with its severe economic problems. The Labour government was also on the defensive in Northern Ireland, where violence between Catholics and Protestants continued to rage. The increasing strength of nationalist sentiment in Scotland and Wales induced Prime Minister Wilson in 1974 to promise some form of "devolution" and the establishment of national legislatures in Scotland and Wales, but legislatures with uncertain powers. And the government also felt compelled, in June 1975, to hold a national referendum on Britain's membership in the European Common Market, thereby threatening the original Common Market countries with withdrawal if British treaty obligations were not substantially revised.

Despite these awesome problems, it is a compliment to the durability and responsibility of British political institutions that few observers anticipated any radical alteration of the British constitution or Britain's long-standing patterns of political decision making. The foundations for political compromise and governmental action remained intact, and along with reference to the parliamentary system itself, this potential for policy making could be explained largely in terms of the structural integrity of British political parties.

Party Organization

A *majority* position in Parliament (whether or not through a coalition of parties) assures the British government of the *institutional* opportunity for implementing its program. This stands in marked contrast to the political process in the United States. It is appropriate to emphasize here that this institutional advantage enjoyed by the British executive is the consequence not only of Parliament's constitutional supremacy, and within Parliament of the effective domination of the House of Commons, but also of the discipline and cohesion of

British political parties, regardless of their majority or minority status.

Originally, the Conservative and Liberal parties were merely aggregates of local party organizations in which the real party authority resided. During the last third of the nineteenth century, national organizations arose to federate and control (loosely) the local associations. This control has grown stronger, in large measure because the Labour party has been setting the pace in this respect.[17] All three parties have built up elaborate central offices in London, which function continuously and are the seat of real power in their respective party organizations. While there are some marked differences, as between the two older parties on the one hand and Labour on the other, each party has an annual party conference (roughly comparable to a national convention in the United States), which is presumably the supreme authority, and a central office. The party conference consists of delegates from the local organizations; it elects party officers and committees and expresses itself on matters of policy, but, with the tentative exception of the Labour party, it does *not* formulate the party's platform or tell its parliamentary members what to do. However, even in the Labour party there is much control by the central office. The cabinet system, by its very nature, requires that a party's parliamentary leadership, in or out of power, be left free to enter into compromises and to adapt the party program as political exigencies demand; this precludes day-to-day control over policy by the rank and file.

Another difference between Labour and the older parties has to do with the selection of parliamentary candidates. The central offices of the Conservative and Liberal parties compile lists of acceptable candidates and make these lists available to local party organizations, but the local organization need not choose its candidates from this list, and its choice does not require approval by the party's national organization. On the other hand, although Labour candidates are initially chosen by local party organizations, they must be formally approved by the national organization, which may—but seldom does—reject them.

The financial support of the Conservative party comes, as might be expected, from wealthy donors. The Labour party derives most of its financial support from individual dues and from fees paid by trade unions and other associations that are affiliated with the party. The Labour party never succeeds in raising nearly as much money as the Conservatives, who also enjoy almost a monopoly of control over the daily press (approximately 90 percent in terms of circulation). The centralization of the press and other communications media in London, the importance of the parties' headquarters in allocating constituencies to party candidates, and the primacy of *party* (rather than candidate) spending in election campaigns, as well as the simple fact that heightened political status comes only through loyal party work, help to explain the high cohesion of the British party system, which in turn is indispensable to responsible government.

Another important feature of British political parties is their continuous activity. While American party organizations tend to relax between the dates fixed for elections, the threat of parliamentary dissolution at any time keeps British party organizations constantly mobilized. Party propaganda, through meetings, lectures, conferences, pamphlets, press editorials, and other media, is constantly bombarding the public, a fact that helps to account for the remarkable political awareness and interest shown by the British electorate.

There is no legal control over British political parties, and hence any group may organize as a party without formalities. This is in marked contrast to the difficulty—and, in some states, the impossibility—of organizing minority or third parties in the United States. This freedom of association, which extends to *all* types of voluntary groups, makes the British two-party system seem all the more remarkable. In contrast to the multiparty systems of the European continent, British politics rests on the assumption that, despite admit-

---

[17]Generally speaking, working-class-oriented parties in all countries have imposed stricter discipline upon their members and elected officials than the more liberal and conservative parties have. The high cohesion and centralization of leftist parties is in part a reflection of their more coherent ideologies, which also call for a more radical break from the status quo. The British Labour party, however, is less ideologically militant than its socialist counterparts on the Continent and therefore less rigid in its organizational structure. These differences may be attributed to the socioeconomic and political characteristics of Great Britain, discussed at the outset of this chapter, and to the Labour party's continuing access to governmental power. The prospects of exercising governmental power are usually a sobering corrective to a more extreme ideological orientation.

ted differences of opinion within the memberships of political parties, such differences can be reconciled and compromised within the opposing parties, one of which is likely to be the government, and the other the Opposition. Britons know that there are more than two sides to a question, political or otherwise, but having evolved a two-party system and based parliamentary organization and procedure upon it, they tend to view minority parties with disfavor. Minority parties, such as Sir Oswald Mosley's Fascists and the British Communist party, have never attracted much popular support. Even in the 1970s Britain seems firmly committed to the two-party system, a commitment which is necessarily reinforced by the electoral system and which in turn means that both Conservatives and Labourites must continue and intensify their policy of appealing to all classes and groups. Neither can afford to be labeled as the party of a particular social class. Hence party platforms seek to widen the areas of agreement among the voters, leaving the more specific aims of interest groups to be sought through the organization and activities of such groups rather than by setting up a separate political party for each group, as is common in continental European politics.

STUDY-GUIDE QUESTIONS

1 How does an "open" aristocratic class contribute to the development of stable democracy? What are the probable effects of a "closed" aristocracy on a nation's political development?
2 How do the institutional forms of parliamentary government in Great Britain differ from those of presidential government in the United States?
3 What has been the political role of the British monarchy? How has the role of the monarchy varied over time, and to what extent has the monarchy contributed to historical continuity and political legitimacy in Great Britain?
4 How would you explain the relatively high political cohesion of British political parties?
5 What is meant by "responsible" government? What explains the relatively high responsibility of government in Great Britain?

REFERENCES

Bagehot, Walter: *The English Constitution,* Cornell University Press, Ithaca, N.Y., 1966.
Blondel, Jean: *Voters, Parties, and Leaders: The Social Fabric of British Politics,* Penguin Books, Inc., Baltimore, 1963.
Butt, R.: *The Power of Parliament,* Constable & Co., Ltd., London, 1967.
Daalder, Hans: *Cabinet Reform in Britain, 1914–1963,* Stanford University Press, Stanford, Calif., 1963.
Jennings, W. Ivor: *Cabinet Government,* 3d ed., The Macmillan Company, New York, 1959.
———: *Parliament,* 2d ed., Cambridge University Press, London, 1969.
King, Anthony (ed.): *The British Prime Minister: A Reader,* Macmillan & Co., Ltd., London, 1969.
McKenzie, Robert T.: *British Political Parties,* rev. ed., St. Martin's Press, Inc., New York, 1963.
Rose, Richard: *Politics in England,* Little, Brown and Company, Boston, 1964.
Sampson, Anthony: *The Anatomy of Britain Today,* Harper & Row, Publishers, Incorporated, New York, 1965.
Verney, Douglas V.: *British Government and Politics,* Harper & Row, Publishers, Incorporated, New York, 1971.

Chapter 12

Politics in Western Europe

Europa was a goddess celebrated in Greek mythology, and her name came to represent the world's geographic center of power and wealth in the modern age. But in looking at Europe on a global map, one sees that it is a relatively small area of the world (extending from the Ural Mountains in Russia to the Atlantic Ocean) that is a curious appendage to the great land mass of Asia. Asia has four times the area and population of Europe, but from the eighteenth century to at least the mid-twentieth century it was Europe, especially Western Europe, that dominated Asia and, indeed, almost all the world. Why?

The peoples of Western Europe were the first to develop on a massive scale the modern technologies of economic and industrial organization. These technological capabilities were applied to the vast deposits of natural resources that fueled Europe's modernizing economies and supported its navies and armies. But as the technologies of production *and* aggression outstripped man's understanding of human nature and social relationships, it was inevitable that sympathy and compassion in the interest of others would be subordinated to the self-assertion of groups and nations at the expense of others.[1]

What is of concern here is the apparent patterns of social relationships that contribute to conflict and stability *within* the countries of Western Europe. The relative detail of the preceding chapter

[1] On this last point, see Konrad Lorenz, *On Aggression*, Harcourt, Brace & World, Inc., New York, 1966.

Table 12.1 Selected Geographic, Demographic, and Economic Characteristics of Major European Democracies

	Area in square miles	Total population (millions, 1973)	GNP (billions U.S. $, 1971)	Annual per capita income (U.S. $, 1969–1972)	Approx. % GNP from industrial production	Number of persons per television receiver (1969–1970)
West Germany	95,959	60.3	235	3,790	55	3.7
United Kingdom	94,211	56.5	115	2,000	35	3.5
Italy	116,313	54.9	104	1,525	39	6.1
France	210,039	52.0	170	2,783	35	5.1
Netherlands	12,961	13.5	35.0	2,600	42	4.4
Belgium	11,780	11.0	26.0	2,680	30	5.5
Sweden	173,666	8.3	36.5	4,400	39*	3.4†
Austria	32,374	7.5	16.8	1,466	30	5.9
Switzerland	15,941	6.4	24.5	2,020	50	5.6
Denmark	16,629	5.0	17.2	2,702	20	4.9
Finland	130,120	4.8	11.2	1,700	31	4.5
Norway	125,182	4.0	13.1	2,880	39	4.7
United States	*3,615,125*	*208.1*	*1,050.0*	*4,400*	*27*	*2.6*

*Percentage working population employed in mining, manufacturing, and construction.
†Includes both radio and television receivers.
Source: The Official Associated Press Almanac 1974, Hammond Incorporated, Maplewood, N.J., 1974.

on Great Britain has served, in part, to highlight the characteristics of the American political process, discussed in Chapters 9 and 10. And, in many respects, it is true that Great Britain is more comparable to the United States than it is to the other countries of Western Europe.

Crossing the English Channel, one moves into a different world of cultural, social, and political relationships. The apparent causes and characteristics of these relationships need to be summarized here, although in less detail than is available from the more elaborate studies of politics in specific European countries. After all, this book is only an *introduction* to the subject matter of political science. However, while much must be left unsaid, this chapter (and the entirety of the text) may at least stimulate the student to undertake further inquiry into those areas of political life which are of particular interest. This chapter may also provide students with a "conceptual framework" for understanding better the politics and societies of some of those countries they read about and visit in the course of their student and adult lives.

Interested and inquiring adults, however, never cease being students of life around them. The problem is to understand it. The following may be of some help in this continuing effort.

A CONCEPTUAL FRAMEWORK

"Conceptual framework" is an unfortunately pompous term for designating a systematic way of looking at things. In this case, a conceptual framework is needed for classifying some of the phenomena of Western European politics and attempting some tentative explanation of the more observable patterns of social and political interaction. The term should not be confused with "model," which rigorously predicts behavior, or "theory," which deductively predicts *and* explains behavior. In part because of the nonquantifiable characteristics of most political phenomena, political science (as compared with physics or economics) is relatively impoverished when it comes to formal theories and models. This deserves to be lamented less than explained. And the problems of systematic conceptualization are all the more complicated when one attempts to deal with a large number of cases with widely varying characteristics—even at the superficial level of observation. (See Table 12.1.)

Social Respect and Social Identity

Some conceptual order may be imposed on the subject matter of the present study if we begin with the following premises or assumptions:

1 Most people want to be respected by their peers (their acquaintances or associates).
2 Fundamental to the acquisition of social respect is an individual's sense of identity.
3 A sense of identity is acquired in various ways: by an individual's place in the family, tribe, village, region, or nation and through his or her association with others who share the same racial, religious, or linguistic characteristics.

Only in very advanced and modernized societies are these *ascriptive* identities subordinated to the *achievement* identities that are exalted in classical liberal and socialist ideologies. According to these ideologies and in societies where achievement norms are dominant, the identity and status of the individual is or ought to be a function of what he does and how he performs. But in most societies, throughout history and in the contemporary world, ascriptive characteristics are the principal source of individuals' social identity and the primary means by which they advance a claim to the respect of others.

It follows that a study of the various patterns of cleavage and consensus along the lines of ascriptive identity will tell us a great deal about the political and social relationships of the world around us.

Race

It has already been pointed out that racial heterogeneity threatens the social and political stability of any society. As immigrants from the West Indies and southern Asia took up residence and found jobs in Great Britain after the late 1950s, race and the immigration policies of the Commonwealth became important issues in British politics. In Western Europe, however, there is a high degree of racial homogeneity, with almost all the population belonging to the anthropologist's category of Caucasoid peoples.

This precise definition of race, however, has not prevented the use of "race" by political leaders and movements to gain political advantage. This is illustrated most obviously by the anti-Semitism of European fascism, especially German national socialism. "Race" has also been used synonymously with "nationality," and it thus has been intended to designate those from "inferior" cultures. As the number of workers immigrating into Switzerland from Spain, Italy, Yugoslavia, Turkey, and North Africa increased throughout the 1960s, new political groups were organized to protest the growing dependency of the Swiss economy on foreign labor. This appeared to be especially troubling as the Swiss economy began to experience the inflationary problems typical of other Western European countries and as Switzerland faced an uncertain period of economic readjustment following the growth and success of the European Common Market (from which Switzerland excluded itself by virtue of its international neutrality). And, in fact, the parliamentary representation of these particular groups, invariably on the extreme right of the Swiss party system, increased dramatically between the elections of 1967 and 1971—from one to eleven seats in the 202-seat National Council, a parliamentary body that is otherwise notable for the long-term continuity and stability of its various partisan groups. Responding to these political pressures, the Swiss federal government, in August 1974, imposed an overall limit on the number of immigrants that would be allowed into the country on a yearly basis; it also declared that the current number of foreigners living in Switzerland was near to the maximum allowable and that the number must be gradually reduced over the next decade.

From these preliminary findings, then, one might generalize that an appeal to racial identity—even in the context of a largely homogeneous racial group—is more likely to arise in times of already existing political instability or in times of relative economic stress and change. Other ascriptive identities no longer suffice, and political leaders, especially those on the margins of the political system, identify race as the vehicle for enhancing their political influence. In effect, they appeal to the lowest common denominator of their targeted clienteles—that of genetic inheritance. They thus attempt to build coalitions of supporters that cut across the other basic sources of ascriptive identity, including the following.

Religion

Even more than racial (or linguistic) homogeneity, a common belief in the moral truths of a particular religion is a powerful source of social and political unity. After the Roman Emperor Constantine's conversion to Christianity in A.D. 312, for example, the Christian faith became the primary source of cultural identity for the peoples of Europe.

Given Christianity's assumption that it was the one true religion, however, and its argument that all those who were not Christian were destined for damnation (with few exceptions), there was bound to be major conflict wherever there appeared competing faiths or interpretations of Scripture—equally absolute in their moral assumptions. In Russia, for example, Leon Trotsky correctly understood that a major source of revolutionary agitation against the tsarist autocracy was to be found among the "Old Believers." The Old Believers numbered one-fourth of Russia's Christian population in the early twentieth century, and they were intensely hostile to the tsarist state largely because of its support of the Russian Orthodox Church. Thus the Old Believers were an important base for revolutionary organization, even where religion was irrelevant to the goals of the revolutionaries. This example again helps to make the point that fundamental differences in ascriptive identity are likely to have major consequences for politics.

Protestants and Catholics But, of course, the principal division within Christianity dates from the sixteenth century and the Protestant Reformation. The suffering and destruction that have resulted from the struggles between Protestants and Roman Catholics are incalculable, and the consequences in terms of cultural cleavage and political instability are obvious even today. In the early 1970s, there were 192 million Roman Catholics living in Europe and 131 million Protestants (there were 93 million of the Eastern Orthodox faith). There were major Catholic political parties in all nine of the continental European countries with competitive party systems and large Catholic populations. And in seven of these nine countries there also were major anticlerical parties. Thus the religious cleavages generated by the Protestant Reformation in the sixteenth century are clearly an important factor in the explanation of political conflict in modern Europe.

Major religious wars broke out in Switzerland in 1529, 1531, 1656, 1712, and 1847. In Switzerland in the early 1970s, 53 percent of the population was Protestant, and 45 percent was Roman Catholic. While overt violence between Switzerland's religious groups has disappeared, a major cleavage according to religious identity continues to distinguish Swiss political parties. Those Swiss voters most fervent in their Catholic beliefs tend to vote for the Christian Democratic party, while the vote of Swiss Protestants is divided along the lines of economic class, but seldom if ever going to the Christian Democrats. These same generalizations apply to Holland, where one of the major cleavage lines drawn through the party system distinguishes Catholics from Protestants, and Orthodox Protestants (mainly of a Calvinist orientation) from the more liberal or latitudinarian Protestants.

The most dramatic and contemporary example of religiously based conflict is provided by the unhappy circumstances of Northern Ireland (or Ulster). A part of the United Kingdom, Northern Ireland remained attached to Great Britain after Irish independence was formally declared in 1922. The Ulster Protestant elite retained its dependent political status largely because it feared being absorbed by the Catholic population of independent Ireland, and it insisted on maintaining its position of domination over the approximately one-third Catholic population that remained in Northern Ireland. This meant the exclusion of the Ulster Catholic minority from the political process of Northern Ireland and the United Kingdom—a servile status for Ulster Catholics that has led to explosive violence since 1969. Between 1969 and the British general elections of February 1974, 1,000 lives were lost in Northern Ireland's religious struggles (including the lives of almost 200 British soldiers sent to Northern Ireland to maintain a semblance of order), 10,000 people were wounded, and property damage was estimated at $100 million. The twelve members of the House of Commons elected from Northern Ireland in 1974 were all Protestants, and all but one were from the extremist Protestant parties bent on perpetuating the status and privileges of Ulster Protestants. And while in Great Britain the 1974 elections were fought over the issues generated by labor agitation and economic crisis, the only issues of importance in Northern Ireland related to religion.

Church and Anti-Church A religious cleavage also marks the politics of those countries nominally classified as almost entirely Catholic. France and Italy, especially the latter, are obvious examples. As political participation and the organization of mass-based political parties developed after the mid-nineteenth century, the Catholic Church proved hostile to republican institutions and politics. Fearing a reduction in its social, economic, and political privileges and the erosion of its influence over the rank-and-file faithful, the church only belatedly met the republican challenge—and then by establishing its own political parties and trade unions.

A major issue in France has been the extent of state subsidies for parochial schools, while in Italy the recent effort to pass legislation sanctioning civil divorce has further troubled the usually shaky coalition of Italy's government parties. The term "radical" as used by many political parties in Western Europe does not refer primarily to issues of economic policy; it in fact derives from the nineteenth century and denotes those republican and anticlerical parties which opposed the pervasive influence of the church in politics and social organization. Radicals, socialists, and communists have been generally agreed on the antirepublican effects of church schools, where young citizens receive an interpretation of national history that regards the periods of republican government as corrupt and periods of monarchical or (as in the case of France) Bonapartist rule as filled with virtue and glory. It probably is no coincidence that, today, the area of primary communist strength in Italy (in the regional center, including Florence and Bologna) is also the historical location of the Papal States, where the church long exerted its control as the major owner of land and principal agent of political administration. Even where there is apparent religious homogeneity, then, it is necessary to look below the surface of the society's culture, where, especially in Catholic countries, basic political cleavages that reflect differences in religious values are likely to be found.

Language

The very basis of an individual's sense of identity with a community derives from a common language—which is essential to the communication of shared values and norms. Where a social order claiming the universal allegiance of European peoples has developed, it has depended on a common language spoken by at least the elites of otherwise culturally disparate groups: Attic Greek in the case of the empire of Alexander the Great, and Latin in the case of European Christianity before the Reformation.

The initial manifestation of *nationalism* (along with religion, the most powerful political force in the modern world) turned on the emergence of national languages, frequently as developed by popular writers inspired by religious convictions: Dante in the case of Italy and, in Germany, Martin Luther, whose translation of the Latin Bible into idiomatic German lent a strong cohering force to early German cultural identity. As cultural identities along linguistic lines differ, then, the probabilities of social and political conflict increase. In contemporary Europe there are at least thirty-nine distinct languages within the single category of the Indo-European language. But, as the history of nationalism and the rise of the nation-state suggest, linguistic homogeneity is a predominant characteristic of most European states. There are, nevertheless, some important exceptions.

In December 1973 the prime minister of Spain was killed by a bomb that had been placed beneath his parked automobile. The assassination was attributed to Basque separatists, who, literally since the time of Julius Caesar, have used violence to attempt to win their cultural and political autonomy. Today there are more than 1½ million Basques living in the north of Spain, and the majority retain their ancient language, which is unrelated to any other language group.

In Switzerland, too, linguistic differences have resulted in violence. In the 1960s French-speaking militants in the predominantly German-speaking canton of Bern used dynamite and, on one occasion, occupied the parliamentary chamber of the Bern cantonal assembly to underline their demands for a separate linguistic region. Their efforts appeared to be indirectly encouraged by French President Charles de Gaulle's support in 1967 for the separatist movement of French-speaking Canadians in Quebec. And, at least superficially, Switzerland would appear to have a major language problem: 75 percent of the Swiss population speaks German, 20 percent speaks French, 4 percent speaks Italian (all three languages are official state languages), and 1 percent speaks Romansh (which is officially accepted as a "vocational language"). As in India and Canada, however, where there also are major linguistic divisions, a *federal* form of government and linguistic homogeneity within each federal jurisdiction appear to have reduced the social and political tensions associated with this type of cultural cleavage.[2]

Linguistic Divisions in Belgium This underlines the importance of recent efforts by Belgian political elites to replace their unitary state with a federal system that would enhance the cultural autonomy of Belgium's two major linguistic communities: the Flemish-speaking Belgians (Flemings), who make up 55 percent of Belgium's population of 11 million, and the French-speaking Walloons, who represent approximately 44 percent of the population.

The frequent violence between these two linguistic groups has periodically threatened the very foundations of the Belgian state, and it has been especially intense in the city of Brussels, where the two groups come into contact through economic and educational institutions. Three of the seven political parties represented in Belgium's Chamber of Representatives are based primarily on linguistic identities. A fourth and major Belgian political party, the Liberals, lost a third of its parliamentary seats in the 1971 elections because of its support for a federalist system. The Liberal party's position on federalism was especially unpopular with the party's French-speaking voters, who viewed federalism as a threat to their existing socioeconomic and political advantages. In these same elections, the language-oriented parties based in Brussels and Wallonia doubled their parliamentary representation, while the Flemish United People's party registered important gains in Flanders. The rate of growth in the parliamentary representation of these parties dropped dramatically in the March 1974 elections, however, while the dominant Christian Socialist and Belgian Socialist parties remained in control of the government. But the importance of the language issue in Belgian politics was again demonstrated by the Socialists, who have attempted to bridge the linguistic division; in 1973 the Belgian Socialist party made the dual-party presidency (consisting of one Fleming and one Walloon) a permanent feature of its party constitution. No study of Belgian politics, then, or of any country with major linguistic divisions, is complete without a careful analysis of the way this particular type of cultural cleavage interacts with political organization and decision making.

Economic Class and Reinforcing Cleavages

The above example of the Belgian Socialists helps to make an important point: In order to understand more fully the characteristics of politics in Western Europe (or, for that matter, in any country), one must determine how the several lines of cultural cleavage in a given society intersect with one another and, ultimately, how these various patterns are affected by existing political institutions. At this point in the elaboration of the conceptual framework it is also necessary to add another dimension of potential cleavage—economic class.

The category of economic class is not a conceptual invention of Karl Marx, although Marx did play an important role in alerting social scientists to the impact of economic relationships on the structures of society and politics. Economic class—in the sense of an individual's relationships to others who perform similar tasks or share similar circumstances in the system of production and distribution—played an important role in social and political life long before Marx focused on the proletariat as the force of the future. Plato identified the struggles between rich and poor as a primary source of instability in the Greek city-state; Aristotle correctly argued that a relatively democratic and stable society depends on the existence of a large middle class; and well before the onset of industrialization, the struggles between landless peasants and a landowning nobility marked an important part of the history of European politics.

---

[2]French-speaking Swiss in the canton of Bern voted by referendum in June 1974 to establish a separate canton. The results of the referendum thus extended the principle of Swiss federalism and laid the basis for eliminating the prolonged conflict between French- and German-speaking Swiss who had previously lived under the same cantonal jurisdiction.

The emergence of an industrial working class, however, immensely complicated the structure of European societies. Our concern here is with the extent to which the several cultural *and* economic cleavages of a particular society overlap and reinforce one another, thereby raising to an especially high point the chances of major social and political conflict.

Reinforcing Cleavages in Northern Ireland and Belgium What lends particular force to the *religious* conflict in Northern Ireland, for example, is the reinforcing cleavage of *economic class*. Not only is the Catholic minority in Northern Ireland discriminated against on the basis of religious belief, but it also lives in the more impoverished ghettos of Belfast and has the lower-paying jobs, a higher rate of unemployment, and—as a consequence of these reinforcing cleavages—virtually no representation in the political process of Northern Ireland or, after the 1974 elections, in the British Parliament. Economic *and* political circumstances thus combine with religious cleavage to present Ulster moderates and British political leaders with an almost insoluble problem. Any effort to improve the political representation or economic conditions of the Catholic minority meets with the entrenched resistance of Ulster Protestants, and as specific reforms are proposed (as in late 1973), the leadership of the Protestant majority gravitates into the hands of the Protestant extremists.

In Belgium, *linguistic* divisions between Walloons and Flemings are reinforced by both *religious* and *economic* group identities. While the Belgian population is predominantly Roman Catholic, there have been major differences (as in Italy and France) over the appropriate social and political role of religious institutions. Belgian cultural and social life is segmented into confessional and nonconfessional subcultures, each with its own patterns of socialization, political parties, interest groups, cultural organizations, and even stores and businesses. The more fervent Catholics are found among the rural Flemish-speaking population, while the more urban and French-speaking population of Belgium is relatively nonconfessional, even anticlerical. The earlier and more rapid industrial development of the southern Walloon region (bordering on France) also meant that the growth of an industrial working class in Belgium initially reinforced the already existing linguistic and religious cleavages; workers in Wallonia could identify with one another in terms of economic class, language (French), and religious orientation (relatively nonconfessional), and this intensified their hostilities toward the more agrarian, Catholic, and Flemish-speaking Belgians in the northern provinces.

Reinforcing Cleavages in the United States and Canada It is appropriate here to refer also to the reinforcing cleavages that intensify cultural and political conflict in the United States and Canada. The same generalizations advanced above with regard to religion in Northern Ireland and language in Belgium apply with equal force to black citizens living in the United States—although the basic cleavage in this instance is racial rather than religious or linguistic. But the *racial* minority status of blacks in the United States is aggravated by their underprivileged *economic* and *political* circumstances—and there is every reason to believe that the latter derive largely from the former. In Canada, *religious* and *linguistic* cleavages reinforce each other; the great majority of French-speaking Canadians are Catholic, and the great majority of English-speaking Canadians are Protestant. Both language and religion thus distinguish the two communities, which are periodically at odds with each other. And it is important to note that the strength of the French-speaking separatists and the highest incidence of separatist violence have been concentrated in Montreal rather than in Quebec City or other areas of French-speaking Canada. Why should this be the case? Apparently the answer is that the English-speaking (and Protestant) community is most prominent in business, banking, and other areas of economic activity in Montreal. Especially in Montreal, then, the identities associated with *economic* role and *religious* affiliation reinforce the more basic cultural cleavage that derives from differences in *language*.

These findings help to illustrate an important point in the study of comparative politics: Where several cleavage lines reinforce one another, marking out in each case the same group in terms of its social identity, the chances of violence and political instability are extremely high.

Cross-cutting Cleavages

It seems reasonable to argue that if Catholics in Northern Ireland were not also discriminated against in terms of economic role and political participation, their understandable hostility toward Ulster Protestants might be reduced from its present level of intensity. And, in fact, the intensity of conflict between Flemings and Walloons in Belgium is moderated to some extent by the presence of strong confessional (Roman Catholic) groups within *both* linguistic communities. While Walloons and Flemings are divided by language, there thus is some basis for a common identity between many Walloons and most Flemings—their common allegiance to Catholicism and their support for the social and political activities of church institutions. And as the Flemish-speaking areas of Belgium have become more industrialized and urbanized, common economic interests have also developed to help bridge the differences between Belgium's linguistic communities. In this way, industrialization and the development of new *economic* classes can help to reduce *cultural* cleavage—if the identities of economic class cut across the cleavage lines of religion, language, or race.[3]

We can speak of this particular pattern of social identification in terms of "cross-cutting cleavages." Where a society's cleavage lines are cross-cutting instead of mutually reinforcing, there is a tendency for social and political instability to decline or to exist at levels of conflict lower than might otherwise be the case. Political competition is less in terms of basic ascriptive identities and more a function of ideological differences that transcend particular social groups. This facilitates bargaining and compromise between the groups and their political representatives.

Cross-cutting Cleavages in the Netherlands In the Netherlands, for example, the potential for conflict along the lines of religious cleavage (between Catholics, Calvinists, and liberal Protestants) is reduced by the cross-cutting cleavage of economic class; workers, farmers, and businessmen are drawn from all the religious groups. A Catholic worker may find his hostility toward a Protestant worker moderated by their common interests in trade union organization, better wages, greater job security, and the election of political leaders sympathetic to working-class interests. Thus the identities of economic class (either proletarian or bourgeois) can transcend cultural cleavage, raising the society's potential for compromise instead of conflict.

At the same time, religious groups in the Netherlands receive support from important segments of all the major categories of economic class; workers, farmers, and businessmen can find a common identity in their religious convictions, thus moderating the hostilities that may derive from their class-consciousness and different economic interests. The Netherlands, in fact, is an almost classic example of a relatively stable and highly democratic society, characteristics that are in part attributable to the Netherlands' various cleavage patterns, which are cross-cutting instead of mutually reinforcing.

Cross-cutting Cleavages in Switzerland These generalizations also apply to Switzerland. It will be recalled that Swiss society is characterized by major cultural cleavages along the lines of both religion (Catholicism and Protestantism) and language (primarily German and French). And yet it also should be remembered that in 1970 an international opinion sample of political and economic elites identified Switzerland as one of the ten best-governed countries of the world.[4] How has it been possible for Switzerland to develop a stable and democratic government of such high repute in the context of a society with major cultural cleavage?

An important part of the answer to this question involves cross-cutting cleavages. (See Table 12.2.) Table 12.2 shows that many Swiss citizens who speak German, French, or Italian share the religious values of Catholicism. German-speaking and

---

[3] In the early stages of modernization, however, the effects of economic growth are likely to be distributed unevenly and along the prevailing lines of cultural cleavage. This is typical of most of the contemporary underdeveloped world. Economic development in Nigeria (after Nigeria's independence from Great Britain in 1960), for example, aggravated the cultural differences between major tribal groups, contributing to the destructive violence and civil war of 1966–1970.

[4] See Chap. 8.

Table 12.2 Cross-cutting Cleavages in Switzerland: Distribution of Cantons According to Religious and Linguistic Characteristics

		Number of cantons where the principal language is:		
		German	French	Italian
Number of cantons where the principal religion is:	Catholic	7	2	1
	Protestant	9	3	—

French-speaking Swiss citizens share the religious values of Protestantism. At the same time, many Catholics and Protestants have a common identity through the language of German and others through the language of French. If *all* Swiss Catholics spoke only German and if *all* Swiss Protestants spoke only French, the lines of cultural cleavage in Switzerland would be mutually reinforcing—and the chances of social conflict and political instability would be much greater than they are. If this were the case, the politics of Switzerland might well resemble the politics of Belgium or Northern Ireland instead of the politics of a stable democracy highly esteemed throughout the world.

The Impact of Politics

It has already been pointed out how governmental institutions can aggravate or moderate the political effects of a society's cultural and economic cleavages. *Federalism* in Switzerland, Canada, India, and perhaps Belgium can lower the intensity of cultural and political conflict by reducing the social interaction of citizens with different group identities. *Political parties* can bridge existing cultural cleavage if they base their appeal on economic class, as in the case of the Belgian Socialists. *Monarchical institutions*, as in the Netherlands, Great Britain, Sweden, and Denmark, can help to establish a national identity for citizens otherwise separated by cultural and economic differences.

The *electoral system* may reinforce existing cleavages by ensuring that each cultural and economic group has its own political representatives (typical of systems of proportional representation). Or it may induce political parties to appeal across cultural and class lines in order to build an electoral majority (typical of the single-member district, simple-majority electoral system). It may also encourage partisan elites to work together in coalition government, or it may reinforce their tendencies toward factional conflict and obstructionism.

The *policy choices* of political elites are also likely to have a major impact on the society's potential for cohesion or fragmentation. As in the case of Switzerland, a foreign policy of neutrality derives less from humanitarian ideals than from the sheer necessity of avoiding the aggravation of cultural cleavage. It is not difficult to imagine the intense domestic conflict that would have resulted from the Swiss government's decision to support either Germany or France during the periodic wars between those two nations from the late nineteenth through the mid-twentieth centuries. In Italy, the decision of governing elites in 1970 to draft a law granting the right of civil divorce—against the wishes of the Catholic Church—threatened the government's always tenuous majority in parliament. And the 1974 referendum campaign waged for and against the divorce law reinforced the continuing cleavage between Italy's clerical and anticlerical factions.

The Netherlands: A Tradition of Compromise But the values and choices of political elites may operate independently of their more immediate and objective circumstances. In the long struggle of the Netherlands against the domination of Spain, England, and France, Dutch political elites came to appreciate the necessity of mutual toleration and compromise among competing groups in order to maintain the unity essential to winning independence from more powerful states.

This spirit of accommodation has marked the politics of modern Holland, where rival political

Table 12.3 Parliamentary Parties and Government Coalitions in Six European Democracies

Country and lower house of parliament	Date of election	Major parties or coalitions	Seats in lower house
West Germany Bundestag (Total seats=496)	Nov. 1972	Social Democrats* Christian Democratic Union and Christian Social Union Free Democrats*	230 225 41
Italy Chamber of Deputies (Total seats=630)	May 1972	Christian Democrats* Communists Socialists Neofascists and Monarchists Social Democrats* Liberals* Republicans†	267 179 61 56 29 21 14
France National Assembly (Total seats=487)	Mar. 1973	Union of Democrats for the Republic (Gaullists)* Social Democrats Communists Independent Republicans* Reformists Democratic and Progressive Center*	184 100 73 54 31 23
Belgium Chamber of Representatives (Total seats=212)	Nov. 1971	Christian Socialists* Socialists* Liberals Flemish United People's party French-speaking Democratic front Walloon party Communists	67 59 34 22 13 12 5
Switzerland National Council (Total seats=202)	Nov. 1971	Radicals* Social Democrats* Catholic Conservatives* Agrarians* Independents Liberals Communists Evangelical Christian party Democrats Extreme right	49 48 44 21 13 6 5 3 2 11
Norway Parliament (Total seats=155)	Sept. 1973	Labor* Conservatives Center party Christian party Socialist-Communist coalition†	62 29 21 20 16

*Indicates a party represented in the government (cabinet) that was formed after the election.
†Indicates a party or coalition not included in the government but voting with the government to ensure its parliamentary majority.

elites recognize the legitimacy of opposing socioeconomic and cultural groups and respect the rights of their political representatives to share in policy making. The inability of a single party to win control of the government requires a coalition of parties; yet these coalitions do not lead to permanent divisions between one faction and another, and instead they appear to reinforce the tendencies toward compromise and bargaining. While one coalition may temporarily dominate national politics (for example, the Catholic People's party and the Anti-Revolutionary party), a different coalition (for example, the Catholic and Liberal parties) may constitute the government of an important municipality or province. Even when their political parties are not included in a governing coalition, the representatives of major subcultural groups in Holland are usually invited to participate in the bargaining associated with important policy decisions.

The Effects of Political Parties Of particular importance to the elaboration of our conceptual framework, then, is the extent to which the major political parties of any given political system aggregate interests from across the various lines of cleavage in the society. In the case of Western European politics, it should already be apparent that we are dealing with a sometimes bewildering variety of political parties and that most European democracies are distinguished from their British and American counterparts by the presence of a *multiparty* political system. (See Table 12.3.)

Political parties may either reinforce or moderate existing cleavages in the society. These particular patterns in turn may reflect the structure of governmental institutions, the nature of the electoral system, the country's rate of industrial development and urbanization, the pace of suffrage reform, and the values of partisan elites. Since political parties are the essential link between citizens and government, the characteristics of their support and the nature of their appeal are likely to have a determining impact on the political process.

Contrasting patterns in Holland and Belgium The cross-cutting characteristics of governing coalitions in the Netherlands, for example, are in turn reinforced by the aggregative characteristics of the major political parties. By advancing the policies and institutions associated with the welfare state and a planned economy, the Dutch Labor party collects support from both Protestant and Catholic workers, thereby moderating cleavages along religious lines. And Protestant and Catholic parties in the Netherlands appeal for support along the lines of religion, thereby moderating the divisions of economic class.

In the recent political history of Belgium, by contrast, the Catholic (Christian Socialist) party has appealed more to Flemish than to Walloon voters and more to rural than to urban economic interests. The Belgian Liberal party has not aggregated interests from across the linguistic divisions of the society, nor has it enjoyed a substantial following from other than the urban-industrial and professional middle classes. Unlike the Labor party in the Netherlands, the Belgian Socialists—despite their appeals to both Walloon and Flemish workers—have not effectively cut across the society's linguistic divisions, nor have they been willing to compromise on the issue of religion (the Socialists in Belgium remain resolutely anticlerical). In Belgium, then, the party system tends to reinforce existing cultural and economic cleavages in the society, thereby lending to the political life of any government an uncertain future. Even the monarchy has failed to ensure Belgium's social and political cohesion, as the pro-Catholic and Flemish population has tended to support monarchical institutions, while they have been opposed by the more anticlerical Walloons.

Partisanship and representation: Switzerland and Belgium In contrast to the nonaggregative characteristics of the Belgian political system, the Radical and Liberal parties of Switzerland (the principal parties in the building of modern Switzerland after 1848) were Protestant-oriented, but they drew support from both French-speaking and German-speaking cantons. And the more contemporary appeal of the Swiss Social Democratic party to voters according to economic interest has helped to moderate the divisions between Swiss citizens in terms of both language and religion. The Swiss electoral system of proportional representation has ensured an impressive continuity of partisan representation in the national government, and the major parties that traditionally constitute the governing coalition have grown accustomed to bargaining and compromise. The list system of Swiss voting (whereby the parties propose several candidates in each election district) even encourages partisan elites to include candidates from competing parties on their own election lists.[5]

In Switzerland, and also in Belgium, government coalitions are carefully constructed to afford representation to major cultural groups. The Swiss Federal Council (the executive branch of government) is usually based on a four-party coalition and is composed of seven councilors elected by the National Council; traditionally, no more than five councilors are German-speaking, and at least two are French-speaking. In the Belgian government formed after the 1968 elections by the Socialist and Christian Socialist parties, fourteen Cabinet members (of a total of twenty-eight) were from the Walloon community, and fourteen Cabinet members were from the Flemish community. Even where cultural conflict agitates the society, then, the bargaining ethic of political elites, parties that aggregate supporters from across the various lines of cultural and economic cleavage, and a balanced structuring of political representation and leadership can help to offset the hostilities kindled by more basic social identities.[6]

These and other characterizations of politics in Western Europe may be illustrated by three case studies. Together, Italy, France, and West Germany account for almost three-quarters of the population and gross national product of the continental European democracies. They also represent striking contrasts in the social, cultural, and political styles of contemporary Western Europe.

---

[5]For example, in a recent cantonal election for the seven-seat executive council in Geneva, the Radical party presented a list of candidates that included not seven Radicals but four Radicals, one Liberal, one Social Democrat, and one Catholic Conservative. The Catholic Conservative party, admitting the dominance of the Radicals in Geneva canton, proposed a list of candidates that included four Radicals (the same four candidates included on the Radicals' list), one Liberal, and *two* Catholic Conservatives. (The voter casts a ballot for only one election list.)

[6]Outside the European context, Canada again provides us with an illustration of a part of our conceptual framework; in the June 1974 national elections, the Canadian Liberal party was returned to power with an absolute parliamentary majority *and* with widespread support from both French- and English-speaking provinces. Thus the Liberals and their bilingual leader, Prime Minister Pierre Elliott Trudeau, may help to moderate cultural cleavages in Canada by bridging the gap between Canada's linguistic communities.

ITALY: CLEAVAGES ALMOST EVERYWHERE

The Effects of History and Culture

Traveling throughout Western Europe, one cannot help but notice some superficial differences from one country to another. These differences, however superficial, are frequently important indicators of more basic variations in the patterns of national development and thus in the contemporary styles of social and political organization.

Is it pure coincidence, for example, that so many of the "castles" of England and France are really country estates without walls and battlements, situated in open valleys or on fertile plains, and that so many of the castles of Germany and Italy are (or were) solid fortifications sitting astride mountain passes or commanding a view of the flow of traffic along major waterways?

Political Unification These curiosities of modern tourism are signs of the timing and extent of political unification. In England, France, and Scandinavia, the state was unified at a relatively early date. Centralizing monarchs reduced or eliminated the prerogatives of the feudal nobility and, in the interests of themselves and a growing bourgeoisie in search of national markets, consolidated territory and extended political control far beyond the streets and buildings of the capital. And it is another curiosity for the modern tourist that in England, France, and the Scandinavian countries, there is one dominant city where politics, culture, and communications are centralized. Italy and Germany, on the other hand, have many major cities with varying architectural styles and cultural traditions and with differences in political heritage.

These rich variations in a country's history exact a heavy price in terms of modern politics. The later the date of political unification, the lower the legitimacy of governing institutions, and the more unstable the country's politics. And where political unity was imposed by force rather than by an evolutionary process of nation building, the loyalty of citizens to governing institutions is more in doubt, especially in the context of economic instability.

In Switzerland, for example, the confederation of cantons into a national state began in 1291 and proceeded slowly over many centuries. But the political unification of Italy dates only from the *Risorgimento* (or "revival") of the nineteenth century, culminated politically and militarily by the elimination of papal control over Rome in 1871. Writing in the midst of the brilliance of Italy's *sovereign* city-states during the Renaissance, Machiavelli and Dante argued in vain for national unity, a national unity that would parallel the cultural identity of the Italian people and help to protect them from the depredations of foreign invaders. (But the geographic circumstances of Italy were, by themselves, an obstacle to early unification.) After the fifteenth century, the continental European powers invaded and reinvaded Italy, and especially Lombardy (in the north, surrounding Milan) served as a continuing battleground for armies whose leaders perpetuated and profited from Italy's fragmentation. Prior to the stunning success of the *Risorgimento*, the Italian south was controlled by the Spanish Bourbon dynasty as the kingdom of the Two Sicilies (with its capital in Naples). The Italian center was ruled by the Catholic Church, through the pope, and was known as the Papal States. In the north, Lombardy and Venice were ruled directly by the Austrian Hapsburgs, while Parma, Modena, and Tuscany were defined as duchies and were under the dominion of Austrian princes.

Only the Savoy dynasty, controlling Piedmont, Genoa, and the island of Sardinia, enjoyed a measure of autonomy from the machinations of the European powers. And it was the House of Savoy, under the leadership of King Victor Emmanuel II and his able prime minister Count Cavour, aided by the military bravura of Giuseppe Garibaldi, that in fact laid the basis for Italian unity in 1861. It was, however, a *political* unity of the Italian south and center that depended on the military and diplomatic triumphs of a dynasty in the Italian north. At this point in Italy's history, another northern leader of the *Risorgimento* (Massimo d'Azeglio) correctly observed: "We have made Italy; now we must make Italians."

Divided Allegiances Making Italians, in the sense of creating a nation of Italian people with common values and allegiances, has not been easy. Nor can it be said to have been accomplished more than a century after political unification. The effects of *region*, as an index of differing cultural and political styles, have been complicated by radical disjunctures between past and present, each with its own peculiar impact on the Italian people according to their regional identities.

Thus the separate sovereignties fragmenting Italy before the *Risorgimento* were replaced suddenly and violently by the constitutional monarchy imposed by the House of Savoy. Benito Mussolini and Italian fascism stamped out the young and struggling institutions of republican politics between 1922 and 1943. The Resistance against Italian fascism and the German occupation of northern Italy raised the hopes of leftist reformers and revolutionaries, who dominated Italian politics immediately after World War II. A national referendum in 1946 eliminated the monarchy, in part because of its identification with the discredited Fascists, but the vote was close, and a majority of the electorate in the Italian south voted to keep the monarchy. It is no coincidence that the subsequent strength of the Monarchist party was largely in the south, where it numbered among its supporters many of the large landowners who sought to maintain their feudal-type control over the peasantry. And, in the 1974 referendum on the law permitting civil divorce, the majority of southerners voted against the law, while the majority of northerners, particularly in the large urban centers, voted in favor of it. The divorce law was upheld, 59 to 41 percent, but at the cost of embittered partisan rivalry and the reinforcement of Italy's divisions between clerical and anticlerical forces.

Italian politics since the war has thus been a constant struggle to maintain republican institutions and a semblance of policy continuity in the context of competing groups, subcultures, and allegiances. The ideological orientation of the many governments may be classified as center, center right, or center left, depending on the most recent election results, the issues raised by political elites, the shifting balance of partisan strength in the Italian parliament, and the intensity of factional conflict within all the major parties.

A Political Culture of Alienation These many conflicts have not helped to build popular support for

Italy's political system. The survey research carried out by Gabriel A. Almond and Sidney Verba in 1959 helps to make the point in a comparative context. In what is now a classic study in political science, Almond and Verba argued that a critical factor in the building of stable democracy is the citizen's sense of "efficacy": Does the citizen believe that he or she can influence the policies of local and national government, either individually or in association with others? In Great Britain, 53 percent of the respondents in the Almond-Verba study thought that they could influence the policies of both local and national government. The comparable figure for respondents in the United States was 44 percent; in Italy it was only 29 percent.[7] Among those respondents who thought that they could influence government, 92 percent in the United States expressed pride in their national political institutions. The comparable figure for respondents in Great Britain was 50 percent; in Italy it was only 3 percent.[8]

Also important to the building of stable democracy are attitudes that express toleration of others and a willingness to cooperate in associational life. But Almond and Verba found that "the picture of Italian political culture that has emerged from our data is one of relatively unrelieved political alienation and of social isolation and distrust."[9] Ironically, the strength of the dominant government party in the Italian republic, the Christian Democrats, rests largely on the support of "politically uninvolved Catholic women." The importance in Italy of sustained economic growth and of the commitment of Italian political elites to democratic values is thus dramatically clear; only in this context is Italy likely to develop the basis for a political culture that supports democratic institutions.

Parties and Politics

But rapid economic growth in Italy, beginning in the late nineteenth century and recurring again as the "Italian economic miracle" of the mid-1950s and early 1960s, further complicated the cultural and class dynamics of Italian politics. Until the 1960s, the geographic extent of industrialization was extremely uneven, and major business activity and industrial production were concentrated in the northern triangle traced by Milan, Genoa, and Turin. The initial development of economic classes along industrial lines and the extent of class conflict between proletariat and bourgeoisie reinforced the regional cleavages between north and south.

Regional Variations in Political Styles In part because of the uneven impact of industrial development, political styles in the north tend to follow the lines of ideological commitment and bureaucratic organization. In the south, the more traditional and agrarian patterns of client-patron relationships prevail. No doubt this personalist style of politics, or *clientelismo,* is characteristic of all Italy, rendering much of Italian political competition between *and* within parties a matter of who knows whom and who has done what for whom. But because of the lower level of industrial development in the south and because of the south's traditional patterns of monarchical and feudal-type social relationships, the system of *clientelismo* does appear to be more characteristic of southern Italian politics. Sidney G. Tarrow writes:

> Strong, ideological groups in the North are reduced in the South to congeries of local notables who mouth the slogans of their party with little sincerity. Politicians change party label at will, and their constituents join them with dispatch.[10]

This is hardly the picture of a stable or responsible party system.

These contrasts between ideological and opportunistic styles of political competition are in many ways cemented into the edifice of Italian politics by the complexity of party competition. And if in viewing the surface of Italian politics one is led to hope that things are not as complex as they seem, disappointment is inevitable: Below the surface, the situation is even more complex. Why?

---

[7] Gabriel A. Almond and Sidney Verba, *The Civic Culture,* Little, Brown and Company, Boston, 1965, table VII.1, p. 181.

[8] Ibid., table VIII.4, p. 199. These data relate to respondents classified as having "high subjective competence."

[9] Ibid., p. 308.

[10] Sidney G. Tarrow, *Peasant Communism in Southern Italy,* Yale University Press, New Haven, Conn., 1967, p. 81. The regional variable as a measure of different political styles may be most relevant to Italian parties on the ideological left. In this context, see also Alan Zuckerman, "Social Structure and Political Competition: The Italian Case," *World Politics,* vol. 24, no. 3, pp. 428–443, April 1972.

Suffrage Reform and Proportional Representation

It has already been noted (in Chapter 8) that political instability is the frequent result of an extension of political participation that outstrips the development of (1) participatory norms among citizens and (2) the capabilities of existing political institutions. Following the political unification of Italy, literacy and property qualifications restricted the suffrage to 2 percent of the population (in 1871). The property qualification was removed in 1882, extending voting rights to a mere 7 percent of the population. But in 1912 universal male suffrage was adopted, and in 1919 an electoral system of proportional representation was instituted: "No informed observer could argue that 1919 was an appropriate time for the introduction of this electoral innovation into Italy."[11]

Chapter 8 also discussed some of the principal effects of the single-member district, simple-majority electoral system—as compared with the effects of proportional representation (PR). The latter, as illustrated by the example of Italy, tends to multiply the number of parties capturing representation in the legislature; parties elect legislators according to the approximate distribution of their support in the electorate. This has several important consequences, plainly evident in Italian politics.

Parliamentary Division and Coalition Government

First, it is very difficult for a single political party to capture a majority of parliamentary seats. Only after the 1948 elections did Italy's dominant political party, the Christian Democrats, enjoy an absolute majority of seats in the Italian Chamber of Deputies. The upper house of the Italian parliament, the Senate, is constitutionally coequal with the lower house, but its smaller representation typically duplicates the partisan division of the Chamber, and it is in the Chamber of Deputies that governments are made and broken. And with the exception of the parliament elected in 1948, the Christian Democrats (who have provided Italy with all its prime ministers since World War II) have had to rely on the cooperation of other parties for the formation and parliamentary support of a government.

As Table 12.3 shows, the government formed after the 1972 elections was composed of Christian Democrats, Social Democrats, and Liberals, with additional parliamentary support coming from the Republicans. Each of the government parties placed its more prominent deputies in the Cabinet, with the number of deputies appointed to ministerial rank determined by the party's parliamentary strength.

The coalition building essential to the formation of a government, however, is usually a long and arduous process. After the 1963 elections, for example, there was a "government crisis" (no government could be formed that was based on a parliamentary majority) that extended for seven months. As the issues confronting the government shift from month to month, or even from day to day, the basis for the coalition may be eliminated, and the government—losing the support of one or more of its coalition partners—falls. A new government coalition must be constructed, usually drawn from the same distribution of partisan strength in the parliament and with due regard for excluding extreme left and extreme right parties from governing status (which further restricts the bargaining options of political leaders). Thus while there were eight national elections in Italy between 1946 and 1972, there have been thirty-six governments since World War II (up to 1974), an average life-span for each government of nine months in office.

In March 1974, for example, Italy's center-left coalition government, with the Christian Democrats' Mariano Rumor as prime minister, collapsed when the government parties failed to agree on the appropriate remedy for Italy's growing economic problems. The Republicans argued for a reduction in government spending and for higher taxes and tighter controls on credit, which were held essential to controlling Italy's skyrocketing inflation. Opposing this strategy were the Socialist ministers (who had been included in the government since the 1972 elections); they argued that the proposals advanced by the Republicans would raise unemployment, slow economic growth, and cut back on welfare benefits to Italy's lower classes. The Socialists also insisted that higher taxes should be accompanied by fundamental tax reform that would shift more of

---

[11] Dante Germino and Stefano Passigli, *The Government and Politics of Contemporary Italy*, Harper & Row, Publishers, Incorporated, New York, 1968, p. 4.

the economic burden onto Italy's wealthier citizens. Divided on these basic issues, the government fell. Within a few days, however, Mariano Rumor had formed a new government, without the Republicans (who nevertheless promised to support the new government in parliament) and including many of the same Socialist, Social Democratic, and Christian Democratic ministers who had served in the previous Cabinet. In this way some executive continuity is maintained (through overlapping personnel), and the making and breaking of governments may be understood in part as a method of finding a tentative majority for a particular policy position.

Reinforcing the Lines of Cleavage This example of coalition building in Italy also shows how PR electoral institutions can reinforce existing cleavages in the society, and not only along the lines of economic class or subcultural cleavage. PR electoral institutions help to ensure that each party will carve out its particular clientele and maintain it over extended periods of time. With only minor fluctuations in voting support and parliamentary representation from one election to another, partisan identities become crystallized and may no longer represent changing interests or divisions within the electorate. There is a widening gap between the fragmentation of the party system and the distribution of interests within the society. But even in terms of Italy's more traditional lines of cleavage, there has been no political party or governing institution that effectively aggregated interests from across the cleavage lines of economic class, region, attitudes toward the legitimacy of the state, or subculture (the last including clerical and anticlerical groups).

Partisan Fragmentation Italian citizens with a strong bias against the role of the Catholic Church and with working-class status are concentrated in the parties of Italy's left. But the Italian left is itself divided between communists and at least one minor and two major socialist parties. In fact, in all Catholic European countries the parties and trade unions of the working class are split into at least two major and, in some cases, three or four minor organizations—thereby adding to the lines of cleavage traced by economic class. The more moderate and unified European working-class movements are found in Protestant countries, where economic class has not been complicated by the clerical issue and where the representatives of the working class have enjoyed frequent access to governing institutions.

As this last point suggests, leftist parties tend to be deradicalized by their experience in government—a process that helps to explain the *non*revolutionary orientation of the Italian Communist party, which has exercised extensive governmental power in the provinces and municipalities of central Italy. But while the Italian Communists dominate the Italian left and are the second largest party in Italy (after the Christian Democrats), they have been excluded from participation in the national government since 1947. They must also contend with other competing parties and trade unions on the Italian left, and it is precisely this fragmentation of the Italian left that works to the advantage of the Christian Democrats.

Presumably united by their proclerical orientation, the Christian Democrats, however, are themselves divided by differences along socioeconomic lines and according to the personalities of individual leaders. It is easy to count at least eight factions *within* the Christian Democratic party, each with its own leader and group of followers. In fact, adding together the relatively institutionalized factions within the four-party coalition that fell in March 1974, one can see that Italian governments may be composed of as many as *fourteen* clearly identifiable factions at a given point in time. Even without a shifting in formal party loyalties, a government may fall simply because one of its faction leaders withdraws support from the dominant coalition within the party.

Responsibility and Opposition This makes the government's, and parliament's, responsibility to the electorate very tenuous indeed, and all the more so because there is no cohesive opposition party that can step into power with an alternative program sanctioned by a majority of voters. In Italy, the more effective political opposition takes place *within* the governing coalition. Major issues thus tend to be ignored because a decisive policy would threaten the government's fragile coalition of supporters, both inside and outside the coalition parties.

It might be argued that this makes contemporary

Italian government an affair of too many doing too little for too few. And the policy immobility of Italian governments places all the more emphasis on the executive continuity that is provided by nonelected civil servants working behind the scenes. This also describes one of the important political transitions traced by France in the years following World War II.

FRANCE: CLEAVAGES IN DECLINE

Compared with Italy, France's cultural variations according to geographic region are relatively slight, and the subordination of all aspects of French social and political affairs to Paris stands in striking contrast to the far less central role in Italian life played by Rome.

In France, there *are* regional differences. A small but militant group of Breton-speaking separatists in Brittany has sought greater cultural and political autonomy from Paris. Voters in the western and eastern regions of France are traditionally more Catholic and conservative. The earlier strength of the anticlerical and republican Radicals was concentrated in the center and south. Socialists and Communists, also anticlerical but more ideologically radical than the Radicals, have found major support in both the agrarian and industrial regions of the south and north.

But the greater regional and cultural homogeneity of France reflects the early development of national unity, a process begun at least in the ninth century with the empire established by Charlemagne and essentially completed by the reign of Louis XI in the fifteenth century. Until the mid-twentieth century, almost all of France outside Paris was provincial. Few, however, could have applied the provincial label to citizens of Venice, Florence, Milan, or Naples.

A History of Revolution

But cultural homogeneity and popular sentiments of national unity are clearly not the only factors essential to the building of stable democracy. Political institutions that reinforce the national identities of citizens must also prove responsive to their interests and demands. The adaptive capabilities of political institutions are tested with particular severity when socioeconomic change mobilizes new sectors of the population who challenge the old ways of distributing wealth, status, and power. And the history of France is an almost classic example of political institutions that failed to adapt to new conditions of social life. Political change in France has, as a consequence, been marked more by revolution than by evolution.

From the late sixteenth to the late eighteenth centuries, the Bourbon dynasty ruled by divine right and resisted any reduction in its absolute authority. Under the reign of Louis XIV, the French nobility was collected together in the expensive grandeur of Versailles. Although the nobles no longer lived on their estates in the provinces, they sought to maintain their feudal prerogatives among the peasantry without providing the services traditional to their responsibilities of noblesse oblige.

A new urban class of citizens was also developing, including the more enterprising artisans of the towns and a new middle class whose wealth was based on commerce and finance. The wealth of the bourgeoisie (or "people of the town") derived from money, not from land (as in the case of the nobility) or from manual labor (as in the case of peasants and the still small class of factory workers). And yet the social status and political influence of the bourgeoisie did not coincide with their growing economic prominence.

Mobilized by the financial crises of a bankrupt monarchy more interested in war than in domestic reform, these several forces converged on the old regime in 1789. Peasants burned the estates of the nobility, while the lawyers, journalists, businessmen, and intellectuals of the middle classes agitated for a new social and political order based on the rights of man—liberty, equality, and fraternity.[12]

Between 1789 and 1792 a constitutional monarchy was established, with Louis XVI struggling to maintain his royal authority against the Constituent Assembly and the representatives of the bourgeoisie. The Assembly's nationalization of the property of the church helped to lay the basis for civil strife between clerical and anticlerical Frenchmen, a divi-

---

[12]See Chap. 5 for a discussion of the precise meaning of these terms in the context of classical liberal ideology. It should also be noted that the universal and absolute quality of these liberal principles made compromise with France's royalist and Catholic factions all the more difficult after the revolution of 1789.

sion in French society that extended well into the twentieth century. The eventual domination of the Assembly, and subsequently the National Convention and the execution of the king in January 1793, also helped to ensure civil war between royalists and revolutionaries. In many respects, these two lines of mutually reinforcing cleavages (clericals and monarchists against anticlericals and republicans) laid the basis for much of France's troubled history: revolutionary violence, unconstitutional seizures of power, and radical departures from the existing regime in:

1792: the First Republic
1797 and *1799:* coups d'état against the executive ministers of the Directory
Again in *1799:* establishment of the Consulate, dominated by Napoleon Bonaparte
1804: the First Empire under Napoleon I
1814–1815: restoration of the Bourbon monarchy under Louis XVIII and, after *1824,* Charles X
1830: the July Revolution and installation of the Orleanist monarchy of Louis-Philippe
1848: the February Revolution, followed by the Second Republic
1852: coup d'état of Louis-Napoleon and his declaration, as Napoleon III, of the Second Empire
1871: inauguration of the Third Republic, following France's defeat in the Franco-Prussian War and the uprising of the Commune of Paris
1940: installation of the French government at Vichy under Marshal Pétain, following Germany's victory over France in 1940
1944: organization of a provisional government under General Charles de Gaulle
1946: adoption of the constitution of the Fourth Republic
1958: adoption of the constitution of the Fifth Republic, following a military revolt in Algeria and the National Assembly's investiture of General de Gaulle as premier; the election of de Gaulle as the first president of the Fifth Republic in December 1958

Depending on the reader's cynicism or conceptual perspective, this brief chronology of France's past may be interpreted as representing a lot of change or only more of the same.

France before de Gaulle
Neither the Third nor the Fourth Republic of France enjoyed an auspicious beginning. The former was officially proclaimed by the constitution adopted in 1875, a republican constitution that issued in part from the disagreement between Orleanist and Bourbon royalists over who should be king. The first draft of the Fourth Republic's constitution was defeated in a national referendum in May 1946. A slightly altered draft was presented to the electorate again in October, and the results prompted General de Gaulle (who had already withdrawn from the political fracas) to remark that the Fourth Republic had been "accepted by nine million voters, rejected by eight million, and ignored by eight million."

De Gaulle and a majority of French citizens had ample reason for concern. The Fourth Republic was in many ways a duplicate of the Third Republic. In both cases, the constitutional form was parliamentary, with the executive (or government) drawn from a shifting coalition of political parties seated in the legislature. Unlike parliamentary government in Great Britain and Scandinavia, where it has meant the control of the legislature by the executive, parliamentary government in pre-Gaullist France (as in Italy) resulted in a weak executive dominated by parliament—and a parliament without either a cohesive majority or opposition. This in turn reflected the multiple lines of cleavage dividing French citizens, and not only in terms of the monarchical-republican and clerical-anticlerical issues.

Class Conflict and Politics Well before the inauguration of the Third Republic, an important new line of cleavage had developed in French society. The old antagonisms between peasant and nobility had been replaced by a simmering conflict between a highly class-conscious proletariat and a very conservative bourgeoisie. The confrontation between these two uncompromising classes occasionally erupted in major political upheaval, as in 1936, when a general strike immediately followed the election victory of Communists, Socialists, and Radicals allied in the "Popular Front." The militancy of French workers had been assured by the intensely ideological style of French political competition, which in turn could be attributed to the socializing effects of a Catholic culture and the continuing controversies initiated by the French Revolution. The workers' hostility to the political system was also reinforced by the French state's long refusal to extend welfare services to the lower classes and to sanction trade union organization.

It was, in fact, only after the success of the Popular Front in 1936 that the French government removed restrictions on trade union organization and encouraged collective bargaining between labor and management. By comparison, trade union organization in Great Britain had been permitted beginning in 1825, and the state's responsibility for providing welfare services was acknowledged in 1601 (the comparable date for France is 1893). It may safely be said that where the working class has been excluded for a prolonged period from the policy-making process of government and industrial management and where the state has shown no concern for the plight of its lower classes, leftist political parties and trade unions will be more militant, and their ideologies more extreme.

In France as in Italy, however, the parties of the left have been divided between reformists and revolutionaries. Even when the latter have ceased to be revolutionary, the division of the left has remained a prominent feature of partisan conflict. In the late nineteenth century, these divisions split the socialists between those who claimed to be the "orthodox" followers of Marx and those "revisionists" who argued that industrial society had changed since Marx had studied the characteristics of capitalism. The revisionists held out hope for reforming capitalism through the institutions of the state, capitalizing on universal suffrage and the nominal majority of the industrial and agricultural working classes. The orthodox socialists continued to mouth the platitudes of revolution, but their progressive deradicalization was hastened by the outbreak of World War I, which found all the socialist parties of Western Europe rallying to the colors of the "bourgeois" state.

After the Bolshevik Revolution in Russia, however, the French (and Italian) left was further divided by the growth of Communist political and trade union influence. But increasingly immersed in the electoral politics and the political games of parliamentary bargaining, the Communists also were bureaucratized and deradicalized, like the orthodox socialists before them, and the biggest question asked only when their revolutionary rhetoric would be altered to match their reformist behavior. Evidence of the Communists' willingness to acknowledge their reformist orientation was already apparent by the mid-1930s. And the prominence of the French Communist party in the Resistance against the German occupation (1940–1944) ensured the Communists of a major political role in the early days of the Fourth Republic.

It was the Communists, Socialists, and more progressive Christian Democrats (in the Popular Republican movement) who wrote the Fourth Republic's constitution. Anxious to guard against a return to France's authoritarian traditions represented by monarchism, Bonapartism, and Marshal Pétain's Vichy France, these three parties sought to institutionalize the dominance of a popular majority committed to social democracy. How could this be accomplished?

Dominance of a Divided Parliament First, the constitution of the Fourth Republic prescribed a bicameral parliament, consisting of the National Assembly and the Council of the Republic. But the National Assembly was clearly the preeminent house of parliament. The Council of the Republic could not permanently block legislation passed by the lower house, nor could it create or oust the government (Cabinet), which was responsible only to the National Assembly. A major instrument for maintaining a semblance of executive authority over the legislature in any parliamentary system is the government's right of dissolution. Even the mere *threat* of dissolving parliament and sending its members back to their constituents for an election contest may be sufficient to ensure the government's continuity in office. But in the Fourth Republic the government's right of dissolution was so hedged about that it ceased to be an effective sanction for disciplining the fractious parliament. And, finally, the framers of the Fourth Republic's constitution—true to their republican and egalitarian ideals—chose proportional representation (PR) as the electoral system for selecting representatives, on the basis of universal suffrage, to the all-powerful National Assembly. The reader can probably guess the result of these institutional arrangements in the context of France's ideological and socioeconomic cleavages.

Between November 1945 and the inauguration of the Fifth Republic in September 1958, there were six national elections and twenty-five governments. The French Communist party, with approximately 26 percent of the popular vote (throughout the history of the Fourth Republic) and thus a major parliamentary party, was excluded from governmental participation after 1947. As in Italy, the exclusion of the Communists restricted coalition building in the parliament and shifted government and public policy toward the center and center right. Major right-wing factions (the Gaullists in 1951 and the Poujadists in 1956) also were unacceptable to the parliamentary majorities that made and broke governments on the average of once every six months. Again as in Italy, the political consequence was policy immobility. And many of the day-to-day decisions that did lay the foundations for France's own spectacular economic recovery after the war (especially after 1953) thus fell into the hands of France's civil servants, particularly the highest administrative echelon represented in the prestigious Council of State. Major economic change in postwar France, then, was well under way before de Gaulle returned to power in 1958.

End of the Fourth Republic It was not economics or even—by itself—governmental instability that dug the grave of the Fourth Republic. The death knell of the Fourth Republic was sounded by the issue of colonialism or, more precisely, decolonization. Italy had been one of the Axis states and a conquered country in World War II, and it thus was spared the devastating problem of determining its relationship to a network of colonial holdings. Had Italy confronted this particular issue, it too might have undergone a right-wing revolution and a drastic restructuring of its political system. It also is a tribute to the cohesion and competence of government in Great Britain that the British were able to dismantle their empire without the threat of intensive factional strife, much less civil war.

But France was continually at war in one or more of its colonies throughout the history of the Fourth Republic. Its governments were committed to maintaining the integrity of the French Empire, especially in Southeast Asia and North Africa. This proved an impossible task in the face of the "winds of change" that swept across the colonial world after World War II. And the apparent inability of a succession of French governments to guarantee Algeria as an integral part of France finally induced civilian extremists and the French Army in Algiers, in May 1958, to challenge the authority of the Fourth Republic.

When the challenge came, there was almost no one on the French left, center, or right who was willing to rush to the defense of the discredited Republic. But waiting in the wings, where he had long pondered the fate of France, was Charles de Gaulle. And after twelve years in political seclusion de Gaulle again assumed the role of France's "man of destiny." His role was not unlike that of the proverbial "legislator" of Greek and Roman antiquity, who was to step into chaos with a clear vision of what is needed to begin anew.

The Gaullist Experiment

The constitution of the Fifth Republic, approved by four voters out of five in September 1958, did not give de Gaulle everything he wanted. But it laid the basis for de Gaulle's efforts to build a strong executive that could counterbalance, even override, the factionalism of parliament.

The President The cornerstone of the Fifth Republic is the presidency. Both the Third and Fourth Republics had presidential institutions whose incumbents (like the president of postwar Italy) were largely ceremonial figures elected for seven years by both houses of parliament. The president's principal task was to appoint a premier-designate who was thus authorized to assemble a government coalition according to the prevailing distribution of partisan strength in the legislature. The president consequently had no real authority for regulating the conflicts characteristic of a multiparty system, and, in fact, his political visibility was directly related to the instability of the government.

According to the constitution of the Fifth Republic, the president is an "arbiter," above the melee of partisan strife, but more closely involved than his predecessors in the policies and activities of government. He appoints the premier and other government ministers. He may dissolve the National Assembly and call for new legislative elections (which de Gaulle did, with stunning success, in 1962 and 1968). He may circumvent the parliament and the parties by going directly to the voters with legislation proposed in the form of a referendum (one of de Gaulle's favorite strategies). He presides over the meetings of the Council of Ministers (the government) and must sign the Council's ordinances and decrees before they become law. The president is commander in chief of the armed forces and, under Article 16 of the constitution, he has dictatorial authority in the event that the state is "threatened in a grave and immediate manner" (a constitutional provision de Gaulle invoked in 1961 following another military coup in Algiers).

While the Fifth Republic's constitution provides the president with far-ranging authority, much of the actual definition of his role depends on the force of his personality, the persuasiveness of his vision, and the nature of the issues confronting the government. In the case of Charles de Gaulle, there was no doubt about the government's subordination to the President throughout his tenure in office, from December 1958 to his abrupt resignation (following a referendum defeat) in April 1969. President de Gaulle was plainly more than an arbiter, and his visions of a stable political system and renewed French grandeur dictated his direct intervention in the policy-making process. The government ministers who served him were clearly his choices, not necessarily those of parliament, and his domination of both government personnel and policy making was probably essential to France's liquidation of its colonial burdens in Algeria, ratified by a national referendum in April 1962.

Ensuring a Strong Presidency The Algerian crisis concluded, de Gaulle's primary concern was to make certain that subsequent presidents would be able to exercise influence over the political process that was less dependent on personality and circumstantial crisis—and more a function of their *institutional* position in the Fifth Republic. How could Gaullist presidential power be institutionalized? Perhaps partly influenced by the characteristics of the American presidency, de Gaulle engineered a referendum victory in October 1962 that instituted the direct and popular election of the president (whose tenure in office remained at seven years). Previously selected by an electoral college of some 81,000 "notables," the president of the Fifth Republic was henceforth the only political figure who could claim the direct popular support of a voting majority of the French nation.[13]

Enjoying a popular mandate from the electorate, the president should be able to enhance his image of remaining aloof from partisan strife. Popular election of the president also enables him to maximize his leverage in exerting influence on the parliamentary factions that threaten the continuity of public policy. And, in at least two important respects, there is a striking resemblance between politics in the United States and politics in the Fifth Republic: The direction and coherence that mark the policy-making process come largely from the presidency, and the principal institution for aggregating interests from across the various cleavage lines in both societies is based on a popularly elected chief executive.

Executive Supremacy But the institutionalization of a strong and popularly elected president was not the only weapon in the Gaullist arsenal for attacking France's perennial instability. The following constitutional and parliamentary reforms instituted by the Fifth Republic are less important than the generalization they support: that "Gaullism" is, in part, an attempt to restructure the political process by manipulating the institutional details of executive-legislative relationships.

1 As already noted, the executive has acquired a potentially effective sanction over parliamentary obstructionism through its authority to dissolve parliament. In both 1962 and 1968, when de Gaulle dissolved the National Assembly and called for new elections, the Gaullists were returned with an enlarged parliamentary majority.

2 The executive's right of dissolution, however, applies only to the National Assembly, not to the Senate—which replaced the Council of the Repub-

[13]A popular majority is assured by the provision of a second-ballot runoff between the two top candidates in the event that no presidential candidate receives an absolute majority on the first ballot. Both de Gaulle in 1965 and Pompidou in 1969 were forced into a second-ballot runoff, which they easily won. Valery Giscard d'Estaing's presidential victory in 1974, however, was by a very narrow margin: 50.8 percent to 49.2 percent for his Socialist opponent, François Mitterrand. Twelve candidates contested the 1974 presidential elections on the first ballot, thereby demonstrating the wisdom of the provision for a second-ballot runoff.

lic in 1958. The Gaullist constitution augmented the legislative role of the upper house of parliament and based its smaller membership on an electoral college that ensured a more conservative parliamentary body. The original intent was to provide another check on the frequently unruly behavior of the popularly elected Assembly and to offset the strength of its leftist parties (mainly the Communists). Thus the Senate can block any constitutional revision (unless it is in the form of a presidential referendum, as in 1962), but while it can check the Assembly, it cannot overthrow the government. And should the Senate prove too obstructionist, the government may overrule it in the National Assembly by declaring a proposed bill "urgent."

3 The role of the executive in parliamentary proceedings is also substantially strengthened. The president's messages to parliament cannot be debated. The government has priority in setting the legislative agenda. There are severe limits on the right of legislators to propose amendments to government bills. The government's budgetary and fiscal proposals must be voted on virtually intact, and the parliament can neither propose bills nor offer amendments that would lower taxes or increase government expenditures. Following the government's response to parliamentary questions, members of parliament have no right to propose a resolution or to vote on the government's declared position.

4 In the Fourth Republic, a vote of censure or no confidence against the government passed if the government failed to receive the support of a parliamentary majority. This contributed to the short tenure of governments in the Fourth Republic because a coalition of opponents was always easier to assemble than a coalition of supporters; and, in effect, abstentions counted against the government (and there usually were many abstentions). In the Fifth Republic, however, the government cannot be removed from office unless a motion of censure (in the National Assembly) receives the support of an absolute majority of the Assembly's total membership. Thus abstentions are votes in favor of the government, and the problem of forming a coalition majority falls on the government's opponents instead of on the government. *And* the National Assembly can initiate only one censure motion during each legislative session.

5 The president's designation of Cabinet ministers is not restricted to members of parliament. (In fact, when President de Gaulle selected Georges Pompidou as his premier in 1962, he chose a banker and a technocrat who was not a member of parliament.) If members of parliament are appointed to the Cabinet, however, they must resign their parliamentary seats. This enhances the government's cohesion and renders individual Cabinet ministers less willing to oppose specific government policies. If dismissed from the government, they do not have a parliamentary seat (and the stipend paid by the government to each deputy) to return to, as they did in the Fourth Republic. Thus they are effectively excluded from the political process, at least until the next parliamentary election.

6 In addition to the government's dominant role in the legislative process, the constitution of the Fifth Republic introduced an entirely new category of law identified as "ordinances." Under a parliamentary grant of authority, the government may promulgate law by decree, and in fact this particular authority has been used extensively by Gaullist governments to implement far-reaching reforms in the socioeconomic relationships of French citizens. It amounts to law making without the direct participation of parliament.

It is especially through its authority to issue ordinances that the Fifth Republic has institutionalized the policy-making role of the French civil service. Long an important influence behind the scenes, the highest echelon of the civil service (the Council of State) is, for the first time in France's constitutional history, cited explicitly in the constitution of the Fifth Republic and granted important consultative authority. That *consultation* can also mean *effective power* is demonstrated by one of the prominent characteristics of the Fifth Republic, both during and after de Gaulle's tenure as president: the elevation of civil servants and technocrats to Cabinet status and their influential participation in the political process behind the facade of presidential charisma and the president's popular majority in the national electorate.

Restructuring the Party System

Karl Marx would have described the Gaullist experiment as an attempt to alter the "infrastructure" by reforming the "superstructure." No doubt that, among history's great political thinkers, Machiavelli also would have found much of interest in Gaullism, and not only in terms of the less noble political tactics that describe many of de Gaulle's political maneuvers. Both Machiavelli and de Gaulle sought to build stable republican institutions in the context of a cleavage-ridden society and, in the process, to reduce the intensity of cleavage-based conflict. And with the tentative exception of the student-worker general strike of May and June 1968, which split the French left to the advantage of the Gaullists, it seems to be the case that President de Gaulle and those who followed him have successfully concluded an important part of the Gaullist experiment. Elected in June 1969, President Georges Pompidou (de Gaulle's premier between 1962 and 1968) continued the Gaullist tradition of strong executive domination of the policy-making process, as has Pompidou's successor, Valery Giscard d'Estaing, elected in May 1974 after Pompidou's sudden death. Giscard, in fact, had been the minister of finance under both de Gaulle and Pompidou and was therefore thoroughly acquainted with the techniques of Gaullist executive control.

In many respects, however, the accomplishments of the Gaullists and their successors have depended less on the reform of executive-legislative relationships than on the dominance and cohesion of the presidential coalition *in parliament.* If and when a parliamentary majority proves unwilling to ratify the president's choice for premier or to legislate the president's program, all the institutional advantages of the chief executive may rapidly dissipate in the atmosphere of revivified party competition. In founding the Fifth Republic, however, the Gaullists were concerned not only to strengthen the executive branch of government but also to restructure the patterns of partisan conflict within the electorate—and thus within parliament. The reader has probably already guessed that efforts in this direction were concentrated on reforming the electoral system.

The Effects of PR As in contemporary Italy, the multiparty tendencies of the Fourth Republic were reinforced by an electoral system of proportional representation (PR). Each of the many election districts was allotted a number of seats (up to seven) according to the district's population, and these seats were distributed to the various parties according to their electoral support in the district. The results demonstrated the almost universal effects of PR electoral institutions: a proliferation of parties represented in the legislature; only slight fluctuations in electoral and parliamentary strength from one election to the next; centralized party structures with cohesive parliamentary delegations; and each party intensely ideological and highly competitive with the other parties, especially to its immediate left and right. How was it possible to reduce the number of parties and to substitute the ethic of compromise for the passions of conflict?

The Double-Ballot Electoral System De Gaulle and his advisers chose the single-member district, *double-ballot* electoral system that had prevailed during the Third Republic. In the Fifth Republic, then, only one candidate can win in each election district. To be elected on the first ballot, a candidate must receive an absolute majority of votes cast (which seldom happens). On the second ballot (held one week after the first), only those candidates can stand for election who received at least 5 percent of the vote on the first ballot, and election is by simple plurality. The first ballot encourages multiple candidacies (as in American presidential primaries) and thereby helps to perpetuate the multiparty characteristics of the political system. But the single-member district and the second ballot place a premium on compromise and bargaining between the parties. Those who do not bargain successfully do not survive, or their existence is seriously threatened. And, in contrast to the electoral politics of the Third Republic, where the same electoral system was operative, in the Fifth Republic there was a new and vital force—the Gaullists—who proved to be an attractive second-ballot ally for the center and center-right parties. (See Table 12.4.)

It is obvious from Table 12.4 that the results of the French parliamentary elections of 1958, the first of the Fifth Republic, drastically distorted the distribution of partisan opinion in the electorate. Seldom has a democratic election had such undemocratic consequences. According to PR, for example, the Gaullists should have received 82 seats in the National Assembly, but their pivotal role in the alliances formed before the second ballot raised their Assembly representation to 189 seats. And instead of the 88 seats the Communists would have

Table 12.4 Elections to the French National Assembly of the Fifth Republic, November 23 and 30, 1958

	Percentage of votes, first ballot	Deputies elected, second ballot	(PR)*
Communists	18.9	10	(88)
Socialists	15.5	45	(72)
Radicals	11.5	40	(41)
Christian Democrats	11.7	57	(42)
Gaullists	17.5	189	(82)
Indeps.-moderates	20.1	132	(93)

*Hypothetical representation according to the PR electoral system of the Fourth Republic.

received under PR, they were reduced to an insignificant faction of only 10 deputies.

Reforming the French Left Because they had only ten deputies, the Communists were unable to form a "parliamentary group" in the National Assembly; a parliamentary group was conveniently defined as requiring at least thirty deputies. The French Communist party consequently lost its representation on the Assembly's committees, its occasional influence in the legislative process on behalf of its working-class supporters, and its access through parliamentary proceedings to the public media. It also suffered a catastrophic reduction in the income the party had traditionally received from the government—in the form of stipends paid to each parliamentary deputy. It was soon thereafter that the Communists terminated their press operations in a number of important working-class municipalities. Why had the French Communists fallen upon such hard times? The answer is that in the 1958 elections, they had been unable and unwilling to form second-ballot alliances. In many election districts, Communist and Socialist candidates confronted each other on the second ballot—to the immense advantage of the Gaullists and their allies.

But the Gaullist electoral challenge also threatened the position of the French Socialists. Like that of the Communists, their party membership had been declining over the past decade, and their propaganda and press operations had been severely handicapped by a substantial drop in party income. By the time of the French municipal elections of March 1959, the Communists and Socialists already were beginning to search for some common ground. The advantages of their cooperation were especially apparent in the parliamentary elections of November 1962; the combined total of their popular vote, compared with that in 1958, increased from 34.4 to 36.8 percent (21.8 percent for the Communists and 15 percent for the Socialists), but their collaboration on the second ballot raised their representation in the National Assembly from a total of 55 to 106 seats (41 for the Communists and 65 for the Socialists). With only a modest increase in their electoral support, the two parties almost doubled their parliamentary representation.

Continued cooperation between French Communists and Socialists, however, and in both electoral and trade union politics, was especially contingent on the Communist party's willingness to repudiate its dogmas and opportunism of the past (it had long ceased to represent a revolutionary threat). In effect, the Communists were forced to demonstrate their allegiance, in words and action, to the bargaining game of reformist politics. The party's growing commitment to cooperation and compromise was dramatized in the presidential elections of both 1965 and 1974; the Communists refused to field their own candidate and instead supported the Socialist candidate, François Mitterrand, who received a very respectable percentage of the second-ballot vote (45 percent in 1965 and 49 percent in 1974).

While the cooperation of Communists and Socialists has not been without serious difficulties (notably in 1968 and 1969), their collective efforts have constituted a major change in the political patterns of postwar French politics. It is one of the more remarkable ironies of Gaullism that in attempting to isolate the French Communist party, the Gaullists and their institutions instead accelerated the revisionist trends of French communism and hastened the party's integration into the political game.

France in the 1970s

In the absence of a major political or economic crisis, then, there is reason to hope for a continued reduction in the ideological intensity and partisan fragmentation of the French party system. This prediction could not have been made with any confidence in the mid-1960s, when the collaboration of Communists and Socialists remained tentative and when the future of the Fifth Republic's institutions *without de Gaulle* was in doubt. Before President de Gaulle's final exit from the stage of France's political dramas (in 1969), there also was reason to question the long-term viability of the Gaullists and their republican allies: Without the spell of de Gaulle's charismatic presence, could they hold themselves together and thereby represent a coherent alternative to a reformed and reformist French left?

At least until President Pompidou's death in 1974, these important questions could be answered in the affirmative. Pompidou succeeded in building a strong grass-roots organization that survived the departure of de Gaulle, and Pompidou himself proved an able executor of the powers bequeathed by the Gaullist presidency. These powers, along with Gaullist parliamentary strength, enabled Pompidou to continue the policies of economic modernization, together with modest social reform, and to maintain France's independent posture in foreign affairs (to the continuing dismay of the United States). The consolidation of France's political factions and the consequent "rationalization" of the party system also continued. For example, on the first ballot of the 1962 parliamentary elections, the Communists, Socialists, and Gaullists received a total of 69 percent of the popular vote; in 1967 their combined total was 79 percent; and in 1973 it was 82 percent. This trend paralleled the decline of the more traditional parties of the Third and Fourth Republics *and also* signified the virtual disappearance of earlier issues that had helped to fragment the party system: the role of the Catholic Church, the appropriate structure of the political system, and the fate of France's colonial empire.

As events proved, however, the critical test of the Gaullist experiment came in 1974. When the results were in, it was clear that the institutions of the Fifth Republic had passed the test, while the Gaullists themselves had failed. Pompidou's sudden death left no one in charge of the Gaullist party organization, and the absence of a designated successor with time to nourish his own sources of support contributed to the Gaullists' disarray in the presidential contest. Competing personalities only grudgingly withdrew in time for a single Gaullist candidate to emerge for the first ballot. However, the Gaullist Jacques Chaban-Delmas received only 15 percent of the presidential vote, and he was therefore excluded from the second round of balloting in favor of the Independent-Republican Valery Giscard d'Estaing (33 percent on the first ballot) and the Socialist-Communist candidate François Mitterrand (43 percent). The election of Giscard on the second ballot, his subsequent appointment of a maverick Gaullist as premier (Jacques Chirac had supported Giscard on the *first* presidential ballot), and the eventual consolidation of Gaullist strength behind Giscard as both candidate and president suggested that the cohesion of the French left and its electoral threat are major factors in holding together a presidential coalition of the French center and center right.

The succession to the presidency of the Fifth Republic of a non-Gaullist (although Giscard is closely associated with Gaullism) also signals the institutionalization of the Gaullist constitution and its widespread acceptance. Even the eventual election of a leftist president (an increasing possibility with the lowering of the voting age) would very probably leave the powers of the presidency intact, and these powers will be all the more essential if the presidential coalition in parliament fails to muster a continuing majority. Politics in France would thus closely resemble the constant bargaining process long characteristic of executive-legislative relationships in the United States. This is also to say that France has moved beyond the period of Gaullism without de Gaulle, and—appropriate to the French liking for irony—it may be well into the period of Gaullism without the Gaullists.

But with continued economic growth, the recent trends toward a more cohesive and responsible party system, and the *embourgeoisement* (or "becoming middle class") of large sectors of the French population, the Gaullist experiment may have succeeded in laying the basis for stable democracy. French politics will then dignify rather than contradict the grandeur of France.

WEST GERMANY: TOWARD STABLE DEMOCRACY

The length and detail of the above discussion of politics in France are justified by the simple fact that the French have tried to reform themselves. The effects of self-conscious choice are important in any context—as is argued by French philosophers in the literature on existentialism. And men who strive to alter their own patterns of behavior in pursuit of noble goals are worthy of more than passing attention.

This also applies to the politics of Germany, but to a lesser extent because at critical junctures in German history the institutions of government and politics have been the result of military intervention from without instead of political reform from within. This contrasting pattern of political change, however, also deserves close attention from the student of comparative politics.

From Unity to Tragedy

Like Italy, Germany was politically unified (in 1871) long after the onset of urbanization and the growth of a cultural sentiment of national unity. These patterns of development appear to coincide with an ideology of intense nationalism that is frequently expressed through international aggression. Emphasis on building the state also is inconsistent with a concern for individual liberty. And wherever patriotism becomes the primary criterion of citizenship, the individual is invariably submerged in a collective mass subordinated to an authoritarian elite.[14]

The Weimar Republic Germany's defeat in World War I thus laid the basis for radical political change that reflected the demands of the victorious Allies and only a minority of German political elites and citizens. Germany's *first* democratic constitution, adopted in Weimar in 1919, introduced universal suffrage (including women in the electorate for the first time) and an electoral system of proportional representation. Suddenly, all German citizens were invited to participate in the political process—and it has already been pointed out that stable democracy is in part the result of a *gradual* expansion of political participation. PR electoral institutions reinforced the multiparty tendencies of Weimar Germany, and the specter of squabbling partisan factions reduced further the legitimacy of a government that had been compelled to accept the settlement dictated by the Allies at Versailles.[15]

Especially after the devastating impact of the Depression (beginning in 1929), the unstable coalition governments of the young republic proved incapable of coping with crisis or of inculcating in German voters a respect for Weimar's institutions. The electorate was increasingly polarized between extreme left and extreme right parties, and PR enabled the Nazis to rapidly become the dominant party in the Reichstag. Although founded in 1919, the Nazis had only 12 seats in the Reichstag in 1928, but with the Depression their representation grew to 107 seats in 1930 and 230 seats after the elections of July 1932. It thus became impossible to build a stable government coalition from among the dwindling forces of the Reichstag's democratic parties. The aging president, General von Hindenburg, convinced that he was acting in the interests of domestic order and the constitution, appointed Adolf Hitler as chancellor in January 1933. Aided by the terroristic tactics of the Nazis' paramilitary units, Hitler proceeded to engineer an election victory and a parliamentary majority that granted him dictatorial power. The death of the Weimar Republic was as abrupt as its birth, but less painful.

Opposition to Democracy The weakness of Weimar institutions may be attributed largely to the

---

[14]See the discussion of fascism in Chap. 7.

[15]See Chap. 7, p. 110, for the effects of the Versailles Treaty on the territorial integrity of Germany.

prevailing authoritarian political culture of Germany in the early twentieth century and to the antidemocratic values of Germany's dominant social classes. The critical institutions of the civilian bureaucracy and military establishment, the aristocracy and large landowners, and the major industrialists and—with the Depression—important sectors of the middle and working classes (both industrial and peasant) were all fundamentally hostile to democracy. In Sweden, at the turn of the century, there also was resistance from the upper social classes to suffrage reform and political democratization. But unlike Germany, Sweden escaped the destruction of World War I, and the effects of the Depression on the Swedish economy were less severe. Thus Sweden was able to evolve toward stable democracy free of the imposition of external authority and without a radical break from the past.

In the case of Germany, however, it took another and even more destructive war to break the back of the old order that opposed social change and the introduction of the lower classes into the political process. It may be argued that, ironically, the Nazi revolution and Germany's subsequent defeat in World War II laid the basis for a society that was both more stable and more democratic.

Redefining the German State

By 1949, if not sooner, it was obvious to the Western Allies that the Soviet Union was not about to relinquish its hold over the occupied territory of East Germany. The Soviet Union's hostility to German reunification should not have puzzled Western diplomats then, nor should it puzzle them now. As a result of German aggression in World Wars I and II, at least *20 million* Russian soldiers and civilians were killed. The comparable figure for the United States is 520,000, and in *both* the Pacific and European theaters for World War II; for Great Britain, 1.2 million; and for France, 2 million. A perpetually divided Germany and an Eastern European buffer zone of states friendly to the Soviet Union (kept in line by force, if necessary) were thus the almost inevitable outcomes of World War II. Western politicians who preferred to interpret the Soviet Union's European policies in terms of "communist subversion" only reinforced the West Germans' long-standing refusal to come to terms with reality and the consequences of their own historical acts.[16]

The Bonn Basic Law Faced with a divided Germany, the United States, Great Britain, and France agreed in 1949 to turn their occupied zones in West Germany over to an indigenous and democratic political elite. The new capital was located in Bonn, on the river Rhine, and the provisions of the Bonn "Basic Law" were put into effect. To have defined the Basic Law as a constitution (which is what it was) would have been equivalent, in the eyes of West Germany's political leaders, to an admission of the permanent division of Germany. Not only was this ideologically unacceptable, but it would also have constituted an immense political liability at the polls. An important measure of how far the West Germans have traveled since 1949, and the principal accomplishment of the Social Democratic government of Chancellor Willy Brandt (between 1969 and 1974), was West Germany's formal recognition of "two states of the German nation" and the Brandt government's success in the early 1970s in normalizing the Federal Republic's relations with East Germany, Eastern Europe, *and* the Soviet Union. The constitution of the Federal Republic of Germany, however, continues to be called the "Basic Law," and its provisions have inevitably played a major role in structuring the political process of the Federal Republic.

The Allies, of course, were anxious to build institutions that would help to prevent a repetition of the dramas that ended the Weimar Republic. They thus established a Constitutional Court with powers of judicial review that could protect civil liberties and overturn any authoritarian legislation issuing from parliament or the executive branch of government. Also following American insistence, the Basic Law instituted a federal system of gov-

---

[16]West Germany is officially known as the Federal Republic of Germany. East Germany is officially known as the German Democratic Republic. It has less than one-half the area and one-third the population of West Germany and far fewer natural resources. East Germany, however, ranks among the world's top ten countries in industrial production. The unification of the two Germanies would thus create an economic and political colossus that the Russians, the East Europeans, and West Germany's Common Market partners are not anxious to confront. Outside West Germany, it is safe to say that almost no one truly supports German reunification.

ernment (as is indicated by the formal name of West Germany); the Federal Republic of Germany is divided into ten states (or *Länder*) with governments and powers distinguished from those of the federal government in Bonn. The Allies thus sought to check Germany's traditions of rigid political and administrative centralization. The upper house of the federal parliament, the Bundesrat, is the exclusive representative of West Germany's state governments, and the Bundesrat has an absolute veto on legislation affecting their organization and authority. (One of Hitler's first acts was to eliminate the autonomy enjoyed by provincial and local government under the Weimar constitution.) And, seeking to prevent a recurrence of presidential authority as exercised by General von Hindenburg, the Allies established a presidency with responsibilities similar to those of the presidents of Italy and the Fourth Republic. The Federal Republic's president has limited powers and is elected by the Bundestag (the lower house of the federal parliament) and an equal number of electors appointed by the state legislatures. Lacking a popular mandate and extensive constitutional authority, the president of the Federal Republic is consequently in no position to play the role of either a von Hindenburg or a de Gaulle.

The Chancellor The political gravity of West German politics is centered in the office of the chancellor (or prime minister). The status and duties of his Cabinet ministers resemble those of the department heads who make up the Cabinet of an American president; they are responsible to the chancellor and not collectively to the parliament (as in Italy and Great Britain). The chancellor is leader of his party in parliament, however, and typically enjoys the support of a majority in the Bundestag. And the Bundestag, with the exception noted above, can usually override the Bundesrat in the legislative process.

Profiting in 1949 from the already apparent record of Cabinet instability in Italy and the Fourth Republic, the Basic Law introduced an ingenious device for limiting turnover in the chancellorship. The Bundestag can overthrow a government only by the vote of an absolute majority of its members (as in the Fifth Republic), but it must at the same time elect a new chancellor—also by an absolute majority. While this constitutional provision (known as the "constructive vote of nonconfidence") has never been implemented, its very existence has helped to strengthen executive government in West Germany, and within the context of the Basic Law's democratic guarantees. Political stability in postwar West Germany, however, and the development of a democratic political process that supports democratic institutions, have depended on more than just the constitutional specifications of the Bonn Basic Law.

Up from the Ashes

It is difficult, perhaps impossible, for new political institutions to acquire legitimacy in the minds of citizens when:

1 There is little or no economic growth.
2 There is no major political party to lend stability to government and continuity to public policy.
3 There is no dominant political leader, enjoying some measure of charismatic authority, who can collect the loyalties of disparate groups and channel them toward governing institutions.

Fortunately for West Germans *and* for all Western Europe, none of these conditions applied to the Federal Republic after 1949.

Rebuilding the Economy Economic recovery was initially aided by West Germany's ample resources, including a large work force that was both skilled and disciplined, and by Allied-imposed restrictions on West Germany's military expenditures. The money that other European states spent on armies and armaments was invested (at least until the mid-1950s) in new and modern industrial facilities. West Germany's productivity soon surpassed that of Great Britain, where the far lower level of destruction caused by World War II meant that industrial modernization was much more difficult (in fact, it still continues at a halting pace). The United States also provided substantial economic aid to West Germany, seeing in a revived West German economy a bulwark against European communism.

Thus throughout the 1950s and early 1960s, economic recovery in the Federal Republic was nothing short of spectacular. Contrary to the myth that West Germany's economic rebirth was the result of free enterprise and capitalism, the government of the Federal Republic has continuously played an important role in postwar economic growth. But government planning in West Germany (because of the obvious socialist implications, the West Germans, like the Americans, are reluctant to call it "planning") and economic controls have inevitably increased as inflation has become a greater problem and as the early potential for basic industrial recovery has been realized.

The Adenauer Era Any explanation of the economic progress and political stability of West Germany must also lean heavily on the role of the Christian Democratic party and its unchallenged leader, Konrad Adenauer. Because of the prominent parliamentary position enjoyed by the Christian Democratic Union (CDU) and its Bavarian allies (the Christian Social Union, or CSU), Adenauer held a virtually impregnable position as party leader and chancellor between 1949 and 1961—a period equal in time to the entirety of Hitler's Third Reich. The CDU-CSU alliance appealed primarily to the religious identification of West German voters, but it also developed into a broad-based party that aggregated interests from across West Germany's lines of socioeconomic *and* religious cleavages. No doubt the CDU-CSU received its strongest support from Catholics and business interests. But its electoral appeal, and the forceful personality of Adenauer, cut deeply into the ranks of Protestants, workers, and all the socioeconomic categories of the West German electorate.[17]

The long domination of Adenauer and the Christian Democrats and the concentration of decision making in the hands of government and interest-group elites in fact troubled many observers who were especially concerned over the absence of an effective political opposition. This prerequisite for responsible democratic government depended on the growth of the West German Social Democratic party (the SPD). But in the 1950s the SPD appeared to be led by a colorless and doctrinaire faction tied to the anachronisms of Marxian socialism. Both the image and the direction of the SPD began to change after 1959, when the party's national congress (convened at Bad Godesberg) abandoned its Marxist heritage and adopted a moderate program more suited to the problems of a modern industrial society. And, in 1960, Mayor Willy Brandt of West Berlin was designated the SPD's candidate for the chancellorship and thus the party's effective leader.

Rise of the Social Democrats In the four national elections between 1961 and 1972, the SPD's popular vote and representation in the Bundestag steadily increased. The weakening position of the CDU-CSU alliance forced it into a government coalition, first with the small Free Democratic party (the FDP), and then in 1966 with the Social Democrats (the so-called grand coalition). Following the elections of 1969, the SPD was able to form a coalition government with the FDP, which, since its inception in 1948, had moved from the ideological right to the center left.

Given a chance to demonstrate to the voters its governing competence, and in the context of the Brandt government's success in foreign affairs, the SPD became the largest party in the Bundestag after the 1972 elections. Subsequent state elections, however, showed that the SPD was as vulnerable to the political fallout of inflation as any other ruling party—socialist or conservative. The essential realization of Brandt's objectives related to *Ostpolitik* (normalizing Bonn's relations with Communist Europe) also predisposed the Chancellor to an early retirement from the rigors of office. But the timing of Brandt's resignation was determined by the revelations of a spy scandal that compromised the Chancellor's judgment if not his integrity. Brandt was replaced in May 1974 by a more conservative SPD leader, Helmut Schmidt, who had distinguished himself as minister of finance. Schmidt also stood higher than Brandt in the public-opinion polls, and his elevation to the chancellorship therefore improved the SPD's prospects for perpetuating its ruling status.

The prospect of a prolonged opposition role has added to the disarray of the Christian Democrats, and there is the possibility that a split between the

---

[17] A national opinion sample in 1964 showed the CDU-CSU alliance receiving the support of 28 percent of West German Protestants (39 percent for the Social Democratic party, or SPD), 45 percent of the votes from Roman Catholics (26 percent for the SPD), 22 percent of the votes from industrial and agricultural workers (50 percent for the SPD), and 48 percent of the votes from the lowest income category (46 percent for the SPD). See Lewis J. Edinger, *Politics in Germany,* Little, Brown and Company, Boston, 1968, table VIII.3, pp. 246–247.

CDU and its Bavarian wing (the CSU, which is more provincial, conservative, Catholic, and nationalistic than the CDU) would reinforce the SPD's dominance in a legislature with two major and two minor parties: the SPD and the CDU, on the one hand, and the FDP and the CSU, on the other. The Free Democrats might then continue to play the role of a small but pivotal party in the shifting of governmental power between the SPD and the CDU. But there is nothing like the possibility of power for keeping a political alliance intact (the CDU and the CSU).

Reducing the Number of Parties The instability associated with a multiparty parliament is, however, a characteristic of neither West Germany's past nor its probable future. Why? Again, the reader should here anticipate a reference to the effects of electoral systems.

In parliamentary elections, West German citizens are organized into 248 constituencies, and each citizen casts two votes. The first vote is for a candidate, and the candidate with the most votes in each constituency is elected to the Bundestag. The citizen's second vote is for a party; the remaining 248 Bundestag seats (for a total of 496) are distributed proportionally to the parties according to the national distribution of this second vote—with two important exceptions: Parties that do not receive at least 5 percent (nationally) of the second vote and parties that fail to capture at least three seats by direct election do not win any seats in the Bundestag.

The "5 percent" provision of the Basic Law is credited with reducing the number of West Germany's political parties, thereby controlling for the extensive partisan fragmentation that helped to undermine the Weimar Republic. In the first Bundestag elected in 1949, there were ten political parties; after the elections of 1953, there were six; there were four after 1957; and there have been only three political parties in the Bundestag since 1961.

As the number of West Germany's parliamentary parties has declined, the more extremist parties (especially on the right) have disappeared, and the remaining parties have moderated the intensity of their ideological differences. This is due in part to the necessity of appealing to similar socioeconomic and cultural groups in the electorate in order to build a political majority in parliament. Thus the religious issue (Protestants *versus* Catholics) is no longer a major determinant of partisan voting. The declining importance of this particular cleavage in West German society is reflected in part by the SPD's increasing strength among Catholic workers and in part by the FDP's support from those urban and professional groups that formerly supported the CDU.

Support for Democracy Parallel with these trends is the emergence of a political culture that supports democratic institutions. This is of fundamental importance in assessing the prospects for democracy in West German politics. In 1953, for example, 57 percent of the West German population expressed support for democracy, while 19 percent (or almost one out of every five citizens) supported monarchy or authoritarian government. In 1960, 74 percent supported democracy, while only 7 percent (less than one in ten) supported monarchy or authoritarian government.[18]

In 1959, Almond and Verba found that West German citizens, whatever their ideological sympathies, had a "passive subject orientation" and, consequently, were relatively withdrawn from the "input" dimensions of the political process.[19] This also appears to have changed, however, and over the years voter participation in national elections has increased significantly (from 78.5 percent in 1949 to 91.2 percent in 1972), and *without* an elevation in the level of ideological intensity. The 1972 elections, in fact, were "widely hailed as evidence that the West Germans had finally come

---

[18]Edinger, op. cit., table IV.3 p. 102. The data collected by Edinger also show important changes in the characteristics of German political elites, in this case with regard to Cabinet ministers serving under the Empire (in 1890), the Weimar Republic, and the Federal Republic (in 1960). Over this extended period there was a substantial decline in the percentage of Cabinet ministers who were large landowners (an important source of antidemocratic sentiment) and major increases in the percentage of Cabinet ministers whose backgrounds were in business and the teaching profession and who were drawn from the working and artisan classes (table IV.4, p. 183). These trends also appear to reinforce the tendencies in West Germany toward democratic government.

[19]Almond and Verba, op. cit., pp. 362–363.

of age politically. . . . West German politics have become markedly and increasingly moderate, pragmatic, and competitive."[20]

These findings suggest that the chances for stable democracy and responsible party politics are *at least* as good in West Germany as they are in any other country of the industrialized world. One measure of informed judgment, however, is sober skepticism when trying to predict the future. The only thing certain about the future is that it is coming, perhaps faster than one would like.

A NOTE ON POLITICS IN THE POST-INDUSTRIAL SOCIETY

Since World War II, Western Europe has undergone what amounts to a second major industrial revolution, with important social and political consequences for both the present and the future. The old aristocracies that opposed democracy have been swept away. The numbers of conservative and reactionary peasants, in the grip of the Catholic Church, have also been substantially reduced. The size of the industrial working class appears to have reached its maximum limit. The most rapidly expanding sector of employment is in the service industries (the tertiary sector of the economy), and white-collar employees represent an ever-larger percentage of the working population. Small business has given way to big business, and independent companies are absorbed by giant corporations increasingly international in their operations and organization.

At the same time, urbanization, the extension of educational opportunities, high rates of literacy, and the diffusion of information through the electronic media have helped to homogenize opinions and values. Old cleavage lines, at least in terms of religion and urban-rural life-styles, have weakened and in some cases disappeared. To return to the categories suggested at the outset of this chapter, we may say that *ascriptive* identities are being replaced by *achievement* identities. Men and women are judged less in terms of the circumstances inherited at their birth and more in terms of the role they play in society—not who they are, but what they do. The great mass of society in the postindustrial world identifies with essentially middle-class values, and an ever-larger majority of citizens (but not everyone) enjoys the symbols and comforts of middle-class existence: adequate housing, schools, secure employment (or unemployment insurance), provisions against infirmity and old age, private or public means of transportation, annual vacations, and that most pervasive sign of *embourgeoisement*—a television set.

That government has played a fundamental role in this process is obvious. But government has also undergone major change. Like all aspects of social life, it has become increasingly bureaucratized. As complex economies require varying degrees of governmental intervention to smooth out the bumps of the economic cycle, a technocratic elite has gradually assumed the role played earlier by partisan elites and legislative institutions. This particular trend, along with others already cited, has helped to reduce the intensity of ideological conflict between groups appealing to specific clienteles.

It no longer is possible, however, to distinguish political parties or partisan elites strictly according to the sociology of their supporters. As the society's values have become more homogeneous, the parties have reached across older lines of class cleavage and have become more heterogeneous in their support. And as the intensity of ideological conflict has declined, it has become increasingly difficult to distinguish the major parties in terms of their promises and performance. Incumbent governments and governmental parties may fall from power less because of what they stand for than because of the economic difficulties that happen to coincide with their tenure in office.

In most of Western Europe after the mid-1960s and in West Germany in the early 1970s, the most troubling economic problem was inflation. It perhaps was no coincidence that in early 1974, two ministers of finance, Giscard d'Estaing in France and Helmut Schmidt in West Germany, became the chief executives of their respective governments; this suggested the intent of both citizens and elites to give government into the hands of those most qualified to deal with what President Ford in the

---

[20]William E. Laux, "West German Political Parties and the 1972 Bundestag Election," *The Western Political Quarterly*, vol. 26, no. 3, pp. 507, 527, September 1973.

United States called "public enemy number one." The same enemy plagued other postindustrial societies, including Japan, but it also threatened the economic ambitions of the underdeveloped countries, which were seeking to minimize the uncertainty of material life for hundreds of millions of people throughout the world. Indeed, the only governments that were immune to the problems of inflation were those with sufficient petroleum resources to make them the world's suppliers of basic energy.

After the worldwide depression of the 1930s it seemed that government had found a way of preventing massive depression and unemployment. Limited inflation, along with industrial development, was also acceptable—even essential to continued economic growth. But the ever-heightening levels of inflation that followed the second industrial revolution have seemed beyond the control of governing elites, regardless of their ideology and no matter how technocratic their composition. Labor-oriented governments, as in Great Britain and West Germany, have been reluctant to impose controls on wages, and their attempts to do so have resulted in labor strikes, a weakening of their trade union support, or both. Unionization of white-collar employees and professionals promises greater leverage for these groups in the economic policy making of government—and thus greater difficulties for governing elites as they attempt to mediate between competing demands. Increased wages for workers and the middle classes have been the only way these groups could hope to keep pace with the escalating cost of living. However, increased wages mean increased costs of production, distribution, and services, and these new costs are inevitably passed along to the consumer—meaning primarily workers and the middle classes. Growing concern for the ecology of the natural environment and the specter of a worldwide energy shortage only complicate the already troubled life of policy makers.

All this may help to explain a noticeable malaise in the body politic, a skepticism about the efficacy of governing institutions, and fundamental doubts about the ability—if not the honesty—of political leaders. Since the early 1960s, even the traditionally more tranquil societies of the postindustrial world have been troubled by increasing violence—riots, political assassinations, kidnappings, and random acts of terrorism. The problems confronting government would appear to be only multiplied as our modern economies move into an age of increased automation and cybernetics control, with machines that run machines and the individual increasingly atomized in an impersonal environment. And yet the problems of our modern economies may be insignificant compared with the worldwide impact of climatic change and substantial reductions in rainfall, of hybrid varieties of crops ever more vulnerable to plant disease and infestation, and of continued population growth, growth that promises to far outstrip the capabilities of natural resources *and* governing institutions. There is only temporary solace in the observation that it is easier to see the problems of the future than it is to see their solutions.

The present patterns of politics may thus undergo profound transformation. Instead of a textbook that will enhance understanding of the present, what is written here may become only a history of the irrelevant past. It is appropriate, then, that the next and final chapter in this section on comparative politics be devoted to a radically different style of political organization.

STUDY-GUIDE QUESTIONS

1 What are "ascriptive identities"? How does the ascriptive identity of religion affect patterns of social interaction and political competition (for example, in Northern Ireland)?
2 What is meant by "cross-cutting cleavages"? Which is the best example of a country with cross-cutting cleavages: Switzerland, the Netherlands, or Belgium? Why?
3 How may *political* institutions and organizations moderate a society's various cleavages?
4 How would you explain the relative political instability of postwar Italy and the French Fourth Republic?
5 What are the institutional, or constitutional, innovations that have contributed to political stability in postwar Germany (the Federal Republic) and the French Fifth Republic?

REFERENCES

Allardt, Erik, and Yrjö Littunen (eds.): *Cleavages, Ideologies and Party Systems,* The Academic Bookstore, Helsinki, 1964.

Almond, Gabriel A., and Sidney Verba: *The Civic Culture: Political Attitudes and Democracy in Five Nations*, Little, Brown and Company, Boston, 1965.

Andrews, William G.: *European Political Institutions*, 2d ed., D. Van Nostrand Company, Inc., Princeton, N.J., 1966.

Blondel, Jean: *The Government of France*, 4th ed., Thomas Y. Crowell Company, 1974.

Dahl, Robert A. (ed.): *Political Oppositions in Western Democracies*, Yale University Press, New Haven, Conn., 1966.

Edinger, Lewis J.: *Politics in Germany*, Little, Brown and Company, Boston, 1968.

Ehrmann, Henry W.: *Politics in France*, 2d ed., Little, Brown and Company, Boston, 1971.

Epstein, Leon: *Political Parties in Western Democracies*, Frederick A. Praeger, Inc., New York, 1967.

Germino, Dante, and Stefano Passigli: *The Government and Politics of Contemporary Italy*, Harper & Row, Publishers, Incorporated, New York, 1968.

Heidenheimer, Arnold J.: *The Governments of Germany*, 3d ed., Thomas Y. Crowell Company, 1971.

Hoffmann, Stanley: *Decline or Renewal: France since the 1930s*, The Viking Press, Inc., New York, 1974.

Kogan, Norman: *A Political History of Postwar Italy*, Frederick A. Praeger, Inc., New York, 1966.

LaPalombara, Joseph: *Interest Groups in Italian Politics*, Princeton University Press, Princeton, N.J., 1964.

—— and Myron Weiner (eds.): *Political Parties and Political Development*, Princeton University Press, Princeton, N.J., 1966.

Lijphart, A.: *The Politics of Accommodation*, University of California Press, Berkeley, 1968.

Lipset, Seymour Martin, and Stein Rokkan (eds.): *Party Systems and Voter Alignments*, The Free Press, New York, 1967.

Loewenberg, G.: *Parliament in the German Political System*, Cornell University Press, Ithaca, N.Y., 1967.

Macrae, Duncan, Jr.: *Parliament, Parties and Society in France, 1946–1958*, St. Martin's Press, Inc., New York, 1967.

Moore, Barrington, Jr.: *Social Origins of Dictatorship and Democracy: Lord and Peasant in the Making of the Modern World*, Beacon Press, Boston, 1966.

Rokkan, Stein, Angus Campbell, Per Torsvik, and Henry Valen: *Citizens, Elections, Parties*, McKay Publishing Company, New York, 1970.

Schoenbaum, David: *Hitler's Social Revolution: Class and Status in Nazi Germany, 1933–1939*, Anchor Books, Doubleday & Company, Inc., Garden City, N.Y., 1967.

Weil, Gordon L.: *The Benelux Nations: The Politics of Small-Country Democracies*, Holt, Rinehart and Winston, Inc., New York, 1970.

Williams, P. M.: *The French Parliament: Politics in the Fifth Republic*, Frederick A. Praeger, Inc., New York, 1968.

Wilson, Frank L.: "Gaullism without de Gaulle," *The Western Political Quarterly*, vol. 26, no. 3, pp. 485–506, September 1973.

Chapter 13

Government in the Soviet Union: Politics or Antipolitics?

"Politics in the United States," "Politics in Great Britain," and "Politics in Western Europe" have been the titles of the preceding chapters. By "politics" we have meant the bargaining and competition that are associated with public policy making, for in these societies the policy-making process is relatively visible, and the struggle for the control of governing institutions and for access to political decision makers is marked by the periodic election of representatives from competing parties. In these particular societies "politics" is very much alive, if not entirely well.

There is no doubt that in the case of the Soviet Union we are dealing with a different kind of political system. The Soviet Union is dramatic proof that in government, as in magic, appearances can be deceiving. The Soviet constitution is highly democratic. There is universal suffrage, and elections are held periodically. There are discernible differences in the structures and functioning of legislative, executive, and judicial institutions. Citizen liberties and rights are constitutionally specified and judicially protected. But.

There is, above all, only one party, and it is doubtful that it deserves to be called a "political" party. Elections, then, are not competitive. There is no institutionalized opposition to the existing elite or its policies. Citizen access to top decision makers is extremely limited, if it exists at all. And no matter how little the student may actually have read about Soviet Russia, he or she is likely to know that much of its history has been characterized by one-man rule, terror, and repression. If there is "politics" in the Soviet Union, then, it exists below the surface and in the nooks and crannies of a regime that is most appropriately labeled "authoritarian."[1]

A CULTURAL POLYGLOT

By now, the reader should be able to give an unambiguous answer to an obvious question: What are the chances of building stable democracy in an extended geographic unit that encompasses many nationalities, religions, and linguistic groups? If we consider only these superficial but fundamental characteristics of Russia—both tsarist and Communist Russia—we are likely to conclude that some form of authoritarian government was and is almost inevitable.

The territorial extent of the United States is 3.6 million square miles (3 million square miles if only the continental forty-eight states are counted); that of China is 3.7 million square miles. But the Soviet Union stretches for 8.6 million square miles from Europe across Asia, covering one-sixth of the world's land surface. This geographic giant was bound to include a diversity of cultural groups.

"Russia," in fact, refers specifically to the dominant language group that, under the Muscovite regime, gradually extended its territorial and political control after the thirteenth century. While Russian is the official language of the Soviet Union, it is the native language of only 60 percent of the population (it is the second language of all other Soviet citizens). "Polyglot" means "many languages," and there are more than sixty other major language groups in the Soviet Union, including Ukrainian, Belorussian, Lithuanian, Latvian, Estonian, Moldavian, Georgian, Armenian, Yiddish, German, Uzbek, Tatar, and Kazakh.

Russians and Ukrainians belong largely to the Orthodox Christian faith. The peoples of Central Asia are Muslim. Other religious groups are Roman Catholic, Protestant, Jewish, and Buddhist. And despite the Bolsheviks' official proclamation of atheism (which was considered more appropriate to a society looking toward the future through science and technology), religion remains an important source of social identity for millions of Soviet citizens—especially in the more provincial and less industrialized areas of the Soviet Union.

When the Bolsheviks came to power in 1917, there were approximately 200 different nationalities that had been subordinated to the authority of the Russian tsars. Reversing the forced assimilationist policies of tsarist government, the Bolsheviks (who adopted the "communist" label after the Revolution) established a federal state that was based on the nationality divisions of Russian society. The formal federalism of the Soviet Union is indicated by its official name—the Union of Soviet Socialist Republics (U.S.S.R.). Less assimilationist than the tsars, the Communists nevertheless laid the basis for a quantitative reduction in nationalist identities. Internal migration, economic growth, natural demographic trends, and the cultural changes effected by modern communications and transportation systems have all contributed to a progressively smaller number of nationality groups: 196 in 1926, 109 in 1956, and 91 in 1970.

But there are today, and there will be far into the foreseeable future, at least seventeen *major* nationality groups. It thus is obvious that the Soviet Union deserves to be classified as a multinational and highly heterogeneous society. And throughout history, in all the great multinational world empires (including the Persian, Roman, Turkish, and Chinese), the state has been ruled by an autocracy that leaned on the administrative capabilities of a far-flung bureaucracy.

CONTINUITY

As this last point suggests, there is more continuity than change between tsarist and Communist Russia. Both are characterized by authoritarian regimes that have ruled their subjects through bureaucratic control. In a culturally heterogeneous society, the unity of the state first symbolized by the tsars is now symbolized by the Communist party. A bureaucracy that once ruled in the name of the tsars now rules in the name of the party. And both tsarist and communist states subordinated religion, or suppressed it, in the interests of the all-powerful state. Both tolerated legislative institutions and

---

[1] See Chap. 3 for a discussion of authoritarianism and totalitarianism and Fig. 3.2, p. 37, for an impressionistic ordering of contemporary states (including the Soviet Union) along a continuum of democracy and authoritarianism.

elections only insofar as they reinforced the policy positions of an entrenched ruling elite. Both insisted on the conformity of intellectuals and artists to the interests and symbols of the regime, and both sought to stamp out dissent. To secure these ends, both tsars and Communists used the repressive powers of secret police, censorship of the arts and media, exile to Siberia, forced labor camps, the execution of political enemies, and the confinement of intellectual dissidents to asylums for the allegedly insane.

Both tsars and Communists built a centralized state that attempted to eliminate or hold within narrow boundaries any manifestations of cultural autonomy (whether from Ukrainians, Lithuanians, Jews, or any other cultural or nationality group). Both attempted to legitimate their autocratic authority in terms *other than* citizen consent, democratic elections, and popular participation in policy making. The tsars appealed to divine right; the Communists appeal to the party's infallible interpretation of historical inevitability. In this sense the basis of political legitimacy for both tsars and Communists has been in terms of supernatural myth, and the absolute and universal qualities of the myth helped to condition both tsarist and Communist elites to think in terms of sweeping change and utopian solutions to prevailing problems.

The Bolsheviks, then, captured control of a society that was, in many respects, tailor-made for the type of system the Communist party proceeded to construct. There was in Russia no political culture or widespread set of values and norms conducive to democratic government. Social change and economic development had been traditionally initiated by the ruling elite and did not derive from the innovative efforts of individual entrepreneurs. And both tsarist and Communist elites emphasized basic economic development in the interests of the state instead of in the interests of heightened standards of living for citizens. The Russian citizen, in fact, has typically been thought of by his rulers as more of a producer in the collective mass than a consumer with legitimate private interests. Thus there has been no political, intellectual, or ideological tradition separating individual rights from the prerogatives of the state. In Russia, any appeal to the notions of social contract, inalienable rights, or the necessary consent of the governed was absurdly out of context with both past and present.

Communism in Russia came to power in a society where there was no middle class to foster the ideas of individual enterprise and humanism. On the contrary, much of traditional Russian society, as represented by the peasant village and even by some of the values and norms of the old aristocracy, was oriented toward collectivist styles of economic production and social organization. In Russia, China, Yugoslavia, and parts of Eastern Europe, communism found some solid foundations on which to build a collectivist society in the name of modern socialism. In all these societies, but especially in Russia, the Communists also inherited a peasant mass, sullen and suspicious, but vulnerable to manipulation by urban elites who perpetuated the exploitation of the peasantry for the greater ends of the state. In the case of Russian communism, there was even more continuity than change with regard to foreign policy: the search for warm-water seaports and an abiding concern to eliminate or neutralize the influence of Western powers in the areas peripheral to the vast Eurasian land mass of Russia.

These dimensions of continuity between tsarist and Communist Russia help to give perspective to the details of Russian history. And after a necessarily brief summary of Russia's development from tsars to commissars, we must also begin to examine the ways in which communism in Russia represents change as well as continuity.[2]

HISTORICAL BACKGROUND

The history of what we call Russia begins during the eighth and ninth centuries A.D., when Viking invaders from the north, led by a warrior named Rurik, imposed their rule upon the disunited Slavic tribes. The Slavs had entered Russia earlier from the south and had intermingled with other peoples

---

[2]The Communist party's designation of state officials as "commissars," after the October Revolution of 1917, reflected the Bolsheviks' conviction that their revolution was in the tradition of the French Revolution of 1789. And there are, in fact, some important points of continuity between the French, Russian, and even the American Revolutions: They all aimed at overthrowing a social system based on aristocratic or inherited privilege, and they all succeeded in replacing it with a new order in which talent rather than birth determined the individual's place in society.

in this region, including the Germans, Lithuanians, Turks, and Finns.

The Kiev State

The Vikings penetrated as far south as the Black Sea and eventually established at Kiev the capital of the first Russian state. Trading and military contacts between Kiev and Constantinople led to a treaty, followed by the Christianization of the Kiev state in 988 A.D. The coming of Christianity marked a turning point; not only Greek priests but also architects and artisans entered Russia, and the Greek alphabet was adapted for Slavic use. Byzantine culture made a deep and lasting imprint on Russian life; the Byzantine pattern of imperial autocracy, including its fusion of church and state, became the model for later Russian tsars.

The Kiev state expanded until it reached from the Baltic to the Black Sea and across the southern plains. It then began to decline because of a variety of problems, including the rise of serfdom and the concentration of land ownership in the hands of the nobility. In 1054, after the death of Prince Yaroslav the Wise, Russia was divided into principalities ruled by his sons. In the thirteenth century Russia was invaded and conquered by the Tatars; in the struggle to drive them back, the grand duchy of Moscow rose to a position of leadership among the Russian principalities. Other invasions of Russia (by the Germans, Lithuanians, and Poles) were followed, in the fifteenth century, by a long period of encirclement and isolation, which served to strengthen feudalism and autocracy.

The Grand Duchy of Moscow

The Muscovite regime, established and extended by military conquest, was despotic from its inception. In the sixteenth century, Ivan IV ("the Terrible") took for himself the title "tsar" (or czar), meaning Caesar. During this same century, the Russians pushed eastward, and in 1639 they reached the Pacific and Alaska. In 1613 an assembly of nobles put the Romanov family on the throne, which had become vacant. In the eighteenth century Peter I ("the Great") began the westernization of Russia, and Catherine II established elective municipal *dumas* (assemblies) and attempted to modernize Russian laws.

However, the essential spirit of representative government remained alien to Russian rulers. The various elective bodies were chosen by landlords, not by workers or peasants; illiteracy was rampant (two-thirds of all Russians were illiterate as late as 1917); the courts were staffed by the tsar's appointees and showed favoritism toward aristocrats and landowners; due process of law was unknown; and censorship, espionage, and harsh punishment were taken for granted. During the nineteenth century, a few tsars experienced moments of liberalism; the most notable was Alexander II (1855–1881), who "abolished" serfdom in 1861, introduced trial by jury, reorganized the courts, and established rural self-governing councils.

However, these reforms either lacked, or soon lost, substance. The abolition of serfdom was illusory; although freed from the arbitrary power of his former landlord, the ex-serf received only a very small plot of land (too small to support his family), for which he had to make substantial payments. His taxes were high, and his land could, under certain circumstances, be taken from him against his will and without compensation. Peasants usually had to hire out to work on their landlords' estates in order to eke out their living. Some 2,000 peasant revolts between 1861 and 1863 testified to the failure of this "reform."

The Failure of Reform

The successors of Alexander II curtailed local self-government, abolished jury trial, set up special courts to try cases involving the peasantry, launched pogroms against the Jews, and intensified the policy of "russifying" the diverse peoples brought within the empire by conquest. To deflect the efforts of these captive peoples to achieve autonomy or independence, the tsars engaged in military adventures in the Near East (against Turkey) and in the Far East (against Japan). Russia's humiliating defeat in the Russo-Japanese War (1904–1905) touched off the revolution of 1905 and forced tsar Nicholas II to grant halfhearted political reforms, which, however, failed to touch the problems and grievances of peasants, captive peoples, or the new class of factory workers brought rapidly into existence during the last third of the nineteenth century.

The Duma created by the tsar's decree of 1905 was not truly representative; most of its members were landlords, many of them elected indirectly and by a restricted electorate from gerrymandered districts. The limited powers of the Duma, to which the ministers were not made responsible (in spite of the tsar's promises that they would be), were further weakened by the creation of an upper legislative chamber (the State Council), half of whose members were appointed by the tsar, which had to consent to any legislation passed by the Duma. Moreover, the tsar retained an unlimited power of veto.

The defeat of feudal, agrarian Russia by industrial England in the Crimean War (1853–1856) had prompted the tsars to take steps to industrialize their backward country. They invited foreign capitalists to finance these undertakings. No concern was shown for the welfare of factory workers, who were really transplanted peasants attracted to the factories by the promise of money wages and the idea of living in the city. But reality fell far short of their expectations. Wages were low, hours long, and factory discipline harsh; trade unions and collective bargaining were illegal, and strikes were punishable by imprisonment or exile to Siberia. A system of factory espionage prevented even the discussion of reforms among the workmen themselves. There was virtually no legislation restraining employers from exploiting their workers, who were, moreover, able to afford only poor, unsanitary housing and lived under conditions of increasing misery and destitution. Under these circumstances, it was scarcely remarkable that the factory laborers grew more and more discontented and radical.

The Rise of Protest Movements

Three main currents of reform developed in Russia during the latter nineteenth century. The first might be called a "middle-class" movement, although Russia did not have a true middle class in the Western sense of the term. It was a small group, made up chiefly of merchants, manufacturers, intellectuals, and lesser government employees; it sought such political reforms as a written constitution, an elective parliament (Duma), a responsible ministry, and civil liberties. In 1905 this movement organized itself as the Constitutional Democratic party (sometimes called the "Kadets").

The second movement was aimed at land reform and directed its appeal principally to the peasants, who constituted four-fifths of the population. These "populists" (*Narodniki*) advocated a type of agrarian socialism; the big landlords were to be expropriated, and their estates merged into a vast peasant commune. Many populists preached violence and recommended acts of terrorism against public officials and prominent members of the nobility. In the 1860s and 1870s the *Narodniki* were the largest radical group in Russia and exerted a strong influence in intellectual circles. In 1900 they organized as the Socialist Revolutionary party.

The Beginnings of Russian Marxism

The third and ultimately most important reform movement was based on the ideas of Karl Marx, whose *Kapital* had been translated into Russian in 1872. This movement began with a small group of Russian exiles, mostly intellectuals, organized in Switzerland in 1883 by Georgi Plekhanov, the "father" of Russian Marxism. In 1895 an underground Marxist group was formed in St. Petersburg under the leadership of Vladimir Ilyich Ulyanov, better known as Lenin. The object of this organization (soon called the Workers' Social Democratic party) was to capitalize on the mounting resentment and class-consciousness of the factory workers, the new industrial proletariat, which, according to Marxist-Leninist doctrine, would constitute the vanguard of all revolutionary forces and groups. Plekhanov, Lenin, J. O. Martov, and the other intellectuals who led the party were dismayed by the fact that the proletariat represented only a very small segment of the Russian population (as did the intellectuals and reformers themselves).

The Split in the Party

In 1903, at a congress of the party held outside Russia, a conflict arose over the tactics to be adopted and also over internal party organization and control. The moderate wing, led by Martov, argued that Russia could not be transformed into a socialist or communist society until capitalism in Russia first flourished and then decayed. The moderates contended that they were adhering strictly to

Marx's theories in this respect. Since much time would obviously be required for this evolutionary process to be completed in Russia, it was futile to plan on an early revolutionary attempt to seize power, and in the meantime the party should be organized along democratic lines. In the interim, the party ought to work cooperatively with other parties and groups to achieve piecemeal reform.

The revolutionary wing of the party, under Lenin's leadership, claimed that Marx had not meant that revolution must be timed in each country according to the stage of capitalist development or decadence in that particular country.[3] Rather, said Lenin, proletarian revolutions should be timed to coincide with the general stage reached by capitalism in the world as a whole. Viewing capitalism as a worldwide system of imperialism through which the advanced industrial nations had achieved domination over the backward areas, Lenin argued that Russia had become a link in the chain of capitalist imperialism—rather like a colony to be exploited—and was perhaps the weakest link in that chain. Lenin viewed world capitalism as already decadent and regarded Russia as ripe for revolution because of its weak, corrupt government, the degree of discontent among the people, and the existence of determined revolutionary leadership (his own faction). Lenin also believed that the party should have a centralized, military type of organization, in view of the imminence of its revolutionary tasks and the difficulties of organizing for revolution among the spies and secret police working for the tsar.

Despite Lenin's efforts to turn the uprising of 1905 into a proletarian revolution, tsarist military forces triumphed, Lenin (again) went into exile, and reactionary policies reigned supreme, despite the existence of a national Duma established by the tsar. Elected by a restricted suffrage in gerrymandered districts, handicapped by a largely appointed upper house, confronted by ministers it could not control or remove, and with negligible legislative powers, the Duma was no more than the ghost of a true parliament. Strikes, demonstrations, peasant uprisings, and student protests between 1907 and 1914 all testified to the existence of a widespread conviction that change in Russia could be achieved only by drastic action.

THE REVOLUTIONS OF 1917

The Russian military collapse during World War I, coupled with disclosures of graft and bungling, charges of treason in high places, the breakdown of transportation, and food shortages, led to the so-called bourgeois revolution of March 1917 (according to the old Russian calendar, February 1917). All factions, from moderates to extremists, helped in giving the final push that ended the tsarist regime.

This revolution did not so much overthrow the government as take advantage of its internal decay. Lenin, who, like so many other revolutionary leaders, had been living in exile, returned to Russia in April 1917. Assuming leadership of the Bolsheviks, he directed an effective campaign of organization and propaganda, which by autumn had given them a majority of the delegates to the second All-Russian Congress of Soviets, which was to meet on November 7. However, instead of waiting until the Congress assembled to secure the adoption of the Bolshevik program, the Bolshevik-indoctrinated soldiers and revolutionaries seized the government by force. The Soviet government was proclaimed on November 8 (October 26 by the old Russian calendar), with Lenin as the president of a Council of People's Commissars. The Council was declared to possess complete governmental power. Trotsky became commissar of foreign affairs, and the remaining posts were filled chiefly by other members of the Central Committee of the Bolshevik party.

No elected legislature was created for several years, and Russian government operated as an executive-administrative dictatorship. Three decrees were now issued: (1) the Decree of Peace, leading to the negotiation of peace with the Central Powers by the Treaty of Brest-Litovsk in March 1918; (2) the Decree of Land, making all land the property of the state; and (3) the Decree of Industry, which nationalized major industries and put workers in nominal control of the industrial plants. Peace was indeed concluded (at the cost of staggering cessions of territory), but the decrees of land and industry required years before they became

---

[3] See Chap. 6 for a discussion of the relationship between Marxism and Leninism and for other variations in communist ideology.

effective over any considerable portions of Russian territory. Counterrevolution, foreign intervention, famine, terror, and inertia all operated to delay the arrival of the Leninist millennium. Still another decree was issued in November 1917: the Declaration of the Rights of the Peoples of Russia. This decree proclaimed the equality of all the races and nationalities included within the old Russian Empire, their right of self-determination (including the right of secession), and the abolition of all special privileges for any nationality. Joseph Stalin, one of Lenin's most loyal supporters in the Bolshevik elite, was appointed the first commissar of nationalities.

THE PERIOD OF WAR COMMUNISM: 1918 TO 1921

During the period of war communism, Russia was invaded by German, Polish, French, British, American, and Japanese armies and ravaged by counterrevolution from within. White (or counterrevolutionary) Russian forces came close to overthrowing the Bolshevik regime, although in the end the White armies were defeated, in large part because of Trotsky's skill in organizing and directing the Red Army. Invading German armies were at first successful, setting up a puppet regime in the Ukraine; after the final defeat of Germany in 1918, an Allied-sponsored (but equally hostile) regime took over that rich and populous area. Russia was forced to cede territory to Poland to end Russo-Polish hostilities in 1921, and the Japanese were not expelled from Siberia until 1922. The old Russian Empire was disintegrating rapidly; many nationalities denied autonomy by the tsars now broke away and in the name of national self-determination set themselves up as independent states. Among these were Finland, Poland, Estonia, Latvia, and Lithuania. Rumania seized the province of Bessarabia, claiming that its population was more Rumanian than Russian. Separatist movements developed in White Russia, the Ukraine, and the Caucasus region. Events immediately following the Bolshevik Revolution thus appeared to confirm the Bolsheviks' ideological conviction that the representatives of capitalism and bourgeois democracy were bent on liquidating the socialist experiment in Russia. The consequent and continued emphasis of Soviet foreign policy has been on massive military preparedness and a system of foreign states surrounding the Soviet Union that would not threaten its national security.

To foreign intervention, counterrevolution, and regional independence movements after 1918 must be added the sharp opposition and conflict inside the government itself. Left-wing elements had opposed the Treaty of Brest-Litovsk, and the Social Revolutionaries (a peasant party) were also so opposed to the coercive policies adopted by Lenin to collectivize agriculture that they finally left the government and sided with the White Russian faction. Even Bukharin, a prominent Bolshevik theorist, opposed the government's policies toward the peasants and nationality groups. An attempt to assassinate Lenin led him to organize the Cheka (secret police) to carry on a terroristic campaign of retaliation and to protect the new regime from counterrevolution.

Vigorous and often violent resistance to the communist regime came also from the Russian Orthodox Church and the peasants. The church, viewed by the Bolsheviks as a pillar of support for tsarist rule and thus an instrument of class exploitation, was subject to terroristic persecution, including the pillaging and burning of churches, the smashing of icons (holy pictures and images), the killing of priests, and the closing of seminaries. The peasants, however, were too stubborn, too numerous, and too economically important to be dealt with in such a ruthless fashion. Peasant uprisings served as a warning to the government, which decided to adopt a more conciliatory policy. The end of civil war and foreign intervention in 1921 permitted the relaxation of many controls, which thus won further support from those peasants who had already begun to accept the Bolshevik regime as a lesser evil than a return to tsarist landlordism.

THE NEW ECONOMIC POLICY: 1921 TO 1927

The failure of forced-draft communization in Russia had become apparent to Lenin by 1921. Without abandoning the ultimate goal of a completely communistic society, the Tenth Party Congress in 1921 adopted Lenin's proposed New Economic Policy, but only after a bitter internal struggle in which Trotsky and others urged continuation of socialist development at home and revolution abroad. The NEP represented a series of important concessions to capitalism. Peasants were now taxed only a certain portion of their crop and were allowed to sell their surpluses on the open market. Private small-scale manufacturing was permitted, and private trading was resumed. Labor was allowed the free choice of jobs, the right to strike, and wider wage differentials, reversing the pre-1921 trend toward wage equality and regimentation in general. The failure of factory management by workers' committees led to a new program to train managers, give them more authority, and provide them with salaries well above those of the lowest-paid workers. Steadily increasing managerial powers over workers and ever-widening differentials in economic reward have persisted as basic features of the Soviet industrial system.

In terms of international relations, the NEP era was marked by a resumption of diplomatic relations with such nations as Germany, Britain, Italy, and France; the conclusion of treaties with various individual states; an effort to establish a zone of neutral states along Russia's boundaries; and the cultivation of credit and trade opportunities abroad. All this stood in marked contrast to earlier attempts to foment worldwide revolution. But, in fact, the Treaty of Brest-Litovsk and, subsequently, Stalin's declaration of "socialism in one country" made it clear that the international revolution had been indefinitely postponed. And Soviet foreign policy has, with remarkable consistency, been more concerned with national defense than with international aggression or revolutionary adventure. It was precisely this conservative orientation and "greatpower chauvinism" that so enraged Trotsky and his supporters after the 1920s, Marshal Tito after World War II, and the Chinese Communists after 1960. It also troubled Fidel Castro until Cuba's dependency on Soviet economic aid reconciled him to a more subdued role in furthering the cause of socialist revolution in Latin America.

THE SOVIET SYSTEM OF GOVERNMENT

The problem of territorial disintegration following the Bolshevik Revolution presented both a practical and an ideological dilemma. The Declaration of Rights of the Peoples of Russia had affirmed the rights of national self-determination and secession; therefore, why should regions aspiring to independence not be allowed to go their own way? Also, in view of the evidence of Bolshevik renunciation of old-style Russian imperialism (such as the treaty with Persia in 1921, giving up all Russian spheres of influence), how could a comparable imperialism be perpetuated *within* the old Russian Empire? However, on the side of practical politics, how could the new rulers of Russia allow such a rich industrial area as the Ukraine to be lost to the new socialist economy, especially when it would almost certainly become a powerful pawn in the hands of hostile powers?

The problem was solved by a combination of pressure and persuasion. Treaties of military and economic union were concluded between the Russian Socialist Federal Soviet Republic (R.S.F.S.R.) and White Russia (1920); the Ukraine (1920); Georgia, Armenia, and Azerbaijan (1921); Turkmenistan (1925); and Tajikistan (1929). In 1924, a treaty of union became the first constitution of the Soviet Union, which then included only four republics: the Russian, White Russian, Ukrainian, and Transcaucasian—the last a merger of Georgia, Armenia, and Azerbaijan. With the addition of the Turkmenistan, Tajikistan, and Uzbek republics, the number of members in this supposedly federal union rose to seven.

The Constitution of 1924

The first constitution of the Soviet Union presented a new and dubious version of federalism; the government of the union held paramount power over all trade, the plan of the national economy, the general principles of education, and the basic labor and land laws. The states (called "republics") were declared to have the right of secession and sovereign authority over residual matters such as the administration of justice, health, education, and social welfare, but in these spheres, as in all others, the policies of the republics were required to conform to those of the union. Laws and decrees issued by the governmental organs of the various republics were subject to repeal by the All-Union Congress. The result was a pattern of complete political and economic centralization, further cemented by the additional controls exercised through the Communist party—the only legal party organization.

The pattern of governmental institutions in both

the union and the republics reflected Lenin's faith in the indispensability of leadership by an elite of intellectual revolutionaries. Elections—based on a restricted suffrage—were, indeed, permitted, but real power remained in the hands of the leaders of the Communist party. Theoretical rule from the bottom up became in fact actual rule from the top down. Elections were held every two years to choose village, town, and factory "soviets" (the Russian word for "councils"), with urban workers electing one deputy for every 25,000 workers, and the peasants electing one deputy for each 125,000 inhabitants. Excluded from the suffrage were those hiring labor for profit, those receiving income not derived from work, private traders, priests, monks, tsarist police officers, and members of the royal family. The ballot was public, not secret.

Eligible voters chose only the members of their local soviet, which in turn elected members of district soviets. These elected deputies to the congress of the particular union republic and also deputies to regional congresses, which in their turn chose delegates to the All-Union Congress of Soviets—theoretically the supreme governing body of the Soviet Union. This sovereign assembly of about 2,000 members (of whom roughly 75 percent were Communists) met only once every two years, and then really for the sole purpose of approving (and applauding) everything that had been done between Congress meetings. The All-Union Congress, at its biennial meeting, elected a Central Executive Committee of some 605 members, who actually wielded *legislative* powers between the brief meetings of the Congress. This Executive Committee was a bicameral parliament consisting of a Council of the Union (414 members) and a Council of Nationalities (191 members). The Council of the Union was based on population; the Council of Nationalities, on a pattern of representation for the republics and regions. This two-house Executive Committee was itself largely a phantom; it met only three times a year and, in turn, delegated its powers to a Presidium of some twenty-seven members (drawn almost entirely from the inner circle of the Communist party and reelected in virtual perpetuity). The Executive Committee also elected the fifteen members of the Council of People's Commissars, heading the various administrative departments, and the judges of the U.S.S.R. Supreme Court.

The primacy of Soviet executive-administrative agencies merely continued an old Russian custom; the notion of legislative supremacy had always been an alien concept. The lack of individual liberty was equally traditional; such Soviet features as a secret police, restrictions on the formation of citizen organizations (including opposing political parties), censorship, denial of religious freedom, and general subordination of the individual had all been anticipated, as we have seen, by the tsarist regime.

The Constitution of 1936

By 1936 the Soviet regime, with Stalin now firmly in control, was faced with a new international and domestic picture. Hitler's capture of power in Germany in 1933 and the spread of fascism elsewhere had led to an abrupt and complete reversal of the party line; Communists in other countries were now instructed to cooperate with liberal and democratic parties to form popular fronts with them to check the rise of fascism. Internationally, the Soviet Union sought collective security with the Western democracies to halt the expansion of Italy, Germany, and Japan. The central theme in Soviet propaganda became the great similarity (suddenly discovered) between Russia and the bourgeois democracies, especially with regard to the goals they were all seeking. Thus Russia said it wanted world peace, sought no additional territory, would support the League of Nations in collective action to check international aggression, and was striving at home toward higher living standards, greater liberty, and more democracy for its people.

Within the Soviet Union, the Communist regime had consolidated its position through its control of education, its censorship and propaganda, its suppression of all criticism and opposition (whether right or left), and its exile or outright liquidation of all real or potential rivals to Stalin. By a ruthless policy of brutality and starvation (see below), the great bulk of the peasantry had been forced into the collective farms. The First and Second Five-Year Plans had mercilessly catapulted the Soviet peoples into the industrial age. Stalin was able to say that enemies at home had been eliminated, that the classless society had arrived, and that it was therefore no longer necessary to disfranchise or discriminate against particular social groups.

Stalin thus proposed in 1936 that a new constitution be adopted. A draft version was circulated and received extensive discussion in meetings of such bodies as regional and local soviets, trade unions, and local Communist party organizations. Only minor changes were made as the result of these supposedly democratic discussions, and the new constitution went into operation in 1937 following the election of deputies to the new Supreme Soviet. It is this constitution which remains in force today and which describes the principles and structure of government in the Soviet Union.

First Principles The constitution begins with a chapter entitled "The Social Structure," in which basic principles and purposes are set forth. The Soviet Union is declared to be a "socialist state of workers and peasants," to whom (as represented by the soviets) "all power in the U.S.S.R. belongs." The constitution does not claim that its system is one of "communism," but only "socialism," which, according to Lenin, was a lower, preliminary stage of evolution. Declaring that the "economic foundation of the U.S.S.R. is the ... socialist ownership of the instruments and means of production," the constitution distinguishes between two forms of "socialist property": "state property," i.e., government-owned, and "collective property," i.e., belonging to collective farms or cooperative societies. Spelling out which kinds of property belong to the state and which to the collectives, the constitution makes it clear that virtually all property belongs to the former, including all land. Collective farms are declared to have the perpetual, free *use* of the lands they occupy, but use is not ownership.

The constitution, however, does permit the right of private property in "incomes and savings from work, ... dwelling houses and subsidiary home enterprises, in articles of domestic economy and use, and articles of personal use and convenience, as well as the right of citizens to inherit personal property." Small-scale private enterprise by individual peasants and handicraftsmen "based on their own labor and precluding the exploitation of the labor of others" is also permitted. Thus the sale of one's own skill and effort, as during one's spare time, is officially sanctioned. Every household belonging to a collective farm also receives the use of a small individual plot of land and actually owns its dwelling, a limited amount of livestock, its poultry, and its tools; this enables a family to supplement its share of the income from the collective farm by the sale of garden vegetables, eggs, poultry, and the like.

"The economic life of the U.S.S.R. is determined and directed by the state national economic plan," and the constitution also declares that its guiding principle "is that of socialism: 'From each according to his ability, to each according to his work.'" The duty of every able-bodied citizen to work is affirmed and is supported by the warning, "He who does not work, neither shall he eat"—a saying long associated with capitalistic individualism rather than socialism.

Federalism Like its 1924 predecessor, the constitution of 1936 establishes an allegedly federal structure, based on a voluntary union of equal Soviet Socialist Republics, which now number fifteen. A long enumeration of the powers of the Soviet Union, however, leaves the republics with even less sovereignty than they enjoyed under the 1924 constitution; each union republic's constitution must be drawn up in full conformity with that of the Soviet Union, and any discrepancies between republic and union laws are resolved in favor of the latter. The "right freely to secede" is repeated, although on several occasions separatist movements have been crushed by force. In 1944 two amendments purported to give each union republic the right to enter into direct relations with foreign states, including the right to conclude treaties and exchange diplomats and consuls and the further right to have its own military forces. However, these rights have no substance and were proclaimed to enable the Soviet Union to argue more plausibly that some or all of its union republics should be accorded the status of full-fledged membership in the United Nations after World War II. The argument succeeded in winning the admission of the Ukraine and White Russia (or Belorussia) into the United Nations—a maneuver that the Soviet Union considered essential to counterbalancing the United Nations voting strength of states whose foreign policies were influenced by the United States. The "federal" structure of the Soviet Union, however, remains more an administrative device that reflects cultural heterogeneity than an effective structure for participation in policy making. This particular function, as will be discussed below in more detail, is reserved exclusively to the Communist party.

Civil Rights and Civil Liberties The most novel and widely publicized feature of the 1936 constitution was its tenth chapter, entitled "Fundamental Rights and Duties of Citizens." Reversing the usual Western sequence, the Soviet constitution proclaims such economic and social rights as those to guaranteed employment, rest and leisure, free medical service, old-age and disability insurance, education, and equality for women in all spheres of economic, government, cultural, political, and other public activity, before listing such traditional civil liberties as freedom of conscience, speech, the press, and assembly; the inviolability of person and home; and the privacy of correspondence. Equality of all citizens irrespective of nationality or race is also proclaimed.

Some of these rights, however, are compromised by the language of the constitution itself; for example, freedom of antireligious propaganda is recognized, but not of *pro*religious propaganda. This is consistent with the Communist party's conviction that religious belief and church organizations threaten the party's monopoly of power and its political legitimacy in the minds of the religious faithful. Also, freedom of speech, the press, and assembly are declared granted in order to strengthen the socialist system—not, obviously, to criticize or overthrow it. Moreover, the privileged position of the Communist party, in which only the most active and politically conscious citizens may unite, is set forth in the very paragraph presumably conferring the right of the people to form public organizations. Clearly, the right of association, like the other rights mentioned above, is neither free nor equal.

Elections Another widely acclaimed feature of the 1936 constitution was its ostensible adoption of universal, equal, and direct suffrage by secret ballot, thus completely reversing the restricted, unequal, indirect, and open voting under the 1924 system. The right to vote was given to all Soviet citizens who had reached the age of eighteen, with no restrictions (e.g., religion, education, sex, race, property status, or past activities) except for insane persons and those convicted, by a court, of crimes involving disfranchisement. Clear-cut as these statements appear, they lose all significance for democracy when it is realized that there is only one legal party, which holds a monopoly of propaganda, prestige, and power. Although trade unions, cooperative societies, and cultural and youth organizations may nominate candidates to compete with party nominees, the latter enjoy such prestige that in no national election since 1937 has more than one candidate's name appeared on the ballot in any district choosing deputies to the Supreme Soviet. Article 79 of the constitution, however, states that "the voter leaves on each ballot the name of the candidate for whom he is voting and strikes out the names of the others."

Perhaps surprisingly, many Soviet citizens have frequently crossed off the name of their local candidate. Failing to receive a majority of votes in their particular districts, 102 candidates were defeated in the 1948 elections, 289 in 1961, 129 in 1967, and 101 in 1971. This is, admittedly, a small percentage of candidates out of a total of some 2 million who stand for election to the various levels of Soviet government. (The fluctuations between 1948 and 1971 appear to coincide with the relative relaxation of political controls that marked the Khrushchev years—from the mid-1950s to 1964.) But defeated candidacies in Soviet elections are also an indirect measure of the extent to which the regime seeks to win popular support for its policies; thus a defeated candidate is replaced by one who can presumably work more closely with his local constituents. And, in many ways, the elected soviet deputy performs the same functions for his constituents that members of the United States Congress perform for theirs: checking on the activities of bureaucrats, especially at the local levels of government, and intervening between citizen and state in order to smooth the administrative process—in the urban neighborhoods, towns, and villages of Soviet society.

It is important to remember, especially in connection with the Soviet Union, that no government can function efficiently or long survive without the willing cooperation of a large majority of its citizens. No doubt, in the *non*communist world, the degree of dissent in the Soviet Union is overemphasized, and the legitimacy that the Soviet government is accorded by most of its citizens is ignored.

From these perspectives, it is clear that one should not evaluate Soviet elections as though they were equivalent to elections in the United States, Great Britain, or any other competitive party system. Elections in the Soviet Union are a national holiday (which helps to account for the very high turnout—typically 99 percent—of Soviet voters). They are a means of registering the citizen's loyalty to the state—and few Russian citizens have ever been faulted for their lack of patriotism for "Mother Russia." While Soviet elections do not have an impact on policy making, they are an important means of communication between citizens and elites; the election "campaign" (usually of two months' duration) offers the elite an opportunity, and an obligation, to explain and justify government policies. This becomes increasingly important as a highly literate citizenry, with access to both domestic and international sources of information, demands ever more plausible interpretations of the regime's activities at home and abroad.

Moreover, approximately one-half of soviet candidates standing at any particular election are nominated by the party and its auxiliary organizations for the first time; they have never before been nominated or elected as government deputies. This sizable turnover in the large number of candidates offers the state an opportunity to single out individuals for honor and distinction and provides many Soviet citizens with the chance of at least formal participation in the governing of the state. Citizen identification with the regime is thus enhanced, and it is in this sense too that elections in the Soviet Union are an important part of Soviet government. The problem is in our tendency to interpret institutions and procedures in the Soviet Union in terms of our own values and experience with government.

THE STRUCTURE OF THE SOVIET STATE

It is already apparent from the above that the Soviet state does not function like the governing institutions of democracy. In the Soviet Union, the Communist party makes policy. The *state*—as distinct from the *party*—is primarily an instrument of administration. Thus the party establishes the policies that are expressed, formally, through legislation passed by the state and administrative decrees implemented by the state bureaucracy. (See Figure 13.1.) Figure 13.1 shows that a Soviet citizen may be represented by, and may elect deputies to, as many as six different levels of government. Each of these levels is defined in terms of the population size and the geographic extent of its jurisdictional authority.

The Supreme Soviet

At the top of the state hierarchy is the Supreme Soviet (a bicameral legislature). As its name suggests, the Supreme Soviet is the highest echelon of legislative authority in the Soviet Union, and its laws may control the legislative and administrative activities of all the lower levels of the state hierarchy.

The "legislative process" of the Soviet Union, however, is essentially one of ratification instead of policy making. The deputies elected to the Supreme Soviet, and those at every level of government, have been nominated by the party because they represent some part of the Soviet ideal—not because they have legislative talents. Nevertheless, elected deputies may and do offer amendments to proposed legislation; they may express criticism of existing laws and suggest needed reforms; and they may criticize the functioning of the bureaucracy and attempt to enhance the responsibility of bureaucrats in their dealings with citizens. But the committee and plenary proceedings of the Supreme Soviet are not notable for debate and controversy, and its deputies are invariably constrained to operate within the parameters already established by the party. In terms of legislation and administrative decrees, the party makes its will known through the executive bodies of the state hierarchy. And at the top of the state hierarchy, these bodies are the Presidium and the Council of Ministers—which are only formally elected by the Supreme Soviet.

The Presidium of the Soviet Union

Although the constitution asserts that "the highest organ of state power in the U.S.S.R. is the Supreme Soviet of the U.S.S.R." (Article 30), it is the Presidium of the Supreme Soviet of the Soviet Union (theoretically elected by the Supreme Soviet every four years) that actually directs and controls it. Moreover, the Supreme Soviet meets only twice each year in brief sessions, between which the Presidium exercises many of the functions assigned

GOVERNMENT IN THE SOVIET UNION: POLITICS OR ANTIPOLITICS?

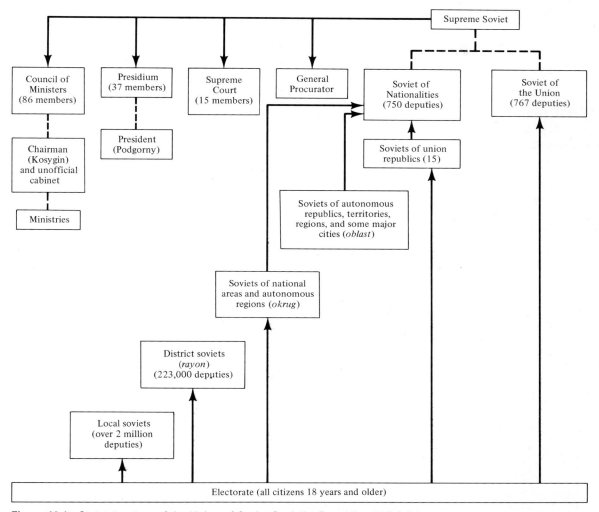

Figure 13.1 State structure of the Union of Soviet Socialist Republics (U.S.S.R.).

to the Supreme Soviet. The Presidium is invested with an impressive list of executive, legislative, and judicial powers. It convenes sessions of the Supreme Soviet; issues decrees having the force of law (and the Supreme Soviet always subsequently grants the required confirmation); interprets the laws of the Soviet Union and annuls union or republic ministerial ordinances deemed in conflict with the Presidium's interpretation; dissolves the Supreme Soviet and orders new elections for both chambers if a deadlock occurs between them (which never happens); may appoint and dismiss ministers of the Soviet Union between sessions of the Supreme Soviet; issues pardons; orders general or partial mobilization; may proclaim a state of war if the Supreme Soviet is not in session; ratifies treaties; sends and receives diplomats and consuls; and proclaims martial law. This concentrated blend of powers is topped by the Presidium's performance of the functions of a titular chief of state; it constitutes, in theory, a collegial executive (of some thirty-odd members), although in practice the chairman of the Presidium often performs many ceremonial duties, such as presiding at state dinners and diplomatic receptions.

The chairman of the Presidium, in fact, is formally identified as "president" of the Soviet Union. In 1974, however, President Nikolai Podgorny was a figure of formidable power and was considered by most observers of Soviet politics to be second-in-command behind Leonid Brezhnev, General Secretary of the Communist party. But it was clear that Podgorny's authority derived less from his presidency of the Soviet Union and chairmanship of the Presidium than it did from his high status *in the Communist party.*

The Council of Ministers of the Soviet Union

This last generalization also applies to the Chairman of the Council of Ministers, Alexei Kosygin. The chairman of the Council of Ministers may be understood as an approximate counterpart to the premier or prime minister of a parliamentary government. But since there are no partisan divisions within the parliament and since the Supreme Soviet has no effective autonomy in policy making, the premier's responsibility as chairman of the Council of Ministers consists primarily in supervising the administration of policies that are established by the party—outside the formal hierarchy of the state.

According to the 1936 constitution of the Soviet Union, the Council of Ministers is elected by, and is responsible to, the Supreme Soviet. When the Supreme Soviet is not in session, the Council of Ministers is responsible to the Presidium. In fact, the lines of actual responsibility are simply reversed. The center of legislative and administrative activity in the Soviet Union is in the Council of Ministers, and the chairman and his informal "inner cabinet" draft almost all the legislation submitted to the Supreme Soviet and supervise the day-to-day operations of the many ministries (or departments) that administer the Soviet state. The Council of Ministers is, in effect, the chief executive authority of the Soviet Union. Thus it was appropriate that President Kennedy, in the early 1960s, addressed his communications to *Chairman* Khrushchev, referring to Khrushchev's leadership position in the *state* hierarchy instead of to his position as first secretary of the Communist party.

Party Control

This already helps to explain how the Communist party supervises the state apparatus of the Soviet Union. There is not only the *ideological norm* of party control, as expressed by the 1936 constitution—the Communist party is "the vanguard of the working people . . . and . . . the leading core of all organizations of the working people, both public and state"—but also an *overlapping of personnel* that unites the top executive offices of the state with the top policy-making organs of the party.

Both Stalin and Khrushchev, for example, eventually came to hold, simultaneously, the positions of chairman of the Council of Ministers and first party secretary. After Khrushchev's removal from his party and state posts in 1964, the party's Central Committee sought to check any revival of this kind of one-man rule by declaring that the two positions could no longer be held by a single individual. It was an important sign of the Communist party's determination to avoid any return to Stalinist-type dictatorship, and it also signaled the party's intent to maintain at least a nominal division of authority at the top.

Since 1964, Leonid Brezhnev has held the position of first party secretary (or general secretary, as the post was renamed in 1966), while Alexei Kosygin has continued as chairman of the Council of Ministers. But Kosygin, like Podgorny, sits in the party's highest body, the Political Bureau (or Politburo). And, in the early 1970s, two other Politburo members (K. T. Mazurov and D. S. Polyansky) occupied the positions of first deputy chairmen of the Council of Ministers, thereby demonstrating the party's intent to intervene directly in the functioning of the state apparatus, in part through overlapping personnel who hold top positions in both the party and the state.

That the undoubted number one man in the Soviet Union was Leonid Brezhnev testified again to the dominance of the Communist party in Soviet government, however formally distinguished the party hierarchy is from that of the state. Thus it now is appropriate to turn directly to the structure and functions of the Communist party of the Soviet Union (CPSU).

THE CPSU

Structure

In any revolutionary effort, the organization that captures power must undergo profound transformation as it attempts to consolidate power and to administer the state. It has already been pointed out that one of the strategic choices of the early Communist elite was to reorganize the state as an instrument of party rule, basing the structure of the state on the system of soviets (councils) that had begun to develop in revolutionary Russia in both 1905 and 1917.

Consolidating Power The CPSU further entrenched its power by means of the following actions:

1 Reorganizing Russia's military establishment around the Red Army
2 Creating a secret-police apparatus, successively referred to as the Cheka (established in December 1917), the OGPU, the NKVD, the MVD, and in 1953 (after the execution of the MVD's chief, L. Beria, and the return of the secret police to the party's control) the KGB
3 Subordinating the trade unions, after the mid-1920s, to the party in order to strengthen the party's control over the workers
4 Establishing a network of auxiliary organizations designed to extend the party's influence beyond the ranks of its immediate membership, for example, among youth and students, the Komsomol, Young Pioneers, and Little Octobrists—each appealing to a different age group, with Komsomol membership (from ages fourteen to twenty-eight) almost a prerequisite for entrance into a university and for eventual leadership of the CPSU itself

But how was the CPSU to control this far-flung apparatus designed to mobilize support for, and accomplish the objectives of, socialist construction? In part, as has already been seen in terms of party-state relationships, it exercises control through ideological leadership and overlapping personnel. In the latter category, one finds the top officials of the army, the secret police, the trade unions, and the party's auxiliary organizations also occupying top policy positions in the party. This in turn, however, has required the elaboration of a party apparatus that duplicates at every level the distribution of state and public responsibilities outside the party's hierarchy. The result is graphically represented in Figure 13.2

The Party Hierarchy The lines that connect the various levels of party organization depicted in Figure 13.2 suggest that party members at the base indirectly elect party elites at the top. Thus it appears that members of the Politburo and Secretariat are elected by, and are responsible to, the Central Committee, which in turn is elected by, and is responsible to, the periodic convocations of the All-Union Party Congress, which is supposed to convene every four years and which in turn is elected by, and is responsible to, the several republican party congresses—and so on down to individual party members collected together in their primary organizations.

One of the principles of political science, however, is that the more indirect the electoral process, the more elitist the result: the greater the opportunities for top executive and policy-making personnel to manipulate nominations and elections in order to entrench their own positions. And, in fact, the actual power relationships within the CPSU are precisely the opposite of those suggested by the lines denoting organizational relationships in Figure 13.2. Each level of the party's organization is subordinate to its immediately superior level, which controls the selection of personnel in the lower body and may intervene in any and all matters of decision making. But the key instrument of central control is in the vertical hierarchy of the party secretariats.

The Party Secretaries Lenin's ruling Politburo consisted largely of intellectuals and professional revolutionaries, most of whom preferred participation in policy making to the humdrum tasks of party organization and the implementation of policy decisions. Among the principal exceptions, however, was Joseph Stalin.

In 1922, Stalin was appointed head of the Secretariat of the party's Central Committee. He already had begun to assemble a far-flung apparatus of administrative control as commissar of the Workers' and Peasants' Inspectorate between 1919 and 1922. But it was especially through his position as first party secretary that Stalin was able to build a cadre of subordinate secretaries throughout the

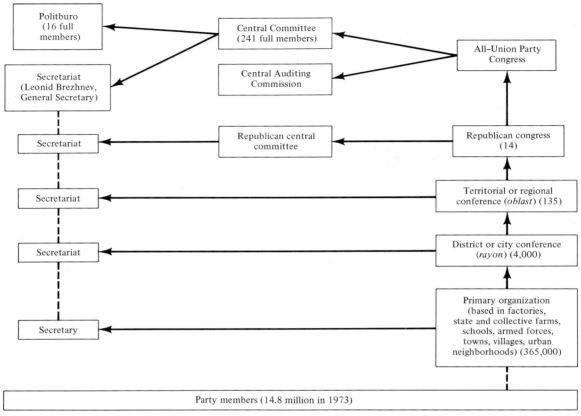

Figure 13.2 Organization of the Communist Party of the Soviet Union (CPSU).

party's hierarchy that proved more loyal to him than to Trotsky or to anyone else after Lenin's death in 1924. The purges of the 1930s, by eliminating almost all the party's cadres with revolutionary experience, further entrenched Stalin's position, and there were ominous signs that a new party purge was being prepared before Stalin's death in 1953. Another measure of Stalin's accumulation of power was his elimination of even the party as an instrument of policy making; no party congress was convened between 1939 and 1952, and after World War II Stalin ignored the Politburo by using only ad hoc committees of loyal subordinates.

It was no coincidence, then, that Stalin's immediate successor, Georgi Malenkov, was also first secretary of the party. But Malenkov resigned his position as first secretary in late 1953, apparently because he chose to concentrate his energies on the premiership as chairman of the Council of Ministers. It was a strategic mistake. Malenkov's successor as first secretary was Nikita Khrushchev, and by 1957 Khrushchev was firmly in command of both the party and state apparatus. And Khrushchev's successor after 1964 was First Secretary Leonid Brezhnev.

This illustrates the important point that the real center of power in the Soviet Union is in the CPSU and that the first or general secretary of the CPSU controls the party through his ability to manipulate the selection of personnel in the Politburo, the Central Committee, and the lower secretariats of the party's hierarchy. Just as General Secretary

Brezhnev exerts controlling influence over the executive organs of the All-Union Party Congress, party secretaries at the republican, *oblast, rayon,* and local levels of party organization exert similar influence over their own respective levels of party organization. The history of the Communist party of the Soviet Union and its prevailing power structure are dramatic confirmation of the argument that whoever controls the implementation of policy also controls the making of policy.

Functions

The primary function of the CPSU is to chart the course of Soviet economic, political, and social development. The party establishes general policy and oversees, through overlapping personnel and close consultation with state and public authorities, the implementation of general policy guidelines. The *state* apparatus of the Soviet Union is responsible for the more detailed elaboration and administration of party policies, thereby freeing the *party* for a broader and supervisory role in socioeconomic development. The party retains the right to intervene at every level of administration, and thus it is the keeper of the conscience and vision that impel Soviet society toward modernization and socialism and, ultimately (according to the regime's own definition), communism.

Responsibilities This means that the individual party member is expected to busy himself or herself (about 22 percent of the CPSU's members are women) with tasks that bring Soviet society closer to the goals established by the party. Party members are responsible for checking on the progress of the local government and economic bureaucracy in meeting the demands of the current economic plan. In agriculture, industry, transport, and housing and new factory construction, in the service sector of the economy, party members must see that planners, managers, and officials meet their assigned quotas. The party member functions as a prodder, agitator, and entrepreneur; he attempts to coordinate the efforts of workers and managers, suppliers and builders, citizens and public officials. It is the party member who sees that the most talented students gain entrance to the university and that the most productive workers in the factory receive their badges of merit and, perhaps, an annual vacation in a workers' resort on the Black Sea. Working mothers who have difficulty finding a day-care nursery for their children may go to their local party representative for help. If citizens in a particular area of the city are not adequately served by existing public transportation or if they lack public utilities, it is the local party personnel who threaten, cajole, convince, and effect compromises in the hope of resolving the problem.

The party member, then, must expect to work long hours without direct compensation. He or she may be temporarily separated from family and friends in response to the party's commitment to build a new factory in an underdeveloped region or to bring under cultivation vast tracts of land in Central Asia. On the collective or state farm, in the office or factory, the party member is expected to set an example for fellow workers by demonstrating constant commitment to the goals of socialist development. In brief, party members must inspire their fellow citizens; they must become models of work and thought that exemplify social consciousness and an unselfish dedication to the welfare of the greater society. Certainly the CPSU constitutes an elite within Soviet society, but it functions as a *mobilization elite* that is responsible for leading the whole society ever upward and onward toward the regime's social and economic goals. In this sense, Lenin's concept of the revolutionary vanguard and the subsequent development of the CPSU represent a major institutional innovation in modern political and social organization.

Motivation The history of the Soviet Union, however, also demonstrates that men and women cannot be constantly motivated by only *ideological zeal.* The correct performance of party tasks has also been motivated, especially in the 1930s, by *fear,* but also by *patriotism* and (an un-Marxist) love of country. This latter finds partial expression in the long-standing Russian passion (dating from at least Peter the Great) for catching up with the West and even for becoming economically like the West without duplicating the West's ideology or social structure. The Soviet population was urged to mobilize against German aggression in World War II not by exhortations to save socialism but through appeals to a deep-seated patriotism and for universal participation in the "great patriotic war." In this and in other less dramatic tasks, party members are expected to take the lead, constantly reminding their fellow citizens of the basic values and strategic goals of the society.

Another and especially strong motivation at work in Soviet society, obvious from the beginning of the First Five-Year Plan in 1928 and increasingly emphasized since World War II, is the familiar Western norm of *private incentive*. Party members (and nonparty workers) are motivated to achieve and excel by the advantages that result from superior performance. Better housing, the purchase and enjoyment of the more preferred articles of personal consumption, higher social status, access to better educational and employment opportunities, *and* influence on policy making are among the rewards that accrue to dedicated party members. It is in this sense, too, that the members of the CPSU constitute an elite of Soviet society.

Membership

The tendency in Western literature on the Soviet Union is to emphasize the elitist position of the Communist party, thereby at least implying the dictatorial rule of the party in Soviet society. As the above suggests, however, the CPSU has come to function as more of a coordinator and leader of Soviet society than as a dictator. Especially in a complex economy, it is more efficient to inspire workers to greater output and to motivate them through incentive than to intimidate them through fear and coercion. The nature of the elitist position of the CPSU thus requires careful analysis and interpretation.

In many respects, those who join the CPSU are self-selected. No one is compelled to join the party against his (or her) will. The party does not want the average citizen or worker. It wants the dedicated, not the self-serving. The student who distinguishes himself in school is likely to be asked to join the Komsomol (which in the early 1970s numbered about 27 million members). The citizen who distinguishes himself in his work is likely to be asked to join the party (which numbered more than 15 million members in 1974). And it is very important to note that CPSU membership has generally increased over the years, both in absolute numbers and as a percentage of the total Soviet population.

Growth At the time of the October Revolution in 1917 there were approximately 200,000 Bolsheviks, who constituted 0.12 percent of Russia's total population (of 160 million). By 1926, CPSU membership was 1,080,000, or 0.74 percent of the total population. Party membership reached 3.5 million in 1933, but Stalin's purges reduced the total to 1.9 million by 1938. New party recruits (and loyal Stalinists) raised the membership to 3.4 million in 1940, or 1.7 percent of the total population. In 1950, CPSU membership was 6.3 million, or 3.5 percent of the total population.

Party membership has consistently risen since Stalin's death in 1953, reflecting in part the liberalizing impact of the Khrushchev years and the elite's concern to broaden the mass base of the party as an agent of social mobilization. Thus by 1960 CPSU membership stood at 8.7 million, or 4.1 percent of the total population. In 1973 there were 14.8 million party members, who constituted almost 6 percent of the total population of the Soviet Union. If one counts only the percentage of the population that was eighteen years or older in the early 1970s, one out of every eleven Soviet citizens (9 percent) was a member of the Communist party.

The Political Activists This helps us to understand better the significance of the CPSU's elite status—and, in this case, from a comparative perspective. It is a truism of political science that government and politics are everywhere the affair of a minority. In the United States, for example, survey research (opinion polling) has found that fewer than one in three citizens participates in national election campaigns—which are, of course, the very heartbeat of any social organism that claims to be democratic. In its study of the 1956 presidential elections, the Survey Research Center of the University of Michigan found that only 29 percent of the population worked for a candidate or party, attended campaign meetings, spoke to friends or acquaintances about the political issues of the day, or even bothered to wear a campaign button.[4] A leading American political scientist, the late V. O. Key, Jr., defined the "political activists" in the United States as "the

---

[4]Angus Campbell, Philip E. Converse, Warren E. Miller, and Donald E. Stokes, *The American Voter*, John Wiley & Sons, Inc., New York, 1960, p. 91.

professional politicians, the semiprofessionals, and the highly placed individuals in corporate, associational, and community life who have political sidelines and connections."[5] Key concluded from his research that the political activists of the United States numbered "probably no more than 10 per cent of the population at the most."[6] And in 1974 a study by Common Cause reported that 1 percent of the United States population accounted for 90 percent of all campaign and election money, thereby ensuring a highly unequal distribution of political access among United States citizens.[7]

From this comparative perspective one might argue that the elite status of the Communist party of the Soviet Union is not at all an uncommon phenomenon of political life, in either relatively authoritarian or relatively democratic regimes. In fact, one perhaps should interpret the CPSU as *an institutionalized aggregation of the political activists and leading citizens of Soviet society.* Such an aggregation is bound to be a small minority of the citizens of any society; what is different about the Soviet Union is that this small minority is highly organized. These characteristics are likely to be found in any society where the ideology calls for rapid social and economic development. What is at issue is the extent to which this inevitable elite is "representative" of the total population.

Sociological Composition

Cultural Characteristics There is no doubt about the domination of the Great Russians, culturally and politically, over the other nationalities that made up tsarist Russia. An important dimension of *change* (rather than *continuity*) is the Communist regime's greater toleration of cultural diversity within the Soviet Union; there has been no officially enforced policy of "russification," and minority languages and traditional customs have not been suppressed, although they are often the vehicle for the Communist party's political communications to the population. And while many Jews may be denied rights enjoyed by Jews in other countries and even by other Soviet citizens, they are no longer herded into their synagogues and burned to death—as occasionally happened under the regime of the tsars.

But the CPSU, as a ruling elite, has itself become culturally diversified and thus more sociologically representative of the whole population of the Soviet Union. In 1965, for example, 62 percent of the CPSU's membership was of Russian nationality (while the Russians, in 1959, represented 55 percent of the Soviet population). Ukrainians constituted 15 percent of CPSU membership (18 percent of the total population); White Russians, 3.3 percent (3.8 percent of the total population); Georgians, 1.7 percent (1.3 percent of the total population); Armenians, 1.6 percent (1.4 percent of the total population); and Kazakhs, 1.5 percent (1.7 percent of the total population). All the other major nationalities have found approximate representation in the political elite according to their distribution in the total population of the Soviet Union.[8]

It also is true that ruling communist parties in Czechoslovakia, Yugoslavia, Albania, North Vietnam, and China have significantly strengthened the political representation of cultural groups that, before communism, were the underrepresented or suppressed populations of these particular societies. This is not to say that the policy-making process of these societies has been democratized. The data show, however, that the new authoritarian (Communist) elites are more culturally representative of the populations they govern than the authoritarian elites that preceded them.

Socioeconomic Characteristics This generalization also applies to the socioeconomic characteristics of Communist party membership. In the Soviet Union, the inspirational and leadership role of the CPSU in all the productive details of Soviet life is reinforced by the great diversity of occupations of party members. In 1967, only 7.4 percent of the CPSU's 12.7 million members were employed by

---

[5]V. O. Key, Jr., *Public Opinion and American Democracy*, Alfred A. Knopf, Inc., New York, 1961, p. 184.
[6]Ibid., p. 357.
[7]Reported in the *Los Angeles Times*, Apr. 21, 1974.

[8]These data are assembled from Soviet sources and are reported by David Lane in *Politics and Society in the USSR*, Random House, Inc., New York, 1971, table 7, p. 134. The membership of the Central Committee of the CPSU and the party's Politburo is also generally representative of the Soviet population's cultural characteristics. See Robert H. Donaldson, "The 1971 Soviet Central Committee: An Assessment of the New Elite," *World Politics*, vol. 24, no. 3, table 2, p. 387, April 1972.

the government or held positions in the party or economic bureaucracies; 13.7 percent held occupations in science, education, health, and culture; 25.2 percent were employed as factory workers; 17.1 percent were employed on collective or state farms; 7 percent were in the military; 6.6 percent were in transportation; 5.2 percent were in construction; and 6 percent were retired citizens living on state pensions. Other party members were employed in services and in other branches of the economy, such as trade or communications, or were students or housewives.[9]

This is hardly a picture of a narrowly based elite, isolated from the population and preoccupied with its own utopian visions of the future. The diversified occupational characteristics of the CPSU are instead appropriate to the party's principal task of social mobilization of the entire population for economic development.

The Elite of the Elite

Looking at the characteristics of the top elite within the CPSU itself, one also finds some important indicators of change over time.

Tsarist elites were drawn primarily from the aristocracy, and their high social status was more a function of ascriptive than achievement norms. The Bolshevik Revolution reversed these trends. Lenin's first government and close party collaborators were distinguished not by noble birth but by their intellectual and organizational abilities. Under Stalin, party elites were notable for their bureaucratic conformity and their skills as coercers as well as organizers, but a trend toward expertise in the management hierarchies of the party and the economy was apparent even during the Stalinist era.

A Managerial Bureaucracy It was especially obvious by the early 1970s that the top elite of the CPSU was made up of highly trained specialists who were skilled in the tasks of economic management. Brezhnev himself was trained in metallurgical engineering; Kosygin was a textile engineer and manager of an industrial plant before his promotion to top posts in the party and state hierarchies; and Podgorny had earned a degree in engineering and was a specialist in agricultural production. In fact,

of the 241 full members of the CPSU Central Committee constituted in 1971, 56 percent had professional management experience in the agricultural or industrial sectors of the economy.[10] And while in 1970 only about 6 percent of the total Soviet population twenty years and older had completed higher education, 92 percent of the 1971 Central Committee's full members had completed higher education (only 10 percent of these had received their education from special party schools); the comparable figure for the 1956 Central Committee was 86 percent.[11]

The organization of the CPSU Central Committee also makes clear the importance of educational and professional competence, as Central Committee members carry out their supervisory functions among ministries and departments of the state; the Central Committee has parallel departments for agriculture, science, higher education, heavy industry, light industry, machine construction, the chemical industry, construction, transportation, trade, finance, and planning.[12] It is obvious that party members, especially in the top elite, have to develop their own areas of expertise if they are to exercise supervisory control over the activities of bureaucrats in the state and economic hierarchies. And continued policy control by the party depends in part on the continuing professionalization of its leadership and cadres.

The Secularization of Power This in turn has important implications for the policy choices of elites, who may be persuaded less by the ideological formulas of earlier days than by the practical requirements of science and industry. Decision making tends to be more pragmatic as the party becomes an elite of technocrats. And ideology tends to be less compelling as the revolutionary experience and the dramas of collectivization and early industrial development recede into the distant past.

In 1962, 39 percent of the CPSU's total membership had less than ten years of party service; by 1965, this figure had increased to 43 percent, and it is by now well over half of the total party membership. Of the 241 full members of the 1971 Central

---

[9]Lane, op. cit., table 8b, p. 135.

[10]Donaldson, op. cit., p. 393.
[11]Ibid., p. 391.
[12]See the complete listing in Lane, op. cit., pp. 210–211.

Committee, 60 percent had been born between 1920 and 1937.[13] Thus there are many party members throughout the CPSU and in the party's top elite who have had no direct experience with either the Revolution or the numbing discipline imposed by Stalin.

These, too, are important measures of change in the Soviet Union, where the party's role in state and society should be understood less in terms of coercion than management. And it well may be that, in this respect, the contemporary Soviet Union only dramatizes the characteristics of all advanced industrial states: rule by bureaucracies and policy making by technocrats.

THE SOVIET PLANNED ECONOMY

There is, however, one fundamental dimension of Soviet society that has not changed and probably never will: the planned economy.

This is understandable because the very definition of socialism in the Soviet Union includes the state's ownership of all the means of production, which necessarily implies the state's supervision of economic activity. *Private* ownership of factories and land, for Marxists and Leninists, means exploitation of those who work by those who own. But if ownership is placed in the hands of the state *and* if the state is representative of all the people, exploitation is abolished. Or so the argument goes.

Soviet experience, however, suggests that this may be more a manipulation of definitions than a fundamental change in the real world of the worker. And Marx and Lenin obviously failed to anticipate the extent to which state ownership of the means of production, as compared with the capitalist system, might entail a more intensified exploitation of the worker: The managers replace the capitalists, the state directs the managers, the party supervises the state, and the demands placed upon the worker are only heightened by the system's identification with the general welfare. The most crushing oppression is typically justified in terms of the will of all the people. But it is important to remember (as was pointed out in Chapter 7) that authoritarianism is not a *necessary* consequence of state ownership and a planned economy. The values of elites and the characteristics of political culture must be taken into account. In the case of the Soviet Union, however, it is understandable that the authoritarianism traditional to Russian society would also find expression in the state's socialization of the means of production and economic planning.

The Five-Year Plans

As was discussed above, the New Economic Policy initiated by Lenin in 1921 was continued until 1928. By this time Stalin had consolidated his power over party and state, and the Soviet economy had recovered from the destruction wrought by World War I, the February and October Revolutions, and the civil war. But the state had continued to play a prominent economic role even during the NEP. Large industries had been controlled by the state as "trusts," and the Supreme Economic Council had fixed prices and appointed the members of boards of directors.

Basic Principles and Goals of Soviet Planning This system of economic control was nevertheless considered inadequate for rapid economic development. The basic assumption was that all details of production and distribution could be rationally planned by the state, and in the context of accelerated growth. In keeping with the primary goals of the national economic plan, resources could be allocated to specific industries, production targets fixed for each factory and every worker, and distribution regulated in terms of the needs of national defense, citizen consumption, and further economic development.

The state commission responsible for devising and administering the plan—"Gosplan," from the Russian syllables making up "State Planning Committee"—had been in place during the NEP. But in 1928 Gosplan was ordered to draw up a five-year plan that would raise dramatically the Soviet Union's production of coal, iron, and steel. The First Five-Year Plan was declared fulfilled in 1932, and the Second Five-Year Plan was launched in 1933. Although the Second Five-Year Plan was devoted to the same objectives of heavy industrialization, it was better organized than its predecessor, and its goals were more realistic. By the time of its completion the Soviet Union had raised its total national product from 70 to 90 percent over the

[13]Donaldson, loc. cit.

relatively short space of ten years. The emphasis on heavy industry worked to the advantage of the Soviet Union in its defense against German aggression during World War II. But heavy industry had been emphasized to the disadvantage of consumer goods production, and it had entailed the subordination of agriculture and the Russian peasantry to the demands of rapid industrialization.

Collectivization It in fact was assumed in 1928 that the agricultural sector of the Soviet economy had to be radically restructured if the goals of the First Five-Year Plan were to be achieved. Food had to be supplied to the growing cities and industrial centers. Thus agricultural production had to be made more efficient and, consequently, mechanized. Mechanization in turn required the consolidation of small peasant holdings into large tracts of land. The resulting surplus of agricultural population would provide more workers for industry. And it was important to break the back of peasant resistance to Communist power, which could be accomplished by eradicating the peasant village.

Stalin thus initiated the collectivization of Soviet agriculture in 1929, and by early 1930 approximately one-half of Russia's peasant farms had been integrated into a system of collective farms *(kolkhozi)*. Reluctant peasants were threatened with death or deportation, and perhaps as many as 5 million lost their lives because of the coercion of the program and the famine that followed the peasants' widespread destruction of livestock and agricultural produce. But by 1934 collectivization was virtually complete, and in 1938, 99 percent of the land was under the cultivation of 240,000 collective farms.

Thus the agricultural sector of the Soviet economy, and the interests of both rural and urban consumers, could continue to be subordinated to the demands of heavy industrial development—which was emphasized in the five-year plans that were launched successively in 1938, 1946 (this plan was delayed by World War II), 1951, and 1956. This last and Sixth Five-Year Plan was discarded in 1957; it was admitted that the plan was overly ambitious, but there also were mounting political and economic problems that demanded serious attention. A Seven-Year Plan was adopted in 1959, but this and subsequent plans (including the plan adopted in 1971) have been increasingly modified on a yearly basis; annual budgetary expenditures and guidelines are more controlling, and there is an apparent trend away from long-range economic projections. This is appropriate to the more advanced stages of development now attained by the Soviet economy *and* to the declining utopian mentality of Soviet leaders. It also suggests again some of the problems characteristic of Soviet planning.

Problems

Soviet experience does argue forcefully for the possibility of rapid economic development, through central planning and rigidly enforced controls, of basic industry.

But once the heavy industrial base has been laid, planning mechanisms must be adjusted to conform to an ever more sophisticated economy. It becomes increasingly difficult to program all the details of a modernizing economy, and insistence on rigid centralization tends to heighten inefficiency, waste, and even corruption. To increase economic efficiency, centralized controls must be relaxed (not necessarily eliminated); more autonomy must be delegated to managers; a system of distribution that adjusts supply to demand (instead of to command) must be introduced in strategic sectors of the economy, especially those related to consumer goods; and more incentive has to be allowed for producers and decision makers throughout the economic hierarchy.

Incentive and the Peasant's Private Plot The problem of incentive is illustrated especially well by the conditions of Soviet agriculture. Russian peasants are organized into either collective or state farms. Peasants on state farms (which now number about 13,400) are salaried employees and are considered the agricultural counterparts to workers in a factory. The larger percentage of peasants live and work on collective farms (which number 35,600), and each peasant household is given a small amount of land (about $1^1/_2$ acres) to farm as it pleases, with the proceeds from the sale of the produce going exclusively to the family. Soviet authorities admit that there has been a constant struggle to induce the peasant to expend as much energy on the collective as he does on his private plot. And while private plots represent about 0.2 percent of all area cultivated in the Soviet Union, they account for about 17 percent of total agricultural output. In 1966 the government newspaper *Izvestia* (*Pravda* is the party's newspaper) reported that private plots accounted for 6 percent of the Soviet Union's crop yield, 42 percent of meat and dairy products, 64 percent of potatoes, 75 percent of poultry products, and almost the entire percentage of fruit production.

Workers and Consumers Soviet planners have also recognized that private incentive is an important source of motivation for industrial workers. In the 1920s and 1930s, wage differentials were increased, and the effects of the piecework system (payment according to units produced instead of time on the job) were exaggerated by bonuses and rewards given to those who exceeded production quotas. The Stakhanovite movement (workers who are aided by fellow workers to vastly overfulfill their quotas) also helped to create an aristocracy of workers, but the disposable income of all workers remained at a low level, and there was not much to buy with even the money that was earned from overfulfilling production quotas. Consumer goods were in short supply and of poor quality, and the *real income* of workers did not regain its 1928 level until 1952. While Soviet workers are much better off than the average person alive in the world today, their per capita consumption is approximately one-half that of citizens in Western Europe and one-fourth that of citizens in the United States,[14] and this in an economy (with great natural resources) that claims to be socialist and in a society that promises its citizens a life that is better than life under capitalism.

The Quota System The distortions worked by rigid central planning, however, are especially obvious in precisely those categories of production and distribution which directly affect the living styles and consumption patterns of Soviet citizens. According to the principles of Soviet economic planning, the needs of consumers are as susceptible to rational calculation as the needs of defense, heavy industry, and the Soviet space program. Gosplan and its many departments and commissions thus determine how many sewing machines or television sets or raincoats should be produced to meet consumer needs according to the outlines of the current plan and anticipated consumer demand. The quantity of goods to be produced is specified, along with the appropriate performance indices, and these specifications are passed along the planning hierarchy to the planning commissions at the republic and *oblast* levels. Further details are added, and production responsibilities are allocated to local units, down to particular factories, worker brigades, and even individual workers.

In a controlled economy it is difficult to measure the total *cost* of production. But it is even more difficult to measure the value of *output*, which is distorted by whatever criterion is adopted. If workers and factories are assigned quotas based on the *quantity* of raincoats produced (for example), the tendency is to manufacture the cheapest and poorest-quality raincoat because more of them can be produced. If *weight* is the measure of paper production, a paper factory will concentrate on producing heavy wrapping paper and will neglect the production of paper suitable for stationery and for other office and consumer use. If *size* is the measure of production for construction siding, the largest panels will be produced, and much will be wasted by cutting and fitting on the construction site.

This still says nothing about the waste and inefficiencies that result when factories hoard materials and supplies so that production schedules can be maintained; when managers falsify reports so that they can receive their bonuses or keep their jobs; when "storming" takes place on the assembly line and construction site at the end of the production period so that quotas can be met; when workers and managers refuse to exceed established quotas by too much because new and higher quotas will be assigned; when cases of inefficiency and corruption are concealed because reports to the authorities would threaten the patronage system of supply and commendation worked out covertly by managers and officials; and so on.

It should quickly be added that most of what we know about the problems of the Soviet economy, particularly in terms of consumer goods production, comes directly from the press and public

---

[14]These and other relevant economic data are summarized by Robert G. Wesson in *The Soviet Russian State*, John Wiley & Sons, Inc., New York, 1972, pp. 82, 236.

officials in the Soviet Union. This at least suggests an abiding concern to correct some of the more flagrant irrationalities of a planning system that is supposed to be rational.

Attempts at Reform

It seems apparent now that Stalin's death in 1953 marked the end of Soviet rule according to the heavy-handed methods of oppression and terror. Well before the Twentieth Congress of the CPSU in 1956, the new Soviet leaders had made it clear that they preferred inducement to coercion, and peaceful coexistence to international tension. But the Twentieth Congress, publicly and semiprivately through Khrushchev's detailed denunciation of Stalin's "crimes," did indeed dramatize the regime's efforts to seek new directions, both at home and abroad.

These efforts were at least in part motivated by the leadership's awareness of the need for economic reform. Stalinist economic controls may have been suitable to the early stages of industrialization and collectivization, but their effectiveness had obviously declined with economic growth. And, too, it was important to pay closer attention to the ideology's specification of life-styles for Soviet citizens that were superior to the standard of living in the West.

After Stalin's death, Malenkov thus came to represent policies that called for greater attention to the consumer goods sector of the economy. Khrushchev, the eventual victor in the struggle for power, also vowed to improve consumer goods production, but he emphasized the importance of solving once and for all the problems of Soviet agriculture. His principal solution was to bring under cultivation the millions of acres of "virgin farmlands" in Central Asia. He also sought to reform the planning and administrative process and to revivify the party—in part by encouraging the turnover of lower-cadre personnel.

By 1964 all these efforts had failed, and Khrushchev consequently lost his majority position in the party's Central Committee. The virgin farmlands were plagued by marginal rainfall, and the harvest of 1963 was so disastrous that large quantities of grain had to be imported. The Soviet Union's foreign exchange was thus expended for bread instead of for the Western equipment and technology needed for advanced industrial development. Khrushchev's attempted reforms of the planning process also threatened the entrenched bureaucracy, and his frequent reorganization of the administration of agriculture (on at least five separate occasions) only confused the already complex lines of bureaucratic responsibility. The Central Committee's vote to remove Khrushchev from office in fact resembled the action of a board of directors that ousts a corporate director for mismanagement. Brezhnev's emergence as the party's new first secretary seems to have been the result of a compromise reached by the Central Committee's members, not the consequence of any play for power by Brezhnev. The entire proceeding was a dramatic comment on the Soviet Union's changing styles of decision making—less command and more bargaining, at least within the top echelons of the party.

Libermanism Khrushchev's successors, however, were also committed to economic reform. The first efforts toward "Libermanism" (following the proposals of Yevsei Liberman and other Soviet professors of economics) were initiated in 1965. The intent was to establish a partial free market in selected consumer goods industries, linking factory production through retailers to consumer demand instead of to the quota system imposed by central planners. Factory managers were given more autonomy in buying their primary materials, in determining the allocation of their work force, and in adjusting wages, and they were encouraged to negotiate directly with retail outlets in the setting of prices. The positive results of these innovations encouraged additional proposals, including the charging of interest on state bank loans to factories. This particular proposal had been previously rejected as an insidious capitalist device, but it now was argued that an interest charge on industrial loans would help to ensure that the money would be put promptly and efficiently to use; previously, loans had been applied for even when there was no immediate prospect for plant expansion or for any other change in the factory's organization of production.

The thrust of these and other economic reforms in the mid-1960s was in the direction of "market socialism" for a limited but important sector of the Soviet economy. The authority of central planners was being reduced to the advantage of managers, retailers, and consumers. The more grandiose promises of the Khrushchev years (including the unrealized projection of spectacular increases in per capita meat consumption and the promise issued by the Twenty-second Party Congress in 1961 that the foundations of communism would be laid by the 1980s) were abandoned or ignored. In agriculture, the Brezhnev-Kosygin emphasis was on more intensive cultivation of existing farmlands, with production yields raised through the use of chemical fertilizers. Reality seemed to be taking over from ideology. But after the ill-fated economic and political reforms attempted in Czechoslovakia before the Soviet-led invasion of 1968, market socialism became a taboo subject in the Soviet Union—and it was explicitly repudiated by Professor Liberman as "un-Leninist." There were, however, even more compelling reasons explaining the derailment of the economic reforms advanced in the mid-1960s.

The Inertia of Bureaucracy The inauguration of the Brezhnev-Kosygin regime in 1964 signaled a reconsolidation of the party's administrative authority, which had been threatened by Khrushchev's reforms. There was also a narrowing of the boundaries of discussion and debate, boundaries that had been broadened in the decade after Stalin's death. And by the early 1970s it seemed that reconstituted party authority and basic economic change had proved to be incompatible. The attempts to decentralize planning, to grant factory managers more autonomy, and to introduce supply-demand mechanisms in place of the quota system of production had undermined the authority of the party and had weakened the position of entrenched bureaucracies in the state and the economy. The point is sufficiently important to merit repetition: In brief, economic reform threatens bureaucratic power, and once the planning system is in place, it develops an inertia of its own that is highly resistant to change.

These generalizations do not apply only to the Soviet Union. In the United States, one of the principal reasons for the failure of the War on Poverty program launched by the Johnson administration in the mid-1960s was the hostility of city and state politicians and administrators; the new federal program threatened their own local bases of power and patronage. In all modern states, however authoritarian or democratic, it is easier to continue with the old than it is to start anew.

TRENDS AND PROJECTIONS

This is not to say that, in the Soviet Union and elsewhere, piecemeal and incremental change does not take place—even though it may be long overdue and only a partial solution to perennial problems. The increasing "technological lag" between the Soviet economy and the advanced industrial economies of the noncommunist world has compelled the Soviet Union to seek closer trading relationships with the West, which means continuation of a foreign policy of peaceful coexistence. By 1974, for example, the Soviet Union and the United States were searching for some common ground in order to negotiate a reduction in armaments, while trading contracts between the Soviet Union and United States suppliers had been or were being negotiated in areas such as commercial jet aircraft, electronics, truck and automobile manufacturing, fertilizers, petroleum, and natural gas. In 1971 United States exports to the Soviet Union totaled $161 million; the figure in 1972 was $547 million, and it was $1 billion in 1973. In July 1973 Soviet Ambassador Dobrynin pointed out that the United States was fast becoming the Soviet Union's number one trading partner.

Nor is the CPSU's monopoly of control over all aspects of the economy a foregone conclusion. In March 1970 the Central Committee admitted the necessity of improving economic efficiency by permitting the organization of vertical industrial corporations, even though such corporations cut across the geographic zones of party control at local and regional levels. In the same year, profitability was introduced as a means of determining wholesale prices on industrial equipment. More recently (in 1974), consumers and retail outlets were given the right to return poor-quality goods or to receive a total refund of their money. Advertising was also encouraged as a means of improving sales and distribution, and Soviet trade officials signed contracts with two Western marketing firms in order to make more attractive the advertising, design, and packaging of Soviet products.

And, for the first time in the history of Soviet planning, the five-year plan initiated in 1971 projected a larger increase in the production of consumer goods (44 to 48 percent) than in the production of producer goods (41 to 45 percent). Meeting the objectives in this former category, however, has always been more difficult than fulfilling the quotas for heavy industry. The 1971 plan nevertheless represented an important change in the priorities of Soviet planners. And if inflation and lagging growth rates in noncommunist states continue to pose insoluble problems for policy makers, it is likely that the quality of life of Soviet citizens will, within the next two or three decades, approximate that of citizens in other industrialized countries of the world. The major issue, then, may be less in terms of "communism" versus "capitalism" than in terms of the rich nations against the poor.

Economics, Politics, and Society

It should be apparent from the preceding sections of this chapter that economic change in the Soviet Union has brought with it important changes in the politics and social structure of Soviet society. Khrushchev's efforts toward de-Stalinization and economic reform reflected, in part, the Soviet economy's growth beyond the stage of basic industrialization. And it is very difficult, and increasingly inefficient, to impose centralized authority and coercive control on a complex economy and an ever more literate and informed citizenry. With economic modernization, decision making becomes more complex; broad social goals are less self-evident and thus more difficult to define; and new types of interests and categories of decision makers tend to emerge.

It has been argued, in fact, that economic development in the Soviet Union has brought about a "pluralization" of the decision-making process. Scientists, educators, economists, new generations of party cadres, state administrators, factory managers, and those whose interests are identified with the military, with heavy industry, or with the consumer goods sector of the economy all claim a role in policy making and may—depending on the issue and the cohesion of the top elite—compete with one another and with the party at a remarkably high level of *political* intensity.

Liberalization As compared with the Stalinist era of fear, secrecy, and repression, there also has been an indisputable liberalization of citizen life. This trend is perhaps best illustrated by basic reforms in Soviet law and jurisprudence. In the 1950s and 1960s, the powers of the secret police were substantially curtailed. Military courts were stripped of most of their powers over civilians. Citizens can no longer be held responsible for the criminal acts of their associates or relatives. The principle that confession alone is proof of complicity in cases of treason has been repudiated. The burden of proof in all court cases now rests upon the prosecution, and Soviet citizens accused of crime—as in most Western countries—are presumed innocent until proved guilty. In some cases of misdemeanor offenses and "antisocialist" behavior, the judicial process has been decentralized, and, since the 1950s, an extensive apparatus of citizen tribunals (or "comrades courts," which now number approximately 300,000) has sprung up at the grass-roots level of Soviet society. In the late 1950s there was a systematic review of all persons convicted of counterrevolutionary crimes during the Stalinist era; the great majority of those who had survived were released from labor camps, and their criminal records were erased. The trend toward procedural due process of law in the Soviet Union has obviously coincided with a marked decline in the use of terror as an instrument of government. And the restricted use of capital punishment for economic crimes (involving black-market operations, hoarding, and corruption) is only a vivid reminder of the different values that support a system appealing to social consciousness instead of private gain.[15]

An equally important measure of liberalization and political change in the Soviet Union is the fate of those who have fallen from power. Many of the old Bolsheviks liquidated by Stalin during the purges were exonerated, and their place in history rehabilitated, during the Khrushchev years. And since the execution of L. Beria and his fellow henchmen in the secret police (between 1953 and 1956), there have been no political executions. The power struggle that ended with Khrushchev's triumph in 1957 was not sealed by the liquidation or exile of Malen-

---

[15]See especially Harold J. Berman, *Justice in the USSR*, Harvard University Press, Cambridge, Mass., 1963.

kov, Molotov, Bulganin, or any of the other defeated contenders. In 1964 Khrushchev was retired with a pension to his country home and was given the use of an apartment in Moscow and a chauffeured limousine. These critical shifts in the allocation of high political power, in both 1957 and 1964, were accompanied by extensive debate and political maneuvering among the hundred or more members of the party's Central Committee. Brezhnev's consolidation of his position in the Politburo in 1971 and in 1973 was accomplished primarily by adding Brezhnev supporters instead of by eliminating his occasional adversaries. With economic development, pluralization, and liberalization, the decision-making process of the Soviet Union has become more competitive—even *political*.

This is not to project a trend in the Soviet Union toward what we might call "democracy." Indeed, from a broad historical perspective, it may be that the viability of democratic institutions and the number and influence of those who subscribe to democratic ideals are on the decline. If this is true, the contemporary Soviet Union may represent in many ways a projection of our own particular future: technocracy; bureaucracy; a greater concern for creature comforts than for popular participation in policy making; a consequent emphasis on consumerism, political stability, and law and order, to the advantage of authoritarian elites who can make good on such demands; the declining relevance of old ideologies and social ideals (whether those of liberalism, socialism, or communism); and an increasingly rigid social structure in which prevailing elites pass on to their children the advantages of education, professional status, and power.

It is important that those who oppose these trends (including the authors of this book) guard the sanctity of their ideals with action as well as words. Effective action, however, also depends on understanding, and the development of a better understanding of the American political process is the intent of the following pages.

STUDY-GUIDE QUESTIONS

1 To what extent does the regime established in Russia by the Bolsheviks represent a continuation of the characteristics and patterns of tsarist rule?
2 How does the CPSU attempt to ensure its control over the policies and administrative activities of the Soviet state?
3 Where in the CPSU is power concentrated, and how is it organized?
4 What are the implications for revolutionary ideology of the professionalization of political elites?
5 What is the meaning of "Libermanism," and what are some of the obstacles to basic economic reform in the Soviet Union?

REFERENCES

Barghoorn, Frederick A.: *Politics in the USSR*, 2d ed., Little, Brown and Company, Boston, 1972.
Berman, Harold J.: *Justice in the USSR*, 2d ed., Harvard University Press, Cambridge, Mass., 1963.
Conquest, Robert (ed.): *Soviet Nationalities Policy in Practice*, Frederick A. Praeger, Inc., New York, 1967.
Dallin, Alexander, and Thomas B. Larson: *Soviet Politics since Khrushchev*, Prentice-Hall, Inc., Englewood Cliffs, N.J., 1968.
────── and Alan F. Westin (eds.): *Politics in the Soviet Union: 7 Cases*, Harcourt, Brace & World, Inc., New York, 1966.
Fainsod, Merle: *How Russia Is Ruled*, Harvard University Press, Cambridge, Mass., 1963.
Lane, David: *Politics and Society in the USSR*, Random House, Inc., New York, 1971.
Meyer, Alfred G.: *The Soviet Political System*, Random House, Inc., New York, 1965.
Nove, Alec: *The Soviet Economy*, 2d ed., Frederick A. Praeger, Inc., New York, 1969.
Schapiro, Leonard: *The Communist Party of the Soviet Union*, 2d ed., Random House, Inc., New York, 1970.
Skilling, H. G., and F. Griffiths: *Interest Groups in Soviet Politics*, Princeton University Press, Princeton, N.J., 1971.
Spulber, Nicholas: *The Soviet Economy: Structure, Principles, Problems*, W. W. Norton & Company, Inc., New York, 1969.
Tatu, Michel: *Power in the Kremlin: From Khrushchev to Kosygin*, The Viking Press, Inc., New York, 1970.
Treadgold, Donald W.: *Twentieth Century Russia*, Rand McNally & Company, Chicago, 1959.
Wesson, Robert G.: *The Soviet Russian State*, John Wiley & Sons, Inc., New York, 1972.

PART THREE

STATE AND CITIZEN: GOVERNMENT IN ACTION

Chapter 14

The Voice of the People: Public Opinion

We turn now to a consideration of the ways and means by which an individual relates to the political environment. The focus of attention is the role that the citizen plays when interacting with other citizens and groups and with the political institutions in society.

The next three chapters seek answers to such questions as the following: How does one develop attitudes and opinions about politics? Are there patterns of conflict and consensus among the myriad of individual opinions expressed by the citizenry? Can these beliefs be related to public policy by governmental action? Why do people behave the way they do in political situations, some willing to participate in the political process and others feeling alienated? What role do groups play in mobilizing opinions to promote certain specific interests? And, finally, how do political parties serve to link the citizen to the governmental apparatus?

Western political democracy was born during the Golden Age of ancient Greece. Whether myth or reality, the inspiring ideal of pure democracy has ever been the robed Greek citizen assembled with his peers in open forum, freely debating the burning issues of the day, challenging the opposition, eloquently stating his own views, and then personally casting his vote to create the law of the land. The early institutional development of democracy is identified with the era of the distinguished Greek general and statesman Pericles, about 500 B.C. Philosophical speculations over democratic principles took place during the next two centuries, long after the institutional framework for direct popular participation in government was on the wane. In his classic commentary *The Republic,* Plato rejected the thesis that the decision-making power of government should rest in the hands of the citizenry, while Aristotle, in *Politics,* endorsed the principle as only the second best of several alternatives.

Pure Democracy: The Rational Model

The sharing of political power by both government and the citizenry through direct popular participation and the universal opportunity to hold public office became the historic symbols of Greek democracy. It is doubtful whether any substantial portion of the Greek citizenry had the leisure time, the economic status, or even the inclination to participate personally in the government. However, the Athenian's conviction that he had a right to formulate and criticize public policy laid the foundation for the belief that in a democratic government, public opinion is the "voice of the people."

The practice of direct democracy virtually disappeared after the Greek experience, to emerge only infrequently in Western history through such institutions as the tiny *Landesgemeinde,* or village assemblies, in Switzerland and the town meetings in early New England. The concept of popular sovereignty and the implicit right of revolution propounded in the writings of John Locke and Thomas Jefferson prepared the way for a revival of the notion of the "will of the people." The growth of the institutions of representative government and the democratization of the suffrage reinforced this belief and prepared the way for an uncritical view of the role of public opinion in a democratic society.

The broadening acceptance of the democratic philosophy led to several generalizations, which, taken together, constituted the prevalent view of the role of public opinion in a representative democracy: (1) that the public was interested in public policy; (2) that the public was informed; (3) that it would deliberate and reach rational conclusions; (4) that rationally conceived individual opinions would tend to be held uniformly throughout the social order; (5) that the public, having reached a conclusion, would make its will known at the polls and elsewhere; (6) that the public's will, or at least the views of the majority, would be enacted into law; and (7) that continued surveillance and constant criticism would ensure the maintenance of an enlightened public opinion and consequently a public policy based upon the principles of social morality and justice.

During the late nineteenth and early twentieth centuries, the rational model of public opinion underwent scrutiny by a number of noted scholars. James Bryce, the British historian, mingled with party workers, political bosses, lobbyists, and the various strata of the American voting public. In his classic studies, *Modern Democracies* and *The American Commonwealth,* he came to the conclusion that the average American citizen is not particularly aware of the prevailing issues of public policy until they are brought to his or her attention by small energetic groups bent upon promoting a specific issue. In *Public Opinion in War and Peace,* A. Lawrence Lowell, a former president of Harvard University, also questioned the concept of an all-embracing public and the possibility of a universally held opinion.

The attack upon the traditional concept of public opinion shifted gradually to a closer examination of the assumption that public opinion is the result of individual personalities, attitudes, and behavior. Walter Lippmann, in two penetrating studies entitled *Public Opinion* and *The Phantom Public,* called attention to the impact of man's environment on the opinion-forming process. Lippmann argued that the individual's political ideas are formulated to a great extent by information and impressions that he receives from the world around him. Because of the complexity of modern civilization, he is dependent upon sources other than personal experience—such as newspapers, radios, pictures, and word-of-mouth accounts by others—for much of his information. According to this view, the individual's opinions are based upon incomplete knowledge of the real world outside, and the combination of memory, imagination, prejudice, emotion, and fragmentary information prevents him from making rational judgments on matters of public policy.

Public Opinion: A Reassessment

In the decades following the close of World War II, political scientists rather belatedly applied many of the findings of psychologists on the nature of man, and of sociologists on the characteristics of groups, to the phenomena of politics. To the research hypotheses viewing man idealistically in terms of how he should behave (normative standards) were added scientific investigations of his actual behavior (empirical data). In a more general sense, attention was diverted from the nature of the state per se to the characteristics of *society* and its *inhabitants*: to the distribution of power, to leadership and followership, to group behavior, and to bureaucracy.[1]

The new assessment produced a redefinition of the nature of public opinion and the relationship of the concept to the decision-making process in government. A realistic view of the voting behavior of the American electorate, for instance, revealed that a substantial number of citizens are uninformed on key issues of public policy upon which they pass judgment, that as many as one-third admit from time to time that they have "no opinion" on legislation of national importance, and that others vote under the misapprehension that candidates agree with their interpretations of partisan issues. It was discovered that policy makers are more often than not inattentive to any of the voices of public opinion, with the exception of those few constituents who help to elect them to office.

The stereotype of a "public" proved to be a myth and has been replaced with the concept of a myriad of "publics," while "opinion" has ceased to be thought of as a disembodied voice but rather as the view of a single individual. Finally, "public opinion" now represents the collectivity of individual opinions of a designated public. It is in this context that the term will be used in this discussion. Indeed, the assumption that public opinion has any measurable effect upon the formulation of public policy has been questioned.

The model of the fictitious "rational man" participating collectively in creating a rational public policy in an ideal state has been placed in proper perspective. The attention of social scientists has turned toward such matters as the nature of the opinion-forming process, the politicization of the individual, the linkage between mobilized segments of the opinion-holding public and the governmental process, and the distribution of power and influence throughout society.

New models such as the "authoritarian-leadership" and "elitist" interpretations of how the public participates in the governing process have been explored. From these new perspectives the role of the individual in the process of governance is being assessed once again. For as Professor V. O. Key, Jr., stated so succinctly, "unless mass views have some place in shaping public policy, all talk about democracy is nonsense."[2]

Most contemporary observers would agree, but the search for the connection between mass views and public policy has proved to be a major challenge. For example, an area of considerable importance to all American citizens is the nature of the constitutional system. A National Opinion Research Center survey concerning the Bill of Rights, released in November 1945, produced the following:[3]

Question:	What do you know about the Bill of Rights?	
Responses:	Never heard of it	28%
	Heard, but don't know what it is	36%
	Know what it is	21%
	Confused	4%
	Wrong	5%
	Part wrong—part right	3%
	Don't know	3%

Almost three decades later, however, the Columbia Broadcasting System polled a different audience about the meaning of the Bill of Rights. The document was not mentioned by name, and the questions asked were in the form of problems relating to its specific provisions. The findings indicated a far greater degree of sophistication. Although the respondents were unwilling to part with certain judi-

---

[1] The approach to public opinion in this chapter is based upon American sources, and the analysis relates to American publics. For a summary and guide to pertinent English, French, and especially German literature on the origin of the expression "public opinion," see Paul A. Palmer, "Public Opinion in Political Theory," in Carl Wittke (ed.), *Essays in History and Political Theory*, Russell and Russell, New York, 1936, p. 236 and passim. See also Hans Speier, "Historical Development of Public Opinion," *American Journal of Sociology*, vol. 55, no. 4, Jan. 1950, pp. 376–388. Early challengers to traditional views included A. Lawrence Lowell in *Public Opinion in War and Peace*, Harvard University Press, Cambridge, Mass., 1923; and Walter Lippmann in *Public Opinion*, Harcourt, Brace and Co., Inc., New York, 1922; and *The Phantom Public*, The Macmillan Co., New York, 1927.

[2] V. O. Key, Jr., *Public Opinion and American Democracy*, Alfred A. Knopf, Inc., New York, 1961, p. 7.

[3] Ibid., p. 51. The CBS survey referred to below is reported in Robert Chandler, *Public Opinion: Changing Attitudes on Contemporary Political and Social Issues*, R. R. Bowker Company, New York, 1972, pp. 4–6.

cial guarantees, such as trial by jury, when described in this manner, more than three-fourths of them were willing to restrict some of the basic freedoms in order to control group protests and vocal dissent when such disruptive activity threatens the established law and order. The groups most frequently opposed to the guaranteed freedoms were identified as women, older people, and the least well educated.

Both studies reveal areas of knowledge and ignorance on the part of individuals constituting the public and illustrate some of the intricacies involved in probing the nature of public opinion. No one can "wish it away." Not only has the practice of polling the public's views become institutionalized in American political society, but the use of polls also is inextricably a part of the popular concept of the democratic political process. The political environment is impregnated with the incantations and rituals of government officials responding to the "will of the people."

We propose to examine briefly some of the findings of scholars who have addressed their attention to this phenomenon called "public opinion" within a specified frame of reference. First, we shall discuss the process of socialization of the individual in political matters—his or her maturation and early relations with the major institutions that bring about politicization. Second, we shall be concerned with the characteristics of personality involved in the formation of attitudes and the holding of opinions. Next, attention will be directed to certain aspects of the public-opinion environment such as "belief systems," social class, group membership (including reference groups), and the effect of the mass media in respect to the "two-step flow" of information. The following section presents the characteristics of publics and opinions as they relate to the distribution patterns of consensus and conflict. Finally, there will be a reexamination of problems of opinion linkage with government in formulating public policy.

POLITICAL SOCIALIZATION

How and where does an individual acquire knowledge about politics? The latest search for "political man" began in the early 1960s with an intensive investigation of the learning process as applied specifically to political phenomena. The two principal modes of inquiry, the study of changes within the individual personality (psychology) and the experiences the individual encounters in the environment (sociology), pointed to the uniqueness of the learning experience.

Political behavior results from the interaction of the individual with his or her environment. The following are some of the principal arenas in which these experiences are derived: (1) the community, where acquaintance is made with the culture patterns of society, a sense of loyalty is developed, and attitudes toward customs and regulations are conditioned; (2) the social institutions, such as the home, school, church, and government, that contribute to a personal sense of values and a belief system; and (3) the realm of political phenomena—political people, agencies, policies, and practices that make up the political culture. In short, the impact of the total personality interacting with the totality of political experience provides the raw materials for the formation of attitudes and the expression of individual opinions.[4]

The Maturation Process

The findings regarding political socialization must be accepted tentatively. A safe assumption is that the escutcheon of the newborn child is quite innocent of political knowledge. Three of the agencies involved in his search for a "political self" are his family, peer group, and school, probably in that order of importance. In a discussion of the political maturation process, Professors Richard E. Dawson and Kenneth Prewitt have listed some of a child's political learning experiences according to chronological age from years five to eighteen.[5]

At the age of five or six the child initially becomes aware of some elements of the political

---

[4]For an excellent introduction to this entire process, see Heinz Eulau, *The Behavioral Persuasion in Politics*, Random House, Inc., New York, 1963; see also William C. Mitchell, "The Socialization of Citizens," in Charles G. Bell (ed.), *Growth and Change: A Reader in Political Socialization*, Dickenson Publishing Company, Inc., Belmont, Calif., 1973, pp. 32–59.

[5]Richard E. Dawson and Kenneth Prewitt, *Political Socialization*, Little, Brown and Company, Boston, 1969, pp. 41–52, provides the basis for this account; see also Fred Greenstein, *Children and Politics*, Yale University Press, New Haven, Conn., 1965; and David Easton and Robert D. Hess, "The Child's Political World," *Midwest Journal of Politics*, vol. 6, no. 3, pp. 231–235, August 1962.

world. There is little informational content to these earliest perceptions. He seems to exhibit some positive emotional attachment to his country, which may be the beginnings of patriotism. His first recognition of symbols of political authority apparently relates to a policeman, a mayor, or possibly the president. He regards these personifications of political eminence in a distinctly friendly light. He can identify a political party. Perhaps one of his most significant accomplishments is to distinguish between the subgroups in his environment and to place them in friendly or unfriendly categories. The child's experiences in relating to rich-poor, black-white, and other social groupings are considered important to later social adjustments as an adult.

Between the ages of seven and thirteen both the child's store of information and his knowledge of the political environment increase notably. He recognizes abstract symbols. The president assumes the character of a role player. It is understood that he may be voted out of office or impeached for improper behavior; indeed, the president becomes both more and less than simply a benevolent individual. This is probably the most significant learning period for a youth.

From age thirteen to age eighteen, it is believed, key attitudes become well established, and many attributes of the political self are finalized. The youth is aware of ideological differentiations and understands important dimensions of both political participation and partisanship. Many of his future political habit patterns have been internalized and integrated with his personality.

Family, Peer Group, and School

To what extent is this experience of early political socialization the root source from which adults derive their basic attitudes? The answer is not known for certain, but there is some indication that a significant legacy persists throughout life. Part of the problem is that of differentiating between socialization per se and political socialization. The following are believed to be some of the contributions of the family to adult political heritage: orientation to the cultural value system; identity with the community (patriotism); an awareness of the meaning of authority; and finally, and most easily developed, an awareness of political party. A substantial majority of the electorate adopts and keeps the party affiliation of the parents.[6]

Peer groups, which establish close social relations with friends, fellow students, and co-workers, are considered of prime importance in the socialization process from youth through adulthood. Young people may follow the advice of their contemporaries rather than that of their parents. Friends reciprocate strong emotional attachments. Ties of regard and affection or fear of ridicule for nonconformity can force an individual to accept group norms including political orientations. Information is exchanged, and views and opinions reinforced, while the comfort and security of one's position is enjoyed through friendly person-to-person contacts. The network of peer-group memberships is considered of prime importance in political orientation.

The school is the formal institution through which society conserves and transmits its culture and value system from one generation to another. Nevertheless, the exact contribution of formal education to political socialization is in dispute. The school makes the student much more aware of the political process, and it imparts information, knowledge, and skills relating to politics. It offers training in many political practices, such as voting in elections, chairing a meeting, exercising leadership, and discussing and debating controversial issues. Occasionally it provides contact with prominent politicians.

One extremely significant aspect of the educational experience is the sudden widening of the child's intellectual horizon. Family values and norms may be compared with alternative ways of viewing the world as expressed by peer-group

---

[6]For this discussion see Robert E. Lane and David O. Sears, *Public Opinion*, Prentice-Hall, Inc., Englewood Cliffs, N.J., 1964, pp. 18–30; Robert D. Hess and Judith V. Torney, "Role of the Family in Political Socialization," in Bell, op. cit., pp. 188–200; M. Kent Jennings and Richard G. Niemi, "The Transmission of Political Values from Parent to Child," in Bell, op. cit., pp. 201–232; Richard E. Renneker, "Some Psychodynamic Aspects of Voting Behavior," in Bell, op. cit., pp. 264–275; James S. Coleman, "Education and Political Socialization," in Bell, op. cit., pp. 281–286; and Kenneth P. Langdon, "Peer Group and School and the Political Socialization Process," in Bell, op. cit., pp. 377–386. For contemporary critiques running counter to some of the conventional wisdom on political socialization, see Fred I. Greenstein, "A Note on the Ambiguity of 'Political Socialization,'" in Bell, op. cit., pp. 63–70; and the editorial comment of Bell, op. cit., and passim.

members and teachers or embodied in the school curriculum. A comparison of different social values and a growing awareness of social- and economic-class status may lead either to reinforcement of early learning or to political rebellion. In either case, the child's opinion pattern is affected. The ultimate outcomes of the maturation process, including influences during early childhood and youth, become evident in adult behavior.[7]

Most citizens are not particularly interested in politics most of the time. We have attempted to show the sources of political information that contribute to an individual's political attitudes as he grows up: His father, mother, brothers, and sisters are "resource persons" within the primary group of the family; his friends are another important source of information because a youth tends to listen to members of his peer group; and, finally, the school gives him some formal instruction in the ways that political parties work, and a teacher whom he regards highly may have a lasting influence upon his political self-image as a liberal, conservative, Democrat, or Republican. The learning that takes place as a consequence of daily living in the environment, however, has a significant impact upon the individual's personality and habit patterns. We turn now to a brief discussion of personality development and the attitudes that form the basis for opinions.

PERSONALITY, ATTITUDES, AND OPINIONS

Up to this point, political socialization has been discussed in terms of the problems the individual encounters in the environment. An important reciprocal development in the explanation of public opinion involves the psychological changes taking place within the individual. Psychologists explain the interaction between the individual and the environment in terms of the theory of stimulus and response. The personality is stimulated by a thought, a sight, a sound, a problem, hunger, or thirst. The individual's response is the result of a combination of psychological reactions such as perception, cognition, reason, and feeling that condition behavior.[8] Over a period of time the individual learns habit patterns of thinking and role playing. He also acquires attitudes, or predispositions to think and behave in ways unique to his personality. In a broad sense, the opinions he expresses are reflections of these attitudes.

A number of key "psychological variables" enter into this stimulus-response, habit-building learning theory. We shall call attention briefly to several of these: perception, cognition, reasoning and feeling, attitudes, and opinions.

Perception Walter Lippmann emphasized a cardinal principle of psychology when he noted the discrepancies between the true nature of the outside world and the pictures of it that people carry around in their heads. This distortion of reality is due in part to the psychological process of perception. The individual is constantly bombarded by impressions or stimuli from the phenomena of his environment: ideas, events, personalities, and objects. He responds to these messages in a selective fashion, being attentive to some and rejecting or ignoring others. By exercising such preferences in his perceptions of reality, he inevitably achieves only a partial view of the world in which he lives. Expressed in terms of a voter's political behavior, his perceptions may lead to the logical support of a candidate and a party because their views do indeed coincide with his own. There is always the possibility, nevertheless, that such dedication is misplaced—that the voter's perceptions of candidate and party have led him astray and that he is supporting those who in reality harbor views diametrically opposite to his own.

Cognition The perceptions experienced by the individual as he interacts with his environment over a period of time develop into a mental picture of what the world looks like to him. Insofar as he is interested in politics, he develops a "cognitive map" of the political world consisting of his likes and dislikes and preferences for candidates, parties, issues, and people wielding political power.[9] Cognition is the method by which the messages and stimuli from the outside world are made meaningful and become part of one's knowledge and thinking processes and a guide to his actions.

---

[7]Bernard C. Hennessy, *Public Opinion*, 2d ed., Wadsworth Publishing Company, Inc., Belmont, Calif., 1970, pp. 247–279, 291–304, discusses group and school influences, as does V. O. Key, Jr., op. cit., pp. 293–343.

[8]Hennessy, op. cit., pp. 198–202.

[9]The term "cognitive map" is attributed to Herbert Hyman, *Political Socialization*, The Free Press of Glencoe, Inc., New York, 1959, p. 18.

Reasoning and Feeling Two other aspects of the learning process that are particularly important to an understanding of the function of opinion behavior are reasoning and feeling. To reason is to think in a logical fashion. It involves arranging the information and thoughts one has developed in a proper and harmonious relationship to one another in order that they will "make sense" in some useful manner. Stimuli received from the environment also produce an emotional reaction, or feeling, which is sometimes pleasant and sometimes unpleasant.

None of these stages in the learning process are one-step operations; they are interrelated and they occur simultaneously. Given the uniqueness of each individual's personality and the uniqueness of his experiences in life, the process indicates in the broadest sense some of the psychological factors involved in the opinions he expresses.

Attitudes A more immediate source of an individual's opinions is his attitudes. As he goes through life accumulating a myriad of experiences, the individual tends to accept some as satisfying and to reject others as unsatisfying. Gradually he develops a complex of habit patterns or attitudes deeply embedded within his personality. *An attitude is a tendency, or a predisposition, to behave in a given manner.*

Attitudinal habit patterns represent a person's outlook on life; they are of central importance to his belief system. They provide signals for a list of priorities concerned with the way in which he should respond to his environment, and they may be regarded as frames of reference for his behavior. Specifically, a person's attitudes assist him in resolving conflicts in demands made upon him from different sources; they help him to make decisions that bring about the most favorable adjustments to such stresses. Attitudes also provide guidelines for understanding the environment; they form the basis of standards for judging the reality and accuracy of one's experiences. The individual needs psychological protection of his self-image, or ego, when he encounters criticism; attitudes provide a defense mechanism by means of which such attacks (be they true or untrue) may be rationalized. Finally, attitudes perform what has been called a "value-expressive" function; they provide the individual with opportunities to express his "central values"

or inner thoughts about the type of person he conceives himself to be, thus greatly facilitating his adjustment to others.[10]

Opinions An opinion is an individual's response to stimulation by the environment. It is the reflection of an attitude or a group or hierarchy of attitudes. It has been referred to as the "focusing" of an attitude. An opinion may express an attitude in a number of ways—by thought, gesture, or words. Most commonly, however, an opinion is the verbalization of an attitude.

An opinion is much less stable than an attitude and may be changed at will. Moreover, for a variety of psychological reasons, an individual may express opinions that either intentionally or unintentionally do not reflect his attitudes. Thus a person's opinions are not necessarily consistent with one another, nor do they always reflect political behavior accurately. An individual may say one thing and do another. Moreover, if circumstances change, opinions are often altered to accommodate the new situation.[11] Why are opinions so volatile and unstable? Why do so many citizens tell pollsters that they have "no opinion"?

In a fascinating study entitled *Political Thinking and Consciousness: The Private Life of the Political Mind*, Robert E. Lane suggests that all personalities are "plural" in that the individual has a "repertoire of identities" or self-images.[12] He displays these at different times and places to accommodate different situations or audiences. He expresses the appropriate opinions to project the preferred image.

M. Brewster Smith and his associates suggest that opinions may be used to serve personality adjustments in three ways: object appraisal, social adjustment, and externalization. In the first instance an individual uses opinions to evaluate objects and events in the environment in relation to his own interests. Opinion serves as a guide to achievement in the outside world. In terms of social

---

[10]Daniel Katz, "The Functional Approach to the Study of Attitudes," *Public Opinion Quarterly*, vol. 24, no. 2, pp. 170–175, Summer 1960. For this section, see also Angus Campbell, Phillip E. Converse, Warren E. Miller, and Donald E. Stokes, *The American Voter*, John Wiley & Sons, Inc., New York, 1960, pp. 42–43, 189–190, 500–503.

[11]William Albig, *Public Opinion*, McGraw-Hill Book Company, New York, 1939, pp. 6ff.

[12]Robert E. Lane, *Political Thinking and Consciousness: The Private Life of the Political Mind*, Markham Publishing Co., Chicago, 1969, pp. 94–97.

adjustment, opinions assist a person in relating to other people and groups, even to the point of expressing hostility. Finally, externalization involves the use of opinions to "live with" oneself by making normally unacceptable feelings acceptable and by reducing anxiety.[13]

An opinion is conceived and held by an individual. It is the way he expresses his likes, dislikes, beliefs, and nonbeliefs. The political scientist is concerned with attitudes and opinions particularly as they relate to political personalities, institutions, ideologies, and processes. One way to study political behavior is to observe and analyze the attitudes individuals have and the opinions they express in public about politics. Political socialization is the process by which the individual is inducted into the political culture. The opinions an individual holds are uniquely the product of his or her own personality. Opinion behavior is the interaction of the total personality with the sum of environmental experience.

A few brief summary observations may be in order. The role a person plays in the political life of a society—whether he is a participant, dashing from one meeting to another to make speeches, raising money, or running for office; whether he is an observer interested but not very active; or whether he is a nonparticipant, divorced entirely from partisan politics—depends in part upon how he perceives the political world. It depends on whether he is moved to respond to the urgings of others that he be a partisan and on his reactions generally to political stimuli.

Perceptions, feelings, and impressions are made meaningful by a process of cognition. They become a "political road map" guiding reactions to political experiences. Eventually the individual develops attitudes, habit patterns, or tendencies to react in certain ways: against corruption in government and for nonintervention in foreign policy; against communism and for "law and order." These attitudes are reflected in opinion responses to the environment, and these opinions serve as psychological "adjustors," either facilitating or disrupting social relations with the members of the community. Since they have many psychological uses, opinions may or may not accurately reflect the individual's attitudes, and thus they may be a faulty guide to his or her belief system.

Does the American public have a belief system? Are there some common denominators in attitudes toward societal goals? In an attempt to identify some basic attitudes common to the American national character, Stuart Chase conducted a survey of the results of a cross section of opinion polls taken largely during the period 1958 to 1961. His findings are summarized in a study entitled *American Credos*.[14] A generalized consensus of poll results indicated that in the field of foreign policy, the American public has abandoned isolationism, supports the United Nations, distrusts the Soviet Union (particularly with respect to disarmament negotiations), and believes that the most significant issue the nation faces is the prevention of nuclear war.

In the area of domestic policy, the public exhibits some ambivalence regarding government action, reacting unfavorably to the concept of the welfare state but favorably toward social security, public housing, federal aid to schools, and medical care for the aged.

THE PUBLIC-OPINION ENVIRONMENT

Political socialization continues throughout life, but adulthood usually brings pronounced environmental changes that have an impact upon behavior, attitudes, and opinions. These include a new job or profession, perhaps in another locality; a move up or down the status ladder to membership in a different social class; marriage to a partner with other experiences of politicization; a different circle of friends; and an identity with an age bracket that will inevitably change as the life cycle progresses.

The most important result of these changes will be in the adult's outlook on life.[15] He may now interpret his experiences to his own satisfaction, and he finds himself in a position to exert some authority over his destiny. Certain childhood influences tend to persist, such as feelings of patriotism and political partisanship, but the adult realizes that

---

[13]M. Brewster Smith, Jerome Bruner, and Robert White, *Opinions and Personality*, John Wiley & Sons, Inc., New York, 1956, pp. 39–41, as cited in Lane, op. cit., pp. 22–23.

[14]Stuart Chase, *American Credos*, Harper & Brothers, New York, 1962, pp. 186–202.
[15]See Dawson and Prewitt, op. cit., pp. 52–62.

he must adjust his life-style and outlook to the prevailing mores. Each person perceives his environment in his own way, depending upon personal experiences and expectations. As a citizen, the individual may exert himself to alter the laws and customs that determine his relationship to society. He is concerned with his self-image and the role he wishes to play: Will he retain his empathy for society and become a conformist, or will he be a cynic and nonconformist, perhaps choosing the role of an alienated person who lacks both knowledge of, and interest in, politics? He must come to terms with the political order. Is the government behaving in a legitimate manner? Is the system dispensing justice? In the inevitable social conflict of a free society, does he side with the electoral consensus on such matters as the availability of economic opportunity, the distribution of wealth, the granting or withholding of civil rights to minorities, détente with the Soviet Union, military support for the country's allies, and economic aid to the developing nations?

The adjustment of the adult individual to the "opinion environment," and thus his own attitudes toward public affairs, will be greatly conditioned by his socioeconomic status (SES), the groups to which he belongs, his exposure to information presented through the media and his interest in absorbing it, and the political leadership provided for him.[16] The first of these phenomena to be considered is the impact of social-class identity.

Social Class

Given an opportunity for self-classification, an overwhelming majority of Americans will claim middle-class status whether they are blue-collar, white-collar, or professionals. Indeed, an individual's self-image helps determine his political role. Nevertheless, using the factors of education, occupation, and income, some gross distinctions can be made between SES categories and political behavior. In general, the higher the educational level, the more information, understanding, and empathy an individual has regarding political matters and the more likely he is to engage in such overt acts as voting, contributing to a campaign, and working for a party. Low-strata individuals are more likely to have "no opinion" on public issues and to consider the immediate, and often material, benefits when voting. Moreover, higher-status individuals tend to be more conservative in their views. Because of the value system of American culture, social-class orientation in the opinion-forming process is not as significant as group membership.[17]

Group Membership

Group membership presents opportunities to exchange views on subjects of common interest, to acquire new ideas and discard old ones, and to stockpile additional information. Moreover, groups usually form norms of behavior and require compliance to sustain membership. If socialization is continued in this manner, will it enhance political sophistication? The answer depends on how close-knit the group is and on whether political concerns are a part of group life.

Social psychologists have identified three classes of groups. *Primary groups,* such as family and friends, are small, and a good deal of social interaction occurs on a face-to-face level. Other examples of primary groups are lodges, service clubs, and church congregations, all of which involve intimate contacts and mutual support. Where membership is voluntary, individuals are likely to share common backgrounds. A high degree of empathy is developed among members, and the pressures to conform are substantial. A certain degree of homogeneity is achieved, and although politics may remain of peripheral interest, the group might be activated for a political cause with considerable success. At any rate, individual attitudes undergo substantial modification as a result of primary-group experiences.[18]

Secondary groups are large segments of the population held together by a major interest, such as the national professional organizations of teachers, doctors, and lawyers and economic groups like the AFL-CIO and the Chamber of Commerce of the United States. Secondary groups encompass large numbers of primary groups, and individual, one-to-one contact is minimal. Members do develop a "we versus they" competitive instinct such as

---

[16]For a discussion of occupation, class, stratification, and groups, see Key, op. cit., pp. 121–152, 182–206, 500–534.

[17]Campbell, et al., op. cit., pp. 333ff.

[18]See Lane and Sears, op. cit., pp. 33–42, for this discussion and the following section.

characterizes the employer-employee syndrome of socioeconomic conflicts. In a broad sense, political mobilization takes place on this level, but the association of members lacks the personal and individualized opinion-forming potential of the primary group. A final classification is *category groups*. These are even larger segments of society wherein individuals associate voluntarily or involuntarily by virtue of belonging to one or more sociological, demographic, or economic categories. Persons of Scottish or Mexican-American descent are examples, as are whites, blacks, the socially elite, and the middle class. In a still broader sense, identity with a social class leads to political orientation and offers opportunities for modification of attitudes toward politics.

Several aspects of the role of groups as sources of the formation of adult political opinion must be stated very briefly. Secondary and category groups are believed to perform a most valuable service to the individual opinion holder whether he is a member, a leader, or merely an observer who holds their activities in high regard. They serve as *reference groups,* or guideposts to his political thinking about politics and issues of public policy. Moreover, the individual may adopt a life-style according to the standards set by a group to which he constantly refers for guidance. A commonly cited example is the laborer who consistently places himself in the middle class in socioeconomic status.[19]

Finally, an individual opinion holder's attitude toward the solution to a problem may well be conditioned by the fact that the primary groups to which he belongs or one or more of his secondary or category groups make conflicting demands on his loyalty. This creates "cross-pressures," and the emotional tug-of-war may sharpen his attitude and modify his opinion on the matter under dispute. If the strain is too great, however, the individual may exercise an option to defer his choice, or indeed he may refuse to make a decision. These group affiliations and the individual's reaction to them are symptomatic of the nature of the problems of political socialization that are encountered by the adult opinion-holding citizen, and to some extent they explain the seeming inconsistencies in his opinions.

[19]Campbell, et al., op. cit., pp. 299ff.

The Dimensions of "Public" and "Opinion"

In order to gain a perspective on the nature of public opinion, we have been discussing some aspects of the sociopsychological process of opinion formation. We now return to a more specific reconsideration of some of the problems of the opinion environment, such as the nature of "public" and "opinion" and the patterns that public opinion assumes in the community.

A public is no longer regarded as a conglomerate, undifferentiated mass of people. A public is essentially a segment of society, and there are many different types of publics. Publics may be identified by a specified geographic base, such as a township, city, county, state, or nation. A public may comprise groups sharing common interests, for example, a service club, a business organization, or a labor union. Some publics are relatively permanent, such as a political party, which has a continuing membership and organization, while others are brought together temporarily by communications facilities, such as a television or radio network. Within this purview a public may be any group of designated individuals. In the pluralistic American society, where groups abound in virtually unlimited numbers, there is an intricate mosaic of publics that can seek to influence government if the spirit moves them.

The other aspect of the concept of public opinion—namely, the nature of opinion—is not quite so readily understood. Among the major properties of an opinion are direction, intensity, stability, and salience. To determine the *direction* of an opinion is to ascertain the extent to which the response to a question indicates approval or disapproval. A simplistic measurement would be to elicit one of three responses: "yes," "no," or "don't know." A more meaningful technique would be to place a response on a continuum representing an attitude scale with "for" at one end and "against" at the other and with gradations of approval in between: "agree strongly," "agree but not strongly," "not sure," "disagree," "disagree strongly." The gradations of response permit qualifications to the general direction of the opinion.

Intensity is a second significant component of opinion: How firmly committed is an individual to a position he has taken? Is he a fanatic, or is he indifferent? Can he be persuaded by logic to change his attitude? Intensity may be related to traits of personality. There is ego-involvement, for instance, in strong advocacy of a position regarding a contentious issue, such as the relationship between church and state or problems of civil liberty or racial discrimination. Professor V. O. Key, Jr., referred to intensity as an aspect of the *quality* of an opinion reflecting the strength with which it is held.[20]

The component of *stability* has to do with whether the direction and intensity of an opinion will remain relatively constant over a period of time. Changes in opinion require the modification of attitudes and reflect the response of the individual to the stimuli presented by the environment. The volatility of public opinion is of great moment to government decision makers and is a constant challenge to political leadership. Finally, *salience* refers to the degree to which an individual prefers one opinion over another. A salient opinion is central to his thinking and behavior; it is the most important among the several opinions he entertains. The salience of a group of opinions clustered around a central theme is of particular interest to pollsters. By gauging the significance of such clusters, for example, it is possible to determine which issues in a campaign are of greatest concern to the electorate.

The Media and the Opinion Environment

The television, radio, and newspaper media are generally accessible to the American public, and the messages carried by these mass media are pervasive throughout society and greatly widen the individual's political horizon. It is possible, for example, to view the proceedings of a national political convention from one's own home. The nature of the impact of the mass media upon the opinion-forming process, however, is still under investigation, although certain generalizations regarding the relationship between the media and the public can be made.

The political content of the media is small in comparison with reporting of crime, sports, social events, and entertainment. The proportion of the public interested in political news or analysis beyond the current-events stage is also minimal. Moreover, the validity and reliability of messages transmitted either over the air or through newspapers, magazines, pamphlets, and books are subject to the variables of partisanship in editorial policies and authors' prejudices. There is no question that the media provide much subject matter for discussion. Psychologists have offered explanations of why people are attentive to such sources of information: the fear of not having an opinion to express when challenged by others, for example, or the desire to share information with acquaintances.

Two characteristics of the process of interaction between media and public in respect to opinion content are particularly significant. Through a psychological process known as "selective perception," an individual tends to ignore information or ideas that do not coincide with his established beliefs and values and to be receptive to those which do. Moreover, that portion of the public already committed to a high degree of political concern contains the most avid users of the media for political information. Thus the net effect of media exposure to political information is to reaffirm the previously held beliefs of the attentive public.

Another aspect of media impact is reflected in the prevalent "two-step-flow" theory of information communication. It is suggested that the original recipient of a media political message is likely to be an opinion leader, since only the committed person tends to follow political affairs. He or she conveys the message, usually in some informal manner such as during a casual conversation, to the members of a primary group. Since group opinion leaders are few in number, their views are respected and their influence is exerted over the group.

There can be no doubt that the media have an impact upon the opinion-forming process. Taken together, the press, motion pictures, radio, and television hold a mirror up to contemporary society, and the images, accurate or inaccurate, are seen by its members. They may view political speakers, party rallies, conventions, parades, "talkathons," press conferences, candidates, and issue debates in all manner of postures, shapes, and forms in the setting of the social milieu. The variables in any analysis of media impact include the differential roles played by the several media, the degree of

---

[20] On "direction" and "intensity," see Key, op. cit., especially p. 208; for topics discussed in this section, see also Lane and Sears, op. cit., pp. 5–16.

authenticity and the quantity and quality of political information purveyed, the character of both the original recipient of the information and those to whom it is relayed, and finally the incorporation of whatever intelligence is received into individual political thought and action.

In summary, the impact of the mass media, particularly television, on the style of American politics is verifiable, but the effect upon the behavior of the individual voter is in doubt. The searching eye of the television camera has eliminated the shambles of the old-style national convention and replaced it with a shortened, streamlined, efficient political event. Media campaigning has replaced barnstorming from the rear platform of a Pullman car. Professional political campaign firms will purvey an artificial candidate image for a price.

On the other hand, how can an individual sort out the impact of a single televised campaign speech from his total experience? With the exception of dramatic events, such as the Kennedy-Nixon presidential campaign debates of 1960, it is probable that any political stimulus is merged with existing attitudes or predispositions; the informed are reinforced in the positions they have taken, and the one-third to one-fourth who are uninformed are probably not attentive. The proposition that a substantial portion of the public receives instantaneous communication and that the modification of political views is reflected within hours in public-opinion polls and ultimately in altered political behavior lacks verification as yet.[21]

DISTRIBUTION PATTERNS: CONSENSUS AND CONFLICT

How are the opinions of the public identified, and how is such information made meaningful to government officials? A vast technology provides many ways to accomplish this objective, but only a few clues need be presented here. The public is reduced to a statistically accurate sample of the "universe."

[21] Harold Mendelsohn and Irving Crespi, *Polls, Television, and the New Politics,* Chandler Publishing Co., Scranton, Pa., 1970, pp. 281–314. For the impact of mass media, see also Robert E. Lane, *Political Life,* The Free Press of Glencoe, Inc., New York, 1959, pp. 275–289; and Key, op. cit., pp. 359ff. For the concept of the two-step flow, see Elihu Katz, "The Two Step Flow of Communication: An Up-to-Date Report on an Hypothesis," *Public Opinion Quarterly,* vol. 21, no. 1, Spring 1957, pp. 61–78.

A survey is taken, and the responses are studied with reference to attitude scales. Opinions may scatter widely along a continuum, bunch in clusters, or both. The configuration is interpreted with reference to the properties of opinion: direction, intensity, stability, and salience.

The aspects of opinion most frequently subject to investigation in a political context are four in number. Issues in public-policy areas probably come first. Typical subjects are unemployment, inflation, recession, law and order, civil liberties, and foreign-affairs topics, particularly those relating to nuclear war and national security. Identification of political personalities, prognostications of election outcomes, and the style and quality of leadership in the local, state, national, and international arenas are subjects of sustained interest. In the highly pluralistic American society the study of group organization and activity yields important information about the dispersal of power and influence in the nation. Finally, the temper of the public regarding the political system—cynical, critical, or enthusiastic—is usually under periodic surveillance.

Two opinion patterns germane to the well-being of a political society are the degree of public support for the regime, or the *consensus* pattern, and a measure of popular discontent, or the *conflict* pattern. In the view of an eminent authority in this field, the late V. O. Key, Jr., there are three variants of consensus.[22] When opinions tend to cluster closely at the positive end of an attitude scale and only a small number are scattered elsewhere, the pattern is said to show a unimodal, or *supportive,* consensus. Presumably, the government's policy has won general support. There is the implied negative connotation, however, that a change in policy might incur disapproval.

The three variations of the consensus pattern are *permissive, decision,* and *multiple* consensus. In the first instance, the majority of the public is prepared in advance to accept government action in a given area. An example would be the widespread approval for acceptance of Hawaii as a state before statehood was actually granted. Consensus of decision describes the reaction of the public to a

[22] See Key, op. cit., pp. 27–76, for these and following distinctions of consensus.

situation rapidly reaching the time of decision, so that the hardening of opinion is a virtual mandate for government to act. Key cites the reversal in attitude of the majority of the American public toward support for Britain in the dark days of 1941. The initial sentiment for noninvolvement changed to marginal endorsement for aid sometime after the successes of the German Army invasions in Europe. The United States government was poised to act when the issue was resolved arbitrarily by the Japanese attack on Pearl Harbor.[23]

In the case of multiple consensus or a concurring majority, initially there is little agreement among major interest groups or within the public generally regarding the solution to a problem. Gradually, various groups and segments of the public, working independently of one another and on separate timetables, reach a common conclusion for diverse reasons. A multiple consensus has been established to support some phase of public policy or government action.

Within the arena of American politics, where free discussion and wide-open advocacy prevail, conflicts in opinion are usually polarized into "for" and "against" groups. Therefore, opinion conflict patterns tend to cluster at the two extremes of the attitude scale and are bimodal in nature. Conflict patterns in opinion develop over public issues, but an important corollary and root cause is found in the group loyalties of an individual, particularly his or her party loyalty. The two-party system in the United States is characterized by a perpetual struggle for political power, and it practically institutionalizes adversary relationships for partisan causes. Party members may identify with the position of their party on an issue or, if they are uninformed, vote out of loyalty.

It has been conjectured that conflicts over major issues center initially in the leadership circles of the two factions and that positions are delineated and disseminated to the adherents.

What interpretations are warranted by application of the consensus model to various facets of American opinion? Certainly it is a test of the democratic theory of self-government and the concept of the "rational man." Key speculates as follows: The American public as a whole has a low degree of interest in politics, a poor record of participation, a paucity of hard information, limited expectations of government performance, and no basic ideological consensus. Yet government acts as though consensus does exist. Why? It does so for two fundamental reasons. First, characteristics of the American people such as self-reliance, pragmatism, optimism, and dedication to individualism generally do not prompt the citizen to demand a government that behaves according to a set of ideological principles; however, there is a demand for support for those specific objectives such as public education and social security for which a broad consensus in the public does exist. Second, there is indeed an ideological consensus in American society, but it exists in the involved, participating influentials—the elite and the leadership. The elite responds to the public's desires, and this produces a consensus wherein the public authenticates the legitimacy of the regime.

Lloyd A. Free and Hadley Cantril, in an interesting study entitled *The Political Beliefs of Americans,* address themselves to somewhat the same problem: the apparent dichotomy between the ideological principles acknowledged by Americans as consensus goals and the demands made upon government, rather than the individual, to solve the critical problems of modern society.[24] They find that the "core of the difference" between liberals and conservatives as revealed in their attitudes and political behavior is a fundamental disagreement on the employment of the power and resources of the national government for the accomplishment of social goals. In general, the American public accepts the conservative philosophy expressed in terms of protecting the status quo, resisting change, and curbing the federal power. On the other hand, the same public demands action programs from government, such as protection of the underprivileged, compulsory education, unemployment insurance, and minimum-wage legislation, which are interpreted as "liberal" objectives because they can be obtained only by greatly increasing the role of government in society and thus disturbing the status quo.

In short, these researchers found the American

[23] Key, op. cit., p. 36.

[24] Lloyd A. Free and Hadley Cantril, *The Political Beliefs of Americans: A Study of Public Opinion,* Simon and Schuster, New York, 1968, pp. 4–7.

public to be ideological conservatives and liberal (or operational) pragmatists. If such a state of affairs persists, social conflict will intensify, consensus will be more difficult to achieve, and any role that public opinion might play in effectuating public policy would be compromised. The dilemma constitutes a genuine challenge to political leadership. Government policy makers must constantly strive to achieve practical solutions to problems and at the same time reconcile operational achievements with ideological goals. We now turn to a consideration of the problems of access of public opinion to the decision-making processes of government.

The Government, Public Opinion, and Public Policy

The ultimate challenge of the empiricist to the rational-man concept of democracy is the question: Does government respond to public opinion when making public policy? In seeking an answer, scholars have examined what David Truman termed the "channels of access" to government and what V. O. Key called the "linkage" between public opinion and the decision-making machinery of government. Others have studied aspects of the problem such as the voting behavior of the public, the performance of elected representatives while in office or of political leaders who make policy decisions, or have focused on the completed decisions and their implementation, the channels of communication between the public and government, or the weapons the public can use to bring recalcitrant legislators in line. Who among the public attempts to gain access to government? What messages are carried? How does the government respond? The problem of the interaction between public opinion and public policy awaits solution. Indeed, its ramifications are so complex that a discussion of only some of its dimensions would be feasible here.

The "Attentive" Public

Only a relatively small proportion of the public is believed to participate directly in the formulation of public policy. The criteria for identifying these "attentives," as they have been called, are information and knowledge about politics, an interest in participating in political action and the motivation to do so, and a social position and status that permit access to government decision makers. In this context the public may be divided into segments: the mass public, which constitutes perhaps 85 percent of the people and generally possesses a low coefficient of concern for public affairs; the attentive public, or the 10 percent harboring a high degree of awareness of the political environment and what goes on there (sometimes referred to as the "opinion holders"); and the thin top layer of "influentials," or "opinion makers," who actually formulate policy.[25]

The role of the masses is a passive one; this segment is not directly involved in the process of transmitting opinion to the public-policy makers except in the broadest sense of exercising preferences for candidates and issues at the polls. By accepting the political regime, by reminding the activists that democracy is supposed to operate on consensus, and by believing that it does, the mass public sets the outer limits of acceptability of public policy. When directly faced by great challenges such as war or depression, the mass public may become aroused, and the resulting reaction may be definitive as far as public policy is concerned.

Separated from the mass public is a much smaller segment of individuals from the higher echelons of socioeconomic status. These are the educated, informed, motivated participants in public affairs. They belong to political parties and interest groups, and they vote fairly regularly. They employ mass communication channels to express their views. They are alert and attentive to issues of public policy, and they are the confirmed opinion holders of the community.

There is some disagreement among scholars about the existence of a third, or top, tier within the public. Some believe that among the influentials are those leaders who actually man the fulcrum of decision-making power in society. This group would include the hierarchy in the political parties, the officeholders in business, labor, and agricultural interest groups, and the elected and appointed officials of government. They are the inner core of the influentials and are designated as opinion mak-

[25] For topics in this section, see James N. Rosenau, *Public Opinion and Foreign Policy*, Random House, Inc., New York, 1961, pp. 27–41; Hennessy, op. cit., pp. 31–56; and Key, op. cit., pp. 359–365, 536–558.

ers of the myriad special publics scattered at random throughout society.

The Government Apparatus

The government is inhabited by people. If only a small elite among the public seeks access to government, to whom do they speak? They exchange views with the official inhabitants of the executive, legislative, judicial, and administrative branches of the government. The inventory of "access points" to the machinery of the governmental process is a very long one. The president, for instance, has a White House staff of several dozen individuals who advise him on public-policy issues, frame proposals for legislation, write his speeches, and so forth. The members of his Cabinet, most of whom are department heads, and the vast bureaucracy of hundreds of officials manning the administrative agencies and bureaus make policy daily under his direction. Congressmen are approached by their constituents and campaign donors, extensive public hearings requiring witnesses are held in framing legislation, and the courts are available for lawsuits to strike legislation from the statute books and to inhibit administrative rulings. On a more personal basis, the attentive public may write letters, make speeches, visit with administrators, compose newspaper editorials, work for political parties, make or withhold campaign contributions, organize public protests, or otherwise dramatize contentious positions on public policy. Indeed, there is a two-way flow of information between government officials and the effective public. Government responses to these public solicitations for attention include newscasts, ceremonial rites, television appearances, motion picture documentaries, public meetings, and an enormous output of published material including bulletins, brochures, commission reports, task-force studies, interviews, and so forth. Government engages constantly in elaborate programs to influence and shape public opinion.

The Policy Output

The interaction of the leader-elite within and outside the government, bent upon meeting or thwarting the desires and needs of the public, produces a veritable flood of laws, decrees, judicial decisions, and rulings that, as public policy, control the social and economic environment: social security, agricultural subsidy, minimum-wage laws, graduated income taxes, publicly supported educational systems, criminal statutes, foreign-aid appropriations, a lower voting age, and limits on campaign expenditures. The key question is: Which transaction through what access channel created, altered, or abolished some phase of public policy?

PATTERNS OF POLITICAL LINKAGE

The relationship between public opinion and policy has been analyzed from several points of view. One approach is to trace the interaction in terms of the *flow of influence* between individuals and groups in society: Who has influence over whom and to what degree, and how is compliance achieved and behavior modified? A second approach is to study the *communications network* to determine how messages are transmitted and received in the policy process. A variation of the first two forms of investigation is to chart the *transmission of opinion* within the public and between the public and government. The presence of influence in the transmission of opinion is not altogether ignored, but no attempt is made in this conceptualization to explain influence in behavioral terms.[26]

An alternative to the attempt to devise a schematic approach to the complexities of linkage would be to view some of the accumulated evidence that seems to bear upon the problem. Research emphasis in this field has centered primarily upon voting behavior, the reciprocal relationships between the individual and his or her legislative representative, and two principal political institutions most active in entering the policy-making arena with government: the political party and the interest group. V. O. Key, Jr., made a pioneering study in this area in 1961 entitled *Public Opinion and American Democracy,* as did David B. Truman in 1951 in *The Governmental Process: Political Interests and Public Opinion.* More recently, Norman R. Luttbeg, in *Public Opinion and Public Policy,* has suggested some "models of political linkage" based upon a collection of studies of the means utilized by political leaders in making gov-

---

[26]See Rosenau, op. cit., pp. 9–18, for this and the statement immediately following.

ernment policy according to the needs and demands of the public.[27]

The *rational-activist model,* referred to earlier in this chapter, depicts the relationship between voters and their legislative representatives in the context of informed, participating individuals making rational choices between clearly perceived alternative courses of action. Studies show that voter behavior in response to candidate image, partisanship, and campaign issues does not fit this model. Presumably, therefore, elections leave a good deal to be desired as devices for linking voters and their representatives and government policy. The *political parties model* assumes that voters will view objectively the proposals of competing political parties, will make a choice, and will be willing to alter their preferences in case their expectations remain unfulfilled. Evidence indicates that because of a lack of information, the public is unable to use a congressman's voting record to judge his responsiveness to its needs. Moreover, party loyalty interferes with an objective evaluation of his performance. Since parties present issue platforms and since they recruit for and also staff key positions in government, these misperceptions seriously compromise the function of providing linkage between public and government.

The *pressure-group model* rests upon the assumption of an American pluralistic society harboring a myriad of groups. Most individuals belong to one or more interest groups whose membership is mobilized to influence government policy in matters of mutual concern. Farm, labor, and business groups compete to press their goals upon government representatives through their leaders. Since group objectives often conflict, the resultant struggle produces negotiations and compromises that eventually become public policy. Even though this model unquestionably represents an important aspect of the policy process, linkage once again may be compromised for a variety of reasons. It is quite possible that the group leader may either intentionally or unintentionally misrepresent the views of the group membership when contacting government agencies. Faulty communication may cause him to perceive incorrectly what his group believes about key issues. Moreover, he may be unable to marshal the votes of the membership in support of a policy position that has been decided upon. In other words, the role of the elected representative may be reduced to simply "counting noses" among influential group leaders and casting his vote accordingly.

Implicit in these points of view characterized by Luttbeg as "models" is the question of whether the elected representative can be made aware of the needs and preferences of the public and, further, whether the public is able properly to reward or penalize him for his performance. There remains the possibility that the various irrationalities of human behavior described herein that intrude between the constituent and his representative may be dealt with. This desirable circumstance of the congruence of views has been characterized by Luttbeg as the "belief-sharing model" (or consensus model) and the "role-playing model." In other words, recognition is made of the possibility that the preferences of all parties concerned coincide because of shared experiences or that the representative follows his constituents' wishes because of a sense of duty. It is presumed that coercion is not a factor in these relationships.

Seen from this perspective, the opinion environment of a democracy throws new light upon the roles of government and citizen. Government is not a highly sensitized reactor to constant expressions of mass opinions. The public speaks with many voices, and it is the duty of government to reconcile or to choose between these disparate views or to ignore them and take its own course. Much of the business of government takes place beyond the reach of public opinion. The number of available

---

[27]Key, op. cit., pp. 411–534. Key's "linkage" categories include elections, representation, political parties, and pressure groups. See also Norman R. Luttbeg (ed.), *Public Opinion and Public Policy,* rev. ed., The Dorsey Press, Homewood, Ill., 1974. Luttbeg adopts a useful frame of reference for the furtherance of a theory of linkage between citizen preferences and public policy. He separates the first three traditional categories of rationalist-activist, political parties, and pressure groups from the last two of sharing and role playing. The classification rests in part upon the absence of reward-punishment coercion exerted by the public upon its representatives by means of elections. Thus in the latter two models congruence is achieved between the public and the representative—in the one instance because, acting upon his own views, he achieves the wishes of his constituents, and in the second because he simply desires to serve his constituents. This discussion is based upon Luttbeg's classifications; see pp. 1–10. The relationships between constituent and representative are the subject of continuing research, and Luttbeg assembles and relates these five categories in a meaningful manner.

channels offer differential access to the decision-making machinery by various publics. Many influences far beyond the scope of public opinion are present when key decisions are made, and some of these are preponderant in a given situation. The citizen plays a unique role in the democratic process, ranging from avid actionist to nonparticipant, and the role may change with each political situation he faces. His behavior is often a source of puzzlement to those in authority because his desires are sometimes inconsistent. He insists upon lower taxes, but with equal vehemence demands national security, roads, and education and welfare programs for which revenue must be collected and spent.

SUMMARY

Has the American citizen, through lack of interest, abandoned the role assigned to him in a democracy? Most authorities agree that there is no mass opinion in a democracy formulated by political man and translated into public policy. Angus Campbell and his associates conclude that the typical voter possesses very limited information on fundamental issues of policy.[28] He has no coherent patterns of belief that would indicate rational, structured political thinking in critical areas such as welfare legislation, foreign policy, federal economic programs, minority rights, and civil liberties. He is confused about the position of the major parties on specific issues, and, finally, he is unable to identify past government policies in major areas or to judge whether his government has acted rationally.

While not disputing most of these allegations, a recently current point of view places the citizen's political behavior in a somewhat more favorable light. Examining the opinion environment of American politics, others believe that the citizen follows leadership from the many publics to which he belongs and that this guides his judgment on policy matters. Surveys of electoral voting habits establish a clear distinction between the great masses of citizens and the relatively small percentage of political activists and opinion makers who are sufficiently informed to make their influence felt in the policy-making machinery of government. This leadership is provided by political activists representing all the social, economic, and cultural strata in society. Lacking detailed knowledge on some issues and uninterested in others, the citizen can and will express himself if and when he perceives a direct correlation between his personal welfare, the issue, and government action. He is guided by those leaders in whom he has confidence, and they in turn represent every segment of the public (the well educated, the ignorant, the rich, those with middle incomes, the poor, the captains of industry, the white- and blue-collar leaders, Protestants, Catholics, Jews, and others).

The opinion-environment thesis rests on the hypothesis that expertise on policy issues is decidedly relative.[29] Even members of the Foreign Service are specialists on only one small segment of the globe or one very limited area of world diplomacy. How can the average citizen possibly have access to the detailed data necessary to pass judgment on a complex issue of international relations? He cannot and does not, but he probably uses his own sources of information, listens to the opinion leaders whom he respects, and thus formulates his opinions. In those particular matters that challenge his imagination, he may have reasonably well-developed inclinations and points of view, which he may express through available channels.

Following this line of reasoning, each issue, each candidate for office, and each election produces its own unique public. The citizen shifts from public to public and from the status of nonparticipant to that of political activist. The interpretation of public opinion in terms of numbers becomes a relative matter. Considering the vast array of voluntary political associations and the complex intergroup relationships in society, the public may be very well represented by the many millions of persons who do vote in any one presidential election and the select few million who are issue-oriented on a specific occasion. Certainly if numbers of involved citizens have any significance, no society in history has ever produced voluntary political participation on such a scale.

In pursuing our objective of exploring the role of the individual citizen as he or she interacts with the

---

[28] Campbell et al., op. cit., pp. 168–187.

[29] This is the general conclusion reached by V. O. Key, Jr., op. cit.

many facets of the political environment, we introduce the subjects of political behavior and interest groups in the next chapter. We shall also consider some of the problems of communication and propaganda as they affect the opportunities and ability of the individual to particpate in the political process.

STUDY-GUIDE QUESTIONS

1 Criticize the concept of the "voice of the people" in a democracy by comparing the traditional characterizations of "public" and "opinion" with the contemporary interpretation of "public opinion."
2 Discuss the process by which a child undergoes political socialization and apply the stages of political development to your own childhood experiences.
3 Explain the significance of a person's political "cognitive road map."
4 Stuart Chase reports in *American Credos* that American citizens have abandoned isolationism, support the United Nations, distrust the Soviet Union (particularly in disarmament negotiations), and believe that the prevention of nuclear war is the most significant issue faced by the nation. Agree or disagree, stating your reasons.
5 What are the connecting links between the people, the government, public opinion, and public policy?

REFERENCES

Bell, Charles G. (ed.): *Growth and Change: A Reader in Political Socialization,* Dickenson Publishing Company, Inc., Belmont, Calif., 1973.
Campbell, Angus, P. E. Converse, W. E. Miller, and D. E. Stokes: *The American Voter,* John Wiley & Sons, Inc., New York, 1960.
Chandler, Robert: *Public Opinion: Changing Attitudes on Contemporary Political and Social Issues,* R. R. Bowker Company, New York, 1972.
Dahl, Robert A.: *Who Governs?* Yale University Press, New Haven, Conn., 1961.
Dawson, Richard E., and Kenneth Prewitt: *Political Socialization,* Little, Brown and Company, Boston, 1969.
Free, Lloyd A., and Hadley Cantril: *The Political Beliefs of Americans,* Simon and Schuster, New York, 1968.
Greenstein, Fred I.: *Personality and Politics,* Markham Publishing Co., Chicago, 1969.
Hennessy, Bernard C.: *Public Opinion,* 2d ed., Wadsworth Publishing Company, Inc., Belmont, Calif., 1970.
Key, V. O., Jr.: *Public Opinion and American Democracy,* Alfred A. Knopf, Inc., New York, 1961.
———: *The Responsible Electorate,* Harvard University Press, Cambridge, Mass., 1966.
Lane, Robert E.: *Political Thinking and Consciousness: The Private Life of the Political Mind,* Markham Publishing Co., Chicago, 1969.
———: *Political Life,* The Free Press, New York, 1972.
——— and David O. Sears: *Public Opinion,* Prentice-Hall, Inc., Englewood Cliffs, N.J., 1964.
Lipsit, Seymour M.: *Political Man,* Doubleday & Company, Inc., Garden City, N.Y., 1960.
Luttbeg, Norman R. (ed.): *Public Opinion and Public Policy,* rev. ed., The Dorsey Press, Homewood, Ill., 1974.
Mendelsohn, Harold, and Irving Crespi: *Polls, Television, and the New Politics,* Chandler Publishing Co., Scranton, Pa., 1970.
Roll, Charles W., Jr., and Albert H. Cantril: *Polls: Their Use and Misuse in Politics,* Basic Books, Inc., Publishers, New York, 1972.
Rosenau, James N.: *Public Opinion and Foreign Policy,* Random House, Inc., New York, 1961.
Truman, David: *The Governmental Process,* Alfred A. Knopf, Inc., New York, 1951.

Chapter 15

Political Participation: The Individual and the Political Environment

Since the days of the ancient Greek philosophers, politics has been discussed in terms of the nature of man, his social relationships, and his environment. In recent years man has come to be thought of less as an abstraction and more as a living, mortal being with emotions, attitudes, traits of personality and character, and conscious and subconscious motivations. Today his behavior is studied in the context of rational and irrational patterns of action. Society is now viewed as the product of the interactions of individual and group relationships; the reciprocal influences of man, society, and environment have become a central concept in the study of political dynamics.

This chapter is concerned briefly with the aspects of political study that have brought this form of analysis to its most advanced stage of development. More extensive consideration will be given to some of the environmental influences that stimulate, modify, and sometimes channel political action, such as the problems in the communication of meaning, the manipulators of political power (such as interest groups, political parties, and professional campaign firms), and, finally, the methods, techniques, and media employed by propagandists. The unit of analysis is still the individual, but the perspective is broadened from his or her "opinion behavior" to other fundamental relationships with the social institutions in the political universe.

THE BEHAVIORAL MOVEMENT IN POLITICAL SCIENCE

Political scientists have long been troubled as to whether the methods they use in analyzing political phenomena and describing the political universe are genuinely scientific. The traditionalists in the discipline have relied heavily upon the historical-descriptive-normative approach to politics, in which research emphasis is placed upon tracing the origin and development of political institutions and practices, discussing the anatomy of governments and other political organizations, and suggesting ways to improve them. A great deal of such research has been of high analytic quality, but it has also had definitely normative overtones; various criteria have been set forth for judging which institutions and practices would produce the best state and society. Empirically minded students of politics have argued that many current descriptions of supposed political reality (of things as they are) are actually unrealistic and do not match the objectivity achieved in some of the other social sciences, for example, in studies of personality and individual behavior by psychologists, in investigations of group structure and organization by sociologists, or in the application of statistical models to social phenomena by mathematicians.

A spirited controversy over social theory and analytic technique raged during the 1950s, instigated in part by the utilization of scientific methodology in the natural and physical sciences for the solution of space-flight and similar problems. Simultaneously, social scientists were engaging in extensive cross-training within their own disciplines and were developing some of the experimental and quantifying techniques employed in other sciences. As a consequence, a movement developed among political scientists which emphasized empirical research and which is now known as the "behavioral school."[1]

The Behavioral Approach

There is substantial agreement among political scientists that a primary goal of the discipline is to define the role of government and describe political phenomena in terms of proved generalizations consonant with widely accepted theories of human nature and society. Behavioralists maintain that this objective may best be achieved by stripping away the myths, legends, dogmas, and prejudices that mark the rationalizations and subjective value judgments of a great deal of contemporary political research. They would seek answers to pragmatic questions such as: What produces the dynamism of politics? What kind of forces, persons, ideas, and conditions cause political action? How do differences in individual personalities affect the way people behave politically? How do political actors, such as legislators, behave? Under what circumstances and by what means does social action become political action? Is there really any such phenomenon as political behavior?

The behavioralist views the political system as an integral part of the general social system. Politics is described in terms of those human relationships in which power, influence, and authority are manifested. The personality structure of the individual, his attitudes, and his general internal physical and psychological environment are of primary importance, as are his overt acts in the external environment. Explanations of the individual's motivations to act are contingent upon an analysis based (as far as feasible) upon empirical evidence of the interaction between the personality and the environment.

This sociopsychological political approach is being tested; new hypotheses and norms are being subjected to verification by a wide variety of empirical techniques. Scientific surveys, based upon statistically accurate probability samples, provide data gathered by means of questionnaires, interviews, and panels. Economists preceded political scientists in adapting many of these techniques to social science data. Psychological research has provided methods of personality analysis, particularly in the areas of attitude formation and motivation; sociology has contributed forms of analysis of group structure and dynamics; and methods for the extensive statistical treatment of data subject to quantification have been borrowed from the field of mathematics. For example, legislative roll-call votes, election results, and judicial decisions, treated statistically, provide subject matter for behavioral research.

Role Playing, Decision Making, and Group Dynamics

Many novel modes of investigation have been devised or adopted, such as the application of

---

[1] See Evron M. Kirkpatrick, "The Impact of the Behavioral Approach on Traditional Political Science," in Austin Ranney (ed.), *Essays on the Behavioral Study of Politics*, The University of Illinois Press, Urbana, 1962, pp. 1–29; Andrew Hacker, *The Study of Politics*, McGraw-Hill Book Company, New York, 1963, pp. 1–28; and Harold Lasswell, *The Future of Political Science*, Atherton Press, New York, 1963.

role-playing theory to identify the individual's behavior in the social matrix. The behavior pattern of a leader or follower is delineated by thinking of the person as an actor cast in a role and playing a part in a political drama. He behaves according to his own motivations and in respect to the expectations of others. Since all individuals have varied interests, they play many different roles in pursuit of both their political and nonpolitical goals. On occasion they will encounter problems that cause their roles to conflict. The behavioralist traces these roles through the complex of interpersonal relations.

Another approach is the view that politics is a decision-making process. Here the analytic tool consists in tracing the procedure utilized by an individual in appraising alternative courses of action. The steps in the procedure of problem solving are studied: recognizing the problem, defining it, considering alternative solutions, testing each for reliability and validity, and selecting the best answer. Other considerations in decision analysis are the consequences that would result from a particular decision, the risk involved in adopting it, and the ultimate value of each course of action. This approach is believed to make the explanation of the reasons supporting a political decision more meaningful.

Behavioralists are also interested in group dynamics. Such matters as why people join groups and the nature of groups themselves—their size, structure, organization, program, and leadership—are analyzed. The relationships of the individual to the group and of one group to another provide a new dimension for the study of social conflict. The analysis of the nature of the struggle between groups searching for the same or mutually exclusive goals enlivens and enlightens the study of political parties and interest groups.

The struggle analyzed in terms of "conflict theory" stipulating competition over values and interests is viewed as the sponsorship of certain preferences that people and groups have among the various rewards society has to offer. Such rewards, sometimes referred to as "resources," are variously described as status, prestige, income, power, influence, or security. Explanations are given of why these rewards are distributed unevenly throughout society, so that some individual preferences are advantaged and gratified, while others are disadvantaged and therefore remain unrecognized.[2]

These modes of analysis, expressed in an unusual vocabulary and symptomatic to some extent of their origin in the related social science disciplines, are provocative, novel, and challenging, and they may well become a permanent part of political science; indeed, their implications have been felt in every area of the discipline. However, any central concept, to be accepted as universally valid, must pass the rigid tests of persistence, consistency, and interrelatedness with other accepted hypotheses. A great deal of experimentation, research, and testing of basic assumptions must be accomplished before this new approach may be accepted as a more valid explanation of political dynamics than other accepted modes of analysis.[3]

Politicization of the Individual

Much can be learned as a result of empirical measurement of the political environment and the incidence of overt political action in its social matrix. A special contribution of the behavioralists, however, is the analysis of human nature in relation to political participation. The individual personality is considered in terms of both inherited and acquired characteristics and from the perspective of the responses of others to the impact of the personality upon society. As each uniquely endowed personality attempts to accommodate to its environment, behavior patterns emerge that can be scientifically observed. Insofar as these patterns relate to political phenomena, they provide interesting tools for the analysis of political behavior.

There is disagreement among psychologists concerning the frame of reference for personality

---

[2] For a helpful introduction to the problems and methodology of the political science discipline, see Stephen L. Wasby, *Political Science: The Discipline and Its Dimensions,* Charles Scribner's Sons, New York, 1970, pp. 3–200. Authoritative presentations of the behavioralist viewpoint may be found in Robert A. Dahl, *Modern Political Analysis,* Prentice-Hall, Inc., Englewood Cliffs, N.J., 1963; and Heinz Eulau, *TheBehavioral Persuasion in Politics,* Random House, Inc., New York, 1963. For the limits of behavioral analysis, see James C. Charlesworth (ed.), "The Limits of Behavioralism in Political Science," *Annals of the American Academy of Political and Social Science,* Philadelphia, October 1962.

[3] Sources illustrative of the behavioral approach are Robert E. Lane, *Political Life,* The Free Press of Glencoe, Inc., New York, 1959; and Seymour M. Lipset, *Political Man,* Doubleday & Company, Inc., Garden City, N.Y., 1960.

analysis; some stress physical aspects, others dwell upon social manifestations, and a third group prefers to describe indigenous character traits.[4] In this last context, individuals are alleged to possess configurations of dominant and submissive character traits. A person with a preponderance of dominant personality traits will strive for a position in society from which he or she can wield authority. Heads of states, generals, members of a church hierarchy, political party leaders, and captains of industry may be placed in this category. A personality wherein submissive traits prevail will tend to comply with the commands of others. A presumably well-adjusted individual has both kinds of characteristics and will lead in some situations and follow in others, without experiencing a strong compulsion to dominate his fellow men.

A second illustration of personality-trait analysis is the theory of extroversion and introversion. Individuals are classified, and their behavior observed, according to whether their personalities are marked by self-centeredness and antisocial tendencies or outgoing, attention-seeking characteristics. A tendency toward extroversion, with the concomitant of gregarious behavior, is claimed to be a distinct asset to a politician running for office.

Psychologists prefer to think in terms of "accommodation" rather than "normality" in evaluating human behavior, but a common denominator for judging personality traits relating to politics is the reaction of the individual to lawfully constituted authority. Most citizens accommodate to court decisions, administrative decrees, and statutory law most of the time. Those who disobey the law frequently and who indulge in excessively aggressive behavior toward society may entertain quite rational objectives, such as a strong desire to substitute their own set of values for the existing mores, or they may have unbalanced or nonintegrated personalities. In his study entitled *The Human Mind,* Dr. Karl A. Menninger suggests that when a person confronts a situation, the result may be success, failure, or compromise.[5] A maladjusted personality who experiences failure may attempt to cope with the situation by violating the law, or perhaps he may become the victim of a nervous breakdown. Dr. Menninger has categorized personality types disposed to failure: (1) the organic-disease type (crippled personality), (2) the hypophrenic type (stupid personality), (3) the isolation type (lonely personality), (4) the schizoid type (queer personality), (5) the cycloid type (moody personality), (6) the neurotic type (frustrated personality), and (7) the antisocial type (perverse personality). Adolf Hitler and Joseph Stalin, with their shared contempt for the dignity of man and a penchant for genocide, were afflicted with one or more of these debilitating personality diseases.

As a background for the interpretation of social action that has political orientation, the behavioralist draws upon the psychologist's investigations into such matters as motivations, value systems, and attitudes to which human beings respond. People are motivated by needs and wants, and this provides the stimulus for action. These needs are divided into two categories: internal needs, such as the needs for food, sex, and shelter, which are basic to physical survival, and external needs, such as the needs for security, status, prestige, and power, which are essential to spiritual well-being. These motivational forces within each individual's personality will be expressed in terms of his set of values about life—matters that he considers important or unimportant, his concepts of good and evil, goals that he thinks are worthy of great effort to achieve or unworthy of attainment, and means and ends that are socially and personally desirable or undesirable to him. His attitudes toward himself and society will provide an index to the mainsprings of his motivations and thus to the rationale of his behavior.

Sometimes the motivations of the individual personality toward political action are based upon conscious decisions, and sometimes they seem to derive from unconscious desires and needs. A person may view political action as an endeavor that will be rewarding in terms of economic gain, social status, and prestige, or perhaps he may think of it as a way of acquiring knowledge of where and how political decisions are made. Such attitudes will make him a power seeker in the community. On the other hand, psychological maladjustments during the maturation period of a human personality

---

[4]For a discussion of personality theory, see Calvin S. Hall and Gardner Lindsey, *Theories of Personality,* John Wiley & Sons, Inc., New York, 1957.

[5]Karl A. Menninger, *The Human Mind,* Alfred A. Knopf, Inc., New York, 1930, p. 17.

may leave deficiencies that drive the adult to seek compensations in a later political life. Without recognizing the source of his motivation, he may attempt to retrieve pride and self-esteem, lost in childhood experiences, by seeking to climb the political status ladder. Emotional deprivation and excessive aggressive tendencies are often legacies of wounded psyches that may seek remedial therapy in political action. Since politics involves social conflict, an individual may indulge in combativeness through argument and disputation on a political partisanship level, thus syphoning off tensions generated while playing other social roles. Political partisanship often constitutes a means of camouflaging bitterness and even hatred associated with social conflict, economic class warfare, and ethnic prejudice. The experience of verbally castigating a president may replace a strong desire to use profanity with a wife, a business superior, or a career rival.

Another interesting area of investigation by the behavioralists concerns the attitudes an individual holds toward politics and the extent of his participation. A person with a strong sense of "political efficacy," or a belief that his participation will actually affect the outcome of a political event, will be much more highly motivated to participate. If he views the rewards of the political game as worthwhile and is sanguine about the prospects that his expectations may be realized, he will usually make an effort to vote, contribute funds, campaign, or perhaps run for office. On the other hand, if a person loses sight of social values and fails to relate his interests to those of society, he may suffer from a sense of "anomie." This syndrome of feelings of anonymity and estrangement from group values and associations results in a lack of interest in political affairs. The individual believes that political leaders are not concerned with his welfare. He may tend to substitute his own goals, such as economic success, for the ends that society finds desirable. Lacking a dedication to social values shared by his fellow citizens, he may become prey to those who would order society along dictatorial lines.[6]

THE GROUP APPROACH

Although there are many approaches to a realistic description of the political process, the study of the individual personality in a role-playing, power-controlling capacity is one of the most fruitful. Others of equal significance include the study of decision making and the implementation of influence in the creation of public policy, as well as the nature and interrelationships of the groups that compose society.

Group analysis also involves a consideration of the nature of the group itself: the reasons for its formation; its history and tradition; the size of its membership; its programs, aims, and goals; and the extent of its involvement in politics. Furthermore, a group may be meaningfully conceived from a sociological viewpoint as a power structure. Treated thus, a group reveals a hierarchical organization of power within which leadership, elites, organizations, and followership may be evaluated. The concept of a power structure also reveals lines of authority, resources, degrees of unity, and the presence of status, prestige, and skills. Among the power structures in society, government is classed as "generalized" since it is vested with sovereignty; other groups are placed in the "specialized" category. Viewing society as a group of interrelated power structures permits a realistic search for institutionalized power and informal authority. Groups may thus be related to the political process by observation of the dynamics of group interaction.[7]

The Group as a Unit of Analysis

As in other areas of the political science discipline, scholars have sought to develop a coherent theory with which to explain and analyze the behavior of groups in the political milieu. Using the group as a unit of analysis, the political environment is explored to ascertain how society is organized and how power is dispersed, whether there is one basic power center or a multiplicity of power centers,

---

[6]On anomie, see Lane, op. cit., pp. 166–169. For an able discussion of some of these problems pertaining to the electorate, see William H. Flanigan, *The Political Behavior of the American Electorate,* 2d ed., Allyn and Bacon, Inc., Boston, 1972.

[7]The group approach, wherein "values are authoritatively allocated in society through the process of the conflict of groups," is discussed in Charles B. Hagan, "The Group in Political Science," in Roland Young (ed.), *Approaches to the Study of Politics,* Northwestern University Press, Evanston, Ill., 1958, pp. 38–51. For a general critique of the behavioral position, see Herbert J. Storing (ed.), *Essays on the Scientific Study of Politics,* Holt, Rinehart and Winston, Inc., New York, 1962.

what patterns emerge when groups interact, how conflict develops when interests clash, in what manner tensions are alleviated and conflicts are resolved, the process through which issues emerge and are formulated into public policy through the decision-making apparatus of government, and, finally, which are the principal factors in the political dynamics of society that produce stability and equilibrium or instability and conflict.[8] The stipulation is made at the outset that groups do not operate in a vacuum. There are several conceptualizations for the organization of contemporary society, emphasizing how groups are interlocked horizontally by class and social status and vertically by hierarchical organization of power relationships.

Pluralism

Among the theories that have been developed to serve as frames of reference for interpreting group behavior is the concept of "pluralism."[9] It is the contention of pluralists that individuals having shared attitudes and values band together voluntarily to promote their common interests and to achieve certain specified goals. Thus there is a multiplicity of groups in society at any one point in time. In fact, there are hundreds or even thousands of relatively independent groups in society, with leaders pursuing the goals their members wish to achieve.

It is the interaction between these groups that provides an important dynamic in social relations. Indeed, a group is conceived of in terms of the activity it engages in, rather than as an assembly of people. Groups express, or "articulate," their goals, and they make "demands" on one another and on government to achieve their objectives. These goals and demands represent their interests, and the means they use to obtain results generate "pressure" on government to act. Inevitably, some of these demands will coincide, and groups with the same goals may join forces to achieve them. Other group interests will clash, and conflict may ensue. The more activity these groups engage in and the greater the urgency with which they express their demands, the more intense intergroup conflict becomes. Inevitably, groups will form coalitions to block the aspirations of competitors or to achieve success in tandem with one another. These concepts of conflict, consensus (general agreement), coalition building, and destruction through negotiation and bargaining are fundamental to an understanding of group behavior. When issues arise in the realm of public policy, demands are made of the decision-making machinery of government, and influence is exerted upon it to pass laws, rules, and regulations complying with group requests. In fact, David Truman explains the meaning of "politics" in terms of the claims that groups make upon the institutions of government, while Earl Latham looks upon politics as the adjustment of conflicting group claims through the use of power.[10]

Group theory supports two versions of how government behaves at this point. The "arena theory" holds that government is one of the groups in a multipower-centered society, but is *primus inter pares* because of its decision-making capacity. For this reason, government's role is to offer an arena within which the group power struggle takes place. In this context it should be noted that groups within government are part of the pluralist conflict theory: Bureaus, legislative committees, judicial councils, administrative departments, and other government agencies are an integral part of the intergroup activity making up the power struggle. In a free democratic society, government responds to group demands. The "umpire theory," on the other hand, stipulates that the power struggle takes place outside the governmental sphere and that the official decision makers of the polity preside over the environmental conflicts as judges.[11]

Whichever role is played by government, some group coalitions prevail over others, and in a democracy a majority is attained, a decision is

---

[8] Several caveats are required in discussing group theory. First, there are other theoretical approaches to the study of interest groups such as role playing and comparative culture analysis; second, some scholars attempt to explain the entire field of political science in terms of group analysis, while others do not; and, finally, some assumptions of the group theorists have been rejected by critics. These variations and nuances are revealed in several sources. See Betty H. Zisk (ed.), *American Political Interest Groups: Readings in Theory and Research*, Wadsworth Publishing Company, Inc., Belmont, Calif., 1969, pp. 1–78ff.

[9] See William E. Connolly (ed.), *The Bias of Pluralism*, Atherton Press, Inc., New York, 1969, pp. 8–13, for this introduction.

[10] David B. Truman, *The Governmental Process*, Alfred A. Knopf, Inc., New York, 1951; and Earl Latham, "The Group Basis of Politics: Notes for a Theory," *American Political Science Review*, vol. 46, no. 2, pp. 376–397, June 1952.

[11] For the distinctions between arena and umpire roles for government, see Connolly, loc. cit.

reached, conflict is abated, and a new "allocation of resources" is achieved. What keeps society from flying apart in the process? Among several reasons is the fact that government is constantly negotiating with groups involved in the public-policy realm. There is a built-in stabilizer at the root of the social order; individuals belong to many groups, and the overlapping membership mitigates the sharpness of the conflict. A general consensus prevails on fundamental principles of the "rules of the game," or what outer limits of conflict are acceptable before other groups enter the contest, and it is largely this wide area of agreement that prevents serious social dislocation. Thus the multipower-centered society persists partly because of the exertion of the countervailing powers by many groups in conflict. Through the achievement of a temporary balance of power, equilibrium is established and social stability is achieved.

Elitism

The "elitist" model of social power differs significantly from the pluralist conception. There are many variations in interpretations of the model, but only the general hypothesis can be introduced here.

Who are the elite? In a political sense an elite is composed of those individuals belonging to the hierarchy of a power structure who participate in making the key decisions in matters of public policy. The model has been applied to the manifestation of power in the local community as well as in the nation-state.

The Community Elite On the community level those who wield power may be identified in several ways: by the nature of the positions they hold, by the reputations they enjoy among their peers, or by the very fact that they do indeed personally participate in the decision-making process. In the first instance the mayor, members of the city council, and the chief of police would be counted among the community elite. In the second instance the elite would be discovered by asking recognized leaders, such as a newspaper editor, bank president, and county judge, among others, to rate the power potential of prominent members in the community according to their reputations. Lastly, the identity of individuals with high status and established reputations would be determined using the single criterion of the influence they exert as actual participants in the decision-making process. Interest-group representatives, private citizens, and others involved in a decision relating to a major issue of public policy would be included in this category.

In short, the answer to the question of "who runs this town" would seem to be that the elite do. They shape, administer, and enforce compliance with the public policies of the community because they are strategically placed to exert influence in the community. The problem of community power-structure analysis is extremely complex, however, and includes careful examination of the processes by which influence is exerted and the substantive choices are made in supporting or opposing specific policy issues. Many aspects of the hypothesis remain in dispute: Do the elite rule on their own behalf or in the interests of the public? Why should the people's elected representatives defer to the nonpolitical powers in the community? Is American society indeed divided into classes? Should the "upper class" rule the community? Is the elite stable, or does the membership circulate?[12]

The Elite in the Nation Such problems achieve far greater significance when the model is applied to society as a whole. In this context there are at least two major approaches to elitist theory: the "single-elite model" and the model for "multiple elites." One of the most widely influential proponents of the first concept was C. Wright Mills. According to his views expressed in *The Power Elite* and other works, society is organized around power structures, the three most important of which are the economic, military, and political communities. Each power structure is manned by a top hierarchy, or elite: corporate presidents and board chairmen, the chiefs of staff of the armed services, and the highest elected or appointed officials in the government, such as the prime minister or the president and his cabinet. Thus a small, powerful group of

---

[12]For an unusually lucid introduction to the controversy over elitist theory consulted for this account, see Arnold M. Rose, *The Power Structure: Political Process in American Society*, Oxford University Press, New York, 1967, pp. 1–10, 255–297. For one view of the community elite, see Floyd Hunter, *Community Power Structure*, The University of North Carolina Press, Chapel Hill, 1953. For the national elite, see C. Wright Mills, *The Power Elite*, Oxford University Press, New York, 1959. Rose, ibid. passim, controverts both interpretations and advances his own hypothesis.

individuals of high status enhanced by prestige or salient position within the hierarchy of the power structure constitutes the elite. More importantly they control and operate the decision-making machinery of the government.

Beneath these top few are the mid-elite—the vice presidents of corporations, the colonels in the army, and the members of congress who participate in the political process on the lower levels. Below these are the teeming masses of society, who are generally apathetic about, or uninterested in, the problems of governance but who can be mobilized in time of extreme crisis to legitimate the actions of the elite.

While conceding the merit of many of Mills's observations, other scholars have been critical of the model representing society as a monolithic power structure. The rationale for its existence, based upon an "economic-elite-dominance" hypothesis akin to the principles of Marxian socialism, has also been questioned. In a penetrating study entitled *The Power Structure,* Arnold M. Rose offers an alternative entitled the "multi-influence hypothesis."

Rose views society as a multiplicity of power structures, each with its own elite prevalent in every organized activity of life and at all political levels: local, state, regional, and national. Elites compete for power within their individual power structures and with other elites in the public-policy arena. Thus the power structure in the United States is highly complex and diversified rather than unitary in nature. Moreover, the political elite is positioned above and not below the economic elite, and therefore analogies to the scientific socialist views of Karl Marx are inapplicable.

The Pluralists versus the Elitists The pluralists and elitists agree that ultimate power rests in the decision-making process. The pluralists find power widely distributed among groups in society eventually finding its way to the sphere of government. The elitists find power being manipulated at the pinnacle of the social structure by a powerful hierarchy of interconnecting elites.

A critical variable in the elite model is the question of the openness of society. If counterelites and new elites have free access to positions in the hierarchy through the political process (openly contested elections, and so forth), the elite model can be and indeed has been used widely to analyze the utilization of power in a democracy. On the other hand, if the elite operates in a closed society, such as existed during the Fascist regime in Italy or the National Socialist regime in Germany, elitism takes on the character of a control device in a totalitarian polity.[13]

Viewed in the context of the pluralist and elitist concepts of power, interest groups play a vital role in the political process. They assist the public in articulating political, social, and economic concerns and demands. They help forge a link between the public, political parties, and the government. They are nongovernmental conveyors of power into the inner circles of the decision-making process. The various models of pluralism and elitism assist in evaluating their role in the policy process. They are prime contenders in the struggle for political power.

INTEREST GROUPS

The group as an analytic tool has some specific disadvantages. For instance, in any one society there are thousands of groups which have such disparate characteristics as those of a legislative committee, a political party, a local service club, or a college student body and which defy classification. Moreover, the individual's motivations for joining a group are difficult to ascertain, and there may be no agreement between the elite and the rank and file upon the basic goals of the organization. However, the application of group analysis to reasonably homogeneous categories has met with some success, particularly in the investigation of interest groups, political parties, and segments of the electorate.

It is difficult to generalize about the multifarious reasons why individuals join political (or politically oriented) groups. Some become members of political groups for social or other nonpolitical reasons. It is probable that political empathy—supported by

---

[13] For an insightful critique of elite theory and an astute rejoinder, see Robert A. Dahl, "A Critique of the Ruling Elite Model," *American Political Science Review,* vol. 52, no. 2, pp. 463–469, June 1958; and Peter Bachrach and Morton S. Baraty, "Two Faces of Power," *American Political Science Review,* vol. 56, no. 4, pp. 947–952, December 1962. See also Norman L. Crockett (ed.), *The Power Elite in America,* D. C. Heath and Company, Boston, 1970.

information about politics, concern for issues of public policy, and belief that activity of this sort will be rewarding—is an important consideration. However, once the interest in identifying with a particular group is generated, it is reasonable to assume that the person believes that he or she is sharing the attitudes of others in the achievement of a common goal. Some interests are shared to a degree by all people. This is generally true of art, science, and culture. Other interests are more private in nature—the benefits of the end product accruing to particular individuals. Economic interests requiring political expression fall into this category.[14]

In the democratic process, the public official nominated by a political party and elected to public office serves as the official channel for the representation of the public's interest at all levels of government. Society and government have become so complex, however, that the lone citizen-voter in an electorate of millions has virtually lost his capability to influence public policy. As the representative of his constituents, the elected official faces equally perplexing problems. For example, in taking a stand on legislation, the two United States senators from California must consider such varied economic interests as those concerned with banks, railroads, motion pictures, television, public utilities, mining, shipping, building, citrus fruit, wine, walnuts, lettuce, and lima beans. Moreover, different segments of a single industry often present conflicting demands, such as the legislative programs of radio, television, and motion pictures in the fiercely competitive entertainment field. This dilemma is partially solved when the individual joins a group of like-minded citizens and makes representations to the legislator from his constituency. The elected official in turn can evaluate the desires of his constituents more effectively through the unofficial channel of interest-group activity.

This phenomenon of group political activity shapes our political institutions, bridges the gap between the individual and government, and is characteristic to some degree of all contemporary democracies and even of totalitarian states. The targets of interest-group activity are the decision-making processes of a political society. Thus the interest-group system in any one state will be shaped by the nature of the government apparatus (whether the executive is of the presidential, cabinet, or dictatorial category) and by the cultural, economic, and social environment (standard of living, distribution of wealth, class structure, and ideological considerations such as the underlying values of fascism, communism, or democracy).

Public policy represents the compromise, achieved in political terms, on the solutions to problems of domestic and foreign policy. It is the result of bargaining, negotiation, and trading between representatives of the public and private sectors of the social order. Statutes, executive orders, court decisions, and administrative rulings all constitute possible channels to the power centers of government. Interest groups apply pressure upon public officials such as legislators, executives, administrators, and members of the judiciary through the electoral and appointive processes by which they obtain and hold their seats of power. Access to the centers of decision making is also achieved by utilizing the opportunities made available through the normal conduct of governmental business, such as questioning the ruling of a regulatory commission in a court action, rendering testimony in legislative hearings, challenging the constitutionality of a statute, or rendering a service to a congressman such as writing speeches or doing research on current issues.

Much interest-group activity is directed toward definition and redefinition of the role of government in society, particularly in the realm of economics. Such activity has a specific frame of reference: to limit government authority, to enlist government support in the promotion of group objectives, or to employ government to restrict the scope of operations of known competitors. Interest groups can rarely achieve their broadest objectives without making demands upon government for positive action. The alternative recourse is to attempt to mobilize public opinion in support of a program in the hope that the electoral process may be employed as a sanction against the prevailing government policy.

---

[14]Robert M. MacIver, *The Web of Government*, The Macmillan Company, New York, 1947, pp. 421ff. For this section, see L. Harmon Zeigler and G. Wayne Peak, *Interest Groups in American Society*, 2d ed., Prentice-Hall, Inc., Englewood Cliffs, N.J., 1972; and Robert H. Salisbury (ed.), *Interest Group Politics in America*, Harper & Row, Publishers, Incorporated, New York, 1970.

The interests that bring a group into being are never isolated from those of other groups. Goals can be achieved only through a process of cooperation and conflict. A power-structured group finds that it must rationalize its own objectives and attack its competitor's programs in terms of the prevailing myths and legends of society.

There are many thousands of interest groups in the United States, with memberships of all the groups together running into the millions. The principal economic groups may be divided into three classes: business, agriculture, and labor. Prominent members of these respective categories are the Chamber of Commerce of the United States and the National Association of Manufacturers; the National Grange, the American Farm Bureau Federation, and the National Farmers' Union; and the American Federation of Labor and Congress of Industrial Organizations (AFL-CIO). All the professions have national associations to further their interests, examples being the American Medical Association, the National Education Association, the National Society of Professional Engineers, and the American Bar Association.

Patriotic societies and veterans' groups are large in numbers and active politically. Some of the best known are the American Legion, the Veterans of Foreign Wars, and the Daughters of the American Revolution. Religious, racial, and reform groups are exemplified by the National Council of Churches of Christ in America, the National Catholic Welfare Conference, the B'nai B'rith, the National Association for the Advancement of Colored People, and the Women's Christian Temperance Union. Finally, one of the best-known women's organizations is the League of Women Voters.

This list is merely indicative of the mosaic of interests around which individuals tend to organize in order to express their opinions and make their influence felt in the social order. The importance of this phenomenon to an understanding of political dynamics, however, is that any interest group may become a political interest group when it concerns itself with public policy and the implementation of political power relationships.

What is the role of government in the matrix of competing interest groups? Government must exercise a stabilizing influence in the midst of the battle of diverse propagandas, sometimes yielding, sometimes overruling, always receptive to special pleading, and ultimately mediating between energetic antagonists. In order to establish a degree of equilibrium in the midst of acrimonious contention and to protect an idealistic, though nebulous, concept termed the "public interest," it is mandatory that government engage in an extensive campaign of counterinfluence.

The special pleading of government, bitterly resented by most groups, is predicted on certain basic necessities in a democracy. It is vital that the most important generalized power structure in society (government) explain its activities for the benefit of all the people. When partisan petitions have been heard, weighed, and evaluated and when decisions have been made on the basis of compromise among the whole spate of special pleadings of all interest groups, it is the responsibility of government to publicize the decision and the reasons that support it. Government can legitimately publicize, through investigations and otherwise, the facts regarding the methods of special pleading used by any particular interest group. The people will then learn of these matters from some source other than the biased fulminations of that group's competitor for power. The idea that representative and responsible government lacks the right to tell the people its story of the social conflict shows a complete misunderstanding of the essence of democracy.

Political Parties, Interest Groups, and Public Policy

Interest groups are an integral part of the political milieu, and their behavior is conditioned by the nature of the party system. There is a fundamental difference between the functions of a political party and those of an interest group. The party selects, nominates, and elects candidates for public office; assumes the responsibility of governing the nation; creates and enforces public policy; and, when out of power, presumably behaves as an alternative government, offering competitive courses of action and criticizing the incumbent opposition. Lacking these responsibilities, the interest group pursues limited objectives with monolithic purpose and considerable intensity of effort. It can raise and spend funds and otherwise initiate political action in ways outside the legal scope of party functions. Some interest groups are closely allied with one of the major parties; others remain independent and seek bipartisan support for their objectives.

Interest Groups in the One-Party State

The pattern of interest-group behavior in a one-party regime is not readily ascertainable. The traditional political habitat for an interest group is the competitive, pluralistic, democratic society blessed with free speech, uninhibited political participation, and access to the power centers of government. The characteristics of a totalitarian society contrast markedly: the uniformity of belief imposed by an all-pervading ideology such as communism, fascism, or national socialism; the fusion of party and government in a hierarchical apparatus that regiments the recruitment of the citizenry into public life and stifles initiatives for alternative courses of public policy; government control of the media, limiting the free exchange of ideas and opportunities to mobilize for political action; and, finally, the implicit and actual employment of fear psychology and violence to intimidate the population into compliance. How much would the accepted definition of "interest group," *sui generis,* have to be distorted to fit the pattern of groups in a dictatorial society?

Sometime after the death of Stalin in 1953, changes in the domestic policies within the Soviet Union gently loosened the severe stringency of internal controls. Greater latitude was permitted in the expression of opinions, and social interaction accelerated between individuals and groups. The search for power, status, and prestige, present in any society, became more apparent in institutional rivalry. Observing these trends, scholars applied the theory of group analysis to political, economic, and sociocultural developments and posed the general hypothesis that interest groups did function in the Soviet environment, albeit in a somewhat more restricted manner.[15]

Because of the pervading presence of the Communist party, the inner recesses of the highest decision-making body—the Politburo—are inaccessible. Nevertheless, it is assumed that conflicting views on public-policy matters are held within and between groups. Groups make demands upon one another and either directly or indirectly upon government. Policy inputs and outcomes undoubtedly have programmatic effects—methods of procedure are altered, goals are modified, and individuals are mobilized to exert influence.

As a result of the complexity of Russian society and the difficulty of conducting empirical research, most studies are limited to the dynamics of political groups. Their operations are viewed as occurring in certain strata of political life and in given echelons of power, e.g., political institutions of the party and government or professional groups of architects. In a study entitled *Politics and Society in the USSR,* one political analyst, David Lane, identifies five such categories: political elites (such as members of the Politburo), institutional groups (trade unions), loyal dissenters (doctors and teachers), amorphous social groupings (peasants and manual workers), and unincorporated or estranged groups (those which are not part of the Soviet apparatus or which are alienated from the regime, such as groups of dissident intellectuals and members of religious sects). Lane suggests that groups in the first three categories can probably communicate their interests to the law-making machinery of Soviet society but that groups in the latter two might not be as effective.[16]

That competition, controversy, and adversary political relationships are prevalent among Soviet elites is beyond question. However, serious questions arise when one regards this activity from the perspective of interest-group behavior. Given the power structure of party-government relations, what is the depth of penetration of interest-group activity into the lower echelons of society, and are demands on those levels articulated and aggregated into meaningful policy goals? What accommodation is made to the ever-changing degree of tolerance of conflict characteristic of a dictatorship? Are the group structures themselves usable when leadership is not elected, but rather appointed from the top? Is it indeed possible for groups in disparate social and political categories to place demands upon one another or even to negotiate or bargain in a meaningful manner?[17] A number of important

---

[15]For an excellent presentation of the approach to interest groups in a dictatorial state, and specifically in the Soviet Union, see H. Gordon Skilling and Franklyn Griffiths (eds.), *Interest Groups in Soviet Politics,* Princeton University Press, Princeton, N.J., 1971. The sections referred to for this discussion are the Skilling chapters, pp. 3–45, 379–416.

[16]David Lane, *Politics and Society in the USSR,* Random House, Inc., New York, 1971, p. 235.

[17]Skilling and Griffiths, op. cit., pp. 379–416.

caveats must be accepted in order to fit intergroup theory to the Soviet scene; perhaps two of the most important are the unwillingness of the Communists to accept serious "deviationism" from the party line and the inevitable consequences to those who persist.

Sometimes distinctions can be made between dictatorships and totalitarian one-party states on the basis of the penetration of the party into the fabric of the society and the degree of coercion present. In a revealing discourse on interest groups in Yugoslavia, Jovan Djordjevic identifies a large number of groups operating in just such a restricted and regimented environment. He categorizes these groups as those participating directly in government, those holding a basic position in the political system, and those representing different interests of the citizens. Djordjevic casts the relationships between the more generic and broader-based "sociological" and the derivative and more narrowly focused "political" interest groups within the philosophical framework of Marxism. He discusses their status and roles in terms of the phenomenon of institutionalization, alleges that they do not possess public rights but that they do have rights to participate in social government, and finally admits that groups organized to influence and manipulate public opinion on their own behalf simply do not exist in Yugoslavia.[18]

A one-party state need not be totalitarian, however, and a new pattern for the articulation and aggregation of interests in an authoritarian but nontotalitarian one-party system is emerging among the newly independent African states; one example must suffice. When Tanganyika gained its status as an independent republic within the British Commonwealth in 1962, its first president, Julius K. Nyerere, headed the African National Union (Tanu) party. Writing subsequent to the formation of the United Republic of Tanzania—the result of the union of Tanganyika and Zanzibar—in 1965, Nyerere justified the maintenance of a one-party state: in the absence of a class-structured society, a multiparty or two-party system was unnecessary; the Tanu party achieved national unity through independence and earned the right to prevail; and the party, *sans interest groups,* represented the demands of the nation as a whole, was freely elected by the people, and therefore provided a firmer basis for democracy than alternative party systems.[19]

Interest Groups in the Multiparty State

The relationships between party, interest group, and government in a multiparty, parliamentary-cabinet state present special problems. Most Western European states have from five to a dozen parties, some closely identified with ideological schools of thought. Organized labor as an interest group in Italy or France, for example, may be closely tied to the Communist or Socialist party apparatus. Interest group and party may virtually lose separate programmatic identity in this context; leadership may overlap, and parliamentary representatives may speak in ideological terms for both groups. Similar relationships exist between business, church, patriotic, or national-minority interest groups and specific political parties.

For example, some of the consequences of ideological politics in the French system are interesting.[20] Theoretically, a party system offering a wide variety of ideological choices spread from left to right across the political spectrum would appear to offer unparalleled advantages to the citizen, the party, and the interest group alike. The well-organized and disciplined ideological party that controls its parliamentary delegation makes a poor ally both for its own similarly oriented interest groups and for nonideological groups. In the first instance it limits the scope of action of closely

---

[18]Jovan Djordjevic, "Interest Groups and the Political System of Yugoslavia," in Henry W. Ehrmann (ed.), *Interest Groups on Four Continents,* The University of Pittsburgh Press, Pittsburgh, 1960, pp. 203–219 and passim. For a pioneering study in comparative interest groups, see Gabriel A. Almond, "Research Note: A Comparative Study of Interest Groups and the Political Process," *American Political Science Review,* vol. 52, no. 1, March 1958, pp. 270–282.

[19]Rupert Emerson, "Parties in National Integration in Africa," in Joseph La Palombara and Myron Weiner (eds.), *Political Parties and Political Development,* Princeton University Press, Princeton, N.J., 1966, pp. 283–285.

[20]George E. Lavau, "Political Pressures by Interest Groups in France," in Ehrmann, op. cit., pp. 68–86 and passim. See also Henry Ehrmann, *Organized Business in France,* Oxford University Press, London, 1958; Lowell G. Noonan, *France: The Politics of Continuity and Change,* Holt, Rinehart and Winston, Inc., New York, 1970, pp. 299–312; and Roy C. Macridis, "France," in Roy C. Macridis and Robert E. Ward (eds.), *Modern Political Systems: Europe,* 3d ed., Prentice-Hall, Inc., Englewood Cliffs, N.J., 1972, pp. 187–191.

related groups in making deals with other parties. In the latter case it refuses to squander the vote of its parliamentary representative in alliance with a non-programmatic group, which may be championing an alien cause. Nonideological groups therefore prefer to negotiate with nonideological parties.

The tenuous relationships established in a multi-party coalition cabinet and its uncertain political life-span offer additional variations to interest-group politics in one-party and two-party states. The lack of effective statutes controlling political expenditures permits French interest groups to spend unspecified, but undoubtedly generous, sums in traditional campaigning at the grass roots. In general, however, greater effort is expended in trying to influence elected and appointed officials. Since the fortunes of a coalition cabinet are constantly in flux and political opportunism is practically a way of life, interest groups may succeed in playing off one ideologically oriented cabinet member against another, thus gaining access to a key decision-making process of the government. This is possible in part through access to the "little cabinets" of officials surrounding each minister. Another area of activity lies within the ranks of the bureaucracy, since the ratio of public officials to the total working population in France is high and the standard of living of public officials is relatively low. The many administrative committees, councils, and commissions actively preparing, interpreting, and enforcing government regulations offer a prime target. Finally, it is alleged that parliamentarians in the National Assembly are brought together as allies of interest groups in *groupes parlementaires d'études* and are put under obligation for the purpose of implementing predetermined strategy and tactics for influencing public policy.

Interest Groups in the Two-Party State

In two-party states, the area of agreement on the general goals of public policy is usually wider; disagreement is likely to center on the ways and means of their implementation. The two major parties represent loose coalitions of a great diversity of economic, cultural, and political interests. Interest-group activity tends to serve as a corollary channel for functional representation in the decision-making process.

In Great Britain, for example, the two-party system has produced nationally organized groups to represent all phases of the economy and most social causes of nationwide significance. The merging of the national interest with special interest takes place through the agency of consultation between the government (Cabinet) and private interest groups. This development has been attributed to the reaching out of government agencies into the community in search of guidance and to the general acceptance by the population of the creative role played by government as the custodian of the national interest. Interest groups in Britain have ready access to such ministries as those of education, labor, transport, agriculture, fisheries, food, and health through regularly constituted Advisory Councils, where their views are solicited.[21] Contact with Parliament is established and maintained in a number of ways. Members of interest groups may be elected to the House of Commons; conversely, members of Parliament (MPs) may be elected to honorary positions on the executive boards of interest groups, and organizations may hire parliamentary agents to represent them or may utilize parliamentary correspondents to keep MPs informed of their views.

Party discipline in the Cabinet and in Parliament is relatively strict and constitutes a genuine barrier to the unrestrained support of special group programs. Conflicts of interest on the part of the MP are generally resolved in favor of the government. A very useful interest-group tactic is the sponsorship or defeat of amendments to proposed or established statutes. Sometimes assurances can be exacted from the government that laws will be enforced in a given manner. There is also an effective liaison between groups with mutual concerns, resulting in patterns of alliances to achieve common legislative and administrative goals. General appeals to public opinion are usually ineffective, but interest groups have learned to win support by campaigning for parliamentary candidates in sympathy with their programs.

Thus interest groups play a vital role in

---

[21] J. D. Stewart, *British Pressure Groups*, Oxford University Press, Fair Lawn, N.J., 1958, p. 18 and passim; see also A. M. Potter, *Organized Groups in British Politics*, Faber & Faber, Ltd., London, 1961; S. H. Beer, *Modern British Politics*, George Allen & Unwin, Ltd., 1960; R. Rose (ed.), *Studies in British Politics*, Macmillan and Co., Ltd., London, 1967; and S. E. Finer, *Anonymous Empire*, 2d ed., Pall Mall Press, London, 1966.

twentieth-century politics. They exist, in some form, in all states as channels for functional representation. They differ in form, depending upon the degree to which the people can organize voluntarily and discuss their views in a particular environment. Their patterns and tactics are conditioned by the nature of the institutional apparatus to which they are attempting to gain access. They succeed, in part, according to the degree of integration of the social order in which they operate and according to the need for functional representation beyond the opportunities provided by the political party system.

ASPECTS OF THE POLITICAL ENVIRONMENT

Social action depends upon the flow of influence among individuals and groups in the community through the process of communication. It is through discussion, criticism, negotiation, debate, compromise, and special pleading that opinions are expressed (and decisions made) that will eventually be marshaled into purposeful public policy.

The conveying of meaning would appear to be a simple operation. The politician clinches an argument by intoning, "The facts speak for themselves." However, the study of the process of communication raises serious questions. Do the facts actually speak for themselves? What does a candidate for office mean when he claims to "stand foursquare on the inviolate and sacred principles of the American way of life"? How can this same candidate be a "true representative of democracy" to his supporters and a "traitor" or a "subversive" to his opponents? How can the federal conservation program be, at one and the same time, "in the great tradition of the general welfare of the American people" and a "diabolically conceived plot of the controllist-socialists to subvert the capitalistic system of free enterprise"?

Apparently, in looking at a set of facts, interpreting a series of circumstances, or evaluating goals and motives, people may come to diametrically opposed conclusions and select a contrasting group of "trigger words" and symbols with which to express their reactions. "Facts" are *not* self-explanatory.

The Communication Process

The basic purpose of communication is the transfer of meaning. During his entire span of life, man is preoccupied with the necessity of making himself understood and of attempting to understand others. Indeed, the character and nature of the individual's personality, the attitudes he develops, the opinions he expresses, and his success or failure in life probably depend upon his mastery of the art of communication. He must effectively convey not only facts, ideas, and ideals but also his emotions, hopes, fears, anxieties, loves, achievements, and frustrations. He must evaluate and represent both the mental and physical environments in which he lives, and he must accurately describe, explain, appreciate, and capitalize upon his life experiences. Failure to effect at least a minimal orientation to life through the communication process will probably result not only in failure to establish a proper social adjustment but possibly also in a breakdown in personality.

Meaning may be transferred through gestures, signs, pictures, or the Morse code and by means of many media such as books, television, radio, newspapers, speech, and the cinema. The most important factor in communication, however, is language. Words serve as symbols of the reality in which we live. Harold Lasswell has given language a special status in the realm of politics. He reasons that the science of politics is the language of power.[22]

Unfortunately, the political milieu of the twentieth century is characterized by a breakdown in communication. Strikes signalize the blockage of negotiations or perhaps a suspension of communication between labor and management; racial prejudice indicates a communication barrier between blacks and certain segments of the white population; religious intolerance shows the severance of communication lines among Jews, Catholics, and Protestants. The absence of the free flow of ideas within and among groups is unquestionably a primary cause of the lack of effective communication on the international level, which intensifies the

---

[22]Harold Lasswell et al., *Language of Politics*, George W. Stewart, Publisher, Inc., South Norwalk, Conn., 1949, p. 8; and William Albig, *Public Opinion*, McGraw-Hill Book Company, New York, 1939, pp. 26–52.

conflict between Russia and its satellites on the one hand and the United States and its allies on the other, as well as between the Soviet Union and Red China.

Communication Channels

The development of the media for mass communication has opened a Pandora's box for the transmission of information (and misinformation) and the conveyance of influence throughout the polity. In a political sense the elite at the fulcrum of the decision-making process may speak to the mid-elite, and the mid-elite to the public as a whole, on matters of public policy. Not only has the potential for leadership been greatly enhanced, but the relationship between candidate and voter in the campaign process has also been permanently altered.

The media of press, radio, motion pictures, and television are regarded in a different light by the public, the owners, and the users for hire. To the public they are sources of entertainment as well as information; to the owners they represent large investments of capital being risked in order to realize a monetary profit; and to the advertisers and propagandists they are a means of influencing millions of people to behave or think in a particular manner.

The number and variety of communications media in the United States and the extent to which they are used are a significant characteristic of twentieth-century civilization. In 1973 there were 932 television broadcasting stations, and about 95 percent of the households were equipped with television sets; the income from the industry surpassed $3.5 billion in 1971. Access of the people of the United States to commercial radio broadcasts from 6,902 stations was practically universal in 1970. In the same year 1,748 daily newspapers enjoyed a circulation of 62.1 million copies.

The advantages of mass media lie in the fact that they make it possible for a uniform message to be repeated indefinitely to a very large audience. But what of the nature of the message? In a nation dedicated to the principle of free speech, are all points of view heard? The mass-media channels are commercial enterprises, owned and operated for profit. Radio and television time is sold to advertisers of merchandise and ideas who are willing to pay the fees. Theoretically, any individual or group may buy time, providing the message to be dispensed is not prejudicial to the national interest.

Advertisers on the airwaves or in the press rarely dictate editorial policy directly. Two factors, however, interfere with the completely free interplay of ideas, theories, and opinions relating to economic, social, and political policy. Advertisers can exert leverage on the content and display of information by exercising the right of free choice in withholding their patronage, and thus they can jeopardize the solvency of a newspaper publisher or radio-station owner. Moreover, insofar as is practicable, such an owner will manage the enterprise in a manner that reflects his personal beliefs. Since ownership involves an investment of millions of dollars, most owners probably hold conservative views on matters of public policy, coinciding with those held by advertisers. Thus the forum for contrary opinions is limited.

The rule of caveat emptor applies in the marketplace of ideas. There is no public interest above and beyond the interests of the thousands of publics that are integrated into a national society. The American way of life is vulnerable to entirely unique and antithetical interpretations by the willful propagandist, be he reactionary, conservative, liberal, or radical. Crime, sex, love, and the struggle for status are the substance of the legends and myths presented to the public. From rags to riches; boy meets, loses, and finally wins girl; truth will and must (according to motion picture censorship codes) prevail over falsehood, good over evil, and the moral over the immoral. The mass media convey and help shape the culture pattern of society. Lacking resources within himself to withstand the calculated onslaught, the individual is the victim of his own limitations in making the most significant decisions affecting his behavior as a citizen.

The individual may be brilliant, moronic, or average in intelligence; widely experienced or a neophyte in economics, politics, and social living; alert and interested in his environment or inattentive and perhaps doomed to a limited intellectual horizon. To an alarming extent, he is potentially at the mercy of all who would use exaggeration, suppression, distortion, irrelevancy, emotional bias, and prejudice to create an image of the public interest for mass consumption.[23]

Communication Theory

Communication theory deals with the flow of information throughout society. The important elements of the communication process are the communicant (the person sending the message), the message itself (the information being conveyed), the channels employed (a person-to-person confrontation, the electronic signals of radio or television, the impulses of computer "hardware," or another individual), the recipient, and the consequences or impact of the message (whether it has progressed through a communications network) and its significance.

Aspects of communication theory dealing with mass communications have special relevance to the political process. The unique role of television in political campaigning; the burgeoning of applicable intelligence, known as the "information revolution"; and the expertise of the professional political campaign firm, capable of utilizing both, have combined to cause a reevaluation of the impact of the media upon democratic processes.

V. O. Key, Jr., in his perceptive study entitled *Public Opinion and American Democracy*, has effectively dealt with a number of concerns regarding the utilization of the media to manipulate the public. Some of these matters have been discussed in Chapter 14, on public opinion, but a brief reference to "mass media" in relationship to "mass opinion" may be pertinent at this point.[24] The assumption that there is necessarily a direct connection between an individual's beliefs and behavior and his or her exposure to the media is challenged upon several grounds. Politics has a low priority in the value system and therefore the attention of a minority of individuals.

The "attentives" to television and the press represent those relatively few persons of high socioeconomic status who are already concerned and have an established partisan commitment. By exercising his prerogatives of "selective attention," not only may the individual choose which, if any, of the media he wishes to be exposed to, but he may also react to what he sees, hears, reads, or is told with total independence. The evidence indicates that individuals exercise selectivity in attention; they tend to entertain only that information which confirms their opinions and to reject contrary views.

According to the two-step-flow theory suggested by Paul F. Lazarsfeld, Bernard Berelson, and Hazel Gaudet, the media-message impact is multiplied many times over because the "influentials" who hear the message may discuss its meaning with others,[25] who depend on friends and "advisers" for their views on public affairs. Another mitigating factor that may intervene between the intent of the message and its ultimate effect is the complex of groups to which the recipient belongs. Groups may act as "filters" of opinions presented to the membership, particularly groups that are dedicated to a cause. The implications of these observations are clear: Any assumption that those in control of the mass media can direct a message to a particular individual at a given time or place and gain confirmation of its acceptance must be empirically proved.

Communication and Semantics

Why is communication today a "network of partial or complete understandings"?[26] Some of the difficulties center in the nature and function of language itself; others lie in the psychological problems affecting the individual; and still more are found in the propaganda process, which intentionally distorts meaning.

---

[23]On mass communications, see Wilbur Schramm (ed.), *Mass Communications*, 2d ed., The University of Illinois Press, Urbana, 1960; *Printer's Ink*; *Editor and Publisher*; *Journalism Quarterly*; Douglas Waples (ed.), *Print, Radio and Film in a Democracy*, The University of Chicago Press, Chicago, 1942; Bernard Berelson and Morris Janowitz (eds.), *Reader in Public Opinion and Communication*, The Free Press of Glencoe, Inc., Chicago, 1950; Joseph T. Klapper, *The Effects of Mass Communication*, The Free Press of Glencoe, Inc., New York, 1960; Robert C. O'Hara, *Media for the Millions*, Random House, Inc., New York, 1961; Lucian W. Pye (ed.), *Communications and Political Development*, Princeton University Press, Princeton, N.J., 1963; and Dan Nimmo, *The Political Persuaders*, Prentice-Hall, Inc., Englewood Cliffs, N.J., 1970, pp. 111–162.

[24]See V. O. Key, Jr., *Public Opinion and American Democracy*, Alfred A. Knopf, Inc., New York, 1961, pp. 344–410, for this discussion.

[25]Paul Lazarsfeld et al., *The People's Choice*, Duell, Sloan & Pearce, Inc., New York, 1944.

[26]Edward Sapir, "Communication," in *Encyclopaedia of the Social Sciences*, The Macmillan Co., New York, 1931, vol. 4, pp. 78–80. See also Edward Sapir, "Language," in *Encyclopaedia of the Social Sciences*, The Macmillan Co., New York, 1933, vol. 9, pp. 155–168.

One branch of the science of communication analysis deals with the meaning and use of language and is popularly referred to as the study of "semantics." Semanticists are interested primarily in the way people use language: the meaning of words, symbols, and signs; the relationships between words and the objects or ideas they represent; and the effect that language has upon human behavior.[27] They have successfully identified many of the barriers and blockages in the processes of communication.

Semanticists have found that the representational quality of language is imperfect. Although the mind is constantly working to translate ideas into words, these words do not necessarily represent thought. Individuals habitually say things they do not mean, such as "Kill the umpire" or "I've had a wonderful time." Words may stand as symbols for thought, or they may be psychological safety valves, relieving the emotional tensions of the moment.

Moreover, the circumstances prevailing at the time the words are uttered may well modify their meaning. Wendell Johnson calls attention to the problem of phonation and articulation of sounds and to the auxiliary functions of gesture, posture, facial expression, and general bodily action as important modifying factors. The time and place of the act of communication, including the setting (which may involve music, flags, lighting, and the like), must be considered. Finally, such hazards as speech defects and anxiety tensions that reflect stage fright or feelings of inferiority cannot be ignored in communication evaluation. Such tensions may result from a too limited vocabulary for adequate expression or from an imperfect fund of information to cope with a situation.[28]

Because of the characteristics of human nature, it is a foregone conclusion that perfect communication will probably not be achieved in contemporary society. Nevertheless, if social science is to perfect the technique of analysis and prediction in matters of human behavior and if the misunderstandings that lead to individual tensions and eventually to social conflict are to be alleviated, some attempt must be made to eliminate the most obvious barriers. The semanticists have attacked both the mechanical and psychological problems with corrective solutions. It is important to recognize the symbolic nature of language. A word represents an object or an idea, but it is not a thing in itself. A person cannot vote for his favorite candidate on the word "ballot." The word, however, does represent a piece of printed paper upon which the voter "puts the cross in the square" on election day. We live in a verbal world made up of word symbols and in a nonverbal world of reality. It is vitally important that our language, which is our verbal world, reflect correctly our nonverbal world of objective reality and our experiences in that nonverbal world.

THE PROCESS, CONTENT, AND TECHNIQUES OF PROPAGANDA

A significant aspect of the relation of the individual to his political environment is his exposure to the influence of propaganda. When it originally gained currency in Western Europe early in the seventeenth century, the word "propaganda" meant the propagation of ideas through promotion, persuasion, and the utilization of influence.

Although the practice of propaganda is centuries old and although there are many excellent studies dealing with specialized aspects of the problem, a completely systematized statement of the process is yet to be made. Most attempts to tell how propaganda functions either describe some of the techniques used or discuss various psychological phases of the interaction between the propaganda and the personality being propagandized.

The Propaganda Process

In its simplest aspect, the propaganda process consists of three factors: the propagandist and his message, the technique and media used, and the

---

[27] Several representative studies in the literature of semantics are C. K. Ogden and I. A. Richards, *The Meaning of Meaning*, 2d ed., Edinburgh University Press, Edinburgh, 1926; Alfred Korzybski, *Science and Sanity*, 2d ed., The International Non-Aristotelian Library Publishing Company, New York, 1941; S. I. Hayakawa, *Language in Action*, Harcourt, Brace and Company, Inc., New York, 1941; I. J. Lee, *Language Habits in Human Affairs*, Harper & Brothers, New York, 1941; and W. Johnson, *People in Quandaries*, Harper & Brothers, New York, 1946.

[28] Wendell Johnson, "The Communication Process and General Semantic Principles," in Wilbur Schramm (ed.), *Mass Communications*, The University of Illinois Press, Urbana, Ill., 1949, pp. 26–74. See also Daniel Katz, "Psychological Barriers to Communication," *The Annals of the American Academy of Political and Social Science*, vol. 250, pp. 17–25, March 1947.

subject exposed to the influence.[29] The propagandist may be any individual, organization, agency, association, or institution that has a message and is interested in influencing the opinions and behavior of the subject. The technique involves the selection of appropriate methods and means to achieve the stated goals. The subject may be any individual or group providing the attitudes and opinions to be influenced in a given situation. Related factors involve the timing and skill employed by the propagandist in the manipulation of technique and, finally, the degree of success achieved in conditioning attitudes, changing behavior patterns, and implanting new clichés, stereotypes, and tabloids in the mind of the subject.

In the analysis of the formation of public opinion, mention was made of the conjuncture of heredity, environment, and experience in the formation of an individual's habits, attitudes, and personality traits. The propagandist wishes to create new habit patterns in the subject and to condition existing attitudes. At the base of the process is the principle of stimulus and response; that is, the propagandist provides carefully selected stimuli in order to elicit the desired response. Utilizing the appropriate psychological skills, the propagandist must first attract attention and then arouse interest, using the proper means so that the individual will perceive and distinguish the propaganda stimulus from among the many stimuli to which his or her senses of sight and hearing are constantly being subjected.[30]

The Technique and Content of Propaganda

A consideration of the technique and content of propaganda involves several factors, of which the following are important: the status of the propagandist, the particular situation invoking attention, and the plan of attack.

Status An inventory of the assets and liabilities of the propagandist will delimit the practical scope of his operations. There is a great difference in the power potential of various special-pleading groups. Among the factors affecting status are numbers, financial resources, internal integration and control, prestige and goodwill, and access to channels of communication. Groups differ notably in the possession of one or more of these assets. The National Association of Manufacturers claims to speak for 14,000 large and small manufacturers; the American Farm Bureau Federation has a membership of over 1.9 million; and the AFL-CIO has 13.6 million members. From the propagandist's point of view, membership may denote voting strength, prestige, a source of income, or, most importantly, channels of influence.

Financial resources may offset numbers as an asset for the propagandist. Money can be converted into minutes of radio time, thousands of news releases, hundreds of pamphlets, and square feet of billboard space. The AFL-CIO may collect $1 apiece from its 13½ million members for the dissemination of propaganda through the Committee on Political Education. The American Medical Association can assess its 219,000 members $25 each to raise approximately $54 million with which to hire a professional political public relations firm to propagandize against government-administered health insurance. It is not necessary, however, for all financial resources to be available in terms of dollars. The use of communication media may be offered free of charge or for greatly reduced fees, and goods and services may be donated without cost.

All interest groups spend a great deal of time and money propagandizing their own members. A closely knit organization such as the AMA, which exercises an unusual degree of control over the professional lives of its members, can propagandize with vigor and singleness of purpose and with reasonable assurance of practically unanimous support or, at least, with minimal outspoken opposition. Devices used by the NAM to win support for its propaganda line have included referenda by questionnaire among the rank and file and a broadly representative standing committee.

The Situation One of the propagandist's most difficult problems is the fact that he rarely controls the situation in which he works. He must deal not only with keen nonpropagandist competition for the subject's attention and interest but also with competing propagandas. Moreover, he always

---

[29]On the topics covered in this section, see David B. Truman, *The Governmental Process*, Alfred A. Knopf, Inc., New York, 1951, pp. 45–65, 213–287; and Leonard Doob, *Public Opinion and Propaganda*, Holt, Rinehart and Winston, Inc., New York, 1948, pp. 283–334.

[30]Doob, op. cit., pp. 310–320 and passim.

faces a dynamic social order with political overtones. The working environment is in a constant state of flux. What is effective propaganda today may be useless or even heretical tomorrow. Finally, changing interests and conditioning experiences are constantly molding the subject's personality. There are so many uncertainties in a fluid situation that Hitler, Mussolini, and Stalin, all of whom employed propaganda on a very wide scale, promptly took steps to manufacture their own situations. They commandeered all the communication channels, clamped down a tight censorship on news sources, and then created propaganda psychologically and quantitatively tailored to their needs.

An integral part of situational analysis is the estimate that must be made of the vulnerability of the subjects to propaganda. Leonard Doob has suggested that vulnerability depends upon perception, favorable habitual predispositions, intellectual capacity (the less intelligent are more vulnerable), and environment (with face-to-face situations preferred).[31] Frequently the propagandist speaks to some desire or felt need of the propagandee, in which case resistance may be negligible or entirely absent.

The Plan of Attack This third phase of technique and content includes selecting goals, planning the strategy of the campaign, devising tactics, and selecting the specific techniques that will offer the greatest rewards. If, as has been alleged, propaganda is both art and science, this phase is certainly the juncture of the two.

Theoretically, the goals of the propagandist are to condition attitudes or evoke overt behavior. Stated more explicitly, the propagandee is expected to buy your product rather than that of a competitor, vote for your candidate, write to his congressman for or against certain legislation, believe that the administration "fumbled the ball" or "took a courageous step," be a prestige symbol or "front man" for your organization, be a "spreader of the gospel," and so forth.

There are many subtle variations in the selection of goals. One interesting tactic, as Harold Lasswell suggests, is to use propaganda as a psychological catharsis. Symbols are manipulated merely to provide emotional release and siphon off tensions that might otherwise reach explosive intensity. Thus an issue or a "whipping-boy" personality might be introduced as a propaganda safety valve. This diversion would serve as a prelude to further emotional exploitation.

It is difficult to generalize about the strategy of a propaganda campaign because of the many variables in any situation. Since propaganda and warfare are closely related activities, the strategy that Lasswell suggested after studying the propaganda used in World War I might serve as a starting point. Lasswell found four basic principles serving as the foundation of strategy in war propaganda: (1) to mobilize hatred for the enemy by characterizing him as a murderous aggressor, having satanic aims and bent upon wanton destruction; (2) to preserve the friendship of allies by stressing mutual war aims, staging ceremonial demonstrations of friendship, and professing mutual devotion to humanitarian ideals; (3) to preserve the friendship of neutrals, gain their cooperation in a nonmilitary capacity, and identify their interests with the defeat of the enemy; and (4) to demoralize the enemy—for example, by making him question the integrity of his leaders.[32]

Transposing the spirit of such admonitions into propaganda strategy for domestic consumption, the principles would involve (1) creating a socially acceptable image of the group in the public mind, (2) explaining the group's behavior to the public's satisfaction, (3) drawing an uncomplimentary verbal picture of one's competitors, and (4) sitting in constant judgment on the behavior of competing groups.

The Tactics of Propaganda

One of the more important tactical considerations of propaganda is *timing*. The propagandist may need immediate results or, on the other hand, be able to build a campaign over weeks or months or, indeed, over an indefinite period. An element in the time factor is the necessity for *consistency*. If a message is to be repeated in a brief time span, it should be consistent. Hitler, who was a fervent

---

[31] Leonard W. Doob, "Propagandists vs. Propagandees," in Alvin W. Gouldner (ed.), *Studies in Leadership,* Harper & Brothers, New York, 1950, pp. 445–447.

[32] Harold D. Lasswell, *Propaganda Technique in the World War,* Alfred A. Knopf, Inc., New York, 1927, p. 191.

practitioner of the "big lie," recommended the spacing of inconsistencies in order to minimize or avoid detection.[33] The day of reckoning may be deferred, but usually not eliminated, by this tactic.

A second tactical principle is the decision *whether to lie or to tell the truth*, although rarely is the issue so clear-cut. Usually the problem is, rather, which facts to use and which to omit. Presumably the truth will be a factual account, while the lie will consist of unfounded generalizations.

A third tactical principle is the choice between the *rational* and the *irrational* approaches. When the former approach is used, the message is logically constructed to appeal to the intellect of the subject. The latter approach appeals directly to the subject's emotions. Professor Bartlett has suggested that an emotional appeal is more effective if it is calculated to arouse a specific emotion in tune with the anticipated behavior of the subject: pride and love, fear and anxiety, or hate and anger.[34]

The basic method for conveying tactical propaganda is by the use of suggestion. There are, however, many different techniques by which the message may be packaged. The problem is to attract attention and drive the point home with the most telling and lasting effect.[35] The *black-white technique*, or the *law of two sides*, is generally considered effective. The subject should not be left in the uncomfortable dilemma of having to consider alternatives because doubts may be raised, and he or she may arrive at an unacceptable conclusion. Conclusions are disseminated with only one possible acceptable answer—the "white" side of the argument. This method is closely akin to the practice of dogmatism, which may be characterized as the presentation of "a conclusion supported by group endorsement." A dogma, however, is made up of opinion rather than fact, whereas it is conceivable, but not usual, for the generalization in the law of two sides to be factually substantiated.

Distortion by selection is also a widely used method. In this instance, all the propagandist's materials may be based on facts. He has, however, selected only those facts which present the picture he wishes to exhibit. It is not often that the propagandist is in a position to monopolize a news source to the point where such a technique would be completely effective. Closely akin to this method is the practice of *slanting*. All the information may be presented, but the comment, discussion, or opinion accompanying the facts may emphasize only one side or aspect of the problem. *Distraction* is a handy weapon in the arsenal of the propagandist. Drawing a "red herring" across the path of factual information can serve to create an erroneous impression.

The propagandist who lies depends upon mass credulity. Successful fabrication is without doubt an exacting art, requiring a great deal of skill. Propaganda is employed in a highly competitive market, and, quite apart from moral or ethical considerations, continued fabrication is regarded as hazardous and in the long run essentially unrewarding.

There remains for consideration one of the most effective devices at the command of the propagandist: the *rumor*. In a definitive study of this phenomenon entitled *The Psychology of Rumor*, authors Allport and Postman attribute three characteristics to this technique: (1) It is a proposition offered for belief, (2) it is usually transmitted orally from person to person, and (3) it lacks substantiating evidence.[36] Rumors may be fear-inspiring, capitalize upon wishful thinking, or thrive upon hate and hostility. They are most effective within a particular "rumor public"—individuals of like interests who are concerned with the subject matter of the rumor. The ambiguity of the information that is conveyed, coupled with either lack of information or credulity on the part of the rumor public, makes this method of attack particularly effective in politics. Few presidential candidates are able to avoid the insidious effects of this propaganda device. Herbert Hoover was said to be unmercifully exploiting cheap Mexican labor on his California

---

[33]F. C. Bartlett, *Political Propaganda,* Cambridge University Press, New York, 1940, p. 85.

[34]Ibid., p. 74.

[35]Various aspects of technique dealt with here are discussed in Albig, op. cit., pp. 312ff.; Bartlett, op. cit., pp. 51–103; Doob, *Public Opinion and Propaganda,* pp. 354–422; Lasswell, *Propaganda Technique in the World War,* p. 191 and passim; Frederick E. Lumley, *The Propaganda Menace,* Appleton-Century-Crofts, Inc., New York, 1933, pp. 107–136; and Sidney Rogerson, *Propaganda in the Next War,* Geoffrey Bles, Ltd., London, 1938, pp. 79–126.

[36]G. W. Allport and L. Postman, *The Psychology of Rumor,* Holt, Rinehart and Winston, Inc., New York, 1947.

ranch, Al Smith was charged with being an agent of the Catholic Church, and Franklin D. Roosevelt was said to have had Jewish ancestry. Some rumors become firmly established in the culture as legend or myth and are transmitted to future generations as fact. Many of the tales relating to the experiences of Washington and Lincoln may have originated in rumor.

The Limitations of Propaganda

Is there any defense against the impact of the propagandist's "paper bullets"? Apparently, several factors tend to inhibit the best-conceived plans to establish thought control over the citizen's mind. The first is a negative influence that is inherent in the cultural environment. There is competition among propagandas. Some of the most brilliantly directed propaganda shafts are blunted upon the subject's conflicting loyalties. Over a period of time a publisher's or radio commentator's biases and prejudices come to be revealed beyond question, and his editorial fulminations are thus clearly labeled. There is a point of psychological tolerance beyond which the propagandee becomes either confused or apathetic toward the influence business. A defense reaction is motivated, particularly when propaganda fails to clear up the ambiguity of a complex situation. The subject develops a profound indifference, becomes actively hostile to psychological pressures, or retreats into the cultural myths and legends which he has previously defined in terms of his own experience and which he craves to have repeatedly reinforced.

A second limitation lies in the formal rules and regulations that govern the dissemination of information in society. The legal obstacles are very broad in character and not particularly confusing to the propagandist. The government exercises formal censorship in matters affecting its vital interests, such as military information, and protects itself against subversive influences by the Sedition Act. The government further offers its services in protecting the individual against personal attacks involving libel, defamation of character, or slander. In a country devoted to the principle of free speech and civil rights, government controls are reserved for crisis situations and do not affect the bulk of propaganda materials and practices. Official censorship is supplemented by the scruples and moral censorship of the individual conscience. It is practically impossible to evaluate the effectiveness of this latter phenomenon.[37]

The best weapons the citizen can employ to protect himself against the competing emotional appeals of the propagandist are an alert, inquiring mind and a keen appreciation of the dynamics of his social environment.[38] A first step in propaganda analysis is the development of an awareness by the analyst of the propaganda potentialities of a situation. A demand, a plea, or even a suggestion that one point of view be adopted and another rejected regarding an issue, an occurrence, or a personality in public life may provide the stimulus for careful investigation. The subject of the promotional campaign should be identified and placed in proper perspective. Is the occurrence unique? Has the issue been divorced from other closely related issues or separated from the context of past events? Why has a particular personality suddenly become the cynosure of all eyes?

The next stage is to direct attention to the propagandist. Who is he? Which group does he represent? What motivates his interest in this situation? Where does he obtain his financial support? Is he a recognized authority on his subject? What goals is he striving to achieve?

The concluding phase of the analysis should be devoted to an attempt to ascertain the reliability of the evidence presented by the propagandist. What is the stated or implied hypothesis of the argument that he has presented? Is the evidence fragmentary or complete? Is it based upon opinion, hearsay, or fact? Does the evidence reveal prejudice or bias on the part of the special pleader?

Since much of the individual's life is dedicated to the interpretation of his mental and physical environment, an accurate appraisal of that which he reads, hears, and sees will greatly aid his orientation to reality. He may attain his goal partly through informal education and vicarious experience and

---

[37]"Propaganda and Censorship," *Psychiatry*, vol. 3, no 4, pp. 628–632, Nov. 1940.
[38]Harold Lasswell, "The Person: Subject and Object of Propaganda," *The Annals of the American Academy of Political and Social Science*, vol. 179, pp. 187–193, May 1935; William Hummel and Keith Huntress, *The Analysis of Propaganda*, The Dryden Press, Inc., New York, 1949, pp. 73–89.

partly through the media of formal education. Certainly one may assume that in a democracy, the educational process will make the student and potential citizen acutely aware of the dynamics of the social process, the motivation for human behavior, the nature of special pleading and its effect on public policy, the pressuring of government, and finally the mechanics of manipulating opinion through propaganda. Once informed, the individual must pick and choose the evidence he wishes to accept according to the goals and value judgments that are important to him.

STUDY-GUIDE QUESTIONS

1 Evaluate the strengths and liabilities of the "traditional" and "behavioral" approaches to the study of politics. Are these methods mutually exclusive in your estimation?
2 Much has been written concerning the elites who presumably dominated the Fascist and National Socialist governments during the 1930s. Do you detect the phenomenon of elitism in American politics?
3 Communication theory deals with the flow of information throughout society. Relate the significance of this process to the problems of a self-governing people in a democratic society.
4 Compare the differences in the mode of operation of an interest group in a democracy and an interest group in a totalitarian state; relate both processes to the concept of pluralism.
5 What are some of the most effective propaganda techniques? Is a democratic government ever justified in using propaganda on its own citizens?

REFERENCES

Alexander, Herbert E.: *Money in Politics*, Public Affairs Press, Washington, 1972.

Bowen, Don R.: *Political Behavior of the American Public*, Charles E. Merrill Company, New York, 1968.

Crockett, Norman L. (ed.): *The Power Elite in America*, D. C. Heath and Company, Boston, 1970.

La Palombara, Joseph: *Interest Groups in Italian Politics*, Princeton University Press, Princeton, N.J., 1964.

Malecki, Edward S., and H. R. Mahood (eds.): *Group Politics: A New Emphasis*, Charles Scribner's Sons, New York, 1972.

Millerath, Lester W.: *Political Participation: How and Why Do People Get Involved in Politics?* Rand McNally & Company, Chicago, 1965.

Nimmo, Dan: *The Political Persuaders*, Prentice-Hall, Inc., Englewood Cliffs, N.J., 1970.

Rose, Richard: *Studies in British Politics*, Macmillan & Co., Ltd., London, 1967.

Skilling, Gordon H., and Franklyn Griffiths (eds.): *Interest Groups in Soviet Politics*, Princeton University Press, Princeton, N.J., 1971.

Zeigler, Harmon L., and G. Wayne Peak: *Interest Groups in American Society*, 2d ed., Prentice-Hall, Inc., Englewood Cliffs, N.J., 1972.

Zisk, Betty H. (ed.): *American Political Interest Groups: Reading in Theory and Research*, Wadsworth Publishing Company, Inc., Belmont, Calif., 1969.

Chapter 16

The Organization of the People: Political Parties

Why are there political parties? Why are some people Democrats, while others are Republicans, Agrarians, Nationalists, Tories, Labourites, Centrists, Royalists, or Popular Fronters? Although the struggle for political power in domestic politics is, as a rule, no longer fought with physical violence, factionalism and rivalry are perpetuated and institutionalized in the activity of political parties. Partisanship and competition are an integral part of the political process because the goals of winning elections are to staff the government, perpetuate an ideology, keep an elite in power, or perhaps control public policy.

This is the third chapter dealing specifically with problems the individual encounters when interacting with his or her political environment. Our concern in Chapter 14, "The Voice of the People: Public Opinion," was a reassessment of the historic and contemporary models of public opinion, the processes of political socialization of the individual, the ways in which people express their views on public policy, and how individual and collective opinions are linked to government action.

In Chapter 15, "Political Participation and the Political Environment," we reviewed briefly the behavioral movement in political science as a background for a discussion of how the individual behaves in a political context, aspects of personality development, role playing, interest-group dynamics, communication problems, and the significance of propaganda in conditioning responses to political stimuli. In the present chapter we discuss the political apparatus with which the individual is most involved as a participant in the electoral process.

Why Political Parties?

The major party systems may best be presented against a background of the primary functions that a party is expected to perform in the political process. It has been suggested that the elusive public is in reality a varied group of economic, social, and cultural publics. Moreover, the individual who is part of the electorate may be indifferent to the obligations of citizenship or perhaps ill informed on the issues of the day. The party constitutes one connecting link between diverse groups in society and members of the electorate attempting to achieve organized political action. The party attempts to stimulate interest with colorful candidates, clubs, personal canvassing, mass meetings, parades, and free entertainment. It uses all the effective media of communication to educate the uninitiated: literature, speeches, radio, television, cartoons, music, and so forth.

In selecting campaign issues, either to build a positive program for future legislative action or to attack the opposition, the party helps crystallize opinion and create a temporary consensus that is the basis for conducting an election. An integral part of this function is the enlistment and grooming of candidates for elective office. The issues constitute the party line, and the candidates convey the message to the electorate.

The party carries on campaigns to win elections and assumes the responsibility of conducting the government when it achieves success at the polls. In the United States, this function acquires added importance because of the principles of the separation of powers and checks and balances and also because of the division of powers inherent in the system of federalism.

As temporary custodian of the national interest, the party in power must answer not only to its ardent supporters but ultimately also to the entire nation by planning and executing public policy. By bridging the economic and geographic gaps of sectionalism, the party seeks a compromise in public policy that will nationalize the interests of the electorate as well as provide a channel for the effective expression of public opinion.[1]

A Historical Note

Political scientists have considerable data on the historical evolution of the party as an institution and on the sociopolitical factors in the environment that conditioned its development.

Party history in Western Europe represents one phase of the growth of constitutional, representative government. The modern democratic party as it is known today is the result of at least two important political developments: the limitation of the authority of the absolute monarchy and the extension of the suffrage to virtually all the adult population. As long as the king enjoyed a monopoly of power and the mass of citizens could not vote, party activity was not only fruitless but also treasonable. Thus it is not surprising to find the historic roots of the party both in the struggle of the legislature to limit the king's prerogative and in the development of groups within the expanded electorate taking sides in the battle or demanding recognition of their interests.

Each nation has developed its own unique party traditions, and those of the United States derive historically from both the great constitutional struggles between king and Parliament in seventeenth- and eighteenth-century England and the indigenous political experience of the colonists.[2]

The colonial period in American history failed to produce political parties in the modern sense.[3] The struggle over the acceptance of the new national constitution brought forth two national parties: the Federalist party, which supported its adoption, and the Antifederalist party, which constituted the opposition. The dispute produced *The Federalist,* one of the great political tracts in American literature. Among the masterly disquisitions on the principles of the constitution authored by Hamilton, Jay, and

---

[1] Herman Finer, *The Theory and Practice of Modern Government,* rev. ed., Holt, Rinehart and Winston, Inc., New York, 1949, pp. 280–282. For two of the best contemporary discussions of parties in the context of the American system, see Frank J. Sorauf, *Party Politics in America,* 2d ed., Little, Brown and Company, Boston, 1972; and Hugh A. Bone, *American Politics and the Party System,* 4th ed., McGraw-Hill Book Company, New York, 1971.

[2] A classic study of this development in England (vol. I) and the United States (vol. II) is M. Ostrogorski, *Democracy and the Organization of Political Parties,* The Macmillan Company, New York, 1908. See also R. T. McKenzie, *British Political Parties,* 2d ed., Frederick A. Praeger, Inc., New York, 1964. This is an authoritative discussion of the British party system with emphasis upon the historic origins of the Conservative and Labour parties.

[3] For interesting interpretations of the historic and contemporary development of the American two-party system, see William N. Chambers, *Political Parties in a New Nation,* Oxford University Press, New York, 1963; and Judson L. James, *American Political Parties in Transition,* Harper & Row, Publishers, Incorporated, New York, 1974.

Madison was the penetrating analysis of factionalism in essay No. 10, by Madison. In foreshadowing the development of both interest groups and parties, he propounded the interest theory as being a fundamental determinant of factions. To him, economic interests were of paramount importance, including the relations of debtor and creditor, property owner and non-property owner, and landed proprietor and manufacturer. "The regulation of these various and interfering interests," he said, "forms the principal task of modern legislation, and involves the spirit of party and faction in the necessary and ordinary operation of government."

Upon the adoption of the Constitution, the issue that had held the Antifederalists together was resolved. A new party alignment developed, despite Washington's famous admonition against factionalism in his Farewell Address. The conservatives, the broad constructionists of federal powers, the advocates of a strong central government, and the more prosperous commercial and agricultural interests gathered around Alexander Hamilton, first secretary of the treasury, in the Federalist party organization. Those favoring popular rights, the strict constructionists of federal powers, the less prosperous farmers, debtors, and laborers rallied under the banner of Thomas Jefferson, first secretary of state, as the Democratic-Republican party. By the close of Washington's second administration, the embryonic American party system was effectively established.

A Contemporary Approach

Empirical research during the past two decades has sought new perspectives from which parties and party systems may be analyzed and better understood in the contemporary environment. Attempts have been made to relate parties to other institutions in society, to groups competing for power, and to categories of classes and individuals seeking their own interests and goals.

Society is viewed as a dynamic organism wherein competition takes place for prestige, status, power, and security. The competition is not aimless, but purposeful; individuals and groups wish to shape the environment and the circumstances that condition their lives. Considered in this context, a political party is merely one of many groups contesting for power. Others include pressure groups in the realms of business, labor, and agriculture; civic organizations; auxiliaries to the parties; the institutions of the family, school, church, and government; and countless others.

Conflict and competition are therefore the natural and inevitable order of daily life while influence is won, utilized, transferred, or lost. A critical factor in the generation and perpetuation of competition is the scarcity of resources that must be mobilized if influence is to be made effective. Wealth, technology, skills, and individual capabilities are distributed unevenly (or differentially) among individuals, groups, organizations, and institutions. This circumstance intensifies the struggle and heightens the competition; the fortunes of both individuals and groups wax and wane.

The search for influence is not just an undifferentiated mass of social activity and group interaction. By limiting the scope of investigation to relationships of political parties and party systems, some verifications regarding the nature of these elements in the political process may be achieved. What are the characteristics of parties? On what basis may they be compared with one another? What are the properties of a party system? How does one compare such systems in different political environments?

THE POLITICAL PARTY

A political party may be described in terms of the purpose for which it was organized, the character of the membership, its structure, or the functions it performs. The English statesman Edmund Burke thought of a party as a group of men who had agreed upon a principle by which the national interest might be served. Others have defined a party as an organized group of individuals seeking to seize the power of government in order to enjoy the benefits to be derived from such control. A political party has also been characterized as a coalition of group interests representing a segment of the social community.

The Party Concept

One of the most general and also flexible definitions of a party in a Western democratic nation is that offered by Leon D. Epstein: "any group, however loosely organized, seeking to elect governmental office-holders under a given label."[4] As Epstein indicates, this would permit a group of office seekers banded together under a label but sans followers to be designated a party; the label or name would be the distinguishing characteristic since size, degree of integration, and number of followers would be immaterial.

The French scholar Maurice Duverger has contributed an important contemporary treatise on political parties.[5] He believes that the distinguishing characteristic of a party is its structure or anatomy, which he discusses in terms of organization, membership, and leadership. He classifies parties according to whether they have a "direct" or an "indirect" structure. In the first instance, members belong to the party as individuals; in the second, membership in the party is achieved by virtue of belonging to some other organization allied to the party by mutual interests. The relationship between the British trade unions and the Labour party is an illustration.

In characterizing membership as an important variable, Duverger distinguishes between a "cadre" and a "mass" party. The former is a carefully selected group of "notables"—skilled, prestigious, politically sophisticated, and influential—whose reputations attract voter support for electoral activity. The latter tends to be great in terms of numbers with an elite leadership selected from the working classes; this large body of dues-paying members is interested in socialist indoctrination as well as electoral activity. Finally, Duverger views party leadership in the context of "titular" as opposed to "real" leaders. He concludes that leadership assumes an oligarchic form featuring a ruling class or an inner circle.[6]

Professor Samuel J. Eldersveld considers the party from a behavioral viewpoint as a "social group" engaging in "patterned activity" within the social matrix. When interpreted as a social organism, the party possesses role-playing individuals within an identifiable social unit, perceiving and attempting to achieve specific goals. A party is also a polity or miniature political system with an authority structure, patterns of power distribution, a representative process, and electoral and decision-making systems.[7]

The Characteristics of a Party

A discussion of the nature of a party should distinguish between the broad mass of members, whose affiliation is only nominal and whose loyalties are somewhat tentative; the professional workers, who hold official positions in the organization; and the elite of the party, who wield the primary power of decision. A distinction should also be made between the function of a party—which is to nominate candidates for office, to campaign, and if successful to assume the responsibilities of governing—and the objective of a pressure group, for instance, that seeks to influence government in order to obtain laws compatible with its own special interests.

In general, a party has the following characteristics: membership, organization and administration, goals and objectives, and resources (to a greater or lesser degree) including funds, talent, electoral strength, charismatic candidates, and so forth. Most schemes for identifying types of parties emphasize one or a combination of these characteristics and fall conveniently into three broad categories: (1) doctrinaire, (2) organizational, and (3) functional.

Some parties place a high priority upon the nurturing and propagation of specific ideologies and value systems, specifying the mode of distribution of power in society; the socialist parties in Western Europe and the communist parties throughout the world immediately come to mind. The predominant characteristics warranting attention in other parties may be their unique structure: the party hierarchy, administrative agencies, career positions, internal

---

[4] Leon D. Epstein, *Political Parties in Western Democracies*, Frederick A. Praeger, Inc., New York, 1967, p. 9.

[5] Maurice Duverger, *Political Parties*, John Wiley & Sons, Inc., New York, 1954.

[6] Ibid., pp. 61–205 and passim.

[7] Samuel J. Eldersveld, *Political Parties: A Behavioral Analysis*, Rand McNally & Company, Chicago, 1964, pp. 1–23. Professors Ranney and Kendall have developed an interesting classification of party systems based upon an estimate of the number of parties and their prospects of winning elections. To the one-party, two-party, and multiparty categories they have added the modified one-party type in which one party is predominantly successful, but a second one wins often enough to maintain a healthy opposition, and the one-party type (to be distinguished from the totalitarian type) in which one party wins consistently, and the second receives a small token vote and is not effective in opposition. Austin Ranney and Willmoore Kendall, *Democracy and the American Party System*, Harcourt, Brace & World, Inc., New York, 1956, pp. 83–115.

discipline, and mode of liaison with other groups. Finally, the party may be viewed in terms of the functions it performs: campaigning, mobilizing the electorate, establishing relationships with the decision-making centers of government, recruiting leaders, and the like.

A Theoretical Frame of Reference

In order to analyze a political party, scholars have sought a frame of reference that would be applicable to any party at any time in any political environment. Are there any general principles, any hypotheses, constituting a party model that are universal in nature—that would be just as valid in describing the Radical Socialists in France, the Liberal Democratic party in Japan, the Conservative party in Britain, or the American Independent party of Governor George Wallace of Alabama? General principles applicable to all parties would serve as "constants" when applied to a particular party, and the "variables," or unique features, of each party or system could then be analyzed and compared for greater enlightenment.

There are no commonly accepted answers to these questions; indeed, one authority has identified nine separate ways in which parties may be classified and six different categories of party systems.[8] Nevertheless, a new way of looking at parties has been devised by describing party functions in relatively abstract terms.

The People-Party Relationship In this model the party is looked upon as an institution or a mechanism that in a sense stands between the public, particularly the voters in a political society, and the government. How does the party relate to the people on the one hand and to the government on the other? It helps the people identify and *articulate their interests.* Assume that the public feels strongly about capital punishment, communism, income taxes, birth control, amnesty for deserters, or détente with the People's Republic of China. The party provides a forum for discussion, a platform of positions on issues, leaders to express views, and propaganda literature "pro" and "con," all representing the interests of some segment of the public. On another echelon, the public's interests are treated as group interests, representing objectives of various segments of the economy and culture. The party serves as a catalyst through which business, agriculture, labor, civil libertarians, doctors, and conservationists represent their concerns to government. The function of identification and articulation of interests is accepted as a constant, whether it happens in Ghana, East Germany, South Vietnam, or Switzerland and even though the specific interests and issues are unique to each country.[9]

Another service rendered by this party model is termed the "aggregation of demands." Individuals and groups constantly make demands upon a political party. An individual may wish to participate in the political process, for example, and request that the party make the opportunity available. More importantly, pressure groups may demand that social reform be effected by means of redistribution of the wealth through a new tax system, that the state go to war because of some alleged affront, that the government grant subsidies for an agricultural crop, or that the party alter its policy regarding membership of minority groups. Demands may be made directly on the party, internally within the party organization, or to the government through the party.

The party sifts, opposes, accepts, mediates, "brokers," negotiates, and otherwise behaves to aggregate these demands. In other words, it attempts to effect a compromise between opposing interests and to establish a consistent position commensurate with the accepted value system of its members. It generally has a set of principles and a program posing solutions to current problems of public policy. Moreover, it may adopt alternative courses of action for which voters express preferences at the polls and elsewhere.

The concept of aggregation of demands is broad in its connotations. It embraces establishment of a

---

[8]There is a vast literature on the empirical approach to parties and party systems; among the best introductions are "Introduction: The History, Functions, and Typology of Parties," in Roy C. Macridis (ed.), *Political Parties: Contemporary Trends and Ideas,* Harper & Row, Publishers, Incorporated, New York, 1967, pp. 9–23 (see p. 20 for the categories); Harry Eckstein, "Party Systems," in *International Encyclopedia of the Social Sciences,* Crowell Collier and Macmillan, Inc., New York, 1968, vol. 11, pp. 436–453; and Epstein, op. cit. All have been consulted for this section.

[9]For a summary of the party from a functional point of view, see Macridis, op. cit., pp. 17–20.

consensus within a party, efforts to deal with opposing views, or perhaps the formation of a coalition of interests in response to conflicting demands. Once it has performed the function of aggregation, the party will usually *mobilize support* for the positions taken, both within and outside the party. By working for a large common area of agreement among the conflicting demands of individuals and groups, the party can fulfill its obligations and functions as an intermediary between people and government.

The Party-Government Relationship As we turn from the party-public to the party-government relationship, certain other generalizations are in order. The most universally recognized duties of the party in this context are the *discovery, recruitment,* and *training* of personnel both to "man" the party and to provide leadership to the government. Party membership is the most widely used door to power positions in government. Moreover, the party runs the electoral process, which is a primary selective mechanism for public service.

Finally, recruitment, training, and selection for government service have but one objective: control of the decision-making machinery that creates public policy. By managing the government, the party has the opportunity to implement its program.

In practice, the application of these "laws," or model specifications, is subject to many modifications, mutations, and exceptions. Moreover, this brief discussion provides merely a glimpse of the sophisticated empirical rationale of party duties and responsibilities. It is evident, nevertheless, that the operation of a party and the basis for a comparison of parties are being placed in a new perspective by such concepts as articulation of interests, aggregation of interests and demands, brokerage (the representative function), recruitment, selection, training of leaders, and formulation and implementation (of policy).

PARTY SYSTEMS

When the analytic perspective is broadened from the criteria for categorization of parties per se to the evaluation and classification of *party systems,* the party concept gains in significance.

The concept of a party system as differentiated from the notion of a party has been utilized as an analytic device to explore both the conditions under which parties exist and their behavior while inhabiting the political environment. The idea of a system assumes that parties are linked horizontally and vertically to other social groups by structure, function, or both. Viewing parties in this manner offers wide latitude to explore degrees of interdependence and interrelatedness as well as patterns of interaction between parties, interest groups, elites in other power structures, and the various political institutions of the governmental apparatus. A party system is itself a subsystem of the larger political system, which in turn is related to the socioeconomic, cultural, and particularly the legal-constitutional life of a state.

Is there a widely accepted theoretical frame of reference for the description of party systems based upon adequately tested generalizations? Leading authorities believe not. Nevertheless, contemporary research has provided useful insights in this area, and some of the most significant will be briefly mentioned.

Harry Eckstein has effectively summarized some basic analytic concepts in party-system analysis, particularly with reference to the problems of comparison and classification.[10] In representative governments the most important and unique function performed by political parties is the operation of the *electoral process:* discovering the interests of the electorate, finding leaders to represent those interests, electing them to office, and eventually making public policy. In performing these tasks, parties within the representative system compete with one another for power. The study of political systems can therefore be accomplished from one important perspective by analyzing the nature of that competition. Answers are sought to the questions of who competes in the electoral process and of how or why they fail or succeed.

Two widely used methods for the identification of "competitive interaction patterns" are a comparison of the structure or anatomy of the parties within the system and a comparison of the functions they perform. Patterns of variation between systems could be discovered by comparing one-

---

[10] For the following discussion of party systems, see Eckstein, op. cit., pp. 438–448 and passim.

party, two-party, and multiparty systems; by measuring the relative competitive strength of the units within the party system in terms of votes and size (major and minor parties); by ascertaining how the units compete in strategy and tactics; by evaluating party performance vis-á-vis other political structures in the environment; or, finally, by investigating the dynamics of the system, e.g., whether it tends toward stability or instability over a period of time.

The remaining two major categories measuring competitive interaction suggested by Eckstein include the determinants of the party system, its relationships with the other aspects of the general political system, the social structure and culture of the larger system, and the unique history of the parties within the system. Finally, the party system may be viewed *in toto* in terms of the impact it makes upon other structures in the political environment.[11]

Problems of Classification

The traditional method of categorizing party systems is to describe them according to the number of parties they contain. For example, the Soviet Union and the People's Republic of China have one-party systems, Britain and the United States have two-party systems, and France and Italy have multiparty systems. Although no other method has received general approval, this so-called typology of counting parties violates the basic concept of competitive interaction patterns. The empiricists are critical of the theoretical dilemmas caused by the "numbers approach" to party systems. They maintain that there cannot be intraparty competition in a one-party state; that, in fact, the United States and many other two-party polities have had viable competitive third-party movements; and that the category of multiparty states is therefore the only acceptable single-party-system pattern.

An able student of political parties, Frank J. Sorauf, suggests that such comparisons offer only one-dimensional measurement and thus overlook ideological rivalries between major and minor parties that do not actually compete electorally; that the range of competition extends to political groups other than parties; that party differences in organization are ignored; and, finally, that the expectations of systems analysis far exceed the product of competitive party electoral analysis per se.[12]

Perhaps the dimensions of the problem can best be illustrated by a brief presentation of other classificatory systems and methods of analysis utilized by several distinguished scholars. Gabriel Almond, applying the concept of the aggregative function described above as a criterion, has established four categories of party systems: (1) authoritarian party systems (with a subcategory called "totalitarian"), (2) dominant nonauthoritarian party systems, (3) competitive two-party systems, and (4) competitive multiparty systems.[13]

Totalitarian parties aggregate interests by deep penetration into the social structure of the nation, and therefore the transmission and aggregation of demands must come through the single-party structure. Authoritarian party systems are more lenient and permit demands to be made openly, but the absence of free elections causes policy to be made through authoritative structures such as the party, the army, and the bureaucracy. Dominant nonauthoritarian party systems emerge when interest groups join in a program of national independence. A loyal opposition is lacking, party cohesion becomes difficult to maintain, and interests are not effectively aggregated, in part because decisions must be postponed. Competitive two-party systems are exemplified by circumstances represented in the United Kingdom and the United States. Multiparty systems are subdivided into "working" and "immobilist" classes. The former, found in the Scandinavian countries, are "broadly aggregative" and homogeneous, permitting a stable majority and opposition coalitions to run the government. The latter, represented by France and Italy, exist in a "fragmented, isolative political culture" wherein political coalitions are fragile.

Another party categorization is that employed by Maurice Duverger, who uses party strength as a criterion.[14] Strength is measured in terms of both voters in the electorate and party seats in the

---

[11]Ibid., pp. 447–448.

[12]Sorauf, op. cit., p. 29.

[13]For both the classification and following summary, see Gabriel A. Almond, "Interest Articulation and the Function of Aggregation," in Charles G. Mayo and Beryl L. Crowe (eds.), *American Political Parties*, Harper & Row, Publishers, Incorporated, New York, 1967, pp. 57–73.

[14]Duverger, op. cit., pp. 281–299.

legislature, although Duverger emphasizes the latter in his presentation. His categories of strength are four in number: (1) parties with a majority bent on commanding an absolute majority in a parliament, which he finds commonly in two-party systems and only exceptionally in multiparty systems; (2) major parties without hope of ever obtaining an absolute majority and forced to accommodate to the necessity of operating as part of a coalition of parties; (3) medium parties incapable of forming a minority government and confined to either following the lead of a major party or keeping the opposition divided; and (4) minority parties unable to play a political role either with government parties or with parties in opposition.

Roy C. Macridis prefers not to distinguish between party and party system when devising his typology or scheme of classification. He employs three criteria.[15] The first is sources of party support, and here he distinguishes between comprehensive parties, which attempt to solicit votes from the entire electorate, and sectarian parties, which seek adherents from a particular class, region, or ideology. The second criterion relates to internal organization: A closed party restricts membership, and an open party permits virtually anyone to join. The third criterion specifies modes of action as specialized or diffused. The former follows conventional procedures for controlling the government for a limited purpose and for a limited time. The latter is pragmatic in utilizing practically any means to come to power, and it stresses permanent and total control.

This has been a brief introductory excursion into the area of the empirical-theory approach to the study of political parties. The change of emphasis from a straightforward description of the party structure and function is strikingly significant. Empirical theory has added an important new dimension to political analysis. It should be stated, nevertheless, that any definitive understanding of the political process must of necessity be factually based. The first obligation of the student is to develop a clear picture of the "nuts and bolts" of the political universe. It is to this factual world that we now return.

[15]Macridis, op. cit., pp. 20–23.

CONTEMPORARY PARTY SYSTEMS

A knowledge of the contemporary political environment is essential to an understanding of parties and politics. Normative analysis of the circumstances that gave birth to a party movement, the constitutional system within which it works, the electoral practices under which it operates, and the people who support it, particularly the personalities who carry its banner into political combat, helps breathe life into the drama that is party politics. We begin on familiar ground, the two-party system in the United States, and proceed to the other major competing patterns—the multiparty and single-party systems. Throughout it is well to remember the empiricists' admonition that each system has both prototypes and sundry mutations.

The Two-Party System in the United States

In brief compass, what are the outstanding characteristics of the American party system? It operates within a strong, prevailing constitutional system. Its "dualism," as V. O. Key, Jr., suggests, is contained in a "moving political consensus" that eschews ideological extremes and is sufficiently flexible to find a middle ground from one historic generation to another.[16] Its weakness as well as its strength is its disjointed organization, which lacks discipline. Competition occurs in the attempt to win support from "switch voters," the independents or the uncommitted in a virtually classless society. It seeks pragmatic solutions to problems through intraparty and interparty coalitions. Not fitting any known ideal model of popular representation, it works.

Many views have been offered to explain the development of the American two-party system. One of the most significant is that the American political process is indigenous to the constitutional framework of government that it serves. The principle of federalism, implemented by the division of powers between national and state governments

[16]V. O. Key, Jr., *Politics, Parties, and Pressure Groups*, 5th ed., Thomas Y. Crowell Company, New York, 1964, pp. 222–225. For an excellent discussion of the development of the American two-party system, see William N. Chambers, "Parties and Nation-Building in America," in Joseph La Palombara and Myron Weiner (eds.), *Political Parties and Political Development*, Princeton University Press, Princeton, N.J., 1966, pp. 89–90.

and the separation of powers among executive, legislative, and judicial authorities, makes party control of government extremely difficult to achieve. A successful presidential campaign can be conducted only by an elaborate nationwide party organization, with access to many millions of dollars and with a program that is devised to weld the diverse economic, social, and sectional interests of the citizens into a winning coalition at the polls.

The structure of the American party is that of a loose federation of national and state agencies. The strength and primary legal control of the system lie in the fifty states, each possessing its own party government and its own electorate. Campaigns must be waged and won in enough individual states to capture the presidency by a majority vote of the electoral college. In order to ensure control of Congress, a sufficient number of votes must be obtained within each state to elect a majority of the House of Representatives and the Senate.

The American electoral system places very real obstacles in the path of a third party attempting to establish its political strength on a national basis. The 435 representatives are elected from single-member districts. Under our plurality system of voting, the candidate who wins the most votes is elected to Congress. Under the two-party system, both the Republicans and the Democrats compete in almost all the congressional districts. No third party has been able to establish an adequate nationwide base of party strength. Thus a third party may marshal a large popular vote in a state, while losing the contest for the single seat in a congressional district. The "lost" votes count for nought, and the minor party is unable to establish its presence in Congress.

The same circumstances militate against a minor party's attempt to win the presidency. In the 1924 campaign, Robert M. La Follette made an impressive showing as leader of the Progressive party, winning one of each six votes cast for the office. His popular vote of 4,831,289 represented slightly over 17 percent of the combined votes of his opponents. Nevertheless, he received only 13 of the 531 electoral-college votes, or 2.4 percent. The electoral college fails to reflect the true popular voting strength of even the major parties.

If the state were made the electoral district and all representatives were elected at large under a system of proportional representation, the popular strength of the third party would be rewarded by the election of one or more nominees to Congress. It would also gain electoral-college votes commensurate with its strength in the electorate.

None of the many minor parties in American politics has won a national election for the presidency. Third parties have been formed to champion particular causes, such as the Liberty and Free Soil movements, which opposed the extension of slavery in the middle of the nineteenth century. The Prohibition party achieved its greatest triumph with the adoption of the Eighteenth Amendment to the federal Constitution.

All minor parties serve as critics of the major parties. Occasionally a third party will wield enough authority with the voters to cause the loss of an election by a major party. The liberal wing of the Republicans formed the Progressive Republican party under the leadership of Theodore Roosevelt in 1912. The split caused the defeat of William Howard Taft as the Republican candidate and the victory of Woodrow Wilson and the Democratic party.

To be successful in a national election requires the reconciliation of conflicting state and national interests, as well as the diverse sectional needs of groups of states in various parts of the country. The two major parties have become so flexible in the matter of accommodating varied interests in a single program that they now embrace a vast and heterogeneous membership. They have also deprived minor parties of both the capacity and the opportunity to construct a national coalition capable of winning control of the federal government.

This flexibility in the platforms of the major parties is derived in part from the fact that the electorate has accepted the basic principles of democracy, thus delimiting the area within which parties may offer alternative solutions to problems of public policy. An overwhelming majority of citizens accept the principles of representative government, civil liberty, separation of church and state, and the economic theory of capitalism as tenets of the American creed. Indeed, the area of agreement is so broad that minor parties are driven to extremes in their programs and cannot gain general public support.

The universal acceptance of certain basic compromises, which enable the political system to operate, does not imply that party factionalism is nonexistent. Conservative Democrats and conservative Republicans share many views on questions of public policy. They also frequently find themselves aligned against the liberal wings of both parties in legislative matters and in respect to presidential leadership. The prevalence of split-party cooperation along liberal-conservative lines during the Truman, Eisenhower, and Kennedy administrations led Prof. James MacGregor Burns to the conclusion that there is a four-party system in the United States.[17] Party behavior in Congress under the influence of presidential legislative leadership would indicate that the Democrats and Republicans each have a congressional and a presidential party. American political leaders are therefore compelled to deal with four possible political elements in the formulation of a coalition in order to govern.

In addition to internal factionalism, each party has been politically harassed from time to time by extremists—the Democrats by left-wing groups of socialists and communists, and the Republicans, more recently, by ultrarightist groups such as the KKK and the John Birch Society. Such alien groups often work within the party organizations, attempting to reach the centers of power where decisions are made on issues and on candidates selected to run for office. Political expediency, coupled with the past failures of the third-party movements, discourages independent political action by these sects outside the framework of the major parties.

A powerful deterrent to the emergence of a multiparty system is the willingness of pressure groups in the fields of business, agriculture, and labor to work with the major parties. By forgoing the responsibilities of staffing and running the government, the pressure group remains in the strategic position of being able to work through the party in power at any given time. This circumstance has conditioned the nature of the power struggle between the parties. Party leaders assume that since only one of two parties can control the government, they will alternate in power.

The expectation of returning to office under conditions of controlled competition makes opposing political leaders somewhat tolerant of one another. Instead of vindictively attempting utterly to destroy the opposition, they operate under the assumption that while the majority rules, the minority has rights and privileges that will be observed. This understanding also explains in part the insistence of the public that no matter how bitter the political battle, both winners and losers in an election display an attitude of good sportsmanship. Leaders of the two major parties often remark that the development of a third party with genuine strength to contend for power would be a catastrophe. Apparently, the overwhelming majority of the electorate shares this view.

An important characteristic of the American party system is the development by party leaders of ways and means to cope effectively with dissident opinion both within and outside the party. Intraparty conflict may be decentralized on local and state levels, and compromises may be effected that will permit a united front when the party faces the nation in an election. However tentative in character, such unity is evidenced in the language of the national platform. Buried beneath its platitudes and broad generalizations are diametrically opposed views on domestic and foreign policy that will be exhumed and aired after the election is safely won. If the internal conflict is irreconcilable, extremists may leave the party voluntarily or be exiled. The former was the fate suffered by the Dixiecrats, and the latter the fate suffered by the Independent Progressives, at the hands of the Democratic party in the 1948 election.

The two major parties constantly sap the strength of minor-party programs by adopting and enacting their more popular platform planks. Also, large groups of voters periodically desert both major parties and become independents, who are then avidly wooed by both. The independent is not deeply partisan in his or her beliefs and to some extent serves as a balance wheel between the Republican and Democratic parties.

---

[17]James MacGregor Burns, *The Deadlock of Democracy: Four-Party Politics in America*, Prentice-Hall, Inc., Englewood Cliffs, N.J., 1963.

Two-party government has been as effective in the British parliamentary system as in the American presidential system—perhaps more so; yet neither has escaped searching criticism.[18] In general, the allegation against the American system is that it is unrepresentative and therefore undemocratic. It is said that the structure of the parties is too loosely knit and that party discipline is lacking, with the result that elected officials are unresponsive to party platforms both before and after election. Moreover, the American public is suspicious of the motivation of politicians; it is unclear whether they wish to serve the body politic or their own more materialistic ends. It has been suggested that two parties present only two alternatives of issues, candidates, and courses of action, in contrast to the range of choice offered by several parties of approximately equal strength. Furthermore, the issues are presented as choices between black and white, "either-or," all-right, or all-wrong alternatives, leaving the voter both confused and frustrated.

All these criticisms contain some element of truth. Undoubtedly an ideal party model would establish clearer lines of obligation and responsibility between voter and representative. Nevertheless, the merits of the system—stability and continuity, consensus and competitiveness—are impressive. In a pragmatic sense it has prevailed, and possibly in respect to the criteria mentioned it best reflects the expectations arising from the American socioeconomic culture.

The Multiparty System

By contrast with the United States and Britain, France has about a dozen parties represented in the National Assembly; Italy, eight major parties in the Chamber of Deputies; West Germany, three major parties in the Bundestag; and Japan, four major groups and a scattering of independent members in the House of Representatives.

What are the origins of the multiparty system? Sigmund Neumann has suggested that one reason for multiple parties is the persistence of deep cleavages in a political society caused by differences in nationality and religion.[19] Divisive forces are often inflamed by irreconcilable elements within the nation or by external revolutionary movements. Another hypothesis is that if political revolution is accompanied by great social transformations, groups in society may differ on both the new goals to be achieved and the means to implement them. Such groups seek differing solutions through the creation of new or separate political parties. It is also possible for a powerful elite to utilize the multiparty system in order to "divide and rule" political society. Once the multiparty system has been entrenched, it can be perpetuated by mechanical and legal devices such as proportional representation (especially the party-list system of voting), party machinery, and electoral laws. Vested interests of individuals, party organizations, and economic and cultural interest groups become firmly established and to a large extent self-perpetuating.

The European party pattern has certain unique characteristics. The first of these is the representation of many facets of the socioeconomic order by separate political parties. Many groups prefer to have direct political representation for a program of specific objectives rather than join a large coalition of many interests, as they would be obliged to do in a two-party system. Thus there are separate parties for peasants, refugees, national minorities, Catholics, laborers, and other similar groups.

In one sense, a large number of parties is consistent with the basic principles of democracy in that the system allows the individual the widest possible choice of alternatives in the realm of public policy. Such was the case in France under the Third and Fourth Republics. Turbulent constitutional struggles left the people in profound disagreement on matters of fundamental policy, such as the extent of public ownership or regulation of business, taxation, church-state relations, and even the fate of democracy itself. On the other hand, government

---

[18] American Political Science Association, "Toward a More Responsible Two-Party System," supplement to *American Political Science Review*, vol. 44, 1950.

[19] Sigmund Neumann, "Toward a Comparative Study of Political Parties," in Sigmund Neumann (ed.), *Modern Political Parties*, The University of Chicago Press, Chicago, 1956, pp. 395–421; for this section, passim. The Neumann study is a highly regarded contribution in this field. For a definitive analysis on political opposition, see Robert A. Dahl (ed.), *Political Oppositions in Western Democracies,* Yale University Press, New Haven, Conn., 1966, particularly chaps. 11–13.

can become impotent if there are too many parties. West Germany and France have passed legislation since World War II to curtail the tendency toward unlimited political factionalism. Switzerland, Sweden, and Norway, all multiparty states, have achieved a stable center of political gravity without either undue political turbulence or an excess of party factionalism.

A second characteristic of the continental European party system is the nature of the party itself. It may vary in size from a few hundred to several million members. In some instances it has no "grass roots" in the electorate, but merely represents a bloc in parliament created by a few partisans hoping to negotiate for committee appointments or a cabinet seat. Only the largest European parties, such as the Christian Democrats in West Germany or the Union for the New Republic in France, possess manpower, organization, or resources comparable to those of either major American party.

By far the most important aspect of the European political system, however, is the fact that rarely can a single party command a majority of the members in the lower chamber of the national legislature. Under the cabinet-type government that prevails, the executive is drawn from the legislature and is responsible to it for the legislative program of the government. Without a parliamentary majority, the cabinet cannot pass essential legislation. Therefore, the process of forming a government requires that the prime minister invite into his cabinet those party leaders whose supporters in the lower house of the legislature are committed (or likely) to vote for the government's program. Thus the typical European cabinet represents a coalition of the representatives of several political parties.

If this plural executive splits—if a member or members of the cabinet whose followers are essential to maintaining the cabinet's parliamentary majority withdraw from the government—the cabinet must resign. In some countries the premier can secure the dissolution of the parliament and precipitate new elections, which he hopes will return him to power; in others he cannot. The Achilles' heel of coalition government is the nature of the commitments that a premier is forced to make in order to get and hold his parliamentary majority. Prospective cabinet members, instructed by their party adherents in the legislature, make diverse and often conflicting demands upon the premier, usually in terms of legislative concessions, as the price for joining his cabinet. If these public-policy issues are not resolved according to prior agreement, the minister may resign, probably forcing a "no confidence" vote in parliament, which requires a new national election.

In contrast to the two-party system, where compromises are usually reached by various intraparty factions *before* the election, compromises in the multiparty system are generally negotiated by the leaders and party blocs *after* the election, beyond the reach of the electorate.

Disagreement between party factions and withdrawal of a party's support from the cabinet may be the result not of principle but of expediency; the dissident leaders may be seeking a better political bargain in a new government. In postwar France before the Fifth Republic, most governments fell in this way, rather than because of votes of no confidence.

When petty partisanship prevails and party support is withdrawn for minor reasons, instability and deadlock result. Between the close of World War II and September 1957, France had twenty-two governments, with an average life of about 6½ months.

The goals of democracy can be achieved just as effectively in a multiparty system as in a biparty system. Coalition government need not be unstable if there is a substantial popular consensus concerning the basic principles of the economic and social order, such as that in the Scandinavian nations. However, in France and Italy, large and powerful radical wings on the extremes of left and right are the real roadblocks to moderate, middle-of-the-road national policies.

The One-Party System

The basic functions of the political party in a one-party system would appear to bear a remote resemblance to those of the two-party and multiparty systems: recruiting candidates, conducting elections, and operating the governmental apparatus. The ultimate goals of the societies in which they operate, however, and the methods utilized to achieve them are in sharp contrast. In general, parties mobilize the support of the public for the regime, educate the citizen, staff the government through elections, and participate in the public-policy decision-making process. The differences in theory and practice between the one-party and the dual and multiparty systems may be dramatized in a comparison of the properties of democracy and dictatorship.

The one-party state is founded on the assumption that the sovereign will of the state reposes in the leader and the political elite. This authoritarian principle found expression first in monarchies and more recently in dictatorships.

Needing a monopoly of power to survive, the modern dictatorship abolishes all opposition parties. The official party takes on the characteristics of an army and is thoroughly integrated with the state. In order to stifle recurring resistance, it is driven to adopt techniques of physical coercion, such as purges and liquidations, and to employ measures of psychological coercion through extensive and vigorous propaganda campaigns.

However, even a dictator must create machinery through which the masses appear to participate in the political process because in the twentieth century, some semblance of popular support seems mandatory. The technique devised by Hitler, Mussolini, and Stalin has been called the "dictated plebiscite." Criticism of the regime (if any) was severely restricted, highly organized, and not representative of the thinking of the electorate. Although "elections" were conducted, the voter was limited to names submitted to him by the party hierarchy. A negative vote was not only extremely hazardous but also virtually futile.

Although a totalitarian, militaristic party organization may appear to be the strongest of all party systems, it is exceedingly vulnerable. In the first place, no successful formula has yet been devised by which one dictator may transfer his authority to a successor. Nor has it been possible completely to sever the bonds of political tradition by substituting new myths and symbols for accepted values through the use of force. Further, it is improbable that an atmosphere of fear and suspicion through coercion and terrorism can be maintained indefinitely. Finally, the ferment of class and group interests in society, with their attendant social tensions, cannot be accommodated without substantial alteration in the rigid, stratified structure of a totalitarian state. Individual loyalties and demands of reciprocity from economic, social, and cultural groups will eventually modify and condition such an artificial apparatus internally, as will the external pressures of the international struggle for survival.

Variant Party Systems

Within the typologies of the two-party, multiparty, and one-party systems certain political mutations occur that are worthy of note in the interest of accurate classification.[20] The one-party system is also found, for example, in countries and areas that are not totalitarian. There are one-party states in the United States, notably in the South. Despite signs of revival of the Republican party in several Southern states and although the South is not as solidly Democratic as it once was, this area has long been characterized by one-party politics. The voter's choices have been restricted to personalities, cliques, and factions; he or she has seldom had a choice between conflicting public policies. Similar situations have existed in some of our largest cities, such as Boston, New York, and Philadelphia.

Moreover, some of the newer nations (e.g., Ghana and Egypt) are one-party states, but fall short of being totalitarian dictatorships in the full sense of that term. They are authoritarian in the sense that many of the totalitarian devices for quashing civil liberty and forcing compliance are present, but the executive or the elite he represents chooses to implement "permissive policies" that allow individuals and groups to render limited criticism of existing programs or offer alternative solutions to proposals. Within limits, factions may develop in the monopolistic party, seeking to promote the careers of competing officials or to achieve certain accepted, specified goals. The situation is likely to occur in newly formed states or when an existing state has undergone a revolution. The monopoly party has not fully penetrated the economic, social, cultural, or political institutions of society, and previously established interest groups with deep roots in the lives of the people are permitted to exist.

[20]For an excellent discussion of these topics as a symposium of authoritative comment, see La Palombara and Weiner, op. cit., particularly the opening and closing chapters by the editors.

Finally, the concepts of *stability* and *change* serve as analytic factors in the evaluation of party systems. The former is exemplified by the length of time that a coalition party government functions, and the latter by the brief excursion of the British electorate into the multiparty system when Labour joined the Conservatives and Liberals after World War I. A two-party system also resembles a one-party polity when competition ceases to exist and the electorate is left virtually without viable alternative programs.

THE PARTY WITHIN THE SYSTEM

There is no universal pattern of political party structure. Parties generally lack the orderly symmetry of government, with its neat pyramid of agencies, each resting in a geographic district and ascending in authority from subordinate to superordinate echelons of command. The party is an intricate institution, possessing both formal and informal agencies with varying stages and degrees of integration with the official apparatus of government. Parties are creatures of their cultural environment, and the machinery with which they perform their functions is shaped by history, tradition, and the electoral process stipulated by constitutional government. The functions within the various systems are reasonably uniform in principle: socialization and education of the citizenry; ascertainment, articulation, and aggregation of interests; mobilization of the voters for the electoral process; translation of demands into public policy; and recruitment and monitorship of political leaders for the public service.

In the United States

In searching for the genre "political party," it is customary to attack the problem in three separate contexts: the organization and structure of the party itself; the "party in the electorate," namely, the grass-roots, popular support of the party; and the "party in government," or the behavior of public officials placed in office by the party to run the government. The key agency in formal party organization in the United States is the committee, operating within a specific geographic area and interlocked with other committees arranged in a hierarchy. At the head of the Democratic party stands the Democratic National Committee, composed of approximately 300 representatives of the fifty state committees and each of the territories, leaders of the Democratic Governor's Conference, party leaders in the United States Senate and House of Representatives, and appointees representing Democratic voters on a national scale.[21]

The Republican party uses a formula calling for one man and one woman from each state and territory, plus the state chairmen from each state in which the party has won a majority of the state delegation to each house of Congress, a gubernatorial victory, or the last presidential election. Thus the membership of the Republican National Committee may vary between 125 and 150. Although nominally elected by the national party convention, which meets every four years to nominate presidential and vice-presidential candidates, the members of the national committee are selected in several different ways: by state party primaries, state conventions, state central committees, or state delegations to the national conventions or by appointment by the national chairperson. A substantial number of committeemen are lawyers or businessmen with some college education, while committeewomen represent a mixture of housewives and career women. The majority of both committeemen and committeewomen have held either a party or government position at one time.[22]

Since a national committee is unwieldy in size, its work is accomplished through an executive committee and a national chairperson chosen by the party's nominee for president. The president is the titular head of his party until a successor is nominated. The defeated party often lacks an official spokesman, although the national chairperson continues to run the party organization through the national committee.

The national committee meets to discuss strategy, policies, and issues in congressional election years. It is also instrumental in organizing the convention during presidential election years. Individual members maintain constant political contact

---

[21]The formula adopted by the 1972 national convention included additional members assigned to a state in proportion to its representation on the standing committees of that convention. The initial appointment of the at-large members included ten from organized labor, eight blacks, and two persons of Spanish-American ancestry.

[22]Bone, op. cit., p. 162.

with the state organizations. The selection of the national chairperson is ratified by the national committee; he or she appoints the executive committee, establishes a party headquarters, and manages the presidential campaign.

Both national parties maintain senatorial and congressional campaign committees, whose principal function is to assist members of Congress or aspirants to campaign in their respective districts.

The highest organ of the state party is the state central committee, selected according to state law by election or appointment. A party chairperson and executive committee usually manage state election campaigns and assist the national committee in presidential and congressional election years.

Party committees exist in most of the over 3,000 counties in the United States. Such committees are usually elected at primary elections, but in a few states they are appointed. The county chairperson is usually a grass-roots politician with patronage to dispense and serves as an important cog in the state, as well as in the local, hierarchy. County committees campaign in state as well as national elections and exhibit an unusual degree of independence in local affairs. In many states party committees also exist for cities, wards, and congressional and other legislative districts, though often such committees rarely meet.

At the very bottom level of the pyramid are thousands of precincts, which are the smallest units in the official party organization. In cities with strong party organizations each precinct will usually have a captain in charge of party affairs, who is sometimes assisted by a committee. But elsewhere the party organization seldom extends down to the precinct.

In some of the largest cities the parties are also organized in each ward, which is presided over by a ward boss and again, perhaps, a committee. Chicago, Baltimore, and New York City, for example, have fully organized local party machines.

An evaluation of the formal party organization should cite the merit of wide popular participation, the relatively democratic process of electing committee personnel, and the enormous amount of party activity on all levels. The debit side is rather imposing, however. It is a truism that politics is actually the preoccupation of the interested few. The structure is too loosely knit, and far from being an integrated organization, it is characterized by localism. The loyalties of both candidate and constituent are local rather than national. The electoral district, be it city, county, or congressional, and the destiny of the candidate from that area are the focal points of political interest.

In presidential election years, national party controls exert a unifying influence on partisan activity, partly because a president can be elected only by a coalition of states. However, the authority of top party officials is compartmentalized by jurisdiction; the national chairman exercises little control over state chairmen. Often the latter have little authority over county chairmen. With the expansion of the principle of civil service selection of government employees, patronage becomes less effective as an instrument of party discipline. In short, the sum of the centrifugal forces in the national party system is greater than the sum of the centripetal forces; the national party organization tends to represent a confederation of agencies rather than a unified, disciplined whole.

Using both the nomenclature and classificatory system introduced into party literature by Maurice Duverger, Frank Sorauf describes the relationship of the American party organization to the party in the electorate and the party in government.[23] In this context the American party organization is a "cadre" (or elite) party rather than a "mass" party. The organization rarely rules the party; it cannot command the electorate, but must woo it; it lacks control devices and discipline over even its own officeholders in government; and it is not a hierarchical organization in the sense that it controls its component parts—the state and local subgroups—but, rather, is managed by a small number of leaders and activists. By contrast, the mass party characteristic of European politics is highly integrated with the party electorate manning the organization and closely in touch with the government officeholders who must report upon their stewardship.

Robert Michels, in his study entitled *Political Parties*, developed an interesting theory relating to party control that attracted considerable attention in the second decade of the twentieth century.[24] He

---

[23]Sorauf, op. cit., pp. 61–64.
[24]Robert Michels, *Political Parties*, The Free Press of Glencoe, Inc., Chicago, 1949 (originally published in 1915).

suggested that after a vigorous youth, a political party is destined to become bureaucratic and to develop oligarchic tendencies. The fashioning of formalized practices and machinery is followed by the creation of an elite, or inner circle, which makes the decisions on party behavior.

Various reasons support this hypothesis. The rank and file of the party abandon control of the machinery by default. The few who are in influential positions simply bypass the normal custom of holding referenda among the whole membership. They issue ready-made decisions that must be obeyed. Party leaders have a monopoly on skills and techniques of party management. Finally, once the oligarchy becomes entrenched, it protects its status by a combination of legal means or graft and deserts the interests of the people.

Although only portions of this hypothesis are acceptable as an explanation of the distribution of power in the American party system, it is undeniably true that American parties have developed some oligarchic tendencies.

In Great Britain

The structure of British parties is relatively simple in comparison with that of parties in the United States. Since the British government is parliamentary and unitary in form, rather than presidential and federal, the national British parties are not called upon to cope with fifty state parties or to compete periodically in a vast nationwide election to select an executive. There are only three elective offices in the United Kingdom. The national office filled by popular vote is that of member of Parliament; in local government, county and borough councilors are elected. There are fewer elections. The small size and compactness of the territory minimize functional and sectional political differences. Discipline, relating both to issues and to the behavior of party representatives, is more specifically defined and enforced than it is in the United States.

The basic unit in the British party is called the "constituency" or "local association," and it speaks for the electoral district from which an MP is sent to the House of Commons. In 1974 England was authorized 516 seats in Parliament; Scotland, 71; Wales, 36; and North Ireland, 12, for a total membership of 635.[25] Membership in the Conservative party is open to those individuals willing to pay nominal dues and to support the principles of the party. Five of every six Labour party members join indirectly through association with groups sympathetic to the party's ideals, such as the trade unions, the Fabian Society, and the cooperative movement. Constituencies have varied considerably in size from perhaps 20,000 to over 120,000 voters scattered among the wards or polling districts. The wards are organized through committees charged with electioneering tasks. There are also many auxiliary societies, clubs, and other politically active organizations operating in various subdivisions of the constituency, which help develop and sustain party interest. Since receiving the vote in 1928, women have become increasingly active in party affairs, particularly at the local level. The youth were enfranchised when the voting age was lowered to eighteen years for the 1970 election.

Party machinery at this level includes an elected Executive Council (Conservatives) or a General Management Committee (Labour), with a chairman, a secretary, and an official known as the "party agent" in charge of administrative activity. Special representation for women and youth organizations is provided on the constituency committee. The party agent is unique in democratic politics. He is a paid professional organizer who obtains his position only after passing an exacting examination. His duties and responsibilities, prescribed and regulated by law, are roughly analogous to those of a combination of county chairman and precinct captain in American politics. During a parliamentary election he manages the party candidate, organizes the constituency, conducts the electioneering, and is responsible for winning the election. He files a detailed report of his activities, including an

[25]For the organization of British party structures, see principally Samuel H. Beer, "Great Britain: From Governing Elite to Organized Mass Politics," in Neumann, op. cit., pp. 9–57. For other topics in this section, see T. Brennan, *Politics and Government in Britain*, Cambridge University Press, London, 1972, pp. 18–49; John D. Lees and Richard Kimber, *Political Parties in Modern Britain*, London, Routledge & Kegan Paul, Ltd., 1972, pp. 63–75; McKenzie, op. cit.; and W. A. Rudlin, "Political Parties: Great Britain," in *Encyclopaedia of the Social Sciences*, The Macmillan Co., New York, 1934, vol. 11, pp. 601–604. George D. Comfort, *Professional Politicians: A Study of British Party Agents*, Public Affairs Press, Washington, 1958, discusses the agent's role.

accounting of campaign expenditures. Since his work is considered a profession, he does not succumb to the two great vices of American politics: patronage and spoils. It is highly unusual for him to become a candidate for public office.

The constituencies form the base of the national party organizational pyramid, with two different but interconnected channels of authority ascending to the party leader in Parliament at the apex of the entire structure. The administrative and professional hierarchy finds constituencies assembled into regional (Labour) and area (Conservative) offices, principally so that the work of the agents may be coordinated on a wider geographic basis. Above the area offices is the Central Office, or national headquarters of the party, presided over by the chairman of the party or the chief national party administrator. An important feature of the Conservative party organization is a series of advisory committees at each principal organizational echelon. The Labour party has advisory groups representing the trade unions, socialist societies, and co-ops similarly situated, resembling a federated structure.

Administrative control of the parties has become increasingly centralized in recent years. The constituency associations depend upon the Central Office for a wide variety of services. Financial support, information, advice, speakers, campaign literature, and propaganda are dispensed from this source. Administrative assistance is rendered by a traveling staff of professional workers who visit the local officials. One of the most important functions of the Central Office is to assist in the selection of parliamentary candidates. Nominations may be supplied from either local or national sources, and the decision to support a candidate—indeed, the decision as to whether the constituency should be contested at all—is the result of a series of consultations on both levels. The significance of the selection procedure lies in the fact that under British practice, the designated candidate is not required to live in the district he intends to represent. Thus it is possible for the local constituents to find themselves voting for a party dignitary of considerable reputation who may not be known to them personally.

Classifying the British parties according to the Duverger typology of elitist-flexible or mass-rigid, depending upon the degree of integration between the electorate, the party organization, and the party in government, presents some problems. Three codicils must accompany the designation of British parties as elitist, cadre types: (1) Both the Labour and Conservative organizations are more highly centralized than others in this category, (2) the party in Parliament is virtually independent of the organizational apparatus, and (3) the Labour party must be placed somewhere within the elitist-mass dichotomy in an "intermediate" category. The special designation of the Labour party rests upon two considerations: Its electoral support extends beyond its membership, to auxiliary groups such as the cooperative societies, and so do its financial resources.

The uniqueness of the British party in a parliamentary-cabinet system is found in the independence of the MPs from the official party organization. The members of Parliament designate their own party leader. If the party in power forms the government, the organization, with its own party chairman, has no control over the "parliamentary party."

Each party does hold an annual conference made up of delegates elected by the constituency organizations. The conference listens to speeches of leaders in and out of Parliament and passes resolutions on party policy. It acts briefly as a sounding board for testing partisan positions on public policy and as a showcase for exhibiting party talent, and it presents an opportunity to rally party support.

In France

French political parties are unique in several important respects. They are heavily doctrinaire in nature and purpose, and with the exception of the Communists, they lack sound organizational structure. As elitist-cadre groups they are top-heavy in leaders, are enfeebled by lack of discipline, and for the most part do not possess a mass-membership base. Thus the system is in a constant state of flux since parties are born, flourish, and frequently either merge with others or simply cease to exist, a fate that befell the once-powerful centrist *Mouvement Républicain Populaire* (MRP) in 1967. In the early 1970s the spectrum, reading from left to center to right, included the Communist party, the Unified

Socialists (PSU), the French Socialists (SFIO), the Radical Socialists, the Democratic Center, the Union of Democrats for the Fifth Republic, the Independent Republicans, and the Independents.

Supplementing the individual parties is an unusual phenomenon, the banding together of parties into "federations," such as the former Federation of the Left, combining the Socialist and Radical Socialist parties, or the more recent Union of Democrats for the Fifth Republic, which included Gaullists of various persuasions. These groups cooperate in numerous ways such as signing electoral agreements to support certain candidates or cooperating on the parliamentary level in the National Assembly.

Since it was at one time large, powerful, and successful, the now-defunct MRP organization will serve as a model or prototype for some of the basic characteristics of a French political party.[26] The smallest local unit, called a "section," had a minimum of ten members on the communal or cantonal levels. These were grouped into regional federations of at least five sections totaling 100 members within a *département*. A departmental federation was run by an executive committee elected from its sections.

The federations in turn elected members to a national congress according to the strength of their respective memberships. The congress met annually and elected an executive committee and the party officers, consisting of a president and a secretary general, who presided over the national party headquarters. Whereas each party shares this relatively standard pattern of organization, the MRP added two rather unique bodies: an executive commission made up of officers of the party serving ex officio, plus members representative of the national committee, and a bureau to serve as liaison between the secretariat and the executive commission by which it was constituted. The executive commission acted as the decision-making mechanism during the interim when the national committee was not in session. The seeming overlap of membership in what may appear to be a rather cumbersome group of national party agencies actually served to bring together the officers of the party, who were nonparliamentarians, with representatives (if any) of the party in the national government and in parliament.

In contrast to the conventional party organization stands the French Communist party, which completely fuses the adherents in the electorate, the organizations, and members in the National Assembly in the classic Soviet pattern of all communist parties. From grass roots to the recognized leader, the echelons are party cell, the section, departmental federations, national congress, Central Committee, Politburo, and Secretariat. Whether because of its militant doctrine or its tightly knit and disciplined apparatus, the Communist party in recent years has consistently been able to mobilize from one-fifth to one-fourth of the French electorate at the polls.[27]

With the resignation of President Charles de Gaulle in 1969 and his death one year later, France reached a watershed in modern political history. De Gaulle's chosen successor, Georges Pompidou, died on April 2, 1974. The Gaullist candidate Chaban Delmas was defeated in the presidential election the following May, and the long reign of the Gaullist Union for a Democratic Republic was ended by a member of the Independent Republican party, Valery Giscard d'Estaing. The victory epitomized the classic struggle between left and right in French politics, for the defeated opponent was François Mitterrand, who ran on a combined Socialist-Communist ticket, with less than 400,000 votes separating the candidates.

THE PARTY AT WORK

Political Auxiliaries

In the mobilization of the electorate the party utilizes a wide variety of auxiliary groups and, in American politics, is itself occasionally the subject of some manipulation by political machines. Peripheral groups provide voting strength, funds, campaign propaganda, and personnel to assist party activities, and they act as sounding boards for the

---

[26]For a more detailed description, see J. A. Laponce, *The Government of the Fifth Republic*, University of California Press, Berkeley, 1961, pp. 93–99; see also Henry W. Ehrmann, *Politics in France*, Little, Brown and Company, Boston, 1968.

[27]Roy C. Macridis, "France," in Roy C. Macridis and Robert E. Ward (eds.), *Modern Political Systems: Europe*, 3d ed., Prentice-Hall, Inc., Englewood Cliffs, N.J., 1972, pp. 192–219.

partisan interpretation of issues. These groups may be divided into several categories.

In the United States there are the youth organizations such as the Young Democrats and Young Republicans. Enthusiasm, volunteer help, and apprenticeship in partisan politics are characteristic contributions from this source. In disillusion over the failures of political parties in parliamentary government during the close of the Fourth Republic and thereafter, a "political club" movement developed in both the political right and left in France. Groups of several hundred party adherents banded together to develop party programs and to recruit and politically socialize members for their cause. The totalitarian states long ago appreciated the necessity of proper indoctrination of the young, and Russia has established a regular hierarchy of youth organizations.

A second classification includes the economic interest groups that are definitely oriented toward one or more of the major parties. Thus the Labour party in Great Britain is closely associated with the Trades Union Congress, the cooperatives, and various socialist organizations. The Republican party in the United States often finds a strong bond of sympathy in the National Association of Manufacturers and the National Grange, while the Democrats are greatly assisted by the AFL-CIO and the National Farmers Union.

Party adherents frequently create auxiliary associations under titles that would indicate a lack of faith in opposition parties and a simulated desertion to the enemy. Examples are "Republicans for . . ." (the Democratic candidate) and "Democrats for . . ." (the Republican candidate).

Finally, many groups operating under a nonpartisan and patriotic banner endorse programs and engage in activities of a highly partisan nature. Two ultraconservative women's groups in this category in the United States are the Liberty Belles and Pro-America, whose views are distinctly oriented toward the Republican party. The Americans for Democratic Action, which finds itself more often than not agreeing with the principles of the Democratic party, is an ultraliberal counterpart with a mixed membership. Party leadership is quick to realize the value of such support, to exploit the propaganda that is gratuitously offered, and to direct auxiliary-group activity toward enlisting voter support.

The Political Machine

Although many laws now regulate party activity, parties have sometimes fallen into the hands of those whose motives and methods of operation are not in the public interest. When people manipulate party machinery illegally and for selfish interests, they are playing "machine politics."

The purpose of the political machine is to mobilize voting strength in order to put "machine candidates" into public office and thus gain access to the power and resources of government. Any electoral district, from the precinct to the state, is utilized as a suitable base of operations. The personnel manning the organization may be public officeholders, party committeemen, interested citizens, or a combination of all three categories. In the informal terminology of the machine organizations, they often hold such titles as "precinct captain," "ward leader," or "state boss." Political machines are indigenous to both major political parties in the United States.

Machine strength lies in the performance of many legitimate services for the voter and sometimes a few illegal ones. A contributing factor is the presence of circumstances in some of the larger cities that make the citizen susceptible to such attentions. In return for his vote on election day, the machine worker will offer the voter such legitimate assistance as processing his application for a civil service examination or helping him to get a driver's license, to qualify for unemployment insurance, or to obtain bail. On the illegal side of the ledger may be found practically any unlawful service such as the use of bribery to raise a score on a civil service examination. In its worst manifestation, the machine may thrive on graft from the negotiation of public contracts and on vice-and-crime-protection payoffs to corrupt government employees. The political machine is gradually disappearing from the American scene. Its greatest strength lay in poverty and public apathy.

Financing Party Activities

Not only is supporting a political party system costly, but it also raises a host of ethical and legal problems. What expenses are legitimate? Should the funds come from public or private sources? How should they be accounted for? If politics is indeed a struggle for power, will the party with the greatest financial resources win? If so, what happens to the vital intraparty competition that is a cornerstone of democracy? Is giving money to a party the ultimate symbol of political participation by the individual citizen?

Most students of party finance believe that, other resources and circumstances being equal, money alone will not necessarily win elections. The skyrocketing costs of electioneering, the increasing sophistication of the public, and the growing tendency toward government regulation coupled with more stringent penalties all conspire to minimize the probabilities of "buying an election." Nevertheless, along with assets essential to electoral success such as technical skill, numbers, favorable ideological position, and charismatic leadership, money is an important variable in conditioning the style of an election and the manner in which it is conducted. Moreover, the dynamics of collecting and spending political money are undergoing significant changes that are impacting public policy.

The sources of political funds and the process by which money is distributed reveal a great deal about the role of parties in the political process. The problem is as complex as it is important; however, the systematic analysis of comparative party finance is in its infancy. Using the "input-output" schematic approach in its broadest sense, Arnold J. Heidenheimer has suggested some generalizations on the subject well worthy of consideration.[28] He adopts two models with which to compare the financing practices of a broad range of political parties in a number of countries. These are the "mass" party, with a large membership, and the smaller, wealthy, elite-like "cadre" party, with few members. Heidenheimer made the assumption that one clue to party strength is the proportion of members willing to contribute to its financial support. The criterion he used to separate the two models was the ability of a party to collect at least two-thirds of its normal, nonelection-year expenses from dues-paying members. The Social Democratic party of West Germany was the only one among eight nations able to qualify as a mass party under this specification. In fact, Heidenheimer discovered that parties with dues-paying members meet only about 20 percent of their nonelection-year budgets in this manner. As a consequence, both mass and cadre parties have been forced to diversify their sources of income, and for this reason their financing patterns are becoming progressively more alike.

Heidenheimer finds that inputs of resource support from interest groups are difficult to identify. Group relationships with parties range all the way from the British Labour party's almost total dependence upon trade union contributions to a similar relationship between a relatively few wealthy businessmen in Japan and the Japanese Liberal Democratic party. In the latter instance, dues income amounts to less than 1 percent of total expenditure in national elections. Interest-group contributions to party support continue to remain substantial, but the trend in party finance is toward diversification of sources, including increased support from government.

Turning to the *output* aspect of party finance, Heidenheimer sought a formula by which the expenditures of political parties might be compared. He decided to relate the total votes cast in an election to the average hourly wage of the male industrial worker during the 1950s and the early 1960s. The mathematical ratio of vote to wage hours produced an "index of expenditure," which represented the cost to the party, beyond personal and institutional contributions, of obtaining voter participation in the electoral process. A comparison of the resulting mathematical ratios or indices placed six of the nations studied in the following order, from lowest to highest: Australia (0.45), Britain, West Germany, the United States, Japan, and Israel (20.5). Heidenheimer concluded that the variables in the index of expenditure as applied to individual countries were partisan politicization, party loyalty, the size of the electorate, the nature of the constituencies, and the availability of public funds for party use.

---

[28] Arnold J. Heidenheimer, "Comparative Party Finance: Notes on Practices and toward a Theory," in Richard Rose and Arnold J. Heidenheimer, "Comparative Studies in Political Finance," *Journal of Politics,* vol. 25, no. 4, pp. 790–801, November 1963. Eight countries are covered by individual authors; this account is based upon Heidenheimer's own contribution to the symposium.

The Cost of Campaigning

Because of its size and political structure, the United States holds more elections than any other nation, and the gross cost is probably the highest in the world. There are over 500,000 elective offices in the nation. In addition to the presidential and congressional elections, campaigns are conducted at least biennially for the governors and legislatures of the fifty states and for officials in over 3,000 counties and many of the 78,000 local governments, including cities (18,000), special districts (21,000), and school districts (22,000). The huge electorate of over 140 million citizens is assembled in about 176,000 precinct polling places staffed with inspectors, registrars, judges, and clerks and frequently equipped with expensive voting machines. No accurate accounting has ever been made of the cost of this aspect of participatory democracy. Educated guesses of the total cost of staging elections during the 1968 presidential election year suggest that $250 million was expended from private sources and about $100 million from public agencies.[29] The sum of $350 million is more than twice the cost of the 1952 election, while preliminary estimates for the 1972 election approximate $400 million.

The legitimate obligations incurred in a national campaign alone are legion. All the expenses immediately concerned with the operation of the many party offices and headquarters must be met, including rent, staff salaries, taxes, stationery and other supplies, and telephone, postage, and telegraph expenses. Publicity and party propaganda must be researched, written, printed, and sent to the voters.

The task of communication is one of the most costly operations in which the party engages. Postage for direct-mail campaigning alone can run into thousands of dollars in a single metropolitan area. A mailing to each of 200,000 registered voters in an average congressional district, for instance, cost $6,000 in 1958, $12,000 in 1968, and $20,000 in 1974. Advertising in newspapers and on billboards is bought at standard rates. Radio and television time is very expensive. Political broadcasting combining television, FM, and AM networks at all levels cost $14,195,000 from September 1 to election day in 1960. In 1962 total expenditures for this purpose advanced to $20 million; in 1966, to $32 million; and in 1968, to $59 million. It has been estimated from data provided in the annual report of the Federal Communications Commission that if production and related costs were added, the total for 1968 would be about $90 million, or roughly one-third of the cost of the entire campaign.[30]

The costs of campaigns for all offices are rising, partly because of inflation and partly because of the application of scientific talent and expensive hardware, such as computers, to electioneering. The 1,116 Senate and House candidates who ran for Congress in the 1972 election reported raising $69.7 million and spending $66.4 million between April 7 and December 31, 1972. The average of $59,498 per contest belies the costliness of close races, which ranged up to $200,000.[31]

By contrast, a candidate for the British House of Commons is prohibited by law from spending more than $2,887 in a campaign in a 60,000-member-county parliamentary constituency. In the 1966 campaign the Conservative constituency expenditures averaged $2,145, and those of Labour averaged $2,033.[32] Each candidate in Britain may have one free mailing of election materials, but is forbidden to purchase television campaign time. Each party receives free air time from the government in proportion to the party membership in the House of Commons. The costs of a general election are not specifically known. When an election was in prospect in 1967, the Conservative party launched a special fund-raising appeal for roughly $5.5 million, and the Labour party appealed for half of that figure.[33] In the mid-1960s a candidate for the

[29]Committee for Economic Development, "Financing a Better Election System," New York, 1968, p. 15.

[30]Herbert E. Alexander and Harold B. Meyers, "A Financial Landslide for the G.O.P.," *Fortune,* March 1970, p. 104. The FCC publishes an annual *Survey of Political Broadcasting.* See also Herbert E. Alexander, *Political Financing,* Burgess Publishing Company, Minneapolis, 1972, p. 11; for campaign financing in the 1960 election in the United States, see Herbert E. Alexander, *Financing the 1960 Election,* Citizens' Research Foundation, Princeton, N.J., 1962. The same author has published works on campaign expenses during the 1968 and 1970 elections.

[31]Georgianna Rathbun (ed.), *Integrity in Politics: Financing of Election Campaigns,* Common Cause, Washington, 1974; and *Report from Washington,* vol. 3, no. 10, p. 13, October 1973.

[32]Peter G. J. Pulzer, *Political Representation and Elections,* Frederick A. Praeger, Inc., New York, 1967, p. 86. These figures do not include between-election costs.

[33]Lees and Kimber, op. cit., p. 64.

French National Assembly spent about $5,000 for a campaign in a major metropolitan district and roughly $10,000 for a contest waged in the suburbs or provinces.[34]

Sources of Funds

One of the least explored and therefore most critically vulnerable areas of party activity relates to the acquisition and disposition of political funds. Lack of information is due in part to the absence of legislation requiring the disclosure of sources and in part to the avoidance or evasion of appropriate regulations.

It is probable that in the democracies with free electoral processes, the principal sources are business, labor, and agricultural groups; wealthy individuals and families; statutory government subsidies; small donations from a large number of party members; and contributions from candidates, in roughly that order. A significant hidden source accrues to the party in power, namely, a subsidy in the form of utilization of government resources for political purposes. The Free Democratic and Socialist parties in West Germany, for example, have maintained that the continued success of the Christian Democratic Union at the polls has been due in no small measure to its refusal to issue a complete financial statement, which would reveal extensive use of government resources for partisan political purposes.[35] Access to free goods and services (e.g., the use of halls, automobiles, and billboard space, otherwise known as "in lieu" benefits) accounts for a substantial portion of the resources of most political parties.

None of the major Western democratic parties are able to subsist solely on dues collected from members.

Despite a constituency membership exceeding 1 million adherents and the support of the trade unions, the British Labour party is constrained to raise money by other means, including the sale of lottery tickets for football pools. A general appeal for funds, aimed at professional middle-class people and asking that they contribute $14 annually, was unsuccessful. In recent years the Conservatives have attempted to build constituency-membership financial support. Party literature cites several main sources for raising money: membership subscriptions and contributions; bazaars, fetes, and social activities; small lotteries, draws, and sweepstakes; and special appeals.[36]

Typical fund-raising activities conducted by literally thousands of committees in both parties throughout the United States include giving testimonial dinners, with tickets priced from $10 to $1,000 each; advertising in party publications, with space costing up to $7,500 or more per page; soliciting for special funds such as Dollars for Democrats (with potential revenue running into hundreds of thousands of dollars); and selling party souvenirs and trinkets.

The greatest fund-raising effort in the history of American politics was conducted by the Republican party and a specially constituted auxiliary, entitled the Committee for the Reelection of the President, in 1971–1972. Approximately $60 million was raised, about one-third before legislation requiring reportage became effective on April 7, 1972. The largest individual donation, $2 million, was given by an insurance tycoon. More than three dozen individuals contributed over $50,000, and about two dozen of these gave $100,000 or more. Both the Democratic and Republican parties were the recipients of interest-group largesse, the AFL-CIO Committee on Political Education dispensing $1.2 million primarily to the former, and the Committee for Thorough Agricultural Political Education (acting for the Associated Milk Producers) giving nearly $1 million to the latter.

The Problem of Controls

Why do individuals and groups give money to political parties? Some give through a sense of civic pride or in the hope that a social or economic philosophy in which they believe will be enacted into public policy. Others demand or at least expect a more substantive reward. In Britain until recently, titles were bestowed upon generous donors, following a practice known as "sale of honors." In the United States, choice ambassadorial posts, such as those in London, Paris, or Rome, have been virtual-

---

[34]Lowell G. Noonan, *France: The Politics of Continuity and Change,* Holt, Rinehart and Winston, Inc., New York, 1970, p. 187; the figures were given in francs: 25,000 and 50,000.

[35]U. W. Kitzinger, *German Electoral Politics,* Oxford University Press, Fair Lawn, N.J., 1960, p. 202.

[36]Lees and Kimber, op. cit., p. 73.

ly auctioned to the highest bidder for sums ranging between $50,000 and $250,000. Business, agriculture, and labor groups almost invariably look forward to favorable treatment at the hands of the legislature in terms of protected subsidies, lower taxes, and the like. They count upon the president to appoint sympathetic administrators to the powerful regulatory commissions, such as Federal Trade, Interstate Commerce, and Security Exchange, or perhaps to influence the ideological orientation of presidential appointments to the Supreme Court. Social groups desire legislation concerning health, education, welfare, civil liberties, and so forth.

The nature of the quid pro quo for a political contribution and the manner in which it is pursued may cause legal, moral, and ethical problems incompatible with both the public interest and the trust the public has placed in its representatives. The so-called Watergate affair of the second Nixon administration raised such grave constitutional questions regarding the responsibility of the chief executive in the face of serious charges of corruption and scandal in his inner administration that the incumbent felt impelled to resign rather than respond to articles of impeachment in preparation by Congress; this was the first presidential resignation in history.

The syndrome of related activities known as "Watergate" may be summarized in terms of the following series of charges and allegations: that members of the inner staff of the Nixon administration planned and executed for political purposes a break-in and attempted espionage of the Democratic party national headquarters; that vast sums of money, running into millions of dollars, were collected and expended in violation of federal laws; and that a conspiracy existed to cover up these acts, in part through the utilization of federal investigatory agencies directly under the jurisdiction of the president, such as the Internal Revenue Service, the Federal Bureau of Investigation, and the Central Intelligence Agency, thus imperiling the civil rights of a substantial number of citizens.[37]

[37]By mid-1975, Mr. Nixon had made no admission of complicity in the activities subsumed under these allegations. Soon after the former chief executive's resignation, President Ford granted him a full and unconditional pardon for any known or yet unknown illegal acts committed in violation of the federal law.

Among the several outcomes of this tragic experience, such as the indictment and conviction of many of the Watergate participants, the reexamination of the executive powers, and the temporary loss of the public's confidence in the character of its political leadership, was a concerted movement toward reform of campaign financing practices. Adopting the principle that public funds should be applied to cover presidential campaign expenses, the Congress passed legislation termed the Federal Elections Campaign Act Amendments of 1974, which became effective January 1, 1975.

In general, the legislation established contribution and spending limits and created a bipartisan Federal Elections Commission to supervise the election laws as well as the public financing program. An individual may contribute $1,000, and a group or organization may contribute $5,000, per candidate for each primary, runoff, and general election. The annual total contribution limit in federal elections is $25,000 for an individual, but there is no limit for an organization. Independent expenditures *on behalf of a candidate* may not exceed $1,000, and no contribution in cash may exceed $100.

Spending limits in presidential primaries are set at $10 million per candidate for all primaries together and at $20 million per presidential candidate in the general election. Other limitations include $2 million for each major-party presidential nominating convention, $100,000 or 8 cents per voter for senatorial primaries ($150,000 or 12 cents for general elections), and $70,000 for House primaries and another $70,000 in the general election. There is no limit, however, to the amount that an organization may contribute annually to a congressional race. Spending limits for all three offices may be increased by a sum of 20 percent of the total allowed through an exemption bonus for the actual costs of fund raising.

Public funding of presidential elections would come from a Presidential Election Campaign Fund created by the voluntary checkoff of a tax dollar from federal income tax returns. Major-party candidates would be eligible for full financing, and minor-party candidates' allotments would be in proportion to the votes they actually received. Public matching funds up to $4.5 million would be available, under certain stipulations, for presidential primary candidates.[38]

It is indeed questionable whether "public morality" may be implemented by legislation. Certain generalizations are warranted, however. First, the cost of election campaigning in the United States has exceeded the capabilities of the candidates and parties to meet their obligations. Second, if limits upon raising and spending money cannot be enforced, the assumption of election costs by the public through government may be the only viable solution.

As the trauma of the Watergate episode so clearly demonstrated to the American public, political corruption on a massive scale bears the potential for tearing apart the very fabric of a democratic society. The maintenance of a free, open, and truly competitive electoral process is the sine qua non of democracy.

STUDY-GUIDE QUESTIONS

1 Compare the strengths and weaknesses of the one-party, two-party, and multiparty systems.
2 The empiricists have added some significant theoretical concepts to the study of political parties. Explain two of these: the "aggregation of demands" and the "articulation of interests."
3 Distinguish between these broad categories of parties: doctrinaire, organizational, and functional.
4 Political auxiliaries are becoming more prevalent in the American political process. Discuss the impact of leftist and rightist group politics upon the functions of the Democratic and Republican parties.
5 Watergate has been characterized as the greatest scandal in American political history. Relate this series of events to the broader issue of ethics in politics.

---

[38]Under the Federal Election Campaigns Act of 1971, donors were required to file periodic reports of campaign expenditures; the key official reports are released by the General Accounting Office. Summaries and analysis of the August 23, 1973, report are made by *Congressional Quarterly*, Weekly Report, vol. 31, no. 40, Oct. 6, 1973; see also *Report from Washington*, op. cit.

REFERENCES

Alexander, Herbert E.: *Money in Politics*, Public Affairs Press, Washington, 1972.

Alexander, Robert J.: *Latin American Political Parties*, Frederick A. Praeger, Inc., New York, 1973.

Almond, Gabriel, and G. Bingham Powell, Jr.: *Comparative Politics: A Developmental Approach*, Little, Brown and Company, Boston, 1967.

Chambers, William N., and Walter D. Burnham (eds.): *The American Party Systems*, Oxford University Press, New York, 1967.

Duverger, Maurice: *Political Parties*, John Wiley & Sons, Inc., New York, 1954.

Eldersveld, Samuel: *Political Parties: A Behavioral Analysis*, Rand McNally & Company, Chicago, 1964.

Epstein, Leon D.: *Political Parties in Western Democracies*, Frederick A. Praeger, Inc., New York, 1967.

Gehlin, Michael P.: *The Communist Party of the Soviet Union*, Indiana University Press, Bloomington, 1969.

La Palombara, Joseph, and Myron Weiner: *Political Parties and Political Development*, Princeton University Press, Princeton, N.J., 1966.

McDonald, Neil A.: *The Study of Political Parties*, Doubleday & Company, Inc., Garden City, N.Y., 1955.

McKenzie, R. T.: *British Political Parties*, 2ded., Frederick A. Praeger, Inc., New York, 1964.

Macridis, Roy C. (ed.): *Political Parties: Contemporary Trends and Ideas*, Harper & Row, Publishers, Incorporated, New York, 1967.

——— and Robert E. Ward (eds.): *Modern Political Systems: Europe*, 3d ed., Prentice-Hall, Inc., Englewood Cliffs, N.J., 1972.

Pierce, Roy: *French Politics and Political Institutions*, 2d ed., Harper & Row, Publishers, Incorporated, New York, 1973.

Scalapino, Robert A., and Junnosuke Masumi: *Parties and Politics in Contemporary Japan*, University of California Press, Berkeley, 1962.

Sorauf, Frank J.: *Party Politics in America*, 2d ed., Little, Brown and Company, Boston, 1972.

Thomas, I. Bulmer: *The Party System in Great Britain*, John Baker (Publishers) Ltd., London, 1966.

Chapter 17

The Impact of Science and Technology: New Challenges and Problems

One may well ask why pure science (with its emphasis on thinking) and technology (with its emphasis on doing) are referred to in an introductory study of political science. The reason is that both are exceptionally powerful forces materially conditioning both man and the nature of his government.

A NEW SOCIAL COMPLEX

The stepped-up scientific and technological output of the twentieth century has brought with it a general (if vague) awareness that nothing is quite as it used to be. The speed and scope of current technological developments set the present age apart from all earlier eras of scientific progress. "Technological change"—a modern-sounding term —has been with us since the dawn of civilization. It is as old as a better Stone Age axe and as new as a transistor radio—as commonplace as a can opener and as complex as a space vehicle. In its simplest sense, technological change may be thought of as a "better way of doing a known job or the discovery of how to do a previously impossible one."[1] Future scientific and technological changes will strike man at a staggering rate. There are, for example, more scientists and technologists living today than have existed throughout all history down to the present. Their output will affect mankind with continuously accelerating and unrelenting force.

Science and technology have significantly altered scores of human relationships. They have especially modified the relationships existing between man

[1]Thomas J. Watson, Jr., "Technological Change," in *Goals for Americans: The Report of the President's Commission on National Goals,* Prentice-Hall, Inc., Englewood Cliffs, N.J., 1960, p. 193.

and man and between man and government. They are primary forces in making modern man (the product of past and present environments) what he is today. They are also primary forces in making modern governments what they are today. A moment's reflection will bring to mind numerous instances of the impact of science and technology upon the role of government. They have brought about vast changes in national defense, industry, agriculture, labor and management, education, economics, transportation, communication, amusements, environments, uses of the ocean, and all aspects of modern life. Also in the wake of science and technology have come food and population problems, space exploration, the invasion of privacy through the use of computers, and a reassessment of national priorities.

Science and technology have led to big government, to which many new and enlarged tasks are assigned. This in turn has led to a vastly increased corps of highly skilled government employees, to legislation regulating or affecting many aspects of daily life, to increased governmental services, and inevitably to vastly increased governmental costs and taxes. A new situation in world affairs, involving vast armaments and large expenditures for foreign aid, has also resulted. Science and technology have produced large metropolitan areas, and rapidly enlarging populations in these areas require fire and police protection, public transportation facilities, and management of water, health, traffic, and land-planning programs (to mention but a few of the traditional problems of the cities). Additionally, there are new needs in the burgeoning metropolis, taking into account critical environmental needs as well as institutional reforms through decentralization and consolidation. In the course of embarking on many new responsibilities, the municipalities have set in motion a sequence of programs affecting policies, officers and employees, revenues, resources, and ultimately, the individual.

Science and technology have virtually revolutionized the role of government in modern society and have greatly altered the relationship between man and government. It will be the purpose of this chapter to offer evidence in support of this view and to discuss the role of science and technology in man's political relationships and their effect upon these relationships.

Science has revealed new technical horizons and new social perspectives. It has challenged man's ingenuity and imagination. It has changed lives in many significant respects. It has brought society within reach of undreamed-of prizes, but at the same time it has created perils so extreme as to cause concern for mankind's very existence.

Technology also has had a powerful influence upon all mankind, touching practically every realm of human behavior and thought. It offers us wonderful tools with which to advance in all fields of human endeavor—including politics. It also offers a newfound leisure in which statecraft can be more closely studied and implemented. However, technology produces weapons. Thus technology's tremendous potentialities point in opposite directions; they may help to perfect man or to destroy him.

Several major questions are presented: Will the scientific-technological developments now unfolding contribute to an environment favorable to the principles of responsible democratic government? Will mankind be able to bridge the ever-widening gap between social understanding and technological inventions? It is generally agreed that changes in patterns of philosophy and politics usually lag behind scientific discoveries. But technological advancement may set the stage for political and moral progress.

Scientific-technological change produces two well-understood results; one is obvious, and the second somewhat less so. The obvious result is the improved material condition of life measured in terms of a standard of living. The other result concerns the world of ideas and produces changes in established doctrines in such significant areas as behavior, ethics, economics, social values, and politics.

Consequently, the need to understand politics is greater than ever. Politics and related social sciences can provide mankind with a perspective and a balanced view of the forces that affect him in an everyday world and in his increasingly not-so-everyday world. A knowledge of politics helps to make one aware of the fact that science and technology have advanced more rapidly than man's understanding of them. It is unquestionably a key responsibility of politics to make the public realize that cultural convictions must be brought abreast of material progress.

In short, our central problem is the effect of scientific-technological change upon political man.

Have such changes been for the better? In reaching an answer, the reader must remember the inescapable fact that the dynamic impact of scientific and technological development cannot be checked or thwarted.

THE TWENTIETH CENTURY AND THE EMERGENCE OF NEW PROBLEMS

The character of the twentieth century has been variously described. Lenin referred to it as the "era of wars and revolutions." American scientists have described it as an "era of basic progress." Many Americans wonder whether our era will ultimately be known as the age of the atom and of nuclear destruction of civilization or whether historians will record it as the age in which a new worldwide ideal was achieved—the kinship of man in a world community with a higher and more civilized standard of living.

Science and technology are capable of providing a vast variety of material goods. Will the possession of such goods induce man to eliminate inequalities and injustices and elevate human and social values? As one of the great authorities in the development of nuclear physics has said, "We shook the tree of knowledge very hard and out of it fell the atomic bomb." However, fear of the bomb has not blinded Americans to the possibilities of peaceful uses of atomic power.

The rewards of science and technology include not only vast arrays of spectacular consumer goods but also significant new ideas. Advances in productivity have aroused higher expectations in the realm of human values. People the world over are now demanding—with ever greater insistence—personal security, better health, the democratic sharing of power, a more equitable distribution of wealth, and individual dignity. Demands for these general values are taking specific form in efforts to improve the role of women and children in society, better the general quality of health care, secure a more equitable sharing of the world's natural resources, provide a more substantial base for better ethnic relationships, extend educational opportunities, improve the conditions in which criminal justice is administered, and stimulate the world's economic activity, including freedom of communication and transportation. There are also demands to reduce or eliminate crime; end environmental pollution, including the destruction of critical ecosystems; stop the profligate using up of the world's natural resources; check excessive growths in the human population; do away with substandard living conditions, especially in the great metropolitan slums; and ameliorate all conditions that constitute limitations on the fullest enjoyment of basic human rights.[2] In some of the more highly developed countries major attention is now being given to the need to concentrate on providing services to the inhabitants. Where there are movements in the direction of a postindustrial society, the efforts of its members are aimed less toward producing consumable items than toward supplying services. Only because of the impact of science and technology has this transition become possible.

Although science and technology have provided most Americans with shorter working hours, more leisure time, an efficient distribution of goods and services, and the challenge to use such special opportunities in a beneficial manner, this good fortune is not a worldwide phenomenon. For millions upon millions of individuals living in the developing nations of the world, technological innovation has created an awareness that material happiness is theoretically within their grasp—even if such benefits more often than not continue to elude them. Their demands for such rewards, in the form of social and political change—if necessary by revolution—constitute one of our age's immediate and serious problems. These peoples show no patience, and temporizing, partial answers no longer appeal to them. In short, science and technology have set the stage in many heavily populated areas of the world for violent behavior if potential benefits are long held in abeyance. As a result, at least in part, of such increasingly forceful demands, institutions (including forms of government) have been modified to assist in the achievement of human objectives.

THE DIFFERENCE BETWEEN PURE SCIENCE AND TECHNOLOGY

Pure science is concerned with obtaining accurate knowledge about the structure and behavior of the physical universe. It deals with universals and with

---

[2] These are set out in the Universal Declaration of Human Rights, which was proclaimed by the United Nations General Assembly on Dec. 10, 1948.

rational analyses of known facts. It is fact-seeking as well as fact-using. It has no axes to grind and no profits to make, and it does not endeavor to prove or disprove any set of theories or convictions. It is neither a mysterious cult nor a mechanical monster. Its sole purpose is to understand the universe and everything in it. It observes the living as well as the inanimate.

Science has been described as an "adventure of the human spirit. It is an essentially artistic enterprise, stimulated largely by curiosity, served largely by disciplined imagination, and based largely on faith in the reasonableness, order, and beauty of the universe of which man is a part."[3] Thus a distinction is drawn between pure science and applied technology.

Technology applies the discoveries of pure science to mankind's practical, immediate needs. It is engineering or applied science. The pure scientist discovers the basic formula; the technologist employs it to establish the assembly line and manufacture the implement. Michael Faraday's studies of electricity and magnetism were applied by Thomas A. Edison in inventing the electric light bulb. However, as Weaver points out, applied researchers uncover much new knowledge, and pure researchers discover many useful and practical things. The distinction between the two is often "more a matter of temperament and motivation than it is of procedure or result."[4]

According to Hubble (one of the world's greatest astronomers), modern technology is about 1,000 years old. Plagues had decimated the population, and it became necessary to find substitutes for manpower (often slave power). The search for machines to do man's work led in turn to the quest for machines to make the needed machinery. Labor-saving devices have replaced scarcity with abundance in the area of basic commodities.

Science and technology affect people as producers, as members of the consuming public, and as citizens of a state or nation. Governments at every level are influenced by these forces. The beneficial influences of science and technology have been distributed primarily among Western peoples, but secondarily and indirectly all around the globe.

Today the populations of the developing nations are fully aware that advances in science and technology are providing opportunities for a richer and more complete life. It is not surprising that scientists and technologists regard their efforts and product as truly international in significance.

It is paradoxical that science and technology have provided us with the highest material standard of living the world has ever seen and have at the same time confronted us with national and international problems of a scope and intensity never before experienced. Even though the survival of mankind has been put in jeopardy, few among us would wish to turn the scientific-technological clock back to the Stone Age. Instead, we are agreed that man must advance his moral, social, and political knowledge and outlook to catch up with his scientific-technological progress.

SCIENCE, TECHNOLOGY, AND BUSINESS

The state, from its earliest beginnings, has concerned itself with the conduct of business activities. Especially since the time of the industrial revolution and the advent of modern technology, government has taken a growing interest in economic affairs. Probably no clearer cause-and-effect relationship exists in the social sciences. As one observer has pointed out, "We live in an age in which advances in science and the growth of industry have been paralleled by an enormous growth of government."[5] Why?

The answer must take into account the following factors. This is the machine age, and those who control machines also control society. Possession of efficient machinery contributes to competitive advantage. As the time required for production of a given item is diminished, a greater total product can be manufactured in a fixed time. The possible abuse of such productive power represents a social problem and has evoked public interest in business practices.

Concurrent with the physical invention of the machine was the social invention of the corporation, trust, business association, and various other legal entities. The major purpose of these combina-

---

[3]Warren Weaver, "A Great Age for Science," in *Goals for Americans*, p. 105.
[4]Ibid., p. 107.

[5]Arthur T. Vanderbilt, "An Example to Emulate," *South Atlantic Quarterly*, vol. 52, no. 4, p. 5, 1953.

tions was to permit the accumulation of large amounts of capital in the hands of a concentrated managerial body. Such capital was then employed in the production or purchase of technological equipment.

The combination of the machine and the corporate device led first to the growth of larger and larger companies and then away from competition and toward monopoly. Some producers developed new ideas and products, crushed their competitors, and became dominant in their respective areas. As a consequence, the relationship between the consumer and the producer was materially altered.

In the United States the general public soon demanded governmental intervention in order to redress the balance of power, which had swung in favor of the industrialist. The demand was most often expressed through pleas for governmental regulation.[6] Farmers, workingmen, and small businessmen secured the enactment of antitrust and other legislation that subjected the new concentrations of economic power to the public interest. National and state laws banned economic concentrations of a monopolistic nature, as well as combinations and conspiracies in restraint of trade. Federal legislation was based on the commerce clause of the Constitution; state laws were based on the police power.

Governmental regulation in some degree and form now applies to virtually every kind of business. The tasks of such regulation have necessitated the enlargement of the civil service. Science and technology have advanced more rapidly than government and have been largely responsible for the expansion of government's regulatory activities. As the powers of government have grown, the private rights of some groups have been reduced, while those of others have been increased; on balance, however, the rights and interests of the general public have been promoted.

Government's interest in industry is not merely negative; it has also assisted industry since the foundation of the republic. High protective tariffs,

[6]There are four main policies that government may pursue toward business: (1) a "hands-off" attitude, (2) control through various regulations, (3) assistance through subsidies or other grants, and (4) public ownership and operation of certain kinds of business. In the United States we have what is often called a "mixed economy," i.e., one in which the government simultaneously pursues all four policies in different sectors of business.

grants of public lands, tax favors and benefits, and subsidies represent the positive side of governmental intervention. A basic responsibility of modern government is that of maintaining a stable economy and preventing wild swings in the business cycle. By seeking to maintain full employment and general prosperity, government also helps business to earn steady profits. Science and technology, by creating huge enterprises and an interdependent economy, have produced a situation fraught with many dangers. Hence government must closely watch business trends in order to ward off depressions, guard against inflation, maintain or restore competition, and prevent the undue concentration of economic power in a few hands. The magnitude of these responsibilities, despite the skills that may be brought to bear on varying situations, places a heavy burden on "big government."

SCIENCE, TECHNOLOGY, AND LABOR

Industrial society was pioneered by dissenters who were not content to accept an earlier orthodoxy, whether theological or technological. The result was invention, new processes, and new products. Even before the industrial revolution, laborers often protested against their working conditions. As early as the year 1500, Sir Thomas More, in his *Utopia,* advocated a nine-hour day—at a time when work from dawn to dusk was commonplace. The coming of modern machines and the factory system transformed the nature of labor, the attitudes of worker and employer, and the relationships of both toward government.

Science and technology have increased the productive capacities of the worker, although workers have been replaced by machines. Automation has become more than a topic for discussion. High productivity has raised living standards and has caused demands for higher wages. The worker believes that as productivity rises in private industry (and sometimes even if his productivity does not increase), his real wages should rise accordingly. Such wage demands raise the question of how increased productivity should be shared as between labor and capital. Clearly, scientific-technological innovations contributed by management are entitled to compensation. Through profits, plants may be modernized and made competitive in national and foreign markets. On the other hand, labor must share in such gains if mass purchasing power is to keep pace with the increased supply of goods being made available.

The task of apportionment is difficult. For example, in the steel industry in 1942, an addition to capital of between $10,000 and $15,000 resulted in expanded plant facilities capable of absorbing one additional worker. In 1952 an addition to capital of $90,000 in such expanded facilities was required before the industry could absorb an additional worker. Today even greater investments are required. Admittedly, the productivity of the worker is greater today than in 1942 or 1952, but the allocation of resulting gains to labor as opposed to management (bearing in mind rapid obsolescence of machinery and higher prospective costs for future equipment) is not an easy task.

The impasse over the distribution of gains has been a major factor in industrial unrest. Experts in labor-management relations have urged the creation of labor-management teams to work out such problems, on the theory that industry is so unified and interdependent that everyone from president to common laborer shares the responsibility that industry owes to the general public. Demands for immediate advantage often seem to ignore this fundamental fact.

For many years, both labor and management have looked to government for assistance and control. Labor wants minimum-wage and maximum-hour laws, additional laws favorable to union activities, and also governmental restrictions on management. Management, conversely, wants government to blunt many of labor's weapons, such as the boycott, the strike, picketing, and the closed union shop. Management and labor may join forces to get government to keep out cheaply produced foreign goods, or they may cooperate in securing the admission of foreign goods where there are mutually advantageous trade conditions. Management, on the other hand, may extend its foreign subsidiaries so as to derive benefits from such trade groupings as the European Common Market or other regional bodies. At the present, goods produced in some of these areas are competitive because of cheaper labor costs as well as tax and tariff advantages. Thus labor and management seek to use the state's power for their own purposes, but both resist the imposition of state control in such matters as the compulsory arbitration of labor-management disputes.

Both labor and management have entered the political arena; both have become politically powerful. Alpheus T. Mason has pointed out that "as if by design, industrial absolutism and political democracy have progressed simultaneously."[7] Business organizations have been confronted by powerful (and wealthy) labor aggregates. Under universal suffrage, the worker-voter refuses to be both sovereign and exploited. Efforts by labor to secure its fair share of scientific-technological advance have led to political awareness and to the formation of political action groups. These have been successful in securing legislation favorable to labor involving compensation and conditions of employment, as well as exemptions from antitrust and antimonopoly laws. Government has been increasingly drawn into the sphere of labor problems; the inexorable march of science and technology will deepen this involvement. Labor-management disputes, especially in industries of nationwide scope, are no longer private quarrels; government must safeguard the public interest.

SCIENCE, TECHNOLOGY, AND HUMAN RELATIONS

Science and technology have transformed the pattern of human relationships—on the job, in the home, in the local community, in the United States, and in the entire world. Shorter working hours have provided both leisure time and the problem of using it in a beneficial manner.

The tempo of the assembly line has demanded younger workers, has displaced older employees, and has led to demands for retirement pensions and annuities. Yet forced retirement at an arbitrary age often means a forced reduction in income and living standards, a personal problem of psychological readjustment, and a loss to society of the services of still vigorous and capable workers. Times of grave national emergency, such as the World War II years, point up the value of elderly workers. Although retirement schemes provide more jobs

---

[7] Alpheus T. Mason, "American Individualism: Fact or Fiction?" *American Political Science Review*, vol. 46, no. 9, p. 1, 1952.

for the young and recreation for the old, the lengthening span of life is producing new ideas on the subject. Today, the trend is toward keeping older workers employed as long as they remain capable and toward delaying the moment of retirement.

Another scientific-technological by-product is the displacement of small entrepreneurs, who are driven into corporate, and frequently regimented, employment. Also, production quotas now replace the historic pride of the artisan in his work. Handicrafts, with their quality of exactness, have given way to mass production, with emphasis on quantity rather than quality. As industrial society has provided greater comforts for the worker, it has also tended to weaken individualism and the sense of personal responsibility.

Workers looked initially to their employers for a certain measure of economic security, and when employers failed to provide such security, they turned to labor unions and to government. Their leisure time has allowed them to take on new political interests; the prospect of personal economic insecurity in a scientific-technological environment has compelled an interest in politics and politicians.

Mass production made the employee a cog in a huge, impersonal, industrial machine. With the advent of a precise division of labor, the individual frequently performed repetitive and highly monotonous tasks. Attendant tensions, frustrations, and feelings of personal insecurity were expressed in class conflict, industrial unrest, a craving for personal recognition and status, and other evidences of discontent.

Where the rate of scientific-technological development has been high, there has been a parallel instability and uncertainty in human relations. As a consequence, adjustment to new situations constantly becomes more difficult. Mental illness has increased substantially. Others, seeking to pursue other values, have quietly opted out of the system.

Responsible business leaders, recognizing this aspect of the machine age, have attempted to reduce the causes of discontent and to eliminate dangerous states of mind flowing from such frustrations and monotony. One major effort has been to rebuild the earlier, closer relationship between managers and workers. This has taken the form of pride in work and the building of a common bond of fraternity in industrial accomplishment and achievement. Individuals are helped to feel that they "belong" to the organization. Management is recognizing that the most important asset of any organization is the human factor, and it is attempting to assess the attitudes of workers toward their work and their overall status. Further, workers have been encouraged to suggest means of improving their relationships with management.

Scientific and technological innovations have produced paradoxical consequences. They have led to economic advance and to the spread of materialism, and yet the fear of nuclear destruction has revived interest in religion. They have contributed to the comforts of family life, and yet they have also emancipated younger members of the family and, through the automobile, the motion picture, and television, have disrupted the family circle. The changing role of the family has brought government into the picture as an agent for the education and protection of the young.

Large-scale unemployment and world depressions are phenomena of the scientific-technological age. So are the tightening controls of both private and governmental groups over the individual. Individuals seek a form of security through joining and associating in groups. Probably science and technology have also contributed to the growing dominance of the national government and the diminishing relative importance of state governments.

Although they have provided opportunities for leisure and for mass education, these new forces have not necessarily caused individuals to develop higher sensibilities or resulted in the equitable distribution of opportunities among them. They have contributed both the blessings and the curses of specialization; they have given us cheaper and more diversified commodities, blighted, however, by the dull standardization of mass production. They have provided facilities for the communication of information and ideas that ought to lead to a better understanding of public issues. Yet when untruths rather than truths are disseminated, the result is popular misunderstanding and confusion. To the degree that such channels of communication broadly disseminate provocative falsehoods (or half-truths), all tensions and conflicts are intensified. Such conditions make political compromise difficult, if not impossible. As a result, the public's interest in the rational settlement of disputes and in responsible methods for shaping public policy is thwarted, and the concept of responsibility in government is endangered. Officials come to regard the public as an adversary, which leads to secrecy, "dirty tricks," and corruption.

Science and technology have been thus far unable to provide the improved social and political organization and control so badly needed to keep pace with invention. Socially and psychologically, we lag far behind the transistors, semiconductors, tape recorders, computers, and other significant improvements that technology has given us. Science and technology have made human want obsolete. However, they cannot give assurance that men everywhere will develop the kind of social intelligence that must exist if human beings are to realize their tremendous possibilities.

SCIENCE, TECHNOLOGY, AND AGRICULTURE

Just as science and technology have increased the productive capacities of the industrial worker, so have they expanded those of the farmer and similarly modified his relationship to the state. The farmer's outlook has been transformed as much as that of any other member of society.

Science and technology in agriculture have widened the farmer's market and enlarged his economic, social, and political problems. In the United States increasing farm productivity has led directly to the vanishing farmer. During the past seventy-five years the population of the United States has more than tripled, and during the past 100 years it has multiplied more than seven times. Yet during this period, owing to mechanized farm equipment and to more efficient farming practices resulting from scientific seed selection, availability of hardy new strains, improved fertilizers and insecticides, soil chemistry, soil conditioners, soil-conservation methods, and techniques of land reclamation and irrigation, the percentage of our population required to feed the nation has been reduced from 84 to less than 10 percent. The number of persons on farms has diminished by about 6 percent in the last few years, but farm surpluses increase continuously.

Science, technology, and government face one of their greatest challenges in the area of agriculture, for if the American experience of producing ever-increasing quantities of food through the efforts of fewer and fewer farmers becomes an international prototype, the underprivileged peoples of the world (assuming there are limits to the present population explosion in the developing nations) may yet achieve adequate nourishment and clothing. If they do, the danger of international communism, which thrives among the chronically underfed and underclothed, will be reduced.

While the United States has been experiencing an extended period of large food surpluses, this has not been true in many other parts of the world. However, because of tariffs and other obstacles to international trade, American surpluses piled up during the 1950s and 1960s, while people in some countries went hungry. During these decades farm surpluses were kept under some measure of control only through an extensive foreign-aid program and through an expensive domestic storage program. To keep up agricultural prices for the farmer, the national government had adopted a comprehensive agricultural program, including subsidies and parity payments designed to keep farm prices balanced against industrial prices. The heavy tax costs to support the farm subsidy programs of that era were a nightmare to our public leaders.[8]

By the 1970s world food shortages were evident—especially in the heavily populated, less developed countries—and the United States, recognizing the political value of its food surpluses and its agricultural potential, terminated policies that had restricted food production. With the sharp increase in the price of foreign oil in the mid-1970s, the United States saw the need to export agricultural products in order to give a measure of stability and protection to its international balance of payments.

The old single-family farm has now been partially displaced by corporate farming—large-scale, highly mechanized, efficient, and impersonal. Obviously, corporations, even when family-owned, are better

---

[8]Once such programs are operational, it is very difficult to correct them. The United States must meet a serious challenge as it searches for a "supply-demand equilibrium to permit the market, with a fair return to farmers, to determine the manpower and capital committed to this sector of the economy." *Goals for Americans*, p. 12.

able to purchase expensive equipment and to acquire huge tracts of land. Farm cooperatives have multiplied. New techniques of processing and preserving food have had a marked impact upon agriculture and upon the dietary habits of the consumer. Science and technology, which have allowed for the replacement of men by machines, plus governmental intervention in the operation of the market, have transformed farming as a way of life. As in other areas (e.g., mining, certain areas of industry, and foreign trade), the government must provide for the education and training or retraining of those who, through no fault of their own, have been obliged to bear the brunt of scientific-technological change.

SCIENCE, TECHNOLOGY, AND NATIONAL DEFENSE

It is in the area of national defense that science and technology have possibly had their largest impact on political society. Here the transition has been from Adam to the atom, and it is now time to ask: Will computers run the war of the future? There are no noncombatants in total war. Each person becomes a soldier, whether in uniform or not. Man's relationship to the state has been sharply altered as a consequence of these modern developments.

The arsenal of scientific-technological monsters is not limited to atom, hydrogen, and cobalt bombs, hideous as these may be. In addition, there are transhemispheric missiles, long-range submersibles, biological agents of destruction, radioactive dusts and fallouts, and toxic gases too horrible to contemplate. It is claimed that modern nuclear weapons would completely poison the atmosphere around the earth. Science and technology have equipped mankind for self-extermination.

The near failure of substantial disarmament and arms-control efforts in recent years is silent but eloquent evidence of the dire conditions confronting modern man.[9] The mere presence of technological methods of warfare, tested but not used, completely transforms the position of the individual in a democratic society. The role of government becomes greater than ever before. The older relationships between national security and individual liberty are in the process of extensive modification. The interest of national security has been accentuated, and the range of individual liberty has been considerably diminished. The concept of the primacy of the free and sovereign individual requires reconsideration and possible restatement in the light of technological weapons and new concepts of warfare.

When democratic governments were established, important individual liberties were declared to be beyond the reach of governmental power. Today, as a result of technology's impact on warfare, the state is compelled to assume many essential powers without the specific consent of the individual. Even if time were to permit consultation of the public via traditional processes, there is no assurance that the technicians would be able to make the problems intelligible to the public, which therefore could not render an informed decision. There is even room for doubt as to whether the technicians and those in government could fully comprehend all the issues and alternative solutions. As Dr. James R. Killian, Jr., a noted American scientist, observed:

> We do not have enough scientists and engineers who have not only a deep understanding of their specialty but, in addition, the cast of mind, the motivation, and the breadth of understanding to serve effectively—and to survive—in policy-making, advisory, and administrative roles in the public service. Government in a technological society requires a reasonable complement of scientists in the public arena if it is to deal wisely with all the great policy matters arising out of science.[10]

The dangers of noncommunication between the scientists and technicians, on the one hand, and the persons holding political office, on the other, and the resultant lack of communication with the public have been portrayed graphically in the writings of Sir Charles P. Snow.[11] Typical efforts to remedy

---

[9]One bright spot has been the Moscow Test-Ban Treaty, signed in August 1963, which provides against testing of nuclear weapons in the atmosphere, in outer space, and underwater. This was followed on July 1, 1968, by the Treaty on the Non-Proliferation of Nuclear Weapons. Since then, the United Nations' Committee on Disarmament has authored important agreements limiting armaments.

[10]*Christian Science Monitor*, Apr. 13, 1961, p. 1. Compare E. Wenk, Jr., *The Politics of the Ocean*, University of Washington Press, Seattle, 1972.

[11]*Science and Government*, Harvard University Press, Cambridge, Mass., 1961; *The Two Cultures and the Scientific Revolution*, Cambridge University Press, New York, 1959.

this situation include the creation by the British government of the post of minister of science, a Cabinet post, and the establishment by President Eisenhower of the office of science adviser to the president and the sub-Cabinet-level Federal Council for Science and Technology. A number of American Cabinet members also have science advisers on their staffs, and in 1962 President Kennedy created an Office of Science and Technology to advise and assist the chief executive in using such forces in the interests of national security and general welfare.

To recognize the existence and nature of the problem is the first step toward its solution. A corps of translators or intermediaries is coming into being—men who can converse in the languages of the natural scientists, the government, and the people. Their role in a scientific and technological society is certain to become increasingly important. In times of extreme crisis—when decisions must be made quickly—the state may be compelled to encroach reluctantly upon the privileges and powers of the individual.

The modification of the role of government has been effected in many other ways: through the extension of its regulatory and prohibitory activities, through a revised interpretation of many civil liberties, through the increased emphasis upon secrecy and the reluctance or refusal of government to tell citizens about new facts and policies, and through a greater concern for security and loyalty. Planning activities have been expanded; political power has been further centralized in the national government; greater authority has been vested in the executive branch of that government; and public ownership of vital resources has grown as the result of our space program. The government's licensing activities have been extended; the defense establishments have been unified; military influence has increased; the idea of total war has been faced with resignation; and civil defense (now a paramilitary function) is receiving some attention. Personnel in the Armed Forces have been increased, as have taxes and budgets; natural resources, including strategic raw materials, are being depleted more rapidly. Predictions of energy shortages have proved to be well-founded.

While the trend is clear, and the reasons behind it apparent, liberty-loving individuals have not permitted these developments to go unchallenged. In recent years the United States Supreme Court has been confronted with many cases requiring it to prick out a line of demarcation between considerations of national security and the constitutional liberties of the American citizen. Such cases place an awesome responsibility upon the Court because they involve the most crucial problem of democracy.[12]

Total war, the product of science and technology, concentrates on the destruction of the enemy's resources, factories, methods of communication and transportation, and civilian morale, rather than merely on his armies in the field. Also, total war includes the period of preparation and the era of cold war. In such a situation, according to Hanson W. Baldwin:

A military observer sees vividly the need for greater military efficiency. He can scarcely oppose reasonable steps to that end. And he recognizes the strength of arguments raised for *absolute* military preparedness—even at the moment when he feels most sure that the United States could achieve this absolute preparedness only at the cost of our whole way of life, our democracy, our liberties. This is the dilemma which the American people face today.[13]

The new weapons are expensive; indeed, their cost is prohibitive for smaller nations. Yet their possession augments national power and prestige. France is now seeking to develop its own atomic arsenal and, despite worldwide protests, has engaged in extended tests in the South Pacific. The People's Republic of China, Egypt, India, and Israel have developed nuclear capabilities, and other countries are making plans. In the United States, defense costs in recent years have exceeded $50 billion a year, and during the years of the Vietnamese war they annually ranged between $70 billion and $78 billion. When one takes into account the cost of national space programs, the monetary costs are even greater. By way of contrast, $40 billion was more than enough to run the national

---

[12]A notable illustration was the 1974 Watergate tapes case, officially entitled *United States v. Richard M. Nixon* and *Richard M. Nixon v. United States,* 94 S. Ct. 3090 (July 24, 1974).

[13]Hanson W. Baldwin, "The Military Move In," *Harper's Magazine,* vol. 195, no. 1171, December 1947, p. 4.

government of the United States from the moment of its first establishment down to the period just before World War I. It is temporarily possible for a healthy economy to produce both guns and butter. However, excessive military costs ultimately produce inflation, waste natural and human resources, and cause a general deterioration of the human condition.

A specific example of the impact of scientific and technological warfare upon governmental structure is the Atomic Energy Commission. This administrative agency was created by the Atomic Energy Act of 1946. The act declares all atomic materials in the United States to be a national monopoly, subject only to public ownership, and to be supervised in the most minute detail by the Commission. While the Commission is permitted to license the use of atomic materials to private persons, it cannot be compelled to make such materials available to anyone outside the government. Subject to definite restrictions designed to safeguard the public interest, the Commission may permit private industrial developments, essentially for the production of commercial power. The importance of this agency was appraised by one of its former chairmen. Gordon Dean once wrote: "The impact of the policies formulated by the Commission would be such as greatly to influence not only our military security and our foreign policy, but in a large measure the whole structure of our society."[14] However, the Commission's policies must be approved by the president and enjoy the support of Congress, which created the agency and can alter or abolish it. Nonetheless, the vesting of such extraordinary powers in an instrumentality of government provides abundant evidence of government's far-ranging influence upon the lives of its citizens.

As pointed out above, the scientist and technologist are more than ever before cast in the role of advisers to the political leaders in government. They are now far more than mere consultants to fighting men. "In the National Defense Research Committee and the Office of Scientific Research and Development, in the Second World War, scientists became full and responsible partners for the first time in the conduct of war."[15] General Bradley has said that "the time has come for scientists to take a greater part in strategic planning. . . . In my opinion, the advice and knowledge of scientists must be contributed to the Joint Staff and to the special committees working for the Joint Chiefs of Staff."[16]

The increasing complexity and cost of modern armament make it slower to manufacture. The increased time lag between drawing board and landing strip or launching pad necessitates clear policy formulation, careful planning, and rigorous fulfillment of production schedules. Otherwise, a military machine may well be obsolete by the time it is built.

An important issue raised by modern war is whether it is possible to adhere in practice to the important democratic principle that there should be civilian control over the military establishment. Another problem is that of shortages of materials that are necessary for technological warfare, such as manganese, nickel, and cobalt; with respect to these the United States is a "have-not" nation.

Can democratic nations support the paraphernalia, and cope with the problems, of total war? Enormous responsibility and enormous authority go together. Although the president becomes the focus of authority, the people must retain the ultimate power to determine basic national policies. Such balancing of concentrated power with popular sovereignty places a new strain on modern democracy. One response has been the 1973 War Powers Resolution, wherein Congress sought to impose limitations on presidential authority in time of military crisis. The resolution was vetoed by President Nixon on the grounds that it was clearly unconstitutional, but the veto was overridden by a fairly narrow margin.

SCIENCE, TECHNOLOGY, AND LAW

Although law is notoriously slow to reflect social changes, it has made several adaptations to the era of technology, notably in the fields of administrative, tort, criminal, constitutional, international, la-

---

[14]Gordon Dean, "The Impact of the Atom on Law," *University of Pittsburgh Law Review*, vol. 12, no. 4, p. 514, 1951.

[15]Vannevar Bush, *Modern Arms and Free Men*, Simon and Schuster, New York, 1949, p. 6.

[16]General Omar N. Bradley, "Soldier's Farewell," *Saturday Evening Post*, Aug. 29, 1953, p. 49.

bor, social security, antitrust, and workmen's compensation law.

Administrative law is a product of the industrial revolution, arising from the need for established procedures covering the relationships between government, as a regulator of conduct, and those being regulated. As government employs administrative agencies to carry out its new functions, new rulings and court decisions emerge concerning the rights and obligations of government and citizen.

The law of torts, the so-called ragbag on the outer periphery of the law, which deals with harms and injuries to persons, has been modified as the result of technological change. With the invention of the automobile, aircraft, and space vehicles, and with the resulting hazards of individual movement, much greater attention has been given to the notion of negligence. In recent years, as respect for human rights has grown, tort law has been much concerned with the right of privacy, which has been increasingly invaded by camera, press, telephone, telegraph, radio, television, and other newer forms of communication.

Professor Hurst has pointed out that whereas "invention itself had been a key invention of the nineteenth century, so, a basic invention of the twentieth might be some effort by law to make technical change mesh in more smoothly with other aspects of life."[17] Legal modifications in response to the atomic era have been rather slow. The workmen's compensation statutes of New Mexico and Tennessee, where huge atomic installations are located, now make provision for radiation injuries. New York has extended the time for filing claims to take account of delayed illnesses, such as radiation sickness and beryllium poisoning. California's Industrial Accident Commission has set up, through administrative regulations, minimum standards for the protection of employees exposed to ionizing radiation. On the national level, the Interstate Commerce Commission has issued new regulations regarding the interstate shipment of radioactive materials. Yet in 1951 it could be said that "the events which have followed the first splitting of the uranium atom up to now have hardly left a dent on the substantive law of this country, on the procedural law, or for that matter on the work habits, the interests, the business or the specialties of the practicing lawyer."[18] Fortunately, within the past decade legislators have perceived the need for extensive protection for persons engaged in extrahazardous activities, including imposing penalties for causing dangerous pollution of the human environment.

SCIENCE, TECHNOLOGY, AND EDUCATION

Inevitably, the age of science and technology has emphasized the scientific and technical side of education, rather than its broader cultural aspects. Public education, particularly in the United States, stresses vocational and practical subjects, and the pattern of public education is reflected in the privately supported schools also.

The atomic era has focused the attention of the national government on scientific research. Before World War II, government sponsorship of such research was confined principally to government-owned installations. Today the pattern is completely different, with the government acting as a research partner with leading universities, setting objectives, establishing work plans, and supplying funds.

In 1950 the National Science Foundation was created, with the statutory responsibility of supporting basic research, encouraging the development of young scientists through the establishment of graduate fellowships, improving the quality of scientific instruction, and broadening the flow of scientific information. However, the National Science Foundation's budget for scientific research doubled in the two years after the Soviet launch of Sputnik in 1957, tripling again in the succeeding five years. By 1972 it had reached $566 million. In the year 1951–1952, Congress appropriated approximately $2.2 billion for scientific activities, including research for all purposes. Of this large sum, only relatively small amounts have been allocated to the National Science Foundation, the largest proportion (53 percent) going to the Department of Defense, and the next largest (36 percent) to the Atomic Energy Commission. In subsequent years, however, increasingly more money has been allo-

---

[17]J. W. Hurst, *The Growth of American Law*, Little, Brown and Company, Boston, 1950, p. 11.

[18]Dean, loc. cit.

cated to basic research in the United States. The Department of Defense continues to receive the lion's share of general allocations. In 1972 it was budgeted $7.8 billion for research and development. Funds for basic research still lag behind expenditures for practical applications. The national government is by far the largest supplier of such funds, but industry, colleges and universities, and nonprofit foundations have also contributed substantially to the support of this kind of research.

In a democracy it is unhealthy if educational opportunities in the social sciences and the humanities do not keep pace with an accelerating interest in the natural sciences and technology. In order that a proper equilibrium between these areas might be maintained, and the public interest be thus preserved and protected, in recent years additional sums have been devoted to the support of the social sciences and the humanities. The latter have found support through governmental appropriations for national defense. The National Science Foundation, whose basic purpose is to support the natural sciences, has allocated funds for research in political science and psychology, among other fields. Great foundations, such as the Ford and Rockefeller institutions, have allocated increasing sums to bolster and upgrade the social sciences—frequently in the areas of law and international affairs. Substantial efforts from many quarters have been dedicated to closing the cultural gap. To further these ends, the National Foundation on the Arts and the Humanities was created in 1965. By 1972 its annual budget had reached $44 million. Present and future generations of students seem likely to gain a substantial opportunity to understand the values of democracy and a wider perspective on their nation, their world, and the universe.

SCIENCE AND TECHNOLOGY IN THE SOVIET UNION

The important rivalries between the United States and the Soviet Union warrant attention to Soviet progress in science and technology. In theory, Soviet science and technology are required to fit into the Marxist frame of reference. However, in practice Russia's scientists and technologists have generally been able to free themselves from political domination. As is well known, Soviet science and technology have long been engaged in a serious challenge to the earlier scientific and technological supremacy of the United States. On the whole, there seems little doubt of this country's continued leadership; although some believe that the Soviets may be ahead in certain limited areas (as much as several years in certain aspects of space technology), American response to the general Soviet challenge has been highly encouraging. For a while, however, there was a widespread fear that the United States might lose the cold war in the classroom—the empty classroom.

The Soviets have taken science and technology very seriously ever since 1917. Stalin, speaking before the Komsomol in 1928, said, "To master science, to forge new cadres of Bolsheviks—specialists in all branches of science, to study, study, study, in the stubbornest fashion—that is the present task, a crusade of revolutionary youth into science—that, comrades, is what we need now." Several years ago an American scientist, Dr. Conway Zirkle, reported that Soviet totalitarianism had adversely affected agriculture, biology, genetics, geology, medicine, pathology, psychology, psychiatry, and physiology. On the other hand, he credited the Soviets with doing excellent work in such areas as astronomy, chemistry, physics, mathematics, and engineering—the areas, it will be noted, that are critical for nuclear inquiry and space activity. This appraisal continues to be valid at the present time.

For many years the United States had a substantial lead over the Soviets in the areas of atomic and nuclear science and technology. However, in 1953 and again in 1955, the Soviets exploded thermonuclear bombs. In each instance this was achieved well before the Western world thought it possible. Then, in 1957, the Soviet Union launched its first satellite, Sputnik, into orbit, and in 1961 Soviet Majors Gagarin and Titov successfully orbited the globe. The United States responded by launching astronauts Shepard and Grissom into suborbital flights in 1961 and by putting Glenn, Carpenter, and Schirra into orbital flights in 1962. Since that time, hundreds of space objects have been orbited by the United States and the Soviet Union. Man in space has lost its novelty, and in July 1975 the joint Apollo-Soyuz test project involving space cooperation between American and Soviet astronauts had become a reality. The details of space competition—and now space cooperation—are exciting. More important to the political scientist, however, are the effects of man's use of the space environment on the processes and problems of government.

On the international level, the United States has signed agreements with seventy countries and with several international organizations to permit the location of United States tracking stations on foreign soil and the exchange of meteorological and magnetic data. Also, the United States has signed agreements with almost fifty nations to facilitate the exchange of information made available by stationary communications satellites. The first such communications satellite, the Early Bird, was put into orbit in 1965 and has made it possible for statesmen, scholars, and publicists to carry on international dialogues and panel discussions. Obviously, such exchanges of information and points of view are of great value for the promotion of international understanding.

The space program has also had a significant effect on the processes of American national government. The National Aeronautics and Space Administration (NASA) created in 1962 an Office of Technology Utilization as a central body to receive, evaluate, and make available to private industry the results of research, new discoveries, and new technology. Because the executive branch of the national government has been strengthened by means of presidential science advisers, committees, and other science agencies, Congress has feared that it was becoming a mere rubber stamp for proposals in the fields of science and technology. Accordingly, the House of Representatives subdivided its space committee to permit more specialization, and the Legislative Reference Service of the Library of Congress has been augmented to provide congressional members and committees with assistance in the field of science policy.

Recent achievements in space include the launch by the United States in 1972 of the Earth Resources Technology Satellite (ERTS-A). It was an earth-sensing satellite, conducted ninety separate data-acquisition projects, and involved cooperation between the United States and thirty-seven other states and two international organizations. Skylab, launched in 1973, conducted an even more extensive monitoring, or sensing, mission. The United States was very generous in the dissemination of acquired data and since that time has been cooperating at the United Nations in seeking an international agreement on activities carried out through remote-sensing-satellite surveys of earth resources. The United States took the lead in securing through the United Nations the 1967 Treaty on Principles Governing the Activities of States in the Exploration and Use of Outer Space Including the Moon and Other Celestial Bodies. In 1972 the United States became a sponsor of the Convention on International Liability for Damage Caused by Space Objects.

The International Geophysical Year, 1957–1958, proved that national scientists and technologists can engage in international cooperation in many subjects common to their universal disciplines. Their cooperative outlooks have brought in their train cooperative efforts on the part of legal and political figures. This collective cooperation has benefited all mankind. These advances have been coupled with a heightened interest in the social sciences and the humanities. This has allowed both the United States and the Soviet Union, as well as many other countries, to make substantial material progress. Such progress allows one to hope that someday states will be able to declare common cause against their common enemies—disease, poverty, ignorance, environmental decay, and war. In the long run, science and technology—suitably managed and equitably distributed throughout the entire world—may contribute to more amicable intergroup and international relations than have existed in the past.

SCIENCE, TECHNOLOGY, AND THE ART OF GOVERNMENT

Man's adjustment to the wonderful and horrible products of science and technology is the critical problem of our time and rests upon ethical and moral as well as political considerations. Thoughtful persons are deeply concerned over the problem of reordering society and individual behavior in the nuclear age. A former member of the Atomic Energy Commission (an engineer) has put the problem as follows:

Atomic bombs are only dangerous because some atomic men cannot be trusted. Science cannot save men from themselves, any more than society can. Rather, it is individual men who must save society and save themselves. The crisis we face today comes from the greed of men and their will to power regardless of conscience. The responsibility for the crisis is man's refusal to submit his behavior to reason and to reason's God.[19]

The American astronaut Col. John H. Glenn, Jr., has expressed substantially the same thought: "As our knowledge of the universe in which we live increases, may God grant us the wisdom and guidance to use it wisely."

Science and technology cannot themselves cope with or solve social and political problems. While science and technology are in vital demand today, there appears to be an even greater present need for those fundamentals of social and religious morality which strengthen man's human qualities—the only characteristics that distinguish him from other members of the animal kingdom. Indeed, there is much evidence that democratic survival depends on the revitalization of these same qualities. Science and technology are quite capable of producing only destruction and anarchy if the spirit of brotherhood is not consciously advanced and if it does not finally predominate. Consequently, it is frequently urged that highly moral individuals are needed as never before to support and manage government so that it in turn can control the destructive forces man has created. It is only this kind of person upon whom the authority to govern should be conferred in the present age. Only such an individual will be able to cope with and develop the art and science of government so that science and technology will mutually provide the abundant harvest of a Golden Age.

Thoughtful observers are obliged to ask where such persons can be found. In a scientific and technological age, out of what field or fields of experience will the moral philosophers, who will be charged with the role of leadership, emerge? Traditional politicians are not well equipped to meet this modern challenge unless they restrain themselves from their tendency to promise more than government can suitably deliver. They must also eradicate some of their commonly held outlooks that allow them so frequently to become enmeshed in sentimental confusion, nostalgia, loyalty to special interests, and fear. The professional moralists, such as philosophers and religious leaders, may not be able to supply the required leadership qualities any more than the traditional politician can. Such persons may be too locked into the perspectives of the past and too far removed from the art and science of modern government. But this is not to suggest that the leadership class of the future will come inevitably from the ranks of science and technology. In 1913 John Burroughs, contemplating the "noon of science," paid tribute to mankind's debt to scientific and technological achievement. He cautioned, however, that "Science without sense may bring us to grief. We cannot have a civilization propelled by machinery without the iron of it in some form entering our souls."[20] Clearly, the leadership group of the future need not come from any particular calling or discipline. Those constituting such a body—large or small—will of necessity be obliged to understand, among other things, the impact of science and technology on the governmental process.

Of critical importance will be the need for leaders and for the entire community to realize that the scientific and technological society is an integrated whole in which everything depends upon everything else and in which many of the sources of its complex machines have been used up and consumed. An atomic or nuclear war would destroy many component elements of the machine; and if the scientific-technological capacity of the nation were ever destroyed, it would be practically impossible to reestablish it in the form in which we now know it. Many distinguished men of science and technology have endeavored to determine the consequences of a nuclear war. The opinions of Edward Teller, Linus C. Pauling, and Hans A. Bethe, among others, vary considerably. The consensus is that the consequences of even limited conflict would be extremely grave and that the result of

---

[19] T. E. Murray, "Some Limitations of Science," *Electrical Engineering*, vol. 71, no. 2, p. 125, 1952. This is also the viewpoint of noted American religious leaders.

[20] *Writings of John Burroughs*, Houghton Mifflin Company, Boston, 1913, Vol. 17, *The Summit of the Years*.

all-out conflict would be destruction of men and materials to a ghastly degree.

World suicide is obviously abhorrent, and when warfare becomes too horrible for man to contemplate, it may be outlawed for this very reason. Democratic states, for defensive purposes, must enlarge their military capacity; even more important, they must reinforce their moral strength. Military strength requires a continuous search for new, effective weapons—useful as deterrents as well as for purposes of attack—but military power alone will not assure peace. Military might should be used only in the cause of right, and it carries the responsibility to promote justice. Might and right can be blended only by a very superior leadership in the science and art of government and in the social sciences as a whole. A sense of world community is also necessary.

The retention of the United States' favored place in the world ultimately requires that it be a moral and intellectual, as well as a scientific-technological, leader. Such ethical heights can be attained only through democracy, which postulates and seeks to realize the dignity and moral worth of man. Science and technology have made the responsibilities of government heavier and more significant than ever before.

As science and technology race across the horizon of man's experiences with rocketlike velocity and titanic impact, a more ethical democracy is required if these constantly accelerating forces are to be kept in their proper place as man's servant, not his master.

STUDY-GUIDE QUESTIONS

1 What do you consider to be the most direct and immediate impact of science and technology on your own relationship with government? Why?
2 Do you believe that the scientific and technological innovations that presently exist in the United States have materially contributed to an enhancement of the democratic system of government?
3 Do you think that the export of science and technology from the United States to developing nations will improve the condition of democracy in such countries? What are your reasons?
4 Can democratic nations support the paraphernalia, and cope with the problems, of total war?
5 Can you offer any suggestions for reducing the costs of government through scientific and technological innovations? What hard evidence are you relying on in support of your suggestions?

REFERENCES

Bush, Vannevar: *Modern Arms and Free Men,* Simon and Schuster, New York, 1949.
Price, Don K.: *Government and Science: Their Dynamic Relation in American Democracy,* New York University Press, New York, 1954.
Ward, Barbara, and René Dubos: *Only One Earth,* W. W. Norton & Company, Inc., New York, 1972.
Wenk, Edward, Jr.: *The Politics of the Ocean,* University of Washington Press, Seattle, 1972.
Wiesner, Jerome B.: *Where Science and Politics Meet,* McGraw-Hill Book Company, New York, 1965.

Chapter 18

Public Administration: Performing the Tasks of the Modern State

THE NATURE OF PUBLIC ADMINISTRATION

The contrast between the economic and social conditions of the eighteenth century, when our governmental system was established, and those of the last quarter of the twentieth century has placed severe stress and strain on democratic government. Today's urbanized, industrialized, technological, and scientific society differs more widely from the society of the Founding Fathers than theirs differed from that of ancient Greece or Rome. Perhaps the greatest miracle of American government has been its gradual modification to meet modern problems without sacrificing either its fundamental structure or the spirit of free government. American national, state, and local governments have shouldered added burdens and met new responsibilities in the course of a gradual evolution that has added hundreds of agencies and millions of officials and employees to the apparatus of government. Significantly, the greatest increase in the numbers of government personnel has occurred at the state and local levels, with the latter state and local governments now vastly outdistancing the federal government as an employer. Of the 9,900,000 persons employed by state and local governments in 1970, some 2,755,000 were employed by the states, and the remaining 7,145,000 by local governments. By

1972 about one out of every fourteen *residents* (men, women, and children) of the United States was employed by government.[1]

Out of these developments a new study or science known as "public administration" and a new profession, that of the trained public administrator, have emerged. Speaking chronologically, government first assumed functions, created new agencies, and expanded its personnel. Then, belatedly, it made the discovery that the new era called for new and improved administrative organization and methods, technically competent personnel chosen on the basis of merit rather than politics, more businesslike administration, and attention to both public and human relations. As a growing field of knowledge and practice, public administration has attempted to meet this challenge. Out of trial and error, experience, and research, students of public administration have arrived at certain basic principles in this field that are considered to be sound guides toward more effective government, though they are not generally held with dogmatic determination and hence are subject to revision in the light of future knowledge.

There is general agreement on certain principles of public administration. First, in earlier times students of public administration were so concerned with freeing administrative processes from the undue political interference then prevalent that they assumed that a sharp distinction could be drawn between politics (policy formulation) and administration (policy execution). They also tended to exaggerate the differences between the two areas. Today there is general agreement that these processes are not—and cannot be—carried on in separate, watertight compartments, but are really two phases of the single, complex process of government. The prevailing view is that *major* public policies in a democracy must be the product of the give-and-take of politics and politicians and that not only administration but also a multitude of *secondary* policy decisions should be entrusted to trained, expert administrators chosen for their competence, not their political affiliation. Not only should such administrators be as free as possible from political pressures, but they should also be invested with both the power and the responsibility to perform the tasks assigned them.

Actually, of course, the expert knowledge of the professional administrator is needed for the formulation of sound public policy; political stereotypes, slogans, and prejudices provide an insecure foundation for legislation. In our national government, the representative, senator, president, and Cabinet officer (all politicians, as they should be) require the expert assistance of administrative specialists, whose knowledge can come to fruition only when translated into active policy through the politician. Neither is complete without the other; yet only in recent years has the contribution of the expert been appreciated.

Second, officials, particularly those holding executive responsibilities, should not be held responsible for the actions of executive or administrative personnel who fall outside the area of their control. Although the president may appoint and remove the members of his Cabinet with no real Senate interference, most state governors are saddled with state executive officers (e.g., the secretary of state, attorney general, auditor, and treasurer) who are directly elected by the voters and whose actions and policies are beyond the reach of the governor. Similarly, most mayors are flanked by comparable municipal officials, elected by the people and thus quite independent of the city's nominal chief executive. The firmly established rule of public administration is that the increasingly important executive branch must be *integrated,* that is, organized in such a way that the chief executive appoints (perhaps with legislative approval), controls, and removes all his principal lieutenants, instead of having such

---

[1] Another way to picture the enormousness of government employment in the United States is to compare the total number of individuals working for all levels of civil government (excluding those in military service) in the United States with the *total civilian employment*:

1954
Total employed: 61,000,000
Working for government: 6,750,000
Ratio: 1 out of 9 works for government
1964
Total employed: 69,300,000
Working for government: 10,000,000
Ratio: 1 out of 7 works for government
1974
Total employed: 86,300,000
Working for government: 14,850,000
Ratio: 1 out of 5.8 works for government

Salaries and wages paid to government employees in 1963 amounted to $49 billion; in 1968, to $87 billion; and in 1973, to $131 billion.

PUBLIC ADMINISTRATION: REFORMING THE TASKS OF THE MODERN STATE

Table 18-1 Number of People Working for Government Each Year

Year	Federal	State and local	Total civilian	Military	Total civilian and military
1930	601,000	2,548,000	3,149,000	256,000	3,405,000
1935	781,000	2,696,000	3,477,000	252,000	3,729,000
1940	1,042,000	3,160,000	4,202,000	458,000	4,660,000
1945	3,816,000	2,128,000	5,944,000	12,124,000	18,068,000
1950	1,961,000	4,065,000	6,026,000	1,460,000	7,486,000
1955	2,397,000	4,517,000	6,914,000	2,935,000	9,849,000
1960	2,270,000	6,083,000	8,353,000	2,476,000	10,829,000
1963	2,050,000	7,300,000	9,350,000	2,700,000	12,050,000
1964	2,200,000	7,850,000	10,050,000	2,685,000	12,735,000
1965	2,378,000	7,700,000	10,078,000	2,653,000	12,731,000
1966	3,000,000	8,600,000	11,600,000	3,092,000	14,692,000
1967	3,100,000	9,000,000	12,100,000	3,377,000	15,477,000
1968	3,100,000	9,500,000	12,600,000	3,548,000	16,148,000
1969	3,000,000	10,000,000	13,000,000	3,459,000	16,459,000
1970	2,705,000	9,900,000	12,605,000	3,066,000	15,671,000
1971	2,800,000	10,200,000	13,000,000	2,714,000	15,714,000
1972	2,800,000	11,000,000	13,800,000	2,392,000	16,192,000
1973	2,600,000	11,300,000	13,900,000	2,358,000	16,258,000

Federal civilian employees by branch of government, 1972

Legislative	33,688
Judicial	8,343
Executive departments	1,704,999
Administrative agencies, boards, commissions, and corporations	1,064,975
Total	2,812,000

officials popularly elected. This is the essence of the city-manager plan of municipal government. This is entirely compatible with democracy, which does not require the direct election of minor administrative officers.

Third, the official's span of control, i.e., the persons or functions subject to his direct supervision, is limited. Although there are numerous exceptions, it has often been suggested that the number of executive departments in a government ought not to exceed ten or twelve. At the present time there are eleven departments in our national government, but suggestions have been made for their consolidations along more functional lines, with a reduction to eight. This proposal, put forward by President Nixon in his second State of the Union Message on January 22, 1971, would retain the Departments of State, Treasury, Defense, and Justice. However, the remaining departments would be consolidated into four functional bodies dealing with human needs, community needs, the physical environment, and the nation's economy. The stated purpose was to "focus and concentrate responsibility for getting problems solved" and to "match our structure to our purposes—to look with a fresh eye, to organize the government by conscious, comprehensive design to meet the new needs of a new era." Such a sweeping reorganization of the executive branch was considered necessary if the government was to "keep up with the times and with the needs of the people." Presumably, if there were fewer executive departments, a chief executive would be better able to keep in touch with them and coordinate them. Moreover, this would allow for a more rational distribution of functions. However, whether the present situation continues or changes are implemented, there will still be a need to relate the independent establishments (boards, commissions, and agencies) to the line departments. Students of public administration are divided as to whether there should be many or few such entities, particularly since they fall outside the range of direct executive supervision and control. It has been suggested that only quasi-legislative or quasi-judicial[2] agencies should enjoy independent status, but even here such immunity from executive control should be strictly confined to their legislative or judicial functions; any executive or administrative activities should be brought under the supervision of the most appropriate executive department. Thus, in 1937, the President's Committee on Administrative Management proposed that the administrative functions of virtually all the more than 100 independent agencies of the national government be placed under one or another of the executive departments, which were to be increased to twelve in number. However, any agency having quasi-legislative or quasi-judicial functions (e.g., the Interstate Commerce Commission, the Federal Trade Commission, and the National Labor Relations Board) was to remain independent in its exercise of such functions.[3]

Fourth, a single executive head is preferable to a board or commission for the performance of administrative duties, although boards may properly be used for quasi-legislative or quasi-judicial functions or to shape policy in a field where goals and methods are still in doubt. Nonetheless, there is a penchant at almost all levels of government for a multitude of independent boards and commissions. Most boards were created to keep particular functions (e.g., education, health, libraries, parks, and fire and police protection) out of politics, but most members of nonpartisan boards show partisanship anyway, and effective administration suffers in any event.

Fifth, most authorities on public administration favor more uniformity in local administration than is found in most states. These authorities do not advocate extreme or rigid centralization of the type found in France, but they believe that more uniform state standards and regulations in such fields as municipal budgeting, accounting, and borrowing; public health; sanitation; police and fire protection; assessment standards; debt limitations; tax structures; and education would be preferable to confused and conflicting local policies in these important matters. Both state and federal grants-in-aid to municipalities seek to secure greater administrative uniformity in fields covered by such subventions.

Sixth, in order to assure that the administrator remains subordinate to the people and their elected representatives, it is agreed that government should have available to it processes for communicating its policies and activities to the public. In Great Britain, the question hour in the House of Commons provides a daily opportunity for any member of the House to ask questions of the ministers. However, in the United States, our literal interpretation of the separation of powers makes this impossible; hence our legislatures depend upon other devices, such as the legislative investigating committee and the possibility, remote though it may be, of impeachment. Both of these, however, tend to be retrospective in operation. Of course it is better to lock the barn door after the horse is stolen than not to lock it at all, but these methods cannot compare with the question hour as a continuous spotlight of publicity playing upon the entire administrative process. In both countries investigative reporting by journalists makes the public aware of governmental dereliction.

Seventh, it is recognized that in order for the administrative process to serve the public interest, the legislature should conduct audits of executive-controlled expenditures. In Britain, a comptroller and auditor general, responsible to Parliament, makes a continuous audit of all disbursements of funds and other financial transactions and submits an annual report to the House of Commons. In the United States, the federal comptroller general, who heads the General Accounting Office (an independent agency under Congress), performs a similar function. The General Accounting Office has audit authority over all the departments and agencies of the federal government. It also assists the Congress in providing legislative control over the receipt, disbursement, and application of public funds.

---

[2]"Quasi" means "as if." In the 1930s it was feared that the administrative agencies, which combined legislative, executive, and judicial functions, violated the constitutional concept of separation of powers. To eliminate this concern and thus to allow such agencies to continue to function, the United States Supreme Court described the powers of such bodies as merely "quasi."

[3]A longer listing of such agencies appears on p. 364, footnote 7.

Hence the comptroller general is not a true auditor, since he exercises accounting and executive control functions. The mingling of accounting and auditing functions is contrary to accepted principles of financial administration. States, counties, and cities also have auditors or controllers, who, however, are frequently directly elected by the voters and hence are not accountable to the legislative body. In a few state and local governments a professional, independent auditing officer is used. Other forms of control over administrators include the recall of elected officials, the popular initiative in legislation, the referendum, the merit system itself, the grand jury, the voluntary citizens' committee, and various legal remedies through the courts. Such legal actions are rather unsatisfactory because incompetence on the part of an administrator is hardly susceptible of proof in court; the mere legality of administrative actions is no guarantee of their wisdom or efficiency. Moreover, the outmoded sovereign immunity rule of American law (now frequently waived by express legislation and increasingly under attack in the courts) that federal and state governments cannot be sued without their consent also militates against the effectiveness of legal remedies in the field of public administration. On the other hand, administrative officers may, in specific instances, be held personally liable for misconduct; e.g., a police officer may be held liable for an unlawful arrest, or a clerk for fraud or embezzlement of funds.

Eighth, the executive should be principally responsible for the preparation of governmental budgets. Moreover, in the field of governmental financial functions there is a need to conserve public resources through the use of centralized purchasing procedures, professional methods of tax assessment, and accurate systems of accounting and public-debt management. Of these, the budget system is the most important. Public administration experts divide the budget process into four stages: preparation or formulation; enactment into law, i.e., passage of appropriation bills; execution, e.g., the actual spending of the sums appropriated, together with accounting records of disbursements; and, finally, a subsequent audit of all such expenditures. These experts agree that the executive branch should prepare the budget plan, that the legislature should pass the appropriation bills embodying the budget (with or without changes), that the disbursement of sums appropriated and the keeping of the public accounting records should be handled by the executive (the treasury or finance department), and that the last step, the postaudit, should be made by an agency responsible to the legislature. The British system of financial administration follows this sequence exactly; Parliament ultimately determines all financial policy, but the details of budget formulation and execution are left to the Cabinet, which delegates these tasks to the Treasury Department but retains collective Cabinet responsibility for policies proposed and disbursements made. The system has worked so well in England that its adaptation to American units of government has been advocated for nearly half a century. The federal budget system established in 1921, as well as many state budget schemes, represents a partial adoption of the British system. In the United States it is the function of the executive to prepare budgets, which are submitted to legislatures through members of legislative committees who are experts in fiscal and budgeting matters. In the United States at the state and local levels, good results have been achieved by giving governors and mayors an item veto over legislative amendments to executive budgets. Many feel that economies would result if the president were given the same power. Lacking such power, American presidents have refused to spend appropriated funds. In the 1970s this alleged presidential prerogative has come under attack.

The ninth principle is that almost all nonelective officers and all employees should qualify for employment through the merit system. Considerable progress in reaching this goal has been made in our national government (where about 92 percent of federal civil servants are now under the merit plan) and also among our cities, but state governments are still lagging.

The term "merit system" means that public employees are to be recruited by examinations (usually competitive) and promoted on the basis either of tests or of some system of rating employee performance; that there shall be a duties classification so that employees' jobs will be properly and comparably titled throughout the various departments and agencies; that salaries shall be standardized and based on the duties classification; and that machinery shall be established to handle employee problems (e.g., dismissal) and to maintain good morale.

The agency charged with administering the merit system is usually called a "civil service commission." It is, as a rule, bipartisan, made up of an odd number of members and independent of any executive department or other administrative agency. Students of public personnel problems favor a single executive personnel director (an expert in this field), who would replace the board or at least take over the actual running of the civil service, leaving the board free to determine broad policies. The United States Civil Service Commission, established in 1883 as a bipartisan body of three members, is an independent establishment; it cannot order the reinstatement of discharged employees, although it can grant them hearings.

The principle that prospective government employees should be tested for their competence is easy to state but hard to implement. Just what is to be tested—intelligence, formal education, mastery of specific skills or bodies of technical knowledge, personality adjustment, maturity, executive ability, experience? Obviously, such qualities as executive ability or administrative aptitude are difficult to measure or even to recognize in the course of an examination, although the oral interview is helpful in this regard.

Much has been accomplished in recent years toward establishing a proper duties classification for civil servants as well as an improved salary scale. A compulsory and contributory pension system is now also in effect. At retirement, an employee's pension is determined by his salary and length of service. Thus a model civil service program would include careful attention to recruitment, retention, and separation. All similarly situated employees would be accorded equality of treatment on the premise of "equal pay for equal work." Because of their professional competence, civil servants are expected to give unqualified loyalty to the existing policies of the political leadership, even though they may not personally be in agreement with such policies. Professional competence and political responsibility are the hallmarks of the ideal civil servant.

In recent years civil servants, especially those providing such services as education, transportation, health care, and police and fire protection, among others, have been in strong disagreement with the pay policies that affect them. This has raised the very difficult question of whether public servants in general, and the ones mentioned above in particular, should be allowed to engage in strikes as a means of making their dissatisfaction known. Fifty years ago it was generally accepted that individuals could not strike if they accepted public employment—especially employment in the field of public order and safety. The legal and moral issues concerning strikes by civil servants are more in flux today than earlier. Nonetheless, the Bureau of Labor Statistics has reported these facts: In 1954 there were 15 strikes involving 7,000 public employees; in 1968 there were 254 involving 201,000; in 1970 there were 412 involving 333,000; in 1972 there were 375 involving 132,000; and in 1973 there were 386 involving 196,000. Many new procedures are being attempted in an effort to solve the problem of conflicting interests of employer and employee—and, of course, to protect the overriding needs of the general public.

THE SCOPE OF PUBLIC ADMINISTRATION

Public administration serves as the ball bearings of government—that part of the vehicle which must function with a minimum of friction if the goals of the state are to be realized. The average citizen is likely to think of public administration primarily in terms of governmental regulation of individual and group conduct, overlooking the vast and varied forms of protection, assistance, and service that government provides. Speaking broadly, public-administration activities fall into four main categories: (1) the protection of society as a whole, e.g., police and fire protection, health care, national defense, education, safeguarding the environment, and conservation of natural resources; (2) promotional activities or assistance to particular economic and social groups, e.g., farmers, factory workers, businessmen, women and children in industry, the aged, and the unemployed; (3) proprietary activities, where a government owns and operates enterprises serving the public, e.g., the post office, the Panama Canal, the Tennessee Valley Authority, or a municipal water or electric-power department; and (4) regulation of particular businesses or activities, through such agencies as the Interstate Commerce Commission, the Federal Reserve Board, the National Labor Relations Board, and others.

Our federal system requires that certain administrative functions be discharged exclusively or mainly by the national government, and others by the states. However, human activities are so intermeshed that there is a vast amount of synchronization, dovetailing, and cooperation among all levels and agencies of government. Indeed, the field of intergovernmental relations is as fascinating as it is complicated. A 1955 study lists an even dozen intergovernmental functional responsibilities: agriculture, civil aviation, civil defense, education, employment security, highways, housing and urban renewal, natural-disaster relief, natural resources and conservation, public health, vocational rehabilitation, and welfare (assistance to the aged, the blind, etc.).[4]

It is manifestly impossible to survey the common aspects of public policy and administration in all these areas. It should be noted that assistance and control usually go hand in hand. In the realm of business, protective tariffs, land grants, subsidies, and tax favors are matched by antitrust laws, rate regulation (in the case of railroads and other public utilities), regulation of interest rates and banking practices, pure food and drug laws, and other forms of social control in the public interest. Publicly provided highways are linked with regulation of freight and passenger transportation by buses and trucks, operators' licenses, and parking restrictions. Public health facilities and services are coupled with health regulations. Building and zoning restrictions accompany governmental efforts to develop more desirable residential conditions in our cities. Growing popular demands for more and better government services (schools, libraries, parks, playgrounds, highways, police protection) result in bigger budgets, higher taxes, new or larger government agencies, and more public officials and employees (popularly dubbed "bureaucrats").

A central problem of public administration in the modern democratic state is that of increasing the efficiency of governmental performance without sacrificing the basic democratic principle that government and its officers and employees must remain responsible to the sovereign people. This task has been harder in the United States, with its vast area and diversity, its federal and presidential system of government, and its traditional distrust of government in general and the executive branch in particular, than in such countries as England or France. However, great progress has been made.

RECENT TRENDS IN GOVERNMENTAL ORGANIZATION

One major development has been the growth and strengthening of the executive organization of the national government. The number of executive departments has been increased from three to eleven, with the Department of Defense containing subordinate departments of the Air Force, Army, and Navy and defense agencies and defense service schools. Frequent reorganization plans have resulted in the transfer of many bureaus and agencies from one department to another in order to achieve greater unity of departmental function.

This trend has been one result of the movement for federal governmental reorganization, which began soon after 1900. In 1937, President Franklin D. Roosevelt's Committee on Administrative Management submitted a comprehensive set of recommendations that were designed to realize some of the principles of public administration set forth at the beginning of this chapter. After much resistance, reorganization acts were passed by Congress in 1939, 1941, 1945, and 1949. The last law was based in part on the recommendations of the Hoover Commission, which made many suggestions that went beyond the executive branch of government. The Commission urged a sharp reduction in the number of federal administrative agencies, the grouping of all agencies (even the regulatory commissions) under departments according to their functions, the creation of a new Cabinet-rank department of education and welfare, greater authority for department heads, and a host of other improvements.

The Reorganization Act of 1949 accepted some, but not all, of the Hoover Commission's recommendations. Significantly, it empowered the president to transfer or abolish administrative agencies (but not executive departments) and to place regulatory commissions under departmental supervi-

---

[4]Commission on Intergovernmental Relations, *A Report to the President for Transmittal to the Congress,* June 1955.

sion; however, either house of Congress may veto such presidential action by vote of a majority of its membership. Many changes have been made under the terms of this law; wide public support for the Hoover Report has been of great help. New Departments of Housing and Urban Development; Health, Education, and Welfare; and Transportation have been created. Obviously, much more remains to be done; indeed, the problem will always be a hardy perennial. It should be emphasized that about thirty states, beginning with Illinois in 1917, have also reorganized their administrative structures, following the direction taken by the national government. Many states (and some cities) have now established Little Hoover Commissions, and the prospects of reform are promising.

Beginning with the Budget and Accounting Act of 1921, the president has been provided with a growing list of staff agencies to strengthen the executive branch and assist him in the discharge of his heavy duties. These agencies include the Office of Management and Budget (until 1970 the Bureau of the Budget), which has wide fiscal responsibilities ranging beyond the preparation of the annual federal budget. Through this office the president endeavors to impose a measure of control over the wide-ranging activities of the federal bureaucracy.[5]

The president's managerial responsibilities have been further institutionalized in the Executive Office of the President, with its numerous secretaries, assistants, deputy assistants, special assistants, special consultants, administrative assistants, military aides, special counsel, presidential physician, and other staff members. The Executive Office includes, among others, the Council of Economic Advisers, to keep the president constantly informed about national economic conditions and trends, some of which might warrant recommendations to Congress; the National Security Council, relating to national defense; the Office of Telecommunications Policy; the Council on Environmental Quality; and the National Aeronautics and Space Council. Such agencies can be created to achieve fixed objectives and then terminated when their goals have been realized or there is a reassignment of function, as in the case of the Marine Sciences Council, which existed from 1966 to 1971.

[5]President Nixon's Message on Reorganization, Mar. 12, 1970, *1970 CO ALMANAC*, pp. 40-A–42-A.

The increasing responsibilities of state governors have also been recognized; they have been given more authority over regulatory and assistance programs and over the state budget. In every state except North Carolina the governor can veto legislation; in all but seven states he can veto items in appropriation bills without necessarily rejecting the entire bill. In a large majority of the states the governor is charged with the chief responsibility for preparing the state budget. Somewhat more than half the states have "strong" governors, which means that many independent administrative agencies have been brought under control by one or another of a small number of departments, which in turn are under the direct supervision of the governor. In New Jersey, under a constitution adopted in 1947, the governor is the only remaining state executive official who is elected; all the others are now appointed by the governor and the Senate.

Some progress has also been made in developing governors' councils or cabinets consisting of heads of departments and other persons. The effectiveness of such an instrumentality is rather limited in most states since the majority of state executive officers are still elected by the voters and feel no sense of loyalty or responsibility to the governor. Sometimes such officers do not even belong to the governor's political party. This situation is hardly conducive to effective executive management.

Mention has already been made of the rise of the city-manager form of government, which applies the idea of separating politics from administration and invests the city manager with power over, and responsibility for, the administration of all city affairs. A movement for municipal reorganization and modernization has paralleled the city-manager movement and has also appeared in cities with the mayor-council form of government.

In cities of the "strong-mayor" type there is a close parallel with recent developments strengthening the office of governor; indeed, mayors generally have broader appointing powers in policy positions than governors. Also, whereas the heads of state departments are often elected, the department heads in cities are usually appointed and are frequently selected through the civil service. Both governors and mayors generally appoint the members of the numerous advisory agencies or commissions that offer suggestions to department heads.

Under the strong-mayor form of government the mayor must distribute his time between his executive, governmental responsibilities and his public-relations or political functions.

In recent years some mayors have been given assistance in the form of a chief administrative officer. The CAO is not directly subordinate to either the mayor or the city council, but stands midway between the two. He makes studies and prepares reports looking toward a more effective organization of the city's business. He is a management consultant. He and his staff make recommendations for changes in government practices. He functions as a kind of efficiency expert with access to all the city's affairs. Normally he has no direct powers, but through research, job and budget studies, and analyses of problem areas, the CAO can assist in the improvement of government services and functions and in the reduction of taxes and other costs to the citizen. In some instances the CAO is also assigned the administrative responsibility of enforcing policies. This last function, of course, takes the CAO out of the area of planning and puts him into the area of operations.

Under the city-manager form of government the manager follows the prototype of the executive vice president or general manager of a large corporation. The city manager is hired by the city council and executes the policies arrived at by the mayor and council, just as in a business organization the manager executes the decisions of the chairman of the board of directors and the members of the board. In recent years an increasing number of counties have adopted similar arrangements. The city-manager plan assumes that the manager will have broad latitude in selecting the means for achieving the desired results. He has broad appointive powers with regard to departmental heads and his own staff, subject generally to civil service requirements.

Prospects for the improvement of governmental administration continue to brighten. Despite popular inertia, the reluctance of legislators to divest themselves of political influence, and a natural tendency on all sides to cling to the status quo, marked progress has been made in recent years, mainly because of the sheer necessity of finding methods adequate for the discharge of government's growing responsibilities.

ADMINISTRATIVE RELATIONSHIPS

Although efficient administration requires that a department head possess authority to match his responsibilities, good administration is a skillful blend of authority and persuasion. The able administrator has the knack of delegating both authority and responsibility and of getting the members of his organization to cooperate with enthusiasm. The cooperative faculty is particularly essential to effective coordination between agencies that are mutually independent. Good administration requires a gift for effective public relations combined with the gentle art of getting people to do what they ought to do in the normal course of their duties.

Good human relations between supervisor and the supervised are now recognized as essential to good administration. Congenial, friendly relationships in a pleasant environment add up to good morale, which is indispensable if an organization is to operate successfully.

Additional requirements include functional unity of organization; a sufficiently narrow span of supervision; the use of staff, line, and housekeeping agencies; and effective communication. All contribute to governmental effectiveness and accountability. Functional organization requires the grouping of related functions or activities in a single department or agency. A proper span of control is based on the realization that one person cannot effectively supervise a large number of persons or agencies. Thus an administrator's range of supervisorial responsibility should be rather narrowly confined.

Staff, line, and housekeeping agencies are essential to the effective organization of government. Staff agencies engage in planning, research, and advice but do not carry on operational or managerial activities. Line agencies perform these basic or substantive functions and are able to accomplish their work more efficiently because they have the benefit of staff studies and housekeeping aids. Housekeeping agencies provide common services for all other agencies, e.g., central purchasing, archives and records services, property management and disposal, automated data and telecommunications services, and printing, legal, financial, custodial, and other kinds of general assistance. On the national level much of this work is now performed by the General Services Administration.

Communication presents a twofold problem. In the first place, the channels must be open, and directives must move promptly through the various levels of the hierarchy to the persons charged with their implementation. Second, orders and instructions must be stated clearly, simply, and understandably. Effective communication is as essential to accomplishment of mission as is the allocation of responsibilities.

ADMINISTRATIVE REGULATION

Basically, government has two functions: rendering services and regulation. Of these, regulation is by far the more difficult. It is much easier to render services to people—to provide assistance and conveniences—than to regulate, restrict, and sometimes prohibit their conduct. Governmental regulations limit individual and group action, restrict uses of property, affect incomes, and generally induce individual behavior to conform to the Congress's definition of the "public interest, convenience, and necessity." Such regulations are imposed (reluctantly, in the United States) to protect and promote the public interest—a concept difficult to define and even more difficult to translate into action in specific situations.[6] It is easier to construct roads, bridges, schools, parks, and playgrounds and to provide water, clean streets, and police and fire protection than it is to reconcile the conflicting interests of management and labor (and the conflicting interests of these two groups and the consumer), to determine railroad or utility rates, or to protect the public against harmful foods or drugs.

Indeed, it is so difficult to regulate economic activities that many people advocate public ownership rather than governmental regulation. The American tradition frowns on public ownership (although some extremely conservative communities operate their municipally owned departments of water and power); hence we cling to the notion that private enterprise can be so effectively regulated by governmental agencies that the public interest will be safeguarded. The record of such regulation tends to refute this popular myth; the members of regulatory agencies frequently acquire the outlook of the businesses they are supposed to regulate, and in some instances they have been politically pressured into acquiescence. If they cling to their convictions, they are sometimes forced to resign.

The Growth of Administrative Regulation

The administrative process, which consists of the "fourth branch of government" in action, has been marked by two important developments. First, administrative agencies perform a combination of legislative, executive, and judicial functions. Second, although they are not being created as rapidly now as they were in the past—about one third were established before 1900, a second third between 1900 and 1930, and the remainder since 1930[7]—there has been a continuous widening of their authority.

In order to overcome the original animosity directed toward them because of the regulatory authority concentrated in them, which constituted a departure from the traditional separation-of-powers doctrine, they have been obliged to prove their capacity to govern fairly. To achieve this result, they have had to demonstrate that they are fully committed to the concept of fairness, which is equivalent to the constitutional concept of due process of law. Moreover, through the recruitment of very highly qualified personnel and the resulting accumulation of expertise, they have established a reputation for objective fact-finding. Wider authority has been conferred on them as they have proved their ability to achieve their statutory goals.

Both federal and state regulatory commissions have certain common features, problems, and limitations. They are independent, in the sense that they are not subject to the direct control of either the executive or legislative branch. Such agencies

---

[6]See Carl J. Friedrich (ed.), *The Public Interest*, Atherton Press, Inc., New York, 1962 (Yearbook V of the American Society for Political and Legal Philosophy).

[7]Kenneth C. Davis, *Administrative Law*, West Publishing Company, St. Paul, Minn., 1951, p. 4. Significant administrative agencies, national in scope and created during both Democratic and Republican administrations, include the following: Civil Service Commission, 1883; Interstate Commerce Commission, 1887; Federal Reserve Board, 1913; Federal Trade Commission, 1914; Federal Power Commission, 1920; Federal Farm Board, 1929; Federal Communications Commission, Federal Housing Administration, Securities and Exchange Commission, 1934; National Labor Relations Board, 1935; Federal Maritime Commission, 1936; Federal Security Agency, 1939; Civil Aeronautics Board, 1940; Atomic Energy Commission, 1946; United States Information Agency, 1953; Foreign Claims Settlement Commission, 1954; and National Aeronautics and Space Administration, 1958.

are bound only by the terms of the legislation which created them and which limited their powers. Executive control is limited to nominating members of the commissions (usually with legislative confirmation), designating chairmen, requiring reports, removing members for causes specified by law, and exercising budgetary supervision. Legislative control is limited to modifying an agency's functions and responsibilities and appropriating money for its maintenance; however, the legislatures that created the commission can also abolish it. Judicial control is applied when cases challenging the constitutionality or legality of administrative acts are presented to the courts. Since the legislation that gives policy direction to an agency is usually vague, a commission enjoys a great deal of freedom in establishing its goals and particularly in implementing specific objectives.

Because of such vagueness and because of the critical impact of these agencies upon many citizens at national, state, and local levels of government, the need was seen for laws that would regulate the regulators. Such laws have been effected in large part through legislation fixing the agencies' internal procedures and allowing for judicial review over their administrative determinations. In 1946, after careful study by special governmental committees and the American Bar Association, the Federal Administrative Procedure Act was unanimously adopted by both houses of Congress. Its preamble proclaimed its purpose: "To improve the administration of justice by prescribing fair administrative procedures."[8] This law has had a substantial impact upon the regularization of the administrative process.

Reasons for Development of Administrative Regulatory Agencies

Several factors account for the growth of the administrative process. During the last 100 years all levels of government have been providing scores of new services to the public. As government embarked upon new tasks, it became necessary to employ practical processes to get jobs done. Many who were called upon to perform the jobs had gained prior practical experience in private business. They quite naturally turned to successful business techniques, unencumbered by fine distinctions between legislative, executive, and judicial functions. As Davis has said, "the early agencies were created because practical men were seeking practical answers to immediate problems."[9]

A second reason is to be found in a notable decision of the United States Supreme Court, which held that the states could not regulate interstate railway rates because of the superior national interest in controlling interstate commerce.[10] This decision led Congress to create, in 1887, the first of the great administrative agencies in the economic field, the Interstate Commerce Commission. This decision further stimulated Congress toward affirmative use of the commerce power, which became the constitutional basis for the great majority of our national regulatory commissions.

Third, it was imperative that governmental regulation be imposed upon unruly, antisocial elements in the American economy. Irresponsible manipulators of economic enterprises required an administrative checkrein. Affirmatively, government has sought to enforce competition.

Fourth, Congress, the courts, and the executive were not well equipped to deal with the existing evils and to protect legitimate enterprise. In order that the manipulators might be constantly watched, it became necessary to build up permanent rather than temporary staffs and to put regulation on a continuing rather than a sporadic basis. The regulation of technical matters required permanent, competent experts.

The traditional branches of government were not staffed with such experts; Congress, in particular, never evidenced the capacity or inclination to concern itself with such details. Elective officials lacked continuity in office and were not, as a rule, competent in technical matters. Committees of Congress often devoted more time and attention to politically motivated inquiries following changes of administration than to the substantial work of the agencies in question. Congress is inherently incapable of supervising the details of administration; moreover, it does not have the time, its members

---

[8]Fifteen years ago only a handful of the states had enacted a state administrative procedure act. Today, with very few exceptions, the Model or Revised Model Administrative Procedure Act is in force in the states. Remaining states have enacted statutes based on the Federal Administrative Procedure Act.

[9]Davis, op. cit., p. 10.
[10]*Wabash, St. L. and P. Ry. Co. v. Illinois*, 118 U.S. 557 (1886).

lack specialized knowledge, it lacks an adequate staff to perform the detailed work, and it is in no position to coordinate staffs or agencies engaged in the intricacies of administration. The decision to create specialized agencies to do work that Congress itself could perform, if at all, only at the expense of its major policy-shaping responsibilities is unquestionably grounded in sound judgment.

The courts, too, have proved unequal to such administrative responsibilities, which is not surprising in view of their passive role and the narrow definition of their duties. Courts hear and decide only those cases which litigants bring to their attention. They lack the authority to search out deserving issues and then decide them. Through the power to issue injunctions they can prevent certain types of conduct from continuing after jurisdiction has been established in a given case,[11] but a court's ability to provide preventive relief is limited. In any event, such relief seeks to prohibit conduct already manifested rather than to prevent objectionable conduct from the very outset. Moreover, judges are specialists in the law rather than in technical facts, and they have lacked the staffs to help them arrive at an intelligent understanding of matters fully comprehended only by carefully schooled experts and specialists.[12]

Other alleged defects of the judicial system may be cited in support of the administrative process. Courts are ill adapted to exercise affirmative, continuous supervision over problems involving shifting social implications; they are more at home in dealing with standardized conflicts involving private rights. Courts are also slow, highly technical, and expensive. As Justice Stone of the United States Supreme Court once pointed out, courts are not the only agency of government that must be assumed to have a capacity to govern.[13]

Fifth, from the affirmative point of view, the administrative agency has had much to offer in its favor. The problems submitted to it are often ill suited to decisions based on rigid rules. When an agency is charged with the allocation of government grants (such as public lands or pensions), the determination of workmen's compensation claims, the setting of utility rates, or the authorization of the sale of bonds by corporations to private investors, the law must be individualized to fit the facts. The administrative process is also capable of greater speed and effectiveness in adjudication.

Further, the administrative agency need not be passive. It has the authority to take preventive measures before serious issues arise and harm is done. After taking jurisdiction, a commission has the power to see the affair through, and it can provide continuing supervision.

One of the strongest reasons advanced for the development of confidence in the administrative process is that capable personnel are being employed by the agencies. Professional standards have been developed among the skilled, technically trained experts who have been attracted to these staffs. Such staffs have generally adhered to the best traditions of the judiciary in their concern for the public interest. Flexibility has not led to substantial inequality, and individualization has produced an almost uniformly high standard of administrative justice.

Criticisms of the Administrative Process

Although the modern legislature has increasingly delegated authority to the executive branch, the traditional American fear of arbitrary executive action has helped to produce a legislative preference for the delegation of authority to the numerous specialized administrative agencies. Such delegation implies that these administrative bodies, with their combination of legislative, executive, and judicial functions, are less likely than the executive to be unfair and capricious.

Because administrative agencies may decide is-

---

[11]An injunction is a court order compelling persons to refrain from certain conduct. It may be worded affirmatively, thus compelling persons to perform specified acts.

[12]Judicial control over administrative behavior is also restricted by the number of appeals that courts are physically equipped to consider. Only about one out of every twenty decisions arrived at by the Securities and Exchange Commission is reviewed by a court, and only one out of every seven hundred decisions of the Interstate Commerce Commission obtains judicial review. Such judicial attention is accorded only to formal administrative proceedings where the agency has conducted hearings and where a decision has been arrived at. Since the bulk of the work of the agencies is carried out informally, it is probable that not more than one case in a thousand is potentially subject to the jurisdiction of the courts. Moreover, such statistics as these must be balanced against the expectation that the courts have previously enunciated wise principles, so that litigants would not receive anything by way of an appeal to a court that had not been previously accorded in the administrative agency.

[13]*United States v. Butler*, 297 U.S. 1, 87 (1936).

sues on an individual basis and may therefore fail at times to adhere to the fundamental equality of treatment prescribed by law, they are definitely subordinated to statutory and constitutional authority. This is frequently referred to as the "supremacy of law."[14] However, the mere legality or constitutionality of administrative action does not guarantee that it will be wise, in line with the broad outlines of governmental policy as a whole, or acceptable to the public.

The absence of uniform rules has exposed commissions to charges of favoritism and arbitrariness. The fear of unchecked administrative power and the possibility of its abuse have resulted in the establishment of statutory checks, particularly with regard to procedural matters.

One of the more serious criticisms of the administrative process relates to its combination of legislative, executive, and judicial functions. Our deeply ingrained traditions of separation of powers and checks and balances give rise to the charge that where such a combination exists, the administrative agency can be prosecutor, judge, and jury.

American insistence on a "government of laws and not of men" reflects our fear of a government by men unrestrained by law. However, administrative agencies are created by law, are governed by it, and must operate within their legal frame of reference. Appeals may be taken from their decisions to the courts, always on questions of law, and sometimes on questions of fact.

Some tradition-minded observers fear the relative informality with which the administrator may arrive at important decisions. This lack of procedural formality always comes as a shock to persons indoctrinated in courtroom procedures. The veteran attorney feels divested of the protective armor of his hard-learned procedural formalisms. A vested interest in traditionalism is always opposed to change.

The administrative process need not adhere to the formal rules of evidence, and certain types of evidence long excluded from court and jury consideration are readily admitted in administrative proceedings. Both processes are, however, equally interested in ascertaining the truth on all material and relevant questions. Neither administrative agencies nor courts wish to arrive at decisions on the basis of guess, gossip, rumor, imagination, or plainly incredible evidence.[15]

An administrative agency's ruling on fact is not subject to the complexities of the judge and jury system. Records showing the grounds for administrative decision are usually but not always kept. Often the hearing officer, sometimes called an "examiner," makes a record of the proceedings in a given case, and such factual material is used by higher officers in arriving at a final decision. Also, an administrative officer often has more discretionary power in the admission of evidence than is granted to a judge. These factors all contribute to the feeling that administrative agencies are not only less formally, but perhaps also less certainly, organized than the court system.

Administrative agencies have also been attacked on the ground that the administrative official is not the equal of the judge in training, experience, impartiality, and political independence. Many Americans are unable to accord the member of a regulatory commission the respect that they habitually render to a judge. Partisan appointments to administrative bodies have not heightened their prestige. Also, many members of regulatory commissions acquire, subconsciously or otherwise, the viewpoint of the very industry they are supposed to regulate. Sometimes the industry being regulated manages to get its own supporters appointed to the regulatory agency. This situation has been quite common with respect to state public utility commissions. Moreover, members of regulatory commissions are appointed for terms of five to seven years, and thus they lack the security enjoyed by federal judges, who hold office during their "good behavior," which means a lifetime appointment.

Some persons have expressed the fear that where administrative rulings are appealed to a higher section of the same agency, the reviewing section will tend to uphold the ruling. However, experience shows that such reviewing sections are frequently willing to reverse the recommendations of trial examiners and lower-echelon employees. In order that a group of persons other than those who

---

[14] John Dickinson, *Administrative Justice and the Supremacy of Law in the United States*, Harvard University Press, Cambridge, Mass., 1927, pp. 76–156.

[15] Walter Gellhorn, *Federal Administrative Proceedings*, The Johns Hopkins Press, Baltimore, 1941, pp. 75–116.

arrived at the original finding may pass upon administrative appeals within the agency itself, provision is often made for separate reviewing authorities. The number of reversals within administrative agencies does not appreciably differ from the ratio found in the operation of appellate review in the courts.

A New Appraisal of the Federal Administrative Process

Periodically, the administrative process—particularly as it applies to the independent regulatory agencies—is subjected to a reappraisal. As the result of personal misconduct on the part of a few commissioners following World War II (such as soliciting personal benefits from industries being regulated), questions have been raised as to the type of person holding such offices. The judiciary has developed the tradition of maintaining a somewhat formal distance between itself and those who come before it seeking justice. Members of administrative commissions have failed, in a few notable instances, to conform to this safeguard. In some instances, commissioners have received social courtesies or other emoluments—sometimes of considerable practical value—from the industries subject to their official supervision. These temptations are especially strong in the case of those regulatory agencies which can allocate highly lucrative franchises to only a small minority of applicants, e.g., the Federal Communications Commission, which must decide which applicant will be licensed to broadcast in a particular area. Commissioners have been known to discuss informally with a party to a case the merits of a matter in the absence of representation from the opposing side, sometimes, it has been reported, at such unofficial gathering places as racetracks, social clubs, and golf courses. Such conversations, of course, have not become a part of the official record of the proceeding, but they have led opposing litigants to the practical conclusion that they must protect themselves by currying similar favors through equally informal activities. Such conduct is indefensible. Excesses by a few have led to criminal conflict-of-interest legislation. Only the appointment of judicially minded individuals who fully appreciate the full extent of their public responsibility can establish a tradition of invulnerability to pressure.

The personnel problem goes deeper than the quality of commissioners. There is a continuing need for the professionalization of agency staffs. The heart of the commission staff is the hearing officer, or trial examiner. The American Bar Association has declared that this position must be made more attractive via status, pay, tenure, privileges and prerogatives, and independence comparable to those enjoyed by a trial judge. The question is often asked: Should the government try to operate its important commissions with examiners who are less competent than counsel for the industries that come before them? A member of the Federal Trade Commission once said: "The real problem in our administrative agencies is to get rid of political hacks and the deadwood, to obtain the finest young men from our law schools and to stimulate and pay them enough to keep them."[16]

While the personnel problem at both the commission and the staff levels is serious in particular instances, the individuals who operate the administrative process compare very favorably with those found in any comparable area of government. Instances of individual wrongdoing do not warrant unfavorable blanket judgments.

A more serious defect in the administrative process has been the slowness with which decisions are arrived at. This has had an enormous impact upon the nation's economic life; without commission approval, industries have not been able to move forward on investment and construction activities. President Kennedy reported to Congress in 1961 that the Federal Power Commission had an $850-million backlog of applications for the construction of natural gas pipelines. The agency's immobilization of jobs, investments, and use of resources was staggering. It was the President's view that the decisions of the agencies "have a profound effect upon the direction and pace of our economic growth."[17] In order to cope with the FPC's backlog, he asked Congress to add two additional members to the Commission and requested additional legislative action to streamline agency procedures.

In the 1950s it became apparent that nonuniform procedures were being employed by many adminis-

---

[16] Former Commissioner Philip Elman, address to the American Bar Association, reported by the *Christian Science Monitor,* Aug. 29, 1961.

[17] *Christian Science Monitor,* Apr. 15, 1961.

trative agencies when dealing with common problems affecting the rights and obligations of private persons and business interests. As a result, Congress in 1964 enacted the Administrative Conference Act, which established a new body called the Administrative Conference of the United States. This body examines administrative procedures used within the national government and makes recommendations for more uniform practices. It may also seek from Congress such legislation as would improve the administrative process.

Legislative gaps in allocating functions to agencies have also been a major defect. These, too, have resulted in economic retrogression, according to James M. Landis, who was appointed as special adviser to President Kennedy in the administrative agency field. According to Mr. Landis, Congress failed in the early 1960s to establish a basic policy for the use and licensing of ultra-high-frequency television stations. Though such facilities were technically feasible, the Federal Communications Commission was slow in authorizing their construction.

Another substantial defect, also chargeable principally to Congress, has been an inability to segregate more specifically the functions of the respective agencies. Overlapping continues, and consolidations, of either functions or agencies, have not taken place. This situation was highlighted in 1959 when Louis J. Hector submitted his resignation from the Civil Aeronautics Board. He recommended that the CAB be abolished as an independent agency and that its functions be turned over to the Department of Commerce, to a new department of transportation, to an administrative court, or to the Department of Justice.

It has also been argued that the agencies are too independent. Those who hold this view contend that the agencies should, like the executive departments, come under the aegis of the executive branch of the government. They are said to be a politically irresponsible "headless fourth branch of government," often seeking to pursue mutually inconsistent policies.

Some contend that such bodies have failed to promote the public interest, convenience, and necessity—the principal reason for their creation. Competing commercial interests—e.g., airline companies seeking air routes—argue before a commission without the presence of spokesmen for the prospective customers, i.e., the public. Some agencies have partially corrected this emphasis by appointing public counsel to represent the interests of the public at large. The perspectives of commissioners can be protected through strong public representation. In recent years, valiant efforts to increase public protection have been made by individuals, such as Ralph Nader, and by law firms engaged in *pro bono publico* perspectives. In some countries a government official known as an "ombudsman" has been appointed to represent a citizen's complaints against administrative incompetence or discrimination. To date, this additional service has received a cool reception in the United States.

In the future there must be constant and long-range evaluation of the administrative process. More attention should be given by the agencies to the problem of advance planning so that delays will not destroy their utility.[18] Greater authority might well be given to the trial examiner. Commission decisions may come to be the product of a single commissioner rather than of the group, as they are at present. Responsibility could be increased by identifying the decision with the name of the commissioner who is responsible for it. Internal organizational changes, permitted under existing legislation, would contribute to the streamlining of the decisional process. If Congress decides that agencies are too independent, it may provide the president with a coordinator. Congress may, alternatively, seek to exercise more congressional control over administrative policy making; this could lead to a legislative-executive stalemate. Probably the best hope is that commissioners will meet the ethical standards of the judiciary; also, they should be relieved of the burden of handling detail and

---

[18] There are several ways in which delays can be eliminated. One is to shorten the "judicialized" procedure for determining policy. A planned approach to the administrative process would resolve this in the following manner: Suppose that two competitors seek to install a pipeline between two cities. This presents two separate questions. First, where should the pipeline run? Second, which of the two companies should be given authority to construct the line? At the present time lengthy courtlike hearings, with witnesses and testimony, are frequently employed to resolve the first question. Many experts now think this question should be resolved by a conference, in which specialists would be likely to agree readily as to the route. The judicialized procedure, of course, would be open to the applicants to prove their superior qualifications for the route. The net result would be a considerable saving of time and money for the government and the claimants and would result in more immediate benefits to the consuming public.

should be supplied with policy guidance by Congress. Adequate staffs are mandatory. If each agency becomes efficient in its own area, the need to achieve coordination of policies among agencies charged with overlapping functions will still remain.

If these criticisms are valid, many administrative establishments must clean house. These defects are remediable and are not inherent in the system. The noticeable trend toward better training of experts in technical fields for service with administrative agencies and also the growing maturity of experts in public administration are encouraging factors in the total picture. Like all human contrivances, the administrative agency is far from perfect. Public vigilance should be constantly focused on commission activities, and only recently have they received the careful scrutiny they deserve.

It is all too easy to criticize, but far more difficult to be constructive. Specific reforms, whether institutional or human, should not be allowed to obscure the almost insoluble complexity of the problem of administrative regulation. Mention must be made of a very important point: Federal regulatory agencies do not merely *regulate;* they also *render services* to their respective industries and, even more importantly, administer the allocation of large government *subsidies.* Recipients of such subsidies include the Civil Aeronautics Board, the Federal Maritime Commission, and the Federal Communications Commission (which grants franchises worth many millions of dollars); yet in dispensing these grants, these agencies are independent of the executive.

Also, many governmental functions, such as the regulation of transportation, energy resources, communications, and protection of the environment, are divided among several agencies; hence the national government can scarcely formulate rational, consistent, overall policies in such areas. Different parts of an industry appeal to different agencies; such competition is wasteful and extremely expensive to both the government and the public.

Procedural Safeguards

Procedural protections surrounding the administrative process have been expanded in recent years. A written record of proceedings is generally kept, and in the event that a full board or commission refuses to accept the recommendations of the hearing officer, the agency generally sets forth the facts that have been developed in the hearing or relied on by the hearing officer as well as the facts established by the agency itself. The losing party can feel assured that he has received a full and fair hearing. Where the decision is in part grounded on official notice (facts accepted as true without supportive testimony because of a past experience), the adverse party is commonly given an opportunity to refute or explain the facts relied on by the hearing officer and derived from such a source. Also, the admissibility of a broader field of evidence than is permitted by the court has not led to prejudicial decisions.

The parties are permitted to substitute written for oral statements in presenting their case. Frequently the face-to-face confrontation and oral testimony so traditional in the judicial process are entirely eliminated. This reduces emotionalism and saves expense.

The decisions of administrative agencies are generally subject to review within the agency. In order to make such reconsideration as fair and impartial as possible, one section of a commission or agency may be charged with issuing rules and regulations, another may conduct hearings and ascertain facts, another may review the findings of the section charged with the ascertainment of facts, while still another may be called upon to enforce the decisions of the adjudication section. When the agency's decisions are appealed to the courts, still another section may be charged with representing the agency's point of view before the courts.

The courts at first resented administrative agencies and viewed them as competitors and interlopers in the administration of justice. Sometimes courts insisted on trying the entire case over again from the very beginning, even though the agency had carefully examined and determined the essential technical facts. Early administrative agencies were turned into "little more than media for the transmission of the evidence to the courts."[19]

The courts soon learned that they were ill equipped to substitute their fact-finding procedures for those of administrative agencies, and they

---

[19] *Final Report, Attorney General's Committee, 1941,* pp. 91–92.

began to accept more gracefully the facts established by such agencies. However, the courts have managed to retain the final power to make independent investigations into fact situations, if and when they deem this to be necessary.

Under the law, if an agency makes a ruling unsupported by substantial evidence on the record considered as a whole, the courts are free to inquire independently into the appropriate facts. They may then decide what new or additional facts should be taken into consideration by the administrative agency after the court has referred the matter back to the agency for action in line with the court's decision. The courts, of course, have always considered it their duty to reverse administrative decisions that have applied the wrong law to the facts.

Objective observers believe that sufficient safeguards have been placed around the administrative process to protect constitutional rights. In addition to judicial review of administrative action, the administrator can be held accountable in claims for money damages in appropriate situations. Also, through the use of extraordinary legal writs the public officer or employee may be compelled to adhere to judicial commands, on penalty of being held in contempt of court and possibly imprisoned.[20]

Administrative officers and employees are, indeed, acutely aware of their legal obligations and hence mindful of the legal rights of those coming under the jurisdiction of the administrative agency. A rapidly growing body of legal principles, standards, and rules known as "administrative law" has secured recognition and serves to make administrative procedures more uniform throughout the United States. It is also likely that the high degree of conformity to norms of fairness demonstrated by most United States administrators derives from their sense of collegiality, which, as Carl Friedrich has suggested, renders each administrator sensitive to the criticism of his professional peers. As it becomes more evident that ours is a government not only of law but also of men, the need for approbation and respect on the part of administrators can serve society's general interest in justice. This intangible but important interest will serve, along with formal procedures and administrative specifications, to protect the individual against governmental excesses.

THE GOVERNMENT CORPORATION

The government corporation is a relatively new but widely used instrumentality of government. Although occasionally employed in earlier periods, it is essentially a twentieth-century device.

Use of the government corporation is not confined to democratic states. It has been used in countries with such diverse governmental structures as the United States, the Soviet Union, the United Kingdom, France, Nazi Germany, Fascist Italy, and Canada. It is a tool of government, not linked to any particular political ideology. In the United States the growth of governmental corporations has been gradual, although accelerated in times of economic or military emergency. Today there are well over 100 nationally owned government corporations in the United States. They are found chiefly in the management of enterprises in the fields of conservation, electric power, finance, foreign affairs, housing, national defense, and transportation. States and municipalities have also established government-owned corporations.

The first Bank of the United States, established in 1791, and the second such bank, set up in 1816, were early examples of the corporate device. The Tennessee Valley Authority, the Reconstruction Finance Corporation (now dissolved), the Panama Canal Company, the Export-Import Bank, the Federal Deposit Insurance Corporation, the St. Lawrence Seaway Development Corporation, and COMSAT indicate the wide federal use of government corporations in the twentieth century.

States have used the corporate form in chartering state universities, state banks, and numerous internal improvement projects such as toll bridges, housing, and electrical and water companies. In California, for example, there are many regional and local government corporations. The Metropolitan Water District, with offices in Los Angeles, brings water from the Colorado River to numerous cities or special districts located in three southern California counties. The members of the board of directors are selected by the member municipalities and special districts. The Port of New York Au-

---

[20]Examples of such writs are mandamus, injunction, quo warranto, and habeas corpus.

thority is a corporate body. Here, through compact, the states of New York and New Jersey have created a bistate corporation that is subject to congressional approval. Pursuant to a comprehensive plan, it operates and builds terminal and transportation facilities within a specified district embracing parts of both states.

A government corporation exists either when there is governmental ownership of all or a controlling part of the shares of stock of an incorporated business entity or where a nonstock entity is declared by law to be a public corporation. The entity may have three basic responsibilities: (1) It may be engaged in providing economic goods or services that otherwise might not be made available to the public; (2) it may regulate by competing, i.e., may provide certain goods or services and thus compel private enterprises to meet the competitive prices or charges of the government corporation; or (3) it may engage in purely regulatory activity.

The principal characteristic of the government corporation is that it is a separate legal entity. It is distinct from the government that created it. It has a corporate charter or franchise, which confers powers upon it. It may do whatever its charter authorizes. However, it must adhere to constitutions, statutes, administrative rules and regulations, and court decisions.

The government corporation is noteworthy for its extreme flexibility, not only of function and operation, but also with regard to the ease with which it can be created and dissolved. Thus it is ideally suited to times of stress and emergency. It may be quickly created by statute or executive order. Where it is necessary to escape from excessively standardized procedures, the government corporation can function within a specified area, unfettered by procedural limitations. When the services of the corporation are no longer required, it may be dissolved with equal facility.

The government corporation has a businesslike structure and is headed by a board of directors having complete and independent control over all its affairs. It engages managers to whom specific responsibilities are allocated. As a separate legal and fiscal entity, it is able to make decisions rapidly and independently. The government corporation can act without securing clearances from innumerable other organizations in the executive hierarchy.

Some but not all government corporations are free from auditing and other government fiscal controls. Some are free to hire their personnel without regard to civil service rules. In such cases the government corporation can hire and fire at will and can secure the services of well-paid but temporary employees who might not have been induced to serve for short periods at conventional government salaries.

The government corporation need not adhere to the separation-of-powers concept. It is organized to get action through the concentration of authority in a small board of directors. It is similarly free from the strictures of the theory of checks and balances.

When first established, a government corporation is dependent upon public funds. However, the corporation may engage in profit-making activities and in conventional buying, selling, and borrowing operations. Its profits may be used to expand its activities or may be returned to the government in order to retire the corporation's debts. It may be given certain advantages not generally granted to private business enterprise; for example, the charter may exempt the corporation from taxation. Government corporations such as the Tennessee Valley Authority often make equivalent contributions to the support of the various areas of government in which they do business. These contributions, in lieu of taxes, generally equal or exceed those assessed against comparable private enterprise.

The government corporation may sue and be sued; it does not share the immunity from suit enjoyed by many governmental instrumentalities. It may be made a defendant in both contract and tort actions.

The government corporation is not without its defects. Its lack of integration with other governmental agencies is a serious handicap to a single, coordinated approach to governmental objectives. Also, government corporations are far from identical in form and structure. However, most federal government corporations are subject to loose managerial supervision by some of the departments of the national government and by the Office of Management and Budget. The TVA is subject to limited executive control because its board of directors is appointed by the president. The Government Corporation Control Act (1945) represents an effort by

Congress to bring such corporations under the watchful eye of the executive branch and Congress.

A corporation's board of directors may change rather rapidly, and such changes may result in shifting and sometimes inconsistent policies. Where a corporation has favors to dispense, such as the lending of huge sums of money to business enterprises, political pressures are heavy. Bribes, lucrative positions, and other temptations are sometimes offered by businesses seeking such favors. But government departments and regulatory commissions are also exposed to such pressures. Fortunately for the nation, very few government corporations have deserved the criticisms at one time directed at certain officers and employees of the Reconstruction Finance Corporation, which resulted in its dissolution by Congress in 1953.

At its best, the public corporation can be a very effective device for efficient government. Its independence from external managerial and financial controls enables it to achieve objectives in the area of business operations that cannot be reached by more conventional departments and administrative agencies. It has hence been increasingly employed for purposes of public regulation of economic activities. It may be used to secure any constitutional objective.

The presence and importance of a far-flung administrative apparatus, including administrative agencies, regulatory commissions, and governmental corporations, make clear the distance traveled since the Founding Fathers first outlined the appropriate structures and functions of government in the United States. If the journey has resulted in substantial changes in some of our most cherished baggage (e.g., the principles of classical liberalism in general and a narrow unworkable view of the separation of powers in particular), it may also be said to have allowed an ever larger majority of citizens to partake in greater opportunities for individual self-development. The growth of the administrative state, in the context of democratic politics, is less an imposition of authority on the people than a practical response to their interests and demands. And as these have become more complex over time, so have the organization, management, and functioning of government.

STUDY-GUIDE QUESTIONS

1 Can you give illustrations supporting the proposition that sharp distinctions cannot be drawn between politics (policy formulation) and administration (policy execution)?
2 What do you consider to be major problems in securing the reorganization of the administrative process?
3 Have you ever considered becoming a civil servant? What are some of the attractions of such a career?
4 What are some of the principal means for keeping those who work for government "honest"? What do you mean by "honest" in this context?
5 Is it a function of those who manage the administrative process at the national level to seek uniform standards throughout the United States, including the standards enforced by the states, concerning such subjects as interstate highways, protection of the environment, fiscal reports, and accounting procedures?

REFERENCES

Davis, Kenneth C.: *Administrative Law,* West Publishing Company, St. Paul, Minn., 1951.
Kohlmeier, L. M., Jr.: *The Regulators,* Harper & Row, Publishers, Incorporated, 1969.
Pfiffner, John M., and R. Vance Presthus: *Public Administration,* 5th ed., The Ronald Press Company, New York, 1967.
Turner, Henry A.: *American Democracy: State and Local Government,* 2d ed., Harper & Row, Publishers, Incorporated, New York, 1970.
Waldo, D. (ed.): *Public Administration in a Time of Turbulence,* Chandler Publishing Co., Scranton, Pa., 1971.

Chapter 19

The Nature of Foreign Policy

In broad terms, foreign policy is the pattern of behavior that one state adopts while pursuing its interests in relations with other states. It is concerned with the process of making decisions to follow specific courses of action. Foreign policy analysis is an attempt to find rational explanations of why nations behave as they do. Succinctly stated: How does a nation set its goals, order priorities, activate the governmental policy-making machinery, and employ its human and natural resources to compete successfully with other nation-states in the international arena? Whereas the study of foreign policy seeks answers to "how" and "why" a course of action is taken, international politics deals with the consequences of the clash of foreign policies in the competitive world environment.

The need to know is urgent if man wishes to avoid retracing the paths leading to two world wars and a worldwide depression within a generation. In this nuclear age, war can no longer be regarded as a catalyst for relieving international tensions. Only by sorting out the tangled skeins of relationships between states can some basis be found for international cooperation and for peace through world order. A starting point is the consideration of the process for formulating and executing foreign policy.

In the first place, foreign policy must be distinguished from the great mass of heterogeneous contacts that individuals, groups, and the government in one state have with their counterparts in other states. There is one standard that may be utilized to separate generalized international contacts from those particularly associated with foreign policy. Within the broad area of international relations, only those matters which originate with, or are overtly or tacitly sponsored by, the government of a state may be considered to belong to its foreign policy. In this sense policy is official, in contrast with haphazard, unsponsored, and unofficial contacts made by individuals or groups. Foreign policy is directed by the government, which is acting as the instrumentality of the state.

Does a state have *a* foreign policy or foreign *policies?* Two approaches may be used in the fractionalization of policy: (1) Reference is made to economic, military, cultural, or financial foreign policy, with the inference that the relations between states may be classified along functional lines, or (2) there is an insistence on the identity of policies based upon geographic area; for example, a state is said to have Latin-American, European, or Asiatic foreign policies. Although the utility of designating certain phases of policy in terms of functional or geographic characteristics may be conceded, foreign policy per se rests upon certain basic principles that provide the frame of reference for a distinctive political concept.

In subsequent sections of this chapter, the relationship of a state's foreign policy to its career in international politics will be investigated by consideration of (1) the underlying principles that shape policy objectives; (2) the factors that condition the formulation of policy; (3) the agencies involved in policy making; (4) the planning process; (5) political dynamics and foreign policy—the role of political parties and interest groups; and (6) the techniques and instruments utilized in policy execution.

PRINCIPLES GOVERNING THE SELECTION OF AIMS AND GOALS

The objectives of a nation's foreign policy are many.[1] They represent the composite desires and wishes of the articulate groups within a state that are interested in some phase of international relations. However, *the one common denominator of all policy goals is the obligation of any politically organized group to maintain the state as an unimpaired entity.* Thus, toward the close of World War II, Winston Churchill met the repeated demands of British colonies for independence with the dramatic statement that he had not become His Majesty's first minister to preside over the liquidation of the British Empire. The necessity of survival not only is the mainspring of foreign policy but also includes many lesser aims dependent upon its achievement. The interpretation of the concept of survival extends considerably beyond the literal connotation of "existence" and embraces certain principles underlying the selection of policy goals. Among the more important of these are the principles of maintaining the integrity of the state, promoting the interests of the economy, providing for the national security, protecting the national prestige, and developing a power potential to prosecute an offensive war if the occasion arises.

Maintaining the Integrity of the State

The concept of internal national unity as opposed to national security includes the administration, control, and governance of the territory and outlying dependencies (if any) of a state, including looking after its citizens both at home and abroad. Not only must jurisdiction over land and people be maintained in any situation wherein national interests touch upon international problems, but the framers of policy must also seek psychological unity in strong public support of action taken in pursuance of negotiations with other countries.

The principle of geographic unity presents three types of problems to the policy makers: (1) maintenance of title to all areas claimed by the state, (2) cession of certain areas, and (3) acquisition of new territories and possessions.

The ideal state might be one that most closely approximated perfect unity in geographic composition, ethnic characteristics, economic balance, religious and cultural mores, historic tradition, and underlying political beliefs. Unfortunately, the present nation-state political pattern, superimposed upon the geographic configuration of the globe, presents a maze of state boundaries violating prac-

---

[1] There is an extensive literature on the nature of foreign policy, the goals sought, the factors conditioning the decision-making process, and methodological problems in policy analysis. Early pioneers seeking realistic explanations were Frank H. Simonds and Brooks Emeny, *The Great Powers in World Politics,* American Book Company, New York, 1937; George T. Renner et al., *Global Geography,* Thomas Y. Crowell Company, New York, 1944 (particularly William F. Christians, "Geography and Nation Making," pp. 561–580); Harold H. Sprout and Margaret Sprout, *Foundations of International Politics,* D. Van Nostrand Company, Inc., Princeton, N.J., 1962; Robert Strausz-Hupé and Stefan T. Possony, *International Relations,* 2d ed., McGraw-Hill Book Company, New York, 1954; and Thorsten V. Kalijarvi (ed.), *Modern World Politics,* 3d ed., Thomas Y. Crowell Company, New York, 1953 (particularly the editor's own article, "The Dynamics of State Existence," pp. 31–60). The best-known contemporary discussion of the normative approach to national power is Hans J. Morganthau, *Politics among Nations,* 5th ed., Alfred A. Knopf, Inc., New York, 1973; an assessment of Morganthau's concept of the national interest by Thomas W. Robinson may be found in James N. Rosenau (ed.), *International Politics and Foreign Policy,* rev. ed., The Free Press, New York, 1969, pp. 182–190, and Rosenau has contributed an essay on the methodological problems of foreign policy analysis, pp. 167–174. All the forgoing sources have contributed to the approach adopted herein.

tically all these ideal specifications. The contrasts in policy reflected in some 148 political entities, each claiming legal autonomy, provide fertile ground for international disagreement.

The principle of unity also extends to control over a state's nationals. In the normal course of events, the consular and diplomatic corps helps to solve the problems of citizens traveling in foreign lands and sifts the immigrant contingents that are permitted to enter the homeland. The significance of the demographic factor in relation to the principle of unity, however, assumes an entirely different aspect when the revisionist governments (1) claim lands to which their countrymen have emigrated, on the theory that all nationals and former nationals have an inalienable right to live under the flag of the country of their origin, or (2) insist that population pressure at home entitles a state to occupy areas that will accommodate the overflow population.

Germany and Italy, under Hitler and Mussolini, persistently claimed suzerainty over their nationals, no matter where they lived in the world. Italy and Japan in the 1930s asserted the right to acquire territory, by force if necessary, in which their "excess" population could settle. The announced objective of this policy was to relieve the economic stress of maintaining the marginal group at home. These designs forced the reorientation of the policies of the states upon which such demands were made.

A third facet of the principle of unity is the necessity for the policy framers to obtain popular support for the direction of policy, including the measures adopted to carry it out. Lacking the necessary approval of a significant percentage of the national population, no foreign policy can be sustained indefinitely or achieve practical and lasting results. This phase of the problem might be termed the "necessity for psychological unity."

Promoting Economic Interests

A second principle underlying the selection of the goals of foreign policy is the obligation of the government to promote the welfare of the state. The economic interdependence of nations has been dramatically evidenced by the world energy and food crisis of the mid-1970s. Even the greatest and most powerful nations of the earth cannot enjoy economic prosperity and maintain a high standard of living while remaining isolated from the channels of world commerce. The prosperity of a state is contingent upon many complex and closely related factors. These may be divided into two categories: (1) the state's assets, including geographic location in relation to the industrial centers of the world, natural resources, climate, and the size and character of the population; and (2) the manner in which these assets are exploited, which is a reflection of the state's cultural status.

Policy goals predicated upon the welfare principle are legion: finding ways and means to attract immigrants to a sparsely settled country, such as Australia; making arrangements for emigration from overpopulated areas, such as Japan; supplementing shortages by trade agreements covering such essential raw materials as copper, rubber, iron, and foodstuffs; locating outlets for capital investments; and exchanging cultural ideas, medical information, and scientific inventions.

In fact, all governmentally directed international activity that augments the economic and social welfare of the population may be subsumed under this basic principle. Not all groups within the state are equally articulate or otherwise capable of making their influence on public policy felt. Therefore, welfare may reflect the restricted objectives of a limited group in society, whether or not such goals redound to the benefit of the nation as a whole. Also, the framers of policy may be forced to adopt aims such as that of national self-sufficiency for military reasons, thus giving security a priority among welfare goals.

Providing for National Security

National security constitutes a third principle underlying the determination of policy aims. The assumption that a nation's foreign policy must be devised to protect it from attack implies the possibility of danger. Because of the slow development of international law and of international agencies to enforce it, each government is dependent largely upon it own resources in case of attack. Thus the framers of policy must provide a defense against any contingency that may arise. Governments wishing to retain their territorial boundaries intact are said to follow *status quo* policies, while those with designs on new territory develop *revisionist* policies. There are two methods by which revisionist policies may be executed: by peaceful negotiations or by force.

The definition of security has undergone complete revision in the light of the experiences of World War II. It now involves at least three phases of preparedness: political, economic, and military.

Political preparedness may be achieved in part by (1) creating a treaty network that will serve the dual purpose of forming strong alliances and commitments with capable allies and consequently of isolating any potential enemy; (2) utilizing international tensions to implement policy; (3) framing and prosecuting a positive, popularly supported, and vigorous foreign policy; (4) avoiding, by negotiation, the precipitation of an overtly hostile act that might cause war; and (5) using international machinery for collective security.

Economic preparedness involves (1) either the possession of essential minerals, foodstuffs, and other raw materials or access to them; (2) industrial capacity; (3) the administrative, industrial, and scientific know-how necessary to create the weapons and other equipment and facilities needed by the military services; and (4) the financial capacity or national wealth to underwrite all the forgoing activities without incurring internal economic collapse.

The military requirements for the maintenance of national security include (1) a long-range strategic plan of attack and defense, supplemented by constant study of possible tactical situations that might develop in encountering potential enemies; (2) the organization and training of a fighting service that can efficiently utilize the modern engines of land, sea, and air power; (3) plans for coordinating civilian personnel and facilities to meet a war situation; and (4) the provision of proper logistical support (i.e., transportation and supply).

A final important factor in national security is psychological preparedness. Whether artificially induced by propaganda or otherwise attained, the morale of the population has become a vital element in the maintenance of national security.[2]

Protecting National Prestige

A fourth fundamental principle guiding the formulation of policy goals is the maintenance of a nation's prestige. Just as individuals are concerned with their personal reputation in the community in which they live, so a state is obliged to consider its influence in relation to other states in international affairs.

What, exactly, is the significance of the term "prestige"?[3] As Harold Nicolson succinctly points out, in the prevailing international order each state possesses the attribute of sovereignty and is thus by legal fiction designated as independent. A state must therefore so conduct its international affairs that its pride and self-respect, or reputation, are maintained intact. When speaking of prestige, Eastern peoples refer to "saving face," and Westerners use the term "national honor."

Since nations, just like individuals, have some difficulty seeing themselves as others see them, most states today would undoubtedly claim the virtues of honesty, chivalry, and objectivity as cornerstones of their national reputations. From a pragmatic viewpoint, however, prestige as a goal of foreign policy is subject to varying interpretations. Under the prevailing standards of international morality, almost any act of diplomatic or military coercion may be justified in terms of protecting national honor. Furthermore, prestige, in a world of power politics, accrues to the nation possessing the greatest military strength. As long as force is the ultimate arbiter of international disputes, the strongest nation will usually enjoy the greatest prestige.

Developing Power

A final vital interest that constitutes a guiding principle in the formulation of policy goals is the acquisition of power. Power exists in social situations involving human relationships. Politics is often described as a struggle for power because in any society, one group is in possession of the government, and another seeks its control. *Political power is the capacity in any human relationship to*

---

[2] On self-sufficiency and military aspects of national security, see Renner, op. cit., pp. 460–477; W. W. Kaufman (ed.), *Military Policy and National Security*, Princeton University Press, Princeton, N.J., 1956; and Samuel P. Huntington (ed.), *Changing Patterns of Military Politics*, The Free Press, New York, 1962.

[3] For this section, see Harold Nicolson, *The Meaning of Prestige*, Cambridge University Press, New York, 1947, and his article by the same title in *The Atlantic Monthly*, July 1937, pp. 11–17.

control behavior and influence thought for the attainment of political goals. There is an infinite number of power situations in society. The power stuggle is characteristic of international as well as domestic politics. In this context, the ruling elite of each state contends for power with those in authority in other states. The objective of the contest is to impose demands, gain concessions, and dictate the terms that govern negotiations with the controlled state. In this sense, power is probably the most universal of all the principles that condition foreign policy goals.

Foreign policy is one means by which power relationships between nations may be established. Each nation is constantly faced with the problem of making its influence felt in the international sphere, and particularly with the necessity not only of being able to defend itself but also of maintaining the capacity for prosecuting offensive warfare. Thus power is considered in terms of a nation's potential to exert psychological and military coercion upon other nations.[4]

Foreign Policy Goals as Variables

The more pragmatically inclined scholars of international relations have become sharply critical of the practice of listing the goals of foreign policy in normative terms.[5] They view individual goals as variables of the time and place at which a particular policy is made. They assume that a nation's aspirations will vary according to its needs from one phase of development to another. They emphasize the many factors conditioning the process of goal selection: the assets and liabilities not only of a particular state but also of the world environment of which it is a part; the fact that some goals are of immediate importance, while others lie in the future, and that some arise from the demands of the citizenry, while others derive from the state's establishment; and, finally, the existence of many inconsistencies in the pursuit of goals. National security, for example, might well be abandoned if surrender was the only road to survival. Stated more succinctly, the procedure for identification and selection of foreign policy goals must be linked more closely to the decision-making processes of foreign policy implementation.

FACTORS CONDITIONING FOREIGN POLICY

In devising its foreign policy, a nation must consider not only the goals it is attempting to achieve but also certain basic facts of existence in the international sphere that affect its status. This frame of reference includes its geographic-strategic situation, population potential, economic endowment, and ideological environment.[6]

The Geographic-Strategic Factor

Two important limitations on policy are the physical environment of the state and the political-military implications of its geographic situation. In the first category, the characteristics of size, climate, topography, and shape are important. An ideal norm would include (1) a size large enough to provide an adequate standard of living for a population that is sufficient to man an adequate conventional military establishment; (2) a climate that is uniform and conducive to physical vigor, preferably either temperate or tropical highland; (3) a topography offering boundaries with natural defense barriers such as mountains, forests, swamps, rivers, deserts, and oceans; and (4) a shape that is relatively easy to defend in conventional warfare.

Few states possess all these advantages, but it is significant that the two that most nearly match such specifications, Russia and the United States, possess the greatest power. *It is the particular variant from the norm that is reflected in the foreign policy of less fortunate countries.* Thus small states must compensate politically in several ways. Switzerland has been fortunate in being able to adopt a policy of neutrality, with the tacit consent of potential ene-

---

[4]See Morganthau, op. cit., pp. 25ff.

[5]See Arnold Wolfers, "The Goals of Foreign Policy," in Naomi Rosenbaum (ed.), *Readings in the International Political System,* Prentice-Hall, Inc., Englewood Cliffs, N.J., 1970, pp. 133–145; and Eugene J. Meehan, "The Concept of Foreign Policy," in Wolfram F. Hanreider (ed.), *Comparative Foreign Policy,* David McKay Company, Inc., New York, 1971, pp. 265–294. See also Richard C. Snyder et al., *Decision-Making as an Approach to the Study of International Politics,* Princeton University Press, Princeton, N.J., 1954. For an interesting reevaluation of the concept of power, see Seyom Brown, "The Changing Essence of Power," *Foreign Affairs,* vol. 51, no. 2, pp. 286–299, January 1973.

[6]This approach was developed by Simonds and Emeny, op. cit.; see also Sprout and Sprout, op. cit., pp. 39–148.

mies, who have found the country valuable as a diplomatic listening post, an administrator of International Red Cross services, a prisoner exchange depot, and headquarters for negotiation between belligerents. China and India, on the other hand, with teeming millions of people widely distributed over many types of terrain and enjoying a varied climate, have demonstrated that mere size and a huge population are not the only ingredients of power.

Before the advent of the modern military machine, favorable topography and terrain, particularly with respect to natural barriers, were great assets in maintaining national security. The Atlantic and Pacific Oceans made American isolationism possible and were responsible for many other phases of policy such as freedom of the seas and the Open Door in Far Eastern trade channels. The great African deserts protected Egypt for centuries, and the Alps on the border between France and Italy have served as a protective barrier for both countries.

The traditional viewpoint regarding the relation of geographic-strategic factors to foreign policy was developed before the demonstration of the importance of air power, augmented by the advent of the atom bomb in World War II. At that time, the importance of the world position of a state depended upon (1) possession of vital resources such as food and minerals, (2) degree of industrialization, and (3) location on or near the major ocean trade routes and world commercial centers. In this sense three areas in the world were the focal points of orientation: Western Europe, including England; the United States; and greater Japan. Each of these power sites had its own regional orbit within which lesser states were located. The United States, for example, was dominant in the Western Hemisphere. All lesser states within its sphere of influence were compelled to take cognizance of the Monroe Doctrine, Pan-Americanism, and the Good Neighbor policy, which were developed to reinforce political hegemony in this region. Moreover, the economic destiny of all the less powerful states was dependent, in large measure, upon the economic policy of the United States.

Although many of these geographic characteristics and their resulting political implications still remain, the advent of air power in the space age has resulted in a complete reevaluation of the importance of world and regional location as a strategic factor in policy formulation. The new dimension of the problem is the use of outer space. Since the Soviet Union launched Sputnik I on October 4, 1957, and the United States placed astronaut Neil Armstrong on the moon on July 20, 1969, the log of orbited manned and unmanned space vehicles has encompassed earth satellites as well as lunar and planetary probes. As the supporting systems of these and future space vehicles become more complicated, they will inevitably be applied to military as well as peaceful purposes, and as the utilization of the boundless areas of space expands the contours of terrestrial geography, security, as a foreign policy goal, will come to depend upon a state's ability to communicate, gather intelligence, and launch military weapons in the new environment.[7]

The Population Factor

The size, the socioeconomic status, and the dynamics of growth or decline of a nation's population will be reflected in the many facets of its foreign policy.[8] Throughout history one important measure of national power has been the size of a state's population. When wars were fought by armies of foot soldiers locked in hand-to-hand combat, the attrition rate that a country was either willing or able to withstand became a significant variable in gauging the strength of its foreign policy. In World War I, for example, Germany mobilized approximately 11.0 million men; Russia, 12.0 million; Britain, 8.9 million; and France, 8.4 million. Casualties in the battle of the Somme alone exceeded 1.2 million.

The advent of the nuclear weapon upon the

---

[7]For the development of the relationships between power, strategy, and geography, see Robert Strausz-Hupé, *Geopolitics: The Struggle for Space and Power,* G. P. Putnam's Sons, New York, 1942; N. J. Spykman, "Geography and Foreign Policy," *American Political Science Review,* vol. 32, no. 1, pp. 28-51, February 1938, and vol. 32, no. 2, pp. 213-237, April 1938; and James Fairgrieve, *Geography and World Power,* 8th ed., E. P. Dutton & Co., Inc., New York, 1941. For a consideration of nuclear weapons as variables, see Herman Kahn, *On Thermonuclear War,* Princeton University Press, Princeton, N.J., 1960; and Bruce M. Russett, "The Calculus of Deterrence," in Rosenau, op. cit., pp. 359-369.

[8]Katherine Organski and A. F. K. Organski, *Population and World Power,* Alfred A. Knopf, Inc., New York, 1961; and Warren S. Thompson, *Population Problems,* 5th ed., McGraw-Hill Book Company, New York, 1965.

contemporary scene has produced a new measure of national power. The size of a nation's population may become less significant than the excellence of its scientific research, technological know-how, and manufacturing capacity. The People's Republic of China, with 800 million inhabitants, and the state of Israel, with 3.1 million, both have the capability of producing atomic weapons. It is doubtful that the United States will ever again mobilize 16.0 million men and women for military service, as was done in World War II. In fact, its military establishment in 1974 consisted of 2.2 million persons, and service was voluntary. Nevertheless, numbers will always play some part in warfare if only because the sophistication of modern weaponry requires logistic support and because a nation with a large population can withstand serious losses through military attrition and still survive as a political entity.

A nation's war-making capability provides a close and dramatic link between the population factor and its foreign policy. Other significant aspects of this relationship stem from the nature of the society itself. The degree of its social integration in the national community and the adequacy of its political institutions are important considerations. The extent of industrialization, which determines the effective use of manpower, and the totality of the goods and services produced in the state (gross national product), are other ingredients of national power. During the last century, for example, Switzerland, with its relatively small population of 6.5 million people, has enjoyed a far greater degree of control over its own destiny in international politics than has India, with almost 600 million inhabitants.

A final consideration linking population to foreign policy is the ratio of its size to the available food and energy supplies needed to sustain it. The key to this relationship is a nation's birthrate. Demographic studies by the United Nations in the mid-1970s revealed that the world's population is increasing at the rate of 2.0 percent annually. Predictions were made that if the same trend continues, the earth's population will double by the year 2006, to a total of 7.0 billion inhabitants.

The rapid growth of the world's population is taking place at a time when there are critical shortages of such essential foodstuffs as wheat, corn, soybeans, and sugar, as well as shortages of oil, an indispensable source of energy. The problem arising from the dilemma of overpopulation in relation to available resources is worldwide in scope, but the impact falls differentially upon individual nations. United Nations statisticians have identified over thirty countries, principally in Latin America, Africa, and Asia, with populations growing more rapidly than the world average and with progressively diminishing resources of fertilizer, money, and petroleum for farm equipment with which to provide food for populations facing starvation.

The historic forms of population control such as war, pestilence, flood, and famine are both unacceptable solutions and of indeterminate occurrence. Moral and religious scruples have seriously complicated the adoption of national policies for birth control. Nevertheless, the international dilemma of the inability of the world to sustain its inhabitants has caused an eruption of "population politics" reflected in the foreign policies of both the "have" and the "have-not" nations. None of these problems appears to be insoluble, but the shifting patterns of foreign-aid programs and political alliances as nations practice the diplomacy of "food strategy" will create international tensions for the foreseeable future.

The Factor of Economic Resources

Of the various factors that influence and shape a state's foreign policy, the nature and condition of its economy are of primary significance. The health of a nation's economy is one index to the vigor and purposefulness it displays in its relations with other states. Informally, the function of an economic system may be described as the utilization of land, labor, capital, and enterprise for the production, distribution, and consumption of goods and services. Normally, the hoped-for outcome of this process is a high standard of living for the people, but whether this goal is achieved may depend upon the nature of the political apparatus under which they live.

The prototype of a powerful state is usually described as one possessing a well-integrated and highly industrialized economy. It is generously endowed with human and natural resources, which are efficiently used to produce goods and services for consumption at home and for export abroad. Its foreign trade meets unfulfilled domestic needs and contributes toward the establishment of a favorable balance of trade with the rest of the world. Surplus capital accumulated from savings is reinvested to replenish the industrial establishment and to undertake new projects. The resulting gross national product may not only produce a high living standard but also support a powerful military capability. The relationship between the two factors will depend upon the national priorities and the resulting policy decisions made by the national government. Totalitarian governments tend to syphon off a disproportionate share of national wealth for military purposes at the expense of consumer comforts.

In any event, the powerful state is typically conceived of as the highly industrialized country that can produce and equip and logistically supply a modern military establishment. Less than a dozen of the approximately 148 nation-states of the world fit the pattern; these include the United States, the Soviet Union, Japan, and possibly Britain and France. Two potential members of the select group are the People's Republic of China and India.

The states of the world are unequally endowed with the human resources of scientific knowledge and technological skills and with natural resources of food, energy, and critical minerals. A nation's foreign policy is formulated, in part, to compensate for deficiencies in the economy. The links between foreign policy and the economic factor are legion: finding ways and means to attract immigrants to a sparsely settled country, making arrangements for emigration from overpopulated areas, supplementing shortages by trade agreements covering essential raw materials, locating outlets for capital investment, promoting multinational corporate business, effecting cultural exchanges with more highly developed countries, and so forth.

A primarily agrarian state such as Argentina must sell its wheat, wool, and beef to an industrial state like England and buy that state's tractors, cloth, and automobiles in return. Even a state with a balanced economy, such as the United States, is dependent upon world trade in some degree for economic prosperity. International economic activity is expressed politically in terms of tariffs, import quotas, trade agreements, and financial arrangements involving the debits and credits of international exchange.

If each nation in the world followed the practice of economic specialization of production and free trade in goods, some equitable adjustment of the economic problem might be effected. However, the doctrine of national self-sufficiency, which implies that each state must develop the maximum war potential, translates economic tensions into political and military action. States may or may not possess such critical raw materials as iron, coal, oil, phosphates, rubber, bauxite, tungsten, uranium, and the many other products essential to warfare. They may or may not be able to utilize their available resources. Foreign policy dictates that the national supply of critical war materials must be hoarded, that deficiencies must be provided for by stockpiling, and that favorable trade agreements must be negotiated in order to deal with deficiencies in resources.

Foreign policy requires not only the protection of foreign investments but also the maintenance of access to critical resources, as the Middle Eastern oil crisis so dramatically illustrated in the fall of 1973 and the winter of 1974. Oil is the most valuable single product in international commerce. Nearly two-thirds of the world's known oil resources and slightly over one-half of the world's oil production capacity are in the possession of twelve Middle Eastern states belonging to a cartel known as the Organization of Petroleum Exporting Countries, or OPEC. In late 1973 and early 1974 OPEC placed a five-month embargo on oil shipments to the United States in retaliation for the latter's pro-Israel foreign policy, threatened to embargo supplies to the world at large, and quadrupled the price of oil to all its customers, thus accumulating an income estimated at $80 billion annually.

The manipulation of both the supply and price of this vital energy resource caused an international crisis among nations utilizing oil for industrial purposes. The entire mechanism of international finance was endangered. The impact on the domestic economies of the nations involved augments a trend toward inflation endangering the stability of domestic banking systems throughout the world. Since oil is also utilized in food production, the food supply of most of the developing nations, many already facing starvation, was placed in jeopardy. The capacity of every major nation to resolve these problems was strongly challenged. The outcomes were reflected in foreign policy negotiations and in terms of the vital interests of national power, welfare, and prestige.

The Ideological Factor

There is a general agreement among scholars that a nation's ideology plays an important role in shaping its domestic affairs, but the degree of impact of ideology upon foreign policy is in dispute.[9] Ideology reflects the belief system of a people—the values they consider important and the ideals they hope to achieve, individually and collectively. It serves to legitimate the existing political system and to reflect the locus and scope of governmental authority. The citizenry is socialized through custom and education to accept ideological goals in justification for domestic policy decisions.

To some degree foreign policy is a statement of a nation's aspirations or the purpose of its existence and therefore reflects its domestic goals. The controversy rests upon the answer to the question: Does ideological dogma influence the foreign policy decision-making process? Is ideology a vital interest of foreign policy?

The issue is readily dramatized when the elite of one nation speaks to the elite of another in terms of "our side" versus "your side"—"democracy" versus "communism." In the early days of the United States–Soviet Union détente, in 1973 and 1974, the foremost Russian ideologue in the Politburo, Mikhail S. Suslov, warned his countrymen that there could be no ideological coexistence between socialism and capitalism. He urged that they maintain "constant vigilance" to rebuff all "intrigues" by aggressive, reactionary circles of imperialism and all hostile "ideological subversions." United States Secretary of State Henry A. Kissinger also stated his views that each nation was committed to its own internal ideological orientation and that such internal arrangements were "nonnegotiable." He admitted, however, that demands of one state upon another for internal changes might be made for "atmospherics," e.g., propaganda purposes. Seemingly, the foreign policy of détente was not to be confused with the internal ideological dogma of communism or democracy.

Historically, hostile ideologies have existed peaceably side by side until competitive economic or national security interests have precipitated open warfare. During the 1930s, for example, fascism, communism, and democracy coexisted. Indeed, the signing of the Hitler-Stalin pact in August 1939 and its repudiation during the summer of 1941, when Germany invaded Russia, proved that *Realpolitik* was more important to the dictators than the conflicting principles of fascism and communism. On the other hand, the alienation of the People's Republic of China from the Soviet-led communist bloc had both ideological and national-security implications. In 1956 Mao Tse-tung accused Nikita Khrushchev of abandoning Marxist orthodoxy both in the internal policies of the Soviet Union and in relations with the communist world. Underlying the ideological dispute were the questions of the worldwide leadership of the communist states and the settlement of claims of national boundaries near the Ussuri River; by 1969 the two nations were engaged in undeclared open warfare in that region.

Tentative conclusions would seem to support the thesis that ideological dogma is not, of itself, a goal of foreign policy. Nevertheless, its principles are utilized to support the domestic regime framing such policy and are widely employed in international propaganda to rationalize and support foreign policy decisions.

THE CONSTITUTIONAL FRAMEWORK: OFFICIAL AGENCIES THAT FORMULATE POLICY

There are at least two important characteristics of governmental structure and practice that have an important bearing upon policy. The first is the arrangement of the internal legal controls that determine the relationships between the executive, legislative, judicial, and administrative authorities. In American presidential government, the executive's power over foreign relations not only is

---

[9]See particularly the selection on values in Joseph Frankel, *The Making of Foreign Policy*, 2d ed., Oxford University Press, London, 1968; Kenneth E. Boulding, "National Images and International Systems," in Hanreider, op. cit., pp. 90–107; Vernon V. Aspaturian, "Soviet Foreign Policy," in Roy C. Macridis (ed.), *Foreign Policy in World Politics*, 3d ed., Prentice-Hall, Inc., Englewood Cliffs, N.J., 1967, pp. 165–172; Chambers Johnson (ed.), *Ideology and Politics in Contemporary China*, University of Washington Press, Seattle, 1973; and Strausz-Hupé and Possony, op. cit., pp. 410–447.

shared by the Senate but also must be exercised within the limitations of the separation-of-powers system and the principle of checks and balances. Under the British cabinet system, although the conduct of foreign relations is still within the prerogative of the sovereign, the prime minister, acting in the name of the crown, is the real executive. His tenure of office rests upon the support of the majority party in Parliament. In the totalitarian countries, policy is usually discussed by an inner clique of the elite, such as the Politburo of the Soviet Union, but the decisions are made by the dictator, whether he is the titular head of the government or not. Thus the constitutional basis of Soviet foreign policy reflects the complete fusion of the executive, legislative, judicial, and administrative powers. Moreover, the Communist party and the government are linked together by a human chain of key officials holding positions in each.

The degree to which popular participation is permitted in the framing of policy is a distinguishing characteristic as between totalitarian and democratic practices. The Soviet Union is a one-party state, and popular endorsement of the government's policy is manufactured by a skillful blending of physical and psychological coercion. By contrast, in the democracies, the citizen may exercise the free franchise as a control device over government. Competing political parties and pressure groups have a profound influence upon the behavior of the elected representatives who share in the formulation and execution of foreign policy.[10]

The Executive and the Administration

The executive department assumes primary responsibility for the formation of foreign policy. The titular executive of a state, be he president, king, or dictator, is charged with a dual responsibility. As chief of state, he is the official spokesman for the government in its relations with other states. As head of the administration of his own government, he supervises the policy-making machinery. Some executives, like the president of the United States, perform many of these duties personally. Others, including the queen of England, because she is above political factionalism, perform the ceremonial functions, but the executive authority remains with the responsible ministers.

In the Federal Republic of West Germany the federal chancellor bears the primary responsibility for the conduct of foreign policy, as Dr. Konrad Adenauer demonstrated during the post–World War II period. With a remarkable exhibition of personal diplomacy, his successor, Willy Brandt, changed the course of German diplomacy with his policy of *Ostpolitik* in the early 1970s. Another variation in practice was provided by Joseph Stalin, who dictated Soviet foreign policy for many years without possessing any official title other than that of secretary general of the Communist party.

The president of the United States can wield great power in making foreign policy. He is the only elected official representing the entire nation. His public utterances characterize policy for the American people. Sometimes his views become policies bearing his name, such as the Monroe Doctrine, the Truman Doctrine, and the Nixon Doctrine. He negotiates treaties, enters into executive agreements, and appoints ambassadors. As commander in chief of the Armed Forces he may plan and direct military operations. He may implement policy by political intervention, as Woodrow Wilson did in his relations with the Mexican government, or by military intervention such as that resorted to by President Harry Truman in Korea in 1950, by President Eisenhower in Lebanon in 1958, by President John Kennedy in Vietnam in 1961, and by President Nixon in Cambodia in 1969. As chief executive, he is responsible for the expenditure of billions of dollars in the foreign-aid programs that constitute a vital part of post–World War II foreign policy. These powers are not unlimited, however, since the Senate must approve treaties, confirm appointments, vote appropriations in conjunction with the House, and, ultimately, sanction executive agreements. The president's authority must be exercised under the scrutiny of a critical opposition party and vigilant public opinion.

A vast administrative hierarchy assists the exec-

---

[10] For topics in this and the following section, see Burton M. Sapin, *The Making of United States Foreign Policy*, Frederick A. Praeger, Inc., New York, for The Brookings Institution, 1966, pp. 34–212; Kenneth N. Waltz, *Foreign Policy and Democratic Politics*, Little, Brown and Company, Boston, 1967, pp. 36–120; and Kenneth W. Thompson and Roy C. Macridis, "The Comparative Study of Foreign Policy," in Macridis, op. cit., pp. 1–27. For a most comprehensive and authoritative presentation of the formulation of Soviet foreign policy, see Vernon V. Aspaturian, *Process and Power in Soviet Foreign Policy*, Little, Brown and Company, Boston, 1971, especially pp. 221–235.

utive in planning and executing policy. Although American presidents sometimes ignore their Cabinets or use them merely as sounding boards, the cabinet in a parliamentary democracy *is* the executive establishment. Following the principle of ministerial responsibility, the cabinet is collectively responsible to parliament for the decisions it makes. The prime minister depends upon the heads of his major administrative departments for advice and political support. The heads of key departments, such as those dealing with foreign affairs, national defense, trade, and economic affairs, are particularly important in the policy-making process. Each major department is staffed with undersecretaries and highly skilled permanent civil servants, who retain their positions regardless of changes in government. They utilize their training and experience to advise the cabinet minister and are effective in influencing the formation and implementation of policy.

The pattern of the decision-making process in totalitarian states offers an interesting contrast. In Communist China policy is formulated by the party, not by the government. The twelve members of the Central Political Bureau constitute the elite of the party. The nine members of the Standing Committee represent the inner elite. From the formation of the People's Republic of China to the mid-1970s, one member of the inner elite, Mao Tse-tung, as chairman of the party, stood at the apex of the policy-making machinery. Mao provided guidelines for the selection and implementation of foreign policy goals through his interpretations of communist doctrine. He employed the National Party Congress of 1,249 members as a sounding board for predetermined decisions. The Central Committee of the party, numbering 195 members, served to clarify existing policy. Although Mao consulted his associates in the Political Bureau, his own views prevailed. In 1964 and 1965 he led his government out of the Soviet communist bloc, and in 1973 he inaugurated a policy of détente with the United States.

The Minister of Foreign Affairs

The secretary or minister in charge of foreign affairs in a democracy is usually the most important official adviser to the executive in matters of foreign relations. In addition to administering his department, he supervises the diplomatic and consular services of the nation and maintains contact with the legislative body. A very important part of the policy-making machinery is directly under his jurisdiction. Since his is usually among the senior cabinet positions, he speaks with considerable authority, although his influence varies according to the role the executive wishes him to play. During his long tenure as president of France, for example, General de Gaulle was, in fact, his own foreign minister. In a dictatorship the minister plays a subordinate role. In the early 1970s, Andrei Gromyko was merely an "errand boy" for General Secretary Leonid Brezhnev. When queried during conferences abroad, his stock answer was, "That must be settled in Moscow."

The foreign office over which the cabinet member presides is itself an elaborate hierarchy. Although the titles of the officials differ from country to country, the functions performed are virtually identical. The pattern of organization includes (1) the minister and his staff, (2) technical and administrative specialists, (3) political or geographic area heads, and (4) specialists in cultural or informational activities. The United States Department of State, for example, is organized on several levels. On the highest level are the secretary of state, his first deputy, the undersecretary of state, undersecretaries for political and economic affairs, and the directors of the Peace Corps, the Agency for International Development, and the Arms Control and Disarmament Agency. The secretary himself is a member of several critically important national agencies such as the National Aeronautics and Space Council (under NASA) and the National Security Council. The heads of the key administrative staffs that provide the supportive services for the Department are the executive secretariat, the inspector general for foreign assistance, and the protocol and press-relations officers.

The secretary's staff includes an ambassador-at-large and several deputy undersecretaries. The administrators representing specialized staff functions report to the undersecretary of state: planning and coordination, inspector general, foreign service, legal adviser, counselor, congressional relations, and political-military affairs.

The deputy secretary presides over several bureaus performing the line functions and field operations of the department of state. Among these are international scientific and technological affairs, intelligence and research, public affairs, educational and cultural affairs, and security and consular affairs.

Finally, the machinery for conducting worldwide political affairs is organized by geographic regions: African, European, East Asian and Pacific, inter-American, Near Eastern and South Asian, and international. Each regional bureau is subdivided into area offices. For example, the bureau for African affairs has charge of offices for Central, South, East, North, and West Africa and Nigeria. Finally, each office is staffed with desk officers in charge of country desks specializing in problems of a single state.

Each nation views the world from a different geographic perspective, and the organizations of foreign ministries therefore offer interesting variations. Communist China has a department for the Soviet Union and Eastern Europe that is concerned with Occidental bloc affairs. Its department for Asian affairs is divided into segments, one dealing with noncommunist Oriental countries and the other with communist Oriental nations. Its Western European department is responsible for noncommunist Europe, and its American and Australasian department is responsible for the Western Hemisphere, Australia, and New Zealand.

The Legislature

The national legislature serves as a policy-forming agent in direct proportion to the extent to which it uses its constitutional powers to support, modify, or defeat the program of the executive. Under a totalitarian regime, the legislative function is limited to unqualified endorsement of whatever portion of the program is submitted to it for consideration. The important functions of foreign policy in Russia are vested in the two houses of the Supreme Soviet, each with a Foreign Affairs Commission. In fact, however, the national legislature meets infrequently and briefly, and such powers as the declaration of war, ratification of treaties, and appointment of diplomatic and military officers are exercised only pro forma.[11] Moreover, totalitarian legislatures are not representative of public opinion. The Communist party of the Soviet Union constituted less than 6 percent of the population in January 1974, and yet an overwhelming majority of the elected members of the Supreme Soviet were party members. Indeed, the national legislatures of dictatorships usually serve only as ratifying agencies for ideas of the ruling elite. Although limited debate is sometimes permitted within the scope of major policy decisions, the policy itself cannot be questioned. Such a challenge would reflect unfavorably upon the integrity of the party hierarchy as well as the government leadership. Neither is the legislature permitted to interfere with any correlative measures, such as appropriations, that may serve to implement policy.

In a democratic regime the legislature assumes a far more active role in shaping policy. Foreign policy must rest upon a basis of domestic law enacted through the legislative process. Legislative committees gather data, listen to the views of specialized interest groups, hold public hearings on important issues, and carefully weigh alternative courses of action. By utilizing the powers of investigation, the legislature can scrutinize the execution of policy by the executive and also instigate a nationwide public debate upon controversial issues, which will enlist the electorate in forming a judgment upon critical questions.

Many democratic legislatures are constitutionally empowered to participate in the shaping of foreign policy. The British House of Commons stages full-dress debates on foreign policy and also utilizes the question hour to gain information and to criticize the government's course of action. In the United States the two key congressional committees that help shape foreign policy are the Senate Foreign Relations Committee and the House Foreign Affairs Committee. The chairmen of these committees from time to time wield considerable influence, both in Congress and in the country at large. The major commitments of the United States after World War II (with the possible exception of the Vietnamese intervention), such as the decision to enter the United Nations, the Marshall Plan, the Point Four program, the North Atlantic Pact, and the Strategic Arms Limitation Treaty with the Soviet Union, required congressional action.

One of the most powerful controls over foreign

---

[11] Aspaturian, "Soviet Foreign Policy," in Macridis, op. cit., pp. 201–203.

policy is the appropriation of funds to implement programs. In the United States the president prepares the federal budget and submits it to Congress. The budget is then assigned to the House and Senate Appropriations Committees for legislative consideration. The Congress is not restricted to presidential recommendations, however, and may increase, decrease, or eliminate any proposed expenditure or substitute proposals of its own. Since the president is not authorized to exercise an item veto in accepting an appropriation bill, Congress has wide latitude in supporting, rejecting, or modifying policy by controlling the purse strings. The various foreign-aid programs, both economic and military, adopted following World War II have been scrutinized and modified by Congress.

The Judiciary

Among the major legal agencies concerned with foreign policy, the judiciary in most states plays a subsidiary and indirect role. In the United States, however, because of the practice of judicial review, the Supreme Court has become the final arbiter in the determination of the constitutional relationships between the major branches of the national government. Although the Court has adopted the self-limiting principle that certain matters, such as the exercise of the president's powers in negotiations with foreign states, may be termed "political" and therefore are not within its jurisdiction, many decisions in other related areas have had a direct bearing on this problem. Typical of the issues with which the Court has been concerned are the following: the relationship between the national foreign-relations power and the reserved powers of the states, the relative powers of the Senate and the president in the treaty-making process, and the constitutional limitation to the treaty-making power.

THE PROCESS OF FORMULATING POLICY

Foreign policy may be regarded as the outcome or end product of an elaborate and intricate decision-making process. The procedure for the formulation of policy includes the following three important functions: (1) information and intelligence gathering; (2) data analysis, or the translation of information into alternative courses of action; and (3) planning, followed by decision making resulting in the adoption of policy guidelines.[12]

The Problem of Information

An effective foreign policy is based in part upon the accuracy and comprehensiveness of the description of the international environment made available to the decision maker. If he has the requisite facts, the other important variable is his ability to interpret them correctly. Because of the wide scope of concerns affecting policy formulation, data must be sought from the fields of agriculture, commerce and industry, labor, and science, as well as military affairs and politics. Most of the executive establishment and a substantial share of a nation's bureaucracy are involved in the process.

The Diplomatic and Consular Corps

One of the important sources of the raw material fed into the decision-making apparatus is the diplomatic and consular corps. In 1973 there were 12,100 Americans and 10,500 foreign nationals working for the State Department. There were 248 embassies, consulates, and missions manned by 3,190 foreign service officers scattered throughout the world. In addition, the Agency for International Development (AID), among many other organizations, employed 11,500 in its global program.

Generally, if specialization is possible, consuls gather economic information, and diplomats interpret political events. Diplomatic missions vary in importance depending upon the significance of the relations between particular states.[13] One distinction between missions is reflected in the rank of the diplomatic staff. The highest diplomatic ranks are those of ambassador (comparable papal officials are known as *nuncios* and *legates*), envoy extraordinary, and minister plenipotentiary, all of equal standing. Lesser ranks are minister resident and chargés d'affaires, in that order. The remaining personnel perform specialized tasks and are vari-

---

[12]For a discussion of these topics, see Sapin, op. cit., pp. 246–366; James L. McCamy, *The Administration of Foreign Affairs*, Alfred A. Knopf, Inc., New York, 1950, pp. 281–307; and Kurt London, *How Foreign Policy Is Made*, 2d ed., D. Van Nostrand Company, Inc., Princeton, N.J., 1950.

[13]For an authoritative description of the diplomatic establishment and the position of the state in international law, see Clyde Eagleton, *International Government*, rev. ed., The Ronald Press Company, New York, 1948, pp. 136–154.

ously designated as agents, attachés, secretaries, and counselors. Frequently, members of the various branches of the armed services and of the commercial departments of the home government are assigned to a mission for liaison purposes.

A major American embassy would include political and economic sections; consular, AID, and public-affairs (USIA) sections; military attachés of the three services; an administrative section; and other attached agencies operating in a particular country.

These "field offices" have a dual function: They represent the state in its relations with the foreign government to which they are accredited, and they provide a constant stream of information on the vital statistics of that nation's political, economic, and cultural life. It is largely this latter function that provides much evidence for policy making by the home state. The ambassador is constantly involved with the business of diplomacy, which is defined as the conduct of political affairs between states by personal representatives. He communicates messages from his government and responds to requests from the host country. He attends endless meetings, many of them of a social nature, representing his government in a public-relations role. He may assist with, or actually conduct, negotiations for treaties or commercial agreements. A vital function is to act as a listening post for current negotiations between other nations and the host state. Meanwhile, in a large embassy, he must supervise the work of from forty to sixty individuals, many of whom are specialists.

Holding a high priority among his obligations is the provision of detailed information about the host nation. Critical questions to be answered in the realm of politics are: How strongly entrenched is the present administration? Does it have substantial legislative support? What is the condition of the executive's health? Who is the political heir apparent? How effective is the opposition to the government? Who are its leaders? Were the last elections fair or fraudulent? What are the major current economic and political problems? What solutions have been suggested? What is the attitude of the administration toward the United States? What factors may bring about a change in this attitude? Intelligence gathered in this manner serves as grist for the policy-making mill.

The collection of economic intelligence is also essential, through a consular section located in an embassy, through a separate network of consulates, or both. The consular branch of the foreign service may be under the jurisdiction of either the department of foreign relations or the department of commerce of the national government. Consular representation is also worldwide in scope. A consulate is staffed by senior officials of varying rank designated as consul general, consul, vice consul, and consular agent. Junior administrators, clerks, and secretaries are assigned various routine or specialized tasks.

The consul is charged with providing information on the economic situation of the country to which he is accredited. Business and trade opportunities are carefully studied and analyzed, and enforcement of any existing commercial treaties is supervised. Other duties involve services rendered to nationals who are traveling through the country or are domiciled there. Finally, the consul reports to his superiors all information, political or otherwise, that he believes to be of significance.

The Intelligence Community

Another primary source of data for policy making is the "intelligence community," referring both to the personnel engaged in gathering information and to the network of agencies involved in the process. Intelligence can be classed as "overt" or "covert." Overt intelligence is publicly available information, obtained from scientific periodicals, government reports, journals of professional societies, and house organs of industrial and manufacturing concerns. Covert intelligence is usually classified or secret information obtained through spying or bribery, and it consists of plans or specifications, usually of a scientific or military nature, belonging to a rival government. Soviet spies, for example, stole many of the plans for the atom bomb from the United States at the close of World War II. The Russians were also able to build a prototype of the supersonic airliner Concorde, the TU-144, on the basis of information taken by an East German spy from British and French manufacturers in the late 1960s.

Little is known publicly of the Soviet intelligence apparatus under the jurisdiction of the State Security Committee, or KGB. Allegedly, it operates successfully from headquarters in Moscow and field offices in embassies and consulates and is worldwide in scope. The First Chief Directorate of international espionage is said to be divided into three sections: information gathering, "disinformation" gathering (lies and rumors), and "wet affairs," or "bloody business." Its chief, Yuri Andropov, was appointed to the Politburo in a reshuffling of personnel in 1974, twenty years after Beria, the most notorious director so honored, was shot.

The United States is engaged in a massive intelligence effort involving over 150,000 individuals in fifteen major agencies and having a budget of well over $6 billion annually. In 1971 President Nixon reorganized the United States intelligence community, restoring a larger measure of civilian control by placing the director of the Central Intelligence Agency (CIA) at the head of a United States Intelligence Board. The principal officers of all the agencies sit on the board as directors to coordinate the work of the community. At the apex of the network rests the National Security Council (NSC), a statutory body created in 1947 by President Truman to achieve some degree of integration between foreign and domestic policies and plans for national security. This vitally important advisory group is composed of the president, the vice president, the secretaries of state and defense, and the director of the Office of Emergency Preparedness. The chairman of the Joint Chiefs of Staff and the director of central intelligence have been made statutory advisers to the Council. The president may designate other officers to attend meetings; President Eisenhower extended such invitations from time to time to the secretary of the treasury, the director of the Bureau of the Budget, the chairman of the Atomic Energy Commission, and the director of the United States Information Agency. The Council is supported by a staff and is located in the executive office of the president.

The Central Intelligence Agency (CIA) has several missions: It is the principal collector of intelligence by clandestine means, indulging in overseas espionage and counterespionage; it conducts covert political and other projects, such as planned interventions in the domestic politics of foreign states, and it serves as the principal evaluator of intelligence data gathered by other agencies. It is closely associated with the work of the NSC. The Department of Defense operates a very large segment of the intelligence community: The National Security Agency staffs the cryptographic command, including the communications code makers and foreign code breakers, and the Defense Intelligence Agency coordinates the vast empire of military intelligence and conducts some spy work for the Army, Navy (ships), and Air Force (satellites). Other agencies of the community include the FBI (domestic counterespionage), the Foreign Intelligence Advisory Board ("blue ribbon" panel), the "Forty Committee" or "303 Group" (a secret panel chaired by Henry A. Kissinger that advises the president on covert operations), the Intelligence Resources Advisory Committee (budget watcher), the State Department Intelligence and Research Bureau, the Atomic Energy Commission (which interprets data on nuclear problems), and the Treasury Department (drugs and economic intelligence).[14]

Planning Policy

Information becomes intelligence through astute study and analysis. Processed information is fed into the decision-making apparatus so that alternative courses of action may be considered, and a plan of execution designed. The basic policy-planning machinery common to most contemporary states includes (1) the executive establishment, (2) top-level consultative agencies, (3) the foreign office professional staff, and (4) the consular and diplomatic corps.[15]

In Britain, for example, the executive establishment for planning purposes would include the

---

[14]For a brief evaluation of the role of the CIA, see "The CIA and the Intelligence Community," in Sheldon Appleton, *United States Foreign Policy*, Little, Brown and Company, Boston, 1968, pp. 244–256; and Chester L. Cooper, "The CIA and Decision-Making," *Foreign Affairs*, vol. 50, no. 2, pp. 223–236, January 1972. For an interesting account of the KGB in action, see "How Russia Spies: A New Game," *Newsweek*, Oct. 11, 1971, pp. 31–34.

[15]For Britain, see Max Beloff, *Foreign Policy and the Democratic Process*, The Johns Hopkins Press, Baltimore, 1955, pp. 62–95; and Leo D. Epstein, "British Foreign Policy," in Macridis, op. cit., pp. 29–61. For the United States, see John P. Leacacos, "Kissinger's Apparat," *Foreign Policy*, no. 5, pp. 3–27, Winter 1971–1972. For a critique of the NSC's alleged neglect of international economic policy, see Harold B. Malmgren, "Managing Economic Foreign Policy," *Foreign Policy*, no. 6, pp. 42–63, Spring 1972. For the thesis that an elite runs United States foreign policy, see Godfrey Hodgson, "The Establishment," *Foreign Policy*, no. 10, pp. 3–40, Spring 1973.

prime minister, the Cabinet, and the top officials of the Foreign Office, particularly the secretary of state for foreign affairs, whose professional "ghosts" are the two ministers of state for foreign affairs and the permanent undersecretary. Top-level policy decisions may be made by the prime minister himself, as Winston Churchill is said to have done at several of the Allied conferences held during World War II. More often these decisions are made as the result of Cabinet discussions, based upon special studies of specific issues made by Cabinet committees, and parliamentary debates. Having a unitary state with a cabinet form of government, backed by a parliamentary majority, the British are not hampered by the problems of separation and division of powers. The executive is in a strong position to make policy decisions and to provide dynamic leadership in foreign affairs. Several characteristics of the British system offer interesting contrasts with that employed in the United States. The personnel of the Foreign Office and diplomatic service are career officers who are relatively immune from partisan politics and political pressure; Parliament rarely "investigates" the Foreign Office for political purposes or attempts to change the course of policy. Moreover, the British public is better informed and more articulate in the realm of foreign affairs.

Foreign policy councils, staffs, or committees exist in all foreign-affairs ministries; however, the informal machinery for making policy is sometimes more important than official agencies. For example, the apparatus constructed by Henry Kissinger as national security adviser for President Nixon superseded the planning process in the Department of State. By 1971 Kissinger had practically institutionalized his advisory function with an organization of 120 persons, 42 of them professionals in the foreign policy field.

The planning agency included two tiers of five study committees each, one bank representing major geographic areas, each headed by an assistant secretary of state (Latin America, Europe, Africa, the Near East, Asia), and the other devoted to substantive policy matters (foreign-aid, trade, monetary, strategic, and military affairs). The topic committees were staffed by officials from the Departments of State, Defense, and the Treasury; the CIA; and other agencies.

The planning staff headed by Kissinger would order studies, critique results, and pass the position papers on to a review board, of which he was also chairman and to which representatives of the Joint Chiefs of Staff, the CIA, and the Departments of State and Defense were assigned. Recommendations were submitted to the National Security Council for consideration and ultimately provided the policy options upon which President Nixon's decisions were based. An undersecretary of state's committee, of which Dr. Kissinger was a member, supervised the implementation of the decision. In less than three years (January 1969 to October 1971) this "informal" planning process produced 138 study memorandums upon which 127 formal foreign policy decisions rested. Another body, the Washington Special Action Group (WSAG), handled sudden crises or emergencies in the national policy area. Members included the director of the CIA, the deputy defense secretary, the chairman of the Joint Chiefs of Staff, and the undersecretary of state for political affairs. Matters of concern to both groups included the Ussuri River crisis (1969), involving China and the Soviet Union; the Cuba–Soviet Union submarine crisis (1969); and the East Pakistan revolt (1971).

POLITICAL DYNAMICS AND FOREIGN POLICY

Foreign policy is not made in a vacuum, and policy planners usually operate within a frame of reference provided by past experience. New policy stems from traditions deeply embedded in a nation's history; it is an extension of past policy, projected in the light of recent experience. One of the most important elements in this process is the impact of public opinion as channeled through political parties and interest groups.[16]

---

[16]For the discussion of political parties and interest groups, the author has consulted Leon D. Epstein, "British Foreign Policy," in Macridis, op. cit., pp. 34–75; Karl W. Deutsch and Lewis J. Edinger, "Foreign Policy of the German Federal Republic," in Macridis, op. cit., pp. 119–173; Vernon V. Aspaturian, "Soviet Foreign Policy," in Macridis, op. cit., pp. 174–237; and Roy C. Macridis, "French Foreign Policy," in Macridis, op. cit., pp. 76–118. See also Lester W. Milbrath, "Interest Groups and Foreign Policy," in James N. Rosenau, *Domestic Sources of Foreign Policy,* The Free Press, New York, 1967, pp. 231–251; and Henry W. Ehrmann (ed.), *Interest Groups on Four Continents,* The University of Pittsburgh Press, Pittsburgh, 1958.

The Political Party

Studies have shown that the various national publics are not well informed about foreign policy. Whatever consensus exists is usually expressed in only the broadest of generalizations, such as "peace," "prosperity," and "survival." As extraconstitutional and nongovernmental agencies, political parties and interest groups are able to mobilize public opinion for or against specific courses of action or perhaps to exert pressure upon the foreign policy decision-making process. The techniques are different in an "open society," where free discussion of issues takes place, and in a "closed society," where compliance with a decision is dictated. The important consideration is that in both democracies and dictatorships, the leaders must ultimately have popular support, or their policies will fail.

In a totalitarian state a single party controls the government, selects its own members for office, harbors no competition, and severely limits public criticism. The government and political party hierarchies overlap. Official government policy is dictated by party policy, and foreign policy is not a debatable issue for the electorate. Hitler, Mussolini, Stalin, and (more recently) Mao Tse-tung, by an artful combination of oratory, ideological propaganda, and coercion, gained acceptance for their foreign policies with their respective publics.

Party systems in a democracy have the advantage of functioning in an environment in which a broad consensus in support of foreign policy already exists. In the British two-party system the electorate may influence foreign policy issues through the local constituency associations that select and campaign for their MP candidates and at the annual meeting of the party conference, where issues are debated. In spite of the agreement on fundamentals, extremists in both the Conservative and Labour parties engender a reexamination of means and ends of specific courses of action.

In Parliament, where party discipline is strong, the MP tends to follow the party line determined by the "establishment." Adversary relationships are formalized by paying Her Majesty's Loyal Opposition, with his "shadow government," to oppose the government and to assume control should the government resign.

Domestic issues have predominated in interparty debate since Britain's world commitments have diminished. Divisive issues of foreign policy in postwar years have included the gradual dismantlement of the Empire, the terms for adherence to the Atlantic Alliance and the Common Market, and the feasibility of developing an independent nuclear capability. Economic necessity as viewed by the establishment, rather than pressure from the party membership, ultimately resolved this issue in favor of the Atlantic Alliance and the Common Market associations and against a nuclear missile program.

In multiparty states requiring coalition governments, the formulation of foreign policy offers unique problems. Theoretically, it is the lack of consensus on basic issues in the electorate that authenticates the existence of a multiparty political system, which permits a variety of views to be brought to bear in the public-policy arena. Experience has demonstrated, however, that often those coalition governments which tend to be dominated by a single party are likely to pursue the most effective and coherent foreign policies. The Congress party in India, the Liberal Democratic party in Japan, and certainly the Popular Republican movement under General de Gaulle in France are examples. The exception would be the extreme instability of both the government and its foreign-affairs policy in Italy under the Christian Democratic party. If a single party dominates a coalition government, the serious debate on foreign policy revision may take place within the factions of that party. Nevertheless, the threat of a new election places at least psychological restrictions on the party in power.

In the United States it is customary for a party platform committee to hold hearings at which pressure groups and interested individuals can present their views. The platform committee, or the subcommittee delegated to consider these proposals, then makes recommendations, which are accepted by the full convention as part of the official party program. The candidates for office then take the "foreign policy plank" to the people during the campaign. In the heat of controversy, each candidate is on his own and may turn or twist the issues in any way necessary to ensure his election. This flexibility in interpreting the meaning of issues gives the isolationists and the internationalists an opportunity to make the maximum appeal to their local constituents and still retain the party label.

Occasionally some aspect of foreign policy becomes a principal issue in a campaign. In 1952 the Republican party charged that the State Department was "honeycombed with subversives, fellow travelers, and incompetents" and that the Democrats had "dropped the ball in Korea" and had "given China to the Communists." The Democratic arguments were more defensive in character, not so spectacular, and therefore not so effective. The situation was reversed in the 1960 campaign, when the Democrats charged the Eisenhower administration with laxity in the national defense effort, permitting a "missile gap" to develop between the Soviet Union and the United States. The nation was so deeply disturbed over continued participation in the Vietnamese war in 1968 and criticism of President Lyndon Johnson from both parties became so violent that he withdrew his candidacy for another term in office. The attack of the "out" party is always more violent and usually more irresponsible than any defense that can be marshaled by those in power. Once the circumstances are reversed, the erstwhile critics are sobered by the responsibilities of formulating and executing policy, as well as of fending off what to them suddenly becomes the "irresponsible attack" of the defeated party.

Party discipline in the United States Congress is notoriously weak. Members are permitted to represent their constituents as they see fit; Democrats tend to favor interventionism—e.g., Korea (the 1950s), Vietnam (the 1960s), and the Middle East (the 1970s)—while Republicans tend to disfavor foreign economic and military aid programs and overinvolvement in international organizations such as the League of Nations and the United Nations. In implementing the legislative committee system involved in the foreign policy process, both parties are prone to invoke the rubric of the "national interest" as a cloak for partisan policy positions.

In the face of crisis, however, it becomes necessary for the two parties to develop an area of agreement in order to support a national policy. At the end of World War II, the external threat of communism caused the Democratic administration in the United States to seek bipartisan support for its policy. Under the leadership of Senator Vandenberg, who asked that "partisan politics cease at the water's edge," the Republican party supported the aid-to-Europe and United Nations policies. In the competitive atmosphere of the party struggle, bipartisanship is not a normal mode of behavior; nevertheless, the ability of party leaders to adopt a common purpose in the national interest is a test of true statesmanship.

The Interest Groups

In a democracy, pressure groups are among the most influential of all extralegal agencies. The pivot of pressure-group activity is self-interest. Religious organizations seek protection for missionaries in foreign lands and are often active in pacifist movements. Business groups may sponsor a high-tariff program or insist upon protection for their foreign investments. Minority groups often attempt to shape government policy toward the land from which they emigrated. Sponsors of world government crusade against policies that tend to impede the attainment of their idealistic goal. Isolationists denounce the United Nations and foreign-aid programs. Group interests are part of the democratic process, which encourages individual and group initiative. Only by tapping the springs of public sentiment can the proper compromises be effected that will ultimately represent a truly national policy.

In all countries the basic objective of interest-group activity is the same: to reach and influence the decision-making agencies of the government toward predetermined goals. In a general sense the categories of interest groups tend to cluster around areas of public policy: the economic interests of business, labor, and agriculture and the consumer and the sociocultural interests of religion, minorities, patriotism, and so forth. There are many variables in a comparison of the roles of interest groups in influencing a state's foreign policy: the arrangement of governmental institutions, the relationship between political parties and the government, and the public's channels of access to the policy-making system are some examples.

West German citizens are granted the right to organize interest groups by the constitution. The pattern of organized interests is similar to that of other democracies: economic groups (employers, employees, farmers, artisans, and those in the professions), religious groups (Roman Catholic and

Protestant), and sociocultural groups (e.g., ethnic groups and veterans). German groups tend to be national in scope, thoroughly institutionalized, and highly disciplined. The interaction between parties and interest groups is close and relatively constant.

In Britain, the highly structured and disciplined party system presents a contrasting environment for interest-group activity. One of the most powerful groups, the trade unions, is closely affiliated with the Labour party, which attempts to implement its goals. Individual members of Parliament are permitted to serve as interest-group agents. Influential leaders of major organizations such as the churches speak out on foreign-affairs problems; other groups, such as the United Nations Association, adopt and promote issues. Finally, the party leaders and members of the British Cabinet often take the initiative in ascertaining the views of groups concerned with foreign policy.

As the prototype of a totalitarian state, the Soviet Union definitely presents a unique environment for pressure-group activity. The communist ideology rejects the concept of competing social classes, and the rivalry for political power must be conducted by factions within the integrated party-government system. One level of competition is that between major institutions of the closed Soviet society: the military (particularly the Army), the Communist party, and the government bureaucracy. Competition is also present among the managers of the various segments of the economy, such as heavy industry, light industry, and agriculture.

Examples of issues under contention within and between these groups that affect foreign policy are the extent to which the ideological goals of world revolution should be implemented and the allocation of economic resources between the various segments of the economy. The decision to produce "guns or butter" vitally affects the Soviet ambition for world recognition and is reflected in cold-war and détente foreign policies. The various interest groups within the system are represented in the party Central Committee and its Presidium, which selects the membership of the Politburo, as well as in government administrative agencies.

By means not altogether clear, the factional pressures generated within the system ultimately reach the decision-making stage in the Politburo. The leadership of this body is reflected, ex post facto, in the foreign policies of the Soviet Union. Despite his protestations favoring international revolution, Stalin's preoccupations were parochial: survival and the security of his satellite empire. Khrushchev's perspective was of global dimensions, but his ambitions overreached his resources, and his style was marked by meaningless braggadocio. Brezhnev parlayed nuclear equality with the United States into true world-power status for the Soviet Union. Each led his nation through the complex machinery of interest-group negotiations to reach the necessary consensus to support his decisions.

THE EXECUTION OF FOREIGN POLICY: INSTRUMENTS AND TACTICS

The capstone of the process of formulating policy is reaching a decision to adopt a course of action. The success achieved by implementing carefully designed plans is one important test of the efficacy of a nation's foreign policy. Where planning is part of the strategic approach to policy formulation, the execution of policy involves the skillful utilization of tactical instruments.

Any legal or extralegal agency or device used to attain policy goals may be classed as a policy instrument. The more widely employed instruments may be categorized as (1) political-legal, (2) economic-financial, (3) military, and (4) propagandistic-ideological.[17]

Political-legal instruments include the use of recognized channels of negotiation such as "good offices" (when one state offers to be the intermediary between two parties in dispute), adjudication (wherein a dispute is submitted to a judicial tribunal, with prior agreement by the contestants to abide by the decision), and de facto and de jure recognition of a newly constituted government. Others are the negotiation of a treaty, a declaration of neutrality, the delivery of a note to the head of a state expressing grave concern over some aspect of

[17] On instruments of policy, see Simonds and Emeny, op. cit., pp. 135–152; Norman D. Palmer and Howard C. Perkins, *International Relations*, Houghton Mifflin Company, Boston, 1953, pp. 155–303; and Charles W. Yost, "The Instruments of American Foreign Policy," *Foreign Affairs*, vol. 50, no.1, pp. 59–68, October 1971. On tactics, see Strausz-Hupé and Possony, op. cit., pp. 210–409; and Frederick L. Schuman, *International Politics*, 5th ed., McGraw-Hill Book Company, New York, 1973, pp. 519–550.

its policy, and the recall of an ambassador or other foreign diplomatic agent.

These legal instrumentalities assume political significance when applied to specific situations. President Wilson gave the Monroe Doctrine a unique interpretation by using the power of recognition in relations with Mexico. The large American investments south of the border made political stability desirable, and the United States developed a policy of not recognizing governments that came into being through military violence. By using the power of recognition, the President coerced the leaders of Mexico into establishing a governmental regime acceptable to this country.

Typical economic-financial instruments include the raising or lowering of tariff barriers or the use of blocked currency, cartels, barter, or the quota system for licensing imports and exports. Embargo and boycott methods were employed effectively as part of Hitler's economic program to establish national self-sufficiency. Direct governmental investment as an adjunct to political control was used by Britain in Middle Eastern oil resources and in the Suez Canal. In 1956 the United States' offer (later withdrawn) of a loan to help finance the Aswan Dam in Egypt provided another example of the use of financial instruments in the execution of foreign policy. Political loans were floated in France and Germany for investment in Russia, Italy, Turkey, and the Balkan countries in the latter part of the nineteenth century and the early part of the twentieth. Another favorite device is the employment of the most-favored-nation clause in commercial treaties. The trade-and-aid policy of the United States was vitally important in achieving the policy goal of reconstituting the economies of the Western European nations.

The world became accustomed to the military instruments of policy that were perfected in the period between the two world wars. The mere announcement of a plan to increase or decrease the size of any branch of the armed services may serve to implement policy. Other examples are the massing of troops on a frontier (as Hitler did while demanding the Sudetenland from Czechoslovakia), the terrorism of the concentration camp, mobilization, and pacific blockade. Before the United States entered World War II, it carried on a policy of militant neutrality with a submarine patrol against Germany in the Atlantic. A show of military strength, such as Britain staged in parading the Mediterranean fleet up and down the Bosporus at the close of World War I, is extremely effective. The engineering of a coup d'état, such as Russia perpetrated upon Czechoslovakia in 1948, is another method. The ultimate military instrument is war, which von Clausewitz called "politics continued by other means."

A final category includes those activities grouped under the general designation "propaganda." With the development of the means of mass communication through radio, the press, motion pictures, and television, the chief limitation on the utilization of propaganda to implement foreign policy would seem to be the ingenuity and resourcefulness of the propagandist. The propaganda instrument has a dual capacity in that it may be as important in rallying domestic support as in influencing the activities of other states.[18]

The main objectives of propaganda in international relations are the justification of a nation's program, the conciliation of friendly states, and the undermining of the position of unfriendly ones. The fundamental principle that is followed is that of dichotomy, namely, leaving the "propagandee" no choice but to favor the "white," "we," or "right" alternative over the "black," "they," or "wrong" side of an issue. The technique is rich in variation: starting false rumors, misrepresenting by skillful selection of facts, changing the semantic content of widely accepted words or ideas, and telling deliberate falsehoods, for example.

The art of propaganda knows no national boundaries and is accepted by the leaders of all states. Hitler was particularly skillful when it came to simplifying and repeating the ideas he wanted to hammer home. He attacked international finance, plutocracy, democracy, bolshevism, the Versailles Treaty, the Jewish people, peace, religion, and a series of personal devils including Churchill, Reynaud, Bevin, Stalin, and Roosevelt. He defended patriotism, duty, work, the leadership principle, *Lebensraum*, national socialism, the superiority of

---

[18]See the symposium in L. John Martin (ed.), "Propaganda in International Affairs," *The Annals of the American Academy of Political and Social Science*, vol. 398, November 1971; for dynamics in general, see Rosenau, op. cit. passim; and Kenneth N. Waltz, *Foreign Policy and Democratic Politics*, Little, Brown and Company, Boston, 1967.

the German "race," and personal heroes, beginning with himself as *der Führer* and including the other notorious proponent of fascism, Mussolini.

The Soviet government has added a new tactic to traditional Western concepts of diplomacy, dramatized by the word *nyet* ("no"). Soviet leaders foresee the inevitable triumph of communism over capitalism; therefore, the obstruction of Western diplomatic maneuvers is a primary objective of Soviet policy. Instead of viewing diplomatic negotiations as a search for areas of agreement through mutual concessions, the Russians too frequently use summit meetings, international conferences, or United Nations debates as forums for political propaganda, bluff, threats, and accusations. However, the limited ban on nuclear testing that was arrived at by treaty in 1963 indicates that when Soviet vital interests are involved, agreement is possible.

One of the most effective propaganda instruments of policy is a nation's ideology. An ideology includes a wide variety of accepted symbols that can be readily manipulated in defending or attacking policy issues. In the United States, democracy is symbolized by the Stars and Stripes, the Statue of Liberty, the blindfolded goddess holding the scales of justice, the American eagle, Uncle Sam, and the colors red, white, and blue. Verbal symbols lie in such phrases as "the American way of life," "due process of law," "in God we trust," "natural rights," "liberty under law," "majority rule," "the dignity of man," and "*e pluribus unum*." Representative Russian Communist symbols have included the hammer and sickle, Lenin's tomb, the color red, and the phrases "dictatorship of the proletariat," "class struggle," "capitalist-fascist," "economic determinism," "workers of the world, unite!" and "decadent capitalism." The struggle for power between the United States and the Soviet Union has often been referred to as a "battle of ideologies," and the issue described as the ultimate triumph of democracy or communism.

Although the fundamental goals of foreign policy remain relatively constant, the tactical employment of the instruments of policy depends upon specific situations that must be met. Tactical maneuvering must take place within the overall strategic plan, according to treaties and other international commitments made in pursuance of major policy objectives, and in the perspective of limitations imposed by the policies of other states immediately concerned. Within the realm of international politics, no situation remains constant. Therefore, the best program of action is one that is flexible enough to meet the dynamics of the international political environment.

Regardless of the accuracy with which an evaluation of any particular situation is made, not all the circumstances can be "cased." Thus any proposed line of action may be upset by the presence of unknown x, or imponderable, factors. To realize the uncertainty of the circumstances surrounding the execution of policy, it is necessary only to recall that Secretary of State Hull was negotiating with the Japanese emissaries while an enemy task force was on its way to Pearl Harbor.

In addition to the hazards of faulty planning, the execution of policy may be hampered by bad judgment, poor timing, uncertainty, vacillation, or inconsistency. France's indecision in the face of Britain's determination to reconstitute Germany as a continental power after World War I was signalized by Hitler's unchallenged march into the Rhineland in 1936. This was followed in 1938 by the abandonment of guarantees to Czechoslovakia at Munich, by the policy of appeasement, and finally by World War II.

The bulk of the tactical maneuvers constituting interstate negotiation may be grouped in three categories: affirmative action, negative action, and anticipatory action. An overt act that affirms a nation's position may be placed in the first category, and most negotiations between states are of this nature.

Any agreement not to exercise certain rights and prerogatives may be classed as a tactic of evasive or negative action. Great Britain and France refused to lead the Council of the League of Nations in using effective economic sanctions against Franco when he overturned the legally constituted government of Spain. Such restraint, however questionable in its effect on the ultimate development of a situation, is a consciously planned, carefully premeditated tactic.

Preventive tactics (with the notable exception of a preventive war) usually occur wholly within the scope of the domestic jurisdiction of a state and serve to implement policy through the interpretation and inference placed upon such behavior by foreign nations. Although Roosevelt initially refused to impose a legal embargo upon shipments to Japan, he did appeal to American manufacturers and shippers to observe a voluntary "moral embargo," which aimed to achieve the same results. Whereas negative action involves the decision not to act, even though legal authorization may be present, preventive action usually involves measures supplementary to, and less extensive than, the limits of legal authorization.

An analysis of the anatomy of foreign policy is an essential prerequisite to an understanding of the dynamics of international politics. The two succeeding chapters will trace the interrelationships of the policies of the major states and the perennial search for peace through international organization.

STUDY-GUIDE QUESTIONS

1 From one perspective a nation's foreign policy may be viewed as the product of its constitutional system. Compare the roles of the British Parliament and the United States Congress in making foreign policy.
2 The growth of a nation's population in relation to its available food resources has caused serious political problems in many states of the world. Discuss population as a factor conditioning the foreign policy of India.
3 The manner in which a nation's ideology affects its foreign policy is constantly in dispute. Explore the relationships between communism and Soviet foreign policy and democracy and the foreign policy of the United States.
4 Sound and effective foreign policy is based upon accurate information or "intelligence" reflecting the realities of world politics. Evaluate the sources of information available to a state in the formulation of its foreign policy and describe how this information is "fed" into the decision-making process.
5 What instruments of foreign policy would you consider using in a game of "power politics"? How? Why?
6 One of the most serious dilemmas of the twentieth century is the great disparity between nations in terms of natural and scientific resources. Can you propose an economic solution for this problem that would be politically acceptable to both "have" and "have-not" states?

REFERENCES

Appleton, Sheldon: *United States Foreign Policy,* Little, Brown and Company, Boston, 1968.
Art, Robert J., and Kenneth N. Waltz (eds.): *The Use of Force: International Politics and Foreign Policy,* Little, Brown and Company, Boston, 1971.
Brzezinski, Zbigniew K.: *Ideology and Power in Soviet Politics,* Frederick A. Praeger, Inc., New York, 1967.
Cohen, Bernard C.: *The Public's Impact on Foreign Policy,* Little, Brown and Company, Boston, 1973.
Deutsch, Karl: *The Analysis of International Relations,* Prentice-Hall, Inc., Englewood Cliffs, N.J., 1967.
Frankel, Joseph: *The Making of Foreign Policy,* 2d ed., Oxford University Press, London, 1968.
———: *National Interest,* Frederick A. Praeger, Inc., New York, 1970.
Hass, Ernst B., and Allan S. Whiting: *Dynamics of International Relations,* McGraw-Hill Book Company, New York, 1956.
Jervis, Robert: *The Logic of Images in International Relations,* Princeton University Press, Princeton, N.J., 1970.
Kahn, Herman, and B. Bruce-Briggs: *Things to Come: Thinking about the Seventies and Eighties,* The Macmillan Company, New York, 1972.
Macridis, Roy C.: *Foreign Policy in World Politics,* 3d ed., Prentice-Hall, Inc., Englewood Cliffs, N.J., 1967.
Morganthau, Hans J.: *Politics among Nations,* 5th ed., Alfred A. Knopf, Inc., New York, 1973.
Nicolson, Harold: *Diplomacy,* 3d ed., Oxford University Press, Fair Lawn, N.J., 1963.
Roberts, Geoffrey K.: *Political Parties and Pressure Groups in Britain,* St. Martin's Press, Inc., New York, 1972.
Rosenau, James N. (ed.): *Domestic Sources of Foreign Policy,* The Free Press, New York, 1967.
Tint, Herbert: *French Foreign Policy since the Second World War,* St. Martin's Press, Inc., New York, 1973.

Chapter 20

Relations between States: The International System

In the last chapter we reviewed the goals and objectives that nations seek in their relations with one another. Our concern was the means of assessment employed by a state in weighing the assets and liabilities that shape its foreign policy. The present chapter is devoted to a discussion of what happens when these various foreign policies meet in the international arena. Since the goals that nations seek are in many respects highly competitive or mutually exclusive, we can anticipate some measure of cooperation, but also a substantial amount of conflict, in interstate relations. A central theme is the politics of international relations, as contrasted with the administrative and legal procedures that states observe in dealing with one another. The following chapter, on international law, will examine the more formal customs, rules, regulations, and laws that regularize the relations between states.

The approach to interstate relations may be briefly stated. The opening discussion highlights some of the recent developments within the community of nations. Next, two contrasting interpretations of the present status of the international system are introduced: the traditional and the contemporary. Attention is then directed to models, or sets of assumptions, that may be utilized in the analysis of international politics: the widely accepted "power model" and the more recently developed counterpoint, the "interdependence model."

From this broad panorama of the field of international politics, the focus of attention is narrowed to a condensed review of the specific strategies and tactics that nations employ in their relations with one another. These categories range along a continuum of behavioral responses from the peaceful art of negotiation through diplomacy to varying degrees of coercion, which culminate occasionally in open warfare.

The field of international politics is examined again to ascertain whether from the welter of interstate transactions any patterns or designs emerge that might make international politics more meaningful. Four concepts are discussed: the balance of power, collective security, power polarization, and deterrence and détente. At this point the student should be forewarned that the concept of power is inextricably associated with the phenomena of international politics; it cannot be dealt with at one time and place and then dismissed. Therefore, although other interpretations of interstate relations are presented, certain facets of political power continue to emerge in various areas of this inquiry.

Finally, this discussion attains a sort of synthesis by incorporating what has gone before into a discussion of the foreign policies of the two most powerful states in the world today, the United States and the Soviet Union.

THE STATE SYSTEM

By the mid-1970s the nations of the world had reached a watershed in their relations with one another. For two decades post–World War II diplomacy had been conducted under the preponderant control of nuclear fusion by the United States. The third decade ushered in several profound changes in the environment of international politics. The Soviet Union attained parity with the United States in terms of ability to use nuclear missiles for military purposes; both states came to the realization that the use of nuclear weapons might destroy civilization as we know it; and the proliferation of nuclear technology to other states had become a reality.

Under the watchful electronic eyes of "close-look, search-and-find" reconnaissance satellites, in orbit twenty-four hours a day, the stockpiles of nuclear weapons of the two major powers maintained a precarious balance. In the meantime, Soviet-American diplomacy sought détente in strategic-arms-limitation treaties, mutually advantageous trade agreements, and the resolution of unresolved territorial problems in Europe and Asia. The "wild card" in the game of international power politics was the intention of the People's Republic of China, whose own stockpile of nuclear weapons would become a foreboding reality before the close of the decade.

Centuries of diplomacy have failed to eliminate war as an instrument of national policy. The aftershocks of the cataclysmic experience of World War II provided a wide variety of targets of opportunity for combat: invasions, such as the Soviet Union perpetrated upon Hungary (1956) and Czechoslovakia (1968); interventions comparable to those of the United States in Korea (1950) and Vietnam (1964 to 1973); civil wars such as the Biafrans waged unsuccessfully against Nigeria (1966) and Bangladesh waged triumphantly over Pakistan (1971); a succession of coups d'état in Greece (1967 and 1973) and Iraq (1963, 1968, and 1973); two actual mini-wars between the Arabs and the Israelis (1967 and 1973); and the continuing conflict along the Ussuri River boundary between the Soviets and the People's Republic of China.

The Community of States

Nevertheless, profound changes were taking place in the very nature of the nation-state system. One of the most important was the proliferation of new states; the size of the international community had doubled in the first half of the century. Of the 148 nation-states recognized as sovereign in the mid-1970s, 74 were relatively new. Of these, 38 were formerly members of the British Empire, 23 owed allegiance to France, and 13 gained freedom from other states: three from Belgium, two each from Japan and Italy, and one each from Australia, Denmark, New Zealand, Pakistan, Spain, and the United States (the Philippines).

The great preponderance of new states originated in Africa (thirty-seven) and Southeast Asia (eight); the rest were scattered from the Mediterranean to Oceania. Among the most important were the (East) German Democratic Republic in Europe, the Republic of India and the Islamic Republic of Pakistan in Asia, the United Arab Republic and the state of Israel in the Middle East, New Zealand in the South Pacific, and the African continental states of Algeria, Libya, and Morocco.

A variety of related causes may be cited for the burgeoning of new states upon the international scene. Population growth and technological change tend to exert pressures upon economic resources, resulting in the bursting of political boundaries. New hegemonies are designed, buffer states are created, former states simply disappear, and old scores of previous hot and cold wars are settled. Major colonial powers reluctantly dismiss their dependencies for the lack of sufficient economic strength to maintain military control over them. The presence of the United Nations on the scene offers a forum for voicing the aspirations of dependent peoples as well as the machinery for monitoring the legal ritual required for independent status. The growth and development of modern technology have greatly broadened the base for the economic infrastructure of neophyte states, providing the sinews for an independent existence.

These changes in the international community have somewhat altered the theoretical perspectives underlying the interpretation of its essential character.[1] The traditional view of the state system originated in the historical experiences of the development of the modern state in Western Europe and has been greatly influenced by the concepts of international law. It envisages the state in rather idealistic terms as a member of the society of states living in a well-ordered world under the aegis of widely accepted rules of international conduct.

The contemporary view of international society is more empirically oriented. Without denying the desirability of a law-ordered community, its advocates dwell upon the actual behavior of individual members of the community and discover many discrepancies between their findings and the prescriptions of the international legal code. These viewpoints will now be characterized more fully.

A Traditional View

The modern state system was born three centuries ago in Western Europe at about the time the treaty of Westphalia was being negotiated, ending the Thirty Years' War (1648). The early states were monarchies, with a king who exercised absolute power over the subjects living within his realm. England, France, Spain, and Italy were among the first members of the system, and they all possessed the requisites of the modern state.[2] Other early members included Switzerland, the Netherlands, Poland, Sweden, and Brandenburg, the forerunner of Prussia.

As the states developed relations with one another, customs, rules, and regulations were devised governing their behavior. Thus from historic experience supplemented by the learned commentary of legal scholars, the body of international law was born. Among the first of these renowned contributors, often termed the "father of international law," was Hugo Grotius of the Netherlands, who wrote the classic *On the Law of War and Peace* (1628). The code of conduct between nations dealt with such matters as the protocol of sending and receiving ambassadors, the legal test to determine the existence of a state, rules for waging war, the diplomacy of peace, the decisions of tribunals, and the conduct of international conferences.

During the eighteenth and nineteenth centuries, the European nations, particularly Great Britain, the Netherlands, France, Germany, and Portugal, built colonial empires spreading throughout the world. The small society of European states gradually expanded to include the new nations in Latin America, Africa, and Asia and became a world community. The practices governing the relations between them were regularized in established codes of international law.

The traditional and largely hypothetical view of the state in the international system may be summarized briefly here because concepts such as international law and sovereignty are dealt with fully in the succeeding chapter. The state is the unit in international politics. It possesses territory, population, government, and legal sovereignty. The characteristic of sovereignty implies that a state has complete control over its internal affairs and is independent from external interference. It is this

---

[1] For two basic approaches that a student may follow in the study of international relations and foreign policy, see Charles A. McClelland, "International Relations: Wisdom or Science?" in James N. Rosenau (ed.), *International Politics and Foreign Policy*, The Free Press, New York, 1969, pp. 3–5.

[2] For an excellent discussion of the origins of the modern state, see Heinz Lubasz, *The Development of the Modern State*, The Macmillan Company, New York, 1964.

aspect that distinguishes it from many other political entities such as colonies, protectorates, trusteeships, and territories, which are classed as dependencies. An independent state is therefore a person in international law, and it possesses rights and assumes duties and obligations toward other states. The chief business of international politics is conducted between sovereign, independent states.

The community of states is held together in part by law, custom, tradition, and precedent, which regularize interstate contact. A state enjoys the right of existence, including the right to take measures to ensure self-preservation; the right of independence; the right to property; and the rights to engage in commerce with other states, to receive and send ambassadors, to negotiate treaties, and (under certain limitations) to receive equality of treatment with other states. In return, the state assumes the responsibility of respecting the rights of other states and the duties attendant upon membership in the international community.

States may join the international system through the legal device of being officially received by member states. By this process of "recognition," other states accept a new member in two stages: a de facto stage and a de jure stage. Tentative, or de facto, recognition is granted when a government has established control within a country and appears able to pursue responsible domestic and foreign policies. Permanent, or de jure, recognition is bestowed upon a government, usually after a substantial trial period, when the continuation of the regime under new auspices seems reasonably assured. Political considerations are often the final determinants in the timing of recognition. On the other hand, states sometimes lose their international personality and leave the system by merging with other states or by failing to maintain their sovereign integrity.[3]

A Contemporary View

The theoretical model of an ideal state behaving according to the prescriptions of international law has never existed in actuality. The contemporary view of international relations does not deny the desirability of maintaining high principles to guide the conduct of states in their interrelations. The empirical approach to the study of international politics, however, insists upon a more searching and realistic description of the world community as it actually exists: Few states are sovereign, an even smaller number are independent, and the inequalities between them are striking and important.[4]

Fewer than a baker's dozen of the major states possess the economic resources, technical proficiency, industrial capacity, or military capability to meet the requirements of the traditional model of sovereign independence. A great number cannot consistently or effectively manage their internal political affairs or their foreign relations. The extent and degree of inequality between states are readily measured by a comparative study of size, population, natural resources, level of education, military hardware, gross national product, or standard of living.

The problem of reconciling the traditional and contemporary perspectives of the nature of the international community may be illustrated by describing one of its newest members. The Republic of Nauru, with a population of 7,500, gained its independence on January 31, 1968, after twenty-one years as a United Nations trust territory. This tiny speck of an island is 12 miles in circumference and 3½ miles wide and is surrounded by a coral reef. It is located just south of the equator and about 1,300 miles northeast of Australia. Its only economic resource is about 60 million tons of valuable phosphate deposits, which experts claim will be exhausted in twenty years. At present, its population enjoys one of the highest per capita incomes in the world. Nevertheless, Nauru does not meet the traditional requirements of statehood, nor do three-fourths of the nations that have received their independence in Asia, the Middle East, and Africa since World War II.

The contemporary view of international politics requires not only a redefinition of the nature of a state but also a reevaluation of the meaning of "international law." The code of conduct for the nation-states has not prevented civil wars, coups d'état, intervention, invasion, violation of treaties,

---

[3]For the traditional view of the state in international law, see Clyde Eagleton, *International Government*, The Ronald Press Company, New York, 1948.

[4]Note especially Hans Rothfels, "The Crisis of the Nation State," in Lubasz, op. cit., pp. 114–129; and John H. Herz, "The Rise and Demise of the Territorial State," in Lubasz, op. cit., pp. 130–151.

seizure of territory, disappearance of sovereign states from the political map, or two world wars within a generation. It is obvious that international law is not law in the conventional sense of an enforceable command issued by a superior to an inferior. No court may force a state to submit to litigation against its will or enforce a sanction without prior agreement of the parties to a suit. The lack of hard-and-fast, enforceable rules permits states to exploit a wide latitude of behavioral options in executing their foreign policies.[5]

TWO MODELS: POLITICAL POWER AND POLITICAL INTERDEPENDENCE

The phenomena of international politics may be analyzed from several different perspectives, two of which will be considered here: the model of "power politics" and the model of "mutual interdependence." For a generation of political scientists the model for analysis was that of the world envisaged as a cockpit, wherein nations were engaged in an eternal struggle for power. Certainly civil strife, revolutions, and war tend to dramatize the rivalries and hostilities in which states indulge and their unceasing efforts to "best" their neighbors. Survival has always been a fundamental, vital interest in international relations, and the power theory seemed ideally suited to explain the competitive relations states had with one another.

Political Power

The community of states rarely inhabits a quiescent environment. Economic, social, cultural, and political tensions of great force are always present, representing an inherent dynamism energizing the ebb and flow of pressures toward peaceful or hostile solutions to problems. The resolution of these pressures into purposeful action may be referred to as the "implementation of political power."

In international relations, *a state's power potential is its capacity to influence or control the behavior of other states for the purpose of promoting its own vital interests*.[6] Power capacity includes skill and technique in the use of consent and constraint, as well as the ability to persuade, threaten, or coerce, to gain ascendancy over another state or states. The situations in which power leverage may be exercised are virtually unlimited in number. There is a degree of power present in any interstate relationship that is imbued with political connotations.

States vary notably in power capacity, which is usually measured in terms of geographic location, manpower, resources, and technological skills or, more specifically, in terms of diplomatic skill, air forces, transportation facilities, food, hydrogen bombs, and quality of propaganda. Power capacities are entirely relative. Belgium and Switzerland are probably evenly matched, as are the United States and the Soviet Union; however, the mismatch between Belgium and the United States is apparent.

Each state has its own pattern of power relationships within the world pattern. Some states are characterized as "haves," and others as "have-nots." The former are well endowed with the assets of power, while the latter seek to better their position at the expense of the haves. This circumstance gives the struggle its essential character. Some states seek to maintain their power position and the elaborate apparatus that supports the status quo. Others, known as "revisionist" states, attempt to alter the network of international commitments in order to improve their power potential or to realize vital objectives.

The concept of power is one useful explanation of the behavior of a nation's leaders in attempting to plan and execute competitive foreign policies in international politics.

The Rationale for the Interdependent Model

Has the "cockpit theory" of international politics remained unchallenged? In the decade from the mid-1960s to the mid-1970s, a hypothesis has been advanced with a counterpoint to the power con-

---

[5] For the view that international law is changing in accommodation to changes in the state system, see William D. Coplin, "International Law and Assumptions about the State System," in Rosenau, op. cit., pp. 142–152.

[6] The concept of power is in contention. See Alan James, "Power Politics," in Bruce L. Sanders and Alan C. Durbin (eds.), *Contemporary International Politics*, John Wiley & Sons, Inc., New York, 1971, pp. 64–74; William G. Carleton, "Realism and World Politics," in Sanders and Durbin, op. cit., pp. 75–83; and K. J. Holsti, "The Concept of Power in the Study of International Relations," in Sanders and Durbin, op. cit., pp. 89–104.

cept. While conceding the inevitability of competition, greater emphasis is placed upon various aspects of the international environment causing the integration of the community of states.[7]

If the logic of events has compromised the stereotype of the independent sovereign state and revealed the tenuousness of international law, so the argument goes, it has also forced a reconsideration of the nature of the international community. The new frame of reference is the model of *interdependence*. From a small society of independent, self-sufficient European states, the international community has developed into a very large, interdependent, international system. The membership of political units has tripled in this century. The world's population of 3.71 billion (1971) will have doubled by the year 2006. The world's nation-states are heavily interdependent in terms of their need for natural resources, which are unevenly distributed: gold in Africa, oil in the Middle East, titanium in Oceania, tin in South America, and technological expertise in the United States, for example. Nations with the largest populations—China, India, and the Soviet Union—must import grain, while the underendowed developing nations, with two-thirds of the world's population, need all the products that the industrialized nations produce.

The mid-twentieth-century world has become more closely knit. Transnational and cross-national reciprocal needs have greatly multiplied the number of transactions between states. Modern communications systems have accelerated the frequency of these contacts.

All nations are attempting to survive. They all have different endowments and capabilities, and no state is self-sufficient. Trade and aid by negotiation and the sharing of resources are the only means by which most of the nation-states can prosper, and a high standard of living is the ultimate objective of all foreign policy. Therefore, mutual recognition by all states of one another's needs and interests provides the only rational terms upon which international politics should be conducted.

The interdependence model copes with war by alleging that historically, war is the exception rather than the rule in the relations between states. Moreover, the monopoly of nuclear fusion has placed the ballistic-missile weapon beyond the reach of all but a few. Recent events have proved that even the Great Powers may not be able to wage conventional war successfully. The United States, for example, was relatively unsuccessful in waging guerrilla war in Vietnam for a variety of reasons: The American military, unfamiliar with guerrilla warfare, was unable to fight the war under constraints imposed by government policy; the impact upon the domestic economy was disastrous; and public opinion at home forced a president to decline to run for office again, while opinion abroad subjected the nation to unprecedented vilification. Moreover, the Nuremberg trials, condemning the leaders of Germany for having committed crimes against humanity during World War II, placed an important new deterrent upon waging unrestricted warfare. In other words, circumstances apart from sheer military strength mitigate the effectiveness of war as an instrument of national policy.

How then do the myths of international law survive the realities of international politics? Proponents of the interdependence model would maintain that most of the transactions between states are in fact negotiated agreements in a peaceful environment. Nations tend to behave habitually according to established custom and tradition. The expectations of world public opinion are that nations will respect one another's rights and that violators may anticipate the sanction of widespread disapproval. By general consensus, nations that are unequal in fact may be treated as equals in international practice. Skillful diplomacy or the threat of a cold war may mitigate the impact of serious disagreements.

Neither the power model nor the interdependence model, when applied to the phenomena of international politics, rejects the concept of interstate competition; however, the terms of the struggle and the ultimate consequences are viewed quite differently.

At the beginning of this discussion of the relations between states, a brief presentation was made of some basic characteristics of the international system. Some of the assumptions underlying the nature of international relations were then stated: the traditional perspective of a community based

---

[7]This section presents only the suggestion that a model could be constructed from the critical literature as a counterpoint to the power thesis. See Seyom Brown, *New Forces in World Politics*, The Brookings Institution, Washington, 1974.

upon sovereign states behaving under the mandate of international law and a contemporary interpretation founded upon a more pragmatic evaluation of the political considerations that motivate interstate relationships. Two models, or sets of assumptions, by which international politics may be assayed were also identified: the power model and the interdependence model.

Our attention is now directed away from these broader generalizations about the international community and toward a closer view of the strategy and tactics employed by states in their dealings with one another. The mode of interaction between states ranges from diplomacy through various stages of coercion to war.

STRATEGY AND TACTICS IN INTERNATIONAL POLITICS

The behavior of states toward one another is sometimes tranquil and often stormy. Internal tensions and external pressures require diplomacy, negotiations effecting agreements, or even understandings to disagree. States maneuver within the international society to attain status, prestige, and security. They often prosecute foreign policy along the classic actions of warfare: surprising the enemy, feinting him out of position, penetrating or encircling his defenses, and destroying his capacity to resist.[8]

The strategy of international politics is usually planned with considerable care. Three strategic plans of action, for example, are *isolation, neutrality,* and *aggression*. A nation may be the manipulator or the pawn in the execution of a policy of political isolation. As the pawn, it discovers that other states have, by treaty agreement between themselves, excluded it from existing alliances. This situation sometimes develops when states are being "punished," as when Germany and Russia were excluded from the League of Nations and when the People's Republic of China was barred from the United Nations. Occasionally, jealousy among the Great Powers will preserve the independence and isolation of a minor country; such was the fate of Abyssinia early in the twentieth century. Japan and China premeditatedly followed a policy of political isolation from Western Europe during most of the nineteenth century. The United States maintained a policy of avoiding entangling alliances well into the twentieth century.

Switzerland is probably the best-known professional neutral in modern political history. Ease of defense, due to natural barriers (no longer so formidable), and a stouthearted determination to resist have been great assets in maintaining this status. During World War II, Switzerland served as a diplomatic listening post for all belligerents and as a Red Cross administration center, thereby proving of greater value to both sides of the conflict as a neutral than as a belligerent.

In the postwar period Jawaharlal Nehru of India served as a self-appointed spokesman for a policy of neutrality for a large bloc of newly created Asian and African states. The policy of noncommitment to either Eastern or Western blocs elicited substantial favors from each without incurring reciprocal obligations.

The strategy of aggression in international politics was clearly illustrated in the events that led to World War II. The Japanese spoke of a new order in greater Eastern Asia; the Germans, of *Lebensraum;* the Italians, of *Italia Irredenta;* and the Russians, of the international communist revolution. Hitler's invasion of Poland in September 1939 and the Japanese attack on Pearl Harbor in December 1941 represented merely the culmination of years of preparatory work to accomplish a grand design of conquest. Planned aggression may be conducted by diplomacy, by coercive acts short of war (sometimes labeled "cold-war tactics"), and by the actual conduct of hostilities with either conventional or nuclear weapons. It is a strategy requiring great resources and involving calculated risks, and it may eventually destroy its creators.

There is great variety in the methods used in the implementation of policy. Some of the more important are political warfare, underground activity, psychological and ideological techniques, and cultural instruments such as education, technology, and science.

Intervention is one of the more commonly employed tactics of political warfare. A fundamental goal of a state is to choose its own form of

---

[8]For the topics in this section, see Robert Strausz-Hupé and Stefan T. Possony, *International Relations*, 2d ed., McGraw-Hill Book Company, New York, 1954, pp. 210–271; and Thorsten V. Kalijarvi (ed.), *Modern World Politics*, 3d ed., Thomas Y. Crowell Company, New York, 1953, chaps. 17, 25.

government. This objective is disregarded when one state interferes in the domestic affairs of another. Frequently cited justifications for this behavior are the protection of nationals, the repression of rebellion, the forestalling of military aggression, or the tipping of the balance in a contest in favor of a satellite. The Soviet government constantly intervened in the affairs of the Central European states after World War II in order to maintain communist elements in power. A particularly brutal example, which invoked the censure of the United Nations, was the slaughter of rebellious Hungarians by tanks in 1956, followed by the establishment of a new puppet government. The United States has a long record of intervention in Latin-American states, particularly at the turn of this century. The instrument of *nonintervention* can be equally effective. There is little question that the United States and the Western powers greatly aided the cause of Franco against the republican government of Spain by following a policy of nonintervention at the very time when Hitler, Mussolini, and Stalin were executing an interventionist policy.

Other illustrations of the techniques of hot and cold warfare include *appeasement, compromise,* and *defensive* or *preventive* war. Appeasement is essentially the granting of concessions, either willingly or as a result of coercion, in order to effect a settlement of a dispute between states. One of the most spectacular examples in modern times was the Munich agreement of 1938. At that time, Britain and France acquiesced in German acquisition of the Sudetenland from Czechoslovakia in order to gain time to prepare for war. On the other hand, compromise as a device of statecraft can often allay tensions that might otherwise lead to war. The logic supporting a preventive war is to strike an enemy before he is ready for offensive action. It is indeed a dangerous maneuver, more adaptable to dictatorial than to democratic diplomacy. The German attack on Russia in 1941 may be placed in this category. Hitler apparently feared that the Soviet Union would steal the fruits of victory if permitted to prepare properly for war with Germany. There has been loose talk in the United States proposing a preventive war against Russia. From the standpoint of power politics, only the certain knowledge that the war could be won would possibly justify any such decision. Viewed in strictly moral terms, such a war would precipitate a profound discussion over ends and means in international diplomacy.

Underground activity has been characteristic of diplomacy throughout the centuries. In recent years secret movements, espionage, sabotage, treachery, subversion, and guerrilla warfare have been developed to a high degree of proficiency.

All the major states operate *intelligence systems* that gather, classify, and evaluate data relating to the plans, capabilities, and behavior of actual and potential enemies. *Espionage* is a vital adjunct to the military and political decision-making process. In April 1961 an attempted invasion of Cuba by anti-Castro exiles failed miserably because of faulty intelligence estimates of Castro's air strength and the capability of insurrectionist leadership within Cuba.

Subversion involves the infiltration of the political processes of a state in order to paralyze its operation and to undermine the loyalty of its citizenry. The Norwegian traitor Quisling prepared the way for the German invasion of his country in 1940. Soviet agents in Czechoslovakia and Poland helped to deliver these governments to the Soviet Union. Communists in the United States have made persistent efforts to interfere with the making and execution of foreign and domestic policy. The term "fifth column" was coined during the Spanish Civil War to refer to the rebels inside the city of Madrid who were to rise up to aid the four Franco columns besieging it.

Guerrilla warfare involves small-scale military operations within enemy territory. The Russians have been particularly successful with this device, setting up temporary puppet communist governments both in northern Greece and in the province of Azerbaijan in Iran shortly after World War II. Guerrilla activity employs terrorism and sabotage to support revolutionary activity against an established government. In 1961 the United States committed military forces to combat Communist-supported, North Vietnam–led efforts to subvert the Kingdom of Laos and to force a capitulation of the Republic of Vietnam by guerrilla warfare.

Direct action of this character can be anticipated and materially supported by effective propaganda and ideological warfare. *A political ideology is a system of ideas purportedly characterizing the nature of the state and the relationship between its government and its citizens.* Such an ideology embraces a set of political, economic, social, cultural, and moral values. Four of the most dynamic ideologies of the twentieth century are communism, fascism, national socialism, and democracy. Several of the newly independent states are formulating ideologies that fit into *none* of these categories. Ideologies reflect varying moral, ethical, and pragmatic standards of behavior, as well as contrasting value patterns. They are often incompatible with one another when they form the basis for political action. This conflict in the value systems subscribed to by different nations causes tensions that frequently lead either to a war of ideas or to actual belligerency. Former Premier Nikita Khrushchev's boast, "We will bury you," epitomized his belief in the superiority of communism over capitalistic democracy.

The doctrine of the sovereign, independent nation-state is supported by the sentiment of *patriotism.* The slogan "My country, right or wrong" symbolizes the importance of the emotions of the people. The struggle for men's minds becomes psychological warfare, and the chief instruments employed are propaganda techniques. The contest between the Soviet Union and the United States over vital interests is often cited as the struggle between communism and democracy.

PATTERNS IN INTERNATIONAL POLITICS

Scholars have long sought to discover recurring patterns in the manner in which states respond to one another in the international political arena. To personalize the concept of a state for a moment, do states display predictable patterns of behavior in their relations with one another? If so, how are these designs established, maintained, or broken up? The following theories seeking to explain various configurations of states in international politics will be presented: the balance-of-power theory, the collective-security theory, the power-polarization theory, and theories of deterrence and détente. A word of explanation regarding these theories: The concept of power, introduced earlier in this discussion, will be treated again, but from a somewhat different perspective. The League of Nations and the United Nations, which are discussed in the next chapter as prime examples of international organizations, will be dealt with here in terms of their respective *political roles* in international relations.

The profile of a power pattern is determined by the extent of distribution and the degree of monopoly of political power within the state system. In an international situation it is assumed that a multiplicity of independent states share the available power in varying degrees, that the power potential of some states is greater than that of others, that all states wish to exercise the maximum power of which they are capable, and that the goals of power are competitively sought by all. It is further assumed that the distribution of power in any one period in history is such that some sort of temporary equilibrium is established. It is impossible to predict the nature or duration of such periods of stability because change is an immutable law of the universe and opposing foreign policies constantly seek either to freeze the status quo or to aggressively modify the existing distribution of power.[9]

The Balance-of-Power Theory

The balance-of-power theory concerns a pattern of interstate relationships closely identified with the politics of Western Europe, particularly in the last century. Central to the concept is the assumption that political equilibrium in a group of states may be maintained if power is distributed among them in such a fashion that no single state or combination of states may gain permanent ascendancy over the rest and in such a way that each may preserve its independence.

One of the able expositors of the patterns that tend to establish such a balance is Hans J. Morganthau. In his *Politics among Nations,*[10] Morganthau stipulates that the two characteristics of international society that invoke a power balance are the multiplicity of states and the antagonisms they harbor toward one another. As states struggle to attain their ambitions, their policies conflict. Their relationships tend to fall into a basic pattern

---

[9] For a uniquely valuable discussion of alternative patterns, see Morton A. Kaplan, "Variants on Six Models of the International System," in Rosenau, op. cit., pp. 291–314.

[10] For the balance-of-power theory presented here, see Hans J. Morganthau, *Politics among Nations,* 5th ed., Alfred A. Knopf, Inc., New York, 1972, pp. 172–221. For a sophisticated discussion of theories of balance and imbalance by Kenneth N. Waltz, Karl W. Deutsch, J. David Singer, Richard N. Rosecrance, and Oran R. Young, see Rosenau, op. cit., pp. 304–345.

of either direct opposition or competition. In the first instance, two states of approximately equal strength stand opposed to each other. State A faces state B with the intent of issuing demands to be met, possibly accompanied by threats of reprisal in the event of noncompliance. State B may respond in several ways: retaliate with reciprocal demands upon state A, attempt to maintain the status quo in their relationships, or increase its own power capacity to cope more effectively with its opponent. It is a situation wherein one state desires to dominate another, and the intended victim resists; thus a precarious balance of power exists between them that is vulnerable to alteration by the turn of events.

A variation of the direct-balance pattern involving the same principle would array state A—the United States, for instance—and its allies against state B, the Soviet Union, and its satellites. Because of the numbers of states on both sides, such an arrangement is more difficult to sustain. Each of the principal states is involved with negotiations with its own affiliates and possibly with its opponent's associates, as well as with the opponent itself.

Morganthau suggests a second pattern of balanced power, the "pattern of competition." Here a third state, state C, is introduced into the relationship, and states A and B may assume several alternative policies with respect to it. Both may strike a balance by agreeing to support the continued independence of state C. Either might form a liaison with the third power as an ally against the other. As another among a wide variety of competitive arrangements to keep the peace, state C, the newcomer to the triumvirate, might be larger than the other two, in which case it holds the balance of power over both.

A more conventional pattern would include a number of states of approximately equal strength maintaining a power balance among themselves. Prompted by complex motives and using an intricate network of commitments and alliances, they check any one or two of their number who adopt aggressive policies, thus upsetting the equilibrium.

The history of European diplomacy during the nineteenth century offers many illustrations of attempts to implement the balance-of-power theory. A classic example is the pattern of British foreign policy. Britain checked the military might of France when Napoleon Bonaparte was crushed at Waterloo. It appeared that the Congress of Vienna, which followed in 1815, had successfully suppressed popular uprisings engendered by the spirit of nationalism. The power relationships that were established supported the status quo and were based upon the principle of political absolutism.

The balance-of-power theory is undoubtedly useful as a partial explanation of the dynamics of international politics; nevertheless, it is vulnerable to attack on several fronts. It is virtually impossible to estimate accurately the power potential of a state or alliance of states. If a true balance does exist, why is history so rich in illustrations of the imbalance caused by war, the search for equilibrium, and the temporary creation of a new balance, which is again destroyed by war?

It would seem that a principal objective of foreign policy is to attain a position of superiority wherein a monopoly, not a balance, of power prevails and then to freeze the status quo, leaving other states in a position of permanent inferiority. The chronic insecurity of a contender for power in the state system today invalidates the utility of a policy of true balance within a stable international environment. In fact, a policy of stability has too many limitations to be useful to a state that is not in a secure or ascendant position. For such a state the only validity of the idea is the temporary gain to be derived in diplomacy from the illusion that balance exists at all.

The traditional theory is also vulnerable today because of the greatly limited scope of technical implementation available to those who would establish or maintain a balance. In this highly integrated world, a state cannot with any degree of assurance fight a localized war, defeat a contender for power, and then gain a voluntary ally to add to the balance. The risk of general war is very great, as illustrated by the confrontation behind the scenes of the United States and the Soviet Union, supporting the respective claims of Israel and Egypt in 1973. Moreover, it becomes progressively more difficult to change sides in a bipolarized world once a commitment is made.

The Collective-Security Theory

During the past few years, the principle of the balance of power has been closely associated with another aspect of the pattern of international politics, known as "collective security." The concept of collective security carries a strong appeal for those who abhor the thought of a group of states struggling to establish a preeminent position over one another at the expense of international morality, ethics, and law. The principle of collective security is to establish mutual responsibility and to pool the resources of the several states in an effort to keep the peace. Thus the maintenance of the status quo becomes a community project instead of a unilateral or bilateral plan of action.

The practice of collective security requires all nations to join one universal alliance instead of two or more balancing alliances. When associated in this manner, each nation adjusts its individual interests in favor of the group interest. When power is shared in an all-for-one and one-for-all alliance, the military and diplomatic resources of the entrire group may be activated to police a misbehaving aggressor.

The League of Nations Two structures to embody the principle of collective security have been fashioned with great care in this century: the League of Nations, in 1920, and the United Nations, in 1945. The apparatus for implementing the policies of these institutions has been elaborately and ingeniously devised: disarmament, economic sanctions, an international police force (not, however, under the League), judicial settlement of disputes, and the invocation and focusing of world public opinion upon recalcitrants.

Unfortunately, the League was handicapped by some of the same procedural problems that later troubled the United Nations. The Council was primarily a meeting of sovereign states, which could not be bound without their consent. On all important questions, particularly those involving concerted action in the application of sanctions, the decision had to be reached by unanimous agreement. It was virtually impossible to achieve unanimity upon critical questions among major powers that were actually following conflicting foreign policies outside the League framework.

The League was born of the Treaty of Versailles, which attempted to freeze the status quo of the pattern of power prevailing at the close of World War I. Why did the League of Nations fail as an instrument of collective security? The explanations are many, varied, and sometimes complex. It may be argued, for example, that the nations of the world were not spiritually, socially, economically, or politically prepared to assume the obligations of international cooperation set forth in the League Covenant. Whether this is wholly true or not, certain prevailing conditions and circumstances militated against such cooperation. The United States refused to join. Powerful states such as Germany, Japan, and the Soviet Union remained (or were kept) outside the framework of the League at the start. However, they were not to be denied the opportunity to achieve status among the nations of the world, with or without League membership. Moreover, the spirit of nationalism and self-determination was strong in the hearts and minds of dependent peoples in Africa, Asia, India, and other parts of the world. To them, the mandate system seemed a poor substitute indeed for the freedom of independence. The League Covenant contained important structural and procedural defects. Its provisions were particularly ambiguous in respect to the vital consideration of outlawing war as an instrument of national policy. Finally, the major powers within the League continued to pursue nationalistic policies both inside and outside the League framework. Plans for collective security rapidly degenerated into the gradual restoration of the balance-of-power system, supported by new alliances.

The United Nations Within twenty years after the signature of the Treaty of Versailles, the world was plunged into a second total war. The United States, France, and Great Britain among the Great Powers faced an alliance of Germany, Italy, and Japan. The Soviet Union joined the Allied nations after a brief association with the Axis states. The war disrupted the old status quo, as the have-not, or *revisionist*, nations made an unsuccessful bid for a new world balance of power.

Inspired by a great victory and motivated by promises made in several declarations during the war, fifty states signed the United Nations Charter on June 26, 1945, in San Francisco. The noble sentiments expressed in the introductory paragraphs of the Charter once again invoked the principle of international cooperation to keep the peace. Building upon the experience of the League of Nations, a concerted effort was made to construct a durable and practical organization to withstand the stresses and strains of international politics leading to breaches of the peace and eventual war. Subsequent events have proved that the machinery of the Security Council, the General Assembly, and the International Court of Justice is adequate but that the spirit of the member nations for its proper operation is lacking.

During the first three decades of its existence, the United Nations has sought to create a role for itself in the realm of international politics. The assumption that the Grand Alliance that won the war would continue to cooperate in harmony during the ensuing peace quickly became an illusion. The economic collapse of Germany, Japan, Britain, France, and Italy in the aftermath of the war toppled these states from the category of Great Powers, revealing the stark two-power rivalry of the United States and the Soviet Union. The ensuing struggle for world influence called the "cold war" demonstrated conclusively that the United Nations could not perform its ideal function of taking custody of the security interests of all nation-states, particularly the Great Powers, by keeping the peace.

Each major state pursued its vital interests, primarily outside the framework of that body, unwilling to permit the 130-odd members to censure its behavior. Members of the Security Council exercised the veto to prevent interference with program and policy objectives; other tactics included refusal to assume assigned financial obligations for United Nations projects, obstructionist procedural maneuvers, noncompliance with adopted policies, and economic and military intervention in the affairs of other states, contrary to the spirit of the Charter.

There are a number of reasons why the United Nations has not lived up to the optimistic expectations of its devoted supporters. It is not an international government, and its members have been reluctant to accept group decisions that placed limitations on their sovereignty or freedom of action. Before the Security Council can act decisively in substantive matters involving the use of sanctions and military force, the Charter requires unanimity among its principal members. This right to veto a course of collective action was the price paid by the founders to gain the support of the Big Five powers in accepting the Charter at San Francisco. Moreover, as the number of members in the Assembly increases, it becomes progressively more difficult to achieve a working majority to endorse controversial policies and to sort out the wide variety of conflicting interests. Thus solutions to the most urgent problems facing the international community, such as control of nuclear fusion and the formation of a viable international police force, are stalemated by lack of unanimity among the Great Powers. The situation invites political gamesmanship with the United Nations machinery. The Russians have played both with the veto power and with voting blocs among the lesser states in order to support or thwart a course of action. The most serious manifestation of this phenomenon was the interjection of the cold-war antagonisms of the United States and the Soviet Union into every phase of the work of the United Nations for the first decade of its existence. Since each power was prosecuting unilateral and conflicting policies based upon miscalculations of the other's intent, the basic mission of the United Nations was sacrificed on the altar of cold-war politics.

Since the United Nations has been unable to implement the principle of collective security, what have been its accomplishments? It has established a "political presence" for the world community. The mighty and the mini-states, the entire membership of the international universe, may sit together, exchange views, evaluate one another's motives, and seek solutions to problems compatible with their diverse interests.[11]

World public opinion has been mobilized from time to time, and history has been recorded through investigative reporting by observer teams of breaches of the peace. Examples include exposure of Communist guerrilla activity in northern Greece (1946–1948); the dispute over Palestinian independence between the Jews, Arabs, and British (1947–1949); the Indian-Pakistani quarrel over Kashmir (1948–1966); and the Hungarian revolt against the Soviet Union (1956).

---

[11]For the position that the United Nations has indeed assumed a specialized role in international politics, see Inis L. Claude, Jr., *The Changing United Nations*, Random House, Inc., New York, 1966; for this discussion, see also Leland M. Goodrich, *The United Nations*, Thomas Y. Crowell Company, New York, 1959; and Morganthau, op. cit.

Lacking an international army able to keep the peace, the United Nations has employed token military and paramilitary forces to "show the flag" when less powerful states skirmished with one another or the tensions of nationalism in the emerging nations exploded into civil war. An example of the former approach was the United Nations presence in the Israeli-Egyptian-French and British dispute over the Suez Canal (1956) and the aftermath of the Israeli-Egyptian-Syrian eighteen-day war in the Sinai (1973–1974); the latter was illustrated by the Katanga uprising against the newly formed Congolese government (1960). The most portentous single military engagement involving entry into the war between North and South Korea in 1950 was made possible because of the boycott of the Security Council by Russia and the willingness of the United States to provide the necessary troops and logistic requirements and funds. These circumstances were fortuitous and are unlikely to occur again.

The Power-Polarization Theory

In the past decade political scientists have sought more sophisticated explanations for the alignment and realignment of states in the international system while seeking accommodation to changing circumstances. Empiricists among them have constructed several theoretical models of power distribution in international politics based upon the polarization of power, two of which are the bipolar and multipolar patterns.[12]

In the aftermath of World War II, Britain, France, Italy, Germany, and Japan were temporarily eliminated as major factors in the power system. They were obliged either to assume the role of satellites or to seek neutral status. Thus the new pattern presented a unique design of bipolarization. The United States and Russia emerged as the major contenders. Each assembled satellites, the world was divided into two vast armed camps, and a new balance appeared. Diplomacy of the 1950s was dominated by a series of confrontations by these two hostile power blocs. Among the more significant issues were the Iranian controversy (1946), the launching of the Marshall Plan (1947), Communist seizure of Czechoslovakia (1948), the Berlin blockade (1948), the NATO pact (1949), the Korean war (1950), Soviet intervention in Hungary (1956), the Quemoy-Matsu incidents (1958), French defeat in Indochina (1954), the Suez attack (1956), the U-2 incident (1960), the Bay of Pigs invasion (1961), and the presence of Soviet missiles in Cuba (1962).

Intensive study and analysis have been made regarding the nature of the coalition welding each group together, the internal and external decision-making processes, the character of transactions between them, the degree of integration and separatism of each coalition at a point in time, the accommodations made to the strategic goals of each, the perception of the adversary's goals, and the varying degrees of tension and hostility that pervaded the relationship.

The era of the 1960s witnessed a change in the distribution of power in international politics when the Western European states, along with the People's Republic of China and Japan, shed their status as satellites and demanded full partnership with the coalition leaders. Moreover, India, Yugoslavia, and other neutral or uncommitted nations joined the developing Southeast Asian and African states in making their wishes known. The new power configuration has been termed a "multipolar system" inasmuch as at least a half dozen states were able effectively to influence the decisions of the two leaders in nuclear warfare.

Theories of Deterrence and Détente

Closely associated with the theory of the polarization of power are the two strategies of deterrence and détente utilized in its implementation.[13] In international politics a policy of deterrence aims to contain the aggressive behavior of a state through fear of retaliation. The concept is at least as old as the relations between the ancient Greek city-states, but it gains relevance today as a military doctrine designed to restrain the use of nuclear fusion for military purposes. After 1945, while the United States enjoyed ascendancy over the Russians in nuclear weaponry, deterrence became the shield by which NATO protected Western Europe. It was the American stockpile of nuclear bombs that gave

---

[12]See Kaplan, op. cit., particularly pp. 296–300.

[13]For the concept of deterrence, see Bruce M. Russett, "The Calculus of Deterrence," in Rosenau, op. cit., pp. 350–368; for détente, see Richard N. Rosecrance, "Bipolarity, Multipolarity and the Future," in Rosenau, op. cit., pp. 325–335.

Secretary of State John Foster Dulles the confidence to speak of going to the "brink of war" with the communist states and of "massive retaliation" in case of Soviet aggression.

A policy of deterrence has serious weaknesses, centered about the credibility of the party threatening to use force; the accuracy of the victim's evaluation of such a threat; the questions of how serious an incident would invite retaliation and of whether the fear of retaliation can be sustained indefinitely; and, most importantly, the miscalculation of either side of the other's motives, which would lead to probable mutual destruction with nuclear missiles.

Détente is a policy for the mutual accommodation of the separate interests of two or more contesting parties leading to the relaxation of tensions between them and the probable avoidance of crises. In international politics when the distribution of power becomes highly polarized, the strategy of détente assumes major significance in the avoidance of war. It implies nonintervention in the internal affairs of the parties, a recognition of established hegemonies, restraint in dealing with intrusions into each other's external affairs, and, in the case of the United States vis-à-vis the Soviet Union, a mutual effort to control nuclear armaments.

These four interpretations of international political patterns conclude our discussion of the various approaches to, and modes of analysis of, international politics. We now turn to a more specific presentation of the dynamics of the international scene with a discussion of the foreign policies of the two great nations who together dominate the mid-twentieth-century universe, the Soviet Union and the United States.

SOVIET FOREIGN POLICY

In the early days of the communist movement, the grand design of Soviet policy was to expand the power of the Soviet Union from the heartland of Eurasia to encompass the world. Ideologically, the communist viewed the world from a perspective of two great warring socioeconomic systems, only one of which would survive. It was assumed, at least in the Communist party dogma, that in this struggle international communism would prevail over the capitalist societies. This destiny bestowed upon the Soviet Union the mission of leading an international conspiracy for world revolution.

In three decades of post–World War II diplomacy, the Soviets have been unable to attain these ideological goals. Their leaders have been forced to alter their priorities to meet the more conventional and realistic objectives of foreign policy: internal and external security for the communist regime, a sound and prosperous economy, great-nation stature, and the military power and prestige to conduct diplomacy on a global scale. Thus the Soviet Union's relationships with the communist community that it purports to lead, as well as its policies toward the rest of the world, have changed.[14]

The three dominant personalities who shaped Soviet policy during this period were Joseph Stalin, who led Russia through the postwar period until his death in March 1953; Nikita Khrushchev, elected premier in March 1958 and deposed in October 1964; and Leonid Brezhnev, chosen first secretary of the Communist party on October 15, 1964. They dealt with several groups of problems that constitute recurring themes of Soviet foreign policy. The first was the status of the communist regime, its legitimacy, its capacity for leadership, and particularly its interpretation of the ideological mission of communism. Another was the changing nature of the relationships between the Soviet Union and the other satellite and nonsatellite communist states. The last of these concerned the Soviet posture toward the noncommunist world. The policies of cooperation and conflict that they pursued resulted in the "globalization" of Russian foreign policy.

The Stalin Era

Stalin's strategy was known as a "continental policy." Internally he maintained a tightly disciplined totalitarian state that eventually produced the technology and industrial capacity to equip the Russians with atomic weaponry. He viewed the world as living in two armed camps, with the United

---

[14]Vernon V. Aspaturian, *Process and Power in Soviet Foreign Policy*, Little, Brown and Company, Boston, 1971. This is an excellent but encyclopedic treatment of various aspects of Soviet foreign policy, consisting of thirty-eight essays (and one documentary excerpt) written principally in the 1960s—twelve by contributors and the remainder by the principal author. See also Alvin Z. Rubenstein (ed.), *Foreign Policy of the Soviet Union*, Alfred A. Knopf, Inc., New York, 1972.

States and its allies attempting to "encircle" the Soviet Union. The tactical execution of his postwar strategy was actually launched before the war ended and during the period of friendly cooperation, when Russia and its allies were fighting a common enemy. The Soviet Union secured its frontiers by the simple expedient of occupying, and later refusing to withdraw its forces from, areas marked for incorporation into the communist satellite system. In the early days of the war, Estonia, Lithuania, Latvia, Bessarabia, Bukovina, and parts of Finland were annexed. Beginning in Eastern Europe in 1944, various degrees of hegemony were established over Albania, Rumania, Bulgaria, Poland, Hungary, and Yugoslavia. In 1948, Czechoslovakia was added to the satellite empire.

Western Europe offered stiff resistance to the predatory ambitions of the Russian Communists, but the division of Germany and the isolation of Berlin left East Germany as a Soviet bastion in that region. Austria was the only occupied country to escape Soviet domination, finding refuge in a status of neutrality confirmed by treaty in 1955. In the Far East, Manchuria, China, North Korea, North Vietnam, and Tibet succumbed to communist infiltration.

Conquest was followed by consolidation through a systematic "Sovietization" of the principal institutions of the communist-bloc countries. In 1947 the Communist Information Bureau, or Cominform, was created as a small-scale substitute for the old Comintern (which had been ostensibly dissolved in 1943). It served to propagandize the satellite leaders concerning the various phases of the world communist movement. In 1949 a Council of Mutual Assistance, or Comecon, was organized to assist in planning the economies of these dependencies and to ensure their integration into the Soviet economic system.

Between 1946 and 1948 an elaborate system of intersatellite treaty alliances was negotiated to secure Soviet boundaries in the west from Germany and in the east from the People's Republic of China. Marshal Tito kept Yugoslavia outside the Russian sphere in 1945, but Czechoslovakia succumbed in 1948. On September 23, 1949, President Truman announced that an atomic explosion had taken place in the Soviet Union. It was later learned that Dr. Klaus J. E. Fuchs, a German-born English physicist, along with a large group of foreign agents had been giving important atomic information to the Soviets by espionage since 1942. Within four years Soviet scientists developed the hydrogen bomb and achieved the potential for equality in thermonuclear weaponry with the United States.

In the eyes of the Russian people, Stalin's accomplishments were monumental: He saved the existence of the state and legitimated the communist regime by emerging victorious from World War II; he outmaneuvered his allies diplomatically by creating an empire of Eurasian satellites to protect the homeland; and he seized every opportunity offered by the cold war to penetrate power vacuums in the Middle East (late 1940s) and Asia (Korea, early 1950s) and among the developing African nations. He ultimately led the Soviets into the United Nations and the atomic era as a great-power rival of the United States. All this was achieved at a frightful cost in human lives and at the expense of a total loss of individual freedom. Life in the Soviet Union was regimented by the terrorism of a police state and the sanctions of the inevitable concentration camp.

The Nikita Khrushchev Interlude

The advent of Nikita Khrushchev to power in 1953 as first secretary of the party Central Committee ushered in a new era in Russian foreign policy. In a seven-hour "secret" speech to the Twentieth Party Congress in 1956, he denounced Stalin as having lost the Marxist vision in creating a "cult of personality." The revived *Weltanschauung,* or image of the world, he offered was of a Soviet state leading the communist community in a "socialist encirclement" of the United States. The "de-Stalinization" of Soviet foreign policy embraced some radical changes in both emphasis and direction. Its mainspring was the creation of a strong economic-technological base at home in order to provide both a higher standard of living for the people and a nuclear-oriented military machine supporting a powerful Soviet presence in the international arena. This was to be accomplished by lessening tensions with the United States through a policy of "peaceful coexistence" and by creating a more hospitable internal environment through abandonment of the extreme coercive practices of Stalin.

Soviet policy during this period was marked by

inconsistency and vacillation between violent confrontations and conciliatory gestures. The Warsaw Pact, negotiated in 1955, tied the Eastern European states to the Soviet Union in a mutual defense treaty countering the North Atlantic Treaty Organization of the Western allies. A year later the Russian Army dealt ruthlessly with rioting in Poland and a rebellion against the communist regime in Hungary. Khrushchev permitted two dangerous crises to develop when the East Germans built the Berlin wall, separating West from East Berlin in 1961. The Russians transported nuclear ballistic missiles to Cuba in October of 1962, forcing President John Kennedy to threaten nuclear war to gain their removal. Less than a year later, however, the United States, Great Britain, and the Soviet Union signed an arms-control treaty banning the testing of nuclear weapons in outer space, the atmosphere, and underwater. During this period Khrushchev engaged in wide-ranging forays of "personal diplomacy" with heads of states while indulging in irresponsible rhetoric promising to free all "suppressed peoples" through "wars of liberation."

By 1962 the East Central European satellites had been integrated with the Soviet Union in several critical policy areas. The leadership of their national communist parties was coordinated with the political leadership of the Soviet Union. Relationships were reviewed and renewed at successive party congresses. Economic integration was advanced by the correlation of the economic plans of the satellites with the Seven-Year Plan of the Russians and was extended to an intricate set of trade-and-aid interrelationships between the Soviet Union and individual members of the bloc. The arrangements were not one-sided, but complementary, and they encompassed Russian monitoring of a worldwide network of trade agreements with noncommunist countries. Some of this trade represents Soviet aid to underdeveloped countries.

Apart from the ideological rhetoric, however, were the clashing nationalist ambitions of the two leaders to head the world communist bloc. China, seeking great-power status, exploded its first atom bomb in 1964 and its first hydrogen bomb in 1967. By 1969 both countries had massed armies facing each other near the Ussuri River and were threatening to fight over disputed national boundaries. The disaffection between the two powers paved the way for President Nixon's détente policies toward both countries.

Brezhnev: A New Epoch

The Brezhnev era began in October 1964 when Khrushchev was suddenly deposed. Whereas Khrushchev had successfully broken out of the confines of containment imposed by United States policy and had given Soviet aspirations global dimensions, he had greatly overreached the resources of Russian power in making his commitments. The new party secretary strove to buy time to build a strong military-industrial base at home and to gain acceptance of the territorial gains made in the postwar period, while establishing credibility in Soviet diplomacy.

The Achilles' heel of Russian diplomacy of this era was the loosening of controls over the satellites and the alienation of the People's Republic of China. The satellites, particularly Czechoslovakia, interpreted de-Stalinization in terms of "desatellization" and proceeded to attempt to liberalize their own rigid rules governing civil rights and civil liberties.[15] This development was accompanied by a theory of "polycentrism" alleging that there were a number of different paths to the achievement of an ideal socialist state. Such views clashed with the orthodox Marxian view of scientific socialism and more particularly with the concept of Soviet hegemony. These developments led eventually to the Russian invasion of Czechoslovakia in 1968 under the so-called Brezhnev doctrine of the right of the Soviet Union to intervene in the business of client states. A dire warning was issued to the other satellites that the only path to socialism was that trod by the Soviets.

There appear to have been two principal causes for the Sino-Soviet split. Mao Tse-tung interpreted the de-Stalinization and peaceful-coexistence policies of Khrushchev to be ideological deviations in domestic and foreign policy from orthodox Marxian principles. He advocated the necessity of war with capitalist countries, rejected Khrushchev's concept of peaceful transition to socialism, and insisted upon application of the communist dialectic to the development of the socialist economy.

In military policy Brezhnev moved to accommo-

---

[15] Aspaturian, op. cit., p. 831.

date the newly won parity in nuclear-weapon capability with the United States to the realities of great-power politics. The Soviets followed the Nuclear Test-Ban Treaty of 1963 with agreements with the United States for the nonproliferation of nuclear weapons (1969), the freezing of the inventory of ICBMs on land and sea, and the limitation of each nation's antiballistic-missile defense systems (SALT) in 1972. These conciliatory actions were interpreted as reflecting concern over the serious implications of the Cuban confrontation and the fact that China was developing its own nuclear capability. Apparently, the Soviet elite clearly understood the implications of total nuclear war.

From 1949 to 1963 Russia created a recurring series of crises over the settlement of the German problem. Its diplomatic objective was to force the Western powers out of Berlin and West Germany, alienate West Germany from NATO and the European Common Market, cause the dissolution of the Western European alliance system, force the military and diplomatic withdrawal of the United States from Western Europe, and destroy the industrial-technological base of the European economy. To maintain the confidence of West Germany, the Western powers refused to recognize the German Democratic Republic as a sovereign state. They did not make any concessions for demilitarization or neutralization or for withdrawal from West Germany.

Brezhnev chose to attempt to alleviate the conditions of stalemate by negotiation with West German Chancellor Willie Brandt, who was prosecuting a policy of *Ostpolitik,* or move toward the East. Soviet initiatives resulted in treaties of friendship between West Germany, the Soviet Union, and Poland in 1970. In 1971 the Soviet Union, Britain, France, and the United States agreed on a plan of Western access to West Berlin over East German territory; later the sovereignty of East Germany was recognized. Twenty-two divisions of Russian troops aided in maintaining stability in Poland and East Germany.

Soviet diplomacy of the Brezhnev period continued a vigorous exploitation of power vacuums in support of client states, utilizing a variety of instruments ranging from treaties of friendship to massive military aid. Examples include support of Bangladesh in its war of liberation from Pakistan (1971–1972), of North Vietnam in the invasion of South Vietnam until the peace treaty of 1973, and of the Egyptians and Syrians in the war with Israel (1972–1973).

By the mid-1970s Soviet foreign policy had apparently achieved a high degree of maturity and sophistication. Members of the Politburo seemed cognizant of the lethal consequences of nuclear war. They were quite willing to employ all available means of conventional warfare to hit targets of political opportunity under the shield of nuclear parity with the United States. Unquestionably, the reach of Soviet power had attained global dimensions, and yet several important goals proved elusive. NATO remained a threat on the Western European front, the "loyalty" of the satellites was measured by the divisions of Soviet troops occupying their territories, and the People's Republic of China fled from Russian hegemony to become a great-power rival.

UNITED STATES FOREIGN POLICY

The grand design of American foreign policy is the establishment and maintenance of a balance of power in international politics that will restrain the ambitions of predatory states and thus ensure a substantial measure of peace and stability in world affairs. The fundamental motivation behind this strategy is not idealism, but self-interest. The basic security of the United States is predicated upon a peaceful world. Although both the Soviet Union and the United States seek security as a prerequisite of self-preservation, their policies present vital differences in both means and ends. Post–World War II American diplomacy may be conveniently divided into four periods: the period of cooperation, 1945 to 1947; the period of containment, 1947 to 1956; the period of competitive coexistence, 1957 to 1960; and the period of nuclear accommodation, 1961 to the mid-1970s.[16]

---

[16]For an excellent summary of this period, see John Spanier, *American Foreign Policy since World War II,* 6th ed., Frederick A. Praeger, Inc., New York, 1973. For an incisive probing of contemporary problems of American foreign policy by thirteen authorities and an editor, assembled by The Brookings Institution, see Henry Owen (ed.), *The Next Phase in Foreign Policy,* The Brookings Institution, Washington, 1973.

The Period of Cooperation

The United States and its allies emerged from World War II after soundly defeating the nations attempting to revise the international status quo. Plans for a peace settlement preceded V-J Day in conferences held at Teheran, Yalta, and Potsdam and found fruition, in part, with the establishment of the United Nations in San Francisco in the spring of 1945. The Soviet Union had been an active participant in these conferences.

Having fought and defeated a common enemy, with the Russians as allies, the United States took a calculated risk that the Soviet Union would be willing to negotiate differences of policy in the postwar settlement. In support of this conviction and in response to the insistent pressure of domestic public opinion, the United States dismantled the greatest military machine the world had ever seen. Soviet diplomacy quickly revealed that the basic decision on postwar Russian strategy had been erroneous. An early signal was the refusal to withdraw occupation troops from Iran in 1946 in compliance with an earlier agreement. Other evidences of Soviet intent accumulated rapidly, including excessive demands for both reparations and territorial concessions from former Axis countries.

The Allies saw plans for the independence of Eastern and Central European states at the Yalta Conference in 1945 violated by the refusal of the Russians to hold free elections or to withdraw their army of occupation. Civil wars in Greece and Yugoslavia were exploited, and unreasonable demands were made upon Turkey for cession of territory and establishment of military bases upon its soil. Whatever goodwill had been generated between the Soviets and their allies during the war and in preliminary peace discussions dissipated within 1½ years of V-J Day in September 1945. With his usual prescience, Winston Churchill identified the Russian strategy first in his Fulton, Missouri, speech early in 1946: "An iron curtain has descended across the continent."[17]

---

[17]Aspaturian, op. cit., pp. 213–285, presents the pros and cons of the dispute between the revisionists and orthodox interpreters of the origins of the cold war.

The Period of Containment: The Truman Doctrine

The revelation that the Soviet Union had decided upon a policy of expansionism and that no Soviet decision supporting the achievement of that goal was negotiable led to a painful reappraisal of American policy objectives. The new American policy of containment was based upon the assumption that since the United States had a monopoly of atomic weapons, the Russians would fight a cold, or nonshooting, war to establish a position of ascendancy rather than equality among the Great Powers. The United States undertook to meet Soviet aggression in all areas (political, economic, and military) and to counter any form of Russian influence around the periphery of the noncommunist world. Soviet strong points were to be met with strength, and weak positions were to be exploited to reveal the inner contradictions of communism. Policy was to remain flexible, offering alternatives that might bring solutions to stalemated situations. Additional implications of the containment policy included the reconstitution of the balance of power in Western Europe and Asia and aid to restore the economies of Great Britain, France, West Germany, Italy, Japan, and China. The ultimate hope was for a change in Soviet policy in response to these external pressures, a possible (but unlikely) internal revolution, economic collapse, a satellite war for independence, or the evolution of a domestic policy that would bring prosperity and mitigate aggressive pressures in international relations.

The implementation of the policy of containment could be effected only in the face of serious obstacles. The United States was relatively inexperienced and unprepared to assume the responsibilities of leading the free world. American diplomacy was denied the ease of unilateral decision based solely upon considerations of *Realpolitik* and the protection of operating behind an iron curtain. Public opinion viewed Russian diplomatic intransigence with utter dismay. A deep feeling of insecurity gripped the nation, prompted in part by ancient isolationist sentiments and by bitter and often irresponsible partisan bickering over questions of loyalty, patriotism, and foreign policy in the national elections between 1946 and 1956.

United States policy, as it developed between 1947 and 1956, encompassed three principal activities: economic assistance to the free peoples, i.e., noncommunist nations; a treaty network among potential allies; and military planning at home and abroad to counteract the Soviet preparations for war. The policy was executed in four principal theaters of operation: Latin America, Western Europe, the Middle East, and the Far East. The new phase of policy was announced before Congress by President Truman on March 12, 1947, in a speech requesting $400 million in aid for Greece and Turkey. The Truman doctrine advocated the reconstitution of the economy of those potential allies which were threatened by Soviet intervention. United States policy, as adopted, progressed through successive stages of development from the Marshall Plan to the Economic Recovery program in 1948 and, finally, in 1951, to the Mutual Security Act.

The recipients of aid under the Marshall Plan and the Economic Recovery program were enlisted in a general program of self-help toward recovery. Under the Mutual Security Act both military and economic aid were emphasized, as well as a Point Four program of technical assistance. It has been estimated that between the close of the war and 1955, the various aspects of the policy were implemented by an expenditure of nearly $60 billion. The recovery of Western Europe under this policy was remarkable. Great Britain, France, and West Germany were elevated to the stature of major powers once again. Other beneficiaries included Italy, the Netherlands, Austria, Belgium, Luxembourg, Denmark, Norway, Turkey, Ireland, Sweden, Yugoslavia, Portugal, Iceland, and Zone A of Trieste.

The second objective of the new strategy required the political commitment of the noncommunist states to the goals of Western nations. This phase of policy was executed by a series of regional pacts permitted by the United Nations Charter. Although the commitments varied, most of these arrangements were directed toward the attainment of mutual understanding and accord among the signatory states in matters affecting their common interests, particularly with respect to threatened aggression and mutual defense plans.

The principal agreement between the United States and the twenty-one Latin-American states in the Western Hemisphere was signed at Bogotá, Colombia, in 1948. The Organization of American States was created as the successor to the Union of American Republics, with headquarters at Washington. A year later the North Atlantic Treaty Organization (NATO) was formed to identify the United States with the protection of Western Europe. Members allied in this venture included Britain, Canada, France, Belgium, the Netherlands, Luxembourg, Norway, Denmark, Iceland, Portugal, Italy, Greece, Turkey, and finally West Germany in 1955. The permanent NATO headquarters was established in Paris, and the top command (known as Supreme Headquarters, Allied Powers of Europe, or SHAPE) was first held by General Dwight D. Eisenhower. This collective defense arrangement was a signal departure from traditional United States policy and served to emphasize the nature of the new global commitments that were undertaken by this nation.

Regional security in the Far East was greatly complicated by the communization of China; the North Korean attack against the Republic of Korea on June 24, 1950; and the defeat of French forces in Indochina in the summer of 1954. Although the Korean conflict was fought in the name of the United Nations, the overwhelming commitment in terms of men, war matériel, and economic cost came from the United States. The end of the conflict found Syngman Rhee, a friend of the Allies, in a very vulnerable situation in South Korea. In August and September of 1951, the United States negotiated a series of pacts creating a treaty network among friendly states in the Pacific area. Agreements included the Japanese peace treaty, a Philippine pact, and the Anzus pact with New Zealand and Australia. Upon the attainment of independent status by Japan in April 1952, special security arrangements were negotiated with the United States.

In the Middle East, United States diplomacy enjoyed only limited success. The withdrawal of British and French interests created a power vacuum exploited by both native nationalism and Russian agents. The Israeli question embittered and temporarily alienated the Arab world. Apart from the incorporation of Greece and Turkey into

NATO, close collaboration was not achieved. Finally, in 1955, a bloc of Middle Eastern states including Britain, Turkey, Iraq, Iran, and Pakistan formed the Middle East Treaty Organization under United States sponsorship.

The military planning phase of postwar American policy was an integral part of the economic assistance and regional security programs. In the summer of 1948, the Soviets blockaded West Germany, isolating Berlin. The Allies retaliated and broke the blockade with the famous airlift Operation Vittles into West Berlin. The next year the United States launched the Mutual Defense Assistance program and passed successive appropriations to furnish assistance and military aid to NATO. American policy was predicated upon the priority of Western Europe over other theaters of operations.

On September 23, 1949, President Truman announced that the Russians had effected an atomic explosion. With the military involvement of the United Nations in the Korean war nine months later, the urgency of effective, long-term military planning on the part of the Allies became painfully apparent.

The military-preparedness program involved the intensification of research and development of atomic weapons by the United States and the rearming of the Allied nations. Reconstituting the political and military strength of West Germany became a high priority after the Federal Republic of Germany achieved independence on May 5, 1955. The isolationist "Fortress America" concept was abandoned. Under the new "Live Frontier" policy, military bases were dispersed throughout the world in such widely separated areas as Spain, Casablanca, Morocco, Alaska, Okinawa, Thailand, and Britain. The USAF Strategic Air Command became the deterrent to Russian aggression because the key industrial centers of the Soviets were brought within American jet-bomber range.

The Period of Competitive Coexistence

The intensification of worldwide political, economic, and military rivalry between the Soviet Union and the United States marked the beginning of the phase of American foreign policy that may aptly be termed the age of "competitive coexistence." Several significant developments around the year 1955 marked the gradual transition away from the policy of containment. The bipolar balance of power between the United States and Russia, which had characterized the postwar years, was altered by the economic revival of Great Britain, France, Japan, West Germany, and Red China. The group of uncommitted states was about to be joined by India and Pakistan. Nationalism was rife in the emergent countries of Asia and Africa; over two dozen were to enter the international arena within the next decade, sounding the death knell of colonialism. The United Nations had lost any opportunity it might have had as a primary agency for the settlement of international disputes; the key decisions in international politics were now being made outside its framework.

Perhaps the most significant developments directly preceding the change in American policy were the effects of the loss in 1949 of the American monopoly on nuclear weapons, the bitter experience of the Korean conflict of 1950–1953, the death of Joseph Stalin in 1953, and the utter failure of the Geneva Conference of the foreign ministers of the United States, the Soviet Union, Great Britain, and France in the fall of 1955. The de-Stalinization policy of the Soviet Union was accompanied by emulation of such American policies as the building of rival political alliances and the launching of substantial trade-and-aid programs with the uncommitted countries and emergent nations.

The initial adjustment of American policy to these altered circumstances coincided with a change of administration in Washington and a shift in military emphasis from manned planes to intercontinental ballistic missiles. John Foster Dulles, the new secretary of state, sought a new formula for coping with the Russian strategy of expansion. He suggested a program of liberation of the communist satellites under a canopy of nuclear-weapon firepower that would constitute a constant threat of massive retaliation. This change of policy posed questions as to the initiation of a nuclear war, the feasibility of retaliation, and the possibility of conducting conventional warfare in a nuclear age. The complete antithesis of such a policy was presented by George F. Kennan, former head of the Policy Planning Staff of the Department of State, in a series of lectures delivered in Great Britain in 1957. Kennan's proposal for disengagement included the withdrawal of all foreign troops from German soil, as well as the disarmament, neutralization, and reunification of East and West Germany.

Neither of these policy extremes proved feasible; hence the middle road of competitive coexistence was chosen. The dominant theme of this position was to launch a vigorous diplomatic offensive on all fronts (political, economic, and military), while constantly seeking a mutually acceptable accommodation of the critical problems dividing the United States and the Soviet Union. The more successful existing policies were retained, refined, and improved.

Nikita Khrushchev countered this strategy with a "hold and probe" policy attempting to heighten international tensions with his own "brinksmanship." He practiced "summitry" with Dwight Eisenhower in Washington (1959) and with John F. Kennedy in Vienna (1961), indulging in extravagant rhetoric such as his remark to the American people: "We shall bury you!"

This was a period of great turbulence in international politics, and extending throughout, like a theme from a Wagnerian tragedy, was the Vietnamese war. Despite massive financial assistance from the United States, France lost Indochina in the battle of Dienbienphu in 1954. The next year President Eisenhower sent a "military advisory group" to train the South Vietnamese Army in warding off attacks from the Viet Minh Communist Army of Ho Chi Minh. Thus began a commitment covering the three succeeding presidential administrations of John Kennedy, Lyndon Johnson, and Richard Nixon and ending in a disastrous war costing 46,000 American lives and between $110 billion and $120 billion. Throughout, the Russians and their client state, North Vietnam, confronted the United States and its client state, South Vietnam.

Typical of other crises of the era of competitive coexistence were the abortive attempt of France, Great Britain, and Israel to use force to prevent the nationalization of the Suez Canal by Gamal Nasser in 1956; the struggle over the Berlin wall between the client states of East and West Germany, lasting from 1958 to 1962; the civil war in the newly formed African Republic of the Congo, in which Russia and the United States chose sides and the United Nations intervened (1960); and, finally, the Cuban situation, wherein the Russians were prevented from placing ballistic missiles within range of the East Coast of the United States by a direct confrontation between President Kennedy and Nikita Khrushchev (1962).

The Period of Nuclear Accommodation: The Nixon Doctrine

In a "swing through the Pacific" on July 25, 1969, from the island of Guam, President Richard Nixon made a speech on American foreign policy for Asia, enunciating a series of principles that have subsequently been interpreted as the "Nixon doctrine." In brief, these guidelines for foreign policy were that the United States would keep its treaty commitments and that it would maintain the nuclear umbrella over its allies, protecting them from external attack and, in return, insisting that they undertake greater responsibility for their own economic well-being and military security. Implicitly, the posture Nixon described came to mean that the United States would gradually phase out a substantial portion of its overseas military establishment and in the future would forgo participation with American troops in "wars of national liberation" such as that in Vietnam.

Less than 2½ years later, the President made his historic "journey for peace," visiting Mao Tse-tung and Chou En-lai in the People's Republic of China in February 1972 and Leonid I. Brezhnev, Aleksei N. Kosygin, and Nikolai V. Podgorny in Moscow in May. The Nixon doctrine thus achieved added clarification during this period of détente or lessening of international tensions. Negotiations led to agreements for trade and cultural exchanges as well as certain political initiatives. Discussions were held on the status of Taiwan and its entry into the United Nations with China, the relationships between Berlin and East and West Germany, and the possibility of arms limitation with the Russians.

A variety of circumstances conspired to make a policy of détente possible. The consequences of the Vietnamese war shocked the American public. Militarily and politically, the nation had overcommitted itself. The struggle took place under circumstances that made victory impossible. Despite the frightful expenditure in lives and money, the public was never truly convinced that the vital interests of the nation were at stake. From the first involvement of combat troops in 1965 to the cease-fire order on January 27, 1973, the divisiveness of the issue betrayed the consensus in American public opinion required of a democracy at war. Labor unrest, student riots, and confrontations between blacks and whites over racial issues seriously challenged the credibility of the government. President Lyndon Johnson was forced to forgo the opportunity to win a second term of office. Clearly, critical domestic issues were demanding the highest priority on the agenda of public policy. Before they could be placed there, however, the international situation required a greater degree of stability.

In the international arena, the nuclear-arms race had reached virtual stalemate, and the cost was seriously compromising the economic stability and resources of the two major powers. Finally, the tense relations between the Soviet Union and Communist China provided a rare opportunity for the United States to seize the initiative to gain concessions from both. Utilizing the diplomatic talents of Assistant to the President for National Security Affairs Henry Kissinger (later secretary of state), President Nixon took the opportunity to practice détente.

What of the future? We turn now from a discussion of the foreign policies of the two titans of the modern world to a consideration of some important dilemmas in international politics faced by all members of the community of nations.

CURRENT PROBLEMS OF INTERNATIONAL POLITICS

The nation-states of the world have trod a tortuous path in their relations with one another during the three decades following World War II. Change is an immutable fact of history, and each generation creates its own problems, seeks its own solutions, and poses its own dilemmas in international politics. Here, briefly stated, are some of the dilemmas of the mid-1970s.[18]

Some Political Dilemmas

The balance of power rests within a multipolar complex. Western Europe, supported by the United States, confronts the Soviet satellite system of Eastern and Central Europe. In Asia, Japan, supported by the United States, faces the People's Republic of China and the Soviet Union, while the two major communist powers interface with each other. The fulcrum of the balance is still the bipolar relationship between the United States and the Soviet Union—their resources, their will to fight if necessary, and their respective evaluations of each other's motives. The United States has the greater leverage at the fulcrum: the cooperation of the two status quo elements, Western Europe and Japan, and détente with the revisionist states of the People's Republic of China and the Soviet Union. An essential element of the balance is the apparent recognition by the two principal states of each other's established political hegemonies.

The balance is precarious, however. Satellites and allies are showing separatist tendencies; China will soon have nuclear military capability, and the question of similarly rearming West Germany and Japan is in controversy; the Common Market countries of Western Europe may become politicized into a confederation or a federation, making their future relationship with the United States uncertain; finally, the American policy of détente may become untenable if the two major communist powers establish rapprochement with each other.

Foreign policy is linked integrally to domestic policy. The survival of the Communist party regimes in China and Russia is an unknown component in the balance-of-power equation. Both countries are faced with generational changes within their elite ruling classes; it is impossible to anticipate the manner in which their successors will view the world's problems. Neither is there any certainty that, lacking the psychological goad of a communist threat while beset with serious internal problems, the American public might not retreat to isolationism, refuse to vote multibillion-dollar defense budgets, and abandon its global commitments.

Without a tradition of political stability and other essential ingredients for statehood, the fledgling, developing nations of the "third world" are caught in the web of great-power politics. They may become client states while fighting over their own nationalistic goals and sorting out their internal power relationships. North Korea, North Vietnam, and Egypt did so while enjoying Soviet paternalism, as did South Korea, South Vietnam, and Israel under a shield provided by the United States. Their

---

[18]Note the interesting essay by Seyom Brown, "New Forces in World Politics," in Owen, op. cit., pp. 281–306.

future is also vulnerable to trade-and-aid programs of the Great Powers and the availability of United Nations support. Their behavior will offer many opportunities to compromise the prevailing power balance. Statehood in the nuclear age faces a precarious existence, the United Nations notwithstanding.

Some Economic Dilemmas

A state's political power is rooted in its economic resources. The ingredients include raw materials, technological know-how, industrial capacity, and trading markets. Together they produce a growing gross national product and a high standard of living, the ultimate objective of foreign policy. Unfortunately, the earth's resources are not equally distributed among nation-states, and access to them has become highly competitive. This is a world of expanding population and shrinking resources concerned with conservation, ecology, air pollution, food, ocean farming, ownership and utilization of airspace, and other essentials of twentieth-century living.

The concept of a policy of national economic self-sufficiency in the name of national security is a will-o'-the-wisp for all but a handful of states. The Soviet Union may follow a policy of détente in order to import the technological know-how and industrial capability of the United States, which fifty years of communism has not provided the Soviet people, but few other states have a quid pro quo to offer in exchange.

The economic dilemma of the era is posed by the clash between the spirit of nationalism, with its mandate for self-sufficiency, and the political terms upon which access to a share in the world's resources will be permitted to all states.

Some Dilemmas of National Security

If change is indeed an immutable law of the universe, can change take place in international relations without war? The application of nuclear fusion to the technology of manufacturing war weapons has rendered the goal of ultimate national security "inoperative" for a large majority of states. The nations with some capability to engage in nuclear war are the United States, the Soviet Union, the People's Republic of China, France, Great Britain, and Israel. Of these, only the arsenals of American democracy and Russian communism have the capability of mass destruction; the United States excels in qualitative nuclear weaponry, and the Soviets excel in quantitative inventory. The rest of the nations of the world either are protected by the nuclear umbrellas of the two superpowers or are relatively, if not totally, defenseless.

A summary of a hypothetical scenario for World War III might read as follows: The Soviets or their satellites will attack Western Europe with conventional weapons; the Allies in NATO will respond; the Russians will be unsuccessful and will retaliate with small, tactical nuclear arms; the Allies will respond in kind; once again unsuccessful, the attackers will resort to intercontinental ballistic missiles; the United States will follow suit.[19] At least 100 million people will be killed in Western Europe, the Soviet Union, and the United States, and large portions of the engaged states will be uninhabitable for an indeterminate period of time. With the advancement of Chinese nuclear capability, the same scenario may be composed covering the other nations of the power-balance configuration in Asia, the Soviet Union, Communist China, Japan, and the United States. Thus the balance of political power is supplemented and augmented by the balance of strategic nuclear power, and therein lie a number of troublesome dilemmas.

The conventional wisdom as to the manner by which these stark eventualities may be interdicted has been expressed as the "doctrine of mutual deterrence." Ideally, the American and Russian capacities to wage offensive and defensive nuclear warfare must be kept in balance, each nation checkmating the other. The two elements in the equation are the offensive strategic first-strike capability and the defensive second-strike, or retaliatory, capability of each state. American military doctrine views the first-strike strategy as not in keeping with the nation's principles and tradition, but adopts both it and second-strike, or defensive, strategy in terms of national survival. Soviet military doctrine makes no such fine distinction and uninhibitedly advocates preparation for nuclear war, *period*. The dilemma: Is the theory of deter-

---

[19]Lord Gladwyn, "The Defense of Western Europe," *Foreign Affairs*, vol. 51, no. 3, April 1973, pp. 588–597.

rence viable in that both states *believe* that neither can use its supersonic bombers, intercontinental ballistic missiles, or multicapped submarine missiles without mutual annihilation?[20]

It was, in part, to maintain deterence as a viable policy that the Soviet Union and the United States agreed to negotiate limits on the production and development of their strategic nuclear weapons system. The first round of the Strategic Arms Limitations Talks (SALT) was held in Helsinki in November 1969. SALT I was followed by SALT II, convened in Geneva in November 1972. But by mid-1975 there were still some critical and unresolved problems. Subsequent negotiations would have to settle differences on the types of missiles to be limited, the identification of missiles with multiple warheads, andappropriate inspection procedures for insuring compliance with any agreement. There also was the issue of regulating the production and deployment of missiles launced from mobile ground stations or from aircraft in flight.

The Dilemma of Peace

Reflection upon the current rivalries, historic animosities, competitive economic interests, and differences in nationality, race, color, creed, and language between the nations of the world leads to the conclusion that "peace" is an ideal rather than a realistic goal of humanity. Nevertheless, a desirable degree of stability in international relations is attainable.

The multipolar balance-of-power formation in the mid-1970s, supported by a viable military doctrine of deterrence, not only made nuclear war untenable but also introduced, however tentatively, the policies of détente. Future shifts in the power balance must accommodate the aspirations of China and Japan in Asia and of the Common Market nations in Europe. The underpinnings of political stability, however, are found in the intricate web of bilateral, multilateral, regional, and broadly international treaties and other agreements that isolate and solve problems at the level of greatest concern to individual nation-states.

[20]Leslie H. Gelb and Arnold M. Kuzmack, "General Purpose Forces," in Owen, op. cit., pp. 203–224; and Jerome H. Kahan, "Strategic Armaments," in Owen, op. cit., pp. 225–246. See also Zbigniew Brzezinski, "U.S.-Soviet Relations," in Owen, op. cit., pp. 113–132.

One of the great international time bombs that can "self-destruct," causing serious world instability, is the economic condition of the emerging nations. The proliferation of nation-states places heavy demands upon the world's resources. On the other hand, economic interdependence, and the dramatic revelation that even the most powerful states must trade resources to survive, bodes well for economic stability through negotiation. Economic prosperity for the peoples of the developing nations would lend powerful support to the creation of political stability in the future.

The general trend of economic and social change in Western civilization has been toward the attainment of a more highly integrated society. The degree and pace of integration vary from one historic period to another, depending upon evolutionary processes. When the nation-states of the world have developed an international society wherein a sound basis for community interest exists, the necessary political formula for integration will follow as a matter of course. Perhaps the United Nations may yet become the "honest broker" for the many dilemmas of the international order.

STUDY-GUIDE QUESTIONS

1 In the mid-1970s the most significant new variable in the international balance of power is the development of the nuclear weapon. Theories of deterrence have been developed to constrain its use either by misadventure or by intent. Develop your own concept of deterrence to cope with this problem.
2 With the proliferation of new states as members of the United Nations, a majority coming from the developing nations of Asia and Africa, it has been alleged that the nature and function of that body have changed drastically. For example, the Soviet Union and the small island of Mauritius in the Indian Ocean each have one vote in the Assembly. Speculate upon the consequences of this new development for the future of the United Nations.
3 Suggestions have been made for the construction of an "interdependence model" for the analysis of international politics. Compare and contrast the assumptions for such a model with those supporting the "power-politics" concept.
4 During the 1970s the United States has seized

upon a rare opportunity to develop a policy of détente with both the People's Republic of China and the Soviet Union. This circumstance came about because the two states were engaged in intense rivalry over ideological and nationalistic interests. Devise policies for both countries that would further the vital interests of the United States.

REFERENCES

Almond, Gabriel A., and James S. Coleman: *Politics of the Developing Areas,* Princeton University Press, Princeton, N.J., 1960.

Aspaturian, Vernon V.: *Process and Power in Soviet Foreign Policy,* Little, Brown and Company, Boston, 1971.

Barnett, Doak A.: *Uncertain Passage: China's Transition to the Post-Mao Era,* The Brookings Institution, Washington, 1974.

Black, C. E.: *The Dynamics of Modernization,* Harper & Row, Publishers, Incorporated, New York, 1966.

Deutsch, Morton: *The Resolution of Conflict: Constructive and Destructive Processes,* Yale University Press, New Haven, Conn., 1973.

Gaddis, John L.: *The United States and the Origins of the Cold War: 1941–1947,* Columbia University Press, New York, 1972.

Gehlen, Michael P.: *The Politics of Coexistence,* Indiana University Press, Bloomington, 1967.

Head, Richard G., and Ervin J. Rokke: *American Defense Policy,* 3d ed., The Johns Hopkins Press, Baltimore, 1974.

Horton, Frank B., III, Anthony C. Rogerson, and Edward L. Warner, III (eds.): *Comparative Defense Policy,* The Johns Hopkins Press, Baltimore, 1974.

Kanet, Roger E.: *The Soviet Union and Developing Nations,* The Johns Hopkins Press, Baltimore, 1974.

Kaplan, Morton A. (ed.): *Great Issues of International Politics,* 2d ed., Aldine Publishing Company, Chicago, 1974.

Langdon, F. C.: *Japan's Foreign Policy,* University of British Columbia Press, Vancouver, 1973.

Legault, Albert, and George Lindsey: *The Dynamics of the Nuclear Balance,* Cornell University Press, Ithaca, N.Y., 1974.

Modelski, George: *Principles of World Politics,* The Free Press, New York, 1972.

Orleans, Leo A.: *Every Fifth Child: The Population of China,* Stanford University Press, Stanford, Calif., 1972.

Owen, Henry (ed.): *The Next Phase in Foreign Policy,* The Brookings Institution, Washington, 1973.

Quester, George: *The Politics of Nuclear Proliferation,* The Johns Hopkins Press, Baltimore, 1973.

Rosenau, James N. (ed.): *International Politics and Foreign Policy,* rev. ed., The Free Press, New York, 1969.

Rustow, Dankwart A.: *A World of Nations: Problems of Modernization,* The Brookings Institution, Washington, 1966.

Spanier, John S.: *American Foreign Policy since World War II,* 6th ed., Frederick A. Praeger, Inc., New York, 1973.

Sprout, Harold, and Margaret Sprout: *Toward a Politics of the Planet Earth,* Van Nostrand, Reinhold, New York, 1971.

Stoessinger, John G.: *Why Nations Go to War,* St. Martin's Press, Inc., New York, 1974.

Chapter 21

International Law and Organization

INTERNATIONAL LAW AND INTERNATIONAL POLITICS

The academic discipline of international relations, as a part of political science, encompasses the more specific fields of international law, international politics, and international organization. International politics emphasizes power and constant maneuver in the international arena. International organization lays greater emphasis on legal and ethical considerations, and its institutions are conducive to orderly and cooperative methods of effecting international change. International law, like all law, rests upon moral and practical foundations. It requires the presence of a responsible and orderly society that is firmly dedicated to the sharing of minimal common values. All three—international politics, organization, and law—operate within the context of power and in a constantly changing environment. All help to explain the external conduct of nation-states. Power as a comprehensive concept is a great deal more than "simple naked force applied by nation-state to nation-state."[1]

International law and international politics are

[1] Myres S. McDougal, "Law and Power," *American Journal of International Law*, vol. 46, no. 1, p. 107, 1952. Moreover, power cannot be separated from reason. As the late Justice Robert H. Jackson has said, "We may go forward on the assumption that reason has power to summon force to its support, confident that acceptable moral standards embodied in law for the governance of nations will appeal to the better natures of men so that somehow they will ultimately vouchsafe the force to make them prevail." See "The Role of Law among Nations," *Proceedings of the American Society of International Law*, p. 17, 1945.

closely related to each other because international politics presumably operates within the framework of international law. In comparison with the expediency of international politics, international law is viewed by some as a firmer, more traditional, and more stabilizing factor in the world community.[2]

International law, in order to keep pace with international politics, is obliged to maintain flexibility in form and substance. Consequently, international law, properly understood, is characterized by its practical, down-to-earth quality. Perhaps the most important point to be made concerning international law, new or old, is that most nation-states normally seek to comply with the concepts of right and wrong contained in existing international law. This is true even though a nation-state, at a particular moment, may not be especially enthusiastic about particular rules of law. Certainly, in times of international crisis, the ready charge of violation of international law supplies adequate evidence of its existence and significance.

INTERNATIONAL LAW AND INTERNATIONAL ORGANIZATION

International law and international organization have been described as opposite sides of a coin. The development of a world environment hospitable to a world community advances both international law and international organization.

Law provides boundaries between permitted and prohibited conduct. Thus international law establishes the rights, duties, powers, and functions of nation-states and of international organizations. Such law may also deal with individuals. With the progressive development of a very large number of international organizations—from the United Nations down—international law and organization have come more and more to house both the maneuver of international politics and the formulation of international policies.

International law, no less than international organization, is goal-oriented and value-conscious. Both interact continuously and effectively upon the decisional process. Both provide means for the integration and achievement of international policies and actions.

National and international goals may be most readily achieved through the balancing or blending of the forces of law, organization, and politics. These goals are more likely to be realized as long as the possible unsettling effect of politics is resisted by law and organization in an effort "to stabilize world peace and order at the middle of the continuum ... of action and reaction, of conflict and compromise."[3]

In summary, international law, organization, and politics have common interests and are part of a larger whole. Each operates on certain principles, and each pursues the art of compromise. Each is dynamic, and each possesses varying perceptions as to values. Each is goal-oriented, but none of them assumes that Utopia will be achieved immediately. All seek to advance the national interest of peace and security, and yet none assumes to be either a grantor or absolute guarantor of long-range international ideals. Working together, they offer a symbol of mankind's inherent unity and diversity and provide a framework within which international challenges can be met.

INTERNATIONAL LAW

Development of International Law

The idea that there should be a form of law governing the behavior of sovereign nation-states may be traced back at least to the time of Grotius (1583–1645), who in 1625 wrote the first influential work on international law, entitled *De jure belli ac pacis*. However, even prior to Grotius, who is known as the father of modern international law, continental and English writers had discussed the need for law governing the conduct of nations.

Grotius's significance lies not only in his own work, which was distributed widely, but also in the stimulus it provided to other thinkers of his era. Books on international law were soon published by Pufendorf (1632–1697), Bynkershoek (1693–1743), Wolff (1679–1754), and Vattel (1714–1767).

Grotius and these later writers were immediately

---

[2] Quincy Wright, "Law and Politics in the World Community," in George A. Lipsky (ed.), *Law and Politics in the World Community,* University of California Press, Berkeley, 1953, pp. 3–14.

[3] Ronald J. Yalem, "Law, Organization, and Politics in the International Community," *1957 Washington University Law Quarterly,* pp. 110, 117.

confronted by a developing concept that has come to be called "sovereignty." They urged that while nation-states might be internally supreme and externally independent, such entities were still subject to a superior law, for without a superior law, such as international law, states would be bound only by their own wills, with resulting international chaos.

Before the emergence of the national state the prevalent notion was that all mankind, as sons of one God and as brothers, owed its duty to a world society having no political boundaries. Individuals were literally citizens of the world, and not of states in the modern sense. After the Reformation, the Renaissance, and the growth of nation-states, individuals were obliged to render allegiance to the nation-state and not to an earlier world community. Society became compartmentalized. This compartmentalization has not been a complete success, and over the years, particularly in the twentieth century, the trend has been generally back toward the concept of a world community.

Thus international law hinges upon the existence of independent nation-states, which are expected to get along with one another subject to the rule of law.[4] International law would not exist in a single world-state managed by a supranational parliament, executive, and judiciary. There must be at least two states before there may be international law. Today there are well over 140 nation-states subject to international law.

The Nature of International Law

Traditionally, international law has been defined as that body of principles and rules[5] generally accepted by civilized nation-states as binding upon their conduct. A leading British writer has defined international law as "the sum of the rights that a state may claim for itself and its nationals from other states, and of the duties which in consequence it must observe toward them."[6]

There is an obvious difference between these two definitions. The traditional one makes nation-states alone the subject of international law. Professor Brierly's definition enlarges upon the traditional view to include individuals.

At the present time it is generally agreed that the principles and rules of international law apply not only to nation-states and to individuals but also to international organizations. Even in earlier days, when the traditional definition was in vogue, individuals were always regarded as proper subjects of international law in special instances. Thus individuals had the duty to refrain from piracy, from engaging in the slave trade, and from carrying contraband (implements of war) to hostile nations. More recently, at Nuremberg, the Nazi war criminals were held personally liable for violation of a personal duty to refrain from engaging in certain antisocial activities. This meant conduct at variance with the postulates of a civilized social order, such as crimes against the peace and against humanity. In earlier days the defendants at Nuremberg might have contended that they were not proper subjects of international law and would then have been excused on the ground that their acts were acts of state. This would have been based on the theory that the German state was the only proper subject of the law. In view of these important changes, and without pausing to cite extensive examples of the status of an international organization as a subject of international law, it seems certain that the traditional, limited view of the subject of international law is clearly bankrupt.[7] The International Court of Justice has held that international organizations are subjects of international law. Its advisory opinion respecting the rights of the United Nations resulting from the death of its representative, Count Folke Bernadotte, in Israel, illustrates this fact. With the recognition of the breadth of international

---

[4] A former president of the American Bar Association has described the rule of law as follows: It means the "rule of reason under the moral standards developed by the experience of man. Traditional moral values underlie law principles. These values have their roots deep in the conscience of humanity." Charles S. Rhyne, "World Peace through Law: A Challenge to the Future Lawyers of America," *The Student Lawyer Journal*, vol. 5, no. 1, p. 6, 1960.

[5] A legal principle is an accepted starting point for legal reasoning. It is broad rather than specific. A universal example is "good faith." Nation-states must conform in good faith to international promises, just as individuals must live up to their contracts. A legal rule is a precise statement of required conduct, plus a penalty for nonconformity. It is detailed rather than general. Under the ancient Salic Code, for example: "If any one shall have called another a fox, he shall be condemned to three shillings."

[6] J. L. Brierly, *The Outlook for International Law*, Oxford University Press, Fair Lawn, N.J., 1944, p. 5.

[7] P. E. Corbett, *The Individual and World Society*, Center for Research on World Political Institutions, Princeton, N.J., 1953, p. 10.

law has come an awareness that it is of greater significance than ever before. Hence an up-to-date definition might read: It is a body of generally accepted principles and rules regulating or controlling the conduct of nation-states, individuals, and international organizations.[8]

Like all law, international law is a form of social control. It is social control based on international consent. It may be expressed in a formal treaty or implied by way of generally accepted conduct. It is generally agreed that such conduct may be the basis for customary international law, which is as binding as express law.

The fact that the methods of creating and enforcing social control on an international level are more primitive than those employed on the national level should not obscure the fact that each, within limits, is able to compel action, secure patterns of conduct, and impose controls on proper subjects. Those who contend that international law does not exist are ignoring the ultimate test of law, namely, that states or peoples more frequently than not, for a variety of reasons, comply with known principles and rules.

The fact that the rules and principles of international law may be less certainly known than those of municipal law[9] and that such rules and principles do not always effectively control the conduct of nation-states, individuals, and international organizations is not a fatal defect. Numerous violations of municipal law do not warrant the conclusion that robbery, for example, is no longer a crime or that law no longer exists. The fact that not all violations of international law are punished does not destroy international law, nor does it justify unlawful conduct.

The means of enforcing law are extremely varied and include physical force (hanging and hostilities) as well as economic means (fines and international boycotts). International law is at its best when it is self-enforcing, that is, when states are aware that it is to their mutual interest or advantage to conform to law.

The Sources of International Law

On the national level there is no difficulty in ascertaining the formal sources of law. Such law flows from highly developed legislative, executive, judicial, and administrative bodies. The people of the community create and amend constitutions. National, state, and local legislative bodies enact statutes and ordinances. Presidents and governors issue executive orders having the force of law. Administrative agencies issue rules and regulations. Courts impart meaning to constitutions, statutes, orders, rules, and regulations, and they legislate in their own right through the processes of the common law. In all these instances there is an explicit and readily ascertainable formal source of law.

While the sources of international law are as well established as those of municipal law, the institutions contributing to its formation and enforcement are neither so highly developed nor so carefully integrated, and occasionally they have not been so well received.

The governing Statute of the International Court of Justice, created by the San Francisco Conference on June 26, 1945, listed six sources of international law.

Treaties The first consists of international conventions or treaties, whether general or particular. Treaties or conventions need not receive universal approval before they become general international law. The Charter of the United Nations, for example, has not been accepted by all the countries of the world. Nonetheless, by reason of the strength and prestige of the members of the United Nations, and as a consequence of the Charter's express provision in Article 2, Section 6, fundamental Charter concepts are considered by some authorities to be binding upon all the nations of the world, whether United Nations members or not.

Treaties have an anomalous quality as a source of international law. On the one hand, it is said that treaties are binding, must be adhered to, and may be enforced. This notion is represented by the Latin phrase *pacta sunt servanda*. This concept accords

---

[8] These principles and rules are generally accepted because they make provision for conditions that are mutually beneficial to those so governed. In this way national interests serve to provide a foundation on which a general system of law may be built. It also means that international law may in many situations be largely self-enforcing, e.g., diplomatic protection, commercial exchanges, and maritime practices.

[9] In this context "municipal law" means the domestic law of any nation-state, such as criminal, contract, mortgage, antitrust, tort, or other forms of locally created laws.

to a treaty the same validity and status that exist for a contract between private persons. Adherence to treaties and contracts is said to contribute to an orderly, predictable (and hence legal) state of affairs.

On the other hand, it is frequently argued that sovereignty and treaty obligations are mutually inconsistent. Those who subscribe to this view regard a treaty as a "scrap of paper" and urge that the sovereignty of a state permits it to disregard and unilaterally disavow a treaty if such action is deemed expedient and in accord with its national interest. Thus it has been argued that a nation-state may voluntarily impose limitations upon itself for the sake of expediency but that later, when the reasons for such self-limitation no longer exist, it may reject what others have come to regard as a solemn covenant. This point of view is destructive not only of treaties as a source of international law but also of international law itself, and the world community has chosen to regard states following such practices as outlaw states.

International Custom A second source of international law is international custom—general practices that have achieved legal standing. Customary law is produced by a continuing course of conduct. As a result, nation-states are legally obliged to conform to given patterns of behavior. Through customary law, practices that at an earlier time were followed only for practical or moral reasons evolve into binding, legal, right-and-duty relationships. The customary law of diplomatic privileges and immunities developed slowly. However, it is possible for customary law to develop quite rapidly, as in the case of the international law of the sea, under which sailing vessels were very quickly accorded a right-of-way over power-driven vessels, following the advent of the latter. Today the practices of states in outer space have contributed to the development of a new legal principle, which calls for freedom in the use and exploration of outer space for peaceful, i.e., nonaggressive and beneficial, purposes.

Generally Recognized Principles of Law A third source of international law consists of the general principles of law recognized by civilized nations. This is the broadest source of international law. In practice it consists of provable precedents and authorities other than treaties, and it is founded upon intelligent international public policy. Examples of general principles include, among others, good faith, respect for acquired rights, and the inherent right of self-preservation.

Judicial Decisions A fourth source of international law consists of judicial decisions by both national and international tribunals. However, under the terms of the Statute of the International Court of Justice, the decisions of the Court have no binding force except between the parties and in respect to each particular case. This is clearly opposed to the notion of precedent as developed in countries adhering to the principles of the common law. The Statute provides that judicial decisions may be regarded only as a subsidiary means for the determination of rules of law.

Writings of Publicists The fifth source of international law is made up of the writings of highly qualified publicists. A publicist is an expert, usually a professor of international law or someone who has had extensive foreign-office experience, who has achieved status as a result of his objective researches into the subject of his specialty. Courts very frequently have recourse to the works of publicists, and there is considerable harmony among their writings. The Statute provides that such writings shall be a subsidiary method for determining the meaning of international law.

Equity Another source of international law is equity, a historic approach to law or its elements, which has for its purpose the mitigation of the harshness of strict law. In international law the doctrine is referred to as *ex aequo et bono,* and under the Statute of the International Court of Justice it may be used as a basis for that Court's decisions, provided the parties agree. To the extent that such decisions may appeal to the intelligence of men, they will be used as precedents in later cases. In this manner recognized principles of justice and fair dealing become a significant part of international law.

Areas of International Law

Traditionally, the substance of international law has been discussed under three major headings: the law of war, the law of peace, and the law of neutrality.

The Law of War International law approaches the problem of war from two essentially different points of view. In the first place, international law governs the creation of a legal state of war; second, it governs the conditions under which such warfare may be conducted.

A legal state of war must be distinguished from the mere use of force as such. The significance of this difference should not be overlooked; war is a *legal* rather than a *factual* condition,[10] which can exist only when at least one of the parties *intends* that war shall actually exist. This state of mind is known as the *animus belligerendi*. Thus if one nation-state intends to engage in a police action, using force short of war, but the other state chooses to regard the action as war, the legal state of war actually exists. It is quite conceivable, further, that a legal state of war might exist temporarily without a display of force and without hostilities. An example was the so-called phony war between the Allies and Germany in 1939, at which time there had been declarations of war, evidencing the intent that a legal state of war should exist, although for months there was little actual combat.

With the establishment of a legal state of war, international law brings into play the rules and principles affecting the rights and duties of the belligerents and, to the extent that neutrality may still exist, the rights and duties of neutrals. Today external subversion is often carried out by forceful means. This has the title of "insurgency" and need not constitute war in the legal sense.

Several highly significant international agreements have materially affected the establishment of the legal state of war or its conduct. Among them were the Hague Conventions of 1907, dealing with the opening of hostilities, the laws and customs of war on land, and bombardment by naval forces in time of war. The Kellogg-Briand Peace Pact of 1928 proclaimed the renunciation of war as an instrument of international policy. The 1949 Geneva Conventions dealt with equally important matters, including the rights and duties of prisoners of war.

The Charter of the United Nations provides, in effect, that war is prohibited, although the pertinent article does not employ the term "war." Thus Article 2, Section 4, provides that "all members shall refrain in their international relations from the threat or use of force against the territorial integrity or political independence of any state, or in any other manner inconsistent with the purposes of the United Nations." This provision withdraws from the members of the United Nations the right to embark unilaterally upon war and upon the aggressive use of warlike force. This provision and others clearly seek to confer upon the United Nations a monopoly of war and warlike force. However, it is a principle of general international law that a nation-state may preserve itself against dangerously hostile conduct by external forces.[11] This principle is recognized in Article 51 of the Charter, which permits a nation-state to engage in individual as well as collective *self-defense*, despite the monopoly of force conferred on the United Nations in Article 2. The wronged state is expected to report the situation to the United Nations. It then becomes the collective duty of the members of that organization—or of a regional organization—to take such action (within the practical range of its capabilities) as is deemed necessary in order to restore international peace and security.

Nation-states frequently engage in forceful acts against other states without the intent to establish the legal condition of war. Such acts are referred to as "force in peace," "force short of war," or "hostile measures short of war." Examples of such use of force include *retortions* (economic pressure in connection with discriminatory tariffs, import and export laws, and boycotts); *reprisals* (acts of force taken against a nation-state because of its earlier violation of the rights of the state engaging in the reprisal, including confiscation of the property of the foreign state or of aliens, embargo, and nonfulfillment of treaty agreements); *pacific blockade* (preventing the shipping of the blockaded

---

[10]Justice Grier in the *Prize Cases*, 2 Black 636 (1862).

[11]Elihu Root, in addressing the American Society of International Law, said in 1914 that each sovereign state has the right "to protect itself by preventing a condition of affairs in which it will be too late to protect itself." "The Real Monroe Doctrine," *American Journal of International Law*, vol. 8, no. 3, p. 432, 1914.

country from entering or leaving its own ports, without a declaration of war); *quarantine* (involving the interdiction of the shipment of offensive war materials); and, in general, forceful intervention of any kind, short of war, in the internal affairs of a friendly nation.

The members of the United Nations illustrated the effectiveness of collective security in the Korean police action. Without considering the serious and extended use of force in Korea to be war, the member states, as well as North Korea and the People's Republic of China, elected to apply the rules of international law to those hostilities. The parties applied the terms of the Geneva Conventions of 1949 relating to the treatment of prisoners of war; the amelioration of the condition of the wounded, sick, and shipwrecked; and the protection of civilian persons in time of war. This was done in spite of the fact that the sixty-odd states that had signed these agreements did not include North Korea or the People's Republic of China. The adherence of those two parties was notably less strict than that of the United Nations' command.

In addition to dealing with the nature of war, the rights of participants, and the conduct of hostilities, the law of war also deals with such public international phenomena as civil war, belligerency, insurgency, the termination of war, and the effect of war on treaties. The law of war also establishes rules as to the right of belligerents to effect blockades, to engage in lawful visit and search of nonbelligerent craft for contraband, and, in the event of its discovery, to establish and make use of prize courts. War also affects private rights. Into this latter area fall such highly important personal matters as the determination of the enemy character of individuals and corporations, the rights of enemy aliens, and the rights of citizens to establish trade and commercial contacts with the enemy.

The international law of war has reached an interesting period in its growth. A vast body of customary and treaty law exists, which recognizes the possibility of the existence of a legal state of war. This body of law also supports the idea that, short of war, a nation-state has the right to engage in forceful acts and that these need not constitute war unless the participants so intend. On the other hand, under certain treaties, including the Charter of the United Nations, the right to engage in war unilaterally, except as an instrumentality of national self-defense, is proscribed. It is clear that the intention of the Charter is to confer an exclusive monopoly over collective international force upon the United Nations or upon regional organizations.

If the United Nations should actually acquire the effective monopoly of force, the law of war relating to the creation by nation-states of a legal condition of war would be substantially modified. States would then be called upon to support wars or police actions as community sanctions under United Nations auspices. In any event, customary and treaty law, as it now exists and as it may be subsequently modified, will continue to govern the conditions under which hostilities may be conducted. The limits of permissive conduct in the course of warfare will continue to be legal limits. Recent conflicts point to the need for a clarification of, and restriction on, the limits of lawful conduct.

The Law of Peace Peace, like war, is a legal condition. It exists when states are not pursuing national rights through war. For our purposes the restless periods of a cold war, in which there may be little international peace of mind, fall technically into the legal orbit of peace. Also, as previously stated, certain types of public coercion may be used in time of peace.

International law regulates or controls scores of peacetime public and private relationships. Public relationships so governed include the recognition of new nation-states and of changes in the form of government of old ones, the law of diplomatic privileges and immunities, acquisition and loss of territory by a state, the right of one nation-state to make use of the courts of another to protect rights, extradition, and the negotiation of treaties and other agreements. Disputes involving private rights may relate to the nationalization by a government of an alien's assets or an alien's right to compensation for personal injury sustained as a consequence of the foreign government's failure to conform to international standards of protection. All such disputes may be resolved through diplomacy. They may also be referred to international courts or arbitral tribunals when a nation-state officially sponsors the claim of its national.

Peacetime international law is confronted by a

complex political-legal situation known as "recognition." Recognition involves the establishment of effective international relations between states and governments and is usually achieved through the exchange of diplomatic representatives. Recognition of governments is accorded on either a de facto or a de jure basis. When de facto, the recognizing state accepts the existence of the other government on a factual basis. When de jure, the recognizing state accepts the existence of the recognized government on a legal basis. Typically, the exchange of diplomatic representatives is reserved for de jure recognition.

National policies, rather than law, determine whether a state will be recognized. The United States, for example, reserves recognition for states that have been able to establish governments which are able to maintain internal law and order and which appear likely to adhere to their international responsibilities. The United States also views nonrecognition as a proper method of indicating moral disapproval of states or governments which have come into being via force or which subscribe to totalitarian principles. Other states usually accord full recognition to any state that is able to establish a reasonably effective government. Refusal to exchange diplomatic representatives prevents the establishment of international political and commercial relations and may lead to resentment on the part of the nonrecognized state or government. On the other hand, the nonrecognizing state may, through the process of nonrecognition, be able to obtain some measure of assurance from the nonrecognized state or government that it will conform to acceptable international standards. When this has been achieved, recognition generally follows.

Among the private relationships controlled by the law of peace are those benefiting individuals rather than the nation-state. For example, treaties of commerce permit aliens, usually on a reciprocal basis, to enter foreign states in order to engage in trade and commerce, to own property, and to return with their profits and goods to their native lands. Treaties prohibiting double taxation and authorizing possession of patents, copyrights, and reciprocal rights of inheritance protect private rights in time of peace.

All treaties, because of the subjects dealt with by treaty, occupy a position of great significance under the United States Constitution. Article 6 states: "This Constitution, and the Laws of the United States which shall be made in Pursuance thereof; and all Treaties made, or which shall be made, under the Authority of the United States, shall be the supreme Law of the Land; and the Judges in every State shall be bound thereby, any Thing in the Constitution or Laws of any State to the Contrary notwithstanding." The Supreme Court of the United States has held that the term "treaty" includes both the formal type of treaty, which has received the approval of two-thirds of the members of the Senate who have given their affirmative advice and consent prior to ratification by the president, and the less formal type of treaty, which has come to be known as an "executive agreement." The latter type of international agreement, when approved by a majority vote in both houses of the Congress and signed by the president, is in reality a joint resolution of the Congress. The formal treaty and the executive agreement described above have equal legal status, and both serve to bind the United States in its external relations.

The formal treaty and the executive agreement must conform to constitutional requirements and are without legal standing if they fail to do so. It is only when these international agreements conform to the provisions of the Constitution that they become the supreme law of the land. This last expression has sometimes been misunderstood. Our Supreme Court long ago held it to mean that while such agreements are inferior to the Constitution of the United States and must conform to the Constitution, when such conformity exists such agreements are superior to earlier national statutes and are superior to state constitutions, laws, and ordinances.

As between a national statute and a treaty, the general rule, subject to minor exceptions (and this exists where the treaty is that special type of an executive agreement that has not received congressional approval), is that the last in point of time is controlling upon the United States and its residents.

In order for formal treaties and congressionally approved executive agreements to be superior to state constitutions, laws, ordinances, and local policies, it is necessary for such undertakings to deal with those matters which fall to the national government under our form of federal government. Thus if the United States entered into an international agreement that clearly dealt with a subject over which a state had exclusive authority, it would be incumbent on the Supreme Court in a proper case to declare that the treaty was in excess of the powers of the national government. In short, all executive agreements and all formal treaties are inferior to the Constitution of the United States, and it is the duty of the Supreme Court to ensure that this principle is respected.

Treaties and customary international law require that a nation-state extend to resident aliens the normal police protections accorded to its own citizens. States failing to accord proper protection may be held liable for breach of duty, just as in the case of individuals who have actually deprived aliens of their rights. All the post–World War II treaties emphasizing human rights fall within this category. Indeed, some of the recent European treaties permit individuals, as individuals, to pursue private remedies against nation-states before international courts and commissions.

The need for clear-cut and stable peacetime rules of international law is apparent. Without such rules the exchange of persons, ideas, goods, and services across international boundaries could not take place. States would then be obliged to live like hermits.

The Problem of Neutrality Neutrality, in the traditional sense, means nonparticipation in existing wars. A neutral state must refrain from giving assistance to warring nation-states which are termed "belligerents." Neutrality imposes duties on the nation-state but not on individuals, who need not be neutral in their private conduct beyond observing the restrictions placed upon them by their own government.

In view of the wholesale collective-security commitments that developed after World War I, the question is frequently raised of whether a nation-state may live up to such commitments and still be neutral. Collective security finds its philosophical basis in the belief that there are just and unjust wars, wars of unjust aggression and just defense. The just-war, or *bellum justum,* concept became a part of the Covenant of the League of Nations, of the Kellogg-Briand Peace Pact, and of the Charter of the United Nations. It is based upon the practical idea that when an arsonist has started a fire, it is to the advantage of the entire community to join in putting it out. The nation-state that fails to assist in putting out the fire may be regarded as an inactive supporter of the arsonist.

The need for concerted self-protection has resulted in the modification of neutrality. The Charter of the United Nations requires members to assist the attacked state against the aggressor, thus giving the concept almost universal support. When the United Nations asked its members to take a stand against the North Korean forces of aggression, the response from its then sixty members was overwhelming. By 1951 some fifty-five members had joined in imposing embargoes upon shipments to the North Koreans, and twenty-six offered to send troops or equipment to the fighting front. Although the United Nations commander found it impossible to accept all the troops and equipment offered (despite his need for even larger quotas of effective men and materials from all sources), the response greatly strengthened the concept of collective security and further dissipated the notion of neutrality. This development means, in the words of a leading writer on international law, that "the rule of general international law, imposing the obligation of impartiality upon neutral states, is superseded by the Charter."[12] The creation of the multimember United Nations peace-keeping forces has not resulted in unneutral conduct by participating states. United Nations members must assist an aggrieved nation-state and abstain from assisting an aggressor. If the Security Council or the Assembly does not call upon all the members for such assistance, it may be assumed that the traditional rules of neutrality would remain applicable to those members not called. Nonetheless, they would have the ultimate duty to assist against any aggressor, and in this sense, neutrality as a concept of international law may be said to be wasting away, if it is not already extinct. However, its utility in the small or brush-war situation, or where the United Nations does not act, is still significant.

The Institutional Approach to International Law

The United Nations is an institution for the creation, development, and implementation of international law. Its large membership, including all the

[12]Hans Kelsen, *Principles of International Law,* Holt, Rinehart and Winston, Inc., New York, 1952, p. 87.

more important nation-states, gives great prestige to the international agreements prepared under its sponsorship. Through the use of the Assembly; various councils, committees, and commissions (including its International Law Commission);[13] and the Secretariat, careful attention has been given to gaps in international law. As the result of the studies undertaken by the United Nations, draft treaties or conventions have been prepared, approved, signed by delegates, and submitted to member states for ratification and enforcement. Its resolutions and recommendations, particularly when unanimous, are now being recognized as having a growing influence.

International Legislation The creation of new rules of international law through the treaty process has been referred to as "international legislation." Of course, the treaty need not be restricted to the establishment of new law, and many treaties affirm that they are merely putting down in specific form the preexisting customary law. For example, the 1958 Convention on the High Seas expressly acknowledged that its provisions were generally declaratory of established principles of international law. The United Nations has been used effectively to facilitate the rapid growth of new rules of international law and for the codification of traditional rules.

International Courts and Tribunals International courts are also institutions for the creation, development, and implementation of international law. The need for a regularized court procedure was recognized after World War I with the creation of the Permanent Court of International Justice. During its effective lifetime (1923–1939) it decided thirty-one cases and rendered twenty-seven advisory opinions. When the San Francisco Conference met in 1945 to create the United Nations, the participating nation-states decided to establish the new International Court of Justice to replace the old court. Since 1945 the International Court of Justice, with headquarters at The Hague, has been called upon to decide important international legal disputes and has rendered about fifty decisions and advisory opinions.

Other international institutions have the duty to apply international law to interstate disputes. Some, like the Tribunal of the Permanent Court of Arbitration at The Hague, established in 1899, are of a permanent nature. Others are temporary, such as the mixed or general claims commissions whereby states, under authority conferred by bilateral treaties, decide claims of their respective nationals.

As individuals have become subjects of international law, international tribunals have been created to hear and decide the rights of persons. Under the International Military Tribunal created in 1945 (the Nuremberg Tribunal), three main types of acts are regarded as crimes carrying individual responsibility: war crimes, crimes against peace, and crimes against humanity.

This Tribunal established as a precedent in international criminal law the rule that the official position of a defendant, whether the head of a nation-state or a responsible official of a government, should not be considered to free such an individual from responsibility for his acts or to justify mitigating his punishment. The Tribunal also laid down the rule that even where the defendant acted pursuant to orders of his government or of a superior officer in that government, he is not thereby freed from personal responsibility. Under such circumstances, however, the Tribunal might (and did) consider such facts in the interest of justice. A similar court, known officially as the International Military Tribunal for the Far East, applied international criminal law to Japanese military commanders and officials. Several of the defendants were found guilty of crimes against humanity. The power of the United States to join in the creation of this international tribunal was affirmed by the United States Supreme Court in the case of *Hirota v. MacArthur, General of the Army*.[14]

The Status of International Law

International law, like all law, must justify its existence by demonstrating its utility. Nation-states, and their nationals, will give force and effect to international law when they perceive that the

---

[13]The International Law Commission is charged with the progressive development of international law. Since 1947 it has prepared for the Assembly draft conventions on such subjects as rights and duties of states, international criminal jurisdiction, the law of treaties, regime of the high seas, regime of the territorial waters, nationality, asylum, diplomatic intercourse and immunities, and other matters. In 1971 it published an analytic "Survey of International Law," *U.N. Document* A/CN.4/245.

[14]338 U.S. 197 (1948).

rule of law is to be preferred over the law of the jungle. Modern international law is neither strange nor exotic. Its practical and dynamic qualities are reflected in the attention now being given by it to such subjects as the environment, human rights— including the rights of those engaged in armed conflict—manned earth-orbiting space objects, multinational business entities, the ocean, and terrorism.

A word of caution is in order at this point. The world community has not reached the same degree of organization that exists within nation-states. The comparative inadequacy of the community's executive, legislative, and judicial institutions has meant that when one contrasts international law with municipal law, the conclusion is reached that international law progresses more slowly. As a result, there has been a slower identification of the customary practices of states as a nascent but real part of customary international law. Although municipal courts have played a larger role in the refinement of legal rules than international tribunals have, with the growing effectiveness of international organizations there has been an enormous increase in the volume of international law. Further, as the world community enlarges, many new opportunities arise for the use of international law and international legal processes.

However, political disagreements often impede action in the United Nations and in other world institutions, and reservations attached to treaties may weaken the effectiveness of international agreements. For example, it is a rather common practice to exclude from the competence of an international court matters regarded by the signatory states as of fundamental importance to themselves, especially matters of domestic jurisdiction or domestic concern.

On the credit side of the ledger, international law has advanced the welfare of mankind and has kept the game of power politics within relatively predictable bounds. Although international law requires a high degree of order in international affairs for it to maximize its values, it can also contribute to the existence of such order while confronted simultaneously with demands for change and for stability.

International law has established rights and duties for states, individuals, and international organizations and has regularized the means whereby disputes are resolved. It has emphasized the fact that there can be legal as well as political disputes, and it has demonstrated that such disputes may be referred to an important body of legal principles, standards, and rules.

We now turn to the subject of international organizations. International law and international organizations are opposite sides of the same coin. Only through the perfection of international organizations can there be a more effective international law—both contributing to the ultimate realization of a more hospitable and harmonious world environment.

INTERNATIONAL ORGANIZATION

Historians have traced the ideal of world cooperation, as a means of achieving peace and human betterment, to the writings of Chinese philosophers who lived more than 1,000 years before Christ. Another early example was the Amphictyonic Council, an organization of Greek cities between the third and first centuries B.C. Efforts toward international cooperation have also been aided by the writings of influential statesmen, including Henry IV of France, William Penn, Simón Bolívar, Woodrow Wilson, and many others.[15]

It has often been said that if we did not have international organizations, we should certainly have to create them. They may be divided into two broad categories: public organizations like the League of Nations and the United Nations and private organizations like the International Chamber of Commerce and the World Council of Churches. Even multinational business entities represent a very powerful type of private international organization. The motives underlying international organizations are as diversified as the interests that appeal to the human mind. Here, however, our attention must be confined to the major public organizations. Their roles continue to increase in importance as foreign policy is increasingly conducted through international organizations.[16]

---

[15] F. H. Hinsley, *Power and Pursuit of Peace,* Cambridge University Press, New York, 1963, chaps. 1–7.

[16] A listing of the specialized international organizations connected with the United Nations appears on p. 435. Other well-known public international organizations include the Organization of American States (OAS), the Organization of African Unity (OAU), the European Economic Community (EEC), and the Council of Europe (COE), with its Commission and Court of Human Rights. The list is a rapidly growing one and could be extended almost indefinitely.

The United Nations: History and Goals

Disheartened by the human misery of recurring wars and encouraged by the hope of achieving a stable peace, the American people, speaking through their government, issued a call in 1945 for an international conference to consider the establishment of a new world organization.[17] The United Nations Conference on International Organization convened at San Francisco on April 25, 1945, and completed its work with the adoption of the Charter and the Statute of the International Court of Justice on June 26. These documents and the goals set out in them have been destined to challenge the whole capacity of men throughout the following years.

It has been a matter of constant concern to world leaders that world public opinion has failed to recognize that it is one thing to establish an international institution dedicated to both practical and idealistic goals, such as the maintenance of international peace and security, and quite another matter to achieve these goals. In any analysis of the United Nations it is important to distinguish between this organization as an instrument of government designed to achieve important social goals and its record of success and failure as it confronts the political issues surfacing in world politics during each succeeding era. As important as the words of the Charter and the Statute are, it is now recognized that international goodwill is an essential ingredient for the resolution of difficult problems. The proof of the United Nations is in its accomplishments, not merely in the goals that were outlined in San Francisco. Since 1945 the United Nations has become an instrument of government. As such, it must be perceived as seeking to achieve identified social goals. It must also be seen as an instrument consigned to human hands—hands that can achieve and hands that can fail.

The nation-states that make up the United Nations have agreed upon three major goals. First, it is dedicated to the building of conditions that will allow for peaceful and friendly relations among peoples. This is to be realized through increased recognition of the dignity and worth of human beings. To this end the United Nations is attempting to raise the world standards of living and to fight hunger, disease, and illiteracy in all corners of the world.

Second, the United Nations seeks to provide formal machinery for the adjustment of international tensions when the normal processes of diplomacy prove ineffective. The many United Nations councils, commissions, and committees afford facilities for rational discussion and debate.

Third, the United Nations is dedicated to the establishment of a program of collective security under which all its members must come to the support of any member victimized by aggression. The United Nations has established machinery whereby diplomatic, economic, and military sanctions may be imposed upon nation-states which have violated treaty commitments or international law or which are a threat to the general peace.

In short, the members of the United Nations are pledged to act *for* peace, security, freedom, understanding, prosperity, health, and education and *against* war, aggression, enslavement, intolerance, poverty, disease, and ignorance. At the final plenary session, in addressing the delegates from the fifty invited nation-states, Secretary of State Stettinius said: "This Charter is a compact born of suffering and of war. With it now rests our hope for good and lasting peace."[18] President Truman said on the same occasion: "This Charter, like our own Constitution, will be expanded and improved as time goes on. No one claims that it is now a final or a perfect instrument. The successful use of this instrument will require the united will and firm determination of the free peoples who have created it. The job will tax the moral strength and fiber of all. It has set up machinery of international cooperation which men and nations of good will can use. . . ."[19] Yet, despite these words of caution, many well-intentioned people assumed that the millennium in international affairs was to be expected overnight, if not sooner. In the words of Sir Winston Churchill, the United Nations "was never conceived as a stairway to Heaven, but as a savior from Hell." Perhaps it should be regarded as neither, but simply as an institution that will further

---

[17] The formal invitation was extended by the government of the United States on behalf of itself and the governments of Great Britain, the Soviet Union, and China.

[18] *U.N. Document* 1209, *Verbatim Minutes*, p. 10.
[19] Ibid.

INTERNATIONAL LAW AND ORGANIZATION

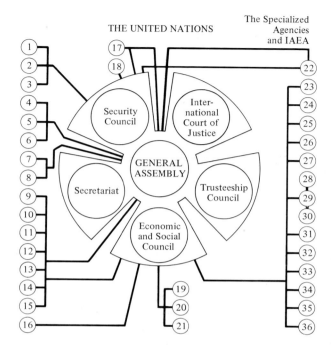

Figure 21.1 The United Nations system.

The United Nations

1. United Nations Truce Supervision Organization in Palestine (UNTSO)
2. United Nations Military Observer Group in India and Pakistan (UNMOGIP)
3. United Nations Peace-keeping Force in Cyprus (UNFICYP)
4. Main Committees
5. Standing and Procedural Committees
6. Other Subsidiary Organs of General Assembly
7. United Nations Relief and Works Agency for Palestine Refugees in the Near East (UNRWA)
8. United Nations Conference on Trade and Development (UNCTAD)
9. Trade and Development Board
10. United Nations Development Programme (UNDP)
11. United Nations Capital Development Fund
12. United Nations Industrial Development Organization (UNIDO)
13. United Nations Institute for Training and Research (UNITAR)
14. United Nations Children's Fund (UNICEF)
15. United Nations High Commissioner for Refugees (UNHCR)
16. Joint United Nations–FAO World Food Programme
17. Disarmament Commission
18. Military Staff Committee
19. Regional Economic Commission
20. Functional Commissions
21. Sessional, Standing and *Ad Hoc* Committees

The Specialized Agencies and IAEA

22	IAEA	International Atomic Energy Agency
23	ILO	International Labour Organization
24	FAO	Food and Agriculture Organization of the United Nations
25	UNESCO	United Nations Educational, Scientific and Cultural Organization
26	WHO	World Health Organization
27	IMF	International Monetary Fund
28	IDA	International Development Association
29	IBRD	International Bank for Reconstruction and Development
30	IFC	International Finance Corporation
31	ICAO	International Civil Aviation Organization
32	UPU	Universal Postal Union
33	ITU	International Telecommunication Union
34	WMO	World Meteorological Organization
35	IMCO	Inter-Governmental Maritime Consultative Organization
36	GATT	General Agreement on Tariffs and Trade

the earthly realization of the higher potentialities of mankind.

The United Nations is made up of seven major components: the General Assembly, the Security Council, the Economic and Social Council, the Trusteeship Council, the Secretariat, the International Court of Justice, and the specialized agencies. (See Figure 21.1.) The responsibilities and functions of each will be explained briefly.

The General Assembly The General Assembly is the major deliberative body of the United Nations.

It is composed of all the member nations (now 138 in number), each having one vote.

Any member of the Assembly may discuss any matter within the scope of the Charter; important measures are adopted by a two-thirds vote, and other questions by majority vote. This is a departure from the rule of unanimity adhered to by the League of Nations and the modified rule of unanimity followed in the Security Council.

The Charter prescribes that important questions shall include (but need not be limited to) recommendations with respect to the maintenance of international peace and security, the election of nonpermanent members of the Security Council, the election of members of the Economic and Social Council, the election of members of the Trusteeship Council, the admission of new members to the United Nations, the suspension of the rights and privileges of membership, the expulsion of members, questions relating to the operation of the trusteeship system, and budgetary matters. The Assembly decides by simple majority vote whether any other subjects are to be considered important. If so, action on such questions then requires a two-thirds majority vote of the members present and voting.

The Assembly has the further responsibility of approving draft treaties and conventions prepared under United Nations auspices, the right to consider the principles governing disarmament, and the right to call dangerous international situations to the attention of the Security Council. The Assembly may discuss any matter within the scope of the Charter or relating to the powers or functions of the United Nations organs. It may also make recommendations to promote the progressive development of international law and its codification; to further international cooperation in the economic, social, cultural, and educational fields; and to advance human rights and fundamental freedoms for all persons without regard to race, sex, language, or religion.

In assessing its responsibilities under the Charter, the General Assembly has contributed to the constitutional growth of the Charter. Just as the Constitution of the United States has been properly termed an "emerging" constitution as a result of its changed meaning and focus over the years, so has the United Nations Charter demonstrated a capacity for constitutional growth. This has taken place as the whole United Nations structure has been obliged to change its stance in order to serve the major purposes for which it was created. One example of the constitutional growth of the General Assembly was the adoption by that body on November 3, 1950, of the famous Uniting for Peace Resolution 377 (V).

The resolution is important from several points of view. In the first place, through it the Assembly specifically conferred upon itself authority to engage in the maintenance of international peace and security, which was not, in specific terms, granted to the Assembly by the Charter. The Charter permits the Assembly to consider such problems and to make recommendations concerning them. Responsibility for the maintenance of peace and security appeared, under the Charter, to have been conferred upon the Security Council, although *exclusive* power was not so assigned. Hence it has been argued that even though the General Assembly had not specifically received this authority under the terms of the Charter, it did in fact and by clear implication possess it.

The Uniting for Peace Resolution resulted from the apparent inability of the Security Council to take effective action in the 1950 Korean crisis. In January 1950 the Soviet Union absented itself from the Security Council. In June 1950, during its absence, the United Nations embarked upon its police action in Korea, which undoubtedly would have been opposed by the Soviet Union had it been present at the time. In August 1950 the Soviet delegate returned and thereafter employed delaying tactics in an effort to prevent effective United Nations assistance to South Korea.

As a result of the resolution, the Assembly, rather than the Security Council, took affirmative steps to maintain the sovereignty of South Korea by recommending that member states join in a collective police action against the aggressor. It thus undertook a new and highly significant function.

This resolution is important because it shows that the Charter is a living document. It is broad enough through interpretation to permit adjustment to crisis situations. The action of the Assembly in 1950 gave notice to the world that members intended to support the concept of collective security, and it also established a striking precedent. With the advent of the Suez crisis in 1956 it was soon seen that the Security Council was unable to take effective peace-keeping action, and the matter was transferred to the General Assembly for authoritative action. Again, when the Congo crisis exploded in 1960, it was the General Assembly—aided on this occasion by decisions of the Security Council—that provided the authority for effective United Nations action. In examining these precedents it should be borne in mind that the pre-1961 General Assembly was a totally different body from the one that exists today. In 1952 only sixty states, and in 1956 only eighty states, had been accorded United Nations membership. It was only in September of 1960 that membership reached 100 with the granting of membership in that year to seventeen newly created African states.

The Security Council: Duties and Functions The Security Council, which is the second principal organ of the United Nations, is charged with the primary responsibility of maintaining international peace and security, including collaboration with the nation-states that are not members of the United Nations. Under Article 39, the Security Council has the duty to determine the existence of any threat to the peace, breach of the peace, or act of aggression and to make recommendations or decide what measures shall be taken to maintain or restore international peace and security.[20] It also has the express responsibility for formulating, with the assistance of the Military Staff Committee, plans for the regulation of national armaments. The Military Staff Committee, as a subsidiary of the Security Council, is required to determine the strength and degree of readiness of plans for the combined action of proposed national air force contingents. National tensions have combined to prevent any effective use of this committee.

The Security Council is also charged with encouraging the pacific settlement of local disputes through regional arrangements or agencies. It may call upon such regional groups, when appropriate, to undertake enforcement action within the area involved. Occasionally, questions arise as to whether a regional organization or the United Nations should be the principal force in the resolution of regional threats to the peace. In the Dominican crisis of 1965, for example, both the United Nations and the Organization of American States considered the problem to fall particularly within their area of concern.

The Security Council also supervises the work of the Disarmament Commission. The Security Council joins with the General Assembly in supervising the work of the International Atomic Energy Agency.

With the 1965 amendment to the Charter, ten members became eligible to Security Council membership for two-year terms. Five are elected each year. Theoretically, the nonpermanent members are selected on the basis of their contributions to the cause of international peace and security. In reality, geographic considerations and bloc politics have been weighty forces. As a result of the amendment, a pattern has emerged allowing two Latin American states, three African states, two Asian states, and three European states to hold membership. Some elasticity in the formula appeared in 1973, when the "European contingent" was represented by one European state, by Australia, and by the Byelorussian Soviet Socialist Republic.

The *voting procedures* within the Security Council depend upon whether the problem presented is one of substance or of procedure. If the issue is *substantive* (e.g., declaring a nation-state to be an aggressor), nine affirmative votes, including those of all five permanent members, are required for passage of the motion. A negative vote by one of the Big Five defeats any substantive motion; this is the veto. The Soviet Union once contended that it could impose a veto by absenting itself from the Council when a substantive issue came to a vote or by abstaining from voting on a substantive issue even if present. Both these contentions have been rejected by the other members as without merit.

At the San Francisco conference the United States favored the introduction of the veto provision in the Charter. It was foreseen that at some future time, the United States might wish to employ

---

[20] In addition to the well-known United Nations Emergency Force (UNEF) in the Middle East, the United Nations Force in the Congo (ONUC), and the Truce Supervision Organization in Palestine (UNTSO), there have also been the following: the Military Observer Group in India and Pakistan (UNMOGIP) and the Peacekeeping Force in Cyprus (UNFICYP).

such a device. Only in the recent past has the United States been placed in a position where it considered that the veto was required to advance its policies. During the 1950s and the early 1960s the issues raised by the Soviet Union were often considered in the General Assembly, where the United States could muster the required votes. The less developed nations did not become members in large numbers until after 1960. During the early years of their membership they did not organize bloc positions, which the United States has now occasionally come to consider to be opposed to its national interest or to the more genuinely valid needs of the world community.

Thus in the years before the decade of the 1970s the veto was essentially a monopoly of the Soviet Union. However, it was also employed by China (Taiwan), France, and the United Kingdom. Also, on several occasions two negative votes were cast, e.g., those of the United Kingdom and France and those of the United Kingdom and the United States. Before casting its first unilateral veto, the United States joined with Britain on several occasions. In March 1970 these two states cast negative votes in order to prevent the adoption of a resolution sponsored by the less developed countries that sought to condemn Britain for its failure to employ force against Southern Rhodesia and for its failure to sever all communications with that territory. Again in 1973 the same states joined in casting negative votes respecting a resolution sponsored by a less developed country and directed toward censuring the Republic of South Africa and Portugal for their failure to comply with Security Council resolutions imposing economic and transportation restrictions on goods and persons transiting from these countries into Southern Rhodesia. In explaining its negative vote, the United States maintained that the resolution was unenforceable, that the sanctions would be ignored, and that it would result in a reduction in the credibility of the United Nations.

Although the United States had threatened a unilateral veto in 1950 at a time when it wished to secure for Secretary General Trygve Lie a second appointment, over the opposition of the Soviet Union, the threat was never implemented. However, in 1972 and 1973 the United States cast three unilateral vetoes in rapid succession.

The vetoes of September 10, 1972, and of July 26, 1973, were cast in the context of the ongoing Middle Eastern crisis. In the first instance the United States wished to link condemnation of terrorism practiced by private terroristic groups against the Jewish athletes who had participated in the 1972 Olympic Games with the governmental activities of the state of Israel involving Jewish aerial attacks upon the occupants of Syrian and Lebanese villages. When the United States was unable to convince the other members of the Security Council of the merits of such a combined condemnation, it vetoed a proposal that would have been condemnatory only of Israel. In the second case the United States cast the sole negative vote on a proposal advanced by eight nonpermanent members of the Council. The latter favored a resolution reaffirming the unanimously adopted Resolution 242 (1967),[21] reaffirming the proposal put forth by United Nations mediator Gunnar Jarring on behalf of the United Nations,[22] favoring the rights and legitimate aspirations of Palestinians, and opposing changes in the occupied territories that might obstruct a settlement or otherwise adversely affect the rights of the inhabitants. The United States urged, in casting the veto, that the draft was partisan in its context and would have overturned the agreement reached in Resolution 242.

Another veto was cast on March 21, 1973, at a meeting of the Security Council held in Panama. Panama, following a presentation to the Council including charges concerning the validity and meaning of the 1903 Isthmian Canal Convention, induced Council members to assert that the United States and Panama should conclude without delay a new treaty for the prompt elimination of the causes of conflict between them. The United States considered that this came close to constituting an interference in its domestic affairs and its security needs. It used the veto to indicate its opposition.

Whether or not one agrees with the considerations that have induced the United States to use the veto with increasing frequency in recent years, one

---

[21]This resolution of the Security Council contained the formula agreeable to both Arab states and Israel for Middle Eastern peace negotiations.
[22]The Jarring proposal linked the Israeli withdrawal pledge to an Egyptian peace pledge and stressed respect for the national sovereignty and territorial integrity for all states in the area.

fact stands out. The United States has been unable to stem the tide of opposition directed toward its international policies. Whether use or threat of use by the United States of the veto will induce other members of the world community to take a balanced approach to the wide-ranging needs and commitments of the United States remains to be seen. Reluctance to use this device should not be confused with its legality.

Decisions on *procedural* matters may be taken by an affirmative vote of any nine of the Council's fifteen members. Procedural matters involve such things as the chairmanship of the Council, items to be placed on the agenda, and dates and times of meetings. Such matters are not subject to the veto.

The Economic and Social Council The Economic and Social Council (ECOSOC), which originally consisted of eighteen members, was enlarged by the 1965 Charter amendment to twenty-seven. The principal work of ECOSOC has been to promote the general welfare of human beings. It is responsible for bringing about those conditions under which mankind can best enjoy the material and spiritual fruits of peace, e.g., economic, social, cultural, educational, health, and related conditions. It promotes respect for, and observance of, human rights and fundamental freedoms for all. It prepares draft declarations and conventions for submission to the Assembly in order to further the above objectives. After having sought for seventeen years to perfect important draft covenants on human rights, success was realized in 1966 with unanimous acceptance by the General Assembly of a Covenant on Civil and Political Rights and a separate Covenant on Economic, Social and Cultural Rights. They have been referred to states for ratification and implementation. The United Nations has given increasingly serious attention to the protection of human rights. In December 1965, for example, the General Assembly adopted and opened for signature a Convention on the Elimination of All Forms of Racial Discrimination. This agreement has entered into force, and the Committee on Racial Discrimination has begun to function. The United Nations has also been engaged in seeking meaningful protection of human rights in time of armed conflict.

Among the other important fields of action pursued through ECOSOC are the rehabilitation of physically handicapped persons, freedom of information, international control of the narcotic drug traffic, programs dealing with drug abuse, protection of the rights of minorities, the rights of children, and improvement in the status of women. In recent years it has made careful studies of the world economic situation, laying stress on economic projections, international economic cooperation, the development of international trade, commodity problems, and improvement in less developed economies.

It is the duty of ECOSOC to assist and supervise the thirteen specialized agencies that work in partnership with the United Nations. ECOSOC also supervises numerous boards, commissions, and programs dealing with economic and social concerns. The commissions include four regional economic commissions for Europe, Asia and the Far East, Latin America, and Africa. ECOSOC has the principal responsibility for the supervision of the United Nations Development Program (UNDP). Located within UNDP are several lesser bodies, including the United Nations Volunteer Program, which is fashioned somewhat along the lines of the Peace Corps in the United States. ECOSOC provides supervision of the United Nations International Children's Fund (UNICEF). ECOSOC supervises bodies engaged in economic development and concerned with training and research. It is the focal point for cooperation between the United Nations and private international organizations. Over the years ECOSOC has become an extremely important arm of the United Nations. Its emphasis on programs has resulted in substantial improvement in many aspects of life, material and otherwise, especially in the less developed countries. Membership in ECOSOC has resulted in substantial benefits to the United States. ECOSOC has made it possible for this country to wage the struggle for the basic economic and social conditions that underlie an effective peace, and it has also enabled the United States to keep old friends and gain new ones. Further, ECOSOC has provided a forum whereby the United States may effectively neutralize the propaganda activities of the Communists.

Technical assistance In 1966 the United Nations consolidated its technical assistance programs in UNDP, whose function is to provide systematic and sustained social, economic, and technical assistance to the less developed countries. Thousands of small-scale grants assist in the formulation of national development plans and in the building of governmental administrative machinery. Larger grants, which may lead to a more efficient use of development capital received from the World Bank, make it possible to conduct resource surveys and research concerning investment opportunities. Such funds are also used to develop competent personnel to carry on development work. During 1971 the United Nations received voluntary pledges and contributions of over $250 million to support UNDP. The United States gave over $86 million, or more than one-third of the UNDP budget.

Possibly the most interesting aspect of the technical assistance program is the fact that many nation-states that are its beneficiaries also supply assistance in other areas of the program. For example, while India, Haiti, Bolivia, and Rhodesia (to list but a few) have received assistance, all have contributed help as well. India has sent many technical experts on varied subjects to other lands (India has recently received Austrian assistance in perfecting its winter ski resorts); Haiti sent a coffee expert to Ethiopia (at the same time, Haiti was being aided by a Chinese expert in fish culture); Bolivia sent a specialist in the control of parasitic diseases to the Philippines; and Rhodesia sent an agricultural statistician to Libya.

Such assistance seeks to raise the technical competence of developing countries, stressing the development of skills that will permit greater and more efficient use of their often abundant resources. Unskilled labor is one such resource. Raw materials, previously wasted or uncaptured, have now become available as the result of technical assistance. In Afghanistan, for example, sugar beet pulp was formerly thrown away; under the guidance of a sugar beet specialist, the pulp has been converted to livestock feed.

The Trusteeship Council By the 1970s the Trusteeship Council had almost terminated the reasons for its existence. Starting with eleven trust territories, it had reduced this number to two by 1974. One, the Trust Territory of the Pacific Islands (Micronesia), was administered by the United States. The second, Papua New Guinea, was under Australian administration. Both states have been cooperating with the local residents in their movement toward full independence, and 1976 has been mentioned as the date for self-government for Papua New Guinea. The United States has indicated it will be guided by the wishes of the inhabitants. Pending the independence of these territories, the Council will continue to supervise the reports submitted by the administering authorities, examine petitions received from residents of the territories, and make periodic inspections at times agreed upon with the administering authorities.

Decolonization and the granting of independence to colonial countries and peoples No account of the work of the United Nations concerning aspirations for self-government would be complete without reference to many other areas that have not achieved independence or self-government. Hundreds of thousands of persons live in Rhodesia, Namibia (formerly South-West Africa), Spanish Sahara, the French Territory of Afars and Issas (formerly French Somaliland), Gibraltar, Belize (formerly British Honduras), the British Virgin Islands, American Samoa, the United States Virgin Islands, Guam, and about thirty other territories. The latter are mostly tiny islands situated in the Caribbean, Indian, and Pacific Oceans. Pursuant to General Assembly Resolution 1514 (XV) of December 14, 1960, states were called upon to implement the independence of such areas and entities "without further delay."

To cope with these areas and their problems, the United Nations established a Special Committee on Decolonization. Efforts have been made through resolutions, consensus positions, and general discussions and debates to secure conformity with the decolonization resolution. For example, in 1973 the special committee adopted a sixteen-power resolution relating to territories under Portuguese administration which reaffirmed that national liberation movements in these areas were the authentic representatives of the inhabitants. The resolution recommended that states, United Nations agencies, and other organizations and bodies within the United Nations system, pending the achievement of independence of such movements, take steps to ensure that liberation-movement representatives be treated as representing such territories. The resolution also made provision for consultation with the Organization of African Unity in bringing about such a result. The special committee, without adopting a resolution, has also demonstrated support for the independence of Namibia, as well as concern for other areas having a colonial status.

Such efforts rely on the provisions of Articles 1 (2) and 55 of the Charter, which refer to equal rights of self-determination of peoples. Such efforts find especially strong support from United Nations members who themselves were once a part of empires and who have secured release from colonial controls. The aspirations of such areas for greater autonomy have followed a steady if somewhat uneven course. The suitable accommodation of competing interests will undoubtedly occupy the close attention of the United Nations for decades ahead. Demands for autonomy frequently find expression in human-rights terms, while support for the status quo is defended in terms of national sovereignty, including economic and security needs.

The International Court of Justice This tribunal is the judicial organ of the United Nations and is located in the Peace Palace in The Hague, Netherlands. Members of the United Nations are automatically members of the International Court of Justice. In addition, Switzerland, Liechtenstein, and San Marino have applied for and have been granted membership in the Court. South Vietnam has limited membership relating to World War II treaties. Under the terms of the Statute of the Court, members are obliged to comply with decisions affecting them.

The Court is charged with two basic responsibilities. In the first place, it must decide cases presented to it. The parties to contentious cases must be states, but such states need not be members of the United Nations. If they are not, their adherence to the Statute will be governed by conditions determined by the General Assembly upon the recommendation of the Security Council. In the second place, the Court may render advisory opinions to the General Assembly or to the Security Council upon request. United Nations organs, specialized agencies, members of the United Nations family, and other parties who are able to obtain either General Assembly or Security Council approval may be granted the right to request such opinions.

The Court has rendered valuable service to the cause of international law and order. Instances include the 1949 decision in the case of *United Kingdom v. Albania* (commonly known as the Corfu Channel case), in which the Court assessed heavy monetary damages against Albania for its unjustified interference with the right of innocent passage of military vessels on the international navigable highway in the Corfu Strait. In the same year the Court rendered an advisory opinion, at the request of the Assembly, concerning the right of the Assembly to seek monetary reparations for injuries and death suffered by Count Folke Bernadotte, United Nations mediator in Israel. The decision took account of the United Nations as a valid subject of international law. In 1951 the Court resolved a dispute between Norway and the United Kingdom as to the extent of Norway's fishing rights in the North Sea. In 1957 the Court handed down an opinion in a case involving the French equivalent of the United States' Connally Reservation, dealing with nationally asserted limitations on the jurisdiction of the Court. In 1962 the Court ruled concerning the duty of United Nations members to pay special assessments, which had been voted by the General Assembly for peace-keeping activities in the Middle East in the 1950s and in the Congo in the early 1960s. Following a very sparse submission of cases to the Court during the 1960s, the General Assembly initiated steps to obtain greater understanding and use of the tribunal. The Court itself initiated procedural reforms, and many thoughtful scholars have suggested changes designed to revitalize the Court. With the decade of the 1970s the Court's work load has been enlarged, although in the fisheries disputes between the United Kingdom and Iceland and between the Federal Republic of Germany and Iceland and in the dispute between Australia and New Zealand and France brought on by the testing of nuclear weapons in the southwestern Pacific, the governments of Iceland and France asserted dubious sovereign prerogatives and refused to appear. However, the Court, after a careful and extensive review of the facts and the legal contentions, decided that it did possess jurisdiction to rule on the merits of the disputes. The successful use of international tribunals has caught the attention of influential persons, and substantial efforts are being made to increase the use of such bodies.

Much will depend upon the acceptance of community outlooks and the presence of a minimum amount of world public order. Reflecting the growing influence in the United Nations of the less developed countries has been the election of three African judges to the Court.

The jurisdiction of the Court is as broad as international law, subject to the provisions of the Charter and Statute. The mere presence of an international court provides stability for the international order. With the passage of time, the confidence of nation-states in the Court will probably increase. The Court has given abundant evidence of its moderation, of its nonpolitical attitude, and of its total dedication to the rule of law in world affairs. Its weakness lies in the fact that many member states have refused to accept its compulsory jurisdiction. Despite strong pressures from American presidents, the American Bar Association, and distinguished groups and individuals, the United States continues to subscribe to a qualified acceptance of the Court's compulsory jurisdiction. Under the Connally Reservation,[23] the United States has declared that it will determine for itself when a matter before the Court is considered to be a matter of American domestic jurisdiction. The reservation has put the United States in an awkward position, since at the time the United States accepted the Statute of the Court, it agreed to permit the Court itself to resolve this precise issue.

The Secretariat The Secretariat of the United Nations is an international civil service, drawing most of its many employees from the almost 140 members of the organization. Headed by the Secretary-General, it now consists of approximately 9,500 persons, of whom about 1,600 were United States nationals in 1973. In addition to the personnel of the Secretariat, the United Nations also employs many others on specialized agencies, commissions, and boards—a preponderance of whom are engaged in seeking to improve economic and social conditions around the world. As in any governmental institution there is a continuing need to attract and retain highly competent individuals with professional skills. The organization requires an impartial international civil service based on merit.

In addition to the Secretariat's permanent offices in New York, other offices are maintained in approximately thirty cities throughout the world. Many of the activities of the United Nations are carried forward in the old League of Nations headquarters in Geneva. However, the headquarters of the new United Nations Environmental Program is located in Nairobi, Kenya.

The Secretary-General's office has achieved an importance hardly anticipated by those who drafted the Charter. The leadership qualities of the incumbent have influenced the achievements of the office. His continuing influence, in the face of some nationalistically inspired disapproval, is in marked contrast to the sparse formal authority granted to him in the Charter. All who have held the office of Secretary-General have come to exercise grave responsibilities. In the political field such responsibilities have been thrust upon him in part because of disagreements as to peace keeping in the Security Council and in the General Assembly. His duties are essentially nonstop—twenty-four hours a day and 365 days each year. Through personal dedication to the principles and purposes of the United Nations the Secretary-General potentially could become one of the most influential personalities on the world scene. His function has come to be regarded as that of providing a kind of international political conscience. To the extent that the Secretary-General is also efficient and wise, public esteem for the United Nations has been enhanced.

The Specialized Agencies Attached to the United Nations are thirteen specialized agencies (some created many years ago), each facilitating international intercourse in a technical field. Additionally, the International Atomic Energy Agency and the bureau of the General Agreement on Tariffs and Trade (GATT) keep a close association with the United Nations. In some respects the achievements of these bodies have been more substantial than those of the United Nations per se. This is due in

---

[23]Indicative of long-ranging dissatisfaction in this country with the conditions under which the United States might have access to the jurisdiction of the World Court as a result of the Connally Reservation have been extended hearings before the Senate Committee on Foreign Relations. *Hearings on S. Res. 94*, 86th Cong., 2d Sess. (1960), and *Hearings on S. Res. 74, 75, 76, 77, and 78*, 93d Cong., 1st Sess. (1973). Government Printing Office, Washington, 1960, 1973.

large part to the low political profile they assume and to the fact that their functions do not normally touch on sensitive security concerns.

The International Atomic Energy Agency, consisting of 103 members, is engaged in securing peaceful uses of the atom and in preventing the diversion of nuclear resources to weapons of mass destruction. GATT, consisting of 82 members, together with 16 other states occupying supporting but informal relationships, seeks to formulate international trade policies conducive to the strengthening of world markets and the elimination of unfair trade advantages.

The International Labor Organization, consisting of 123 members, seeks to improve wages and working conditions all over the world. The Food and Agriculture Organization, consisting of 125 members, is engaged in expanding agricultural production and in improving opportunities for basic nutritional needs. The United Nations Educational, Scientific and Cultural Organization, consisting of 130 members and 1 associate member, has long combated illiteracy and ignorance and has engaged in the promotion of international understanding. In recent years it has furthered the expansion of scientific communication and has sought to protect the world's cultural heritage. The World Health Organization, consisting of 135 members and 2 associate members (although the associate membership of Southern Rhodesia is regarded as in suspense), has taken the world lead in seeking the elimination of communicable diseases and the improvement of health care standards. The International Bank for Reconstruction and Development (World Bank), consisting of 122 members, has supplied capital funds to states so that they might strengthen their national economic systems. The International Finance Corporation, consisting of 97 members, has encouraged the growth of productive private enterprise, especially in the less developed countries. The International Development Association, consisting of 111 members, has assisted in the economic development of poor states by making loans designed to be less burdensome on balance of payments than conventional loans. The International Monetary Fund, consisting of 125 members, assists in the stabilization of national currencies. The International Civil Aviation Organization, consisting of 124 members, advances effective measures for safe and efficient international air travel. The Universal Postal Union, consisting of 146 members, promotes uniformity of postal rates and conditions favorable to the safe and prompt delivery of the mail. The International Telecommunication Union, consisting of 143 members, systematizes communication by telephone, telegraph, and radio. The World Meteorological Organization, consisting of 136 members (of which 124 are states and 12 are additional territories), facilitates the gathering, the interpretation, and the dissemination of data on world weather conditions. The Inter-Governmental Maritime Consultative Organization, consisting of 74 members and 1 associate member, regularizes shipping practices and recently has been much concerned with the prevention of pollution in the marine environment. Despite the essentially universal membership in many of the specialized agencies, the Soviet Union has not joined the Food and Agriculture Organization, GATT, or the four bodies dealing with fiscal and monetary matters.

The specialized agencies have demonstrated considerable flexibility in the assessment of their functions. As new issues have arisen, such as concern for the human, global, and marine environments, the agencies have moved to deal constructively with them. The specialized agencies and other members of the United Nations family work quietly and efficiently. In seeking to understand the United Nations it is well to keep in mind that the greater number of its activities are not spectacular, nor are they in areas where goals are to be achieved easily or immediately. Only through long-range planning and continuing effort will their humanitarian goals be realized.

Problems Confronting the United Nations

The United Nations, as an international institution, faces two key problems: (1) solvency and (2) the effective operation of its component parts. In fact, these are the only real problems of the *organization;* all the rest are problems of the *nation-states* of which it is comprised.

Fiscal Solvency and Financial Arrangements The United Nations is supported by financial contributions from its members. The organization's continuing crisis concerning solvency has stemmed from nonpayment of assessments made against the Soviet Union, France, and several other states in connection with peace-keeping costs in the Congo and the Middle East; from the fact that many states do not meet in a timely fashion their shares of the annual budget; and from the fact that some governments pay their assessments in nonconvertible currencies for which the organization has only limited needs. A further consideration is the fact that United Nations costs, like all other costs over the years, have increased, but there has not been a willingness on the part of the members to vote assessments to meet these higher costs.

It has been the practice of the organization to separate its expenses for routine costs (reflected in the regular annual budget and supported by general assessments) from its expenditures necessitated by its peace-keeping operations (which have been frequently referred to as "special assessments"). However, both are inseparable parts of the financial contributions mentioned in Article 19 of the Charter. At the present, members make voluntary pledges and contributions to support current peace-keeping, humanitarian, and educational activities.

Shortly after the establishment of the United Nations and before important peace-keeping responsibilities arose, the regular annual budget was in the neighborhood of $30 million. By 1957 it averaged about $50 million, by 1961 it was just over $69 million, and by 1965 it exceeded $105 million. At the beginning of the decade of the 1970s, the regular annual budget had risen to $159.8 million.

The share of the United States in 1961 was a little over $22 million and by 1965 had reached slightly more than $35 million. For 1970 it was $50.3 million. The United States, from the beginning of the United Nations through 1964, was accountable for 32.02 percent of the whole budget. For 1965 the proportionate share of the United States was slightly reduced to 31.91 percent of the whole. In 1970 it had fallen to 31.52 percent. Pursuant to a 1972 decision of the United States, which was supported by the General Assembly on January 1, 1974, the regular annual assessment of the United States will not exceed 25 percent of the budget.

That the costs to the United States are trivial may be seen by comparing total United States payments, including both the assessments mentioned above and very substantial voluntary contributions to all United Nations agencies and programs, with the annual cost of operating New York City's fire department. The latter is a more costly activity. From another point of view, the annual cost to each citizen of the United States for the regular assessed United Nations budget was less than 20 cents in 1965 and less than 25 cents in 1970.

In 1961 the cost to each American for the regular annual assessment for the United Nations amounted to less than 12.5 cents; the cost for the United Nations peace-keeping forces, to less than 21 cents; the cost for the specialized agencies, to less than 12 cents; and the cost for supporting the special voluntary programs, to less than 44 cents. Thus the total per capita cost to Americans in 1961 was about 89 cents.

In 1971 each American paid about 24 cents for the regular assessments for the United Nations, less than 3 cents for the United Nations peace-keeping forces in Cyprus, less than 30 cents for the specialized agencies (including IAEA), and about $1.70 for the special voluntary programs. Thus the total per capita cost in 1971 was less than $2.27. Both the 1971 and the 1961 figures approximated the annual per capita expenditure in the United States for the purchase of lipstick.

Particularly as a result of ongoing peace-keeping costs, the finances of the United Nations continue to be critically vulnerable. Many states allow arrearages to occur, and thus sound financial forecasting is next to impossible. Inflation plays no favorites, and this has restricted new programs at a time when new funds to support basic human needs are required. Increased membership has produced larger costs than revenues, and numerous states that contribute next to nothing to the treasury take a cavalier attitude when it comes to the voting of expenditures. Considering its slender regular budget, the United Nations deficit of about $70 million at the end of 1972 was quite alarming.

Effective Operation Critics of the United Nations who are engrossed in fine details can supply a lengthy laundry list of operational defects. These include a bureaucracy possessing uneven training and skills, occasional disloyalty to the organization, difficulties in the assessment and assignment of functions, multitudinous functions requiring extremely perceptive coordinational skills, and ill-considered past proposals such as that of the Soviet Union for a troika-type procedure in the office of the Secretary-General.

Occasioned by the United Nations' twenty-fifth anniversary in 1971, an enormous literature suggested strengthening of the organization. Major proposals included restricting membership to states able to honor the monetary assessments placed on them; allowing poor states to have associate membership without a vote; streamlining existing committee structures; identifying criteria to allow for more representative nonpermanent members of the Security Council; establishing formulas to bring to satisfactory settlement the accounts owed by the Soviet Union, France, and others because of nonpayment of peace-keeping assessments; imposing interest charges on states in arrears in their assessments; building a working capital fund; allowing the United Nations to have special sources of income from areas of the world falling within the common-heritage concept (ocean areas and outer space); instituting United Nations surcharges on international letters, cables, broadcasts, and transportation; and soliciting contributions from private persons, business entities, and charitable foundations. There is a need not only for the United Nations to make basic reforms respecting its internal structure and procedures but also for all international institutions, which are still proliferating, to find ways to coordinate both their separate functions and their many shared, even duplicated, activities.

The Work of the United Nations: Consensus among Members

The United Nations has been described as a twentieth-century social phenomenon. As is true of all human institutions, the members are constantly confronted with the problem of whether it will be possible to manifest the will and provide the resources to achieve stated goals or objectives.

The goals and objectives of the United Nations are set out in the preamble to the Charter. Speaking in the name of the "peoples of the United Nations," rather than governments, a creed, both starkly realistic and idealistic, was identified:

WE THE PEOPLES OF THE UNITED NATIONS DETERMINED

To save succeeding generations from the scourge of war, which twice in our lifetime has brought untold sorrow to mankind and

to reaffirm faith in fundamental human rights, in the dignity and worth of the human person, in the equal rights of men and women and of nations large and small, and

to establish conditions under which justice and respect for the obligations arising from treaties and other sources of international law can be maintained, and

to promote social progress and better standards of life in larger freedom,

AND FOR THESE ENDS

to practice tolerance and live together in peace with one another as good neighbors, and

to unite our strength to maintain international peace and security, and

to ensure, by the acceptance of principles and the institution of methods, that armed force shall not be used, save in the common interest, and

to employ international machinery for the promotion of the economic and social advancement of all peoples,

HAVE RESOLVED TO COMBINE OUR EFFORTS TO ACCOMPLISH THESE AIMS.

Some members, in assessing the role of the United Nations, look upon it as a permanent (or temporary) international conference. Others conceive of it as an ongoing international institution. For many, who feel that there is a need for an effective international forum for the whole complex of political, social, legal, economic, and military problems, it is a beacon leading slowly but inevitably to a better and brighter world.

Those holding this point of view have come to compare the United Nations to a giant iceberg, only a scant amount of which is visible. The portion that can be seen is likened to the political disagreements that attract worldwide attention. The submerged base is compared to the important human-rights, health, humanitarian, educational, social, and economic activities, carried on in large part through ECOSOC and the specialized agencies of the United Nations. The fact is that the United Nations is both a moral ideal and a limited institution of government.

The twentieth century is in fact a paradox. Nationalism has become intensified at the very time when all peoples yearn for progress beyond nationalism to the "wider, larger, and admittedly vaguer community of mankind."[24] Under these circumstances demands have been raised to "look at our world not through a haze of national emotions but see it as it is, in cold, hard reality."[25] An element of this reality is the common membership of the United States and socialist states—possessing varying degrees of militancy—of old states and new states, of rich states and poor states, and of states equipped with advanced science and technology and the less developed countries, coupled in each instance with the problems created by such proximity. Through joint membership—which in the past has not been an unmixed blessing—each country receives sharper perceptions respecting its opponents' principles and policies. Although states are frequently unable to convince their adversaries of the rectitude of their particular ways, this forum nonetheless provides the process for national engagement and disengagement—at a nonviolent level of discourse. Mutual perception of national goals has contributed to the contemplation of détente between cold-war adversaries during the 1970s. With the presence of the People's Republic of China in the United Nations since 1971, when it emerged from outer darkness onto the center of the world's stage, China's policies have been ventilated. This has modified the United Nations and also has substantially influenced the balance of world order.

For the Western democracies in attendance at the United Nations this forum provides an opportunity for their delineation of the world of the future. Their goals are both nationally oriented and world-community oriented. Many see both short-range and long-term objectives best achieved through a vital and strengthened United Nations. Many have come to regard it as the common instrument for the building of a genuine community at the world level—a community based largely on Western values. Others regard it as an obstacle to national action—an impediment to unlimited sovereignty.

Most democracies hope that in the long run, through the United Nations, the rule of law—at least as to some nations and for some subjects—may replace the resort to force in international affairs. The result for the social sciences would be as startling and dramatic as man's current conquests of the natural universe. The world is quietly building in this direction.

The Western democracies, the Soviet bloc, and the developing countries, including China, accept change as the central characteristic of human affairs. The Western democracies have displayed a greater respect for, and commitment to, peaceful change than the communist states. The former assume that their mutual interest in legal change *is shared* and can best be achieved through mutual confidence, good faith, diligent effort, and support for the benefits of world community.

Within this context the members of the United Nations continue to be confronted with the problems of assimilating new members, establishing a program of effective peace keeping, organizing aid for refugees and deprived children, mobilizing atomic energy for peacetime purposes, furthering decolonization and assistance to the less developed countries, preserving and protecting the environment, and building a more firmly based international legal system, as well as facing such issues as disarmament, human rights (including the prevention of terrorism), the veto, and Charter revision—to mention but a few. Of importance is the fact that as new and critical issues rise on the world scene, the United Nations is asked to deal with them.

The problem of new members rests primarily in the hands of the Big Five of the Security Council. The Soviet veto has been employed to keep nation-states out of the United Nations more frequently than for any other single purpose. The Soviet roadblock was circumvented in a striking fashion in 1955 when a "package deal" was worked out with the United States. This resulted in the admission of sixteen new members. Cooperation between the United States and the Soviets resulted in the admission of seventeen new members in 1960. The population explosion of new states during the 1960s has resulted in a rapid augmentation in United Nations membership, and there was also a

---

[24] Barbara Ward, *Five Ideas That Changed the World*, W. W. Norton & Company, Inc., New York, 1957, p. 152.
[25] Ibid.

major readjustment in 1971 when the People's Republic of China took the seat allocated to China in the Security Council and in the General Assembly.

A program of effective peace keeping depends on several basic considerations: whether peace keeping is to be a function of the General Assembly or of the Security Council, whether members will adhere to their solemn commitments, and whether an effective military force can be organized to check prospective aggressors. The existence of a permanent international military force would deter would-be aggressors and would hasten consideration of a workable disarmament program. Through the United Nations the use of outer space has been reserved exclusively for peaceful purposes.

One of the United Nations' major and continuing contributions has been to focus world attention upon human rights, always of great concern to Americans. During World War II, President Roosevelt proclaimed the four freedoms: freedom of speech, freedom of worship, freedom from want, and freedom from fear. The last two were reaffirmed in the Atlantic Charter and were restated on January 1, 1942, in the Joint Declaration of the United Nations. The adoption of the Universal Declaration of Human Rights on December 10, 1948, was a historic act. The Declaration has exercised a powerful influence upon human behavior and has served as a basis for treaties, statutes, national constitutions, and judicial decisions.

World attention was focused during the 1960s on the deterioration of the human environment. The principal causes had enormous consequences for the entire globe. In 1972 the United Nations convened a Conference on the Human Environment, which asserted that states would have to conform to world standards restricting detrimental dissemination of pollutants. To monitor national behavior, the United Nations established a subordinate agency in 1972 known as the United Nations Environmental Program.

Although Charter revision is frequently cited as an area of importance to the success of the United Nations, the fact is that skilled minds have applied a practical interpretative gloss to the Charter. As a result, demands for formal Charter revision are no longer regarded as urgent. The United Nations can be strengthened without Charter revision (1) by a sincere effort on the part of members to live up to their Charter obligations; (2) by the continued development of informal practices and procedures dedicated to the achievement of the fundamental purposes of the organization; (3) by piecemeal amendment, as in the case of the size of the Security Council; and (4) by the use of authorized regional agreements, within the framework of the Charter.

It is possible for the world consensus to emerge from a conscientious use of the United Nations organization. Several significant requirements must be met, however, if basic human expectations are to be served by the United Nations. States in their interrelationships should seek to be law-abiding and to avoid violence. They should respect the integrity and independence of other members of the community. They should be guided by a spirit of cooperation in order to resolve the common problems of an ever-shrinking and increasingly interdependent world. Internally they must recognize the importance of the individual and maintain an orderly government to protect and advance the higher hopes of mankind.

It is only with these factors in mind, and with a full appreciation of national values and aspirations, that one can understand the United Nations today. In a very real sense the United Nations is a mirror of the real world. It is also possible to be quite sure about one additional fact: The United Nations is a far different institution today from what it was at its birth in 1945. It has suffered trials and tribulations along with its numerous successes. For the moment, it has put to rout those critics who have asked whether it is worth saving.

The United Nations in Transition

Adlai E. Stevenson, as United States Ambassador to the United Nations, once said, "The United Nations is right to be brave." Will its members prove worthy of the same accolade? Or will the final historian report that it failed, as others before have failed—that it was simply another imperfect institution in an imperfect world, reflecting the troubles of an old and weary universe?

Several of the issues presented in these questions deserve brief attention. First, the organization has passed through several phases of development. Post–World War II relations, before the Korean police action, proceeded on a fairly even keel. With the Korean conflict, the United Nations (or at least a number of its important members) demonstrated the capacity to mount and to maintain a form of effective collective security. During this period the internal balance of power moved from the Security Council to the General Assembly by means of the Uniting for Peace Resolution. The latent conflict between the Soviet bloc and the free world was fully disclosed.

The second period extended from the cessation of the Korean hostilities to the death of Secretary General Dag Hammarskjold in 1961. This, in retrospect, may have been the organization's brightest hour, for it was during this period that the office of Secretary-General developed profound influence in the affairs of nations. Hammarskjold's personal qualities and the confidence they elicited led to the view, when problems seemed insurmountable: "Leave it to Dag."

During his incumbency the office of Secretary-General expanded markedly, and the United Nations "presence" in the form of the Secretary-General or his representative was noticed in many troubled areas of the world. Almost always the presence resulted in more stable conditions.

With the tragic death of Mr. Hammarskjold, while he was engaged in bringing peace to the Congo, a new era confronted the United Nations. This was the period of approaching universal membership. New nation-states with strong nationalist drives sought an elevated status through membership. Whether all these new members can be fully participating members is open to doubt. Despite their equal rights as members, including a vote, their new and somewhat uninformed condition has led them to form into area blocs in order to allow for the broadest dissemination of acquired data and insights. On numerous issues of policy they have been able to combine around the fact that they are in need of development and see the mature states as being able to supply this resource. Just as the United Nations and the world are in transition, so too are these new members, and the result may be that time and maturity will make them capable of contributing valuable additions to the community perspectives of the organization. A major concern is that the new states, with their bloc orientation, may be induced through their majority control of the General Assembly to take decisions that will have no actual significance in the real world. They must remain aware that impractical majority decisions may not have much influence in areas beyond the very room in which the General Assembly conducts its deliberations and takes its votes.

In its most recent exegesis, spanning the late 1960s and the 1970s, the United Nations has played inconsistent roles. This has been a period of profound soul-searching, partly because of the United Nations' exclusion from the Southeast Asian conflict and its initial ineffectiveness in the Middle East disputes. As a result of its having been left standing unceremoniously in the wings during the Vietnam affair, the impression was created that its peacekeeping inadequacies had blighted all its constructive work. Although this occurred at a time when, in fact, the United Nations was achieving valuable goals, an observer had to be either incurably optimistic or in the possession of a long view of history before he could hold out much hope for it as a viable institution. Yet the United Nations has survived, and it has been a moderating force in troubled waters. Its recent history suggests that its utility may be greatest when real dangers are most threatening.

The Soviet Union and the United Nations

The generally negative or hostile attitude of the Soviet bloc toward the United Nations during the first twenty-five years of its existence is a matter of record. This has been observed on a large number of separate occasions.

The excess use of the veto in the past by the Soviet Union demonstrated disregard for the concept of international cooperation. It also provided evidence of the Soviets' determination to "have it their way," even in areas where their national interest was not a critical issue.

Contrary to the terms of Article 2 of the Charter, in the early 1950s the Soviets gave support to the Red Chinese, who attacked the United Nations command in Korea. Their desire to profit—at the expense of the organization—through an artificially created chaos in the Congo was another Soviet tactic. Having been prevented from sending volunteers to the area by an alert Secretary-General, the Soviets sought to retaliate through the troika proposal. And when the ONUC did bring some order out of chaos and established some semblance of harmony, the Soviets declined with continuing insistence, down to the present, to be bound by the Assembly vote calling for special assessments to cover the cost of the expedition. Soviet policy toward the United Nations has meandered between efforts to dominate it, to render it impotent, and more recently to live with it, as Soviet policy has weaved its way uncertainly in the direction of détente with the West. The Soviet view of United Nations membership for the People's Republic of China is a case in point. It has varied from early outright support and formal sponsorship, to a tongue-in-cheek and unenthusiastic posture, to the admission of major concern over the caustic militancy of China's spokesmen. In the end this has clearly demonstrated the demise of any assumed monolithic relationship between the socialist states. In the 1960s the late Ambassador Adlai S. Stevenson observed that the United Nations not only had been "severely attacked" by the Soviet Union but also had been obliged to shoulder the vituperation of "some Americans—men and women who do not understand the real meaning and importance of the world body." Perhaps the People's Republic of China has now assumed the role of leading critic of the United Nations. In any event, in the 1970s the Soviets have adopted a posture of being less overtly at odds with Charter principles. This condition is manifestly influenced by a variety of pragmatic perceptions of the present trend in international relations.

The United States and the United Nations

To the American public the United Nations is many things. Through the United Nations, said Harry S Truman, we shall have "our supreme chance to establish a world-wide rule of reason." Dwight D. Eisenhower termed it "the soundest hope for peace in the world." John F. Kennedy, in his Inaugural Address, described it as "our last hope" in the age of the atom, and he pledged the United States to "enlarge the area in which its writ may run." Presidents Johnson and Nixon also pledged that their administrations would give, at least at the same verbal level, unconditional support to the United Nations.

A great debate has long engaged the attention of influential Americans. What, they ask, should be the American role in the United Nations? Should the United Nations be the cornerstone for the conduct of American foreign policy? This question takes on added meaning when it is remembered that beginning in 1961, approximately ninety items were entered on the annual agenda of the Assembly. In recent years the agenda has been even longer, with each subject being of importance to at least several members. Additionally, for many nations membership in the United Nations constitutes their sole international involvement, whereas for the United States and many other countries, it is only one of many international organizations through which business can be transacted. A recent count indicates that the United States participates in more than sixty international agencies, up from around fifty a few years ago.

The basic question is a serious one, for it asks whether the United States can afford to be merely equal (in a legal and moral sense) in a forum of widely unequal (in a practical and physical sense) nation-states. The initial responses seem to be threefold. One view is that the United Nations is a mere caricature of the League of Nations and that just as the League could not save the world from World War II, so will the United Nations fail to protect mankind from nuclear incineration at some future date. This group favors a limited or general superstate.

Another group, which has been considerably less influential, occasionally calls for a fortress America. These people, entrenched in frustration or hungering for total victory, would wholly withdraw from international involvements and concede the uncommitted nations, as well as many of the weak but free ones, to the forces of despotism and desolation.

A third group, like the first, seeks to create a new organization, composed exclusively of free nations, or, alternatively, to form a loose association of like-minded states within the United Nations tent. Suggestions have been made for a concert of powers. While not regarded as a superstate, it would have extensive powers and would be employed at least in part as a substitute for the United Nations. Its sponsors, apparently, would let the present United Nations continue its nonpolitical interests and would give up the ideal of a universal political organization. Such an organization would create opposing ideological blocs and probably would advance their direct confrontation. This policy is quite the reverse of that advanced through the United Nations—one designed to permit disengagement or confrontation in the presence of third parties.

In recent years the United States has lost its dominant position within the General Assembly. As the developing nations have secured vast influence in this body, the United States has turned, as other powerful states have in the past, to the Security Council for the implementation of its policies. As the United States seeks to identify its United Nations–oriented policy of the future, it has analyzed the range of its foreign policy options. These include the prospect of empire—a new Pax Americana, chaos, or a legally and politically oriented world community. Since the first two alternatives are unacceptable, the United States has sought to implement its world community orientation through the United Nations. The United States is also acting through additional and supplementary institutions, both universal and regional, that are dedicated—or in the future may become dedicated—to the basic values of our Western society.

The United Nations in Perspective

The United Nations was born in an atmosphere of high—indeed extravagant—hopes that it could promptly establish and permanently maintain a just international peace with security. At the close of both world wars, world public opinion clamored for international organizations that would relegate war to the museum of antiquities. In both instances, people expected too much of the newly created League of Nations and of the United Nations, and many were bitterly disappointed when miracles did not promptly materialize. Frequently such persons failed to distinguish carefully enough the powers of the new entity from the retained powers and prejudices of the nation-states that composed it. The United Nations, in retrospect, seems to have been oversold to the American public in 1945. Time has provided more mature perspectives. It is neither the fearsome supranational monster that some extreme nationalists have denounced nor the beneficent worker of wonders that certain idealistic internationalists seemed to expect it to be. Impatience has been responsible for much current criticism.

Outstanding leaders the world over believe that the United Nations provides greater potential power for uniting the moral and material strength of the world community, for maintaining peace, for resisting aggression, and for advancing the cause of humanity than any other method known to mankind. Hence the United States has supported, as a matter of highest governmental policy, the United Nations as a growing force for world peace and as a practical means for securing worldwide cooperation between nations. In the long run such a policy is based on the hope that through such an organization, it may be possible to achieve an orderly world built on law and reason.

Our State Department has said that the United States supports the United Nations "because we believe it is the best mechanism yet devised for harmonizing the actions of nations in order to maintain peace and security."[26] With this kind of commitment the United States is in a position to employ its enormous resources to achieve these goals.

The United Nations was established by military allies in a period of general friendliness and relative good feeling. Later international tensions and misunderstandings materially affected its work. Although it often appears as an instrumentality to emphasize the differences between nation-states, the United Nations is the world's greatest sounding board for the expression of international public opinion. It is also the forum in which the free world consolidates its forces and becomes aware of its common problems.

Far from dominating the United Nations by its vetoes and other tactics, the Soviet Union in effect has "a bear by the tail." Our former United Nations delegate, Henry Cabot Lodge, Jr., once pointed out that the Soviet Union, never able to muster a respectable number of votes for its views, could not control the United Nations, could not destroy it, and dared not leave it. On the other hand, the United States, in the present as in the past, has been able to reap substantial dividends from its membership by developing and uniting public opinion in its

---

[26] *The U.N.: Meeting Place of Nations*, U.S. Department of State Publication 7246, Government Printing Office, Washington, 1961, p. 1.

favor and by using United Nations facilities to measure the support given to its views by other members. Further, the United States has enjoyed a vantage point from which to observe communist tactics in the war of ideas. And through membership in the United Nations the United States has been able, by immediate recitals of truth, to counteract Soviet and other communist propaganda.

In conclusion, the United Nations has as its primary task the restraining of nation-states through peace-keeping and other measures and through the establishment of respect for the rule of law in world affairs. These are the great goals of international peace and security. Its second task is to mitigate human suffering and to secure to individuals throughout the world community the freedoms and the opportunities needed for the full development of their potentialities. With the establishment of respect for international law and order, the progressive work of alleviating poverty and sickness and illiteracy, terrorism, and fear may be carried forward.

While the United Nations may not be the best and most ideal international organization man is capable of producing (an imperfect institution in an imperfect world), it is nonetheless the best that man has yet devised. Best of all, "It is alive with the spirit of the age to come."[27]

STUDY-GUIDE QUESTIONS

1 What are valid arguments for or against the proposition that international law has been an instrument for the development of a higher degree of world community?

[27] Adlai E. Stevenson, "Past, Present, Future of the U.N.," *The New York Times Magazine,* Jan. 14, 1962, p. 68.

2 Have you ever considered seeking employment in a public international organization such as the United Nations? What kind of educational background would be helpful in obtaining such employment?
3 Prepare a study in which you assess the utility and effectiveness of several of the peace-keeping activities of the United Nations, such as in the Middle East and Cyprus.
4 It was suggested that membership in the United Nations resulted in substantial dividends to the United States. Give examples of such dividends. Has the United States also suffered because of its membership?
5 What do you think of the use by the United States of a veto in the Security Council?

REFERENCES

Brierly, J. L.: *The Law of Nations,* 6th ed., Oxford University Press, Fair Lawn, N.J., 1963.
Dallin, A.: *The Soviet Union at the United Nations,* Frederick A. Praeger, Inc., New York, 1962.
Kay, D. A.: *The New Nations in the United Nations, 1960–1967,* Columbia University Press, New York, 1970.
O'Connell, D. P.: *International Law,* 2d ed., Stevens & Sons, Ltd., London, 1970, 2 vols.
Riggs, R. E.: *US/UN,* Appleton Century Crofts, New York, 1971.
Rosenne, S.: *The Law and Practice of the International Court,* Sythoff, Leyden, 1965, 2 vols.
Russell, R. B.: *A History of the United Nations Charter,* The Brookings Institution, Washington, 1958.
Yearbook of International Organizations, Union of International Associations, Brussels, published annually.
Yearbook of the United Nations, United Nations, Office of Public Information, New York, published annually.

Index

Academic state socialists, 100
Achievement identities and norms, 32, 213, 241, 264
Action groups, labor, 344
Acton, Lord, 95
Adams, Samuel, 139, 140, 143
Adenauer, Konrad, 239, 384
Administration (*see* Executive branch of government)
Administrative agencies, 370–371
 (*See also* Regulatory commissions)
Administrative Conference Act (1964), 369
Administrative organization and behavior, as subdiscipline of political science, 7
Administrative practices:
 auditing and control functions, 359
 legislative controls, 358–359
Administrative process, 365–371
 and courts, 365–366
Administrative regulation, 364–371
 appraisal, 368–371
 criticisms, 366–368

Administrative regulation:
 development, 364–366
Administrative relationships, 363–364
Administrative responsibility, concentration of, 358
Africa, authoritarianism in, 120
Agency for International Development (AID), 387, 388
Agnew, Spiro, 156, 175
Agriculture:
 and less developed nations, 346
 and science and technology, 346–347
Alexander II, Tsar, 248
Alexander the Great, 215
Algeria and French colonialism, 230, 231
Alienation:
 in Italian political culture, 223–224
 in Marxism, 75, 78, 94
Allport, G. W., 312
Almond, Gabriel A., 224, 240, 321
American Institute of Public Opinion (AIPO), 117

Anarchism, 92–94
Anomie (*see* Political behavior)
Anti-trust laws, 343–344
Apollo-Soyuz Test Project, 351
Appointive function, 356–357
Aristocracy, 32–33
 in continental Europe, 189
 in France, 227
 in Germany, 237
 in Great Britain, 33, 98, 189
Aristotle, 2, 4, 5, 11, 20, 27, 30, 63, 66, 67, 141, 189, 216, 276
Articles of Confederation, 130
 colonial problems under, 139, 163
Ascriptive identities and norms, 32, 213, 241, 264
Asquith, H. H., 200
Athens, city-state of, 35, 36, 122
Atlantic Alliance, 391
 (*See also* North Atlantic Treaty Organization)
Atomic Energy Act (1946), 349
Atomic Energy Commission, 349–350
Attentive public, 288

453

Attitudes and public opinion, 281
Austin, John, 47, 51
Authoritarianism:
  accomplishments of, 33
  characteristics, 33–34
  defined, 27
  and fascism, 111
  ideological assumptions, 62–63
  in Russia, 245, 246
  in the underdeveloped world, 120–121
Ayub Khan, 39

Bacon, Francis, 46
Baker v. Carr (1962), 123*n*., 149, 183
Bakunin, Mikhail, 92, 93
Balance of power, 405
Baldwin, Stanley, 197–198
Basic research, funding of, 350–351
Basques, 215
Batista, Fulgencio, 87, 88
Beard, Charles A., 140*n*., 141*n*.
Behavior (*see* Political behavior)
Behavioralism in political science, 11–12
Belgian Congo, crisis in, 437
Belgium:
  culture and politics in, 216–219, 221–222
  political parties in, table, 220
Belief system, 282
Bentham, Jeremy, 47, 105
Berelson, Bernard, 308
Beria, Lavrenti, 84, 259, 270
Bernstein, Eduard, 97
Bethe, Hans A., 353
Bible, the, and communism, 73–74
Bicameralism, 126–128
  in U.S., 139, 148
Bill of Rights:
  in Great Britain, 138, 191
  in U.S., 174
  (*See also* Civil liberties; Civil rights)
Black, Justice Hugo, 149
Bodin, Jean:
  on sovereignty, 24–26
  state, view of, 2
Bolsheviks, 79, 250
  (*See also* Communist party, of the Soviet Union)
Bonn Basic Law, 237–238

Bradley, General Omar N., 349
Brandeis-Goldmark brief, 135
Brandt, Willy, 237, 239, 384, 413
Brecht, Bertolt, 121*n*.
Brest-Litovsk, treaty of, 250, 252
Brezhnev, Leonid I., 84, 258, 260–261, 264, 268, 269, 271, 385, 393
  foreign policy of, 412–413, 417
Bricker amendment, 162
Bryce, Lord James, 184, 276
Bryce Report (1918), 200
Budget and Accounting Act (1921), 162
Budgets, governmental, 359
Bukharin, Nikolai, 82, 251
Bulganin, Nikolai, 84, 271
Bureaucracy, study of, 6–7
Burger, Chief Justice Warren E., 177
Burke, Edmund, 20, 106, 108, 126
Burns, James MacGregor, 324
Burr, Aaron, 180
Burroughs, John, 353
Bush, Vannevar, 349
Business, science and technology, 342–343
Byrd, Harry, 161

Cabinet:
  in Great Britain, 193–195, 200, 202, 203, 209
  (*See also* Executive branch of government, in Great Britain)
  in parliamentary government, 37–38
  in U.S. national government, 163–164
  in West Germany, 238
Calvin, John, 64
Calvinism:
  in colonial America, 138
  and liberalism, 104–105
  in the Netherlands, 214, 218
  and social contract theory, 5
Campaign financing:
  in Great Britain, 198–199, 209
  in U.S., 159–161, 263
Campaigning:
  in Great Britain, 198–199
  in U.S., 159–161, 319, 323, 329, 335
Campbell, Angus, 291
Canada, 216, 217, 222*n*.

Cantril, Hadley, 287
Capitalism:
  development of, 74–75, 99–100
  in early U.S., 143
  in Great Britain, 189
  as viewed by Marx, 77–78
Cardozo, Justice Benjamin N., 55
Carl XVI Gustaf, King, 31
Castro, Fidel, 88, 252
Castro, Raul, 88
Castroism, 87–89
Catholicism:
  and censorship, 176
  and cultural cleavage in Western Europe, 214–215, 226
  and fascism, 111
  social philosophy of, 100–101
Cavour, Count Camillo, 223
Censorship in U.S., 175–176
Censure, vote of: in France, 232
  in Great Britain, 203
  in West Germany, 238
Central Intelligence Agency (CIA), 178, 389
Chaban-Delmas, Jacques, 235
Chamber of Commerce, U.S., 148
Chancellor of the Exchequer, 195
Chancellor of West Germany, 238
Charismatic authority in fascist movements, 111–112
Charlemagne, 227
Charles II of England, 191
Charles X of France, 228
Chartist movement, 98
Chase, Stuart, 282
Checks and balances, 5, 129, 134, 138, 139, 141–142, 170–171
Cheka, 251, 259
Chiang Kai-shek, 86
China, People's Republic of, 85–87
  foreign policy of, 381, 382, 385, 386, 412, 417
  and United Nations, 446–447, 449
Chinese Nationalists, 86
Chirac, Jacques, 235
Chou En-lai, 417
Christian Democratic party:
  of Italy, 224–226
  of West Germany, 239, 240
Christian Social Union, 239, 240
Christianity:
  and communism, 74

Christianity:
    and cultural cleavage in Western Europe, 214–215
    social philosophy of the Church, 100–101
    view of man, 62
    view of the state, 27, 73
    as viewed by Marx, 76n.
Churchill, Sir Winston, 70, 99, 376, 390, 394
Cicero, 4, 5, 30
Civil law, 52–53
Civil liberties, 173–176
    and national defense, 348
Civil rights, 173–176
Civil Rights Act (1964), 122, 150
Civil service system:
    in France, 230, 232
    in Great Britain, 196–199
    in Italy, 227
    in U.S. local government, 184
    in U.S. national government, 359–360
Classical law, 51–52
Classical liberalism, 63–64
    in U.S., 101
Classifying governments, 29–30, 36–37
    figures, 30, 37
Cleavage (see Culture; Political culture)
Cleveland, Grover, 179
Client states, 22
Clientelismo in Italian politics, 224
Climate, effects of, on the state, 23
Code Napoléon, 52
Cognition, 280
Cohesion:
    in British political parties, 190, 194, 198, 199, 203–204
    in U.S. political parties, 158
Cold war, 348, 408
Collective farms in the Soviet Union, 266–267
Collective security, 406–407
Colonialism, 121
    effects on politics of: in France, 230, 231
        in Great Britain, 230
        in Italy, 230
    of Great Britain in early America, 138–139
    and political violence, 119

Columbia Broadcasting System opinion survey, 277
Cominform, 83, 85
Comintern, 81–83, 86
Commerce clause of U.S. Constitution, 135, 143, 343
Common Cause, 263
Common law, 53–56, 134–135, 426
    defined, 25
    in early American history, 137
Common Market, 22n., 344, 391, 420
    and German reunification, 237n.
    and Great Britain, 207–209
    and Switzerland, 213
Commonwealth of Nations, 24, 193n.
Commune of Paris, 228
Communism, 73–90, 94–95
    compared with fascism, 112
    effects of economic development on, 94–95, 269–271
    view of human nature, 62
Communist Information Bureau, 83, 85
Communist International, 81–83, 86
Communist Manifesto, 74, 76n., 78
    (*See also* Marxism)
Communist party:
    of China, 85–86
    of Cuba, 88
    of France, 229, 230, 233–235
    of Great Britain, 210
    of Italy, 215, 226, 229
    role of, 94
    of the Soviet Union, 79, 80, 84, 259–265
        Central Committee, 84, 263n., 264–265
            figure, 260
        compared with political activists in U.S., 262–263
        functions, 261–262, 264
        membership, 262–263
        organization, 259–261
            figure, 260
        Politburo, 259, 263n.
            figure, 260
        secretariats, 259–261
        sociological composition, 263–264
        and state, 258, 261
        Tenth Congress (1921), 251–252
        Twentieth Congress (1956), 84, 268

Communist party:
    of the Soviet Union: Twenty-second Congress (1961), 85, 269
        Twenty-fourth Congress (1971), 84
Community and law, 58
Comparative politics, as subdiscipline of political science, 9
Confidence, vote of: in France, 232
    in Great Britain, 202, 203
    in West Germany, 238
Conflict patterns and public opinion, 286–287
Conflict theory, 295
Congress, U.S., 148–155
    Conference committee, 154
    party cohesion in, 158
    powers of, 142
    and the Supreme Court, 170–172, 176–178
Congressional Budget Office, 171
Connally reservation, 442
Consensus patterns and public opinion, 286–287
Conservatism, 20, 106–109
Conservative party in Great Britain, 98, 108, 198–200, 204–210
Constantine, 214
Constitution:
    of France, 230–232
    of Great Britain, 191–192
    of the Soviet Union: of 1924, 252–253
        of 1936, 253–256
    of U.S., 36, 66, 135
        amending process, 142
        commerce clause, 135, 143, 343
        and judicial system, 167–169
        origins and development, 139–144
        and treaties, 430–431
        (*See also* Checks and balances; Separation of powers)
    of West Germany, 237–238
Constitutional Democratic party of Russia, 249
Continental Congress, 139
Coolidge, Calvin, 162, 170, 179
Corpus juris civilis, 52
Council of Economic Advisors, 362
Council of Environmental Quality, 362
Council of State in France, 230, 232

Council on Wage and Price Stability, 148
Cromwell, Oliver, 191
Cross-cutting cleavages, 218–219
Cuba, 87–89, 252
Cult of the personality:
  in China, 87
  in the Soviet Union, 84
Cultural norms, values, and public opinion, 279–280
Cultural revolution:
  in China, 86–87
  in Marxism, 78
Culture:
  and politics: in Great Britain, 188–189
  in Russia, 246
  in Western Europe, 213–222
  and the state, 21–22
  (*See also* Political culture)
Czechoslovakia, 269

Dante Alighieri, 215, 223
Darwin, Charles, 5
Data, sources of, in political science, 11–12
Davis, John W., 159
Dawson, Richard E., 278
d'Azeglio, Massimo, 223
Dean, Gordon, 349
Debray, Régis, 89
Declaration of Independence, 6, 63, 139, 174
Declaration of the Rights of Man, 63
Defense, national, and science and technology, 347–349
de Gaulle, Charles, 40, 216, 228, 230–232, 332, 391
de Jouvenel, Bertrand, 108
de Lolme, J. L., 197
de Medici, Lorenzo, 26
Democracy:
  and centralization of power, 147
  conditions necessary for success of, 66–68
  criticisms of, 68–70
  direct, 35, 122, 130
  and liberal ideology, 61–70
  philosophic assumptions of, 4
  and private property, 66–67
  rational model of, 276
  representative, 35–36

Democracy:
  stable: characteristics of, 118
    institutions of, 121–136, 245
    and political culture, 224
  and technology, 69, 339–354
  (*See also* Liberalism)
Democratic party, U.S., 147, 179–182, 329, 333
  and presidential selection, 157–161
  (*See also* Political parties, U.S.)
Democratic socialism, 98–104
Demonstration effect, 120
Department of State, U.S., 385–386
Descartes, René, 5
d'Estaing, Valery Giscard, 231n., 233, 235, 241, 332
De-Stalinization in the Soviet Union, 82–85, 270–271
Détente, 383, 410
  (*See also* Union of Soviet Socialist Republics, foreign policy)
Determinism in Marxism, 76–77
Deterrence in international politics, 409–410
de Tocqueville, Alexis, 35
Dialectic:
  and extremism, 111
  in Marxism, 76–77
Dictatorship (*see* Authoritarianism)
Dictatorship of the proletariat, 78
Diplomatic recognition, 400
Dirksen, Everett McKinley, 109
Dissolution of parliament, 37–38
  in France, 229, 230, 231
  in Great Britain, 198
Divine right of kings, 18
  in England, 191
  in Russia, 32, 247
Djordjevic, Jovan, 304
Dobrynin, Anatoly F., 269
Doctrinaire socialism, 95–97
Dodd, Thomas, 152
Dominican Republic, crisis in, 437
Doob, Leonard, 311
Dred Scott decision (1857), 170
Droit, 59
Dulles, John Foster, 410, 416
Durkheim, Émile, 75
Duverger, Maurice, 318, 321, 322, 329, 331

Earth Resources Technology Satellite, 352

East Germany, 237n.
Eckstein, Harry, 320, 321
Economic class:
  and cultural cleavage, 216–218, 226
  in France, 228–229
  in Italy, 224
  in Marxism, 75, 76
Economic development:
  effects of, 91, 94–95, 118–121, 175, 241–242
  in France, 227
  in Great Britain, 188, 189, 204
  in Italy, 224
  in Nigeria, 218n.
  in the Soviet Union, 246, 264, 266, 269–271
  in Western Europe, 211, 213, 241–242
  and fascism, 111
Economic Stabilization Act (1970), 147
Edison, Thomas A., 342
Education, science and technology, 350
Efficacy and political culture, 224
Ehrlich, Eugen, 48
Eisenhower, Dwight D., 102, 147, 159, 162, 171, 179, 180
Eldersveld, Samuel J., 318
Election campaigns in the U.S., 159–161, 319, 323, 329, 335
Elections:
  in parliamentary systems, 38
  in the Soviet Union, 253, 255–256
  (*See also* Electoral systems)
Electoral college, 156–157, 161, 179, 181
Electoral systems:
  double-ballot, 233–234
  in France, 229–230, 231n., 233–234
  functional representation, 125–126
  geographic representation, 123–124
  in Italy, 225–226
  proportional representation (PR), 124–125, 225, 226, 229–230, 233–234, 236
  single-member district, simple plurality (majority), 123–124, 179
  in Switzerland, 221–222
  in U.S. presidential elections, 161, 179
  in Weimar Germany, 236
  in West Germany, 240
  (*See also* Suffrage)

INDEX

Elites:
  in conservative ideology, 108
  in the executive, 7
  in liberal ideology, 63–64
  representativeness of, 36
  (*See also* Political participation)
Elizabeth I of England, 191
Empirical method, 3, 5
Employment, governmental, 355–358
Engels, Friedrich, 74, 75*n*.
  (*See also* Marxism)
Enlightenment, 63
Epstein, Leon D., 317, 318
Equality:
  in anarchism, 93
  in liberalism, 63
Equity, 58, 168
Ervin, Sam J., Jr., 177
Ethics:
  and justice, 48–50
  and law, 49–50
European Economic Community (*see* Common Market)
Executive branch of government, 130–133
  concentration of power in, 343, 358
  in France, 228, 230–233
  in Great Britain, 192–197, 202–204
  in Italy, 225
  relations with legislative branch, 37–39, 129–130, 132–133, 161, 170–171, 228, 230–231
  in U.S., 161–164
  in West Germany, 238
Executive process, as subdiscipline of political science, 6–7

Fabian socialism, 98
Fair Deal, 102
Faraday, Michael, 342
Farming, corporate, 346
Fascism, 109–112, 213
  and communist parties, 253
  in Germany, 110, 112
  in Great Britain, 210
  human nature, view of, 62
  in Italy, 223
Federal Administrative Procedure Act (1946), 365
Federal Bureau of Investigation (FBI), 178
Federal Communications Commission, 368–369
Federal Council for Science and Technology, 348
Federal Power Commission, 368
Federal Republic of Germany, 236–241
  constitution, 237–238
  executive branch, 238
  parliament, 238
  political culture, 236–237, 240–241
  political parties, 237, 239–240
  table, 220
Federal-state relations in U.S., 182
Federal states, 41–42
  centralizing trends in, 42
Federalism:
  and cultural cleavage, 216, 219
  and sovereignty, 25
  in the Soviet Union, 246, 252, 254–255
  in U.S., 143–148
  in West Germany, 237–238
Federalist, The, 131, 141–143, 178, 316–317
Federalist party, 179, 317
Feudalism, as viewed by Marx, table, 77
Filibuster in U.S. Senate, 151, 153, 155
First International, 81*n*.
Food and Agriculture Organization, 443
Food and world order, 346
Ford, Gerald R., 148, 160, 163, 241
Foreign policy, 375–421
  conditioning factors: demographic, 380
    economic, 381
    geographic-strategic, 379–380
    ideological, 383
  and constitutional framework of government, 383–384
  definition of, 375–376
  diplomacy and execution of, 393–395
  execution and administration of, 384–385
  instruments and tactics of: economic and financial, 394
    military, 394
    political and legal, 393
    propagandistic and ideological, 394–396
  and the judiciary, 387
  and the legislature, 386
Foreign policy:
  and policy planning, 389–390
  and political dynamics, 390–393
  and political parties, 391, 392
  and power, 378–379
  principles, aims and goals, 376–379
Foreign service, 387
Forms of government, 29–42
Forty Committee, 389
Founding Fathers, 140–143, 151
  and constitutional liberties, 174
Fourier, Charles, 74
Fourth International, 81
France, 227–236
  constitutions, 175, 229
  Economic and Social Council, 126
  executive branch, 228, 230–233
  Fifth Republic, 230–236
  Fourth Republic, 228–230
  historical chronology, 228
  monarchy, 63, 227–228
  parliament, 127*n*., 228–232
    figure, 92
  political parties, 92, 228–230, 233–234, 331–332
    tables, 220, 234
  presidential government, 40, 230–232
  religious cleavages, 215, 227–228
  Revolution of 1789, 92, 227–228, 247*n*.
  Third Republic, 228
Franco, Francisco, 31, 110
Franklin, Benjamin, 140
Free, Lloyd A., 287
Free Democratic party, 239, 240
Free Soil party, 180
Freedom, according to anarchism, 93
  (*See also* Liberalism)
French Revolution of 1789, 92, 227–228, 247*n*.
  ideology of, 63
Fulbright, J. William, 70*n*.

Gallup, George, 117, 179
Garibaldi, Giusseppe, 223
Gaudet, Hazel, 308
Gaullists, 230, 232, 233
General Accounting Office, 358
General Agreement on Tariffs and Trade, 442–443
General Services Administration, 363
Geneva Conventions, 428–429

Geography, effects on the state, 23–24
George, David Lloyd, 99
German Democratic Republic (East Germany), 237n.
Germany:
   Democratic Republic of, 237n.
   Federal Republic of, 236–241
   Nazism in, 110, 112, 236
   political culture of, 236–237, 240–241
Gerrymandering, 124, 149
Giscard d'Estaing, Valery, 231n., 233, 235, 241
Glenn, John H., Jr., 353
Glorious Revolution (1688), 191
Godwin, William, 93
Goldwater, Barry, 102, 108–109, 151, 181
Gosplan, 265, 267
Government:
   changing role of, 91, 145–148
   distinguished from state, 24
   forms of, 29–42
   role of, in American capitalist development, 101–102
   and science and technology, 352–354
Government Corporation Control Act (1945), 372
Government corporations, 371–373
Governmental assistance programs, 343–344
Grant, Ulysses S., 170
Great Britain, 187–210
   aristocracy, 32–33, 189, 199
   constitution, 191–192
   culture and politics, 188–189, 213
   democratic socialism, 98–99
   Empire and Commonwealth, 24, 193n.
   executive branch, 192–197, 202–204, 209
   historical background, 187–188, 190–191
   liberties, 172, 174
   monarchy, 31, 192–193
   Parliament, 31, 127, 128, 190–191, 197–204
   table, 206
   political parties, 181, 193–194, 204–210, 330–331
Great Leap Forward (in Communist China), 86

Great Society program, 102
Greece, 375
Greeks, ancient: definition of politics, 2
   view of elections, 36
Gromyko, Andrei, 385
Gross national product:
   in selected European democracies, table, 212
   and total imports in Italy, the United Kingdom, and U.S., figure, 23
Grotius, Hugo, 24, 26, 399, 424–425
Group theory, 298–299
Groups in social organization, 283–285
   category groups, 284
   membership, 283
   primary groups, 283
   reference groups, 284–285
   secondary groups, 283
Guerrilla warfare:
   in China, 86
   in Cuba, 88
   ideology, 404–405
   in Latin America, 89
Guesde, Jules, 95
Guevara, Che, 88, 89
Gulf of Tonkin Resolution (1964), 132

Hague Convention (1907), 428
Hamilton, Alexander, 101, 140–142
Hammarskjold, Dag, 448
Hancock, John, 140, 143
Harding, Warren, 170, 179
Hare system of voting, 124
Harlan, Justice John M., 149
Harrington, James, 138
Hayden, Carl, 152
Heath, Edward, 188, 207, 208
Heidenheimer, Arnold J., 334
Helvétius, Claude, 105
Henry VII of England, 191
Henry VIII of England, 191
Henry, Patrick, 140
Hindenburg, Paul von, 236
Hitler, Adolph, 110, 236
   on race, 22
Hobbes, Thomas, 11, 19, 120
Holland (*see* Netherlands)
Holmes, Justice Oliver Wendell, 46, 57
Hoover, Herbert C., 179, 180

Hoover Commission, 361
House of Commons in Great Britain, 201–204
   (*See also* Parliament)
House of Lords in Great Britain, 199–200
   (*See also* Parliament)
House of Representatives in U.S., 148–150, 152–155
Human nature:
   according to fascist ideology, 112
   according to socialist ideology, 95
   as viewed by authoritarian and democratic ideologies, 62, 70
Human relations, science and technology, 344–346
Humphrey, Hubert, 179
Hurst, J. W., 350
Hypotheses, 3
   as tested cross-culturally, 9

Idealists, British, 20, 99, 100
Ideology, 91–113
   continuum of ideologies, table, 93
   defined, 61
   functions of, 61–62
   as viewed by Marxism, 76–77
Impeachment process in U.S., 39, 129n.
Imperialism, according to Lenin, 80, 250
   (*See also* Colonialism)
India, 121, 216
Industrial revolution, 343
   (*See also* Economic development)
Initiative, 130
Injunction, 366
Intelligence community and foreign policy, 387–389, 404
Interest groups, 179, 300–305
   and foreign policy, 392, 393
   in multiparty states, 304
   in one-party states, 303
   and political parties and public policy, 303
   role of, in government, 301
   study of, 8
   in two-party states, 305
   and U.S. Congress, 151
Inter-Governmental Maritime Consultative Organization, 443
International Atomic Energy Agency, 443

INDEX

International Bank for Reconstruction and Development, 443
International Civil Aviation Organization, 443
International Court of Justice, 425, 432, 441–442
International Development Association, 443
International Finance Corporation, 443
International Geophysical Year, 352
International Labor Organization, 443
International law, 51, 58, 423–433
  institutional approach, 431–432
  and international relations, 400–401
  and neutrality, 22, 431–432
  and peace, 429–431
  present status of, 432–433
  and rights of states, 22
  sources of: equity, 427
    international custom, 427
    judicial decisions, 427
    treaties, 426–427
    writings of publicists, 427
  and the state, 24
  and war, 428–429
International Law Commission, 432
International legislation, 432
International military tribunals:
  Far East, 432
  Nuremberg, 425, 432
International Monetary Fund, 443
International organization, 423–424, 433–451
  study of, 10
International politics, 423–425, 433, 448
  and the executive branch, 132
  models of, 401–402
  sovereignty and, 26
  as subdiscipline of political science, 11
  (See also International relations)
International relations, 397–421
  current problems, 418–420
  and developing countries, 398–399
  and diplomatic recognition, 400
  and international law, 400–401
  patterns in, 405–410
  and population explosion, 402
  and the state system, 398–400
  strategies and tactics of, 403–405

International Telecommunications Union, 443
International Workingmen's Association, 81*n.*
Interstate Commerce Commission, 350, 365, 366
Ireland, home rule in, 205
Israel:
  electoral system, 124
  kibbutzim, 35
Italia irredenta, 403
Italy, 219, 222–227
  Christian Democratic party, 224–226
  Communist party, 215, 226, 229
  constitution, 175
  fascism, 109–110, 112, 126
  parliament, 124
  peasant anarchism, 93
  political parties, 224–227
    table, 220
Item veto, 182, 359

Jackson, Andrew, 70, 179
Jackson, Justice Robert H., 57, 423
Japan, 242
  and communist revolution in China, 86
  foreign policy, 382, 391
Jaurès, Jean, 97
Javits, Jacob, 151, 181
Jefferson, Thomas, 6, 66, 140, 143–145, 147, 180, 276
Jeffersonian Democratic-Republican party, 145, 179
Johnson, Lyndon B., 102, 132, 154, 156, 161, 171, 179, 184, 202, 418
Johnson, Wendell, 309
Joint Chiefs of Staff, 389
Judicial branch, U.S., 133–136, 167–178
  (*See also* Supreme Court, U.S.; United States)
Judicial and legal process, 134–135
  as subdiscipline of political science, 6
Judicial process and administrative regulations, 366–367
Judicial review, 69, 135, 136, 141, 172–173
Justice:
  and ethics, 48–50
  and law, 49–50

Justinian Code, 52

Kautsky, Karl, 95, 96
Kellogg-Briand Peace Pact (1928), 428, 431
Kelsen, Hans, 47
Kennan, George F., 416–417
Kennedy, John F., 102, 132, 156, 159, 161, 162, 171, 179, 258
Key, V. O., Jr., 262, 277, 285, 286, 288, 289, 308, 322
KGB (State Security Committee), 388, 389
Khrushchev, Nikita S., 84, 94, 255, 258, 260, 268–271, 383, 393
  foreign policy of, 405, 411–412, 417
Killian, James R., Jr., 347
Kissinger, Henry A., 383, 389, 390, 418
Komsomol, 259, 262, 351
Korean crisis (1950), 436
Kosygin, Alexei N., 84, 258, 264, 269, 417
Kropotkin, Piotr, 93–94

Labor, science, and technology, 343
Labor-management relations, 344
Labor theory of value, 77, 95, 105, 106
Labour party in Great Britain, 99, 108, 198–200, 205–210
LaFollette, Robert M., 323
Laissez faire, 63
  absence of, in continental Europe, 99
  in U.S., 99, 101, 143, 148
  of U.S. Supreme Court, 135
  as viewed by John Stuart Mill, 105–106
Lane, David, 303
Lane, Robert E., 281
Language and cultural cleavage, 215–216
Lassalle, Ferdinand, 97
Lasswell, Harold, 306, 311
Latham, Earl, 298
Law, 45–59
  characteristics, 56–58
  definition, 59
  and government, 45–59
  international, 51, 58, 423–433
  Marxist view of, 76–77

Law:
   and power, 423–424
   as protection of interests, 58–59
   schools: functional, 48
      historical, 47–48
      philosophical, 48
      positivist, 47
      pure science of law, 47
      sociological, 48
   science, and technology, 349
   sources, 50–51, 57
   stages of development, 51
   supremacy of, in U.S., 144
   types of: administrative, 350, 371
      equity, 168
      positive, 50–51, 57
      primitive, 51
      private, 54
      public, 54
      Roman, 52
      tort, 350
Lazarsfeld, Paul F., 308
League of Nations, 292, 403, 405, 407
Lebensraum in international politics, 403
Legal conflicts, 57–58
Legal development, 51
Legal fictions, 51
Legal order, 58
Legal paradoxes, 57
Legal principles, 46, 57, 425
Legal rules, 46, 57, 425
Legal sanctions, 57
Legal standards, 46, 57
Legal systems, 51–56
Legislative branch, 126–130
   functions of, 8
   relations with executive branch: in Great Britain, 202, 204
      in U.S., 37–39, 129–130, 132–133
Legislative investigating committees, 176–178
Legislative politics, study of, 7–8
Legislative process:
   in Great Britain, 200–204
   in U.S., 141, 152–155
Legitimacy, 120, 121, 238
   in Great Britain, 188
   and power, 61
   in Russia, 247, 255
   in Weimar Germany, 236
   in West Germany, 238
Lenin, V.I., 79–80, 95, 249–251, 253, 259, 265

Leninism, 79–80, 250
Levelers, 138
Liberal party in Great Britain, 98, 198, 199, 205–209
Liberalism, 61–70, 104–106, 184
Libermanism in the Soviet Union, 268–269
Liberty:
   equality, and fraternity, 63
   in Great Britain, 172, 174
   in U.S., 173–176
   (*See also* Liberalism)
Library of Congress, 352
Life Peerages Act (1958), 200
Lincoln, Abraham, 163–164, 179
Linkage patterns and public opinion, 289–291
Lippmann, Walter, 276
Literacy and democracy, 68
Local government, U.S., 183–184
Locke, John, 104, 276
   influence in America, 138
   natural right of property, 64
   social contract, 19, 174
Lodge, Henry Cabot, Jr., 450
Louis Napoleon, 133, 228
Louisiana Purchase, 145
Low, David, 208
Lowell, A. Lawrence, 276
Loyalty review in U.S., 176–177
Luther, Martin, 215
Lutheranism, and social contract theory, 5
   (*See also* Protestantism; Reformation)
Luttbeg, Norman R., 289, 290

McCarthy, Joseph R., 152
McGovern, George, 157, 159, 181
Machiavelli, Niccolò, 4–5, 9, 11, 26, 30, 223, 232
McKinley, William, 92
Macridis, Roy C., 322
Madison, James, 140
   on factions, 66, 131, 178
Magna Carta, 137, 174, 190
Majority rule in classical liberal ideology, 105*n.*
Malenkov, G. M., 84, 260, 268, 270–271
Management procedures, municipal, 363
Maoism, 85–87

Mao Tse-tung, 86, 87, 383, 385, 390, 412, 417
Marine Sciences Council, 362
Market socialism in the Soviet Union, 268–269
Marshall, Chief Justice John, 135, 142, 145, 170
Marshall Plan, 386, 415
Martov, J. O., 249
Marx, Karl, 66, 74, 75*n.*, 103, 232, 265
   contributions to political science, 5, 11, 216
   (*See also* Marxism)
Marxism, 66, 74–79, 89, 94, 95
   and European politics, 229
   in Russia, 249–250
Mason, Alpheus T., 344
Matano, Robert S., 120
Materialism in Marxism, 75–76
Mather, Cotton, 138
Mather, Increase, 138
Matthews, Donald R., 158
Mature law, 51
Mayflower Compact, 138
Mazurov, K. T., 258
Media and public opinion, 285
Menninger, Dr. Karl A., 296
Mensheviks, 79
Methodology in political science, 11–12
Mexico, presidential government in, 39
Michels, Robert, 32, 329
Military, civilian control over, 349
Mill, John Stuart, 105–106, 126
Mills, C. Wright, 299
Minority parties, 180
Mitterrand, Francois, 231*n.*, 234, 235, 332
Mobocracy, 4, 30
Models in political science, defined, 212
Modernization and revolution, 118–121
   (*See also* Economic development)
Molotov, V. M., 84, 271
Monarchist party in Italy, 223
Monarchy, 31–32
   in France, 63, 227–228
   in Great Britain, 192–193
   in Italy, 223
   and political unification, 222
Monopolies, 343

Montesquieu, Baron de, 2, 30, 138
More, Sir Thomas, 343
Morgenthau, Hans J., 405
Mosca, Gaetano, 32
Moscow Test-Ban Treaty (1963), 87, 347, 413
Moseley, Sir Oswald, 210
Municipal government, U.S., 183–184, 362
Municipal law, 426
Mussolini, Benito, 110, 112, 223

Nader, Ralph, 369
Napoleon Bonaparte, 228
National Aeronautics and Space Administration, 352, 385
National Aeronautics and Space Council, 362
National Defense Research Committee, 349
National Foundation on the Arts and the Humanities, 351
National Opinion Research Center, 277
National Recovery Administration, 126
National Science Foundation, 350–351
National Security Council, 362, 385, 389, 390
National Socialist German Workers' party (Nazi), 110, 236
Nationalism, 21–22, 96, 215
  effects on Marxist predictions, 79, 81n.
  and fascism, 110–111, 236
Nationalization of industry in Great Britain, 99, 207
Natural law, 26, 50–51, 57, 138
Natural rights, 4, 5, 19, 20, 26, 62, 64, 174
  in colonial America, 138
  in the Declaration of Independence, 6
Nauru, Republic of, 400
Nehru, Jawaharlal, 121
Neoliberalism, 64–66
Netherlands, culture and politics in, 214, 218–221
Neumann, Sigmund, 325
New Deal, 64, 102, 126
  principles of, 102
  and the Supreme Court, 146, 170

New Economic Policy (NEP) in the Soviet Union, 81, 251–252, 265
New England town government, 35–36, 122, 138
New Frontier, 102
New York City, 184
  electoral systems in, 124n.
Newton, Isaac, 5
Nicholas II, Tsar, 32, 248
Nicolson, Harold, 378
Nigeria, 218n.
Nixon, Richard M., 39, 102, 132, 147, 148, 156, 159, 160, 161, 163, 170, 171, 177–178, 179, 180, 183, 202
  foreign policy of, 177, 384, 390
  (See also Watergate affair)
Nominating convention, U.S., 157–159
Normative propositions:
  defined, 6
  in political philosophy, 11
North Atlantic Treaty Organization, 386, 409, 412, 415–416
Northern Ireland, 188, 208
  culture and politics in, 215, 217, 218
Nuclear Test-Ban Treaty (1963), 87, 347, 413
Nuncios and legates, 387

Office of Management and Budget, 362, 372
Office of Science and Technology, 348
Office of Scientific Research and Development, 349
Office of Telecommunications Policy, 362
Old Believers in Russia, 214
Oligarchy, 32
Ombudsman, 369
Opinion polls (see Public opinion polls)
Opposition, role of, in British Parliament, 194, 201–204
Organic concept of the state, 20, 100
  (See also State, natural theory of)
Organization in government, recent trends, 361–363
Organization of Petroleum Exporting Countries (OPEC), 382
Ortega y Gasset, José, 107
Ostpolitik, 237, 239, 384, 413

Outer space:
  law of, 351–352
  treaties, 352
Owen, Robert, 74

Pacific blockade, 428
Paine, Thomas, 18, 73, 139, 140
Papal States, 215, 223
Parliamentary system, 37–38
  compared with presidential system, 38, 202
  development of, 126–127
  in France, 228, 229–232
  in Great Britain, 127, 128, 190–191, 197–204
  table, 206
  parliamentary representation in selected Western European countries, table, 220
  in Italy, 225–226
  in the Soviet Union, 256
  in tsarist Russia, 249
  in West Germany, 238
  (See also Legislative branch)
Participation (see Political participation)
Paton, George W., 51
Patronage in presidential appointments, 162
Pauling, Linus C., 353
Peace Corps, 385
Penn, William, 138
Perception, 280, 282
Percy, Charles, 181
Permanent Court of Arbitration, 432
Permanent revolution, according to Trotsky, 80–81
Personality and attitudes, 280–281
Personality analysis (see Political behavior)
Pétain, Henri Philippe, 228
Philosophy, as distinguished from theory in political science, 11
  (See also Political philosophy)
Planning, military, 349
Plato, 4, 5, 11, 27, 30, 31, 62–64, 141, 156, 216, 276
Plekhanov, Georgi, 249
Pluralism (see Political participation)
Plutocracy, 32, 33
Pocket veto, 154
Podgorny, Nikolai, 258, 264, 417
Police power of U.S. states, 343

Policy formulation as distinguished from policy execution, 356
Policy outputs and public opinion, 289
Political adaptation:
    and aristocratic government, 32–33
    in France, 227, 228–229
    in Great Britain, 189–190
    in India, 121
    and monarchy, 31–32
    and political violence, 119
    and working-class demands, 97, 98
Political behavior, 292
    and anomie, 297
    behavioral approach, 294
    behavioral movement in political science, 292
    and decision-making, 294
    and group dynamics, 294, 297
    and personality trait analysis, 296
    and political efficacy, 297
    and politicization, 295
    and role playing, 294
Political communication, 307–308
Political culture, 9
    and democracy, 67–68
    and fascism, 111
    in Western Europe, 211–242
        France, 227–228, 235
        Germany, 236–237, 240–241
        Italy, 223–224
Political development, 119–121
    as subdiscipline of political science, 10
    (See also Economic development; Political adaptation)
Political environment, 306
Political instability, 119–120
Political interest groups (see Interest groups)
Political leadership and science and technology, 353
Political machines and political parties, 333
Political participation, 293–314
Political parties:
    auxiliaries of, 332–333
    and citizens, 319
    classification of, 321
    and coalitions, 326
    cohesion of, 158, 190, 194, 198, 199, 203–204
    and cultural cleavage, 219, 221–222
    definition of, 317–318

Political parties:
    and democratic government, 178
    and election campaigns, 319, 323, 329, 335
    financing of, 159–161, 198–199, 319, 329, 333–338
    in France, 92, 228–230, 233–234, 331–332
        tables, 220, 234
    and government, 319
    in Great Britain, 181, 193–194, 198–200, 204–210, 330–331
        and U.S., 201, 209
    historical development of, 316
    in Italy, 224–227
    and legislative process in U.S., 155
    minority parties, 323
    party systems: multiparty, 124, 180, 325–326
        table, 220
        one-party, 33–34, 326–327
        two-party, 323
        variant, 327–328
    and political machines, 333
    and proportional representation, 225, 226
    structure and characteristics of, 317–318
    study of, 8
    in U.S., 131, 155, 157–160, 178–182, 322–325, 329, 333
    in West Germany, 237, 239–240
    in Western Europe, 211–242
        table, 220
    (See also Electoral systems)
Political philosophy, 4
    defined, 11
    as subdiscipline of political science, 5–6
Political power and U.S. president, 155, 161–164
Political propaganda, 309–314
Political responsibility:
    in Great Britain, 178, 190, 194, 201–202, 208
    in U.S., 155, 158, 160–161, 178, 184, 201–202, 208
Political science:
    compared with other social sciences, 3
    definitions, 1–4, 17
    goals and uses, 12
    history, 4–5
    methods, 3, 4, 9, 117

Political science:
    as science, 1–4
    subdisciplines, 5–11
Political socialization, 9, 278–279
Political system, defined, 2
Political theory, defined, 11, 212
Political unification, timing of, 222–223
    in France, 227
    in Germany, 236
    in Italy, 222–223
    in Switzerland, 222–223
Political violence, 119–120
Polity, according to Aristotle, 63
Polyansky, D. S., 258
Polybius, 30
Pompidou, Georges, 231n., 233, 235, 332
Pope Leo XIII, 100–101
Pope Pius XI, 101
Popular front:
    and communist parties, 253
    in France, 228–229
Popular sovereignty, 191
Population and the state, 20–22
Populist party, U.S., 180
Populists in Russia, 249
Positive law, 50–51, 57
Post-industrial society, 241–242
Postman, L., 312
Poujadists, 230
Pound, Roscoe, 48
President:
    in France, 230–232
    in U.S., 131, 155–164
        functions of, 39
        and legislative process, 154
    in West Germany, 238
    (See also Executive branch)
President, Executive Office of the (U.S.), 362
Presidential government, 38–40
    compared with parliamentary government in Great Britain, 201
Presidential primaries, 157
President's Committee on Administrative Management, 358, 361
Press conference in U.S. government compared with question hour in British Parliament, 202–203
Pressure groups (see Interest groups)
Prewitt, Kenneth, 278
Prime minister:
    in Great Britain, table, 203

Prime minister:
  in parliamentary government, 37, 38
  (*See also* Executive branch of government, in Great Britain)
Primitive law, 51
Primogeniture, effects of: in continental Europe, 33, 189
  in England, 33, 189
Private law, 54
Progressive movement in U.S., 102, 180
Propaganda, political, 309–314
Proportional representation (*see* Electoral systems)
Protestantism:
  and Calvinism, 104
  and cultural cleavage in Western Europe, 214–215, 226
  the elect, concept of, 64
  and stable democracy, 118
  (*See also* Reformation)
Proudhon, Pierre, 93
Public administration, 355–373
  nature of, 355–360
  principles of, 356–360
  scope of, 360–361
  as subdiscipline of political science, 7
Public law, 54
  judicial and legal process, 134–135
  as subdiscipline of political science, 6
Public opinion, 275–292
  characteristics, 284–285
  conflict and consensus patterns, 286–287
  and culture, 279–280
  defined, 275, 281, 284
  linkage patterns, 289–291
  and the media, 285
  and perception, 280, 282
  and social class, 283
  study of, 8–9
  and the Supreme Court, 171–172, 175, 177, 178
Public opinion polls, 278
  and democracy, 123
  and party identification in U.S., 179
  and ten best governed nations, 117–118
Puritan revolution, 191
Puritanism in New England, 137

Puritanism in New England:
  and censorship, 176
  (*See also* Calvinism)

Quarantine, maritime, 429
Question hour in British Parliament, 202

Race, effects on politics, 213–214, 217
Racial discrimination in U.S. voting, 122
Radical parties in Western Europe, 215
Realpolitik in international politics, 383
Recognition in international law, 429–430
Red Guards in Communist China, 86
Referendum, 130
Reformation, 25, 64
  effects on European politics, 214–215
  effects on the state, 4, 18
Regulatory commissions, 130, 163, 370–371
Reinforcing cleavages, 216–218
  in France, 228
  in Italy, 226
Religion:
  in colonial America, 137–138
  effects on culture and politics: in Italy, 223, 226
    in Western Europe, 214–215
    in the Soviet Union, 245, 255
  as viewed by Marx, 76*n*.
  (*See also* Christianity; Protestantism)
Renaissance and political science, 4
Reorganization of federal government, U.S., 357–358
Representation:
  as delegation of popular sovereignty, 19
  in democratic governments, 122–126
  in U.S. Congress, 148–150
  (*See also* Electoral systems)
Reprisals, 428
Republican form of government, 36
Republican party:
  in Italy, 225
  in U.S., 108–109, 147, 179–182

Republican party:
  in U.S. presidential selection, 157–161
  (*See also* Political parties, in U.S.)
Resources, effects of, on the state, 23
Retorsion in international law, 428
Revenue-sharing programs, U.S., 183
Revisionist socialism, 96–98
Revolution:
  in China, 85–86
  in Cuba, 87–88
  in France, 92, 227–228
  in Marxist theory, 77–78
  and modernization, 118–121
  in Russia, 79–80, 248, 250–251
Reynolds v. Sims (1964), 149
Rhee, Syngman, 415
Rhode Island, colonial government in, 138
Risorgimento, 223
Rockefeller, Nelson, A., 155, 156, 181
Roman law, 52
Roosevelt, Franklin D., 64, 102, 155, 159, 162, 170, 179
Roosevelt, Theodore, 101, 162, 170
Rose, Arnold M., 300
Rosenau, James N., 289
"Rotten boroughs" in Great Britain, 197
Rousseau, Jean-Jacques, 19, 26, 93, 123
Rule of law, 45, 59, 425
Rules Committee, U.S. House of Representatives, 153, 154
Rumor, Mariano, 225, 226
Russia:
  monarchy in, 32
  political culture in, 247
  tsarist policies toward lower classes, 98
  (*See also* Union of Soviet Socialist Republics)
Russian Social Democratic Labor party, 79

Saint Augustine, 46
Saint-Simon, 74
Salmond, Sir John, 49
Savigny, F. C. von, 48
Schmidt, Helmut, 239, 241
Science:
  applied, 342
  concept of, 339

Science:
  pure science and technology, 341–342
  and technology, political impact of, 339–354
Scientific method, 3
Second International, 81*n.*
Self-defense in international law, 428
Self-determination, 21, 22
Senate:
  in France, 231–232
  in Italy, 225
  in U.S., 150–155
Seniority in U.S. Congress, 153, 155
Separation of powers, 38–39, 129, 133, 134, 138, 139, 141–142, 153, 163, 358, 372–373
  according to Montesquieu, 2
  historical background, 2, 5
  and legislative investigations, 176
  and the Supreme Court, 170–172
  and Watergate, 177–178
Shadow cabinet in Great Britain, 194
Single-member districts (*see* Electoral systems)
Sino-Soviet conflict, 87
  (*See also* Union of Soviet Socialist Republics, foreign policy of)
Sirica, Judge John J., 178
Size of the state, effects of, 22
Skylab satellite, 352
Smith, Adam, 64, 101, 105, 131, 143
Smith, Brewster M., 281
Snow, Sir Charles P., 347
Social class and public opinion, 283
Social contract theory of the state, 19, 20, 174
  in colonial America, 138, 139
  during religious wars, 5
Social Democratic party:
  in pre-war Germany, 96
  in Russia, 79
  in West Germany, 237, 239, 240
Social Revolutionary party in Russia, 249, 251
Socialism, 95–104
  according to Marx, 77, 78
  according to Stalin, 82, 254
  in one country, according to Stalin, 82, 252
Socialist parties in Europe, 100
Socialist party:
  in France, 234, 235
  in Italy, 225

Socialist Workers party, U.S., 81
Sorauf, Frank J., 321, 329
Sorokin, P. A., 118–119
South Carolina v. Katzenbach (1966), 150
South Vietnam, 121
  and U.S. politics, 132, 162, 179
Sovereign immunity, 359
Sovereignty, 25–27, 425, 427
  according to Rousseau, 123
  and international relations, 399–400
Spain:
  and Basque separatism, 215
  peasant anarchism in, 93
Specialized agencies, 442–443
Spencer, Herbert, 20, 93, 105
Sputnik, 351
Stakhanovite workers in the Soviet Union, 267
Stalin, Joseph, 81, 82, 251–253, 258–260, 265, 266, 268, 393, 394
  foreign policy of, 81, 252, 410–411
Stalinism, 80–83
State:
  according to anarchism, 93, 94
  according to Aristotle, 2
  according to Christianity, 27
  according to communism, 94
  according to Marxism, 76–77
  according to socialism, 97
  concepts and characteristics of, 17–28
  essential elements of, 20–26
  evaluation of, 27–28
  in international law, 24
  organic view of, 20, 100
  origins of, 18–20
  and the Reformation, 4
State government, U.S., 146–147, 182–183
Statute of Westminster (1931), 192
Steffens, Lincoln, 184
Stevenson, Adlai, 159, 447, 449
Stoicism, 4, 27, 93, 174
Stone, Justice Harlan F., 171
Strategic Arms Limitation Talks (SALT), 386, 413, 420
Structural-functionalism in political science, 12
Succession in U.S. presidency, 155–156
Sudan, 188
Suez crisis (1956), 437, 448
Suffrage, 121–122

Suffrage:
  in colonial America, 138, 139
  in France, 189
  in Germany, 189
  in Great Britain, 189, 197
  in Italy, 225
  in Russia, 189
  in the Soviet Union, 253, 255
  in U.S., 141, 142, 147, 150, 181
  (*See also* Electoral systems; Representation)
Supreme Court, U.S., 141, 146, 149, 150, 169–173, 182, 183
  role of, 123*n.*, 134–136
  and suffrage reform, 122, 123
Surplus value in Marxist ideology, 77
Survey research, uses of, 8, 9, 11
  (*See also* Public opinion polls)
Suslov, Mikhail S., 383
Sweden, 237
Switzerland:
  culture and politics, 22, 213–215, 218–222
  table, 219
  landesgemeinde, 276
  political parties, table, 220
  political unification, 222–223
Systems theory, 12

Taft, William Howard, 162
Taft-Hartley Act, 103
Taiwan and Chinese Nationalists, 86
Tammany Hall, 180, 181
Taney, Chief Justice Roger B., 135, 145, 170
Tarrow, Sidney G., 224
Tax Foundation, Inc., report of, 148
Technology:
  and democracy, 69
  effects on the state, 21–23, 339–340
  and science, political and social impact of, 339–354
  (*See also* Economic development)
Television and public opinion, 285
Teller, Edward, 353
Tennessee Valley Authority, 371–372
Theory in political science, 11
Third International, 81–83, 86
Third party movements, 180
Third world, law in, 51
Tito, Josip Broz, 82–84, 133
Titoism, 82–84

INDEX

Tories, British, 33, 108, 204, 205
  (*See also* Conservative party in Great Britain)
Totalitarianism, 34–35
Trade unions:
  in France and Great Britain, 229
  in the Soviet Union, 259
  in tsarist Russia, 249
  (*See also* Interest groups)
Traditionalists and behavioralists in political science, 11–12
Treasury control in Great Britain, 195
Treaties, relation of, to U.S. Constitution, 430–431
Trotsky, Leon, 80–82, 214, 250–252
Trotskyism, 80–81
Trudeau, Pierre Elliott, 222*n*.
Truman, David, 288, 289, 298
Truman, Harry S, 102, 179, 180
Two-step flow, 285

Ulster (*see* Northern Ireland)
Un-American activities investigating committees, U.S. Congress, 176–178
Underdeveloped countries:
  law in, 51
  politics in, 120–121
Unicameralism, 126–128
Union of Soviet Socialist Republics (USSR; Soviet Union):
  civil rights and civil liberties, 255
  collectivization of agriculture, 266–267
  Communist party of the Soviet Union, 259–265
    (*See also* Communist party, of the Soviet Union)
  comrades courts, 270
  Constitution of 1924, 252–253
  Constitution of 1936, 253–256
  Council of Ministers, 258, 264
  de-Stalinization, 84–85, 268, 270
  dumas (parliaments), 248–250
  economic development, effects of, 85, 264, 266, 269–271
  economic planning, 265–269
  elections, 253, 255–256
  federalism, 246, 252, 254–255
  five-year plans, 82, 265–266, 270
  foreign policy, 247, 251–253, 380, 382–384, 386, 390, 410–413, 417
  and Eastern Europe, 237

Union of Soviet Socialist Republics:
  foreign policy: and peaceful coexistence, 84, 85, 87, 269
    under Stalin, 81, 84, 85, 87
  Gosplan, 265, 267
  government structure, 252–258
  historical background, 247–252
  KGB, 388, 389
  Komsomol, 259, 262, 351
  law, 56
  law reform, 270
  liberalization, 82, 85, 268, 270–271
  New Economic Policy (NEP), 81, 251–252
  party and state relations, 258, 261
  Politburo, 259
    figure, 260
  political culture, 247
  president, 258
  Presidium, 256–258
  revolution of 1905, 248
  revolutions of 1917, 250–251
  science and technology, 351–352
  soviet deputy, functions of, 255
  state structure, 256–258
    figure, 257
  Supreme Soviet, 256
  Trotskyite view of, 81
  and the United Nations, 254, 448–449
Unitary states, 40–41
United Kingdom (*see* Great Britain)
United Nations, 381, 392, 405, 407–410
  costs, 443–444
  and decolonization, 440–441
  Economic and Social Council, 439–441
  Educational, Scientific and Cultural Organization, 443
  effective operation of, 444–445, 448
  General Assembly, 435–437
  history and goals, 434–435
  and human rights, 439, 447
  International Court of Justice, 441–442
  problems, 443–445, 447–448
  Secretariat, 442
  Security Council, 437–439
    veto, 437–439
    voting procedures, 437
  summary view of, 450–451
United Nations Conference on the Human Environment, 447

United Nations Emergency Forces, 437
United States, 137–164, 167–184
  Cabinet, 163–164
  capitalism, development of, 101
  colonial beginnings, 137–138
  compared with other countries, 118
    figure, 37
  Congress, 142, 148–155
  conservatism in, 108–109, 141
  Constitution, 36, 66, 135
    commerce clause, 343
    development of, 139–144
    (*See also* Separation of powers)
  culture, effects of, 22
  democratic socialism in, 101–103
  foreign policy, 414–417
  geographic security, effects of, 23–24
  judicial system, 167–178
  legislative process, 141, 152–155
  political parties, 131, 178–182, 322–325
    compared with parties in Great Britain, 194
  population changes in, 183
  presidency, 39, 155–164
  racial cleavages, 217
  revolutionary era, 138–139
  sovereignty in, 26–27
  state and local government, 146–147, 182–184
  Supreme Court (*see* Supreme Court, U.S.)
  treaties, 430–431
  and the United Nations, 449–450
United States Chamber of Commerce, 148
United States Information Agency (USIA), 388–389
United States v. Richard M. Nixon (1974), 177
Uniting for Peace Resolution, 436, 448
Universal Postal Union, 443
Utilitarianism, 105
Utopian socialists, 74, 77

Values:
  in authoritarian and democratic ideologies, 62–63
  in political philosophy, 6, 11
  in science and technology, 341

Vare machine, 181
Variable, defined, 3
Verba, Sidney, 224, 241
Veto:
  item, 182, 359
  presidential, 154, 162, 182
Victor Emmanuel II, 223
Vietnam, 417
  (*See also* South Vietnam)
von Hindenburg, Paul, 236
Voter turnout in U.S. and Great Britain, 198
Voting, study of, 8–9
  (*See also* Suffrage)
Voting Rights Act (1965), 122, 150, 182*n*.

Wallace, George, 179
War:
  new concepts of, 347
  nuclear, 353–354
  total, 348
War communism, 251
War on Poverty Program, 184

War Powers Resolution (1973), 349
Warren, Chief Justice Earl, 59
Washington Special Action Group (WSAG), 390
Watergate affair, 163, 202, 337–338, 348
  and Richard Nixon, 156, 171, 177–178
  and the Supreme Court, 144
Weakest link in Leninist ideology, 80
Wealth, distribution of, and democracy, 66
  in Great Britain, 208
  in U.S., 66*n*.
Weapons, scientific and technological, 344, 347
Webster, Daniel, 167
Weimar Republic, 236–237
Welfare state in Great Britain, 195
  (*See also* Democratic socialism)
Wesberry v. Sanders (1964), 123*n*., 149
West Germany (*see* Federal Republic of Germany)
Western Europe, politics in, 211–243

Whig party:
  in Great Britain, 98, 204, 205
  in U.S., 179
William and Mary, 191
Williams, Roger, 138
Wilson, Harold, 188, 207, 208
Wilson, Woodrow, 101, 162, 170, 179, 180
Women's suffrage, 122
Workers' councils in Yugoslavia, 83
Workers' Social Democratic party in Russia, 249
World community, 425, 433, 446
World Health Organization, 443
World Meteorological Organization, 443
World War II, 402–404, 409

Yugoslavia, 82–84

Zeno of Citium, 93
Zhdanov, Andrei, 83
Zirkle, Dr. Conway, 351